Triumph 1050 Sprint, Speed Triple & Tiger
Service and Repair Manual

by Matthew Coombs

(4796 - 336 - 8AM2)

Models covered

Sprint ST. 1050cc. 2005 to 2011
Sprint GT. 1050cc. 2011-on
Speed Triple. 1050cc. 2005-on
Speed Triple R. 1050cc. 2012-on
Tiger. 1050cc. 2007 to 2011
Tiger SE. 1050cc. 2010-on
Tiger Sport. 1050cc. 2013-on

ABS and Special Edition versions included

© Haynes Publishing 2014

ABCDE
FGHIJ
KLMNO
P

A book in the **Haynes Service and Repair Manual Series**

All rights reserved. No part of this book may be reproduced or transmitted in any form or by any means, electronic or mechanical, including photocopying, recording or by any information storage or retrieval system, without permission in writing from the copyright holder.

ISBN 978 0 85733 876 1

British Library Cataloguing in Publication Data
A catalogue record for this book is available from the British Library

Library of Congress Control Number 2013948066

Printed in the USA

Haynes Publishing
Sparkford, Yeovil, Somerset BA22 7JJ, England

Haynes North America, Inc
861 Lawrence Drive, Newbury Park, California 91320, USA

Haynes Publishing Nordiska AB
Box 1504, 751 45 Uppsala, Sweden

Printed using 33-lb Resolute Book 65 4.0 from Resolute Forest Products Calhoun, TN mill. Resolute is a member of World Wildlife Fund's Climate Savers programme committed to significantly reducing GHG emissions. This paper uses 50% less wood fibre than traditional offset. The Calhoun Mill is certified to the following sustainable forest management and chain of custody standards: SFI, PEFC and FSC Controlled Wood.

Contents

LIVING WITH YOUR TRIUMPH

Introduction

A Phoenix from the ashes	Page	0•4
Acknowledgements	Page	0•7
About this Manual	Page	0•7
Identification numbers	Page	0•8
Buying spare parts	Page	0•8
Safety first!	Page	0•9

Pre-ride checks

Coolant level	Page	0•10
Engine oil level	Page	0•11
Brake fluid levels	Page	0•12
Tyres	Page	0•15
Suspension, steering and drive chain	Page	0•15
Legal and safety checks	Page	0•15
Bike spec	Page	0•16
Model development	Page	0•18

MAINTENANCE

Routine maintenance and servicing

Specifications	Page	1•1
Lubricants and fluids	Page	1•2
Maintenance schedule	Page	1•3
Component locations	Page	1•4
Maintenance procedures	Page	1•10

Contents

REPAIRS AND OVERHAUL

Engine, transmission and associated systems

Engine, clutch and transmission	Page	**2•1**
Cooling system	Page	**3•1**
Engine management system (fuel and ignition)	Page	**4•1**

Chassis components

Frame and suspension	Page	**5•1**
Brakes, wheels and final drive	Page	**6•1**
Fairing and bodywork	Page	**7•1**

Electrical system

	Page	**8•1**

Wiring diagrams

	Page	**8•38**

REFERENCE

Security	Page	**REF•2**
Lubricants and fluids	Page	**REF•5**
MOT Test Checks	Page	**REF•8**
Conversion Factors	Page	**REF•13**
Tools and Workshop Tips	Page	**REF•14**
Storage	Page	**REF•33**
Fault Finding	Page	**REF•37**
Technical Terms Explained	Page	**REF•48**

Index

	Page	**REF•53**

A Phoenix from the ashes

by Julian Ryder

Where is the most modern motorcycle factory in the World? Tokyo? Berlin? Turin, maybe? No, it's in Hinckley, Leicestershire. Unlikely as it may seem, the Triumph factory in the Midlands of England is a more advanced production facility than anything the mighty Japanese industry, German efficiency or Italian flair can boast. Since the marquee was reborn in 1991, Triumph has grown into a big player on the world stage and is now the only volume manufacturer of automotive transport that can call itself truly British.

It's important to realise that the new Triumph company has very little to do with the company that was a giant on the world stage in the post-war years when British motorcycle makers dominated the global markets. It is true that new owner John Bloor bought the patents, manufacturing rights and, most importantly, trademarks when the old factory's assets were sold in 1983, but the products of the old and new companies bear no relation at all to one another. Apart, of course, from the name on the tanks. Bloor's research-and-development team started work in Collier Street, Coventry and in 1985 work started on the ten-acre green-field factory site, which was occupied for the first time the following year.

The reborn Triumphs

The R & D team soon dispensed with the old Meriden factory's project for a modern DOHC, eight-valve twin known within the factory as the Diana project (after Princess Di) but shown at the NEC International Bike Show in 1982 as the Phoenix. The world got to see the real new Triumphs for the first time at the Cologne Show in late 1990. The company was obviously anxious to distance itself from the old, leaky, unreliable image of the British motorcycle, but it was equally anxious not to engage in a head-on technology war with the big four Japanese factories. The watchword was 'proven technology', the new engines were in-line triples and housed in a universal steel chassis with a large-diameter tubular backbone. Seemingly contrary to the company's desire to distance itself from the past, the new bikes would all carry famous model names from Triumph's past.

But if Triumph's technology wasn't exactly path-breaking it was certainly very clever. The key concept was the modular design of the motor based around long and short-throw crankshafts in three and four-cylinder configurations. Every engine used the common 76 mm bore with either 55 or 65 mm throw cranks so that the short-stroke engine would be 750 cc in three-cylinder form and 1000 cc as a four. Put the long-stroke crank in and you get a 900 cc triple and a 1200 cc four. The first bike to hit the shops was the 1200 Trophy, a four-cylinder sports tourer which was immediately competitive in a very strong class. There was also a 900 cc, three-cylinder Trophy. The 750 and 1000 Daytonas used the short-stroke motor in three and four-cylinder forms in what were intended to be the sportsters of the range. The other two models, 750 and 900 cc three-cylinder Tridents, cashed in on the early-'90s fad for naked retro bikes that followed the world-wide success of the Kawasaki Zephyr.

The reborn Triumphs were received with acclaim from the motorcycle press – tinged with not a little surprise. They really were very good motorcycles, the big Trophy was a match for the Japanese opposition in a class full of very accomplished machinery. The fact it could live with a modern day classic like the Yamaha FJ1200 straight off the drawing board was a tribute to John Bloor's designers and production engineers. The bike was big, fast, heavy and quite high, but it worked and

The 2007 Sprint ST

Introduction 0•5

The 2007 Speed Triple

The 2007 Tiger

worked well. And it didn't leak oil or break down, it was obvious that whatever else people were going to say about Triumphs they weren't going to able to resurrect the old jokes about British bangers leaving puddles of lubricant under them. As the rest of the range arrived and tests of them got into print, the star of the show emerged; it was the long-stroke, three-cylinder, 900 cc motor. It didn't matter how it was dressed up, the big triple had that indefinable quality – character. It was the motor the Japanese would never have made, very torquey but with a hint of vibration that endears rather than annoys. Somewhere among the modern, water-cooled, multi-valve technology, the 900-triple had the genes of the old air-cooled OHV Triumph Tridents that appeared in 1969 and stayed in production until '75.

Model development

The range stayed basically unchanged until the Cologne Show of '92. Looking back at the first range it is now easy to see – hindsight again – that the identity of all the models was far too close. The sports tourer Trophy models were reckoned to be a little too sporting, the basic Tridents still had the handlebar and footrest positions of faired bikes. Triumph management later agreed that the first range evinced a certain lack of confidence; that was certainly not the case with the revamped 1993 range.

Visitors to the Cologne Show in September '92 agreed that the Triumphs were the stars, any lack of confidence there may have been two years earlier was completely gone. Any shyness the management may have felt about the Triumph name's past was shaken off as the new Tridents went retro style. Overall, the identities of the original bikes became more individual and more obviously separated; the Trophy models became more touring oriented, the Daytona more sporty looking and the Trident models more traditional. The factory even had the confidence to put small Union Flag emblems on the side panels of each model, no more apologising for the imagined shortcomings of British engineering. Despite this spreading of the range's appeal, all these bikes were still built on the original modular concept.

There was, however, an exception to this rule of uniformity in the shape of a brand new bike, the Tiger 900. This model was in the enduro/desert-racer style much favoured in Continental Europe but not at all popular at home in the UK. Here was a Triumph with a 19-inch front tyre, wire wheels and a lower power output than the other 900s. Both the chassis and engine parts were slightly different from the rest of the range. Judging their market as cleverly as ever, the factory held back another new model for the International Bike Show at the Birmingham NEC. This was the Daytona 1200, an out and out speed machine with a hidden political agenda. Its high-compression, 147 PS engine gave it brutal straight-line performance in much the same way as the big Kawasakis

The 2011 Sprint GT

0•6 Introduction

The 2012 Speed Triple R

of the mid-'80s, and like them it wasn't too clever in the corners because of its weight and length. The bike was built as much to show that Triumph could do it as to sell in big numbers, it also had the secondary function of thumbing the corporate nose at the UK importers' gentlemen's agreement not to bring in bikes of over 125 PS.

Next year's NEC show saw two more new Triumphs, both reworkings of what was now regarded as a modern classic, the 900 triple. The Speed Triple was a clever reincarnation of the British cafe racer style, complete with clip-on handlebars and rear-set footrests. The big three-cylinder engine in standard tune got an all-black finish with black chrome pipes and silencers for the appropriately mean look. Black wheel rims and new bodywork completed a superbly styled bike available with black or yellow bodywork, the Speed Triple was the star of the show, a bike with an attitude.

The other newcomer was a more radical project, the Daytona Super III. Externally the motor looked like the usual 900 three, but a lot of work by Cosworth Engineering was hidden under the cases. The result was 115 PS as opposed to the standard 900 Daytona's 98 PS.

Triumphs in America

Triumph's next big step was into the US market, where the old company was so strong in the post-war years when the only competition was Harley-Davidson and where there is considerable affection for the marque. The name Triumph chose to spearhead this new challenge was Thunderbird, a trademark sourced in Native American mythology. This time the famous name adorned yet another version of the 900 triple but this time heavily restyled and in a retro package. Dummy cooling fins give it the look of an air-cooled motor, the logo was cast into the clutch cover, and there were soft edges and large expanses of polished alloy. Inside those restyled cases, the motor was retuned even more than the Tiger's for a very user-friendly dose of low-down punch and mid-range power. The cycle parts were given an equally radical redesign, although the retro style stopped short of giving the Thunderbird twin rear shock absorbers. But everything else, the shape of the tank, the chrome headlight and countless other details, harks back to the original Thunderbird and nothing does so as shamelessly as the 'mouth-organ' tank badge, a classic icon if ever there was one.

The first Thunderbird derivative, the Adventurer, appeared for 1996 with a different rear subframe and rear-end styling including a sissy bar and single seat. That same year, the short-stroke 750 cc motor bowed out of the range, but it went with a bang not a whimper not in a final batch of Tridents but in a limited-edition run of 750 Speed Triples. The bigger Speed Triple's motor was inserted in the Sprint and the result called the Sprint Sport. The reason for using up all those motors was the advent of the new range of fuel-injected and heavily revised three-cylinder engines that first powered the T509 Speed Triple and T595 Daytona of 1997.

Fuel Injection

The first fuel-injected Triumph, the Daytona T595, was a major milestone for the Factory. It represented a change of policy, the first time Triumph would venture to confront their opposition on the cutting edge of technology. In early 1997, the Honda FireBlade and Ducati 916 ruled. The T595 was able to play in the same ball park. Only on a race track could the Japanese and Italian machines be shown to be better. In the real world the T595 was at least as good a bike. The old long stroke of 65 mm was retained but everything else was new, it was a radical departure from the modular concept that had dominated production until now. You could see how the new motor was a lightened version of the old triple, but fuel injection was new and the frame was a radical departure from previous practice. Serpentine tubing ran from steering head to swingarm pivot and it was aluminium. Bodywork looked tasty too. Despite what Triumph had said about not taking on the Japanese back in 1991, the T595 came out of comparative tests with the 'Blade and 916 on equal terms. The new bike was also given the Speed Triple treatment and adorned with bug-eyed twin headlights in the fashionable 'streetfighter' style.

The trouble with the Supersports end of the market is that the goal posts keep moving, so Triumph hedged their bets by softening the 955i's nominal 128 PS to 108, housing it in a simpler twin-beam frame and calling the result the Sprint ST. This continuation of the original Sprint concept was one of the hits of 1999. As a sports tourer, the fuel-injected Sprint ST was right up there with Honda's classic class leader, the VFR. Some magazines even preferred the British bike. High praise. The Tiger got the fuel-injected 855 cc motor in '99. The result was a much more svelte machine than the original carburetted model, but Britain still refused to fall in love with the concept. Not that development of the carburetted bikes was neglected. Triumph got a Thunderbird derivative right in 1998 with the Thunderbird Sport.

Up to 1999 Triumph concentrated on big bikes but then they took another giant step towards the big time by taking on the Japanese in the most competitive market sector of them all, Supersports 600, with the TT600. For 2001 the most famous name of all was bought out of retirement: Bonneville. And it was an air-cooled twin! From a standing start in 1991, the Hinckley factory was competing in all the major motorcycle market sectors. Much bigger production volumes meant the original modular concept was no longer a necessity. By the dawn of the 21st Century Triumph had sold over 100,000 motorcycles.

Then the factory was struck by one of the

Introduction

biggest fires ever at a British industrial site. In March 2002 the production line, moulding shop and stores were destroyed and many other parts of the plant severely damaged. Just six months later the rebuilt factory was running at full capacity. The first new product out of the doors was the Daytona 600, a replacement for the TT600. Where the first Supersports 600 Triumph had failed to compete with the Japanese this one was good enough to win a TT in the hands of Kiwi Isle of Man hero Bruce Anstey.

With an eye on America Triumph Triumph then unleashed their most audacious bike yet: the Rocket III. (Whisper it, but Rocket III was actually a BSA model name back in the 1970s.) They call it a cruiser but behemoth would be a better description, it's the first production bike to boast a capacity of over two litres and the only thing on the roads that can make a Harley V-Rod look shy and retiring.

In total contrast to the Rocket III, Triumph got serious about the supersports sector in 2006 with the 675cc Daytona triple. Use of the hallmark three-cylinder layout allowed the bike to race against 600cc fours in Supersport competition despite its capacity advantage. It has had success on the track at national level and has been far from disgraced in the World Supersport Championship. However, the Daytona has dominated its sector in the annual Masterbike test that brings journalists from all over the world to test the leading sports bikes from every manufacturer. It is by common consent one of the best middleweights on the market.

The twins first went from 790 to 865cc before getting fuel injection in 2008. The Thunderbird name came back (for the second time) in 2009 for a 1600cc twin as the range's Cruisers were aimed more and more at the American market. The Modern Classics, as Triumph call the Bonneville and its derivatives, cater more for the British and European traditions, with the Thruxton being a modern take on the classic café racer so beloved of the rockers of the 1960s.

Triumph use the label Urban Sports for the triples, but that phrase covers a range of applications. For 2007 Triumph's signature triple motor was stroked to up capacity to 1050cc and the engine powers Triumph's top-of-the-range trio: the Sprint, which is as good a sports tourer as you can buy; the Tiger, now with aluminium frame, is right up there with the GS BMW as an all-rounder/go-anywhere machine; and the Speed Triple is – well, it's the Speed Triple.

Acknowledgements

Our thanks are due to Fowlers Motorcycles of Bristol who supplied the machines featured in the illustrations throughout this manual. We would also like to thank NGK Spark Plugs (UK) Ltd for supplying the colour spark plug condition photographs, the Avon Rubber Company for supplying information on tyre fitting, and Draper Tools for supplying many of the tools shown in the photographs.

Thanks are also due to Julian Ryder for providing the introductory copy – A Phoenix from the ashes. We would also like to extend thanks to Triumph Motorcycles, Hinckley, for permission to use pictures of the Triumph models. Triumph Motorcycles Limited bears no responsibility for the content of this book, having had no part in its origination or preparation.

About this manual

The aim of this manual is to help you get the best value from your motorcycle. It can do so in several ways. It can help you decide what work must be done, even if you choose to have it done by a dealer; it provides information and procedures for routine maintenance and servicing; and it offers diagnostic and repair procedures to follow when trouble occurs.

We hope you use the manual to tackle the work yourself. For many simpler jobs, doing it yourself may be quicker than arranging an appointment to get the motorcycle into a dealer and making the trips to leave it and pick it up. More importantly, a lot of money can be saved by avoiding the expense the shop must pass on to you to cover its labour and overhead costs. An added benefit is the sense of satisfaction and accomplishment that you feel after doing the job yourself.

References to the left or right side of the motorcycle assume you are sitting on the seat, facing forward.

We take great pride in the accuracy of information given in this manual, but motorcycle manufacturers make alterations and design changes during the production run of a particular motorcycle of which they do not inform us. No liability can be accepted by the authors or publishers for loss, damage or injury caused by any errors in, or omissions from, the information given.

Illegal Copying

It is the policy of Haynes Publishing to actively protect its Copyrights and Trade Marks. Legal action will be taken against anyone who unlawfully copies the cover or contents of this Manual. This includes all forms of unauthorised copying including digital, mechanical, and electronic in any form. Authorisation from Haynes Publishing will only be provided expressly and in writing. Illegal copying will also be reported to the appropriate statutory authorities.

The 2013 Tiger Sport

0•8 Identification numbers

Frame and engine numbers

The engine number is stamped into the top of the crankcase on the right-hand side of the engine. The VIN (vehicle identification number) is stamped into the right-hand side of the steering head and is duplicated on a plate riveted to the left-hand side of the frame just behind the steering head. These numbers should be recorded and kept in a safe place so they can be furnished to law enforcement officials in the event of a theft.

The VIN, engine number, and model code should be recorded and kept in a handy place (such as with your driver's licence) so that they are always available when purchasing or ordering parts for your machine.

The procedures in this manual identify the bikes by model (e.g. Sprint ST, Speed Triple). If a model has been modified during its production life, then either the VIN, engine number, or the model year, or whether it is fitted for example with ABS, is used to differentiate between the versions, as appropriate.

Buying spare parts

Once you have found the identification numbers, record them for reference when buying parts. Since the manufacturers change specifications, parts and vendors (companies that manufacture various components on the machine), providing the ID numbers is the only way to be reasonably sure that you are buying the correct parts.

Whenever possible, take the worn part to the dealer so direct comparison with the new component can be made. Along the trail from the manufacturer to the parts shelf, there are numerous places that the part can end up with the wrong number or be listed incorrectly.

The two places to purchase new parts for your motorcycle – the accessory store and the franchised dealer – differ in the type of parts they carry. While dealers can obtain virtually every part for your motorcycle, the accessory dealer is usually limited to normal high wear items such as shock absorbers, tune-up parts, various engine gaskets, cables, chains, brake parts, etc. Rarely will an accessory outlet have major suspension components, cylinders, transmission gears, or cases.

Used parts can be obtained for roughly half the price of new ones, but you can't always be sure of what you're getting. Once again, take your worn part to the breaker's yard for direct comparison.

Whether buying new, used or rebuilt parts, the best course is to deal directly with someone who specialises in parts for your particular make.

The engine number is stamped into the crankcase on the right-hand side of the engine

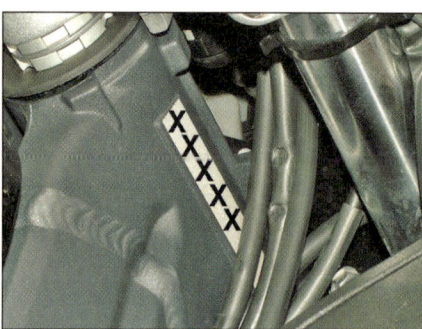

The VIN is stamped into the right-hand side of the steering head

The VIN is duplicated on an information plate (arrowed) on the front of the steering head

Safety first! 0•9

Professional mechanics are trained in safe working procedures. However enthusiastic you may be about getting on with the job at hand, take the time to ensure that your safety is not put at risk. A moment's lack of attention can result in an accident, as can failure to observe simple precautions.

There will always be new ways of having accidents, and the following is not a comprehensive list of all dangers; it is intended rather to make you aware of the risks and to encourage a safe approach to all work you carry out on your bike.

Asbestos

● Certain friction, insulating, sealing and other products - such as brake pads, clutch linings, gaskets, etc. - contain asbestos. Extreme care must be taken to avoid inhalation of dust from such products since it is hazardous to health. If in doubt, assume that they do contain asbestos.

Fire

● Remember at all times that petrol is highly flammable. Never smoke or have any kind of naked flame around, when working on the vehicle. But the risk does not end there - a spark caused by an electrical short-circuit, by two metal surfaces contacting each other, by careless use of tools, or even by static electricity built up in your body under certain conditions, can ignite petrol vapour, which in a confined space is highly explosive. Never use petrol as a cleaning solvent. Use an approved safety solvent.

● Always disconnect the battery earth terminal before working on any part of the fuel or electrical system, and never risk spilling fuel on to a hot engine or exhaust.

● It is recommended that a fire extinguisher of a type suitable for fuel and electrical fires is kept handy in the garage or workplace at all times. Never try to extinguish a fuel or electrical fire with water.

Fumes

● Certain fumes are highly toxic and can quickly cause unconsciousness and even death if inhaled to any extent. Petrol vapour comes into this category, as do the vapours from certain solvents such as trichloro-ethylene. Any draining or pouring of such volatile fluids should be done in a well ventilated area.

● When using cleaning fluids and solvents, read the instructions carefully. Never use materials from unmarked containers - they may give off poisonous vapours.

● Never run the engine of a motor vehicle in an enclosed space such as a garage. Exhaust fumes contain carbon monoxide which is extremely poisonous; if you need to run the engine, always do so in the open air or at least have the rear of the vehicle outside the workplace.

The battery

● Never cause a spark, or allow a naked light near the vehicle's battery. It will normally be giving off a certain amount of hydrogen gas, which is highly explosive.

● Always disconnect the battery ground (earth) terminal before working on the fuel or electrical systems (except where noted).

● If possible, loosen the filler plugs or cover when charging the battery from an external source. Do not charge at an excessive rate or the battery may burst.

● Take care when topping up, cleaning or carrying the battery. The acid electrolyte, evenwhen diluted, is very corrosive and should not be allowed to contact the eyes or skin. Always wear rubber gloves and goggles or a face shield. If you ever need to prepare electrolyte yourself, always add the acid slowly to the water; never add the water to the acid.

Electricity

● When using an electric power tool, inspection light etc., always ensure that the appliance is correctly connected to its plug and that, where necessary, it is properly grounded (earthed). Do not use such appliances in damp conditions and, again, beware of creating a spark or applying excessive heat in the vicinity of fuel or fuel vapour. Also ensure that the appliances meet national safety standards.

● A severe electric shock can result from touching certain parts of the electrical system, such as the spark plug wires (HT leads), when the engine is running or being cranked, particularly if components are damp or the insulation is defective. Where an electronic ignition system is used, the secondary (HT) voltage is much higher and could prove fatal.

Remember...

✗ **Don't** start the engine without first ascertaining that the transmission is in neutral.

✗ **Don't** suddenly remove the pressure cap from a hot cooling system - cover it with a cloth and release the pressure gradually first, or you may get scalded by escaping coolant.

✗ **Don't** attempt to drain oil until you are sure it has cooled sufficiently to avoid scalding you.

✗ **Don't** grasp any part of the engine or exhaust system without first ascertaining that it is cool enough not to burn you.

✗ **Don't** allow brake fluid or antifreeze to contact the machine's paintwork or plastic components.

✗ **Don't** siphon toxic liquids such as fuel, hydraulic fluid or antifreeze by mouth, or allow them to remain on your skin.

✗ **Don't** inhale dust - it may be injurious to health (see Asbestos heading).

✗ **Don't** allow any spilled oil or grease to remain on the floor - wipe it up right away, before someone slips on it.

✗ **Don't** use ill-fitting spanners or other tools which may slip and cause injury.

✗ **Don't** lift a heavy component which may be beyond your capability - get assistance.

✗ **Don't** rush to finish a job or take unverified short cuts.

✗ **Don't** allow children or animals in or around an unattended vehicle.

✗ **Don't** inflate a tyre above the recommended pressure. Apart from overstressing the carcass, in extreme cases the tyre may blow off forcibly.

✔ **Do** ensure that the machine is supported securely at all times. This is especially important when the machine is blocked up to aid wheel or fork removal.

✔ **Do** take care when attempting to loosen a stubborn nut or bolt. It is generally better to pull on a spanner, rather than push, so that if you slip, you fall away from the machine rather than onto it.

✔ **Do** wear eye protection when using power tools such as drill, sander, bench grinder etc.

✔ **Do** use a barrier cream on your hands prior to undertaking dirty jobs - it will protect your skin from infection as well as making the dirt easier to remove afterwards; but make sure your hands aren't left slippery. Note that long-term contact with used engine oil can be a health hazard.

✔ **Do** keep loose clothing (cuffs, ties etc. and long hair) well out of the way of moving mechanical parts.

✔ **Do** remove rings, wristwatch etc., before working on the vehicle - especially the electrical system.

✔ **Do** keep your work area tidy - it is only too easy to fall over articles left lying around.

✔ **Do** exercise caution when compressing springs for removal or installation. Ensure that the tension is applied and released in a controlled manner, using suitable tools which preclude the possibility of the spring escaping violently.

✔ **Do** ensure that any lifting tackle used has a safe working load rating adequate for the job.

✔ **Do** get someone to check periodically that all is well, when working alone on the vehicle.

✔ **Do** carry out work in a logical sequence and check that everything is correctly assembled and tightened afterwards.

✔ **Do** remember that your vehicle's safety affects that of yourself and others. If in doubt on any point, get professional advice.

● If in spite of following these precautions, you are unfortunate enough to injure yourself, seek medical attention as soon as possible.

Pre-ride checks

Coolant level

> **Warning: DO NOT remove the radiator pressure cap to add coolant. Topping up is done via the coolant reservoir tank filler. DO NOT leave open containers of coolant about, as it is poisonous.**

Before you start:

✔ Make sure you have a supply of coolant available – a mixture of 50% distilled water and 50% corrosion inhibited ethylene glycol anti-freeze is needed.
✔ Always check the coolant level when the engine is cold.
✔ Support the motorcycle in an upright position on level ground, using an auxiliary stand if required.

Bike care:

● Use only the specified coolant mixture. It is important that anti-freeze is used in the system all year round, and not just in the winter. Do not top the system up using only water, as the system will become too diluted.
● Do not overfill the reservoir. If the coolant is significantly above the MAX level line at any time, the surplus should be siphoned or drained off to prevent the possibility of it being expelled out of the overflow hose.
● If the coolant level falls steadily, check the system for leaks (see Chapter 1). If no leaks are found and the level continues to fall, it is recommended that the machine be taken to a Triumph dealer for a pressure test.

SPRINT

1 The reservoir is mounted inside the fairing on the left-hand side, and is visible by looking up between the left-hand front fork and the fairing – turn the steering as required for best view. The coolant MAX and MIN level lines (arrowed) are marked on the reservoir.

2 If the coolant level does not lie between the MAX and MIN level lines, remove the upper and lower cockpit trim panels on the left-hand side (see Chapter 7). Remove the reservoir filler cap.

3 Top the coolant level up with the recommended coolant mixture. Fit the cap securely, then install the trim panels (see Chapter 7).

SPEED TRIPLE – 2005 to 2010 models (up to VIN 461331)

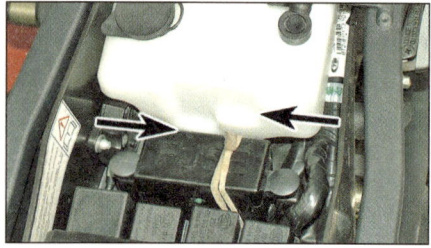

1 Remove the seat (see Chapter 7). The coolant MAX and MIN levels are marked on the reservoir on 2005 to 2007 models, and are at the formed steps (arrowed) on the reservoir on 2008 to 2010 models.

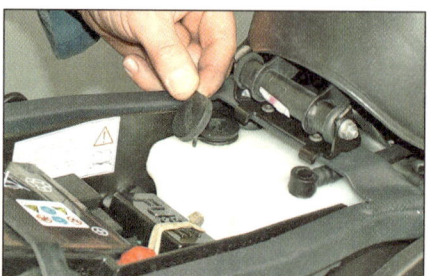

2 If the coolant level does not lie between the MAX and MIN level lines, remove the reservoir filler cap.

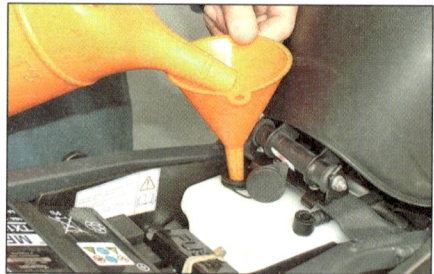

3 Top the coolant level up with the recommended coolant mixture. Fit the cap securely, then install the seat (see Chapter 7).

SPEED TRIPLE – 2011-on models (from VIN 461332)

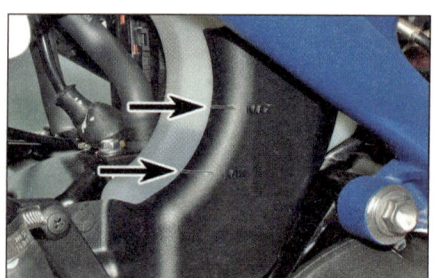

1 The coolant MAX and MIN level lines (arrowed) are marked on the reservoir.

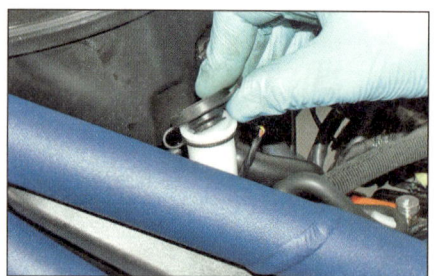

2 If the coolant level does not lie between the MAX and MIN level lines, raise the fuel tank (see Chapter 4), then remove the reservoir filler cap.

3 Top the coolant level up with the recommended coolant mixture. Fit the cap securely, then lower the tank (see Chapter 4).

Pre-ride checks 0•11

TIGER

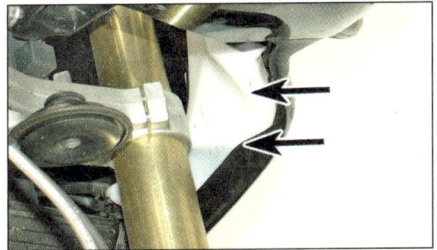

1 The reservoir is mounted inside the fairing on the left-hand side, and is visible by looking up between the left-hand front fork and the fairing – turn the steering as required for best view. The coolant MAX and MIN level lines (arrowed) are marked on the reservoir.

2 If the coolant level does not lie between the MAX and MIN level lines, remove the left-hand cockpit trim panel (see Chapter 7). Remove the reservoir filler cap.

3 Top the coolant level up with the recommended coolant mixture. Fit the cap securely.

Engine oil level

Before you start:
✔ Support the motorcycle in an upright position on level ground – don't check the oil level with the bike on its sidestand.
✔ Start the engine and let it idle for several minutes to allow it to reach normal operating temperature.
Caution: Do not run the engine in an enclosed space such as a garage or workshop.
✔ Stop the engine and leave the motorcycle undisturbed for a few minutes to allow the oil level to stabilise.

Bike care:
● If you have to add oil frequently, you should check whether you have any oil leaks. If there is no sign of oil leakage from the joints and gaskets the engine could be burning oil (see Fault Finding).

The correct oil
● Modern, high-revving engines place great demands on their oil. It is very important that the correct oil for your bike is used.
● Always top up with a good quality oil of the specified type and viscosity and do not overfill the engine. Triumph recommend using Mobil 1 Racing 4T oil.
Caution: Do not mix any chemical additives with the oil, however good they may sound, as they could cause clutch slip. Never use mineral, vegetable, non-detergent or castor based oils.

Oil type	Semi or fully synthetic motorcycle engine oil, API grade SH or higher and JASO MA
Oil viscosity	SAE 10W/40 or 15W/50

1 Unscrew the oil filler dipstick on the rear of the clutch cover on the right-hand side of the engine.

2 Wipe off the oil, screw the cap fully home, then unscrew it again . . .

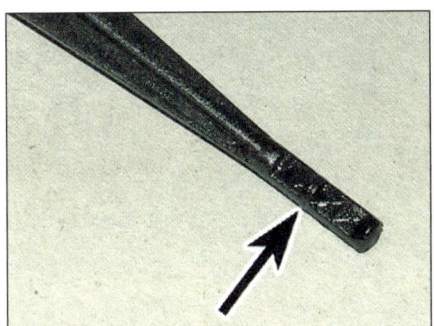

3 . . . and check that the oil is visible up to the top of the hatched area (arrowed) at the bottom of the dipstick.

4 If required, top up the engine oil to the correct level with the recommended grade and type of oil.

Pre-ride checks

Brake fluid levels

Before you start:
✔ Make sure you have the correct hydraulic fluid. DOT 4 is recommended.
✔ Support the motorcycle in an upright position, using an auxiliary stand if required. Turn the handlebars until the top of the front master cylinder is as level as possible.
✔ The rear master cylinder reservoir is located on the right-hand side.
✔ Wrap a rag around the reservoir being worked on to ensure that any spillage does not come into contact with painted surfaces.

Bike care:
● The fluid in the front and rear brake master cylinder reservoirs will drop slightly as the brake pads wear down.
● If any fluid reservoir requires repeated topping-up this is an indication of an hydraulic leak somewhere in the system, which should be investigated immediately.
● Check for signs of fluid leakage from the hydraulic hoses and brake system components – if found, rectify immediately (see Chapter 6).
● Check the operation of both brakes before taking the machine on the road; if there is evidence of air in the system (spongy feel to lever or pedal), it must be bled as described in Chapter 6.

> **Warning: Brake hydraulic fluid can harm your eyes and damage painted surfaces, so use extreme caution when handling and pouring it and cover surrounding surfaces with rag. Do not use fluid that has been standing open for some time, as it absorbs moisture from the air which can cause a dangerous loss of braking effectiveness.**

FRONT BRAKE FLUID LEVEL – SPRINT, 2005 to 2010 SPEED TRIPLE (up to VIN 461331), TIGER

1 The front brake fluid level must be between the UPPER and LOWER level lines (arrowed).

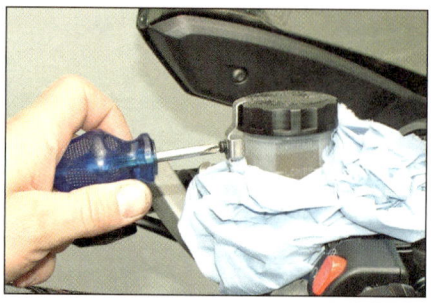

2 To top up, undo the reservoir cap clamp screw and remove the clamp . . .

3 . . . then unscrew the cap and remove the plate and diaphragm.

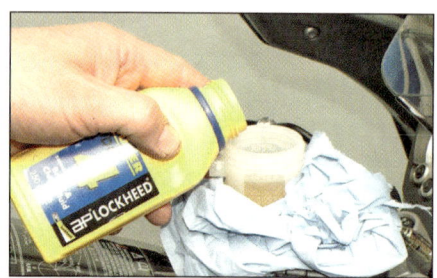

4 Top up with DOT 4 hydraulic fluid, until the level is between the LOWER and UPPER level lines – do not overfill. Avoid spills (see **Warning** on page 0•13).

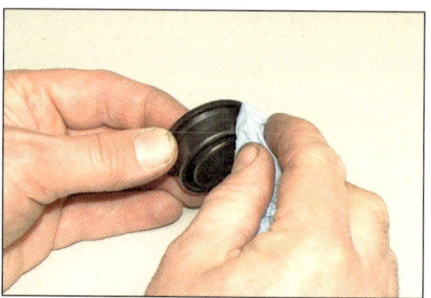

5 Wipe any moisture off the diaphragm, opening it out to access the folds.

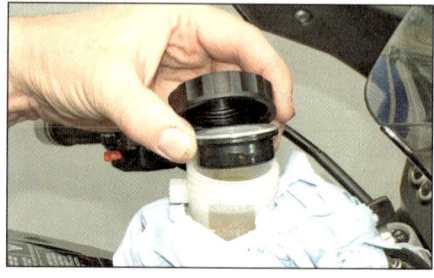

6 Ensure that the diaphragm is correctly seated before installing the plate and cap. Secure the cap with its clamp.

Pre-ride checks 0•13

FRONT BRAKE FLUID LEVEL – 2011-on SPEED TRIPLE (from VIN 461332)

1 The front brake fluid level must be between the MAX and MIN level lines (arrowed).

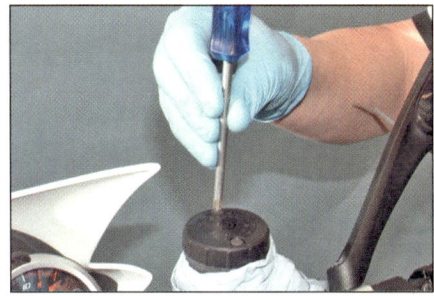

2 To top up, undo the reservoir cap screws and remove the cap and diaphragm.

3 Top up with new DOT 4 hydraulic fluid, until the level is between the MAX and MIN level lines – do not overfill. Take care to avoid spills (see **Warning** on page 0.12).

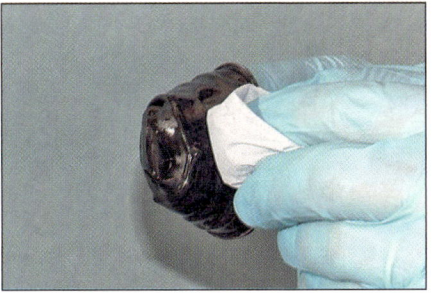

4 Wipe any moisture off of the diaphragm, opening it out to access the folds.

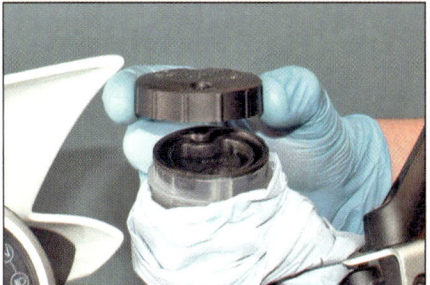

5 Ensure that the diaphragm is correctly seated before fitting the cap. Secure the cap with its screws.

REAR BRAKE FLUID LEVEL – SPRINT ST

1 The rear brake fluid level is visible through the reservoir body – it must be between the UPPER and LOWER level lines (arrowed).

2 If the level is below the LOWER level line, remove the seat (see Chapter 7), then displace the starter relay from its mount.

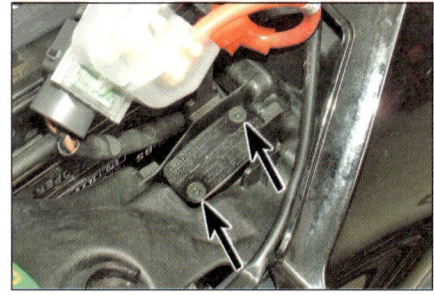

3 Undo the reservoir cover screws (arrowed) and remove the cover and the diaphragm.

4 Top up with DOT 4 hydraulic fluid, until the level is between the LOWER and UPPER level lines – do not overfill. Avoid spills (see **Warning** on page 0•12).

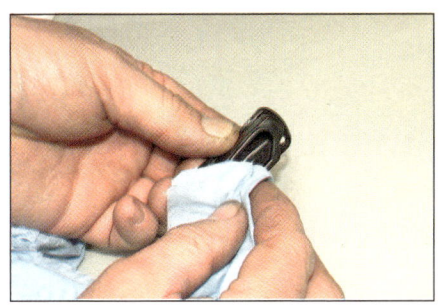

5 Wipe any moisture off the diaphragm, opening it out to access the folds.

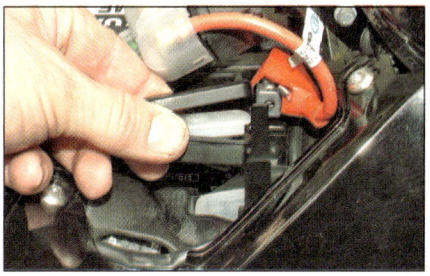

6 Ensure that the diaphragm is correctly seated before fitting the cover. Secure the cover with its screws. Remount the starter relay and fit the seat (see Chapter 7).

Pre-ride checks

REAR BRAKE FLUID LEVEL – 2005 to 2010 SPEED TRIPLE (up to VIN 461331)

1 The rear brake fluid level is visible through the reservoir body – it must be between the UPPER and LOWER level lines (arrowed).

2 If the level is below the LOWER level line undo the reservoir cover screws and remove the cover and the diaphragm.

3 Top up with DOT 4 hydraulic fluid, until the level is between the LOWER and UPPER level lines – do not overfill. Avoid spills (see **Warning** on page 0•12).

4 Wipe any moisture off the diaphragm, opening it out to access the folds.

5 Ensure that the diaphragm is correctly seated before installing the cover. Secure the cover with its screws.

REAR BRAKE FLUID LEVEL – SPRINT GT, 2011-on SPEED TRIPLE (from VIN 461332) and TIGER

1 On Sprint GT models remove the seat (see Chapter 7). On all models the rear brake fluid level is visible through the reservoir body – it must be between the UPPER and LOWER level lines (arrowed).

2 If the level is low on Tiger models, slacken the reservoir bolt sufficiently to allow the reservoir to be tilted.

3 On all models undo the reservoir cap and remove the plate and diaphragm.

4 Top up with DOT 4 hydraulic fluid, until the level is between the LOWER and UPPER level lines – do not overfill. Avoid spills (see **Warning** on page 0•12).

5 Wipe any moisture off the diaphragm, opening it out to access the folds.

6 Ensure that the diaphragm is correctly seated before installing the plate and cap. Tighten the cap securely. On Tiger models tighten the reservoir bolt. On Sprint GT models fit the seat (see Chapter 7).

Pre-ride checks

Tyres

The correct pressures
- The tyres must be checked when cold, not immediately after riding. Note that low tyre pressures may cause the tyre to slip on the rim or come off. High tyre pressures will cause abnormal tread wear and unsafe handling.

1 Remove the cap from the valve – if it is missing fit a new one.

- Use an accurate pressure gauge. Many garage forecourt gauges are wildly inaccurate. If you buy your own, spend as much as you can justify on a quality gauge.
- Correct air pressure will increase tyre life and provide maximum stability, handling capability and ride comfort.

Tyre care
- Check the tyres carefully for cuts, tears, embedded nails or other sharp objects and excessive wear. Operation of the motorcycle with excessively worn tyres is extremely hazardous, as traction and handling are directly affected. Also check the wheels for signs of damage and distortion.
- Check the condition of the tyre valve and ensure the dust cap is in place.
- Pick out any stones or nails which may have become embedded in the tyre tread. If left, they will eventually penetrate through the casing and cause a puncture.
- If tyre damage is apparent, or unexplained loss of pressure is experienced, seek the advice of a tyre fitting specialist without delay.

Tyre tread depth
- At the time of writing UK law requires that tread depth must be at least 1 mm over 3/4 of the tread breadth all the way around the tyre, with no bald patches. Many riders, however, consider 2 mm tread depth minimum to be a safer limit. Triumph recommend a minimum of 2 mm for normal riding, or 3 mm on the rear tyre for high speed riding (over 80 mph, 130 km/h).
- Many tyres now incorporate wear indicators in the tread. Identify the triangular pointer or TWI mark on the tyre sidewall to locate the indicator bar and renew the tyre if the tread has worn down to the bar.

	Front	Rear
Sprint	36 psi (2.50 Bar)	42 psi (2.90 Bar)
Speed Triple and Tiger	34 psi (2.35 Bar)	42 psi (2.90 Bar)

2 Check the tyre pressures when the tyres are cold and keep them properly inflated.

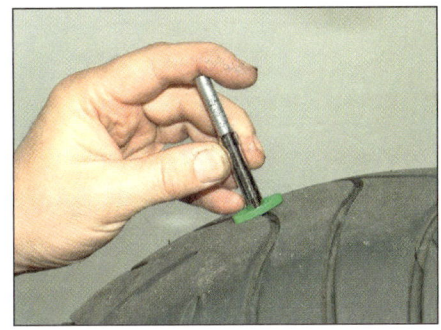

3 Measure tread depth at the centre of the tyre using a tread depth gauge.

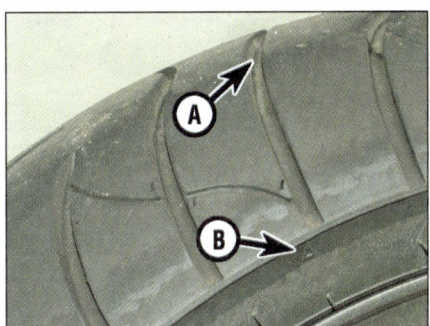

4 Tyre tread wear indicator bar A and its location marking B (usually either an arrow, a triangle or the letters TWI) on the sidewall.

Suspension, steering and final drive

Suspension and Steering
- Check that the front and rear suspension operates smoothly without binding. Check that there are no fluid leaks from the front fork seals or rear shock absorber.
- Check that the suspension is adjusted as required (see Chapter 5).
- Check that the steering moves smoothly from lock-to-lock.

Final drive
- Check that the chain slack isn't excessive, and adjust it if necessary (see Chapter 1).
- If the chain looks dry, lubricate it (see Chapter 1).

Legal and safety

Lighting and signalling
- Take a minute to check that the headlight, tail light, brake light, instrument lights and turn signals all work correctly.
- Check that the horn sounds when the button is pushed.
- A working speedometer graduated in mph is a statutory requirement in the UK.

Safety
- Check that the throttle grip rotates smoothly and snaps shut when released, in all steering positions. Also check for the correct amount of freeplay (see Chapter 1).
- Check that the engine shuts off when the kill switch is operated.
- Check that sidestand (and centrestand on Sprint ST models) return spring holds the stand securely up when retracted.
- Check that the clutch cable is working smoothly and with the correct freeplay (see Chapter 1).
- Check for any nuts and bolts that may have worked loose.

Fuel
- This may seem obvious, but check that you have enough fuel to complete your journey. Check for signs of fuel leakage – if any are found, rectify the cause immediately.
- Ensure you use the correct grade fuel – see Chapter 4 Specifications.

0•16 Bike spec

Weights and dimensions

Sprint ST
Overall length . . . . 2114 mm
Overall width. . . . . 750 mm
Overall height
   Low windshield . . . . 1145 mm
   High windshield . . . . 1215 mm
Wheelbase . . . . 1457 mm
Seat height . . . . 805 mm
Dry weight (no fuel and oil)
   No ABS . . . . 210 kg
   With ABS . . . . 213 kg
Max. payload (rider, passenger, luggage, accessories) . . . . 215 kg

Sprint GT
Overall length . . . . 2260 mm
Overall width. . . . . 940 mm
Overall height . . . . 1210 mm
Wheelbase . . . . 1565 mm
Seat height . . . . 815 mm
Wet weight . . . . 268 kg
Max. payload (rider, passenger, luggage, accessories) . . . . 215 kg

Speed Triple up to VIN 461331
Overall length . . . . 2115 mm
Overall width. . . . . 780 mm
Overall height . . . . 1250 mm
Wheelbase . . . . 1429 mm
Seat height . . . . 815 mm
Dry weight (no fuel and oil) . . . . 189 kg
Max. payload (rider, passenger, luggage, accessories) . . . . 185 kg

Speed Triple from VIN 461332-on
Overall length . . . . 2100 mm
Overall width. . . . . 795 mm
Overall height . . . . 1110 mm
Wheelbase . . . . 1435 mm
Seat height . . . . 825.5 mm
Wet weight . . . . 214 kg
Max. payload (rider, passenger, luggage, accessories) . . . . 195 kg

Tiger
Overall length . . . . 2110 mm
Overall width. . . . . 840 mm
Overall height . . . . 1320 mm
Wheelbase . . . . 1510 mm
Seat height . . . . 835 mm
Dry weight (no fuel and oil)
   No ABS . . . . 198 kg
   With ABS . . . . 202 kg
Max. payload (rider, passenger, luggage, accessories) . . . . 200 kg

Tiger Sport
Overall length . . . . 2150 mm
Overall width. . . . . 835 mm
Overall height . . . . 1310 mm
Wheelbase . . . . 1540 mm
Seat height . . . . 830 mm
Wet weight . . . . 235 kg
Max. payload (rider, passenger, luggage, accessories) . . . . 222 kg

Bike spec

Chassis

Frame type	Twin spar aluminium
Rake and trail	
Sprint	24.0°, 90.0 mm
Speed Triple	23.5°, 84.0 mm
Tiger	23.2°, 87.7 mm
Front suspension	
Sprint	43 mm cartridge forks with spring preload adjustment
Speed Triple and Tiger	43 mm upside-down cartridge forks with spring preload, rebound and compression damping adjustment
Rear suspension	
Sprint	Single-sided swingarm, single shock with rising-rate linkage and spring pre-load and rebound damping adjustment
Speed Triple	Single-sided swingarm, single shock with rising-rate linkage and spring pre-load, rebound and compression damping adjustment
Tiger	Twin-sided swingarm, single shock with rising-rate linkage and spring pre-load and rebound damping adjustment
Wheels	
Sprint	5-spoke cast alloy – Front 17 x 3.5, Rear 17 x 5.5
Speed Triple	
2005 to 2007 models	5-spoke cast alloy – Front 17 x 3.5, Rear 17 x 5.5
2008 to 2010 models (up to VIN 461331)	multi-spoke cast alloy – Front 17 x 3.5", Rear 17 x 5.5
2011-on models (from VIN 461332)	multi-spoke cast alloy – Front 17 x 3.5", Rear 17 x 6.0
Tiger	10-spoke cast alloy – Front 17 x 3.5, Rear 17 x 5.5
Tyres*	
Sprint, Speed Triple up to VIN 461331, Tiger	Front – 120/70-17, Rear – 180/55-17
Speed Triple from VIN 461332-on	Front – 120/70-17, Rear – 190/55-17

*Refer to your owners handbook, the tyre information label on the machine, a Triumph dealer or tyre specialist for approved tyre brands

Front brakes	
Sprint	2 x 320 mm discs with 4-piston calipers
Speed Triple and Tiger	2 x 320 mm discs with 4-piston radial calipers
Rear brake	
Speed Triple up to VIN 461331	1 x 220 mm disc with 2-piston sliding caliper
Speed Triple from VIN 461332-on, Sprint and Tiger	1 x 255 mm disc with 2-piston sliding caliper

Engine

Type	Liquid-cooled, 12 valve in-line three cylinder
Capacity (bore x stroke)	1050 cc (79 x 71.4 mm)
Compression ratio	12.0 to 1
Camshafts	DOHC, chain-driven from the right-hand end of the crankshaft
Engine management system	Multipoint sequential fuel injection, digital inductive ignition
Clutch	Wet multi-plate, cable-operated
Gearbox	6-speed constant mesh
Final drive	Chain and sprockets

Model development

Sprint

The Sprint ST was introduced in 1999 as an all-round sports tourer and immediately superseded the previous carburettor-engined Sprint model which had run from 1993 to 1998.

At that time the ST used the 955i engine from the T595 Daytona, de-tuned to ensure better mid-range performance with the loss of a little top-end power. This was achieved by changes to cam lift, valve timing, fuel injection mapping and exhaust design. Also cast pistons and steel liners replaced the forged pistons and coated aluminium liners used on the higher performance models.

The ST's all-new aluminium twin-spar frame had a longer wheelbase than the wrap-around frame of the Daytona and provided better straight-line stability. Suspension was of Showa manufacture with conventional telescopic forks (adjustable for pre-load) at the front and a single shock and linkage at the rear. It shared the single-sided swingarm and brake components used on the Daytona.

A redesigned 955 cc engine was fitted in 2002, together with many other uprated ancillary components and the model continued until 2004.

In 2005 the larger 1050 cc engine, with revised gearbox and gearchange mechanism, was fitted into a new frame providing a shorter wheelbase, along with revised front and rear suspension, underseat exhausts and new instruments.

In 2006 an anti-lock braking system (ABS) became available as an option.

In 2007 a new electronic control module (ECM) was fitted for Euro 3 compliance, improved starting and greater fuel economy. Styling and ergonomics were addressed by fitting a taller screen as standard (previously available as an option), higher handlebars set further back for a more relaxed ride, restyled side panels and re-profiled seat, and panniers fitted as standard.

In 2008 the performance of the headlight was improved, and the footrests were modified.

The ST remained unchanged from 2009 to 2011, and was then replaced by the Sprint GT.

The Sprint GT has a longer wheelbase provided by extending the swingarm, has a side mounted silencer and panniers fitted as standard, and a taller top gear, all of which give it a slight bias towards the touring aspect of a sports/tourer. ABS is fitted as standard and stopping power has been improved by using a new pad compound, and the engine has more power and torque from the new exhaust and a remap of the ECM, but both improvements are offset by the need to shift more weight. To complement the extended rear end a new rear sub-frame, side covers and tail assembly are fitted, all suspended by a new rear shock absorber and linkage.

Speed Triple

Introduced first as the 885-engined 900 Speed Triple in 1994, this model represented Triumph's attempt at creating a machine in the Streetfighter image. Three years later the 885cc engine received fuel injection and a name change to T509.

Although essentially a Daytona T595 without the fairing, the most significant difference between the two models was the Speed Triple's smaller 885 cc engine, de-tuned for more mid-range power. Apart from having a different oil cooler and the option of either one-piece handlebars or clip-ons, in all other respects the Speed Triple used the same components as the Daytona.

The T509's engine was uprated to 955 cc for the 1999 model year and the model was renamed 955i Speed Triple.

A redesigned 955i engine was fitted in 2002, together with all the other uprated ancillary components. An all-black special edition Speed Triple was available in 2004, the final year for the 955-engined Speed Triple.

In 2005 the larger 1050 cc engine, with revised gearbox and gearchange mechanism, was fitted into a new frame, along with upside down forks and radial brakes at the front and revised swingarm and suspension at the rear, stubby underseat exhausts and new instruments.

In 2007 a new electronic control module (ECM) was fitted for Euro 3 compliance, improved starting and greater fuel economy.

In 2008 Brembo calipers and radial master cylinder replaced the Nissin components. New multi-spoke wheels and a redesigned rear sub-frame, seat and seat cowling were fitted, along with new footrests and radiator shrouds.

There were no changes for 2009, although a special edition SE models was available to celebrate the 15th anniversary of the Speed Triple model. Special features of the SE were Phantom black paintwork with red decals (including John Bloor's signature) including red pinstriping on its black wheels, a gel seat, belly pan and flyscreen.

In 2011 a major update sees a new frame and swingarm, new fuel tank, new wheels, modified forks, a new rear shock absorber, new headlights, new silencers, and new bodywork.

In 2012 the Speed Triple R was introduced, the main differences being the use of Brembo monobloc front brake calipers, and Ohlins suspension front and rear, along with forged wheels, a smattering of carbon fibre and different colour handlebars and rear sub-frame.

Tiger

The fuel-injected Tiger introduced for the 1999 model year bore little resemblance to its carburettor-engine predecessor which had been around since 1993 – it was a completely new model which used a re-tuned version of the 885i engine from the T509 Speed Triple. The engine was housed in a steel tube perimeter frame.

Suspension was taken care of by non-adjustable, 43 mm conventional front forks, and a single rear shock which had a remote preload adjuster and rebound damping adjuster. There was no suspension linkage as on the other models, the rear shock connecting directly to the frame and conventional twin-sided swingarm with integral eccentric drive chain adjusters. Brakes were of Nissin manufacture, although two-piston sliding calipers were used at the front rather than the four-piston type fitted to all other models.

The 24 litre fuel tank ensured a good touring range. Rider comfort and protection from the elements was provided by a handlebar fairing with small fly screen, hand guards over the levers, three-position adjustable seat height and a small luggage rack. Instrumentation was from the Sprint ST.

In 2001, an early variant of the redesigned 955i engine was fitted on the Tiger models. This combined the existing design of cylinder head, fuel and exhaust systems, used with the revised crankcases, alternator and starter motor set-up that were to be introduced on the Daytona, Speed Triple and Sprint models the following year.

In 2005 the 955i Tiger's wire-spoked wheels were replaced by 14-spoke cast aluminium wheels designed to take tubeless tyres and the frame dimensions and suspension set-up were altered to enhance the bike's off-road performance. A new design of swingarm was fitted with conventional chain adjusters.

The 2007 model was all new, featuring the larger 1050 cc engine that has been in the Sprint ST and Speed Triple since 2005, with its revised gearbox and gearchange mechanism, fitted into a new frame, along with upside-down forks and radial brakes at the front and revised swingarm and suspension at the rear, underseat exhausts, new fairing, headlights and instruments. Rider comfort and all-round ability are strong features of the bike.

The bike remained unchanged for 2008 and 2009, although a special SE edition was available in 2009 with ABS and panniers colour-coded in matt graphite grey and black to match the tank and hand guards.

In 2010 the Tiger SE was introduced, and is the same as the standard model but comes with panniers and ABS fitted as standard.

In 2013 the Tiger Sport was introduced, the main differences being the use of the single sided swingarm taken from the 2011 Speed Triple, a new exhaust system, new handlebar switches, revised suspension internals, a new 4-bulb headlight and different bodywork.

Chapter 1
Routine maintenance and Servicing

Contents

	Section number
Air filter	18
Battery	28
Battery removal, charging and installation	see Chapter 8
Brake fluid change	25
Brake fluid level check	see Pre-ride checks
Brake pad wear check	9
Brake system checks	10
Clutch check	13
Coolant change	24
Coolant level check	see Pre-ride checks
Cooling system checks	6
Drive chain and sprockets wear and stretch check	2
Drive chain check, adjustment, cleaning and lubrication	1
Drive chain slider check	14
Engine management system check	4
Engine oil and filter change	3
Engine oil level check	see Pre-ride checks
Engine wear assessment	see Chapter 2

	Section number
Front fork oil change	26
Fuel system checks	7
Headlight aim	see Chapter 8
Idle speed adjustment	16
Nuts and bolts tightness check	11
Rear wheel bearing lubrication – Sprint and Speed Triple	22
Secondary air injection system (SAIS) check	19
Spark plugs	15
Stand(s) and safety interlock circuit	27
Stand, lever pivots and cable lubrication	23
Steering head bearings	17
Suspension checks	8
Throttle body synchronisation	16
Throttle cable check	5
Tyre pressures and tread depth	see Pre-ride checks
Valve clearance check	20
Wheel bearing check	21
Wheels and tyres check	12

Degrees of difficulty

Easy, suitable for novice with little experience	**Fairly easy,** suitable for beginner with some experience	**Fairly difficult,** suitable for competent DIY mechanic	**Difficult,** suitable for experienced DIY mechanic	**Very difficult,** suitable for expert DIY or professional

Specifications

Engine
Spark plugs

  Type
    Sprint ST 2010-on, Sprint GT . . . . NGK CR8EK
    Speed Triple models from VIN 461332 . . . . NGK CR8EK
    Tiger SE and Tiger Sport . . . . NGK CR8EK
    All earlier models . . . . NGK CR9EK
  Electrode gap . . . . 0.7 mm

Engine idle speed
  Sprint ST and Speed Triple. . . . . 1200 rpm
  Tiger and Sprint GT . . . . 1170 rpm

Cylinder identification . . . . numbered 1 to 3 from left to right

Valve clearances (COLD engine)
  Intake valves. . . . . 0.10 to 0.20 mm
  Exhaust valves . . . . 0.20 to 0.30 mm

Specifications

Cycle parts
Brake pad minimum thickness	1.5 mm
Drive chain slack (on sidestand)	
Sprint ST 2005 to 2009	35 to 40 mm
Sprint ST 2010-on	25 to 35 mm
Sprint GT	26 to 38 mm
Speed Triple up to VIN461331	35 to 40 mm
Speed Triple from VIN 461332	21 to 30 mm
Tiger	35 to 40 mm
Tiger SE	32 to 42 mm
Tiger Sport	28 to 38 mm
Chain stretch limit (see Section 2)	
Sprint and Speed Triple	321 mm
Tiger	320 mm
Tiger SE and Tiger Sport	319 mm
Throttle opening cable freeplay (at twistgrip flange)	2 to 3 mm
Throttle closing cable freeplay (deflection)	2 to 3 mm
Clutch cable freeplay (at lever stock)	2 to 3 mm
Tyre pressures (cold)	see Pre-ride checks

Lubricants and fluids
Engine oil type	Semi or fully synthetic motorcycle engine oil, SAE 10W/40 or 15W/50, API grade SH or higher with JASO MA – Triumph recommend Mobil 1 Racing 4T oil
Engine oil capacity	
Tiger Sport	
Dry engine, new filter	3.6 litres
Wet fill with new filter	3.3 litres
Wet fill without new filter	3.1 litres
All other models	
Dry engine, new filter	3.5 litres
Wet fill with new filter	3.2 litres
Wet fill without new filter	3.0 litres
Coolant type	50% distilled water, 50% corrosion inhibited ethylene glycol anti-freeze, or pre-mix coolant
Coolant capacity	
Sprint, and Speed Triple up to VIN 461331	2.8 litres
Speed Triple models VIN 461332	2.4 litres
Tiger	2.3 litres
Brake fluid	DOT 4
Drive chain	Chain lubricant suitable for O-ring chains – Triumph recommend Mobil Chain Spray or Mobilube HD 80
Steering head bearings	Mobil Grease HP 222 or Lithium-based multi-purpose grease
Swingarm pivot and bearings, suspension linkage bearings	Mobil Grease HP 222 or Lithium-based multi-purpose grease
Wheel bearings and seal lips	Mobil Grease HP 222 or Lithium-based multi-purpose grease
Gearchange lever/clutch lever/front brake lever/rear brake pedal/sidestand pivots	Mobil Grease HP 222 or Lithium-based multi-purpose grease
Cables	Aerosol cable lubricant
Throttle grip	Multi-purpose grease or dry film lubricant

Torque wrench settings
Drive chain adjuster clamp bolt – Sprint and Speed Triple	55 Nm
Fork clamp bolts (top yoke)	20 Nm
Fuel pump mounting plate bolts	9 Nm
Handlebar clamp bolts – Sprint	26 Nm
Oil drain plug	25 Nm
Oil filter	10 Nm
Rear axle nut – Tiger	110 Nm
Steering head bearing adjuster nut	
Initial (pre-load) setting	40 Nm
Final setting	15 Nm
Steering head bearing adjuster locknut	40 Nm
Steering stem nut	
Sprint	65 Nm
Speed Triple and Tiger	90 Nm
Secondary air injection reed valve cover bolts	9 Nm
Cooling system cylinder drain plug	
Speed Triple models from VIN 461332-on, Tiger SE, Tiger Sport	8 Nm
All other models	13 Nm

Maintenance schedule

Note: *The Pre-ride checks outlined in the owner's manual, and described in detail at the front of this manual, covers those items which should be inspected on a daily basis. Always perform the pre-ride inspection at every maintenance interval (in addition to the procedures listed). The intervals listed below are the intervals recommended by the manufacturer.*

Pre-ride
- [ ] See *Pre-ride checks* at the beginning of this manual.

After the initial 500 miles (800 km)
Note: *This check is usually performed by a Triumph dealer after the first 500 miles (800 km) from new. Thereafter, maintenance is carried out according to the following intervals of the schedule.*

Every 200 miles (300 km)
- [ ] Check, adjust, clean and lubricate the drive chain (Section 1)

Every 500 miles (800 km)
- [ ] Check the drive chain for wear and stretch and the sprockets for wear (Section 2)

Every 6000 miles (10,000 km) or 12 months (whichever comes sooner)
- [ ] Change the engine oil and filter and check the oil cooler (Section 3)
- [ ] Check the engine management system (Section 4)
- [ ] Check and adjust the throttle cable (Section 5)
- [ ] Check the cooling system (Section 6)
- [ ] Check the fuel system (Section 7)
- [ ] Check the suspension (Section 8)
- [ ] Check the brake pads (Section 9)
- [ ] Check the brake system and brake light switch operation (Section 10)
- [ ] Check the tightness of all nuts, bolts and fasteners (Section 11)
- [ ] Check the condition of the wheels and tyres (Section 12)
- [ ] Check the clutch (Section 13)
- [ ] Check the drive chain slider (Section 14)
- [ ] Check the spark plugs (Section 15)
- [ ] Check/adjust the throttle body synchronisation (Section 16)
- [ ] Check and adjust the steering head bearings (Section 17)

Every 12,000 miles (20,000 km) or two years (whichever comes sooner)
Carry out all the items under the 6000 mile (10,000 km) check, plus the following
- [ ] Renew the air filter element (Section 18)
- [ ] Check the secondary air injection system (Section 19)
- [ ] Check and adjust the valve clearances (Section 20)
- [ ] Lubricate the steering head bearings (Section 17)
- [ ] Lubricate the swingarm and suspension linkage bearings (Section 8)
- [ ] Check the wheel bearings (Section 21)
- [ ] Lubricate the rear wheel bearings – Sprint ST and Speed Triple (Section 22)
- [ ] Lubricate the clutch and brake levers, gearchange lever linkage, brake pedal pivot and sidestand pivots and the throttle and clutch cables (Section 23)
- [ ] Change the coolant (Section 24)
- [ ] Fit new spark plugs (Section 15)

Every two years
- [ ] Change the brake fluid (Section 25)

Every 24,000 miles (40,000 km) or four years (whichever comes sooner)
Carry out all the items under the 12,000 mile (20,000 km) check, plus the following
- [ ] Change the front fork oil (Section 26)
- [ ] Fit new EVAP system hoses – California models only (see Chapter 4)

Non-scheduled maintenance
- [ ] Renew the fuel system hoses (Section 7)
- [ ] Renew the brake master cylinder and caliper seals (see Section 10)
- [ ] Renew the brake hoses (Section 10)
- [ ] Check the stand(s) (Section 27)
- [ ] Check the battery (Section 28)
- [ ] Check and adjust the headlight aim (Chapter 8)
- [ ] Check the cylinder compression and engine oil pressure (Chapter 2, Section 3)

1•4 Routine maintenance and Servicing

Component locations on left side Sprint ST

1. Steering head bearing adjuster
2. Air filter element
3. Drive chain adjuster and lockbolt
4. Drive chain slider
5. Engine oil drain bolt
6. Coolant hose, disconnection point for coolant drain
7. Coolant drain plug in cylinder jacket
8. Fork oil seals
9. Radiator pressure cap
10. Coolant reservoir
11. Upper clutch adjuster

Component locations on right side Sprint ST

1. Battery
2. Rear brake fluid reservoir
3. Clutch cable adjuster at lower end
4. SAIS solenoid valve
5. Front brake fluid reservoir
6. Throttle opening cable adjuster
7. Coolant bleed bolt screw
8. Fork oil seal
9. Oil cooler
10. Engine oil filter
11. Engine oil filler cap/dipstick

Routine maintenance and Servicing

Component locations on left side Sprint GT

1. Coolant reservoir
2. Upper clutch adjuster
3. Steering head bearing adjuster
4. Air filter element
5. Drive chain adjuster and lockbolt
6. Drive chain slider
7. Engine oil drain bolt
8. Coolant hose, disconnection point for coolant drain
9. Coolant drain plug in cylinder jacket
10. Radiator pressure cap
11. Fork oil seals

Component locations on right side Sprint GT

1. Rear brake fluid reservoir
2. Battery
3. Clutch cable adjuster at lower end
4. SAIS solenoid valve
5. Front brake fluid reservoir
6. Throttle opening cable adjuster
7. Fork oil seal
8. Coolant bleed bolt screw
9. Oil cooler
10. Engine oil filter
11. Engine oil filler cap/dipstick

1•6 Routine maintenance and Servicing

Component locations on left side 2005 to 2010 Speed Triple

1. Clutch cable upper adjuster
2. SAIS solenoid valve
3. Air filter element
4. Coolant reservoir
5. Battery
6. Drive chain adjuster and lockbolt
7. Drive chain slider
8. Engine oil drain bolt
9. Coolant hose disconnection point for coolant drain
10. Coolant drain plug in cylinder jacket
11. Fork oil seal
12. Radiator pressure cap

Component locations on right side 2005 to 2010 Speed Triple

1. Rear brake fluid reservoir
2. Clutch cable adjuster at lower end
3. Steering head bearing adjuster
4. Front brake fluid reservoir
5. Throttle opening cable adjuster
6. Coolant bleed bolt
7. Fork oil seal
8. Oil cooler
9. Engine oil filter
10. Engine oil filler cap/dipstick
11. Rear brake light switch

Routine maintenance and Servicing

Component locations on left side 2011-on Speed Triple

1 Clutch cable upper adjuster
2 Air filter element
3 SAIS solenoid valve
4 Coolant reservoir
5 Battery
6 Drive chain adjuster and lockbolt
7 Drive chain slider
8 Engine oil drain bolt
9 Coolant hose disconnection point for coolant drain
10 Coolant drain plug in cylinder jacket
11 Radiator pressure cap
12 Fork oil seal

Component locations on right side 2011-on Speed Triple

1 Rear brake fluid reservoir
2 Clutch cable adjuster at lower end
3 Steering head bearing adjuster
4 Front brake fluid reservoir
5 Throttle opening cable adjuster
6 Fork oil seal
7 Coolant bleed bolt
8 Oil cooler
9 Engine oil filter
10 Engine oil filler cap/ dipstick

1•8 Routine maintenance and Servicing

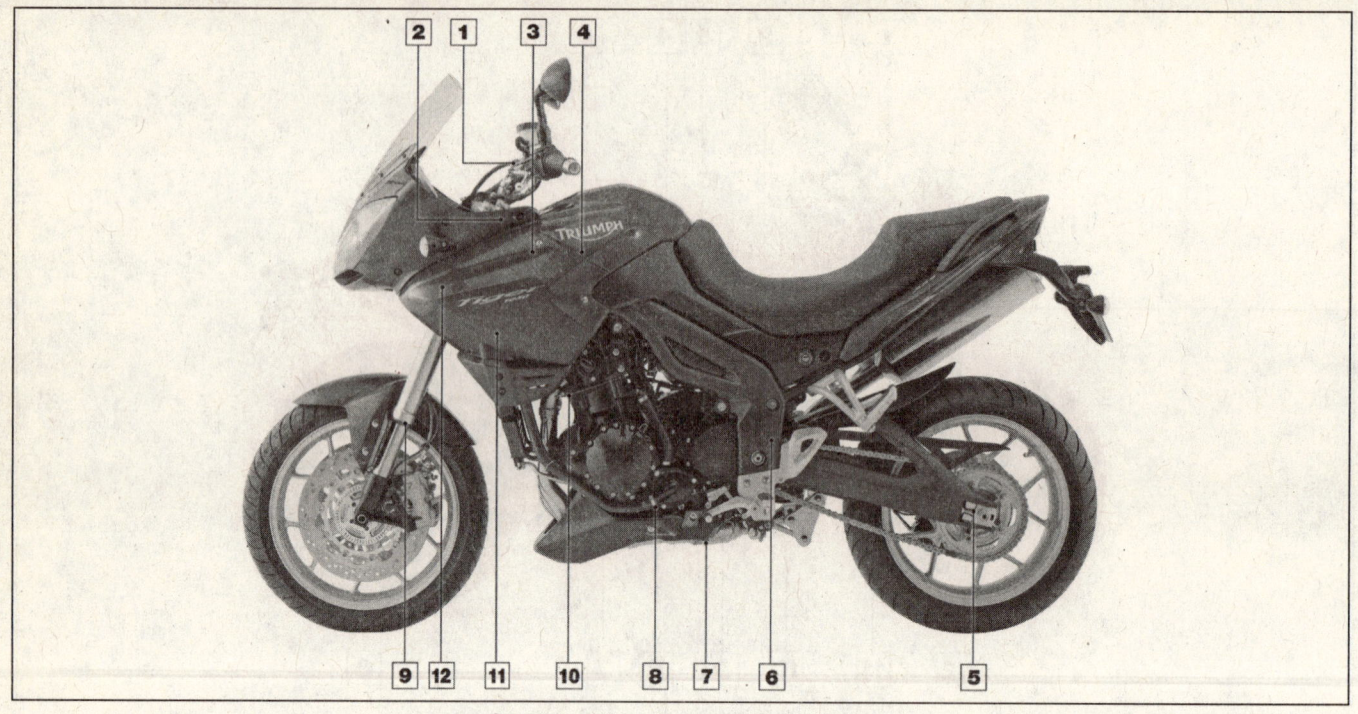

Component locations on left side Tiger

1. Clutch cable adjuster at upper end
2. Steering head bearing adjuster
3. SAIS solenoid valve
4. Air filter element
5. Drive chain adjuster
6. Drive chain slider
7. Engine oil drain bolt
8. Coolant hose disconnection point for coolant drain
9. Fork oil seal
10. Coolant drain plug in cylinder jacket
11. Radiator pressure cap
12. Coolant reservoir

Component locations on right side Tiger

1. Battery
2. Rear brake fluid reservoir
3. Clutch cable lower adjuster
4. Front brake fluid reservoir
5. Throttle opening cable adjuster
6. Coolant bleed bolt
7. Fork oil seal
8. Oil cooler
9. Engine oil filter
10. Engine oil filler cap/dipstick
11. Drive chain adjuster

Routine maintenance and Servicing 1•9

Component locations on left side Tiger Sport

1. Steering head bearing adjuster
2. Clutch cable adjuster at upper end
3. SAIS solenoid valve
4. Air filter element
5. Drive chain adjuster and lockbolt
6. Drive chain slider
7. Engine oil drain bolt
8. Coolant hose disconnection point for coolant drain
9. Coolant drain plug in cylinder jacket
10. Radiator pressure cap
11. Coolant reservoir
12. Fork oil seal

Component locations on right side Tiger Sport

1. Battery
2. Rear brake fluid reservoir
3. Clutch cable lower adjuster
4. Front brake fluid reservoir
5. Throttle opening cable adjuster
6. Fork oil seal
7. Coolant bleed bolt
8. Oil cooler
9. Engine oil filter
10. Engine oil filler cap/dipstick

1•10 Routine maintenance and Servicing

Introduction

1 This Chapter is designed to help the home mechanic maintain his/her motorcycle for safety, economy, long life and peak performance.

2 Deciding where to start or plug into the routine maintenance schedule depends on several factors. If the warranty period on your motorcycle has just expired, and if it has been maintained according to the warranty standards, you may want to pick up routine maintenance as it coincides with the next mileage or calendar interval. If you have owned the machine for some time but have never performed any maintenance on it, then you may want to start at the beginning and include all frequent procedures to ensure that nothing important is overlooked. If you have just had a major engine overhaul, then you should start the engine maintenance routines from the beginning. If you have a used machine and have no knowledge of its history or maintenance record, you should combine all the checks into one large initial service and then settle into the maintenance schedule prescribed.

3 Before beginning any maintenance or repair, the machine should be cleaned thoroughly, especially around the oil filter, valve cover, side panels, etc. Cleaning will help ensure that dirt does not contaminate the engine and will allow you to detect wear and damage that could otherwise easily go unnoticed.

4 Many of the bolts used in the building of the engine are of the Torx type. Unless you are already equipped with a good range of Torx bits, you are advised to obtain a set. Make sure you get bits that can be used in conjunction with a socket set so that a torque wrench can be applied – a Torx key set will not be adequate on its own, though will be useful in addition to the bits.

5 Certain maintenance information is sometimes printed on decals attached to the motorcycle. If any information on the decals differs from that included here, use the information on the decal.

6 Note that in many cases, Triumph use the machine's VIN number as a means of identification rather than the year of manufacture. Always check the VIN number against the details given in this manual to ensure you follow the correct procedure.

Maintenance procedures

1 Drive chain check, adjustment and lubrication

Check

1 As the chain stretches with wear, adjustment will periodically be necessary. A neglected drive chain won't last long and can quickly damage the sprockets. Routine chain adjustment and lubrication isn't difficult and will ensure maximum chain and sprocket life.

2 To check the chain the bike should be on the sidestand with no extra weight on it. Make sure the transmission is in neutral.

3 Push up on the bottom run of the chain and measure the slack midway between the two sprockets **(see illustration)**, then compare your measurement to that listed in this Chapter's Specifications. Since the chain will rarely wear evenly, resulting in a tight spot, move the bike so that another section of chain can be checked – do this several times to check the entire length of chain. Any adjustment should be based upon the measurement taken at the tightest point.

4 In some cases where lubrication has been neglected, corrosion and galling may cause the links to bind and kink, which effectively shortens the chain's length **(see illustration)**. Any such links should be thoroughly cleaned and worked free. If the chain is tight between the sprockets, rusty or kinked, it's time to replace it with a new one. If you find a tight area, clean off the oil and dirt, mark it with felt pen or paint, and repeat the measurement after the bike has been ridden. If the chain's still tight in the same area, it may be damaged or worn. Because a tight or kinked chain can damage the transmission output shaft bearing, it's a good idea to renew it (see Chapter 6).

Adjustment

5 Make sure the transmission is in neutral. Position the bike so the tightest point of the chain is at the centre of its bottom run.

Sprint, Speed Triple and Tiger Sport

6 Slacken the adjuster clamp bolt **(see illustration)**.

7 Locate the C-spanner supplied in the bike's toolkit, or a suitable alternative, into the notches in the eccentric adjuster in the hub and turn it until the amount of freeplay specified at the beginning of the Chapter is obtained at the centre of the bottom run of the chain **(see illustration)**. If you are tightening

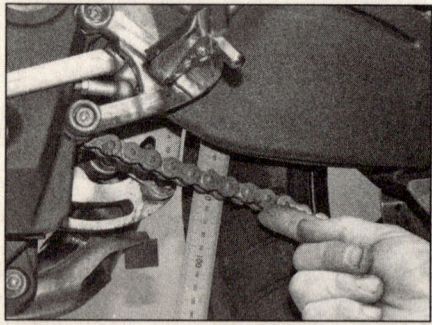

1.3 Push up on the chain and measure the slack

1.4 Neglect has caused the links in this chain to kink

1.6 Chain adjuster clamp bolt (arrowed)

1.7a This adjustment tool is supplied in the bike's toolkit, and locates into the notches in the adjuster

Routine maintenance and Servicing

1.7b Turn the adjuster anti-clockwise to tighten the chain

1.9 Slacken the rear axle nut (arrowed)

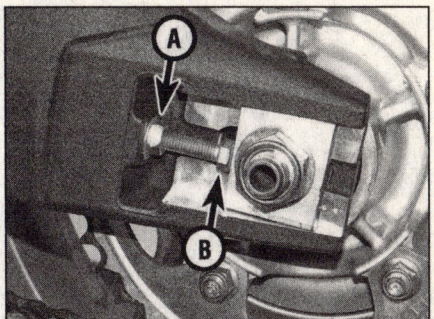

1.10a Slacken the locknut (A) and turn the adjuster (B) as required

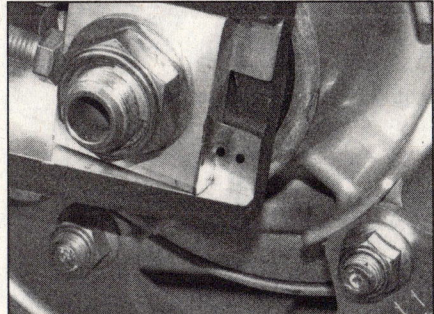

1.10b Check the relative position of the back edge of each adjustment marker with the marks on the swingarm

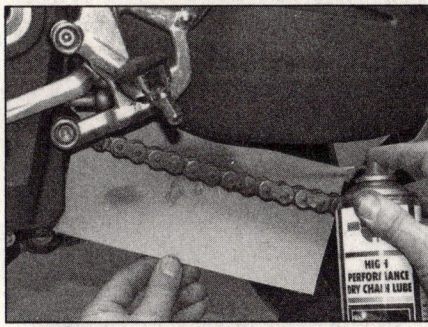

1.12 Tighten the axle nut to the specified torque setting

the chain, locate the tool on the underside of the adjuster and turn it anti-clockwise **(see illustration)**. If you are slackening the chain, locate the tool on the top of the adjuster and turn it clockwise.

8 When the correct amount of freeplay is obtained, tighten the adjuster clamp bolt to the torque setting specified at the beginning of the Chapter **(see illustration 1.6)**. Rotate the rear wheel and recheck the adjustment.

Tiger

9 Slacken the axle nut **(see illustration)**.
10 Slacken the adjuster locknut on each side of the swingarm, then turn the adjusters evenly until the amount of freeplay specified at the beginning of the Chapter is obtained at the centre of the bottom run of the chain **(see illustration)**. Following chain adjustment,

check that the back edge of each chain adjustment marker is in the same position in relation to the marks on the swingarm **(see illustration)**. It is important each adjuster aligns with the same mark; if not, the rear wheel will be out of alignment with the front. Also check that there is no clearance between the head of each adjuster and the front of each adjustment marker – push or kick the wheel forwards to eliminate any freeplay.

 **Refer to Chapter 6 for information on checking wheel alignment.**

11 If there is a discrepancy in the chain adjuster positions, adjust one of them so that its position is exactly the same as the other.

Check the chain freeplay as described above and readjust if necessary.
12 Tighten the axle nut to the torque setting specified at the beginning of the Chapter, then tighten the adjuster locknuts **(see illustration)**. Recheck the adjustment.

Cleaning and lubrication

13 If required, wash the chain in paraffin (kerosene), then wipe it off and allow it to dry, using compressed air if available **(see illustration)**. If the chain is excessively dirty remove it and soak it in a suitable container filled with paraffin (see Chapter 5).
Caution: Don't use petrol (gasoline), solvent or other cleaning fluids which might damage the internal sealing properties of the chain. Don't use high-pressure water. The entire process shouldn't take longer than ten minutes – if it does, the O-rings in the chain rollers could be damaged.
14 The best time to lubricate the chain is after the motorcycle has been ridden. When the chain is warm, the lubricant will penetrate the joints between the side plates better than when cold. **Note:** *Use chain lube which is marked as being suitable for O-ring chains; other types may contain solvents that could damage the O-rings.* Apply the lubricant to the area where the side plates overlap – not the middle of the rollers **(see illustration)**. **Note:** *Triumph recommend that the bike should not be ridden for 8 hours after applying lubricant to allow it to penetrate between the chain components so it's a good idea to do this at the end of the day.*

 Apply the lubricant to the top of the lower chain run, so centrifugal force will work it into the chain when the bike is moving. After applying the lubricant, let it soak in for a few minutes, then wipe off any excess.

1.13 Specially shaped chain cleaning brushes are available from good suppliers

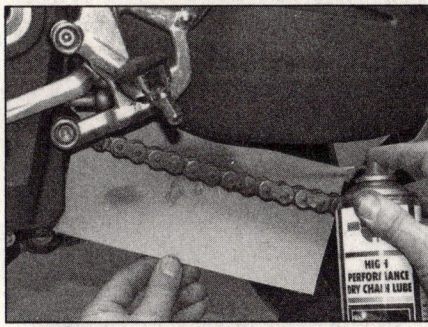

1.14 Apply the lubricant to the overlap between the sideplates

2 Drive chain and sprockets wear and stretch check

1 Make sure the transmission is in neutral. Position the bike so the tightest point of

1•12 Routine maintenance and Servicing

2.2a On Sprint and Speed Triple models up to VIN 461331 undo the screws (arrowed) to release the brake hose cover . . .

2.2b . . . then undo the screw (arrowed) on the outside . . .

2.2c . . . and the screws (arrowed) on the inside and remove the chainguard

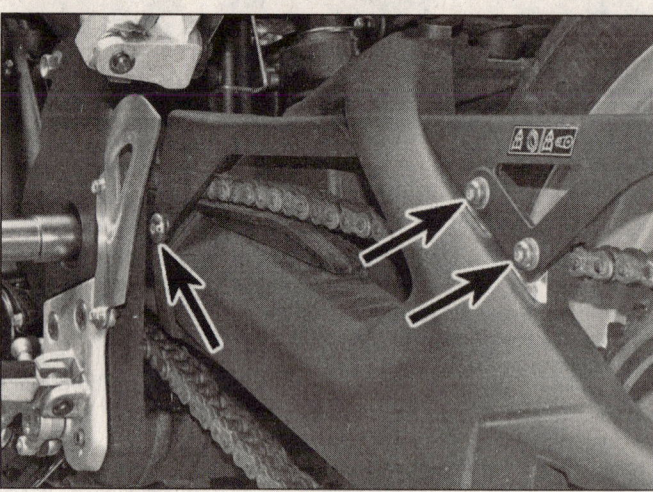

2.2d On Tiger models unscrew the bolts (arrowed) and remove the chainguard

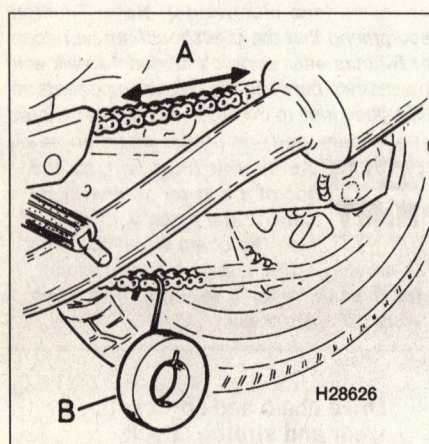

2.4 Check the amount of stretch using a weight (10 to 20 kg) and by measuring as shown

A 21 pin length   B Weight

the chain is at the centre of its bottom run. Support the bike on its sidestand.

2 Remove the chainguard **(see illustrations)**.
3 Check the entire length of the chain for damaged rollers, loose links and pins, and missing O-rings. Fit a new chain if damage is found (see Chapter 6). **Note:** *Never fit a new*

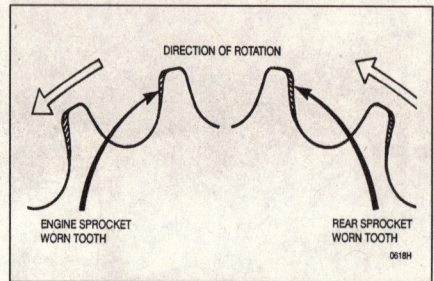

2.5 Check the sprockets in the areas indicated to see if they are worn excessively

chain onto old sprockets, and never use the old chain if you fit new sprockets – replace the chain and sprockets as a set.
4 To check the amount of chain wear (stretch), obtain a 10 to 20 kg (20 to 40 lb) weight and hang it from the middle of the bottom run of the chain **(see illustration)**. Measure along the top run the length of 20 links (from the centre of the 1st pin to the centre of the 21st pin) and compare the result with the service limit specified at the beginning of the Chapter. Rotate the wheel so that several sections of the chain are measured, then calculate the average. If the chain exceeds the service limit it must be replaced with a new one (see Chapter 6).
5 Remove the front sprocket cover (see Chapter 6). Check the teeth on the front and rear sprockets for wear **(see illustration)**.
6 Refer to Section 14 and inspect the drive chain slider on the swingarm for wear (see Section 14).

Routine maintenance and Servicing

3.3 Remove the oil filler cap from the clutch cover

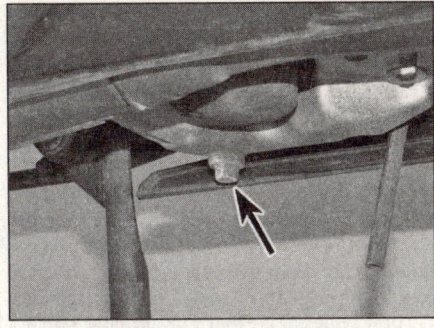

3.4a Unscrew the oil drain plug (arrowed) . . .

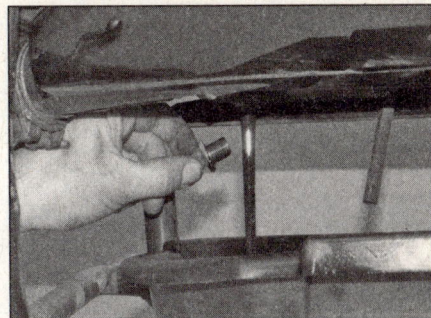

3.4b . . . and allow the oil to drain

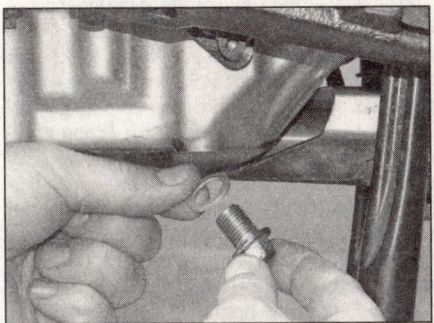

3.5 Fit the drain plug using a new sealing washer and tighten it to the specified torque

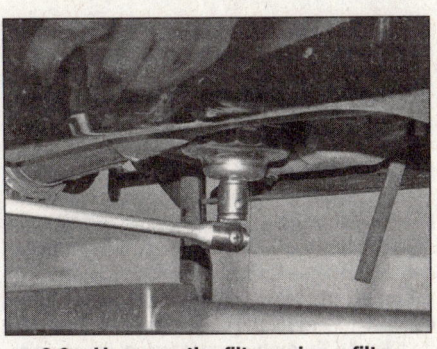

3.6a Unscrew the filter using a filter removal socket . . .

3 Engine oil and filter change

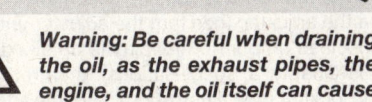

⚠ **Warning: Be careful when draining the oil, as the exhaust pipes, the engine, and the oil itself can cause severe burns.**

1 Consistent routine oil and filter changes are the single most important maintenance procedure you can perform on a motorcycle. The oil not only lubricates the internal parts of the engine, transmission and clutch, but it also acts as a coolant, a cleaner, a sealant, and a protector. Because of these demands, the oil takes a terrific amount of abuse and should be changed often with new oil of the recommended grade and type. Saving a little money on the difference in cost between a good oil and a cheap oil won't pay off if the engine is damaged. The oil filter should be changed with every oil change.

2 Before changing the oil, warm up the engine so the oil will drain easily. Support the motorcycle upright on level ground using an auxiliary stand or the centrestand (Sprint only), making sure it is secure.

3 Position a clean drain tray below the engine. Unscrew the oil filler cap from the clutch cover to vent it and to act as a reminder that there is no oil in the engine **(see illustration)**.

4 Unscrew the oil drain plug from the underside of the engine and allow the oil to flow into the drain tray **(see illustrations)**. Note that the oil drain plug position varies between models; refer to the Component Location views at the front of this Chapter. Discard the sealing washer on the drain plug as a new one must be fitted.

5 When the oil has completely drained, fit the plug into the crankcase using a new sealing washer and tighten it to the torque setting specified at the beginning of the Chapter **(see illustrations)**. Avoid overtightening, as you will damage the sump.

6 Now place the drain tray below the oil filter, which is also under the engine. Unscrew the filter using a filter removal socket or a strap wrench and tip any residual oil into the drain tray **(see illustrations)**. Triumph provides a suitable oil filter tool (Part No. T3880312 for Speed Triple and Tiger models or T3880313 for Sprint models).

7 Pre-fill the new filter with new engine oil and smear some onto the rubber seal, then screw the filter onto the engine until the seal just seats **(see illustrations)**. If a filter socket is available, tighten the filter to the torque setting specified at the beginning of the Chapter. Otherwise, tighten the filter as tight as possible by hand, or by the number of turns specified on the filter or its packaging. **Note:** *Do not use a strap or chain type removing tool to tighten the filter as you will damage the filter body.*

8 Refill the engine to the correct level using the recommended type and amount of oil (see Specifications and *Pre-ride checks*). Install the filler cap, using a new O-ring if the old one is damaged, deformed or deteriorated

3.6b . . . and drain it into the tray

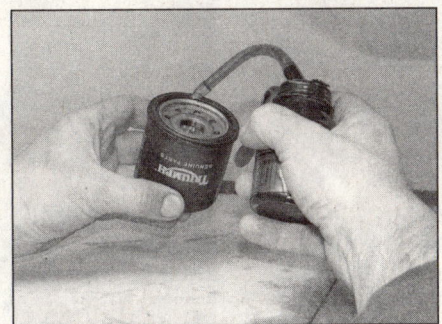

3.7a Smear some clean oil onto the seal . . .

3.7b . . . then thread the filter into the engine and tighten it as described

1•14 Routine maintenance and Servicing

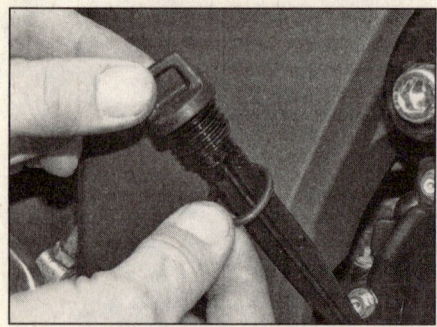

3.8 Check the condition of the cap O-ring and replace with a new one if necessary

Note: It is illegal and anti-social to dump oil down the drain. To find the location of your local oil recycling bank in the UK, call 08708 506 506 or visit www.oilbankline.org.uk

(see illustration). Start the engine and let it run for two or three minutes. Stop the engine, wait a few minutes, then check the oil level. If necessary, add more oil to bring the level up to the top of the hatched area on the dipstick. Check that there are no leaks around the drain plug. Similarly check the filter and tighten it some more if there are leaks.

9 Refer to Chapter 2, Section 6, and check the oil cooler and its hoses for damage and leaks. Renew any components as necessary – if detached, always use new O-rings on the hose unions.

10 The old oil drained from the engine cannot be re-used and should be disposed of properly. Check with your local refuse disposal company, disposal facility or environmental agency to see whether they will accept the used oil for recycling. Don't pour used oil into drains or onto the ground. Remember to drain all the old oil from the filter (you can punch a hole in the filter to ensure it drains fully) into the drain pan. Note that the old filter should be taken to the oil disposal facility rather than disposed of with the household rubbish.

 **HAYNES HINT** *Check the old oil carefully – if it is very metallic coloured, then the engine is experiencing wear from break-in (new engine) or from insufficient lubrication. If there are flakes or chips of metal in the oil, then something is drastically wrong internally and the engine will have to be disassembled for inspection and repair. If there are pieces of fibre-like material in the oil, the clutch is experiencing excessive wear and should be checked.*

4 Engine management system check

Note: The idle speed is controlled by the idle air control valve, which in turn is controlled by the electronic control module (ECM). Idle speed cannot be manually adjusted – it can only be done using the diagnostic tool.

1 The engine management system should be checked for any stored diagnostic fault codes. To do this, the Triumph diagnostic tool is essential. Take your machine to a dealer and have them check the system – it should not take them long. Note that this task is not an option for the DIY mechanic, not only because the diagnostic tool would be prohibitively expensive, but because an authorisation code is required to operate it and these are only available to Triumph dealers.

2 If any problems with the system occur during use, the malfunction indicator light (MIL) in the instrument cluster will illuminate. If this happens, the management system switches itself into 'limp home' mode, so that in theory you should not be left stranded. Depending on the problem, it is possible that you will notice no difference in the running of the motorcycle. In order to diagnose the fault and to turn the MIL off, the diagnostic tool is essential, so again the machine must be taken to a Triumph dealer.

3 Further information on the system, including all tests and checks that can be performed without the Triumph diagnostic tool, is contained in Chapter 4.

5 Throttle cable check

1 Make sure the throttle twistgrip rotates easily from fully closed to fully open with the front wheel turned at various angles. The twistgrip should return automatically from fully open to fully closed when released.

2 If the throttle sticks, this is probably due to a cable fault. Remove the cable (see Chapter 4) and lubricate it (see Section 23). If the inner cable still does not run smoothly in the outer cable, fit a new cable. With the cable removed, check that the twistgrip runs smoothly and freely around the handlebar – dirt and debris combined with a lack of lubrication can cause the action to be stiff. Install the lubricated or new cable, making sure it is correctly routed (see Chapter 4). If this fails to improve the operation of the throttle, the fault could lie in the throttle bodies. Remove the airbox and check the action of the throttle linkage and butterflies (see Chapter 4).

3 With the throttle operating smoothly, check for a small amount of freeplay in the opening cable. This is measured in terms of the amount of twistgrip rotation before the throttle opens. Compare the amount to that listed in this Chapter's Specifications. If it's incorrect, adjust the cables as follows.

4 An adjuster is incorporated at the twistgrip end of the opening cable. Slacken the locknut on the adjuster, then turn the adjuster until the specified amount of freeplay is obtained (see this Chapter's Specifications), then retighten the locknut **(see illustration)**. Turn the adjuster in to increase freeplay and out to reduce it.

5 If the opening cable adjuster has reached its limit of adjustment, reset it so that it is halfway along its adjustment limit, then adjust both cables at the throttle body end as follows. Remove the fuel tank and the airbox (see Chapter 4).

6 Fully slacken the locknut holding the opening (lower) cable in the bracket to free the adjuster nut from its holding tabs **(see illustration)**.

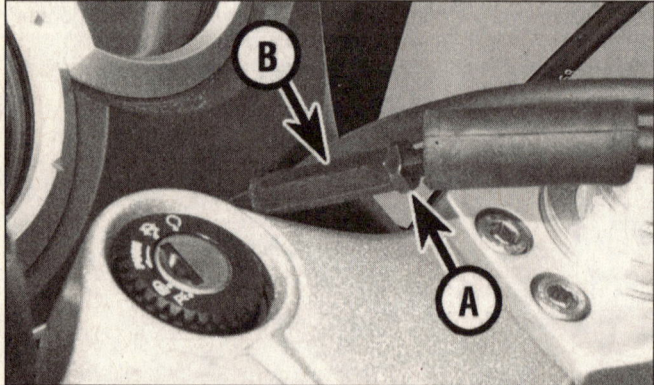

5.4 Pull back the rubber boot to expose the opening throttle cable adjuster locknut (A) and adjuster (B) – Sprint shown

5.6a Throttle opening cable locknut (A) and adjuster nut (B)

Routine maintenance and Servicing

5.6b Throttle closing cable deflection measurement point (arrowed). Locknut (A) and adjuster nut (B)

6.3 Squeeze the hoses to check for cracks, deterioration and hardening

Thread the adjuster nut up the cable to increase freeplay, and down to decrease it, then draw it up against the bracket and check the freeplay, readjusting as required until the specified amount of freeplay is obtained. Tighten the locknut onto the bracket on completion. With the throttle fully closed, ensure that there is the specified amount of freeplay (measured as total deflection of the cable inner wire) in the closing cable and adjust it at the bracket in the same way **(see illustration)**.

7 Further adjustments can now be made at the twistgrip end. If the cables cannot be adjusted as specified, replace them with new ones (see Chapter 4).

8 Check that the throttle twistgrip operates smoothly and snaps shut quickly when released. Install the airbox and fuel tank (see Chapter 4).

⚠ **Warning: Turn the handlebars all the way through their travel with the engine idling. Idle speed should not change. If it does, the cable may be routed incorrectly. Correct this condition before riding the bike.**

6 Cooling system checks

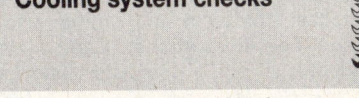

⚠ **Warning: The engine must be cool before beginning this procedure.**

1 Check the coolant level in the reservoir (see *Pre-ride checks*).

2 On Sprint and Tiger models remove both fairing side panels (see Chapter 7).
3 Check the entire cooling system for evidence of leaks. Examine each rubber coolant hose along its entire length. Look for cracks, abrasions and other damage. Squeeze each hose at various points **(see illustration)**. They should feel firm, yet pliable, and return to their original shape when released. If they are dried out or hard, replace them with new ones.
4 Check for evidence of leaks at each cooling system joint. If necessary, tighten the hose clips carefully to prevent future leaks.
5 To prevent leakage of water from the cooling system to the lubrication system and vice versa, two seals are fitted on the water pump shaft. There is a drain hole between the seals in the seal housing section of the pump **(see illustration)**. If either seal fails, the drain allows the coolant or oil to escape and prevents them mixing. The seal on the water pump side is of the mechanical type which bears on the rear face of the impeller. The second seal, which is mounted behind the mechanical seal is of the normal feathered lip type. If on inspection the drain hole shows signs of coolant leakage, remove the pump and replace it with a new one (see Chapter 3) – the seals are not available separately.
6 Check the radiator for leaks and other damage **(see illustration)**. Leaks in the radiator leave tell-tale scale deposits or coolant stains on the outside of the core below the leak. If leaks are noted, remove the radiator (see Chapter 3) and either have it repaired by a professional or replace it with a new one.

Caution: Do not use a liquid leak stopping compound to try to repair leaks.

7 Check the radiator fins for mud, dirt and insects, which may impede the flow of air through the radiator. If the fins are dirty, remove the radiator (see Chapter 3) and clean it using water or low pressure compressed air directed through the fins from the rear face of the radiator. If the fins are bent or distorted, straighten them carefully with a screwdriver. If airflow is restricted by bent or damaged fins over more than 30% of the radiator's surface area, fit a new radiator.
8 On Speed Triple models undo the screw securing the radiator pressure cap.
9 On all models, remove the pressure cap from the filler neck in the radiator as follows: turn the cap anti-clockwise until it reaches a stop – if you hear a hissing sound (indicating there is still pressure in the system), wait until it stops; now press down on the cap and continue turning it until it can be removed **(see illustration)**. Check the condition of the coolant in the system. If it is rust-coloured or if accumulations of scale are visible, drain, flush and refill the system with new coolant (See Section 24). Check the cap seals for cracks and other damage – maintaining a good seal to retain the pressure in the cooling system is essential to the efficient function of the system. If in doubt about the pressure cap's condition, have it tested by a Triumph dealer or replace it with a new one – the expense is minimal. Fit the cap by turning it clockwise until it reaches the first stop, then push down on it and continue turning until it reaches the main stop.
10 Check the antifreeze content of the coolant with an antifreeze hydrometer. Sometimes coolant looks like it's in good condition, but might be too weak to offer adequate protection. If the hydrometer indicates a weak mixture, drain, flush and refill the system (see Section 24).
11 Start the engine and let it reach normal operating temperature, then check for leaks again. As the coolant temperature increases

6.5 Check the drainage hole (arrowed) on the pump (shown removed) for signs of leakage

6.6 Check the radiator fins for damage and leakage

6.9 Remove the pressure cap from the radiator filler neck as described

Routine maintenance and Servicing

beyond normal, the fan should come on automatically and the temperature should begin to drop. If it doesn't, refer to Chapter 3 and check the fan motor, relay and fan circuit carefully, then if the fan still does not work, refer to Chapter 4 and check the engine coolant temperature sensor and the engine management system, which control the fan. Note that if the engine is switched off while the fan is running, the fan should continue to run until the coolant temperature has dropped to a normal level.

12 If the coolant level is consistently low, and no evidence of leaks can be found, have the entire system pressure checked by a Triumph dealer.

7 Fuel system checks

⚠ **Warning:** *Petrol (gasoline) is extremely flammable, so take extra precautions when you work on any part of the fuel system. Don't smoke or allow open flames or bare light bulbs near the work area, and don't work in a garage where a natural gas-type appliance is present. If you spill any fuel on your skin, rinse it off immediately with soap and water. When you perform any kind of work on the fuel system, wear safety glasses and have a fire extinguisher suitable for a Class B type fire (flammable liquids) on hand.*

General checks

1 Remove the fuel tank (see Chapter 4). Check the entire system for signs of leaks, deterioration or damage; in particular check that there are no leaks from the fuel feed hose and its connectors, the fuel rail and injectors, and from the fuel pump assembly gasket on the underside of the fuel tank. Also check the condition of the fuel tank drain and breather hoses and the airbox hoses. Replace any hoses which are cracked or have deteriorated (see below).

2 Refer to Chapter 4 for removal of the fuel rail if fuel leakage is evident.

3 If the tank has been leaking from the fuel pump gasket, tightening the mounting plate bolts may help – remove the tank (see Chapter 4), then rest it upside down on some rag to do this. To ensure the plate is evenly seated, slacken the bolts a little first, then tighten them evenly and a little at a time in a criss-cross pattern to the torque setting specified at the beginning of the Chapter. If leaks persists, remove the pump assembly and replace the seal with a new one (see Chapter 4).

4 Check all throttle body hoses for loose connections, cracks and deterioration, and replace them with new ones if necessary.

5 Check the secondary air injection system hoses (see Section 19).

6 On California models, check the EVAP system hoses for loose connections, cracks and deterioration and replace them with new ones if necessary.

Fuel strainer and filter

7 A fuel filter is incorporated in the fuel pump assembly inside the tank on all models. Additionally on Speed Triple models up to VIN 305059 (Jet black and Neon blue models), VIN 305222 (Roulette green models), or VIN 305251 (Fusion white models) a fuel strainer is also incorporated in the fuel pump assembly. On those Speed triple models cleaning of the strainer is advised after a high mileage has been covered. It is also necessary if fuel starvation is suspected. Remove the fuel pump assembly (see Chapter 4). Clean the gauze strainer to remove all traces of dirt and fuel sediment. If the strainer is dirty, check the condition of the inside of the tank – if there is evidence of rust, drain and clean the tank (see Chapter 4).

8 If fuel starvation occurs and no other fault can be found it is possible the filter is blocked. On those Speed Triple models mentioned in Step 7 the filter is available – refer to Chapter 4 for removal and disassembly of the pump. On all Sprint and Tiger models, and on Speed Triples with a VIN number later than those mentioned it is part of the fuel pump assembly and is not available separately, so a new pump must be fitted.

Hose renewal

9 Remove the fuel tank, and if necessary the airbox, as required for access to the hose(s) being replaced (see Chapter 4). Refer to the procedure in the relevant Section of Chapter 4 and detach the hose at each end, noting how it is secured and its routing. When fitting the new hose make sure it is correctly routed and secured as before.

10 Run the engine and check that there are no leaks before taking the machine out on the road.

8 Suspension checks

1 The suspension components must be maintained in top operating condition to ensure rider safety. Loose, worn or damaged suspension parts decrease the motorcycle's stability and control.

Front suspension

2 While standing alongside the motorcycle, apply the front brake and push on the handlebars to compress the forks several times. See if they move up-and-down smoothly without binding. If binding is felt, the forks should be disassembled and inspected (see Chapter 5).

3 Inspect the fork inner tube for signs of scratches, corrosion and pitting, and oil leakage **(see illustrations)**. Carefully lever the dust seal out of the outer tube using

8.3a On Sprint models check the fork inner tube (arrowed) above the seal for leaks, pitting and corrosion

8.3b On Speed Triple and Tiger models check the fork inner tube (arrowed) below the seal for leaks, pitting and corrosion

Routine maintenance and Servicing

8.5 Check for leakage on the damper rod (arrowed)

8.7a Checking for play in the swingarm bearings

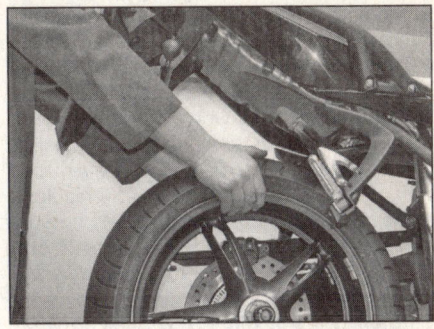

8.7b Checking for play in the suspension linkage bearings

a flat-bladed screwdriver and inspect the area around the fork oil seal. Any scratches, corrosion and pitting in the area of fork travel will cause premature seal failure. If the damage is excessive new tubes should be installed (see Chapter 5). If oil leaks are evident, new oil seals must be fitted (see Chapter 5).

4 Check the tightness of all suspension nuts and bolts to be sure none have worked loose, referring to the torque settings specified at the beginning of Chapter 5.

Rear suspension

5 Inspect the rear shock absorber for fluid leaks at the top of the damper rod (see illustration). If leaks are found, a new shock should be installed (see Chapter 5).

6 With the aid of an assistant to support the bike, compress the rear suspension several times. It should move up and down freely without binding. If any binding is felt, the worn or faulty component must be identified and replaced with a new one. The problem could be due to the shock absorber, the suspension linkage components or the swingarm.

7 Support the motorcycle using an auxiliary stand so that the rear wheel is off the ground. Grab the swingarm and rock it from side to side – there should be no discernible movement at the rear (see illustration). If there's a little movement or a slight clicking can be heard, inspect the tightness of all the rear suspension mounting bolts and nuts, referring to the torque settings specified at the beginning of Chapter 5, and re-check for movement. Next, grasp the top of the rear wheel and pull it upwards – there should be no discernible freeplay before the shock absorber begins to compress (see illustration). Any freeplay felt in either check indicates worn bearings in the suspension linkage or swingarm, or worn shock absorber mountings. The worn components must be renewed (see Chapter 5).

8 To make an accurate assessment of the swingarm bearings, remove the rear wheel (see Chapter 6) and the bolt securing the suspension drop link to the swingarm (see Chapter 5). Grasp the rear of the swingarm with one hand and place your other hand at the junction of the swingarm and the frame. Try to move the rear of the swingarm from side-to-side. Any wear (play) in the bearings should be felt as movement between the swingarm and the frame at the front. If there is any play the swingarm will be felt to move forward and backward at the front (not from side-to-side). Next, move the swingarm up and down through its full travel. It should move freely, without any binding or rough spots. If any play in the swingarm is noted or if the swingarm does not move freely, remove the swingarm and inspect the bearings (see Chapter 5).

9 Check the tightness of all suspension nuts and bolts to be sure none have worked loose, referring to the torque settings specified at the beginning of Chapter 5.

Swingarm and suspension linkage bearing lubrication

10 Over a period of time the grease will harden and dirt will penetrate the bearings.

11 The rear suspension components are not equipped with grease nipples. Remove the swingarm and the suspension linkage as described in Chapter 5 for re-greasing of the bearings.

9 Brake pad wear check

1 Each brake pad has wear indicators that can be viewed without removing the pads from the caliper (see illustrations). Note that on some models it may be necessary to displace the caliper to check pad wear (see Chapter 6). If the pads are dirty, or you are in doubt as

9.1a Front brake pad wear indicator groove (arrowed) – Sprint shown

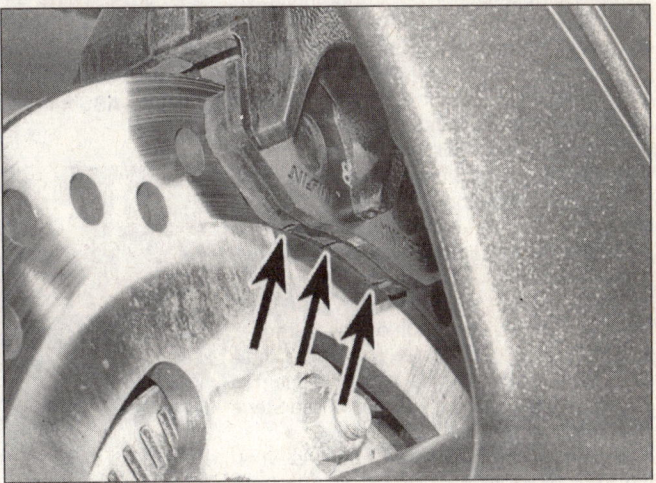

9.1b Rear brake pad wear indicator grooves (arrowed)

1•18 Routine maintenance and Servicing

to the amount of friction material remaining, remove them for inspection (see Chapter 6).

2 The grooves in the brake pad friction material form the wear indicators – when the friction material has worn to the bottom of the grooves (i.e. the grooves are only just or no longer visible), the pads must be replaced with new ones **(see illustration)**. If required, measure the amount of friction material remaining – the minimum is 1.5 mm. **Note:** *Some after-market pads may use different indicators.*

Caution: Do not allow the pads to wear beyond the wear limit indicator or minimum thickness.

3 Always renew brake pads in sets and renew the pads in both front brake calipers at the same time. If the pads appear to be wearing unevenly it is likely that a piston is sticking or has seized – remove the caliper and the pads and check the operation of each piston (see Chapter 6).

10 Brake system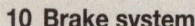

General check

1 A routine general check of the brake system will ensure that any problems are discovered and remedied before the rider's safety is jeopardised.

2 Check the brake lever and pedal for looseness, improper or rough action, excessive play, bends, and other damage. Replace any damaged parts with new ones (see Chapter 5). Clean and lubricate the lever and pedal pivots if their action is stiff or rough (see Section 23).

3 Make sure all brake component fasteners are tight. Check the brake pads for wear (see Section 9) and make sure the fluid level in the reservoirs is correct (see *Pre-ride checks*). Check that there is no sign of fluid leakage at the hose connections and that the hoses between the calipers and master cylinders are not cracked or damaged. On Sprint and Tiger models with ABS remove the fuel tank (see Chapter 4), and check the brake pipes from the calipers to the master cylinders via the pipe joints and the ABS modulator for signs of fluid leakage and for any dents or cracks in the pipes **(see illustrations)**. If the lever or pedal is spongy bleed the brakes (see Chapter 6). The brake fluid should be changed every two years (see Section 25) and the hoses renewed if they deteriorate, or about every four years irrespective of their condition (see Steps 8 and 9). The master cylinder and caliper seals should be renewed if leakage from them is evident or if their action is impaired (see Steps 10 and 11).

4 Make sure the brake light operates when the front brake lever is pulled in. The front brake light switch, mounted on the underside of the lever bracket, is not adjustable. If it fails to operate properly, check it (see Chapter 8).

5 Make sure the brake light is activated just before the rear brake takes effect. On Sprint, Tiger and 2011-on Speed Triple models, the switch is operated hydraulically and is not adjustable. If it fails to operate properly, check it (see Chapter 8). On early Speed Triple models, the switch is operated mechanically by a spring connected to the brake pedal. If it fails to operate properly, first check that the spring is still attached to both the pedal and the switch pullrod. If adjustment is necessary, hold the switch and turn the adjuster nut on the switch body until the brake light is activated when required **(see illustration)**. If the brake light comes on too late, turn the nut clockwise. If the brake light comes on too soon or is permanently on, turn the nut anti-clockwise.

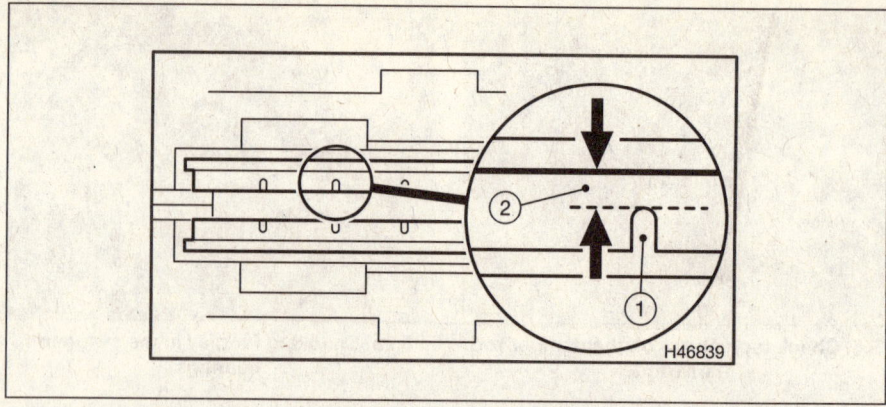

9.2 Brake pad wear indicator groove (1) and minimum thickness (2)

If the switch doesn't operate the brake light, check it (see Chapter 8).

6 The front brake lever has a span adjuster which alters the distance of the lever from the handlebar to suit different hand sizes. On all models except 2011-on Speed Triple models (from VIN 461332) each setting is identified by a number on the adjuster which aligns with the arrow on the lever bracket. Pull the lever away from the handlebar and turn the adjuster ring until the setting which best suits the rider is obtained **(see illustration)**. There are four settings – setting 1 gives the largest span, and setting 4 the smallest. When making adjustment ensure that the pin set in the lever bracket is engaged in its detent in the adjuster. On 2011-on Speed Triple models (from VIN 461332) the adjuster has no marked settings,

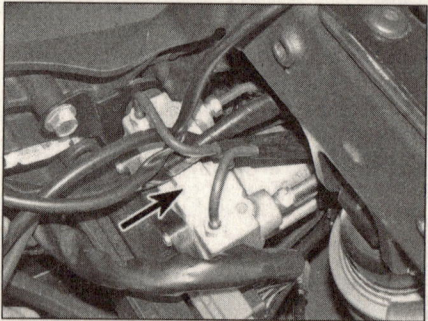

10.3a ABS modulator (arrowed) - Sprint

10.3b ABS modulator (arrowed) - Tiger

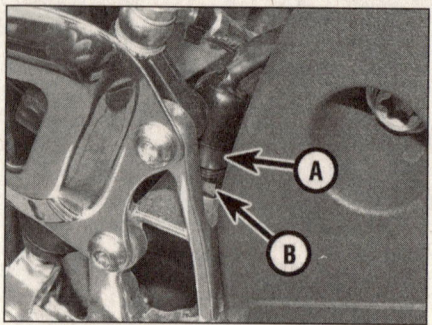

10.5 Hold the brake light switch (A) and turn the adjuster nut (B)

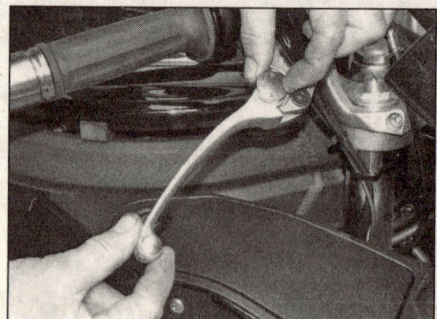

10.6a Adjusting the front brake lever span

Routine maintenance and Servicing 1•19

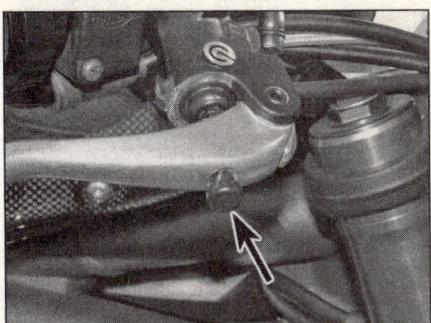

10.6b Span adjuster (arrowed) – Speed Triple from VIN 461332

but each setting is defined by feel as you turn the adjuster **(see illustration)**.
7 On models with ABS, refer to Chapter 6 for information on the system.

Brake hoses

8 The hoses will deteriorate with age and should be replaced with new ones approximately every four years regardless of their apparent condition (see Chapter 6).
9 Always replace the banjo union sealing washers with new ones when fitting new hoses. Refill the system with new brake fluid and bleed the system as described in Chapter 6.

Brake caliper and master cylinder seals

10 Brake system seals will deteriorate with age and lose their effectiveness, leading to sticky operation of the brake master cylinders or the pistons in the brake calipers, or fluid loss. They should be replaced with new ones at the prescribed interval and particularly if fluid leakage or a sticking action is apparent.
11 Replace all the seals in each caliper and master cylinder as a set; master cylinder seals are supplied as a kit along with a new piston and spring (see Chapter 6).

11 Nuts and bolts tightness check

1 Since vibration of the machine tends to loosen fasteners, all nuts, bolts, screws, etc.

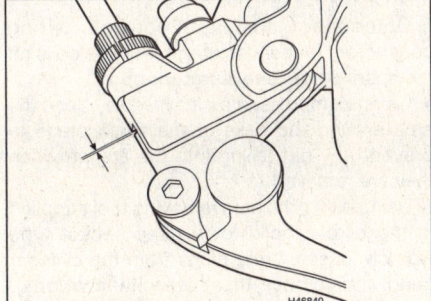

13.3 Clutch cable freeplay is measured at gap between lever stock and bracket

should be periodically checked for proper tightness. If you feel the engine vibrating more than usual, check all the mountings before assuming there are extensive internal problems.
2 Pay particular attention to the following:
Spark plugs
Engine oil drain plug
Gearchange lever, brake and clutch lever, and brake pedal bolts
Footrest and stand bolts
Engine mounting bolts
Shock absorber and suspension linkage bolts and swingarm pivot bolts
Handlebar clamp bolts
Front axle and axle clamp bolts
Front fork clamp bolts (top and bottom yoke)
Rear axle nut
Brake caliper mounting bolts
Brake hose banjo bolts and caliper bleed valves
Brake disc bolts
Exhaust system bolts/nuts
3 If a torque wrench is available, use it along with the torque specifications at the beginning of this and other Chapters.

12 Wheels and tyres check

Tyres

1 Check the tyre condition and tread depth thoroughly – see *Pre-ride checks*.

Wheels

2 The cast wheels are virtually maintenance free, but they should be kept clean and checked periodically for cracks and other damage. Also check the wheel runout and alignment (see Chapter 6).
3 Never attempt to repair damaged cast wheels – they must be replaced with new ones. Check the valve rubber for signs of damage or deterioration and have it renewed by a motorcycle tyre fitting specialist if necessary. Also, make sure the valve stem cap is in place and tight.

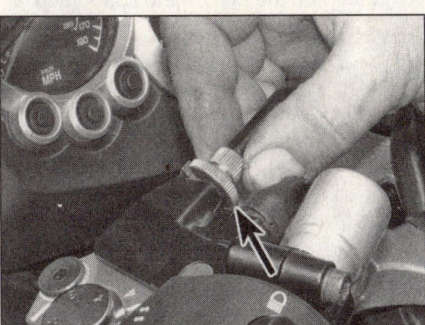

13.4a On Sprint and early Speed Triple models slacken the lockring (arrowed) then turn the adjuster to set the correct freeplay

13 Clutch check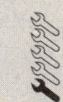

1 Check that the clutch lever operates smoothly and easily.
2 If the lever action is heavy or stiff, remove the cable (see Chapter 2) and lubricate it (see Section 23). If the inner cable still does not run smoothly in the outer cable, replace it with a new one. Install the lubricated or new cable (see Chapter 2). If the action is still stiff, remove the lever and check for damage or distortion, or any other cause, and remedy as necessary. Clean and lubricate the pivot and contact areas (see Section 23). If the lever is good, refer to Chapter 2 and check the release mechanism in the cover and the clutch itself.
3 With the cable operating smoothly, check that it is correctly adjusted. Periodic adjustment is necessary to compensate for wear in the clutch plates and stretch of the cable. Check that the amount of freeplay in the cable is within the specifications listed at the beginning of the Chapter – freeplay is measured in terms of the clearance between the inner end of the lever (stock) and its bracket before the clutch is actuated **(see illustration)**.
4 If adjustment is required, on Sprint and 2005 to 2007 Speed Triple models slacken the adjuster lockring **(see illustration)**. On all models turn the adjuster in or out until the required amount of freeplay is obtained **(see illustration)**. To increase freeplay, turn the adjuster clockwise (into the lever bracket). To reduce freeplay, turn the adjuster anti-clockwise (out of the lever bracket). On Sprint and Speed Triple models tighten the lockring securely.
5 If all the adjustment has been taken up at the lever, reset the adjuster to give the maximum amount of freeplay by screwing it fully into the bracket (make sure the cable release slot in the adjuster does not align with that in the bracket – turn it out some if necessary), then set freeplay to between 2 to 3 mm using the adjuster nuts on each end of the threaded section in the cable bracket on the right-hand

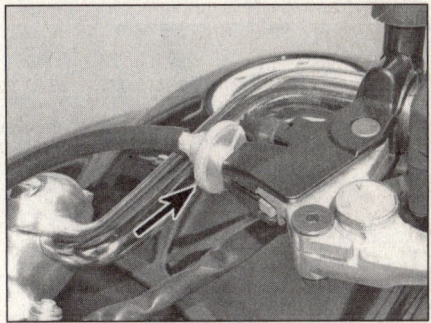

13.4b On Tiger and later Speed Triple models just turn the adjuster (arrowed)

1•20 Routine maintenance and Servicing

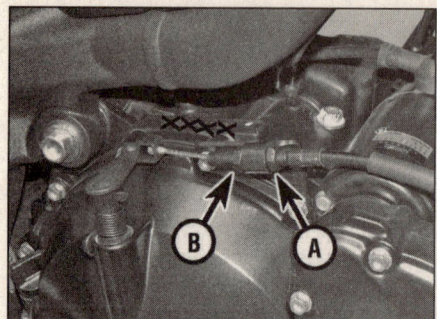

13.5 Front nut (A), rear nut (B)

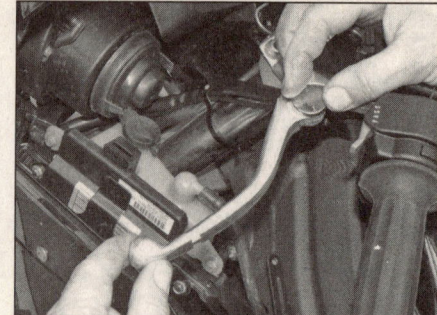

13.6 Adjusting the clutch lever span

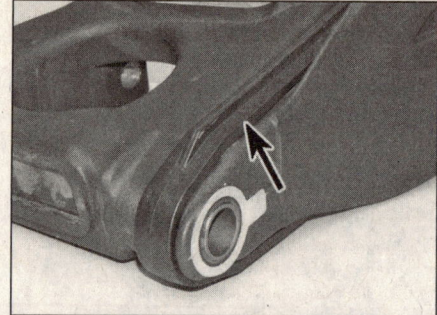

14.2 Clean the chain slider (arrowed) and check for wear

side of the engine. On Sprint models remove the right-hand fairing side panel to access it (see Chapter 7). To increase freeplay, slacken the front nut, then thread the rear nut up the cable until the freeplay is correct (see illustration). To decrease freeplay, slacken the rear nut, then thread the front nut down the cable towards the bracket until the freeplay is correct. Now use the adjuster at the clutch lever bracket to set the specified clearance between the clutch lever and its bracket.

Caution: *The specified clearance is very small and care must be taken to ensure that there is actually some freeplay in the cable, albeit a small amount, otherwise the clutch may slip.*

6 The clutch lever has a span adjuster which alters the distance of the lever from the handlebar to suit different hand sizes. Each setting is identified by a number on the adjuster which aligns with the arrow on the lever bracket. Pull the lever away from the handlebar and turn the adjuster ring until the setting which best suits the rider is obtained (see illustration). There are four settings – setting 1 gives the largest span, and setting 4 the smallest. When making adjustment ensure that the pin set in the lever bracket is engaged in its detent in the adjuster.

14 Drive chain slider check

1 Remove the chainguard (see illustrations 2.2a, b and c, or 2.2d). Create maximum slack in the chain (see Section 1). Clean the chain slider with a suitable solvent to remove all traces of grease and road dirt.
2 Inspect the surface of the slider – if it is deeply grooved or damaged it must be replaced with a new one (see illustration).
3 On Sprint and Speed triple models remove the front sprocket (see Chapter 6). Undo the bolts securing the slider to the swingarm – there is one bolt on the top edge and one bolt on the underside. Draw the slider forwards off the swingarm.
4 On Tiger models the slider is retained by the front chainguard bolt, which has already been removed. Release the slider ends, noting how they locate, then draw it rearwards off the swingarm.
5 Installation is the reverse of removal.

15 Spark plugs

Check and adjustment

1 Make sure your spark plug socket is the correct size before attempting to remove the plugs – a suitable one is supplied in the motorcycle's toolkit which is stored in a compartment in the right-hand side of the cockpit on Sprint models and is opened using the ignition key, in a storage box under the seat on the Speed Triple, and strapped to the underside of the seat on the Tiger. Make sure the ignition is switched OFF. Remove the fuel tank and airbox (see Chapter 4). On all models, the ignition coil is integral with the spark plug cap.
2 Clean the area around the coils to prevent any dirt falling into the spark plug channels. Check that the cylinder location is marked on each ignition coil wiring connector and mark them accordingly if not.
3 Disconnect the ignition coil wiring connectors (see illustration). Pull the coils off the spark plugs (see illustration).
4 Using compressed air if available, clean the area around the base of the spark plugs to prevent any dirt falling into the engine when they are removed.
5 Using either the plug removing tool supplied in the bike's toolkit or a deep socket type wrench, unscrew the plugs from the cylinder head and remove them (see illustrations). Lay each plug out in relation to its cylinder – if any plug shows up a problem it will then be easy to identify the troublesome cylinder.
6 Inspect the electrodes for wear. Both the

15.3a Disconnect the wiring connector

15.3b Pull the coil off the spark plug

15.5a Unscrew the plug . . .

15.5b . . . and remove it from the head

Routine maintenance and Servicing

centre and side electrodes should have square edges and the side electrodes should be of uniform thickness. Look for excessive deposits and evidence of a cracked or chipped insulator around the centre electrode. Compare your spark plugs to the colour spark plug reading chart on the inside rear cover of this manual. Check the threads, the washer and the ceramic insulator body for cracks and other damage.

7 If the electrodes are not excessively worn, and if the deposits can be easily removed with a wire brush, and there are no cracks or chips visible in the insulator, the plugs can be re-gapped and re-used. If in doubt concerning the condition of the plugs, replace them with new ones, as the expense is minimal.

8 Cleaning spark plugs by sandblasting is permitted, provided you clean the plugs with a high flash-point solvent afterwards.

9 Before installing the plugs, make sure they are the correct type and heat range and check the gap between the electrodes **(see illustrations)**. Compare the gap to that specified and adjust as necessary. If the gap must be adjusted, bend the side electrodes carefully and be very careful not to chip or crack the insulator nose **(see illustration)**. Make sure the sealing washer is in place on the plug before installing it.

10 Since the cylinder head is made of aluminium, which is soft and easily damaged, thread the plugs into the head turning the tool by hand **(see illustration 15.5b)**. Once the plugs have seated and are finger-tight, tighten them by 1/4 to 1/2 turn more, using the tool supplied or a socket drive **(see illustration 15.5a)**. Do not over-tighten them.

 **HAYNES HiNT** *As the plugs are quite deeply recessed, you can slip a short length of hose over the end of the plug to use as a tool to thread it into place. The hose will grip the plug well enough to turn it, but will start to slip if the plug begins to cross-thread in the hole – this will prevent damaged threads.*

11 Check the condition of the seal around the top of each coil, directly below the connector socket, and replace it with a new one if necessary – Triumph changed the design of the seal in early 2007 (it has a larger flange – see illustration 15.3b), and recommend that if the original ones are still fitted on 2005 and 2006 models they be replaced with the upgraded ones. Remove the old seal by hand and discard it **(see illustration)**. Clean off any old powder from the coil. When removing the old seal it is possible the outer case of the coil will slide down with it – reposition it by sliding it back up to the seal locating tabs until a click is heard. Fit the new seal with the wide flange uppermost, setting the dimples on top in line with the socket, and making sure the groove on the inside seats over the locating tabs **(see**

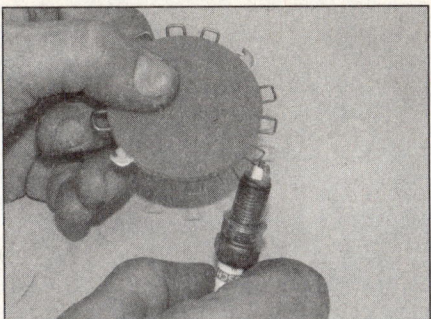

15.9a Using a wire type gauge to measure the spark plug electrode gap

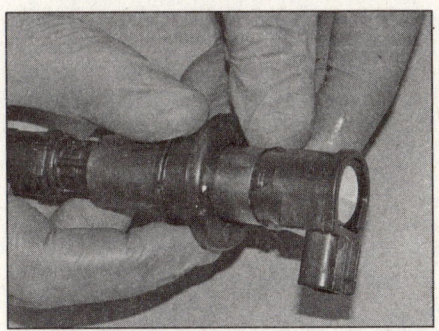

15.11a Slide the old seal down and off the coil

illustration). Make sure the cap for the spark plug is correctly in position on the bottom of the coil.

12 Fit the coils onto the spark plugs **(see illustration 15.3b)**. Connect the coil wiring connectors, making sure each goes to its correct cylinder **(see illustration 15.3a)**.

13 Install the airbox and fuel tank (see Chapter 4).

 **HAYNES HiNT** *Stripped plug threads in the cylinder head can be repaired with a Heli-Coil thread insert – see 'Tools and Workshop Tips' in the Reference section.*

Renewal

14 Remove the old spark plugs as described above and install new ones.

16 Idle speed and throttle body synchronisation

Idle speed

1 The engine idle speed cannot be adjusted in the conventional way. It can only be adjusted using the Triumph engine management system diagnostic tool (see Section 4). If the idle speed is incorrect (see Specifications at the beginning of the Chapter), first check the idle air control valve (see Chapter 4). If that is good take the bike to a Triumph dealer.

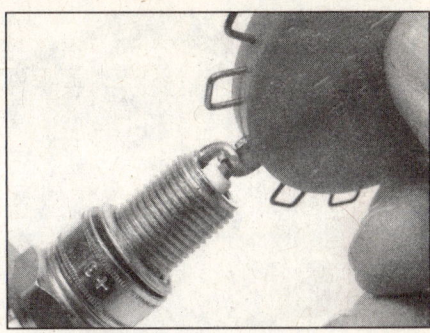

15.9b Adjust the electrode gap by bending the side electrode only

15.11b Make sure the seal is seated as described and with the dimples (arrowed) positioned as shown

Throttle body synchronisation

2 Throttle body synchronisation is the process of adjusting the throttle bodies so they pass the same amount of fuel/air mixture to each cylinder. Throttle bodies that are out of synchronisation will result in decreased fuel mileage, increased engine temperature, less than ideal throttle response and higher vibration levels.

3 The throttle bodies cannot be synchronised in the normal way by measuring the vacuum present in each throttle body using a set of vacuum gauges or a manometer. They can only be synchronised using the Triumph engine management system diagnostic tool. Take the bike to a Triumph dealer.

17 Steering head bearings

1 Steering head bearings can become dented, rough or loose during normal use of the machine – wear or damage will be noticeable in the way the bike handles. In extreme cases, worn or loose steering head bearings can cause steering wobble – a condition that is potentially dangerous. It is good practice to check the bearings on a regular basis and adjust them if necessary as described below.

Check

2 Using an auxiliary stand, support the motorcycle in an upright position so that the front wheel is off the ground.

1•22 Routine maintenance and Servicing

17.4 Checking for play in the steering head bearings

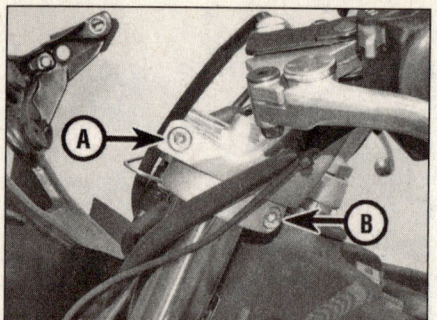

17.6 Handlebar clamp bolt (A) and fork clamp bolt (B) – Sprint models

17.7 Slacken the clamp bolt (arrowed) on each side

3 Point the front wheel straight-ahead and slowly move the handlebars from side-to-side. Any dents or roughness in the bearing races will be felt and the bars will not move smoothly and freely. Again point the wheel straight-ahead, and tap the front of the wheel to one side. The wheel should 'fall' under its own weight to the limit of its lock, indicating that the bearings are not too tight (take into account the restriction that cables and wiring may have). Check for similar movement to the other side.

4 Next, grasp the forks and try to pull and push them forward and backward **(see illustration)**. Any looseness in the steering head bearings will be felt as front-to-rear movement of the forks. If play is felt in the bearings, adjust the steering head as follows.

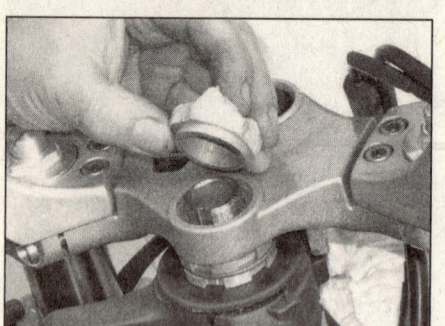

17.8 Unscrew the steering stem nut

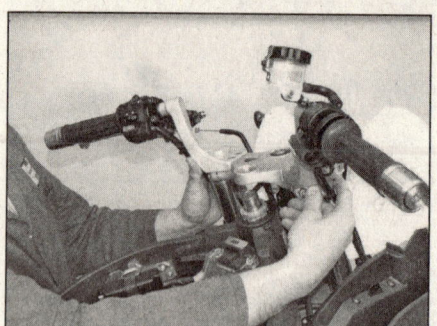

17.9a Lift the top yoke up . . .

HAYNES HiNT *Make sure you are not mistaking any movement between the bike and stand, or between the stand and the ground, for freeplay in the bearings. Do not pull and push the forks too hard – a gentle movement is all that is needed. Freeplay between the fork tubes due to worn bushes can also be misinterpreted as steering head bearing play – do not confuse the two.*

Adjustment

Caution: Take great care not to apply excessive pressure when adjusting the bearings because this will cause premature bearing failure.

5 Remove the fuel tank (see Chapter 4) and, where fitted, the fairing (see Chapter 7). **Note:** *Although it is not strictly necessary to remove the fuel tank and fairing, doing so will prevent the possibility of damage should a tool slip.*

6 On Sprint models slacken the handlebar clamp bolt and the fork clamp bolt on each side **(see illustration)**.

7 On Speed Triple and Tiger models, displace the handlebars from the top yoke (see Chapter 5). Slacken the fork clamp bolts in the top yoke **(see illustration)**.

8 Unscrew the steering stem nut **(see illustration)**.

9 Ease the top yoke up off the forks and lay it clear of the steering stem on some rag **(see illustrations)**.

10 Unscrew the locknut, then lift off the tabbed washer **(see illustrations)**.

11 Triumph specify a torque setting for the adjuster nut, which can only be applied using their service tool (Part No. T3880023 for Sprint models and T3880024 for Speed Triple and Tiger) or you could fabricate a tool to fit the adjuster nut slots **(see illustration)**. Slacken the adjuster nut slightly, then with the tool

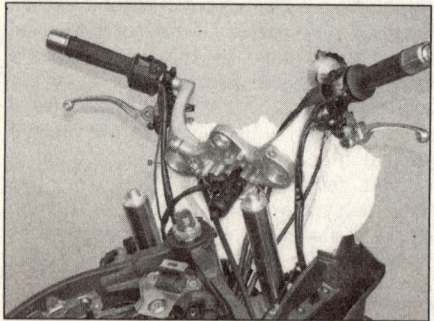

17.9b . . . and rest it aside on some rag

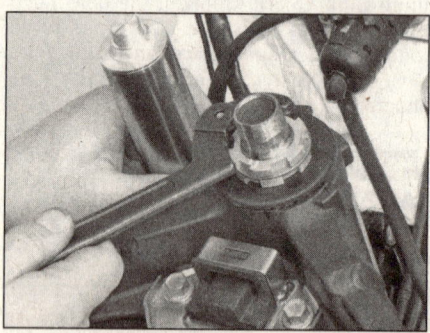

17.10a Unscrew the locknut using a C-spanner . . .

17.10b . . . and remove the tabbed washer

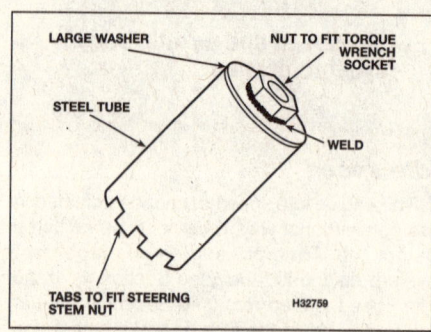

17.11 Home-made version of the Triumph service tool

Routine maintenance and Servicing 1•23

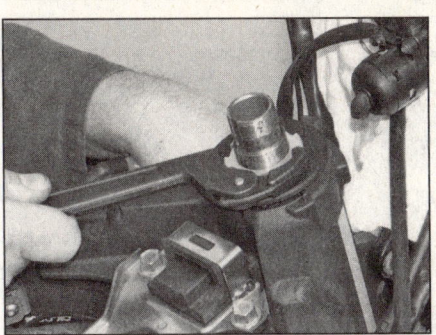

17.12 Using a C-spanner to adjust the steering head bearings

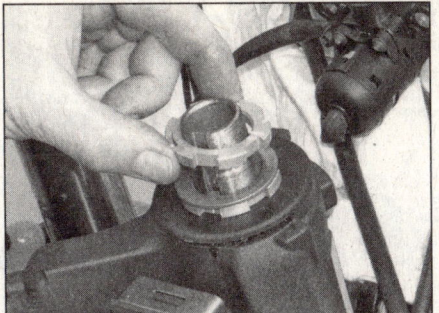

17.13a Fit the locknut . . .

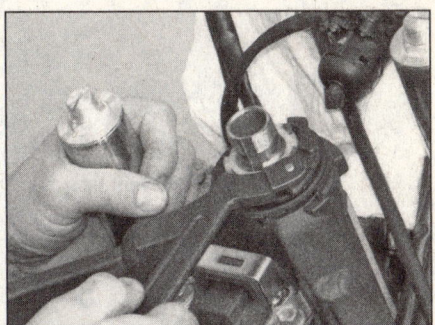

17.13b . . . and tighten to the specified torque

fitted to a torque wrench, apply a torque of 40 Nm to the adjuster nut – this will preload the bearings. Now slacken the nut and tighten it to the final torque setting of 15 Nm.

12 If the service tool isn't available slacken the adjuster nut slightly using a C-spanner until pressure is just released, then tighten it until all freeplay is removed, then tighten it a little more **(see illustration)**. This pre-loads the bearings. Now slacken the nut, then tighten it again, setting it so that all freeplay is just removed yet the steering is able to move freely from side to side. To do this tighten the nut only a little at a time, and after each tightening repeat the checks outlined above (see Steps 3 and 4) until the bearings are correctly set. The object is to set the adjuster nut so that the bearings are under a very light loading, just enough to remove any freeplay.

13 Fit the tabbed washer, locating the tab in the slot **(see illustration 17.10b)**. Fit the locknut and tighten it to 40 Nm if the tool is available, or using a C-spanner if not **(see illustrations)** – make sure the adjuster nut does not turn with it, though it shouldn't as the tabbed lockwasher is there to prevent it doing so (if it does you will have to repeat the adjustment procedure).

14 Fit the top yoke onto the steering stem **(see illustration 17.9a)**. Fit the steering stem nut and tighten it to the specified torque **(see illustration)**. Now tighten the fork clamp bolts to the specified torque **(see illustration 17.6 or 7)**.

15 On Sprint models tighten the handlebar clamp bolts to the specified torque **(see illustration 17.6)**.

16 On Speed Triple and Tiger models install the handlebars (see Chapter 5).

17 Install the fuel tank and fairing as required.

Lubrication

18 Triumph specify that the steering head bearings must be re-greased at every second check and adjustment service interval. Re-greasing involves removing the steering stem – follow the procedure in Chapter 5 to remove and install the stem and adjust the bearings as described above on reassembly.

18 Air filter

Sprint, 2005 to 2010 Speed Triple models (up to VIN 461331), Tiger

1 Remove the fuel tank (see Chapter 4).
2 Disconnect the intake air temperature (IAT) sensor wiring connector **(see illustration)**. Undo the manifold absolute pressure (MAP) sensor screw, then displace the sensor and free the hose from its guide in the airbox **(see illustrations)**. On Tiger Sport disconnect the immobiliser wiring connector.

17.14 Tighten the steering stem nut to the specified torque

18.2a Push the clip in and disconnect the IAT sensor wiring connector

HAYNES HiNT

If the motorcycle is constantly used in dirty or dusty conditions (such as a Tiger used off-road), it is worth cleaning the element between renewal intervals. Remove it as described above, and tap it on a hard surface to dislodge any large particles of dirt. If compressed air is available, use it to clean the element, directing the air in the opposite direction of normal flow. If the element is torn or cannot be cleaned, or is obviously beyond further use, replace it with a new one.

18.2b Displace the MAP sensor . . .

18.2c . . . and free its hose

Routine maintenance and Servicing

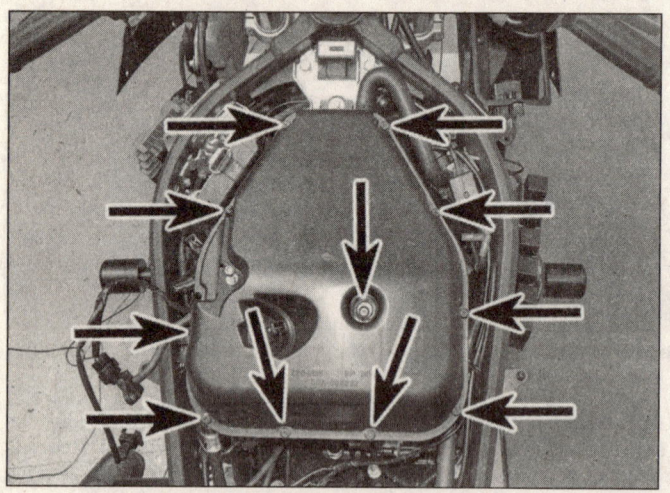

18.3a Undo the screws (arrowed) . . .

18.3b . . . remove the cover . . .

3 Undo the screws securing the top of the airbox and lift it off – don't forget to remove the central screw – then lift out the filter element **(see illustrations)**.

4 Clean the inside of the airbox. Check the condition of the top sealing ring and replace it with a new one if it is damaged, deformed or deteriorated **(see illustration)**.

5 Fit the new filter element into the airbox **(see illustration 18.3c)**. Fit the top, making sure the rubber seal is in place, and secure it with the screws **(see illustrations 18.3b and a)**.

6 Connect the IAT sensor wiring connector **(see illustration 18.2a)**. Fit the MAP sensor hose in its guide and secure the sensor on the airbox cover **(see illustrations 18.2c and b)**.

7 Install the fuel tank (see Chapter 4).

2011-on Speed Triple models (from VIN 461332)

8 Remove the fuel tank (see Chapter 4).
9 Release the battery strap **(see illustration)**.
10 Note the routing of the battery leads. Undo the air filter holder screws, lift the holder out and remove the filter element from it **(see illustrations)**.
11 Clean the inside of the airbox.
12 Fit the new filter element into the holder **(see illustration 18.10c)**. Fit the holder, making sure the leads are correctly routed under its right-hand end, and secure it with the screws **(see illustrations 18.10b and a)**.
13 Hook up the battery strap **(see illustration 18.9)**.
14 Install the fuel tank (see Chapter 4).

19 Secondary air injection system (SAIS) check

1 The system consists of an electrically actuated solenoid valve located at the front of the airbox and three reed valves (one per cylinder) in the top of the valve cover, with

18.3c . . . and lift the filter out of the airbox

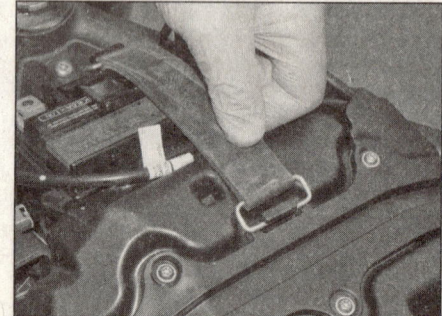

18.4 Check the sealing ring and make sure it is properly seated

18.9 Unhook the battery strap

18.10a Undo the screws (arrowed) . . .

18.10b . . . lift the holder out . . .

18.10c . . . and remove the filter from it

Routine maintenance and Servicing 1•25

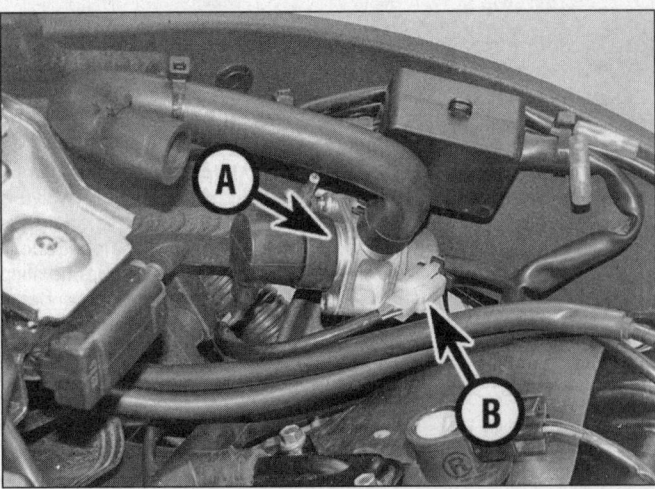

19.1a SAIS solenoid valve (A) and its wiring connector (B) – Sprint models

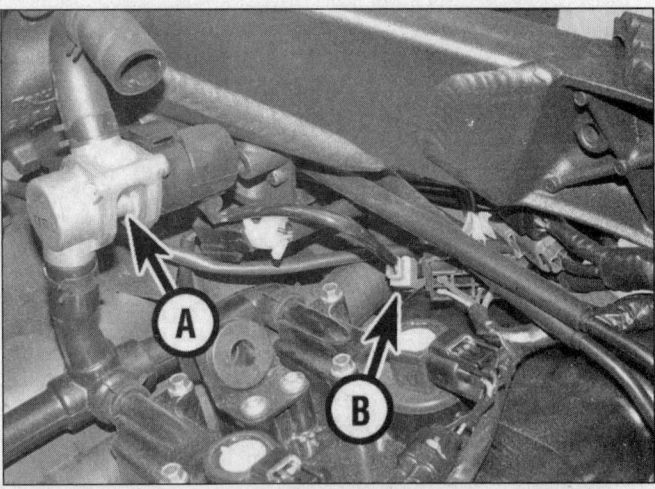

19.1b SAIS solenoid valve (A) and its wiring connector (B) – Speed Triple up to VIN 461331 and Tiger models

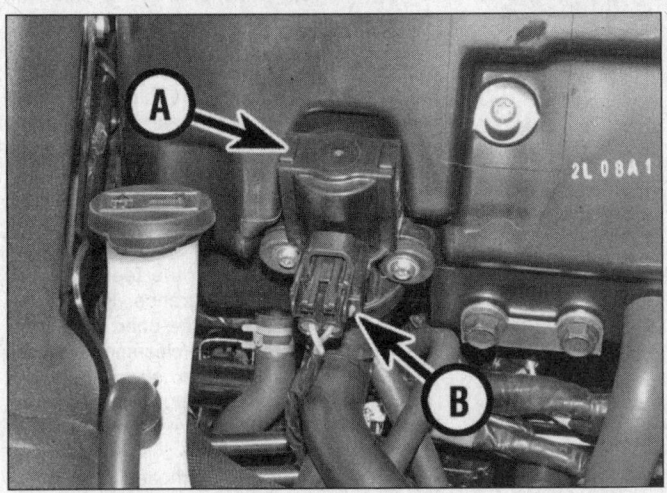

19.1c SAIS solenoid valve (A) and its wiring connector (B) – Speed Triple from VIN 461332

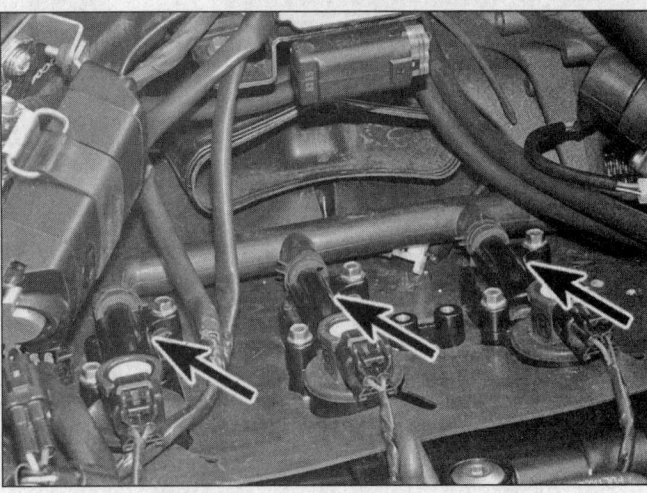

19.1d Reed valve housings (arrowed)

a hose system supplying air from the airbox via the solenoid valve to the reed valves (see illustrations). At certain engine speeds, the electronic control module (ECM) opens the solenoid valve and air is drawn into the exhaust ports via the reed valves. The introduced air promotes further combustion of the exhaust gases, reducing the level of pollutants. The reed valves prevent exhaust gases blowing back into the airbox.

Solenoid valve and hoses

2 Remove the airbox (see Chapter 4).
3 Check the system hoses for loose connections, cracks and deterioration, and replace them with new ones if necessary.
4 A faulty solenoid valve should be indicated by the malfunction indicator lamp in the instrument cluster, although it is impossible to access fault codes without the use of the Triumph engine management system diagnostic tool (see Chapter 4). Triumph provide no test procedure for the valve, however its function can be checked as follows.

5 On all models except the Speed Triple from VIN 461332 disconnect the valve wiring connector (see illustration 19.1a or b). Release the clip and disconnect the air outlet hose. Remove the valve, noting how it locates. On Speed Triple models from VIN 461332 remove the valve from the airbox.
6 First blow into the valve inlet union and ensure no air comes out the outlet union – the valve is closed (see illustration). Now, using a fully charged 12 volt battery and two insulated jumper wires, connect the positive (+) battery terminal to the yellow/orange wire terminal in the valve wiring connector and the negative (-) battery terminal to the brown/pink wire terminal. Check that the valve has opened by again blowing into the inlet union – air should now flow through the valve and out the outlet union. If the valve does not function as described, replace it with a new one.
7 Installation is the reverse of removal. Ensure that the wiring connector terminals are clean and that the connector is firm.

Reed valves

8 Remove the airbox (see Chapter 4).
9 Remove the ignition coils (see Section 15).
10 Mark the air hoses to aid installation, then release the clips and pull the hoses off the unions on the reed valve covers, noting how they fit (see illustration 19.1c).
11 Undo the bolts securing the reed

19.6 Air should only flow through the valve when voltage is applied as described

1•26 Routine maintenance and Servicing

19.11a Unscrew the bolts (arrowed) . . .

19.11b . . . remove the cover . . .

19.11c . . . and lift the reed valve out

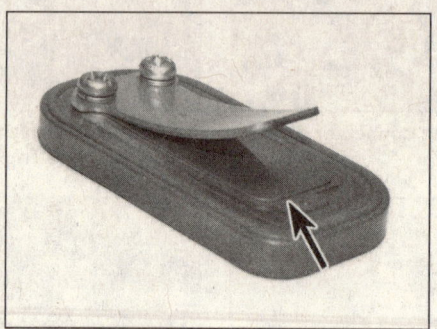

19.12 Make sure there is no gap between the reed and its seat (arrowed)

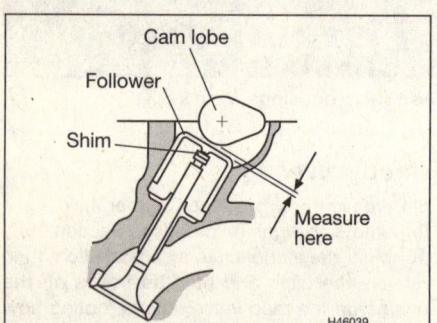

20.5 Measure the valve clearance with a feeler gauge

20.10a Lift out the cam follower . . .

20.10b . . . and retrieve the shim (arrowed)

valve covers and lift off the covers **(see illustrations)**. The reed valves may come off with the covers or they may remain in the valve cover; lift them out carefully, noting which way round they fit **(see illustration)**.

12 If required, clean any carbon deposits off the reeds and stopper plates with a suitable solvent, taking care not to distort the reeds. Inspect the seats – if they are damaged or deteriorated, renew the reed assemblies. Hold each valve up to the light and check that there is no gap between the reed and the seat **(see illustration)**.

13 Installation is the reverse of removal. Ensure the reeds are fitted the correct way round and tighten the cover bolts to the specified torque setting.

14 Ensure the air hoses are clipped securely to the cover unions and correctly positioned before the airbox is installed.

20 Valve clearance check

Check

1 The engine must be completely cool for this maintenance procedure, so let the machine sit overnight before beginning.

2 Remove the spark plugs (see Section 15).

3 Remove the valve cover (see Chapter 2). The cylinders are numbered 1 to 3 from left to right. Make a chart or sketch of all valve positions so that a note of each clearance can be made against the relevant valve.

4 The clearance for a particular valve can be measured when the cam lobe for that valve is pointing away from it, and there is one point during the engine cycle when all the lobes above the valves for a particular cylinder are pointing up – this is when the piston in that cylinder is at top dead centre (TDC) on the compression stroke, and all its valves are closed. To turn the camshafts, place the motorcycle on an auxiliary stand (or on its centrestand on Sprint models) so that the rear wheel is off the ground, select a high gear, and rotate the rear wheel by hand in its normal direction of rotation until the lobes above the cylinder being checked are all pointing away from the valves.

5 Turn the rear wheel until all the camshaft lobes above the No. 1 cylinder are pointing away from the valves. The No. 1 cylinder is now at TDC on the compression stroke. Insert a feeler gauge of the same thickness as the correct valve clearance (see Specifications at the beginning of the Chapter) between the base of the camshaft lobe and the cam follower of each valve in turn and check that it is a firm sliding fit – you should feel a slight drag when the you pull the gauge out **(see illustration)**. If not, use the feeler gauges to obtain the exact clearance. Record the measured clearance on the chart. Note that there is a difference in the clearance between the intake valves and the exhaust valves.

6 Now turn the rear wheel until the camshaft lobes for the No. 2 cylinder are facing away from the valves. The No. 2 cylinder is now at TDC on the compression stroke. Measure the clearances of the valves using the method described in Step 5.

7 Now turn the rear wheel until the camshaft lobes for the No. 3 cylinder are facing away from the valves. The No. 3 cylinder is now at TDC on the compression stroke. Measure the clearances of the valves using the method described in Step 5.

8 When all clearances have been measured and charted, identify whether the clearance on any valve falls outside the range specified. If it does, the valve shim on that particular valve must be replaced with one of a thickness which will restore the correct clearance.

9 Changing the shims requires removal of the camshafts (see Chapter 2). Place rags over the spark plug holes and the cam chain tunnel to prevent a shim dropping into the engine on removal.

10 With the camshaft removed, remove the cam follower of the valve in question **(see illustration)**. Retrieve the shim from either the inside of the follower or pick it out of the top of the valve using a magnet or a small screwdriver with a dab of grease on it (the shim will stick to the grease) **(see illustration)**. Do not allow the shim to fall into the engine.

Routine maintenance and Servicing

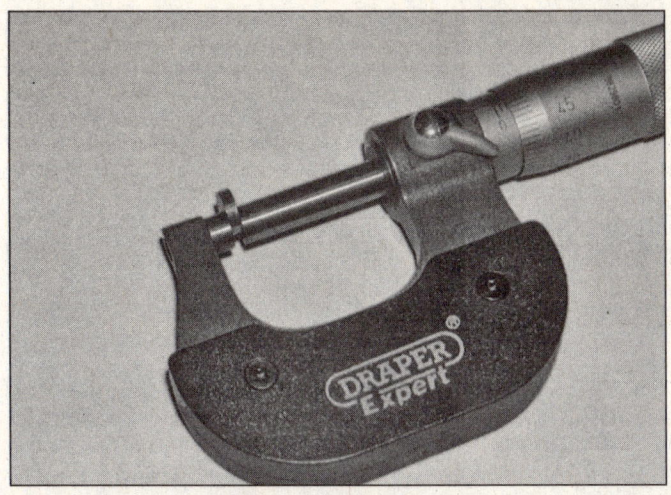

20.11 Measure the shim using a micrometer to confirm its size

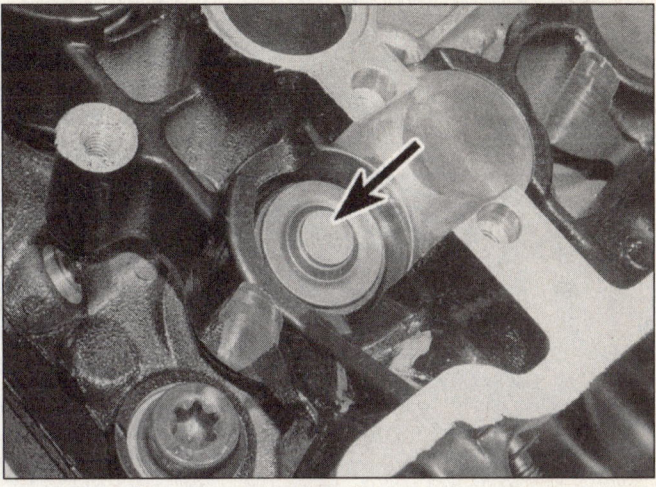

20.16 Fit the shim into its recess (arrowed)

11 The shim size may be marked on one face, but the shim should be measured with a micrometer to check that it has not worn **(see illustration)**. If the shim has worn undersize, this must be taken into account when calculating the valve clearance.

12 The new shim thickness required can be calculated as follows – always aim to get the clearance at the mid-point of the specified range.

13 If the valve clearance is less than specified, subtract the measured clearance from the specified clearance then deduct the result from the original shim thickness. For example:

Sample calculation – intake valve clearance too small

Specified clearance: 0.15 mm
    (0.10 to 0.20 mm)
Measured clearance: 0.08 mm
Difference: 0.07 mm
Shim thickness fitted: 2.575 mm
Correct shim thickness required is
    2.575 – 0.07 = 2.505 mm

14 If the valve clearance is greater than specified, subtract the specified clearance from the measured clearance, and add the result to the thickness of the original shim. For example:

Sample calculation – exhaust valve clearance too large

Specified clearance: 0.25 mm
    (0.20 to 0.30 mm)
Measured clearance: 0.37 mm
Difference: 0.12 mm
Shim thickness fitted: 1.975 mm
Correct shim thickness required is
    1.975 + 0.12 = 2.095 mm

15 Obtain the correct thickness shim(s) from a Triumph dealer. Where the required thickness is not equal to the available shim thickness, round off the measurement to the nearest available size. Shims are available in 0.025 mm increments from 1.70 mm to 3.00 mm. **Note:** *If the required replacement shim is greater than 3.00 mm (the largest available), the valve is probably not seating correctly due to a build-up of carbon deposits or valve damage. Remove the valve for checking (see Chapter 2).*

16 Lubricate the new shim with clean engine oil or molybdenum disulphide oil (a 50/50 mixture of molybdenum disulphide grease and engine oil) and fit it into its recess in the top of the valve **(see illustration)**. Check that the shim is correctly seated, then lubricate the follower with engine oil or molybdenum disulphide oil and fit it onto the valve. Repeat the procedure for any other valves as required, then install the camshafts (see Chapter 2).

17 Rotate the rear wheel several turns to seat the new shim(s), then check the clearances again.

18 Install the valve cover and spark plugs.

21 Wheel bearing check

1 Wheel bearings will wear over a period of time and result in handling problems.

2 Support the motorcycle upright using an auxiliary stand (or the centrestand on Sprint models) and so that the wheel being checked is off the ground. Check for any play in the bearings by pushing and pulling the wheel against the hub **(see illustration)**. Also spin the wheel and check that it rotates smoothly.

3 If any play is detected in the wheel hub, or if the wheel does not rotate smoothly (and this is not due to brake or transmission drag), the wheel must be removed and the bearings inspected for wear or damage (see Chapter 6). Note that on Sprint and Speed Triple models, the rear wheel bearings are housing in the hub rather than the wheel itself (see Section 22). Do not remove the needle roller bearing on these models unless it is going to be replaced with a new one.

22 Rear wheel bearing lubrication – Sprint, Speed Triple and Tiger Sport

1 On Sprint, Speed Triple and Tiger Sport models the rear wheel bearings should be lubricated at the specified service interval.

2 Refer to Chapter 6, Section 16 and remove the hub assembly. If required, remove the grease seal from the right-hand side of the hub and discard it if it is damaged or deteriorated.

3 Clean off the old grease and inspect the condition of the bearings as described in Chapter 6 – note that if the left-hand bearing is sealed on both sides it cannot be cleaned or re-greased.

4 Lubricate the bearings with the grease specified at the beginning of this Chapter. If required, fit a new seal to the right-hand side of the hub, then follow the procedure in Chapter 6 and install the hub assembly.

23 Stand, lever pivots and cable lubrication

1 Since the controls, cables and various other components of a motorcycle are exposed

21.2 Checking for play in the wheel bearings

1•28 Routine maintenance and Servicing

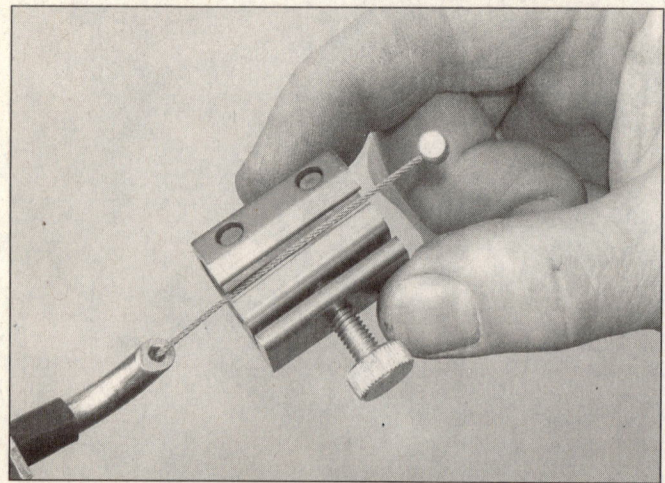

23.3a Fit the cable into the adapter . . .

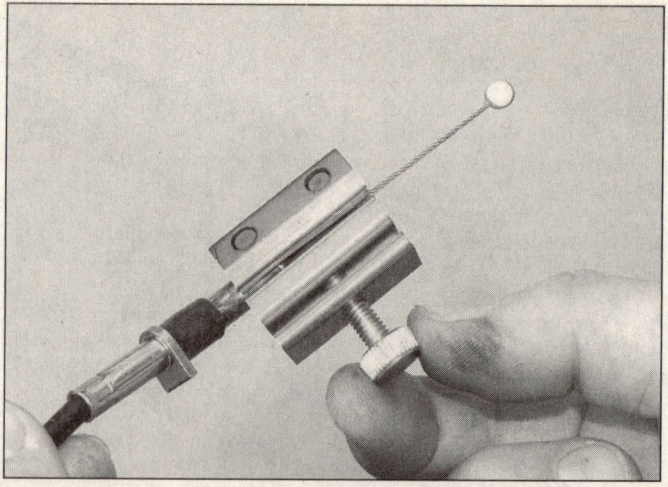

23.3b . . . and tighten the screw to seal it in . . .

to the elements, they should be lubricated periodically to ensure safe and trouble-free operation.

2 The footrests, clutch and brake levers, brake pedal, gearchange lever linkage and stand pivot(s) should be lubricated frequently. In order for the lubricant to be applied where it will do the most good, the component should be disassembled (see Chapter 5) and the recommended lubricant applied (see Specifications). However, if an aerosol spray lubricant is used, it can be applied to the pivot joint gaps and will usually work its way into the areas where friction occurs.

3 To lubricate the throttle and clutch cables, disconnect the relevant cable at its upper end, then lubricate the cable with a pressure adapter (see illustrations). See Chapter 4 for the throttle cable removal procedures, and Chapter 2 for the clutch cable.

24 Coolant change

Warning: Allow the engine to cool completely before performing this maintenance operation. Also, don't allow antifreeze to come into contact with your skin or the painted surfaces of the motorcycle. Rinse off spills immediately with plenty of water. Antifreeze is highly toxic if ingested. Never leave antifreeze lying around in an open container or in puddles on the floor; children and pets are attracted by its sweet smell and may drink it. Check with local authorities (councils) about disposing of antifreeze. Many communities have collection centres which will see that antifreeze is disposed of safely. Antifreeze is also combustible, so don't store it near open flames.

Draining

1 On Sprint and Tiger models remove the left and right-hand fairing side panels (see Chapter 7).

2 On 2011-on Speed Triple models (from VIN 461332) remove the radiator cowls (see Chapter 7). On 2005 to 2010 Speed Triple models (up to VIN 461331) undo the screw securing the radiator pressure cap.

3 Remove the pressure cap from the filler neck in the radiator by turning it anti-clockwise until it reaches a stop (see illustration 6.9). If you hear a hissing sound (indicating there is still pressure in the system), wait until it stops. Now press down on the cap and continue turning it until it can be removed. Also remove the filler cap from the coolant reservoir.

4 Unscrew the bleed-hole bolt on the right-hand end of the radiator (see illustration).

5 Position a suitable container beneath the water pump on the left-hand side of the

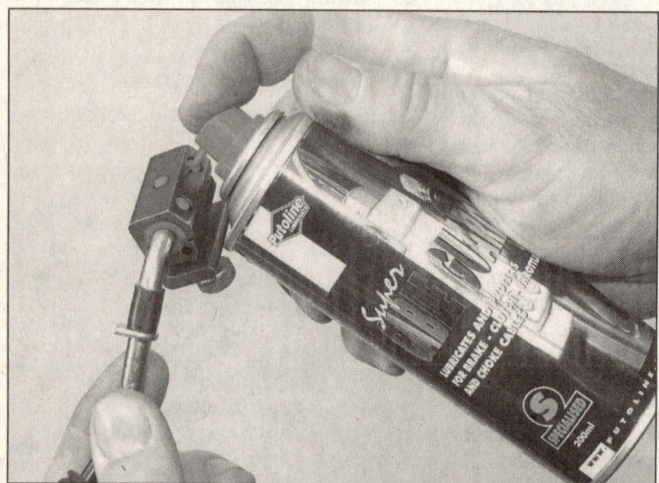

23.3c . . . then apply the lubricant using the nozzle provided inserted in the hole in the adapter

24.4 Remove the bleed bolt (arrowed) from the top of the radiator

Routine maintenance and Servicing

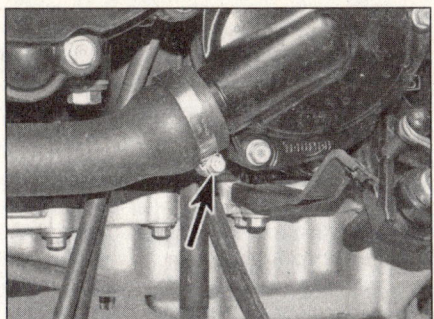

24.5a Slacken the clamp (arrowed) ...

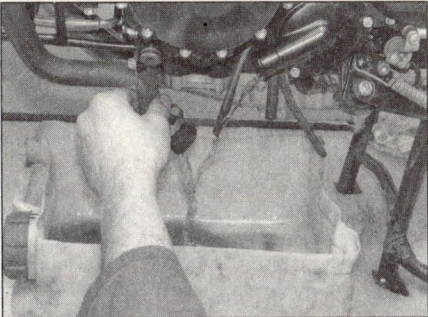

24.5b ... then detach the hose and allow the coolant to drain

24.6a Unscrew the drain plug (arrowed) ...

engine. Slacken the clamp securing the bottom coolant hose to the water pump and detach it, then point it down into the container and allow the coolant to completely drain **(see illustrations)**.

6 Position the container beneath the cylinder drain plug on the left-hand side of the engine. Unscrew the plug and allow the remaining coolant to completely drain **(see illustrations)**. If you are going to flush the system using a flushing compound retain the old sealing washer for use during flushing.

7 Run the system through with clean tap water by inserting a garden hose in the filler neck. Allow water to run through until it flows out clear. If the radiator is extremely corroded, remove it (see Chapter 3) and have it cleaned professionally.

Flushing

8 Clean the cylinder drain hole then fit the drain plug using the old sealing washer. Attach the coolant hose to the water pump and tighten the clamp **(see illustration 24.5a)**.

9 Fill the cooling system with clean water mixed with a flushing compound **(see illustration 24.15)**. Make sure the flushing compound is compatible with aluminium components, and follow the manufacturer's instructions carefully.

10 Fit the pressure cap and the bleed-hole bolt **(see illustration 24.4)**. Start the engine and allow it to reach normal operating temperature. Let it run for about ten minutes.

11 Stop the engine and let it cool for a while. Cover the pressure cap with a heavy rag and turn it anti-clockwise to the first stop, releasing any pressure that may be present in the system. Once the hissing stops, push down on the cap and remove it completely.

12 Drain the system.

13 Fill the system with clean water and repeat the procedure in Steps 10 to 12.

Refilling

14 Fit a new sealing washer onto the cylinder drain plug and tighten it to the torque setting specified at the beginning of the Chapter **(see illustration 24.6a)**. Attach the coolant hose to the water pump and tighten the clamp **(see illustration 24.5a)**.

15 Fill the system via the filler neck with the

24.6b ... and drain the cylinder jacket

proper coolant mixture (see this Chapter's Specifications) **(see illustration)**. Note: *Pour the coolant in slowly to minimise the amount of air entering the system.* When the system appears full, take the bike off its stand and shake it slightly to dissipate the coolant, then place the bike back on the stand and top the system up. Check that there is coolant visible in the bleed-hole. If there isn't, but the filler neck appears full, there is an air-lock somewhere. Try shaking the bike again to disperse it. If that doesn't work you will need to siphon the coolant through the radiator using a vacuum pump – these are commercially available. Alternatively you may be able to form a sufficient seal using a piece of clear flexible tubing that fits tightly into the bleed hole, then sucking on the end of the tube – the reason the tube must be clear is so you can see the coolant when it exits the bleed hole and enters the tube, at which point stop sucking. DO NOT use tubing you can't see through – coolant does not taste very nice and is not good for you. If you cannot get coolant through to the bleed hole it is possible the radiator is blocked, and so must be replaced with a new one.

16 Fit the bleed-hole bolt, using a new sealing washer if the old one is damaged, deformed or deteriorated, and tighten it **(see illustration 24.4)**. Fit the pressure cap.

17 Fill the coolant reservoir to the MAX level line (see *Pre-ride checks*).

18 Start the engine and allow it to idle for 2 to 3 minutes. Flick the throttle twistgrip part open 3 or 4 times, so that the engine speed

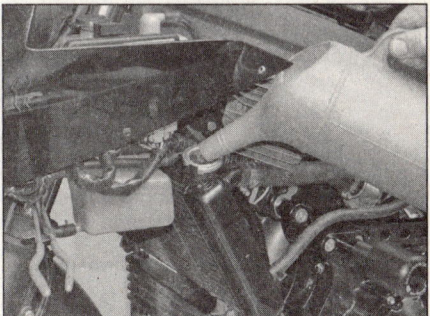

24.15 Fill the system using the correct mixture as described

rises to approximately 4000 – 5000 rpm, then stop the engine. Any air trapped in the system should have bled back to the filler neck.

19 Let the engine cool then remove the pressure cap as described in Step 3. Check that the coolant level is still up to the top of the filler neck. If it's low, add the specified mixture until it reaches the top. Refit the pressure cap. On Speed Triple secure the cap with the screw.

20 Check the coolant level in the reservoir and top up if necessary (see *Pre-ride checks*).

21 Check the system for leaks.

22 Do not dispose of the old coolant by pouring it down the drain. Instead pour it into a heavy plastic container, cap it tightly and take it into an authorised disposal site or service station – see **Warning** at the beginning of this Section.

23 On Sprint and Tiger models install the fairing side panels (see Chapter 7). On Speed Triple models fit the pressure cap screw.

25 Brake fluid change

1 The brake fluid should be changed at the prescribed interval or whenever a master cylinder or caliper overhaul is carried out. Refer to Chapter 6, Section 10 for details. Ensure that all the old fluid is pumped from the hydraulic system and that the level in the fluid reservoir is checked and the brakes tested before riding the motorcycle.

Routine maintenance and Servicing

26 Front fork oil change

1 Fork oil degrades over a period of time and loses its damping qualities.
2 Remove the front forks from the yokes as described in Chapter 5, Section 6, then change the oil as described in Chapter 5, Section 7.
3 Fork oil quantity, level and oil type are given in the Specifications at the beginning of Chapter 5.

27 Stand(s) and safety interlock circuit

1 The sidestand return spring (and centrestand return spring on Sprint models) must be capable of retracting the stand fully and holding the stand retracted when the motorcycle is in use. If a spring is sagged or broken it must be replaced with a new one.
2 Lubricate the stand pivot regularly (see Section 23).
3 The sidestand switch prevents the motorcycle being started if it is in gear and the stand is down, and cuts the engine if the stand is put down while it is running and in gear. Check its operation by shifting the transmission into neutral, retracting the stand, pulling the clutch lever in and starting the engine. Pull in the clutch lever again and select a gear. Extend the sidestand. The engine should stop as the sidestand is extended. If the sidestand switch does not operate as described, check its circuit (see Chapter 8). The neutral and clutch switches are also part of the same circuit – to check them, make sure the engine can be started with the sidestand in either position, as long as the transmission is in neutral and the clutch is pulled in, and cannot be started with the transmission in gear, even with the stand up and the clutch pulled in. If any of the situations are not as stated, check the circuit (see Chapter 8).

28 Battery checks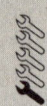

1 All models are fitted with a maintenance-free (sealed) battery which requires no maintenance. **Note:** *Do not attempt to remove the battery caps to check the electrolyte level or battery specific gravity. Removal will damage the caps, resulting in electrolyte leakage and battery damage.* All that should be done is to check that the terminals are clean and tight and that the casing is not damaged or leaking. See Chapter 8 for further details
Caution: Be extremely careful when handling or working around the battery. The electrolyte is very caustic and an explosive gas (hydrogen) is given off when the battery is charging.
2 If the machine is not in regular use, disconnect the battery and give it a refresher charge every month to six weeks (see Chapter 8).

Chapter 2
Engine, clutch and transmission

Contents

	Section number		Section number
Alternator	see Chapter 8	Engine wear assessment	3
Balancer shaft	27	Gearchange mechanism	20
Cam chain and tensioner/guide blades	11	General information	1
Cam chain tensioner	8	Main and connecting rod bearing information	24
Camshafts and followers	9	Oil and filter change	see Chapter 1
Clutch	16	Oil cooler and hoses	6
Clutch cable	17	Oil level check	see Pre-ride checks
Clutch checks	see Chapter 1	Oil pump and oil pressure relief valve	19
Component access	2	Pistons and piston rings	15
Connecting rods	25	Recommended running-in procedure	30
Crankcase inspection	23	Selector drum and forks	21
Crankcase separation and reassembly	22	Starter clutch	10
Crankshaft and main bearings	26	Starter motor	see Chapter 8
Cylinder head and valve overhaul	13	Sump and oil strainer	18
Cylinder head removal and installation	12	Transmission shaft overhaul	29
Cylinder liners	14	Transmission shaft removal and installation	28
Engine overhaul information	5	Valve clearance check	see Chapter 1
Engine removal and installation	4	Valve cover	7

Degrees of difficulty

Easy, suitable for novice with little experience	**Fairly easy**, suitable for beginner with some experience	**Fairly difficult**, suitable for competent DIY mechanic 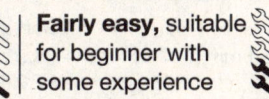	**Difficult**, suitable for experienced DIY mechanic	**Very difficult**, suitable for expert DIY or professional 

Specifications

General
Capacity	1050 cc
Bore	79.0 mm
Stroke	71.4 mm
Compression ratio	12.0 to 1
Cylinder numbering (from left side to right side of the bike)	1-2-3
Firing order	1-2-3

Camshafts, followers and camchain
Camshaft runout	0.05 mm max.
Camshaft end-float	
Standard	0.03 to 0.12 mm
Maximum	0.2 mm
Camshaft bearing oil clearance	
Standard	
Main holder	0.040 to 0.091 mm
Outrigger holder	0.044 to 0.068 mm
Service limit (max)	0.13 mm
Camshaft journal diameter – all journals except outrigger	22.930 to 22.960 mm
Camshaft journal diameter – outrigger journals (cam chain end)	22.953 to 22.956 mm
Camshaft bearing bore diameter	23.000 to 23.021 mm
Follower outside diameter	
Standard	28.476 to 28.490 mm
Service limit	28.549 mm
Follower bore diameter	
Standard	28.515 to 28.535 mm
Service limit	28.468 mm
Cam chain stretch limit	150.14 mm

Valves, guides and springs

Intake valve stem diameter
    Standard.. 4.975 to 4.990 mm
    Service limit .... 4.965 mm
Exhaust valve stem diameter
    Standard.. 4.955 to 4.990 mm
    Service limit .... 4.945 mm
Intake valve guide bore diameter
    Standard.. 5.000 to 5.015 mm
    Service limit .... 5.043 mm
Exhaust valve guide bore diameter
    Standard.. 5.000 to 5.015 mm
    Service limit .... 5.063 mm
Valve stem-to-guide clearance
    Intake .... 0.01 to 0.04 mm
    Exhaust... 0.03 to 0.06 mm
Intake valve seat width (in head)
    Standard.. 0.9 to 1.1 mm
    Service limit .... 1.5 mm
Exhaust valve seat width (in head)
    Standard.. 1.1 to 1.3 mm
    Service limit .... 1.7 mm
Valve seat width (on valve) .... 1.5 to 1.9 mm
Valve spring load at length................................ 440 to 500 N at 26.3 mm

Cylinder liners

Cylinder liner ID
    Standard.. 79.040 to 79.060 mm
    Service limit .... 79.110 mm
Cylinder compression...................................... 150 to 180 psi (10.3 to 12.4 Bar)

Pistons

	Standard	Service limit
Piston OD (measured 5 mm up from skirt, at 90° to piston pin axis)	78.970 to 78.980 mm	78.930 mm
Piston pin bore diameter in piston	16.993 to 17.001 mm	17.029 mm
Piston pin diameter	16.984 to 16.989 mm	16.974 mm
Connecting rod small-end diameter	17.005 to 17.018 mm	17.028 mm

Piston rings

Ring-to-groove clearance (top and second rings)
    Standard.. 0.02 to 0.06 mm
    Service limit .... 0.075 mm
End gap (installed)
    Top ring
        Standard.. 0.28 to 0.49 mm
        Service limit .... 0.61 mm
    Second ring
        Standard.. 0.43 to 0.64 mm
        Service limit .... 0.76 mm
    Oil control ring side rails
        Standard.. 0.33 to 0.89 mm
        Service limit .... 1.03 mm

Clutch

Friction plates
    Quantity 10
    Thickness (inner and outer plate)
        Standard.. 3.8 mm
        Service limit .... 3.6 mm
    Thickness (all other plates)
        Standard.. 3.3 mm
        Service limit .... 3.1 mm
Plain plates
    Quantity 9
    Warpage (service limit) .... 0.20 mm
Clutch cable freeplay .... see Chapter 1

Engine, clutch and transmission

Lubrication system

Oil pressure @ 5000 rpm	40 psi (2.76 Bar), oil at 80°C
Oil pump rotor tip-to-outer rotor clearance	
Standard	0.15 mm
Service limit	0.20 mm
Oil pump outer rotor-to-body clearance	
Standard	0.15 to 0.22 mm
Service limit	0.35 mm
Oil pump rotor end-float	
Standard	0.02 to 0.07 mm
Service limit	0.10 mm

Connecting rods and bearings

	Standard	Service limit
Connecting rod side clearance	0.15 to 0.30 mm	0.50 mm
Connecting rod big-end bearing oil clearance		
All Sprint and Tiger models, Speed Triple models with 'old condition' crankshaft (see Note below)	0.036 to 0.066 mm	0.10 mm
Speed Triple models with 'new condition' crankshaft (see Note below)	0.030 to 0.056 mm	0.10 mm
Connecting rod big-end journal diameter		
All Sprint and Tiger models, Speed Triple models with 'old condition' crankshaft (see Note below)	34.984 to 35.000 mm	34.960 mm
Speed Triple models with 'new condition' crankshaft (see Note below)	35.002 to 35.018 mm	34.978 mm

Note: *The old condition crankshaft is fitted to all Speed Triples up to engine No. 506365, and on the following later Nos.: 513923, 514367, 514684, 514729, 514746, 514848, 514868, 514956, 514978, 515007, 515069, 515103, 515123, 515177, 515560, 515811, 516237, 516392, 516563, 516951, 516989, 517127, 517135, 517217, 517284, 517300, 517613*

Crankshaft and main bearings

	Standard	Service limit
Main bearing oil clearance	0.019 to 0.044 mm	0.07 mm
Main bearing journal diameter	37.960 to 37.976 mm	37.936 mm
Crankshaft end-float	0.05 to 0.20 mm	0.40 mm
Crankshaft run-out	0.02 mm or less	0.05 mm

Transmission

Primary reduction ratio	1.75 to 1 (105/60)
Gear ratios (No. of teeth)	
First gear	2.733 to 1 (41/15)
Second gear	1.947 to 1 (37/19)
Third gear	1.545 to 1 (34/22)
Fourth gear	1.292 to 1 (31/24)
Fifth gear	1.154 to 1 (30/26)
Sixth gear	
Sprint ST and Speed Triple	1.074 to 1 (29/27)
Tiger and Sprint GT	1:100 to 1 (28/28)
Tiger Sport	1.037 to 1 (28/27)
Final reduction ratio	
Sprint	2.210 to 1 (42/19)
Speed Triple models	
Up to VIN 461331	2.333 to 1 (42/18)
From VIN 461332	2.339 to 1 (43/18)
Tiger	2.444 to 1 (44/18)
Tiger Sport	2.500 to 1 (45/18)

Selector drum and forks

Selector fork end width	
Standard	5.8 to 5.9 mm
Service limit	5.7 mm
Selector fork groove width in gears	
Standard	6.0 to 6.1 mm
Service limit	6.25 mm
Selector fork-to-groove clearance	0.55 mm maximum

Torque settings

Alternator cover bolts	
Sprint	10 Nm
Speed Triple and Tiger	9 Nm
Alternator rotor bolt	105 Nm

Torque settings (continued)

Balancer shaft end cap	60 Nm
Cam chain guide blade pivot bolt	18 Nm
Cam chain support bolt	10 Nm
Cam chain tensioner end bolt	23 Nm
Cam chain tensioner mounting bolts	9 Nm
Cam chain tensioner blade pivot bolt	18 Nm
Cam chain upper guide bolts	10 Nm
Camshaft cap and holder bolts	10 Nm
Camshaft sprocket bolts	15 Nm
Clutch centre nut	
Up to engine number 502589	105 Nm
From engine number 502590, and earlier engines retro-fitted with the new nut (see text)	150 Nm
Clutch cover bolts	
Sprint	10 Nm
Speed Triple to VIN 461331, Tiger	9 Nm
Speed Triple from VIN 461332, Tiger SE and Tiger Sport	8 Nm
Clutch pressure plate bolts	10 Nm
Connecting rod cap nuts	see Section 25
Crankcase 6 mm bolts (see text)	12 Nm
Crankcase 8 mm bolts (see text)	32 Nm
Crankcase cover bolts	
Sprint	10 Nm
Speed Triple and Tiger	9 Nm
Cylinder head bolts	
Stage 1	20 Nm
Stage 2	40 Nm
Stage 3	Angle-tighten 90°
Cylinder head-to-cylinder block screws	10 Nm
Engine mounting bolts	
Sprint models	
Mounting bolts	80 Nm
Upper rear and front adjusters on GT models	5 Nm
All other adjusters	3 Nm
Adjuster bolt locknuts	55 Nm
Swingarm spindle adjuster	15 Nm
Swingarm spindle adjuster lock ring	30 Nm
Swingarm pivot bolt	60 Nm
Suspension drag link-to-frame bolt	48 Nm
Speed Triple models up to VIN 461331	
Engine mounting bracket-to-cylinder head bolts	30 Nm
All other mounting bolts	80 Nm
Swingarm spindle adjuster	15 Nm
Swingarm spindle adjuster lock ring	30 Nm
Swingarm pivot bolt	60 Nm
Suspension drag link-to-frame bolt	90 Nm
Speed Triple models from VIN 461332	
Engine mounting bracket-to-cylinder head bolts	30 Nm
All other mounting bolts (but see text)	80 Nm
Front mounting adjuster	3 Nm
Middle and rear mounting adjusters	5 Nm
Tiger and Tiger SE models	
Engine mounting bracket-to-cylinder head bolts	30 Nm
Adjusters (see text)	
Initial setting – all bolts, Tiger	20 Nm
Initial setting – all bolts, Tiger SE	30 Nm
Left-hand side mounting bolts	
Initial setting – all bolts	20 Nm
Final setting – upper rear bolt	85 Nm
Final setting – front bolt	80 Nm
Final setting – lower rear bolt	80 Nm
Final setting – bracket-to-frame bolt	85 Nm
Right-hand side mounting bolts	
Upper rear bolt	85 Nm
Front bolt	80 Nm
Lower rear bolt	80 Nm
Middle bolt	85 Nm

Torque settings (continued)

Engine mounting bolts (continued)
- Tiger Sport models
  - Engine mounting bracket-to-cylinder head bolts .... 30 Nm
  - Adjusters .... 5 Nm
  - Left-hand side mounting bolts
    - Initial setting – all bolts .... 30 Nm
    - Final setting – upper rear bolt .... 100 Nm
    - Final setting – bracket-to-frame bolt .... 85 Nm
    - Final setting – front bolt .... 100 Nm
    - Final setting – lower rear bolt .... 100 Nm
  - Right-hand side mounting bolts
    - Upper rear bolt .... 85 Nm
    - Lower rear bolt .... 85 Nm
    - Front bolt .... 85 Nm
    - Middle bolt .... 85 Nm

External oil hose banjo bolts to cylinder head .... 25 Nm
Gearchange mechanism centralising spring locating pin .... 23 Nm
Internal oil pipe banjo bolts .... 8 Nm
Oil cooler hose union bolts .... 9 Nm
Oil cooler mounting bolts/nuts .... 9 Nm
Oil pressure relief valve .... 15 Nm
Oil pump driven sprocket bolt .... 15 Nm
Oil pump mounting bolts .... 12 Nm
Selector drum bearing retainer bolt .... 12 Nm
Selector drum cam plate bolt .... 12 Nm
Selector fork shaft retainer plate bolt .... 12 Nm
Starter clutch bolt .... 54 Nm
Starter cover bolts
- Sprint .... 10 Nm
- Speed Triple and Tiger .... 9 Nm

Stopper arm pivot bolt .... 12 Nm
Sump bolts .... 12 Nm
Timing inspection cap .... 18 Nm
Valve cover bolts .... 14 Nm

1 General information

The engine/transmission is a water-cooled, in-line three-cylinder design, fitted across the frame. The twelve valves are operated by double overhead camshafts, chain driven off the right-hand end of the crankshaft. The pistons run in removable liners, surrounded by a water jacket. A single balancer shaft is driven directly off a gear on the right-hand end of the crankshaft.

The engine/transmission unit is constructed in aluminium alloy with the crankcase divided horizontally. The crankcase incorporates a wet sump, pressure fed lubrication system. An external oil feed pipe supplies oil to the cylinder head and cam components. The oil pump is chain driven off the back of the clutch housing and in turn drives the water pump.

The clutch is of the wet, multi-plate type and is gear driven off the crankshaft. The alternator is mounted on the left-hand end of the crankshaft.

The transmission is of the six-speed constant mesh type. Final drive to the rear wheel is by chain and sprockets.

Many of the bolts used on Triumph motorcycles are of the Torx type. Unless you are already equipped with a good range of Torx bits, you are advised to purchase a set before attempting work on the engine. Make sure you get bits that can be used in conjunction with a socket set so that a torque wrench can be applied – a Torx key set will not be adequate on its own, though will be a useful addition to the bits.

2 Component access

Operations possible with the engine in the frame

The components and assemblies listed below can be removed without having to remove the engine/transmission assembly from the frame. If however, a number of areas require attention at the same time, removal of the engine is recommended.

Valve cover
Cam chain tensioner
Camshafts and followers
Cam chain and tensioner blade (not guide blade)
Starter motor
Starter clutch
Alternator
Water pump
Clutch
Gearchange mechanism (selector arm/shaft, stopper arm and detent cam plate)
Oil pump
Oil cooler
Sump and oil strainer

Operations requiring engine removal

It is necessary to remove the engine/transmission assembly from the frame to gain access to the following components.

Cylinder head
Cam chain guide blade
Cylinder liners and pistons
Connecting rods and bearings
Crankshaft and bearings
Balancer shaft
Transmission shafts
Selector drum and forks
Oil pressure relief valve

3 Engine wear assessment

Cylinder compression check

Note: *Turning the engine over with the ignition coils removed will generate a fault code in the engine management system – to clear this you will need to see a Triumph dealer equipped with the Diagnostic tool.*

1 Among other things, poor engine performance may be caused by leaking valves, incorrect valve clearances, a leaking head gasket, or worn pistons, rings and/or cylinder liners. A cylinder compression check will help pinpoint these conditions and can also indicate the presence of excessive carbon deposits in the cylinder heads.

2 The only tools required are a compression gauge and a spark plug wrench. A compression gauge with a threaded end to fit into the spark plug hole is preferable to one with a rubber cone end that has to held pressed against the hole. Depending on the outcome of the initial test, a squirt-type oil can may also be needed.

3 Make sure the valve clearances are correctly set (see Chapter 1).

4 Run the engine until it is at normal operating temperature. Remove the spark plugs (see Chapter 1).

5 Fit the gauge into the No. 1 cylinder spark plug hole. If the rubber cone type is used keep the gauge pressed hard onto the hole throughout the test to maintain a good seal – it is a good idea to have an assistant to do this as you also need to pull the clutch lever in and hold the throttle wide open while turning the engine over on the starter motor to do the test.

6 With the ignition switch ON, the kill switch set to RUN, the clutch lever pulled in and the throttle held fully open, turn the engine over on the starter motor until the gauge reading has built up and stabilised **(see illustration)**.

7 Record the reading, then repeat for the remaining cylinders.

8 Generally a range of 150 to 180 psi (10 to 12.5 Bar) is normal, while much above or below this can be considered high or low and should be investigated. Also, there should be no more than about 25 psi (1.7 Bar) difference between any of the cylinders, even if the figures for all cylinders are within the general limits.

9 If the reading is low, it could be due to a worn cylinder bore, piston or rings, failure of the head gasket, or worn valve seats. To determine which is the cause, pour a small quantity of engine oil into the spark plug hole to seal the rings, then repeat the compression test. If the figures are noticeably higher the cause is worn cylinder, piston or rings. If there is no change the cause is a leaking head gasket or worn valve seats.

10 If the reading is high there could be a build-up of carbon deposits in the combustion chamber, or the cylinder head gasket is too thin. Remove the cylinder head and scrape all deposits off the piston and the cylinder head, and on installation fit a new gasket.

Oil pressure check

11 To check the oil pressure, a suitable gauge and adapter that screws into the oil pressure switch will be needed. Triumph do not list an adapter as a spare part, but it is worth checking with a dealer as to availability. Otherwise, remove the pressure switch (see Chapter 8), and take it to an accessory dealer to match it up – If you are buying a pressure gauge, it may well come with a range of adapters. Refit the pressure switch before running the engine.

12 Warm the engine up to normal operating temperature then stop it. On Sprint models remove the right-hand fairing side panel (see Chapter 7).

13 Remove the oil pressure switch (see Chapter 8) and screw the adapter in its place. Connect the gauge to the adapter.

14 Start the engine and increase the engine speed to 5000 rpm whilst watching the gauge reading. The oil pressure should be similar to that given in the Specifications at the start of this Chapter.

15 If the pressure is significantly lower than the standard, the relief valve is stuck open, the oil pump is faulty, the oil pump pick-up strainer is blocked or there is other engine damage. Begin diagnosis by checking the oil pump pick-up strainer (see Section 18), then the oil pump. If those items check out okay, chances are the bearing oil clearances are excessive and the engine needs to be overhauled.

16 If the pressure is too high, the relief valve is stuck closed. To check it, see Section 19.

17 Stop the engine and unscrew the gauge and adapter from the crankcase. Install the oil pressure switch (see Chapter 8).

18 On Sprint models install the fairing side panel (see Chapter 7).

4 Engine removal and installation

Caution: The engine is very heavy. Engine removal and installation should be carried out with the aid of at least one assistant. Personal injury or damage could occur if the engine falls or is dropped. A hydraulic or mechanical floor jack should be used to support and lower or raise the engine if possible.

Removal

1 Position the bike on its centrestand on Sprint models and on an auxiliary stand on Speed Triple and Tiger models, so that it is supported in an upright position, making sure it is secure. On Sprint and Speed Triple models note that the swingarm pivot must be slackened before removing the engine to allow expansion of the frame, so if you have a stand that locates in the pivot points, slacken the pivot before fitting the stand (see Step 27). Lock the front brake on by fitting a cable-tie around the handlebar and brake lever. Work can be made easier by raising the machine to a suitable height on an hydraulic ramp.

2 If the engine is dirty, particularly around its mountings, wash it thoroughly before starting any major dismantling. This will make work much easier and rule out the possibility of caked-on lumps of dirt falling into some vital component.

3 Remove the seat (see Chapter 7). Remove the battery (see Chapter 8).

4 On all Sprint models remove the fairing side panels, on ST models remove the seat cowling, on GT models remove the side covers (see Chapter 7).

5 On Speed Triple models remove the side panels (See Chapter 7). On 2011-on models (from VIN 461332) remove the radiator cowls (see Chapter 7), then remove the left-hand cowl bracket **(see illustration)**.

6 On Tiger models remove the fairing side panels, side panels, seat cowling and belly-pan (see Chapter 7). On Tiger Sport remove the engine cover on the left-hand side by pulling it away to release the pegs from the grommets **(see illustration)**.

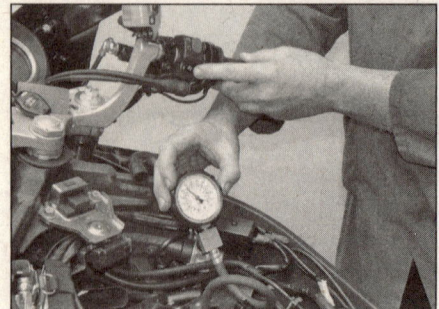

3.6 Checking cylinder compression

4.5 Unscrew the bolts (arrowed) and remove the bracket

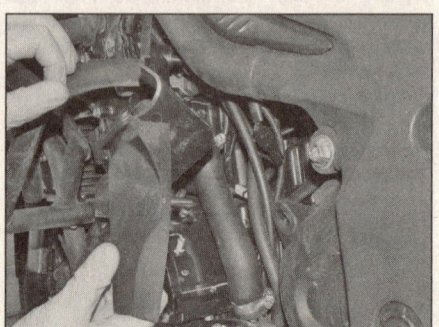

4.6 Release and remove the engine cover

Engine, clutch and transmission 2•7

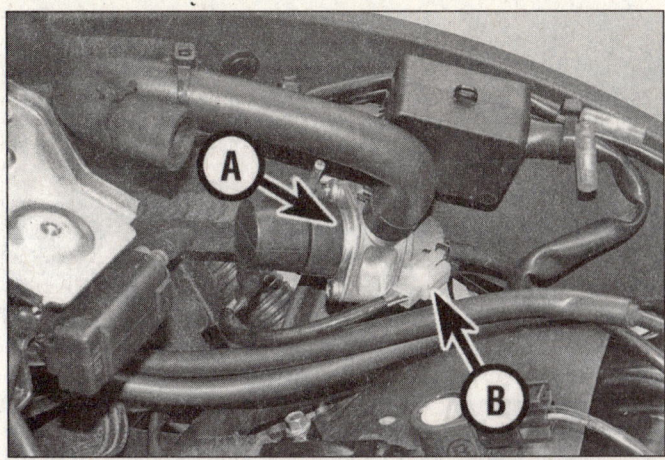

4.7a SAIS solenoid valve (A) and its wiring connector (B) – Sprint models

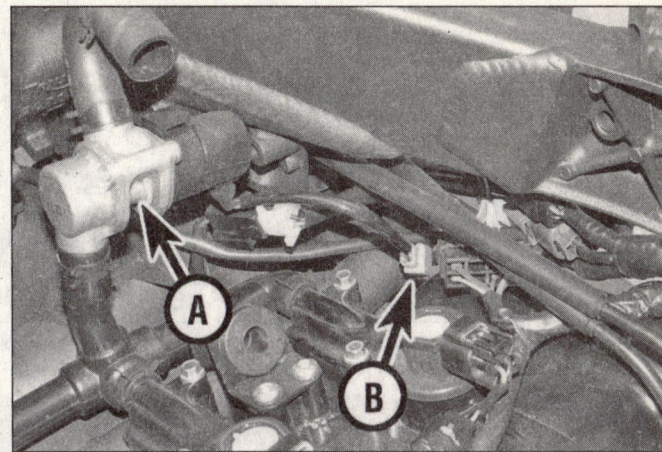

4.7b SAIS solenoid valve (A) and its wiring connector (B) – Speed Triple up to VIN 461331 and Tiger models

4.7c Detach the hoses (arrowed) and remove the valve

4.13 Note the alignment, then unscrew the bolt (arrowed) and slide the arm or lever off the shaft

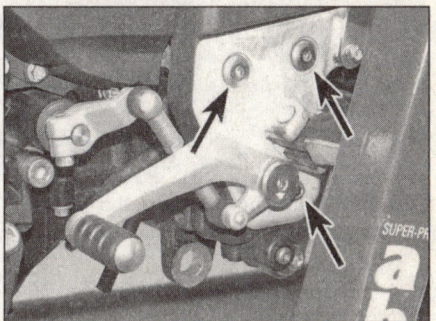

4.14 Unscrew the three bolts (arrowed) securing each footrest bracket

7 Remove the fuel tank and the airbox (see Chapter 4). On all models except 2011-on Speed Triple models (from VIN 461332) trace the wiring from the secondary air injection system solenoid valve and disconnect it at the connector **(see illustrations)**. On all models release the clips and disconnect the air hoses from the valve cover and remove the valve along with the hoses, noting how it locates **(see illustration)**.
8 Drain the engine oil (see Chapter 1). Remove the oil cooler along with its hoses (see Section 6).
9 Drain the coolant (see Chapter 1).
10 Remove the radiator along with all the coolant hoses (i.e. detaching them from the engine rather than the radiator), noting their routing (see Chapter 3). It is advisable to tag the end of each hose using masking tape, then write the location of the hose on the tape. On Sprint models remove the air intake duct – it will probably drop out as the radiator is removed.
11 Remove the exhaust system (Chapter 4).
12 Remove the front sprocket (see Chapter 6).
13 Note the alignment of the punch mark on the gearchange shaft end with that on the lever or linkage arm clamp (according to model) – if the punch marks are not visible make your own mark where the slot in the lever or arm aligns with the shaft. Unscrew the pinch bolt and slide the lever or arm off the shaft **(see illustration)**.
14 On Tiger models, remove the brake pedal (see Chapter 5). Unscrew the three bolts securing each footrest bracket, then detach it from the frame, on the left-hand side along with the gearchange lever and linkage **(see illustration)**.
15 Detach the clutch cable from the release lever on the clutch cover (see Section 17).

4.16 Unscrew the nut and detach the lead from the starter motor

16 If required, remove the starter motor (see Chapter 8). If it is not being removed, pull back the rubber boot on the terminal, them unscrew the nut and detach the lead **(see illustration)**.
17 If the starter motor was not removed, disconnect the wiring connector from the oil pressure switch **(see illustration)** – on early models lift the rubber boot to access the connector.
18 Trace the wiring from the top of the alternator cover on the left-hand side of the engine and disconnect it at the connector

4.17 Disconnect the oil pressure switch wiring connector (late model type switch shown)

4.18a Alternator wiring connector (arrowed) – Sprint

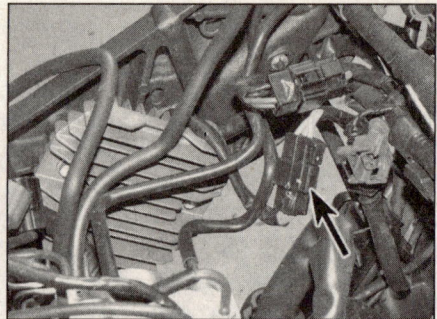

4.18b Alternator wiring connector (arrowed) – Speed Triple

4.18c Alternator wiring connector (arrowed) – Tiger

4.22 Detach the wire from the neutral switch

4.25 Unscrew the bolt (arrowed) and disconnect the earth leads from the crankcase

with the three yellow wires **(see illustrations)**.

19 Remove the sidestand, and if required its bracket along with the sidestand switch (see Chapter 5).

20 Trace the wiring from the speed sensor, which is in the top of the crankcase on the left-hand side, and disconnect it at the connector.

21 Trace the wiring from the crankshaft position sensor, which comes out of the crankcase at the same point as the alternator wiring, and disconnect it at the connector.

22 Detach the wire from the neutral switch **(see illustration)**.

23 Either displace the throttle body assembly from the cylinder head and rest it on some rag clear of the engine (if you do this it is not necessary to detach the throttle cables), or if preferred remove the throttle body assembly completely (see Chapter 4). Plug the intake manifold joints with clean rags to prevent anything dropping inside. Remove the fuel rail and injectors (see Chapter 4).

24 Trace the wiring from the engine coolant temperature sensor, which is in the back of the cylinder head on the left-hand side, and disconnect it at the connector.

25 Detach the earth leads from the engine **(see illustration)**.

26 Remove the ignition coils **(see illustrations 7.4a and b)**.

27 On Sprint models, and Speed Triple models up to VIN 461331, unscrew the bolt from the right-hand end of the swingarm pivot **(see illustration)**. Unscrew the swingarm spindle adjuster locknut on the right-hand side using either the Triumph special tool (Part No. T3880295) or a suitable peg spanner **(see illustration)**. Thread the swingarm spindle adjuster a little way out of the frame on the right-hand side, again using either the Triumph special tool (Part No. T3880290) or a suitable peg spanner **(see illustration)**. Slacken the nut on the bolt securing the suspension drag link to the frame **(see illustrations)**.

4.27a Unscrew the bolt (arrowed)

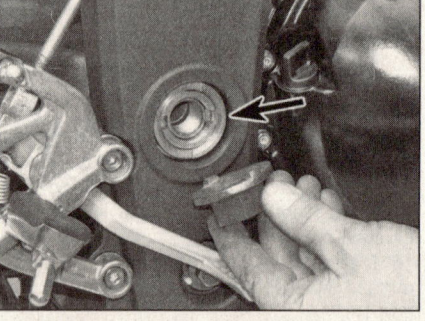

4.27b Unscrew the locknut (arrowed) – this is a tool we made

4.27c Slacken the adjuster – this is a tool made by cutting into an old socket

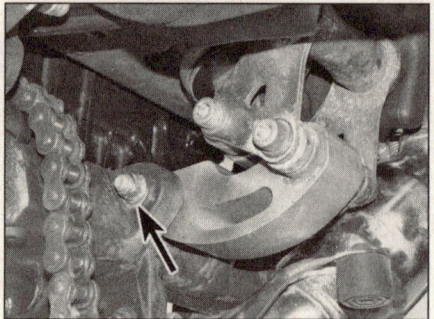

4.27d Drag link bolt nut (arrowed) – Sprint

4.27e Drag link bolt nut (arrowed) – Speed Triple

Engine, clutch and transmission

4.31a The engine is held by three bolts (arrowed) on each side

4.31b Note how the brackets are fitted

28 At this point, position an hydraulic jack under the engine with a block of wood between the jack head and sump. Make sure the jack is centrally positioned so the engine will not topple in any direction when the last mounting bolt is removed. Take the weight of the engine on the jack.

29 Unless you are using a ramp with a front wheel clamp, also place a block of wood under the rear wheel to prevent the bike tilting back when the engine is removed. Check that all wiring, cables and hoses are disconnected and clear of the engine. Remove the fairing/belly-pan and/or oil cooler mounting brackets as required according to model – this can be done after removing the engine if preferred, but take care not to rest the engine on them at any point as they will bend.

30 When removing the engine mounting bolts, retrieve all nuts, washers and spacers from the mountings and slip them back on the bolts in their correct order for safekeeping, noting carefully where each fits.

31 On Sprint models, have an assistant steady the engine then unscrew and remove the nuts on the inner ends of the engine mounting bolts – three on each side **(see illustration)**. Note how the radiator/oil cooler brackets are secured by the nuts on the front mounting bolts **(see illustration)**. Withdraw the upper and lower rear bolts and retrieve the drive chain rubbing block held between the engine and frame by the lower rear bolt on the left-hand side, noting how it fits **(see illustration)**. Slip the drive chain off the output shaft **(see illustration)**. Lower the engine on the jack, allowing it to pivot down on the front bolts **(see illustration)**. Remove the jack from under the engine and lower the engine until it rests, then support it, withdraw the front bolts and manoeuvre the engine clear of the frame and onto the work surface. Unscrew the engine mounting adjuster locknuts on the right-hand side using either the Triumph special tool (Part No. T3880088) or a suitable peg spanner **(see illustration 4.41)**. Thread the engine mounting adjusters out of the frame until they no longer protrude on the inside **(see illustration 4.34a)**.

32 On Speed Triple models, undo the bolts securing the frame-to-cylinder head mounting bracket on the left-hand side and remove the

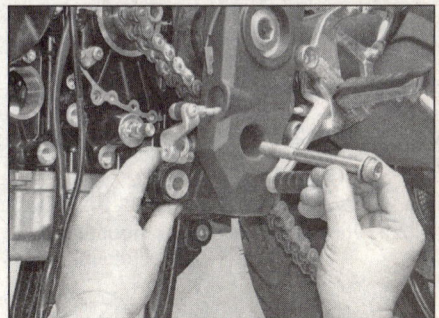

4.31c Retrieve the chain rubbing block when removing the left-hand lower rear bolt

4.31d Slip the chain off the end of the shaft

4.31e Pivot the engine down on the front bolts, then withdraw the bolts and remove the engine

2•10 Engine, clutch and transmission

4.32a Unscrew the bolts (arrowed) and remove the bracket

4.32b Engine mounting bolts – right-hand side

4.32c Upper and lower rear mounting bolts (arrowed) – left-hand side

4.32d Front mounting bolt (arrowed) – left-hand side

bracket, noting how it fits **(see illustration)**. Have an assistant steady the engine and remove the remaining mounting bolts and nuts, on models up to VIN 461331 noting any spacers fitted with the bolts on the right-hand side, and on 2011-on models (from VIN 461332) retrieving the chain rubbing block from between the engine and frame with the lower bolt on the left-hand side **(see illustration)**. On 2011-on models (from VIN 461332) thread the four engine mounting adjusters on the right-hand side out of the frame until they no longer protrude on the inside using tool T3880377 or equivalent. Lower the engine on the jack and slip the drive chain off the output shaft **(see illustration 4.31d)**. Manoeuvre the engine clear of the frame, then lift it off the jack and onto the work surface. On 2011-on models (from VIN 461332) note that Triumph specify to use new nuts when installing the engine.

33 On Tiger models, undo the bolts securing the frame-to-cylinder head mounting bracket on the left-hand side and remove the bracket, noting how it fits **(see illustration)**. Unscrew the nuts on the upper and lower rear and middle mounting bolts on the right-hand side, then remove the bolts **(see illustration)**. Thread

4.33a Unscrew the bolts (arrowed) and remove the bracket

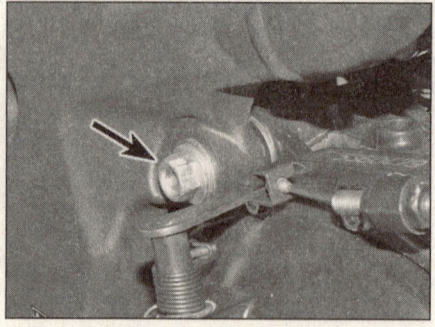

4.33b Upper rear mounting bolt (arrowed) – right-hand side

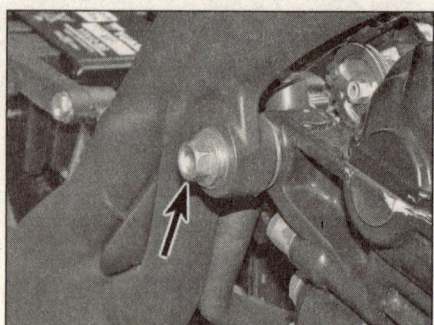

4.33c Middle mounting bolt (arrowed) – right-hand side

Engine, clutch and transmission 2•11

4.33d Lower rear bolt – left-hand side

4.33e Front mounting bolt (arrowed) – right-hand side

the three engine mounting adjusters away from the engine using the Triumph tool (Part No. T3880377). Unscrew the nuts on the upper and lower rear mounting bolts on the left-hand side, then remove the bolts and retrieve the chain rubbing block from between the engine and frame with the lower bolt (see illustrations). Slacken the front mounting bolt on each side. Have an assistant steady the engine, then lower the engine on the jack, allowing it to pivot around the front mounting bolts, and slip the drive chain off the output shaft. Remove the front mounting bolts and manoeuvre the engine clear of the frame, then lift it off the jack and onto the work surface. Thread the front engine mounting adjuster on the right-hand side away from the engine using the Triumph tool (Part No. T3880377). Discard the stainless steel bolts for the upper rear mount on each side, the middle mount on the right and the bracket-to-frame bolt on the left, and discard all the nuts fitted with all the mounting bolts – new ones must be used when installing the engine.

⚠ Warning: The engine is heavy and may cause injury if it falls.

Installation
Sprint

34 Make sure the engine mounting adjusters do not protrude from the inside of the frame (see illustrations).

35 With the aid of an assistant place the engine under the frame and carefully raise the front as shown until the front mounting bolt holes align, then insert the bolts, not forgetting the washer with the left-hand bolt (see illustration 4.31e). Now raise the back of the engine, using a jack if required, slipping the drive chain around the output shaft as you do, until all the rear mounting holes align (see illustration 4.31d). Make sure no wires, cables or hoses become trapped between the engine and the frame. Now follow the correct procedure to install and tighten the mounting bolts as detailed below.

Caution: The engine mounting bolts must be tightened in the correct sequence. Failure to do so could leave the engine incorrectly aligned in the frame, placing undue stress on it, which could lead to severe damage.

36 Fit the washers on the left-hand rear mounting bolts then fit them through the frame and engine, fitting the chain rubbing block between the engine and frame with the lower rear bolt (see illustration 4.31c). Install the right-hand mounting bolts (see illustration 4.31a). Fit the mounting bolt nuts loosely, securing the radiator/oil cooler brackets on the front bolts (see illustration 4.31b).

37 Lower the jack if used and remove it.

38 Tighten the left-hand upper rear mounting bolt, then the left-hand lower rear mounting bolt, and then the left-hand front mounting bolt, to the torque setting specified at the beginning of the Chapter – counter-hold the nut on the inner end of each bolt as you tighten them.

39 Tighten the three engine mounting adjusters on the right-hand side to the specified torque setting using the Triumph tool or suitable hex bit (see illustration).

40 Tighten the right-hand front mounting bolt, then the right-hand lower rear mounting bolt, then the right-hand upper rear mounting bolt, to the specified torque setting, counter-holding the nuts on the inner ends, and making sure that the adjuster bolts do not turn with them – by making a couple of reference marks between the adjuster bolt and the frame you will be able to tell whether the adjuster bolts have moved.

41 Fit the engine mounting adjuster locknuts and tighten them to the specified torque

4.34a Make sure the upper and lower rear adjusters (arrowed) . . .

4.34b . . . and the front adjuster (arrowed) are flush with the inside of the frame

4.39 Tighten the adjuster bolts using a large hex key as shown

4.41 Fit the locknuts onto the adjusters and tighten them using a peg spanner

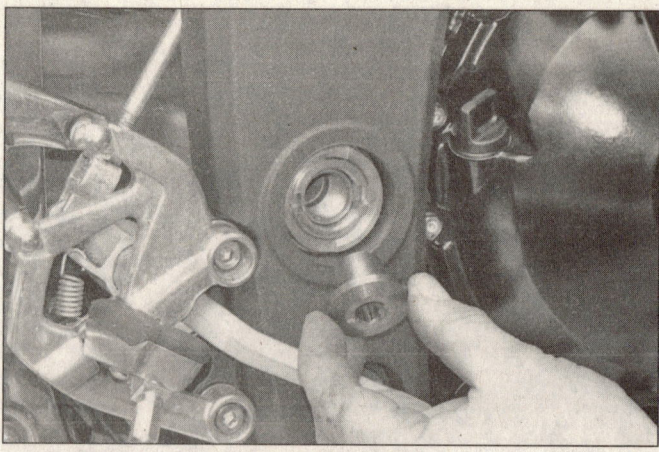

4.43 Fit the swingarm pivot bolt and tighten it to the specified torque

setting using the Triumph tool or suitable peg spanner **(see illustration)**.

42 Tighten the swingarm spindle adjuster, then fit and tighten the adjuster lockring, to the specified torque settings using the Triumph tools or suitable peg spanner **(see illustrations 4.27c and b)**.

43 Fit and tighten the swingarm pivot bolt to the specified torque setting **(see illustration)**. Tighten the drag link bolt nut to the specified torque **(see illustration 4.27d)**.

44 The remainder of the installation procedure is a direct reversal of the removal sequence, noting the following points.
- Tighten all nuts and bolts to the specified torque settings (where given).
- Align the previously made mark on the gearchange linkage arm or lever with that on the gearchange shaft end **(see illustration 4.13)**.
- Make sure all wires, cables and hoses are correctly routed and connected, and secured by any clips or ties.
- Adjust the drive chain as described in Chapter 1.
- Use new gaskets on the exhaust pipe connections, and new O-rings and sealing washers on the coolant and oil connections, as appropriate.
- Refill the engine with oil and coolant (see Chapter 1).
- Adjust the throttle and clutch cable freeplay (see Chapter 1).
- Adjust the drive chain slack (see Chapter 1).
- Start the engine and check that there are no oil or coolant leaks before installing the body panels.

Speed Triple –
2005 to 2010 models up to VIN 461331

45 With the aid of an assistant place the engine on top of the jack and block of wood and carefully raise it into position in the frame, slipping the drive chain around the output shaft as you do so **(see illustration 4.31d)**. Manoeuvre the engine as required so that all mounting holes align. Make sure no wires, cables or hoses become trapped between the engine and the frame.

46 Fit the washers on the mounting bolts then fit them through the frame and engine, along with any spacers previously fitted with the right-hand bolts **(see illustrations 4.32b, c and d)**. **Note:** *Triumph specify that spacers must be fitted on the right-hand mounting bolts to eliminate gaps between the frame and the engine unit (see Step 50).* Fit the mounting bolt nuts loosely.

Caution: The engine mounting bolts must be tightened in the correct sequence. Failure to do so could leave the engine incorrectly aligned in the frame, placing undue stress on it, which could lead to severe damage.

47 Fit the frame-to-cylinder head bracket on the left-hand side, and tighten the two bracket-to-cylinder head bolts to the torque setting specified at the beginning of the Chapter **(see illustration 4.32a)**. **Note:** *Do not tighten the bracket-to-frame bolt at this stage (see Step 53).* Remove the jack from under the engine. Now follow the correct tightening procedure as detailed below.

48 Counter-hold the nut and tighten the left-hand front mounting bolt to the specified torque setting.

49 Counter-hold the nuts and tighten the left-hand upper rear mounting bolt, then tighten the left-hand lower rear mounting bolt, to the specified torque setting.

50 Check for gaps between the frame and the engine unit at all right-hand mounting locations – if spacers were fitted originally they should eliminate any gaps. However, if necessary, spacers are available in 0.5, 1.0, 1.5 and 2.0 mm thicknesses from Triumph dealers. Spacers must be fitted to avoid straining the frame when the mounting bolts are tightened. **Note:** *If a spacer is needed for the right-hand lower rear engine mounting bolt an equivalent sized spacer (part No. T3550355) must be fitted on the bolt that secures the suspension drag link to the frame.*

51 Counter-hold the nuts and tighten the right-hand front mounting bolt, then tighten the right-hand middle mounting bolt to the specified torque setting.

52 Counter-hold the nuts and tighten the right-hand upper rear mounting bolt, then tighten the right-hand lower rear mounting bolt to the specified torque setting.

53 Tighten the left-hand bracket-to-frame bolt to the specified torque setting.

54 Tighten the swingarm spindle adjuster, then fit the adjuster lockring to the specified torque settings using the Triumph tool or suitable peg spanner **(see illustrations 4.27c and b)**.

55 Fit and tighten the swingarm pivot bolt to the specified torque setting **(see illustration 4.43)**. Tighten the drag link bolt nut to the specified torque **(see illustration 4.27e)**.

56 The remainder of the installation procedure is a direct reversal of the removal sequence, noting the points in Step 44.

Speed Triple –
2011-on models from VIN 461332

57 Make sure the engine mounting adjusters do not protrude from the inside of the frame. Fit the frame-to-cylinder head bracket to the left-hand side of the head, and tighten the bolts finger-tight.

58 With the aid of an assistant place the engine on top of the jack and block of wood and carefully raise it into position in the frame, slipping the drive chain around the output shaft as you do so **(see illustration 4.31d)**. Manoeuvre the engine as required so that all mounting holes align. Make sure no wires, cables or hoses become trapped between the engine and the frame.

59 Fit the washers on the mounting bolts then fit them through the frame and engine, not forgetting the chain rubbing block between the engine and frame with the lower bolt on the left-hand side. Fit the new mounting bolt nuts loosely to the bolts on the left-hand side. Now follow the correct tightening procedure as detailed below.

Caution: The engine mounting bolts must be tightened in the correct sequence. Failure to do so could leave the engine incorrectly aligned in the frame, placing undue stress on it, which could lead to severe damage.

60 Tighten the two bracket-to-cylinder head bolts to the torque setting specified at the beginning of the Chapter **(see illustration)**.

61 Counter-hold the nut on the left-hand front mounting and tighten the bolt to 20 Nm **(see illustration 4.32d)**.

62 Remove the middle mounting bolt with its washer from the right-hand side **(see illustration)**. Using tool T3880377 or equivalent, tighten the middle mounting adjuster to the specified torque setting. Apply a smear of copper grease to the threads of the bolt then refit it with its washer. Fit a new nut onto the bolt and tighten finger-tight.

63 Remove the lower rear mounting bolt with its washer from the right-hand side and tighten the adjuster to the specified torque setting. Refit the bolt with its washer (do not apply grease). Fit a new nut onto the bolt and tighten finger-tight.

64 Remove the upper rear mounting bolt with its washer from the right-hand side and tighten the adjuster to the specified torque setting. Refit the bolt with its washer. Fit a new nut onto the bolt and tighten finger-tight.

65 Remove the front mounting bolt with its washer from the right-hand side and tighten the adjuster to the specified torque setting, noting the lower setting. Refit the bolt with its washer. Fit a new nut onto the bolt and tighten finger-tight.

66 Remove the jack from under the engine.

67 On the left-hand side, tighten the upper rear mounting bolt, then the middle mounting bolt, then the front mounting bolt, then the lower rear mounting bolt, to the specified torque setting **(see illustration)** – counter-hold the nuts as you tighten the bolts.

68 On the right-hand side, tighten the upper rear mounting bolt, then the lower rear mounting bolt, then the front mounting bolt, then the middle mounting bolt, to the specified torque setting **(see illustration 4.62)** – counter-hold the nuts as you tighten the bolts.

69 The remainder of the installation procedure is a direct reversal of the removal sequence, noting the points in Step 44.

Tiger

Note: *If the upper rear, bracket-to-frame (LHS) and middle (RHS) mounting bolts on your bike have Torx heads, Triumph specify to replace them with new Hex head bolts (part Nos. T3334610, T3334620 and T3151011) along with new nuts.*

70 Make sure the engine mounting adjusters do not protrude from the inside of the frame.

71 With the aid of an assistant place the engine under the frame and carefully raise the front until the front mounting bolts align, then insert them. Fit a new nut onto the left-hand front bolt only and tighten it finger-tight. Now raise the back of the engine, using a jack if required, slipping the drive chain around the output shaft as you do **(see illustration 4.31d)**, until all the rear mounting holes align. Make sure no wires, cables or hoses become trapped between the engine and the frame. Now follow the correct procedure to install and tighten the mounting bolts as detailed below.

Caution: The engine mounting bolts must be tightened in the correct sequence. Failure to do so could leave the engine incorrectly aligned in the frame, placing undue stress on it, which could lead to severe damage.

72 Fit the lower rear bolt on the left-hand side, locating the chain rubbing block between the engine and frame **(see illustration 4.33d)**. Fit a new nut onto the bolt and tighten it finger-tight.

73 Fit the lower rear bolt on the right-hand side, but do not yet fit the nut.

74 Fit the two new hex head bolts for the upper rear mount on each side **(see illustration 4.33b)**. Fit a new nut onto the left-hand bolt only and tighten it finger-tight.

75 Fit the new hex head bolt for the middle mount on the right-hand side **(see illustration 4.33c)**.

76 Fit the frame-to-cylinder head bracket on the left-hand side and tighten the two bracket-to-cylinder head bolts finger-tight **(see illustration 4.33a)**. Fit the new hex head bolt for the bracket-to-frame mount and tighten it finger-tight. Now tighten the two bracket-to-cylinder head bolts to the torque setting specified at the beginning of the Chapter.

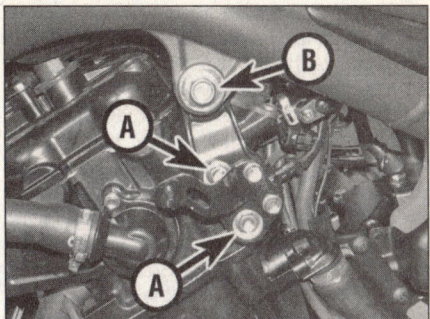

4.60 Bracket-to-cylinder head bolts (A), bracket-to-frame bolt (B)

77 Now tighten the upper rear bolt on the left-hand side, then the front bolt on the left, then the lower rear bolt on the left, then the bracket-to-frame bolt, to the initial torque setting specified at the beginning of the chapter for your model.

78 Working on each right-hand bolt in turn (four in all), but only one at a time, remove the bolt then thread the adjuster into the frame until it just contacts the engine, using the Triumph tool. Once the adjuster contacts the engine tighten it further by half a turn (180°) on Tiger models, and to 5 Nm on Tiger SE and Tiger Sport models. Fit the bolt back through the adjuster, frame and engine, then fit a new nut onto it and tighten it finger-tight.

79 On Tiger models now tighten the upper rear bolt on the left-hand side, then the front bolt on the left, then the lower rear bolt on the left, then the bracket-to-frame bolt, to the final torque setting specified at the beginning of the chapter for each bolt.

80 On Tiger SE and Tiger Sport models now tighten the upper rear bolt on the left-hand side, then the bracket-to-frame bolt, then the front bolt

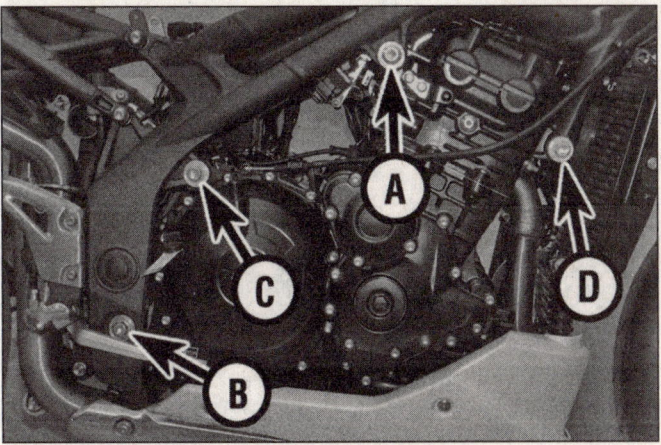

4.62 Middle mounting bolt (A), lower rear bolt (B), upper rear bolt (C), front bolt (D) – right-hand side

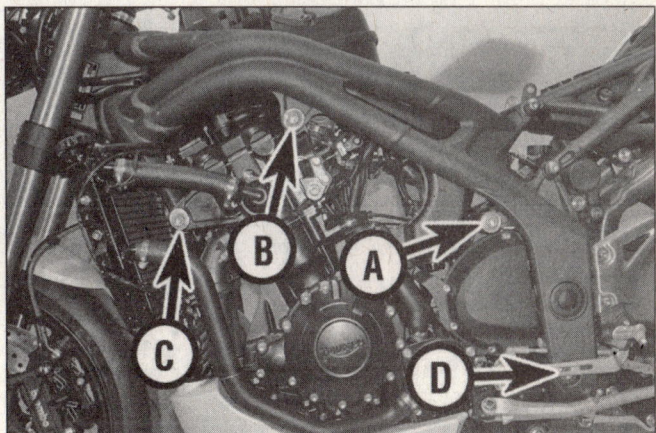

4.67 Upper rear mounting bolt (A), middle bolt (B), front bolt (C), lower rear bolt (D) – left-hand side

2•14 Engine, clutch and transmission

on the left, then the lower rear bolt on the left, to the final torque setting specified at the beginning of the chapter for each bolt for your model.

81 Remove the jack from under the engine.

82 On Tiger models now tighten the upper rear bolt on the right-hand side, then the front bolt on the right, then the lower rear bolt on the right, then the middle bolt on the right, to the torque setting specified at the beginning of the chapter for each bolt.

83 On Tiger SE and Tiger Sport models now tighten the upper rear bolt on the right-hand side, then the lower rear bolt on the right, then the front bolt on the right, then the middle bolt on the right, to the torque setting specified at the beginning of the chapter for each bolt for your model.

84 The remainder of the installation procedure is a direct reversal of the removal sequence, noting the points in Step 44.

5 Engine overhaul information

1 Before beginning the engine overhaul, read through the related procedures to familiarise yourself with the scope and requirements of the job. Overhauling an engine is not all that difficult, but it is time consuming. Check on the availability of parts and make sure that any necessary special tools are obtained in advance.

2 Most work can be done with a decent set of typical workshop hand tools, although a number of precision measuring tools are required for inspecting parts to determine if they are worn.

3 To ensure maximum life and minimum trouble from a rebuilt engine, everything must be assembled with care in a spotlessly clean environment.

Disassembly

4 Before disassembling the engine, thoroughly clean and degrease its external surfaces. This will prevent contamination of the engine internals, and will also make the job a lot easier and cleaner. A high flash-point solvent, such as paraffin (kerosene) can be used, or better still, a proprietary engine degreaser such as Gunk. Use old paintbrushes and toothbrushes to work the solvent into the various recesses of the casings. Take care to exclude solvent or water from the electrical components and intake and exhaust ports.

 Warning: The use of petrol (gasoline) as a cleaning agent should be avoided because of the risk of fire.

5 When clean and dry, position the engine on the workbench, leaving suitable clear area for working. Gather a selection of small containers, plastic bags and some labels so that parts can be grouped together in an easily identifiable manner. Also get some paper and a pen so that notes can be taken. You will also need a supply of clean rag, which should be as absorbent as possible.

6 Before commencing work, read through the appropriate section so that some idea of the necessary procedure can be gained. When removing components note that great force is seldom required, unless specified (checking the specified torque setting of the particular bolt being removed will indicate how tight it is, and therefore how much force should be needed). In many cases, a component's reluctance to be removed is indicative of an incorrect approach or removal method – if in any doubt, re-check with the text.

7 When disassembling the engine, keep 'mated' parts that have been in contact with each other during engine operation together – i.e. cylinder bores, pistons and rings, connecting rods, valves, etc,). These 'mated' parts must not be mixed up and must be installed in their original location.

8 Engine/transmission disassembly should be done in the following general order with reference to the appropriate Sections.

Remove the camshafts
Remove the cam chain/tensioner blade
Remove the cylinder head and cam chain guide blade
Remove the cylinder liners and pistons
Remove the starter motor (see Chapter 8)
Remove the clutch
Remove the oil pump
Remove the alternator (see Chapter 8)
Remove the starter motor (see Chapter 8)
Remove the water pump (see Chapter 3)
Remove the sump
Remove the gearchange mechanism
Remove the selector drum and forks
Separate the crankcase halves
Remove the crankshaft/connecting rods
Remove the balancer shaft
Remove the transmission shafts

Reassembly

9 Reassembly is accomplished by reversing the general disassembly sequence.

6 Oil cooler and hoses

Note: *The oil cooler can be removed with the engine in the frame. If work is being carried out with the engine removed ignore the preliminary steps.*

Removal

1 On Sprint models remove the fairing side panels (see Chapter 7). On Tiger models, if you are detaching the hoses from the engine, remove the belly-pan (see Chapter 7).

2 Drain the engine oil (see Chapter 1). Keep the container below the sump to catch any residual oil in the cooler and hoses.

3 On early Sprint and Speed Triple models the pipes from the cooler connect to the sump. On all other models the hoses connect to the crankcase at the front and on the right-hand side. To detach the pipes or hoses from either the engine or the cooler, unscrew the union bolts and detach the pipes or hoses, noting which fits where **(see illustration)**. Discard the O-rings as new ones must be used **(see illustration 6.7)**.

4 To remove the cooler, first detach the hoses from either the sump or the cooler as required. Unscrew the nuts and/or bolts (according to model) securing the oil cooler, noting the

6.3 Oil cooler hose unions (arrowed) – engine side

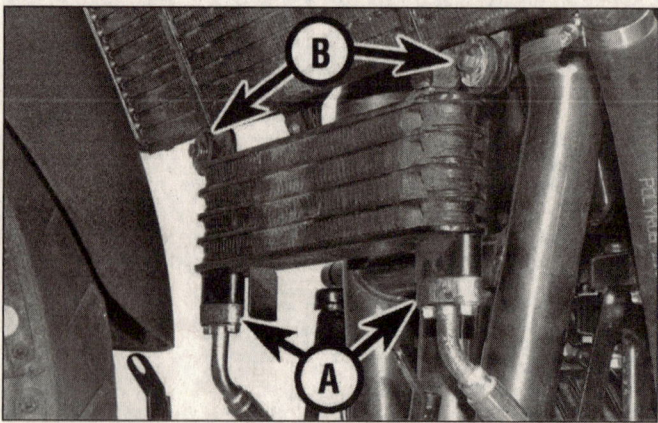

6.4a Oil cooler hose unions (A) and cooler mounting bolts (B) – Sprint models

Engine, clutch and transmission 2•15

6.4b Oil cooler mounting bolts (arrowed) – Speed Triple models

6.4c Note the trim panel (arrowed) secured by the upper bolts on Tiger models

arrangement of the collars and grommets, the guide fitted with the upper right-hand bolt on early Speed Triple models, and the trim panel on Tigers, and remove the cooler **(see illustrations)**.

5 If required remove the cooler mounting bracket(s).

6 Check the cooler for leaks and other damage. Check the cooler fins for mud, dirt and insects, which will impede the flow of air through it. If the fins are dirty, clean them using water or low pressure compressed air directed through from the rear face. If the fins are bent or distorted, straighten them carefully with a screwdriver. If the air flow is restricted by bent or damaged fins over more than 30% of the cooler's surface area, or if the cooler is leaking, replace it with a new one.

Installation

7 Installation is a reverse of the removal procedure, noting the following:
- *Use a new O-ring on each pipe or hose union, according to model **(see illustration)**.*
- *On Speed Triple models clean the threads of the hose union bolts and apply some fresh threadlock.*
- *Tighten the pipe banjo bolt or hose union bolts and the cooler mounting bolts/nuts to the torque settings specified at the beginning of the chapter.*
- *Refill the engine with oil (see Chapter 1 and Pre-ride checks). Make sure there are no leaks from the oil cooler hose unions when the engine is run.*

7 Valve cover

Note: *The valve cover can be removed with the engine in the frame. If the engine has been removed, ignore the steps which do not apply.*

Removal

1 Remove the seat and disconnect the battery negative lead (see Chapter 8).

2 On Sprint and Tiger models remove the fairing side panels (see Chapter 7). On 2011-on Speed Triple models (from VIN 461332) displace the throttle bodies from the intakes so they are clear of the valve cover (See Chapter 4).

3 Remove the fuel tank and the airbox (see Chapter 4).

4 Disconnect the ignition coil wiring

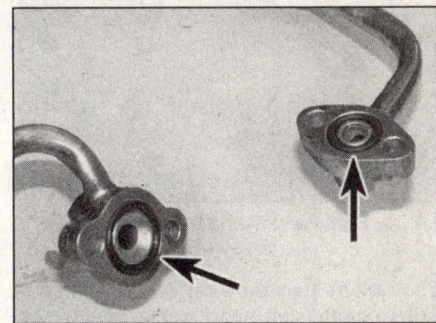

6.7 Always fit new O-rings (arrowed) onto the unions

connectors and pull the coils off the spark plugs **(see illustrations)**.

5 On all models except 2011-on Speed Triple models (from VIN 461332) trace the wiring from the secondary air injection system solenoid valve and disconnect it at the connector **(see illustration 4.7a or b)**. On all models release the clips and disconnect the air hoses from the valve cover and remove the valve along with the hoses, noting how it locates **(see illustration 4.7c)**.

6 On Sprint models lift the rubber heat shield off the valve cover, noting how it locates **(see**

7.4a Disconnect the coil wiring connectors . . .

7.4b . . . then pull the coils off the spark plugs

2•16 Engine, clutch and transmission

7.6a Lift the rubber heat shield (arrowed) off the cover

7.6b Release and displace the alarm unit (arrowed)

7.7a Undo the screws (arrowed) and displace the airbox bracket

7.7b Left-hand frame trim panel screw (arrowed)

7.7c Detach the hose (arrowed) from the reservoir . . .

7.7d . . . then draw it forwards, noting its routing (arrowed)

illustration). Release and displace the alarm unit from the left-hand frame beam (see illustration).

7 On Speed Triple and Tiger models undo the airbox bracket screws and displace the

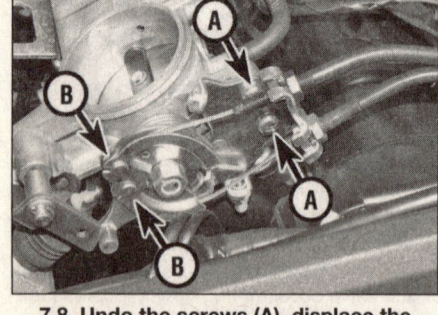

7.8 Undo the screws (A), displace the bracket, then free the cable ends (B) from the cam

bracket (see illustration). On Speed Triple models disconnect and move aside any wiring that is in the way. On 2011-on Speed Triples (from VIN 461332) remove the frame trim panel from each inner side of the frame, then disconnect the coolant hose from the reservoir and position it clear of the valve cover, noting its routing (see illustrations).

8 Undo the throttle cable bracket screws and detach the cable ends from the cam (see illustration). Move the cables aside.

9 Undo the valve cover bolts evenly and a little at a time in a criss-cross sequence, noting which fit where (see illustration). Remove the bolts with their seals, then lift the valve cover off the cylinder head and remove from the left-hand side – where necessary, move the coolant hoses to clear the cover (see illustration). *Note: If the cover is stuck, do not try to lever it off with a screwdriver. Tap it gently around the sides with a rubber*

hammer or block of wood to dislodge it.

10 Note the location of the dowels in the secondary air holes (see illustration 7.14a) – they may remain in the head or come off with the cover. Remove them for safekeeping if they are loose.

11 Examine the valve cover gasket and plug bore seals for signs of damage or deterioration – remove them and replace them with new ones if necessary (see illustrations 7.14b and 7.13). Check the seals on the cover bolts for cracks, hardening and deterioration and replace them with new ones if necessary.

Installation

12 Clean the mating surfaces of the cylinder head and the valve cover with a suitable solvent. If the original gasket is being used, remove any traces of old glue or sealant.

13 Fit the spark plug seals onto the camshaft holder (see illustration).

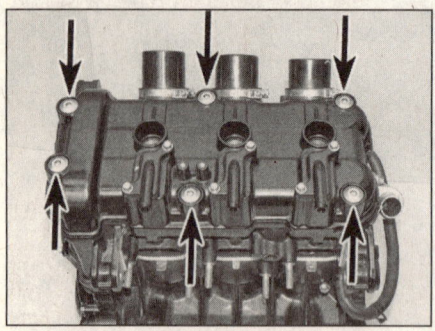

7.9a Unscrew the bolts (arrowed) . . .

7.9b . . . and remove the cover

7.13 Locate the cut-outs in the spark plug seals over the ridges on the cam holder

Engine, clutch and transmission 2•17

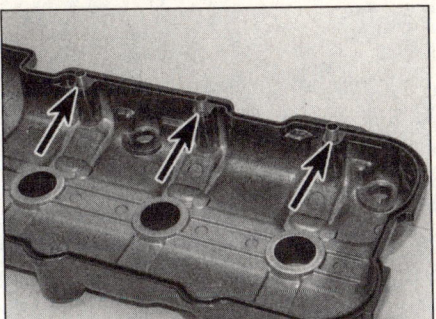
7.14a Fit the dowels (arrowed) if removed

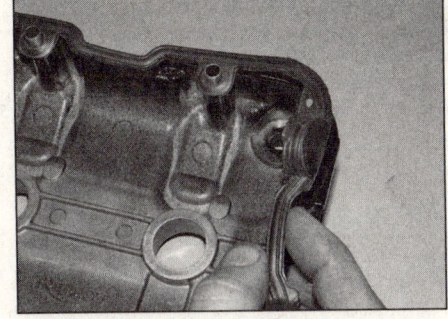
7.14b Fit the gasket over the dowels and into the groove

7.15 Apply sealant to the half-circle cutouts in the head

14 Fit the secondary air injection dowels into the air holes in the cover (see illustration). Fit the gasket into the valve cover, making sure it locates correctly into the groove (see illustration). Use a few dabs of grease to keep the gasket in place while the cover is fitted.

15 Apply a suitable silicone sealant to the corners of the cut-outs in the cylinder head where the gasket half-circles fit (see illustration).

16 Position the valve cover on the cylinder head, making sure the gasket stays in place (see illustration 7.9b). Lubricate the cover bolt seals with engine oil and fit them onto the cover. Fit the cover bolts – the two with the longer shouldered section fit at the cam chain end (see illustration). Tighten the bolts in the sequence shown and to the torque setting specified at the beginning of the Chapter (see illustration).

17 Install the remaining components in the reverse order of removal.

8 Cam chain tensioner

Note: *The cam chain tensioner can be removed with the engine in the frame. If the engine has been removed, ignore the steps which do not apply.*

Removal

1 Remove the valve cover (see Section 7). Remove the spark plugs (see Chapter 1).

7.16a Fit the sealing washers and bolts, locating the two long-shouldered bolts in the right-hand end

2 Unscrew the timing inspection cap from the right-hand crankcase cover (see illustration). Note the cap O-ring – if it is damaged or deformed a new one must be fitted on reassembly.

3 Using an Allen socket in the end of the starter clutch bolt, rotate the crankshaft clockwise until the T1 mark on the starter clutch is aligned with the index mark in the inspection hole and the arrow marks on the camshaft sprockets face inwards towards each other, parallel with the top of the cylinder head (see illustrations). In this position, the No. 1 cylinder is at TDC. If the arrows face away from each other when the T1 mark aligns, turn the crankshaft clockwise one full turn so that the T1 mark again aligns with the index mark – the arrows on the camshaft sprockets will now be facing towards each other.

4 When the tensioner is withdrawn from

7.16b Valve cover bolt tightening sequence

the cylinder head, the cam chain will be untensioned, and could jump a tooth on the intake cam sprocket. To prevent this, fit a

8.2 Remove the timing inspection cap, noting the O-ring (arrowed)

8.3a Turn the engine clockwise using the bolt (A) . . .

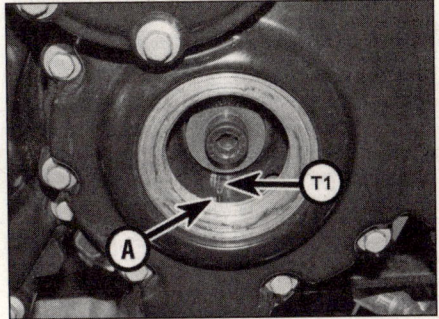
8.3b . . . until the T1 mark aligns with the index mark (A) . . .

8.3c . . . and the arrow on each sprocket points in and is parallel with the head mating surface

2•18 Engine, clutch and transmission

8.4 Cable-tie the chain to each sprocket to prevent the possibility of it jumping a tooth

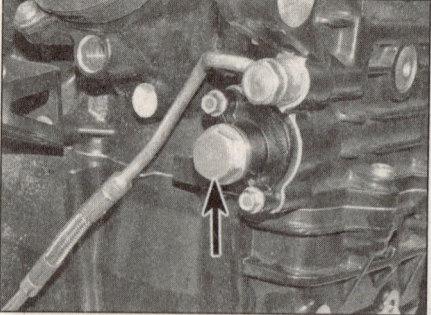

8.5 Unscrew the end bolt (arrowed) and remove the sealing washer and spring

8.6 Unscrew the bolts (arrowed) and withdraw the tensioner from the head

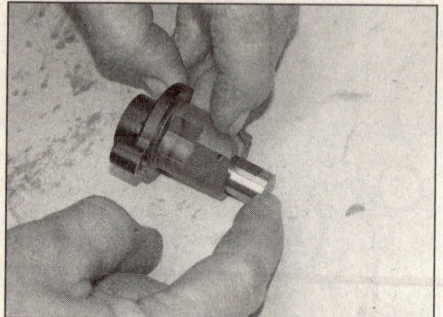

8.7 Release the catch and check the plunger moves freely in and out

8.10 Fit the tensioner using a new gasket

8.11 Fit the end bolt and spring, using a new sealing washer

cable-tie through a hole and around the chain on each sprocket as shown **(see illustration)**.
5 Undo the large end bolt from the tensioner and withdraw the spring, noting that it will be under tension **(see illustration)**. Remove the sealing washer and discard it as a new one must be used.
6 Remove the two mounting bolts and withdraw the tensioner **(see illustration)**. Discard its gasket as a new one must be used.

Inspection

7 Examine the tensioner components for signs of wear or damage. Lift the catch on the tensioner body and move the plunger in and out – if it doesn't move smoothly and freely, replace the tensioner with a new one **(see illustration)**.
8 Check the condition of the spring – if it is obviously deformed replace the tensioner with a new one.

Installation

9 If a new tensioner is being fitted, it must be disassembled as follows prior to installation. The end bolt will not be fully tightened – turn the bolt clockwise until the plunger springs out, then undo the bolt and withdraw the spring.
10 Lift the catch and push the plunger in until it engages with the first tooth on the plunger ratchet in the fully retracted position **(see illustration 8.7)**. Fit a new gasket on the tensioner body, then fit the tensioner and tighten the mounting bolts to the torque setting specified at the beginning of the Chapter **(see illustration)**.
11 Fit a new sealing washer onto the end bolt. Fit the spring and end bolt into the tensioner body **(see illustration)**. Tighten the end bolt to the specified torque setting – as you fit the spring and tighten the bolt the plunger should be heard clicking over the ratchet mechanism as it extends against the tensioner blade and takes up the slack in the chain.
12 Check that the tensioner plunger is correctly located in the middle of the tensioner blade when viewed from above, and that the chain is tensioned. Remove the cable-ties from around the sprockets.
13 Rotate the engine clockwise several times and recheck the timing marks (see Step 3). If the cam chain has jumped whilst the tensioner

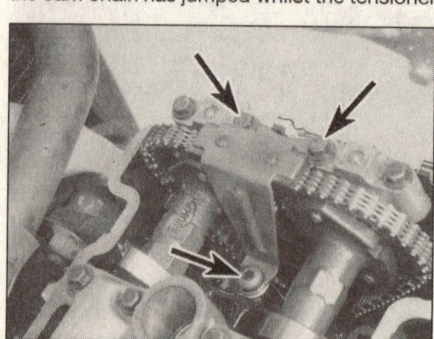

9.2 Undo the bolts (arrowed) and remove the guide

was removed, remove the tensioner again to provide slack in the chain, then reposition the intake camshaft using a spanner on the hex behind the sprocket to turn it while feeding the chain around the sprocket, until the timing marks are correctly aligned.
14 Install the spark plugs (see Chapter 1) and valve cover (see Section 7).
15 Fit the timing inspection cap using a new O-ring if necessary and tighten it to the specified torque **(see illustration 8.2)**.

9 Camshafts and followers

Note: *This procedure can be carried out with the engine in the frame.*

Removal

1 Remove the cam chain tensioner (see Section 8). Note that it is not necessary to cable-tie the cam chain to the sprockets.
2 Remove the bolts securing the cam chain upper guide and lift it off **(see illustration)**.
3 The camshaft outrigger caps and camshaft holder must be matched up to their original journals and fitted the same way round on installation. Check for identification and orientation markings scribed on the caps and holder – if you can't see any markings, or they are unclear, make your own.
4 Undo the remaining bolts securing the camshaft caps and remove them **(see illustration)**.

Engine, clutch and transmission 2•19

9.4 Remove the camshaft caps

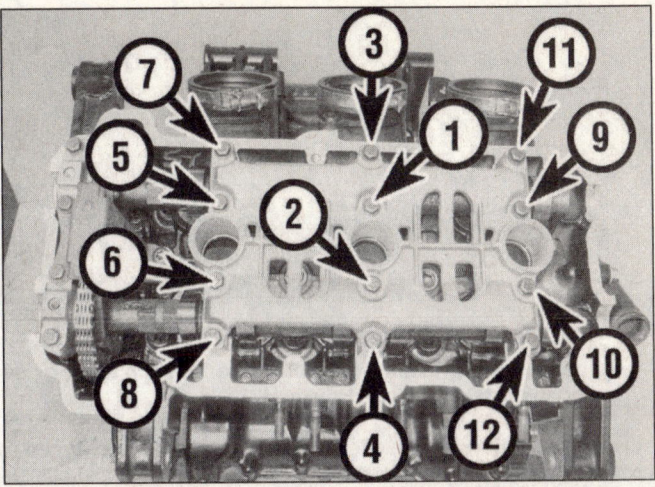
9.5a Remove the bolts in the order shown

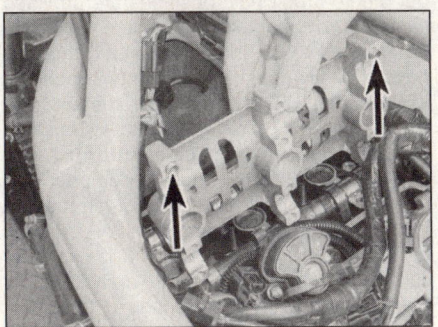
9.5b Note the location of the dowels (arrowed) . . .

9.5c . . . and the location of the O-rings

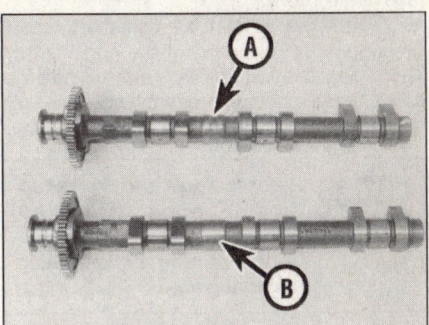
9.7 Intake camshaft has groove (A), exhaust camshaft is plain (B)

5 Undo the camshaft holder bolts evenly and a little at a time in the order shown (see illustration). Remove the bolts, then lift the holder off. Note the location of the dowels and remove them for safekeeping if they are loose (see illustration). Note the location of the camshaft holder O-rings and remove them (see illustration).
Caution: *A camshaft could break if the holder bolts are not slackened as described and the pressure from a depressed valve causes the shaft to bend. Also, if the holder does not come squarely away from the head, the holder is likely to break. If this happens the cylinder head must be renewed; the holders are matched to the head and cannot be obtained separately.*

6 Lift the cam chain off the intake camshaft sprocket and remove the camshaft (see illustration 9.24).
7 Repeat the procedure for the exhaust camshaft (see illustration 9.23). The cam chain can be left to rest on its support bolt in the tunnel. Note that the intake camshaft has a groove in its centre section and a single hex cast into its right-hand end, while the centre section on the exhaust camshaft is plain and there is a twin hex cast into it (see illustration).
8 If the followers and shims are being removed from the cylinder head, obtain a container which is divided into twelve compartments. Label each compartment with the location of its corresponding valve in the cylinder head and

whether it belongs with an intake or an exhaust valve. If a container is not available, use labelled plastic bags (egg cartons also work very well!). Remove the cam follower of the valve in question (see illustration). Retrieve the shim from either the inside of the follower or pick it out of the top of the valve using a magnet or a small screwdriver with a dab of grease on it (the shim will stick to the grease) (see illustration). Do not allow the shim to fall into the engine.

Inspection

9 Inspect the cam bearing surfaces of the cylinder head, caps and camshaft holder (see illustration). Look for score marks, deep scratches and evidence of spalling (a pitted

9.8a Remove the cam follower . . .

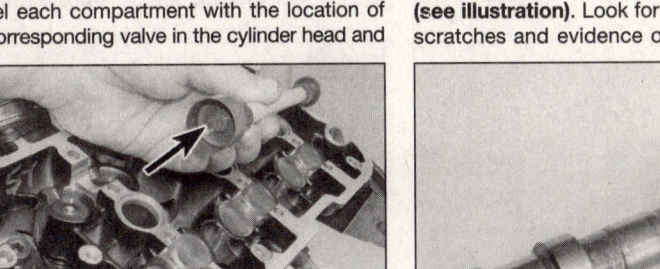
9.8b . . . and retrieve the shim (arrowed)

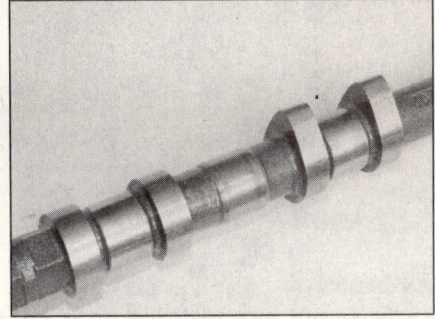
9.9a Inspect the bearing surfaces for scratches or wear

2•20 Engine, clutch and transmission

9.9b Check the lobes of the camshaft for wear – here's an example of damage requiring camshaft repair or renewal

9.13 Lay a strip of Plastigauge across each bearing journal, parallel with the camshaft centreline

 **HAYNES HiNT** Before renewing the camshafts, cylinder head/ caps because of damage, check with local machine shops specialising in motorcycle engine work. In the case of the camshafts, it may be possible for cam lobes to be welded, reground and hardened, at a cost far lower than that of a new camshaft. If the bearing surfaces in the head or holders are damaged, it may be possible for them to be bored out to accept bearing inserts. Due to the cost of new components it is recommended that all options are explored!

appearance). Check the camshaft lobes for heat discoloration (blue appearance), score marks, chipped areas, flat spots and spalling **(see illustration)**.

10 Check the amount of camshaft runout by supporting each end of the camshaft on V-blocks, and measuring any runout using a dial gauge. If the runout exceeds the specified limit the camshaft must be replaced with a new one.

 HAYNES HiNT Refer to Tools and Workshop Tips (Section 3) in the Reference section for details of how to read a micrometer and dial gauge.

11 Next, check the camshaft bearing oil clearances, using a product called Plastigauge. Check each camshaft in turn rather than both at the same time.

12 Clean the camshaft journals, the bearing surfaces in the cylinder head and the caps and camshaft holder with a clean, lint-free cloth, then lay the camshaft in place in the cylinder head – there is no need to engage the chain on the sprocket. Ensure the camshaft is positioned as for removal (see Section 8, Step 3). Apply a smear of grease to each journal and a smear of silicone release agent to each cap and bearing surface in the holder.

13 Cut strips of Plastigauge and lay one piece on each camshaft journal, parallel with the camshaft centreline **(see illustration)**.

Make sure the dowels are installed then fit the caps and camshaft holder in their proper positions (see Step 3). Fit the cap/holder bolts and tighten them finger-tight. Ensuring that the camshafts are not rotated at all, tighten the bolts evenly and a little at a time in the correct sequence **(see illustration 9.27)**, until the specified torque setting is reached.

14 Now unscrew the bolts evenly and a little at a time in the same sequence and carefully lift off the caps and holder, again making sure the camshaft does rotate.

15 To determine the oil clearance, compare the crushed Plastigauge (at its widest point) on each journal to the scale printed on the Plastigauge container **(see illustration)**. Compare the results to this Chapter's Specifications. If the oil clearance is greater than specified, measure the diameter of the camshaft journal with a micrometer **(see illustration)**. If the journal diameter is less than the specified limit, replace the camshaft with a new one and recheck the clearance. If the clearance is still too great, or if the camshaft journal is within its limit, replace the cylinder head and caps/holder as a set with new ones – individual components are not available. Note that if specialist measuring tools are available, the camshaft bearing bore inside diameter can be compared with the specified limit.

16 Repeat the oil clearance check on the other camshaft.

17 Check the camshaft sprockets for wear, cracks and other damage, replacing them with new ones if necessary. The same design sprocket is used for each camshaft, but different bolt hole positions are provided for fitting to the intake or exhaust camshaft. When fitted to the intake camshaft, the hole next to the IN marking and its corresponding opposite should be used; for the exhaust camshaft, use the hole next to the EX marking and its opposite **(see illustration)**. Apply non-permanent thread locking compound to the sprocket bolt threads and tighten them to the specified torque setting.

18 If the sprockets are worn, it is likely the cam chain and sprocket on the crankshaft will be worn as well. Refer to Section 11 for details of how to check the cam chain for wear.

19 Inspect the outer surfaces of the followers for evidence of scoring or other damage. If a follower is in poor condition, it is probable that the bore in which it works is also damaged. Measure the outside diameter of the followers and the inside diameter of the bores and compare the results to the limits in the Specifications at the beginning of this Chapter. If the bores are seriously out-of-round or tapered, the cylinder head and the followers must be renewed.

Installation

Note: *It is important that the followers and shims are returned to their original valves otherwise the valve clearances will be inaccurate.*

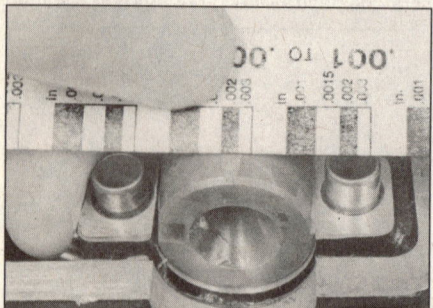

9.15a Compare the width of the crushed Plastigauge to the scale printed on the Plastigauge container

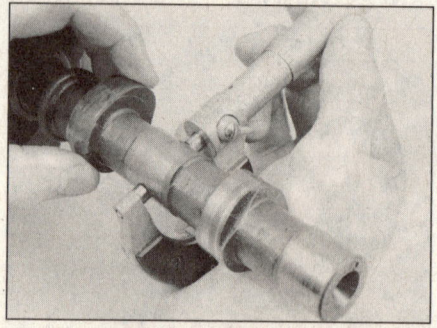

9.15b Measure the cam bearing journals with a micrometer

9.17 Bolt location on intake camshaft (A) and exhaust camshaft (B)

Engine, clutch and transmission 2•21

9.21 Fit each shim (arrowed) on the top of the valve assembly

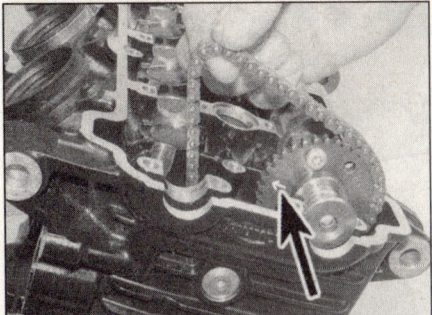

9.23 Keeping the front run of the chain taut, install the exhaust camshaft with the arrow pointing rearwards

9.24 Lay the intake camshaft in the head, making sure the chain is taut between the sprockets

20 Make sure the bearing surfaces in the cylinder head, on the camshafts and in the outrigger caps and holders are clean, then liberally apply molybdenum disulphide oil (a 50/50 mixture of molybdenum disulphide grease and engine oil) to each of them. Also apply oil to the camshaft lobes and the followers.

21 If removed, lubricate each shim and fit it into its recess in the top of the valve (see illustration). Check that the shims are correctly seated, then fit the followers (see illustration 9.8a).

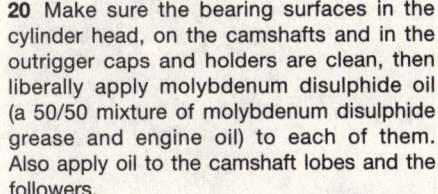

9.25a Install the camshaft holder as noted on removal

22 Check that the crankshaft is positioned as described in Section 8, Step 3.

23 Hook the cam chain up from its tunnel and make sure that it is engaged around the lower sprocket teeth on the crankshaft. Keeping the front run of the chain taut, lay the exhaust camshaft in position so that the arrow mark on its sprocket points rearwards and is parallel with the top mating surface of the cylinder head, then engage the chain on the sprocket teeth (see illustration).

24 Slip the intake camshaft through the cam chain so that the arrow mark on its sprocket points forwards and is parallel with the head (see illustration). Engage the chain fully on the sprocket teeth, making sure that the chain is tight between the camshafts, with any slack lying in the rear run where it will be taken up by the tensioner. Check that the T1 mark on the starter clutch is still aligned with the index mark in the inspection hole.

25 Check the camshaft holder O-rings and replace them with new ones if they are deformed or damaged (see illustration 9.5c). Ensure that the camshaft outrigger cap and holder dowels are installed and fit the caps and holder in their proper positions and way round (see Step 3) (see illustration). Clean

and lightly oil the camshaft holder and cap bolt threads. Fit the bolts, fitting the cam chain upper guide as well, and tighten them finger-tight (see illustration).

26 In order to prevent the cam chain jumping a tooth as the camshafts are tightened down, apply light pressure through the tensioner hole.

27 Tighten the bolts evenly and a little at a time in the sequence shown until the specified torque setting is reached (see illustration).

28 With all bolts tightened down, check that the timing marks still align (see Section 8, Step 3). If the chain has jumped a tooth, release the pressure on the tensioner blade (if applied), then slip the cam chain off the sprockets (there should be enough slack in the rear run to do this easily without having to displace the camshafts). Turn the camshaft(s) as required using a spanner on the cast hex until their alignment is correct. With the timing set up correctly, check that each camshaft is not pinched by turning it a few degrees in each direction with a spanner on the hex.

29 Install the cam chain tensioner (Section 8).

30 Check the valve clearances (see Chapter 1).

9.25b Install the cam chain upper guide

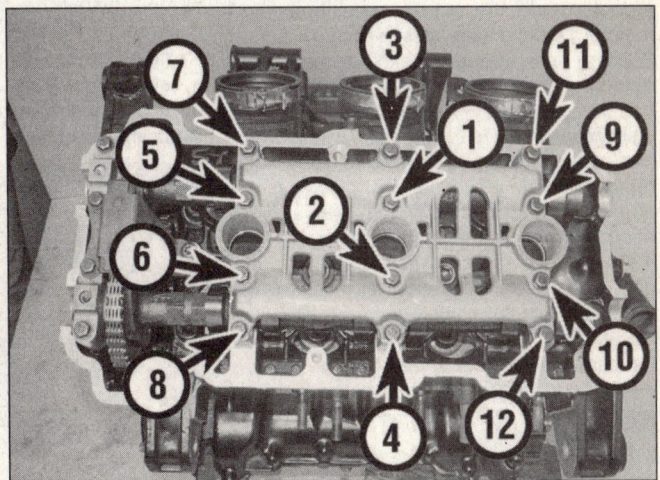

9.27 Camshaft holder and cap bolt tightening sequence

2•22 Engine, clutch and transmission

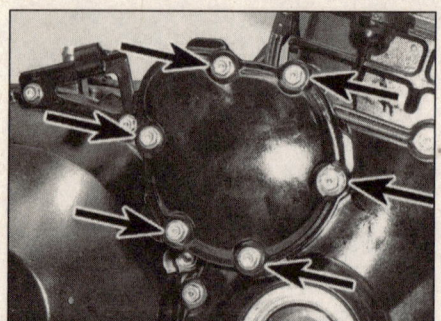

10.2 Unscrew the bolts (arrowed) and remove the cover

10.3a Remove the wave washer and plain washer (where fitted) . . .

10.3b . . . then draw off the idler gear and its bearing

10.8a Unscrew the bolts (arrowed) and remove the cover . . .

10.8b . . . noting the clutch cable guide on Speed Triple and Tiger models (arrowed)

10.9 Remove the wave washer (where fitted) then withdraw the shaft and the intermediate gear

10 Starter clutch

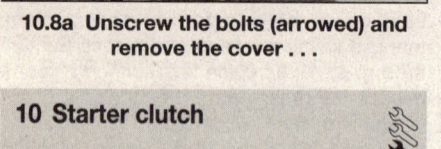

Note: *The starter clutch can be removed with the engine in the frame. If the engine has been removed, ignore the steps which do not apply.*

Starter clutch check

1 If you suspect the starter clutch of being faulty, a simple check can be performed as follows.
2 On Sprint models remove the right-hand fairing side panel (see Chapter 7). On all models, undo the starter cover bolts and remove the cover **(see illustration)**.
3 Using your finger, check that the starter reduction gear turns anti-clockwise (you will be turning the starter motor as well, so some resistance will be felt), and locks when turned clockwise. If not, on engines up to No. 487366 remove the wave washer and plain washer, and on all models draw the gear and its bearing off the shaft **(see illustrations)**.
4 Now check to see that the intermediate gear turns freely clockwise, and locks when turned anti-clockwise. If it does, it is likely the starter motor is faulty and should be removed for inspection (see Chapter 8). If not, remove the starter clutch for further investigation.

Removal

5 Place the bike on its sidestand – this will prevent having to drain the engine oil. If you prefer to have the bike upright drain the oil (see Chapter 1). If not already done, follow Steps 2

and 3 and remove the starter reduction gear and bearing.
6 Remove the reduction gear shaft, and on engines up to No. 487366 the thrust washer **(see illustrations 10.20b and a)**.
7 Remove the starter cover gasket and discard it as a new one must be used, then remove the dowels for safekeeping if they are loose **(see illustration 10.21a)**.
8 Undo the bolts securing the right-hand crankcase cover, noting the sealing washer on the uppermost bolt, and lift off the cover, being prepared to catch any residual oil **(see illustration)**. On Speed Triple and Tiger models also note the clutch cable guide secured by the top bolt **(see illustration)**. Remove the cover gasket and discard it as a new one must be used, then remove the dowels for safekeeping if they are loose **(see illustration 10.19a)**.

9 On engines up to No. 496387 remove the wave washer from the end of the idle gear shaft. On all models withdraw the shaft and the gear, noting which way round it fits **(see illustration)**.
10 To loosen the starter clutch bolt, the crankshaft must be locked to prevent it turning. If the engine is in the frame, engage 2nd gear and have an assistant hold the rear brake on hard with the rear tyre in firm contact with the ground. Alternatively, and if the engine has been removed, Triumph produces a service tool (Part No. T3880017) to do this. Alternatively, a commercially available clutch holding tool located in the holes on the face of the starter clutch can be used as shown **(see illustrations)**. Remove the bolt and washer and draw the starter clutch off, noting how the master spline locates on the shaft **(see illustrations 10.17a and 10.16b)**. Remove the thrust washer from the shaft **(see illustration 10.16a)**.

10.10a Fit the pegs on the tool into the holes in the starter clutch . . .

10.10b . . . then hold the tool and unscrew the bolt

Engine, clutch and transmission 2•23

10.11a Starter clutch gear should turn freely clockwise

10.11b Lift the gear . . .

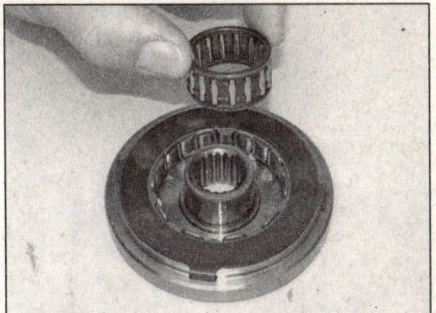

10.11c . . . and the needle bearing out of the starter clutch body

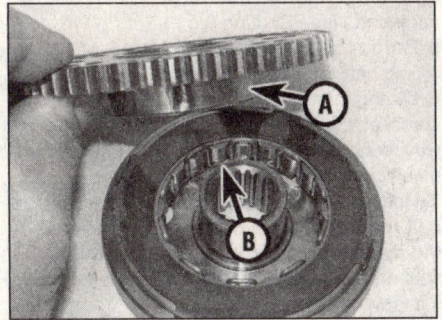

10.12 Check the surface of the hub (A) and the sprags (B) for wear and damage

10.16a Slide the thrust washer on . . .

10.16b . . . then fit the starter clutch, aligning the wide splines

Inspection

11 With the starter clutch body face down on the work surface check that the starter driven gear turns freely clockwise, and locks when turned anti-clockwise (see illustration). If not, lift out the gear then lift out the needle roller bearing (see illustrations).

12 Examine the bearing surface of the gear hub and the condition of the sprags inside the clutch body (see illustration). If the hub or sprags show signs of excessive wear or are damaged, replace them with new parts. Check the condition of the bearing rollers and fit a new bearing if necessary – refer to *Tools and Workshop Tips* in the Reference Section for details of bearing checks.

13 Examine the teeth of the idle and reduction gears and the corresponding teeth of the starter driven gear and starter motor driveshaft. Replace the gears and/or starter motor with new ones if worn or chipped teeth are discovered on related gears. Also check the idle and reduction gear shafts for damage, and check the reduction gear needle roller bearing. Replace any components that are worn or damaged with new ones.

Installation

14 Clean all old gasket and sealant from the covers and crankcase. Clean any old thread locking compound off the threads of the starter clutch bolt.

15 Lubricate the starter clutch sprags, the needle bearing and the hub of the starter clutch gear with clean engine oil. Fit the bearing and then lower the gear into the clutch, rotating it clockwise as you do so to spread the sprags and allow the hub of the gear to enter (see illustration 10.11c and b).

16 If removed, slide the thrust washer onto the crankshaft (see illustration). Align the master splines on the shaft and starter clutch and slide the clutch assembly on (see illustration).

17 Apply a suitable non-permanent thread locking compound to the starter clutch bolt, then fit the bolt with its washer (see illustration). Using the method employed on removal to stop the crankshaft from turning, tighten the bolt to the torque setting specified at the beginning of the Chapter (see illustration).

18 Lubricate the idle gear shaft with clean oil. Position the gear in the crankcase and slide the shaft fully into place, then on engines up to No. 496387 fit the wave washer (see illustration 10.9).

19 If removed, fit the crankcase cover dowels, then fit the new gasket, making sure it locates correctly onto the dowels (see illustration). Fit the cover and tighten the bolts to the

10.17a Fit the bolt with its washer . . .

10.17b . . . and tighten it to the specified torque

10.19a Fit the gasket onto the dowels (arrowed) . . .

10.19b . . . then fit the cover

10.20a Fit the shaft into its bore . . .

10.20b . . . then, where fitted, slide the thrust washer on

10.21a Fit the gasket onto the dowels (arrowed) . . .

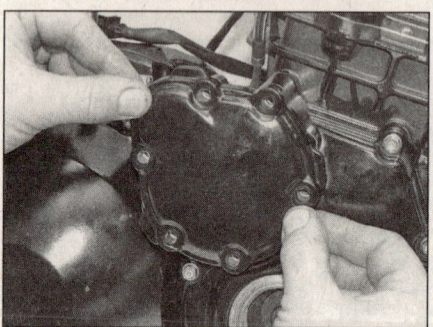

10.21b . . . then fit the cover

torque setting specified at the beginning of the Chapter, using a new sealing washer with the uppermost bolt, and not forgetting the clutch cable guide on Speed Triple and Tiger models **(see illustration and 10.8b)**.

20 Fit the reduction gear shaft and on engines up to No. 487366 the thrust washer **(see illustrations)**. Lubricate the needle bearing with clean engine oil and fit the bearing and reduction gear **(see illustration 10.3b)**. On engines up to No. 487366 fit the outer plain washer then the wave washer **(see illustration 10.3a)**.

21 If removed, fit the starter cover dowels, then fit the new gasket, making sure it locates correctly onto the dowels **(see illustration)**. Fit the cover and tighten the bolts to the specified torque setting **(see illustration)**.

22 On Sprint models install the right-hand fairing side panel (see Chapter 7).

23 If you drained the engine oil, replenish it (see Chapter 1).

11.6 Draw the sprocket off the crankshaft, noting which way round it fits

11 Cam chain and tensioner/ guide blades

Note: *The cam chain and tensioner blade can be removed with the engine in the frame.*

Cam chain upper guide

1 Remove the valve cover (see Section 7).
2 Remove the bolts securing the cam chain upper guide and lift off **(see illustration 9.2)**.
3 Installation is the reverse of removal.

Cam chain and crankshaft sprocket

Removal

4 Remove the valve cover (see Section 7). Unless a new chain is being fitted mark some of the outer facing links in the chain so it can be refitted to run with the same direction of

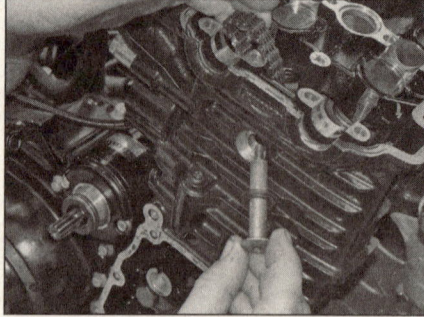

11.7 Remove the cam chain support bolt then lift the chain out of the engine

drive to reduce the rate of wear. Remove the camshafts (see Section 9).
5 Remove the starter clutch and the crankshaft thrust washer (see Section 10).
6 Disengage the cam chain from the crankshaft sprocket and slide the sprocket off, noting which way round it fits **(see illustration)**. Note how the master spline locates on the shaft.
7 Hold the cam chain and remove the support bolt from the centre of the right-hand side of the cylinder head **(see illustration)**. Note the seal on the bolt and replace it with a new one if it is worn or damaged.
8 Slip the chain off the crankshaft and lift it out.

Inspection

9 Check the cam chain for binding and obvious damage and replace it with a new one if necessary. Inspect the crankshaft and camshaft sprockets for worn, chipped or missing teeth. If the chain and sprockets show signs of extensive wear renew them as a complete set.
10 If the chain appears to be in good condition, check it for stretch as follows. Hang the chain from a hook and attach a 13 kg (28 lb) weight to its lower end.
11 Measure the length of 24 pins (from the outer edge of the 1st pin to the outer edge of the 24th pin) and compare the result to the service limit specified at the beginning of the Chapter. If the chain exceeds the service limit it must be replaced with a new one.

Installation

12 Installation is a reverse of removal, noting the following:
● Unless a new chain is being fitted make sure the marks made on removal face out. Hold the chain in position and tighten the cam chain support bolt to the specified torque setting.
● Align the master splines on the shaft and the crankshaft sprocket and ensure the sprocket is fitted the right way round **(see illustration 11.6)**.
● Do not forget to fit the crankshaft thrust washer (see Section 10).

Cam chain tensioner blade

Removal

13 Remove the cam chain tensioner (see Section 8).
14 Undo the tensioner blade pivot bolt – retrieve the washer from between the blade

Engine, clutch and transmission 2•25

and the crankcase as you withdraw the bolt **(see illustration)**. Manoeuvre the blade out of the bottom of the cam chain tunnel **(see illustration)**.

15 Check the tensioner blade for wear, cracking and other damage, and replace it with a new one if necessary.

Installation

16 Installation is the reverse of removal. Clean the pivot bolt threads and apply some fresh threadlock. Don't forget to fit the washer on the pivot bolt between the blade and the crankcase **(see illustration 11.14a)**. Tighten the bolt to the specified torque setting.

Cam chain guide blade

Removal

17 The upper end of the cam chain guide blade locates in a slot in the front edge of the cam chain tunnel and is retained by the cylinder head – it cannot be removed unless the head is off (see Section 12).

18 Undo the guide blade bolt – retrieve the washer from between the blade and the crankcase as you withdraw the bolt **(see illustration)**. Lift the blade out of the top of the cam chain tunnel, noting how it locates **(see illustration)**.

19 Check the guide blade for wear, cracking and other damage, and replace it with a new one if necessary.

Installation

20 Fit the cam chain guide blade into the front of the tunnel and locate it correctly in its seat and in its cut-out in the top of the crankcase **(see illustration 11.18b)**.

21 Clean the bolt threads and apply some fresh threadlock. Insert the bolt and fit the washer onto it between the blade and the crankcase. Tighten the pivot bolt to the specified torque setting.

22 Install the remaining components in the reverse order of removal.

12 Cylinder head removal and installation

Note: *To remove the cylinder head the engine must be removed from the frame.*

Removal

1 Remove the engine from the frame (see Section 4).

2 Remove the camshafts and followers (see Section 9).

3 Remove the cam chain support bolt from the right-hand side of the cylinder head **(see illustration 11.7)**.

4 Unscrew the banjo bolt securing the external oil hose to the cylinder head and position the hose aside **(see illustration)**. Discard the sealing washers as new ones must be fitted on installation.

5 Remove the two screws from the right-hand end of the cylinder head-to-crankcase joint **(see illustration)**.

11.14a Unscrew the bolt, noting the washer behind the tensioner blade . . .

11.14b . . . and manoeuvre the blade out from the cam chain tunnel

11.18a Unscrew the bolt (arrowed) and retrieve the inner washer . . .

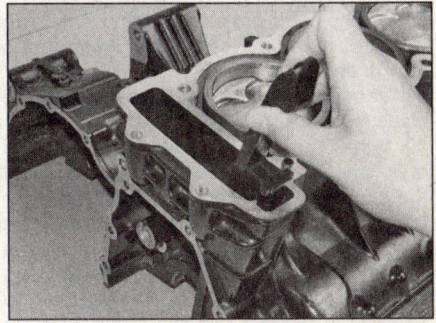

11.18b . . . then lift out the guide blade

12.4 Unscrew the banjo bolt (arrowed) and displace the oil hose

12.5 Remove the two screws (arrowed) from the right-hand end of the head

6 Slacken the eight cylinder head bolts by half a turn at a time in the specified sequence shown **(see illustration)**.

7 Tap around the joint faces of the cylinder head with a soft-faced mallet to free the head.

Don't attempt to free the head by inserting a screwdriver between the head and cylinder block – you'll damage the sealing surfaces.

8 Carefully lift the head off the block, and remove it from the engine **(see illustration)**.

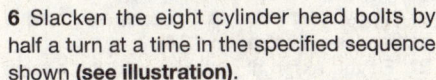

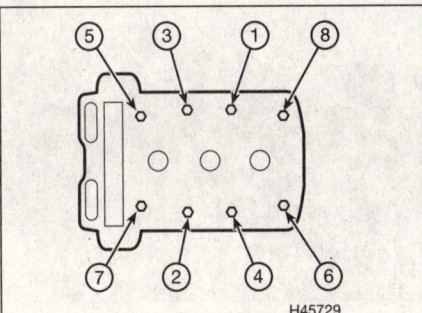

12.6 Sequence for loosening and tightening the cylinder head bolts

12.8 Carefully lift the cylinder head up off the engine block

12.15a Install the dowels (arrowed) . . .

12.15b . . . then fit the head gasket as described

Lift off the head gasket and remove the two dowels if they are loose **(see illustrations 12.15b and a)**.

9 If required, remove the cam chain guide blade **(see illustration 11.18b)**.

10 If the crankshaft is rotated with the head off it is possible that the liners may move and the seal between them and the crankcase be broken, causing coolant from the cylinder block water jacket to seep into the crankcase. If this happens the cylinder liners must be removed and resealed. Refer to Section 14 for liner removal and installation details.

11 Inspect the cylinder head gasket and the mating surfaces for signs of leakage, which could indicate that the head is distorted. If necessary, check the cylinder head with a straight-edge. Discard the old head gasket as a new one must be fitted on reassembly.

Installation

12 Clean the mating surfaces of the cylinder head and block with a suitable solvent to remove all traces of old gasket. If a scraper is used, take care not to scratch or gouge the soft aluminium. Ensure none of the old gasket material falls into the crankcase.

 **HAYNES HiNT** *Refer to Tools and Workshop Tips for details of gasket removal methods.*

12.19a Tighten the cylinder head bolts as described to the specified torque settings . . .

13 Check that the bolt holes in the block are clean and dry. Clean the threads of the head bolts and lubricate them with a smear of clean engine oil.

14 If removed fit and seal the liners in the cylinder block (see Section 15).

15 If removed, fit the two dowels in the block and fit the new head gasket **(see illustration)**. If one side of the gasket is marked TOP this should face uppermost. Check that the gasket locates over the dowels and that all the holes are correctly aligned **(see illustration)**.

16 If removed, fit the cam chain guide blade into the front of the tunnel and locate it correctly in its seat and in its cut-out in the top of the crankcase **(see illustration 11.18b)**.

17 Carefully lower the cylinder head onto the block **(see illustration 12.8)**.

18 Fit the cylinder head bolts with their washers and tighten them finger-tight only at this stage.

19 Tighten the cylinder head bolts in the correct numerical sequence **(see illustration 12.6)** to the stage 1 torque setting **(see illustration)**. Repeat to the stage 2 torque setting. Finally, attach a degree disc to the torque wrench and angle-tighten each bolt 90° following the same sequence **(see illustration)**.

20 Tighten the screws on the right-hand end of the cylinder head to the specified torque setting **(see illustration 12.5)**.

21 Fit the external oil hose onto the engine using new sealing washers on each side of

12.19b . . . and then through the specified angle using a degree disc

the union, and tighten the banjo bolt to the specified torque setting **(see illustration 12.4)**.

22 Install the remaining components in the reverse order of removal.

13 Cylinder head and valve overhaul

1 Because of the complex nature of this job and the special tools and equipment required, most owners leave servicing of the valves, valve seats and valve guides to a Triumph dealer or head specialist. However, you can make an initial assessment of whether the valves are seating correctly, and therefore sealing, by pouring a small amount of solvent into each of the valve ports. If the solvent leaks past any valve into the combustion chamber area the valve is not seating correctly and sealing.

2 With the correct tools (a valve spring compressor is essential – make sure it is suitable for motorcycle work), you can also remove the valves and associated components from the cylinder head, clean them and check them for wear to assess the extent of the work needed, and, unless seat cutting or guide replacement is required, reassemble them in the head.

3 A dealer service department or specialist can replace the guides and re-cut the valve seats.

4 After the valve service has been performed, be sure to clean it very thoroughly before installation on the engine to remove any metal particles or abrasive grit that may still be present from the valve service operations. Use compressed air, if available, to blow out all the holes and passages.

Disassembly

5 Remove the followers and their shims if you haven't already done so (see Section 9). Store the components in such a way that they can be returned to their original locations without getting mixed up.

6 Carefully scrape all carbon deposits out of the combustion chamber area. A hand held wire brush or a piece of fine emery cloth can be used once the majority of deposits have been scraped away. Do not use a wire brush mounted in a drill motor, or one with extremely stiff bristles, as the head material is soft and may be eroded away or scratched by the wire brush.

7 Arrange to label and store the valves along with their related components so they can be kept separate and reinstalled in the same valve guides they are removed from (labelled plastic bags work well for this).

8 Compress the valve spring on the first valve with a spring compressor, then remove the collets from the valve assembly **(see**

Engine, clutch and transmission 2•27

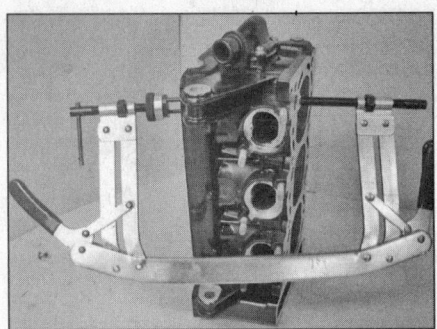

13.8a Compressing the valve springs using a valve spring compressor

13.8b Make sure the compressor is a good fit both on the top . . .

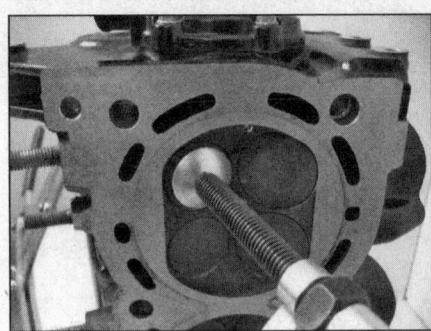

13.8c . . . and the bottom of the valve assembly

illustrations). **Note:** *Take great care not to mark the follower bore with the spring compressor. Do not compress the springs any more than is necessary.* Carefully release the valve spring compressor, then remove the spring retainer and the spring **(see illustrations 13.24c and b)**. Push the valve stem down and draw the valve out from the underside of the head **(see illustration 13.24a)** – if the valve binds in the guide (won't pull through), push it back into the head and deburr the area around the collet groove with a very fine file or whetstone **(see illustration)**.

9 Pull the valve stem seal off the top of the valve guide with pliers and discard it (the old seal should never be reused) **(see illustration)**. Remove the spring seat – using a magnet is the easiest way to lift the seat off the head **(see illustration)**.

10 Repeat the procedure for the other valves. Keep the parts for each valve together so they can be reinstalled in the same location.

11 Next, clean the cylinder head with solvent and dry it thoroughly. Compressed air will speed the drying process and ensure that all holes and recessed areas are clean. Clean any traces of old gasket material from the cylinder head. If a scraper is used, take care not to scratch or gouge the soft aluminium.

 *Refer to Tools and Workshop Tips (Section 7) for details of gasket removal methods.*

13.8d Remove the collets with needle-nose pliers, tweezers, a magnet or a screwdriver with a dab of grease on it

12 Clean all of the valve springs, collets, retainers and spring seats with solvent and dry them thoroughly. Do the parts from one valve at a time so that no mixing of parts between valves occurs.

13 Scrape off any deposits that may have formed on each valve face, head and stem. Again, make sure the valves do not get mixed up.

Inspection

14 Inspect the head very carefully for cracks and other damage. If cracks are found, a new head will be required. Check the cam bearing surfaces for wear and evidence of seizure. Check the camshafts for wear as well (see Section 9).

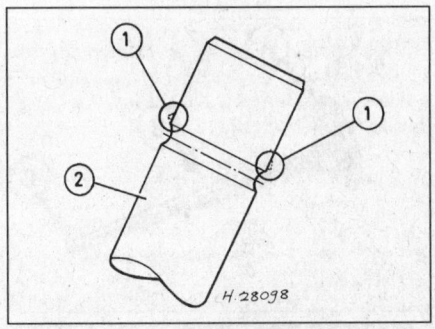

13.8e If the valve stem (2) won't pull through the guide, deburr the area above the collet groove (1)

15 Using a precision straight-edge and a feeler gauge, check the head gasket mating surface for warpage. Refer to *Tools and Workshop Tips* (Section 3) in the Reference section for details of how to use the straight-edge. If the head is warped, but not excessively so, a specialist repair shop should be able to resurface it. If the head is excessively warped, replace it with a new one.

16 Examine the valve seats in the combustion chamber. If they are pitted, cracked or burned, the head will require work beyond the scope of the home mechanic. Measure the valve seat width and compare it to this Chapter's Specifications **(see illustration)**. If it exceeds the service limit, or if it varies around its circumference, valve seat overhaul is required.

13.9a Pull the seal off the top of the guide . . .

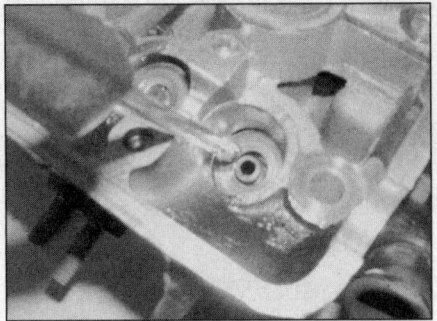

13.9b . . . then remove the spring seat

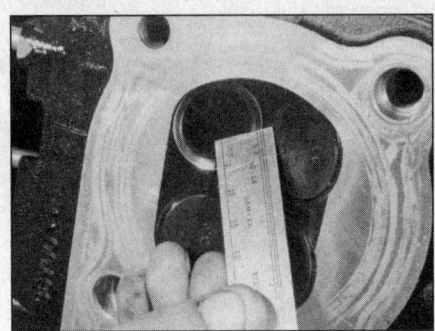

13.16 Measure the valve seat width with a ruler (or for greater precision use a Vernier caliper)

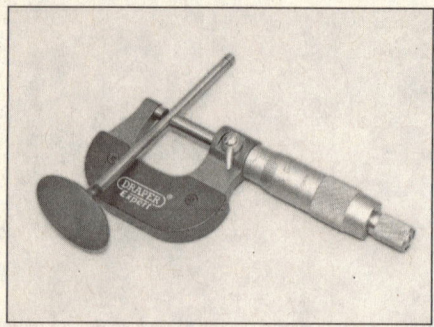

13.17a Measure the valve stem diameter with a micrometer

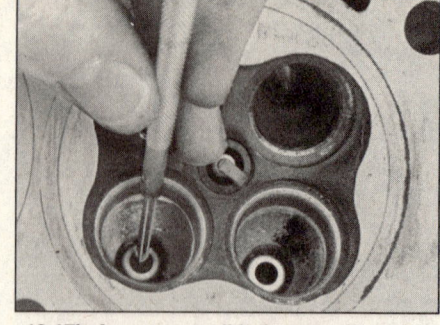

13.17b Insert a small hole gauge into the valve guide and expand it so there's a slight drag when it's pulled out

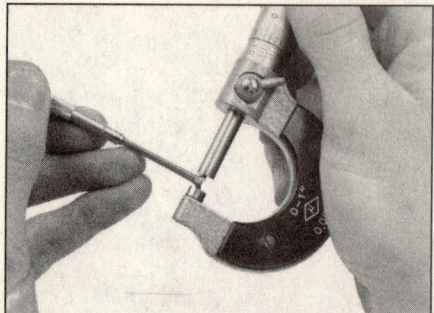

13.17c Measure the small hole gauge with a micrometer

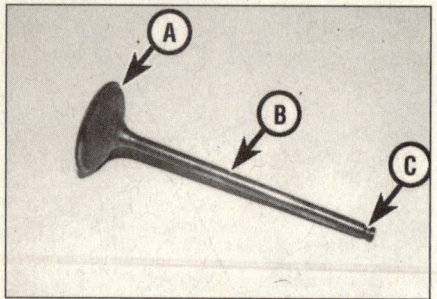

13.18 Check the valve face (A), stem (B) and collet groove (C) for signs of wear and damage

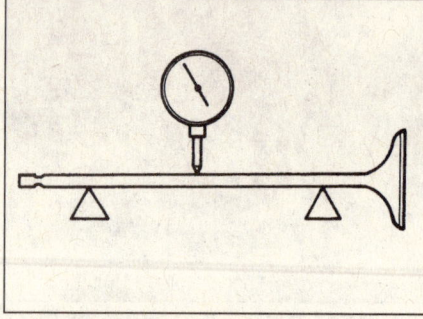

13.19 Check the valve stem for runout using V-blocks and a dial gauge

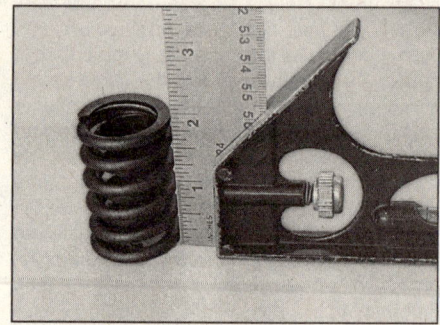

13.20 Check the valve springs for squareness

17 Measure the valve stem diameter (see illustration). Clean the valve guides to remove any carbon build-up, then measure the inside diameters of the guides (at both ends and the centre of the guide) with a small hole gauge and micrometer (see illustrations). The guides are measured at the ends and at the centre to determine if they are worn in a bell-mouth pattern (more wear at the ends). Subtract the stem diameter from the valve guide diameter to obtain the valve stem-to-guide clearance. If the stem-to-guide clearance is greater than listed in this Chapter's Specifications, and fitting new valves will restore the clearance, fit new valves. If the guides are excessively worn, or worn unevenly, a new head will have to be fitted.

HAYNES HiNT *Refer to Tools and Workshop Tips in the Reference Section for details on how to use a micrometer.*

18 Carefully inspect each valve face, stem and collet groove area for cracks, pits and burned spots (see illustration).

19 Rotate the valve and check for any obvious indication that it is bent. Use V-blocks and a dial gauge if available (see illustration). If the valve is bent, it must be replaced with a new one. Check the end of the stem for pitting and excessive wear. The presence of any of the above conditions indicates the need for valve servicing. The stem end can be ground down, provided that the amount of stem above the collet groove after grinding is sufficient.

20 Check the end of each valve spring for wear and pitting. Measure the spring length with the specified load on it (see Specifications) and compare it to that listed. If any spring compresses further than specified it has sagged and must be replaced – it is a good policy to renew the springs on all valves at the same time. Also place the spring upright on a flat surface and check it for bend by placing a ruler against it (see illustration). If the bend in any spring is excessive, it must be replaced with a new one.

21 Check the spring retainers and collets for obvious wear and cracks. Any questionable parts should not be reused, as extensive damage will occur in the event of failure during engine operation.

22 If the inspection indicates that no overhaul work is required, the valve components can be reinstalled in the head.

Reassembly

23 Working on one valve at a time, lay the spring seat in place in the cylinder head (see illustration). Fit a new valve stem seal onto the guide (see illustration). Use an appropriate size deep socket to push the seal over the end of the valve guide, then push further until

13.23a Fit the spring seat . . .

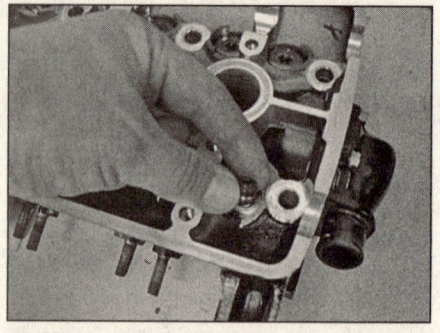

13.23b . . . followed by the valve stem seal

13.23c Press the seal into position using a suitable deep socket

Engine, clutch and transmission 2•29

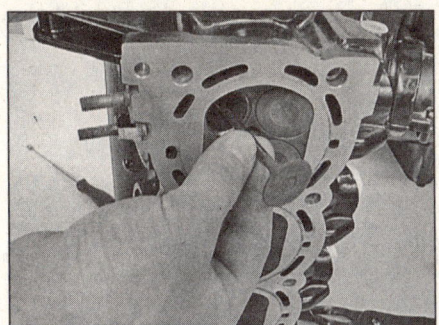
13.24a Lubricate the stem and slide the valve into its correct location

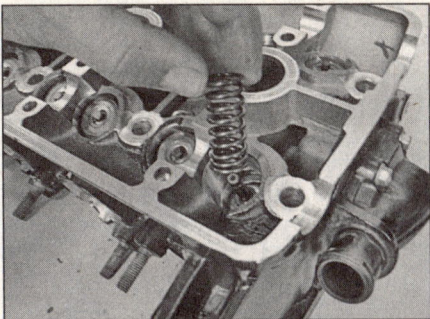
13.24b Fit the valve spring with the closer-wound coils facing down . . .

13.24c . . . then fit the spring retainer

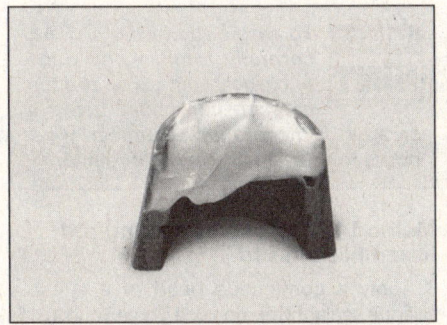
13.25a A small dab of grease will help to keep the collets in place on the valve while the spring is released

13.25b Compress the springs and install the collets, making sure they locate in the groove

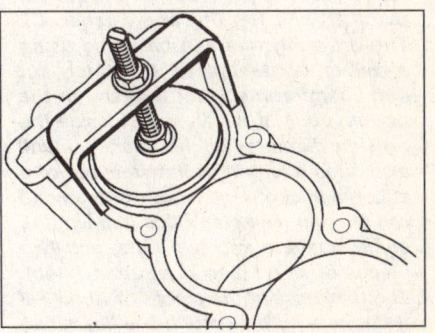
14.3 Extracting a liner using the Triumph tool

it is felt to clip into place **(see illustration)**. Don't twist or cock the seal, or it will not seal properly against the valve stem. Also, don't remove it again or it will be damaged.

24 Coat the valve stem with molybdenum disulphide oil (a 50/50 mixture of molybdenum disulphide grease and engine oil), then fit it into its guide, rotating it slowly to avoid damaging the seal **(see illustration)**. Check that the valve moves up and down freely in the guide. Fit the spring with its closer-wound coils facing down into the cylinder head **(see illustration)**. Now fit the spring retainer, with its shouldered side facing down so that it fits into the top of the springs **(see illustration)**.

25 Apply a small amount of grease to the inside of the collets – this will help to help hold them in place as the pressure is released from the spring **(see illustration)**. Compress the spring with the valve spring compressor and fit the collets **(see illustration)**. When compressing the spring, do so only as far as is necessary to slip the collets into place. Make certain that the collets are securely locked in the retaining groove when releasing the compressor.

26 Support the cylinder head on blocks so the valves can't contact the workbench top, then very gently tap the top of the valve stem to help seat the collets in the groove.

27 Repeat the procedure for the remaining valves. Remember to keep the parts for each valve together and separate from the other valves so they can be reinstalled in the same location.

> **HAYNES HiNT** Check for proper sealing of the valves by pouring a small amount of solvent into each of the valve ports. If the solvent leaks past any valve into the combustion chamber area the valve grinding operation on that valve should be repeated.

14 Cylinder liners

Note: *The cylinder liners can be removed with the pistons in situ, following removal of the cylinder head. However to do this requires the use of a Triumph special tool, Part No. T3880315, to extract the liners. It may be possible to purchase a universal liner extractor from a good automotive tool supplier, but first make sure it is suitable for the size of the engine. A suitable home-made tool can be used to release the liners, but as it uses the drawbolt principle it is necessary to remove the engine, separate the crankcase halves, then remove the crankshaft, connecting rods and pistons before it can be applied. If the liners are being removed as part of a complete engine overhaul and the engine is therefore removed anyway, then no extra work is involved, apart from making up the tool.*

Removal

1 If the Triumph special tool or a liner extractor is being used, just remove the cylinder head (see Section 12). Otherwise, separate the crankcase halves, then remove the crankshaft, connecting rods and pistons, referring to the relevant Sections of this Chapter.

2 Before removing the liners, mark the top edge of each liner at the front with a felt marker pen or similar, which will not damage the gasket surfaces. Indicate the cylinder number and front face of each liner.

3 If the Triumph tool or a liner extractor is being used, turn the engine so that the piston in the liner being removed is at bottom dead centre (i.e. the bottom of its stroke). Gently draw each liner out of the cylinder block **(see illustration)**. The purpose of the extractor is to break the seal between the liner and the crankcase; once this has been achieved, the liner can be lifted out by hand. Do not attempt to lever the liners out because the gasket surfaces will be damaged. As each liner is removed, stuff the crankcase aperture with clean rag to cushion the piston and prevent anything falling into the crankcase.

4 If the home-made drawbolt tool is being used (see **Tool Tip overleaf**), assemble the tool as shown. The bottom plate must be accurately fitted so that is bears on the bottom edge of the liner only – there must be no danger of it cocking sideways or slipping off the edge and scratching the inner surface of the liner **(see illustration)**. Also note that the bottom plate must locate inside the outside

2•30 Engine, clutch and transmission

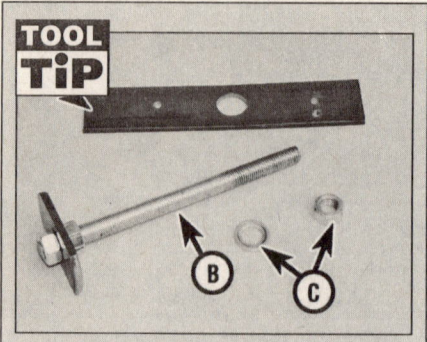

TOOL TIP

Components of the home-made drawbolt tool; steel strap (A), drawbolt and bottom plate (B) and top nut and washer (C). The drawbolt tool can be made using a section of steel plate, accurately cut and chamfered so that it bears on the bottom edge of the liner, just inside the outside diameter of the liner. You will also need a length of flat steel bar of a suitable thickness, a length of threaded rod (15 mm diameter x 200 mm length), some washers and two nuts, and two pieces of wood (see illustration 14.4b). The thickness of the pieces of wood will determine by how much the liners can be extracted before they contact the flat steel bar, so make sure they are thick enough to allow the seal on the liner to be broken, and thus enable the liners to be removed by hand. Assemble the tool as described in Step 4.

14.4a Make sure the bottom plate is accurately cut and fitted

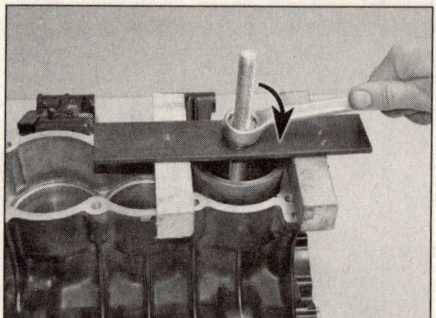

14.4b Turn the top nut clockwise and draw the liner up until the seal is broken

HAYNES HINT *To ease entry of the pistons, carefully remove any ridge of carbon built up on the top of each liner bore using a scraper. If there is a pronounced wear ridge, remove it using a ridge reamer.*

diameter of the liner and have no sharp edges that will score the block as the liner is drawn out. Tighten the top nut and gently draw the liner out of the cylinder block **(see illustration)**. Do not attempt to lever the liners out.

Inspection

5 Check the liner walls carefully for scratches and score marks. Using telescoping gauges and a micrometer (see Section 3 of *Tools and Workshop Tips*), check the dimensions of each cylinder to assess the amount of wear. Measure near the top (but below the level of the top piston ring at TDC), centre and bottom (but above the level of the oil ring at BDC) of the bore, both parallel to and across the crankshaft axis **(see illustration)**. Compare the results to the specifications at the beginning of the Chapter. If the precision measuring tools are not available, take the liners to a Triumph dealer or specialist motorcycle repair shop for assessment and advice. If the liners are worn beyond the service limit, or badly scratched, scuffed or scored, replace them with new ones. The liners cannot be re-bored.

6 Note that the cylinder liners must not be honed.

Installation

Note: *If the crankcases were separated and the piston/connecting rod assemblies removed in order to remove the liners, you can either fit the piston/connecting rod assemblies into the liners before the liners are installed, then install them as an assembly (method 2) – or you can install the liners, then fit the piston/connecting rod assemblies into them afterwards (method 3).*

7 Remove all traces of old sealant from the mating surfaces of the liners and the crankcase. If the connecting rods and pistons are still in situ, this will be tricky because you must avoid old sealant dropping into the sump. Remove any rag from the crankcase and make sure the mating surfaces of the liner and crankcase are clean, oil-free and dry. Check that the piston rings are correctly positioned in relation to the front of the engine **(see illustration 15.28)**.

Method 1 – piston/connecting rod assemblies in situ

8 Apply a continuous bead of a suitable silicone sealant (Triumph use ThreeBond 1215) to the liner mating surface as shown, following any instructions on the sealant package regarding use **(see illustration 14.14)**.

9 Lubricate the bore surface of the liner with engine oil. Make sure that the No. 1 liner is matched with the No. 1 piston/connecting rod assembly and so on, and that it is installed with the previously made mark at the front (see Step 2). Make sure that the piston is at top dead centre (i.e. at the top of its stroke).

10 Slip the liner over the piston, compressing each ring with your fingers as it enters the liner, and use a gentle rocking motion as the liner is pushed downwards **(see illustration)**. The liner has a chamfered lead-in to enable the piston to be installed without the use of ring compressors. Press the liner fully down until it is felt to seat. Clamp the liner in place using suitable bolts, nuts and soft washers threaded into the head bolt holes as shown to prevent it lifting **(see illustration)** – do not overtighten the clamps and do not use steel washers as the mating surface of the head could be

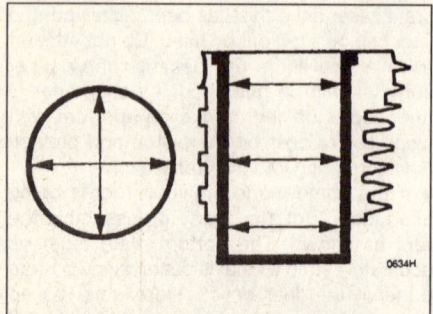

14.5 Measure the cylinder bore in the directions shown with a telescoping gauge, then measure the gauge with a micrometer

14.10a Carefully fit the liner down over the piston, making sure the rings enter correctly

14.10b Assemble a bolt, nut and washers as shown to clamp the liners

Engine, clutch and transmission 2•31

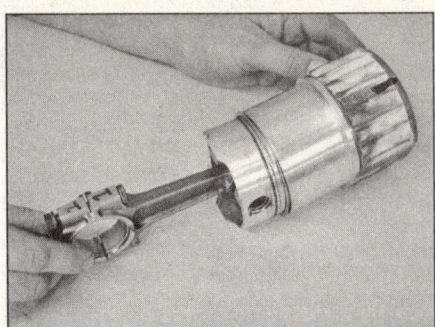

14.13 Carefully feed the piston into the liner, making sure the rings enter correctly

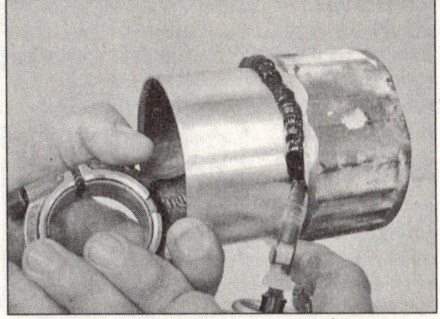

14.14 Apply the silicone sealant as shown ...

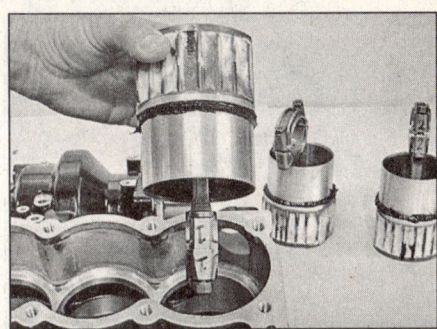

14.15 ... then fit the liner into the crankcase

indented, causing leakage and compression problems.

11 Turn the crankshaft to position the next piston at TDC, then install the other liners in the same way. As the crankshaft is rotated, make sure that the installed liner does not lift off its seating. If this happens, the liner must be removed, cleaned and fresh sealant applied.

Method 2 – piston/connecting rod assemblies removed

12 Lubricate the bore surface of the liner with engine oil. Make sure that the No. 1 piston/connecting rod assembly is matched with the No. 1 liner and so on, and that they are installed the correct way round – the arrow or dot on the piston crown must point to the front of the liner and the front of the engine.
13 Slip the piston into the liner, compressing each ring with your fingers as it enters, and use a gentle rocking motion as the liner is pushed downwards **(see illustration)**. The liner has a chamfered lead-in to enable the piston to be installed without the use of ring compressors. Position the piston near the top of the liner.
14 Apply a continuous bead of a suitable silicone sealant (Triumph use ThreeBond 1215) to the liner mating surface as shown, following any instructions on the sealant package regarding use **(see illustration)**.
15 Fit the liner into the crankcase and press it down until it is felt to seat **(see illustration)**. Clamp the liner in place using suitable bolts, nuts and soft washers threaded into the head bolt holes as shown to prevent it lifting **(see**

illustration 14.10b) – do not overtighten the clamps and do not use steel washers as the mating surface of the head could be indented, causing leakage and compression problems.
16 Install the other liners in the same way. Note that if the cylinder head is being installed immediately, there is no need to clamp the individual liners in place.

Method 3 – piston/connecting rod assemblies removed

17 Apply a continuous bead of a suitable silicone sealant (Triumph use ThreeBond 1215) to the liner mating surface as shown, following any instructions on the sealant package regarding use **(see illustration 14.14)**.
18 Fit the liner into the crankcase and press it down until it is felt to seat. Clamp the liner in place using suitable bolts, nuts and soft washers threaded into the head bolt holes as shown to prevent it lifting **(see illustration 14.10b)** – do not overtighten the clamps and do not use steel washers as the mating surface of the head could be indented, causing leakage and compression problems.
19 Lubricate the bore surface of the liner with engine oil. Make sure that the No. 1 piston/connecting rod assembly is matched with the No. 1 liner and so on, and that they are installed the correct way round – the arrow or dot on the piston crown must point to the front of the liner and the front of the engine.
20 Slip the piston into the liner, making sure the connecting rod does not scratch the surface, then carefully compress and feed each piston ring into the liner until the piston crown is flush with the top **(see illustrations)**.

If available, a piston ring compressor makes installation a lot easier.
21 Install the other liners in the same way.

All methods

22 When all liners are installed, check that their top surfaces are all exactly level with the cylinder block using a precision straight-edge as shown **(see illustration)**.
23 Install the cylinder head soon after installing the liners to avoid crankshaft movement accidentally breaking the seals.
24 Install the remaining components in the reverse order of removal, referring to the relevant Sections of the Chapter.

15 Pistons and piston rings

Removal

1 Remove the cylinder head (see Section 12).
2 If the crankcases have not been separated and a cylinder liner extractor is available, remove the cylinder liners (see Section 14). Make sure that all apertures into the crankcase are well blocked with clean rag.
3 If the engine has been removed and the crankcases are being separated, follow the procedure in Section 25 and separate the connecting rods from the crankshaft, then remove the rods with the pistons from the tops of the liners.
4 Before removing the pistons, mark the cylinder number on the crown of each piston.

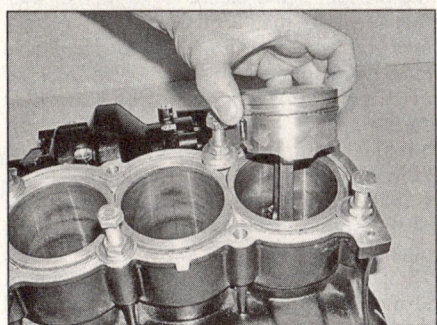

14.20a Carefully lower the connecting rod and piston into the liner ...

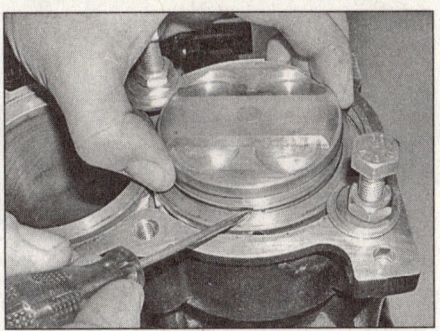

14.20b ... feeding each ring in as you do

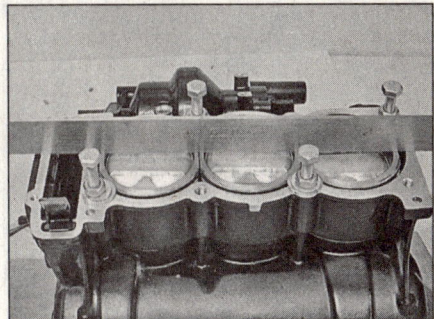

14.22 Check that the liners are all flush using a straight-edge

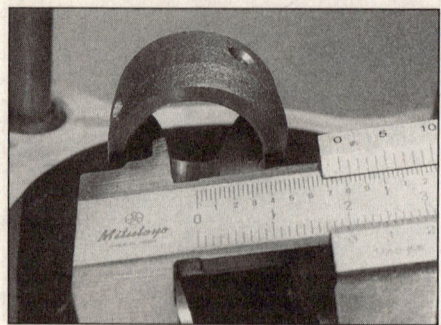

15.5a Use a small screwdriver or pointed instrument inserted in the notch (arrowed) . . .

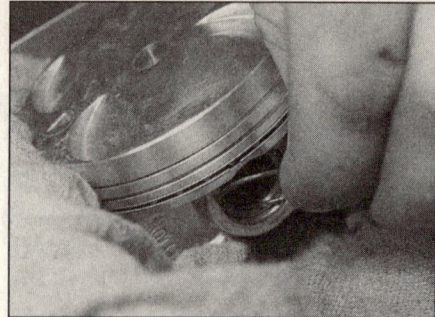

15.5b . . . to lever out the circlip

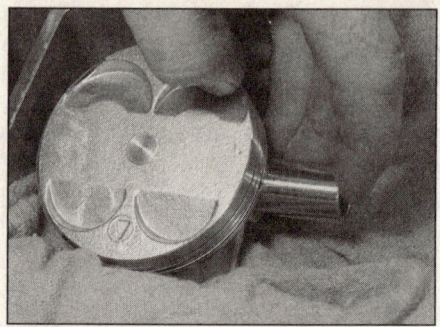

15.5c Withdraw the pin and remove the piston

Also note the arrow or dot on each crown which points to the front of the engine – if the mark is not visible, make your own as the piston must be installed the correct way round. If the connecting rods have been removed, also note and mark which way round they are fitted – the manufacturer's rod size and weight grade markings face the front, the same way as the piston mark.

5 If the connecting rods are still in the engine, rotate the crankshaft so that the best access is obtained for each piston, and on the outer pistons extract the pins inwards. Carefully prise out the circlip on one side of the piston using needle-nose pliers or a small flat-bladed screwdriver inserted into the notch (see illustrations). Push the piston pin out from the other side to free the piston from the connecting rod (see illustration). Remove the other circlip and discard them as new ones must be used. When the piston has been removed, fit its pin back into its bore so that related parts do not get mixed up. Remember the importance of the rag in preventing dropped circlips from falling into the crankcase.

 HAYNES HINT *To prevent the circlip from pinging away, pass a rod or screwdriver, which has a diameter greater than the gap between the circlip ends, through the piston pin. This will trap the circlip if it springs out.*

15.7 Removing the piston rings using a ring removal and installation tool

 **HAYNES HINT** *If a piston pin is a tight fit in the piston bosses, use a heat gun to expand the alloy piston sufficiently to release its grip of the pin. Alternatively purchase (or make up) a piston pin drawbolt tool – see 'Tools and Workshop Tips' in the Reference section.*

Inspection

Pistons

6 Before the inspection process can be carried out, remove the piston rings and clean the pistons.

7 Using your thumbs or a piston ring removal and installation tool, carefully remove the rings from the pistons (see illustration). Do not nick or gouge the pistons in the process. Carefully note which way up each ring fits and in which groove as they must be installed in their original positions if being re-used. The upper surface of the top and second rings should be marked N and 2 N respectively – if the mark on each ring is different, note which mark is for the top ring and which is for the second. The rings can also be distinguished by their different profiles (see illustration 15.26a).

8 Scrape all traces of carbon from the tops of the pistons. A hand-held wire brush or a piece of fine emery cloth can be used once most of the deposits have been scraped away. Do not, under any circumstances, use a wire brush mounted in a drill motor to remove deposits from the pistons; the piston material is soft

15.13 Measure the piston ring-to-groove clearance with a feeler gauge

and will be eroded away by the wire brush.

9 Use a piston ring groove cleaning tool to remove any carbon deposits from the ring grooves. If a tool is not available, a piece broken off an old ring will do the job. Be very careful to remove only the carbon deposits. Do not remove any metal and do not nick or gouge the sides of the ring grooves.

10 Once the deposits have been removed, clean the pistons with solvent and dry them thoroughly. Make sure the oil return holes below the oil ring groove are clear.

11 Carefully inspect each piston for cracks around the skirt, at the pin bosses and at the ring lands. Normal piston wear appears as even, vertical wear on the thrust surfaces of the piston and slight looseness of the top ring in its groove. If the skirt is scored or scuffed, the engine may have been suffering from overheating and/or abnormal combustion, which caused excessively high operating temperatures. The oil pump and cooling systems should be checked thoroughly.

12 A hole in the piston crown, an extreme to be sure, is an indication that abnormal combustion (pre-ignition) was occurring. Burned areas at the edge of the piston crown are usually evidence of spark knock (detonation). If any of the above problems exist, the causes must be corrected or the damage will occur again.

13 Measure the piston ring-to-groove clearance by laying a new piston ring in the ring groove and slipping a feeler blade in beside it (see illustration). Check the clearance at three or four locations around the groove. If the clearance is greater than that specified, the piston is worn. **Note:** *Make sure you have the correct ring for the groove – the two compression rings can be identified by their markings and profile (see illustration 15.26a).*

14 Measure the piston diameter 5 mm up from the bottom of the skirt and at 90° to the piston pin axis (see illustration). If outside of the specified figure, the piston must be renewed.

15 If the necessary measuring equipment is available, measure the connecting rod small-end bore diameter, the piston pin outside diameter and the inside diameter of the pin bores in the piston (see illustrations).

Engine, clutch and transmission 2•33

15.14 Measure the piston diameter with a micrometer at the specified distance from the bottom of the skirt

15.15a Measure the internal diameter of the small-end bore . . .

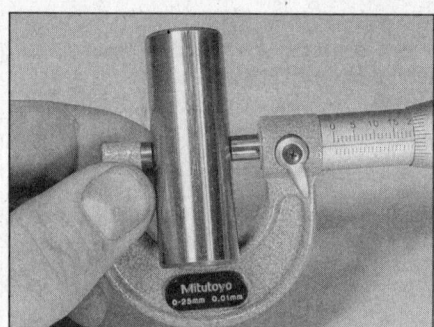

15.15b . . . the external diameter of the pin . . .

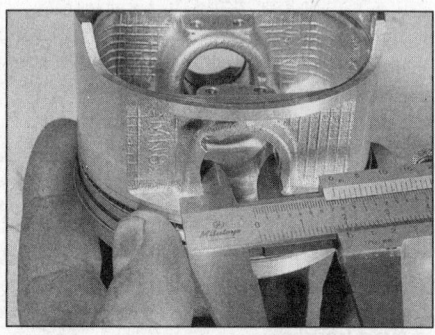

15.15c . . . and the internal diameter of the bore in the piston

15.18 Measuring piston ring installed end gap

Replace any component that has worn beyond the specified limits with a new one.

Piston rings

16 It is good practice to use new piston rings when an engine is being overhauled. Before fitting the new rings, the ring end gaps must be checked.

17 Lay out the pistons and the new ring sets so the rings will be matched with the same piston and cylinder during the end gap measurement procedure and engine assembly.

18 Fit the top ring into the top of the first liner and square it up with the cylinder walls by pushing it in with the top of the piston until the third ring on the piston is level with and parallel all the way round to the top of the liner. To measure the end gap, slip a feeler blade between the ends of the ring and compare the measurement to the Specification **(see illustration)**.

19 If the gap is larger or smaller than specified, double check to make sure that you have the correct rings before proceeding.

20 If the gap is too small, check the liner for distortion (see Section 14) – DO NOT try to increase the end gap by filing the ends of the rings.

21 If the end gap exceeds the service limit specified with the old rings, fit new rings engine and check again. If it is still excessive check the liner for wear (see Section 14).

22 Repeat the procedure for each ring that will be installed in the first cylinder and for each ring in the remaining cylinders. Remember to keep the rings, pistons and cylinders matched up.

23 Once the ring end gaps have been checked/corrected, the rings can be fitted onto the pistons.

24 The oil control ring (lowest on the piston) is installed first. It is composed of three separate components, the expander and the upper and lower side rails. First slip the expander into the groove, making sure the ends butt against each other and do not overlap. Next fit the upper side rail, then the lower **(see illustrations)**. The side rails can be fitted either way up – do not use a piston ring installation tool on the side rails as they may be damaged. Instead, place one end of the side rail into the groove between the expander and the ring land. Hold it firmly in place and slide a finger around the piston while pushing the rail into the groove.

25 After the three oil ring components have been installed, check to make sure that both the upper and lower side rails can be turned smoothly in the ring groove.

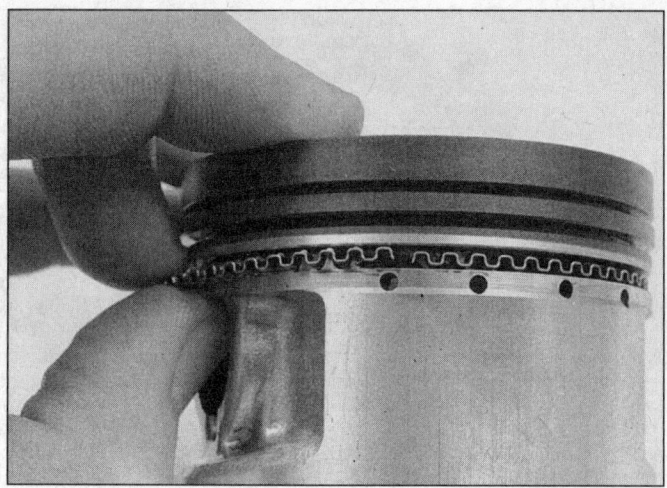

15.24a Fit the oil ring expander in its groove . . .

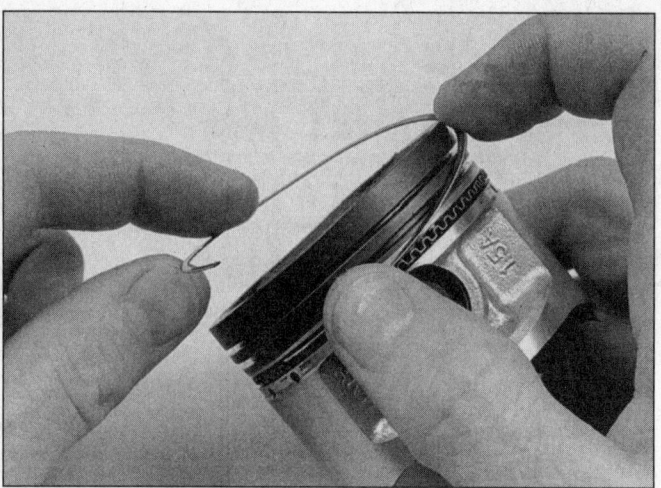

15.24b . . . then fit the lower side rail and the upper side rail each side of it. The oil ring components must be installed by hand

2•34 Engine, clutch and transmission

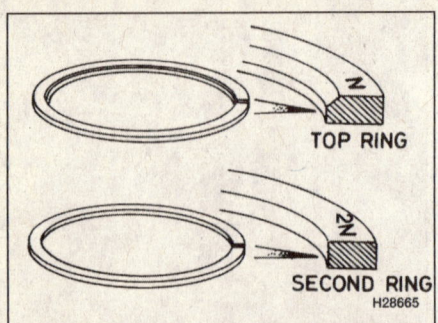

15.26a The rings can be identified by their different profiles – the N or 2N mark must face up

26 Fit the second (middle) ring next – it should be marked 2N at one end, and this mark must face up. **Note:** *If no mark is visible the second ring and top rings can be distinguished by their different profiles* **(see illustration)** – *make sure you have the correct ring*. Fit the ring into the middle groove on the piston. Either use your thumbs to hold the ring ends apart when installing the ring over the piston, or slip

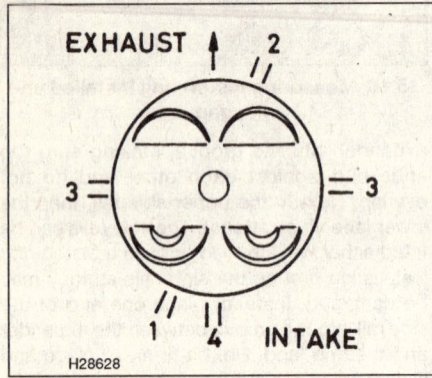

15.28 Stagger the ring end gaps as shown
1 Top ring end gap
2 Second (middle) ring end gap
3 Oil ring side rail end gaps
4 Oil ring expander ends

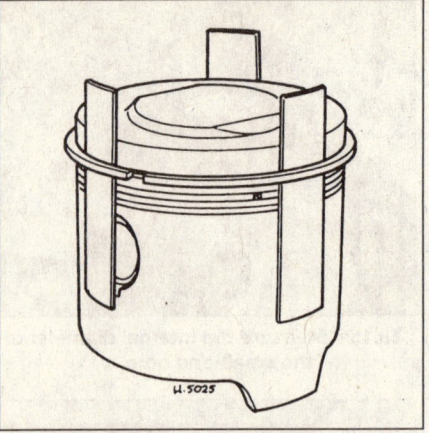

15.26b Old pieces of feeler gauge blade can be used to guide the ring over the piston

sections of old feeler gauge blades between the ring and piston to guide it into its groove **(see illustration)**, or use a ring removal/installation tool **(see illustration 15.7)**.

Caution: Do not expand the ring any more than is necessary to slide it into place – the ring material is brittle and is easily broken if overstressed.

27 Finally, fit the top ring in the same manner. Make sure the letter N near the end gap is facing up.
28 Position the ring end gaps around the piston as shown **(see illustration)**.

Installation

29 If the connecting rods have not been removed from the engine, stuff clean rag into the crankcase mouth to prevent any dropped circlips falling in. Lubricate the connecting rod small-end bore with engine oil.
30 Fit a new circlip into the groove in one side of the piston bore (the outer side for the outer pistons if the connecting rods have not been removed). Locate the piston on its rod so that the arrow or dot marking on its crown is facing forwards, the same way as the manufacturer's rod size and weight grade markings. Push the piston pin fully into the piston and secure with a second new circlip – make sure the circlip is fully seated in its groove **(see illustrations 15.5c, b and a)**.
31 Install the other pistons in the same way. If the connecting rods have not been removed from the engine, rotate the crankshaft to gain the best access.
32 Check that the piston rings are still correctly positioned in relation to the front of the engine **(see illustration 15.28)**.
33 Install all components and assemblies according to your removal procedure, referring to the relevant Sections of the Chapter.

16 Clutch

Note: *The clutch can be removed with the engine in the frame. If the engine has already been removed, ignore the steps which don't apply.*

Removal

1 On Sprint models, remove the right-hand fairing side panel (see Chapter 7). On Tiger models remove the belly pan (see Chapter 7).
2 Place the bike on its sidestand – this will prevent having to drain the engine oil. If you prefer to have the bike upright drain the oil (see Chapter 1).
3 Detach the clutch cable from the release mechanism arm on the clutch cover (see Section 17).
4 Follow the procedure in Section 10 and remove the starter cover, reduction and idle gears and the right-hand crankcase cover to gain access to the right-hand clutch cover bolt.
5 Working in a criss-cross pattern, slacken the clutch cover bolts evenly, noting how the cable bracket is secured **(see illustration)**. Lift the

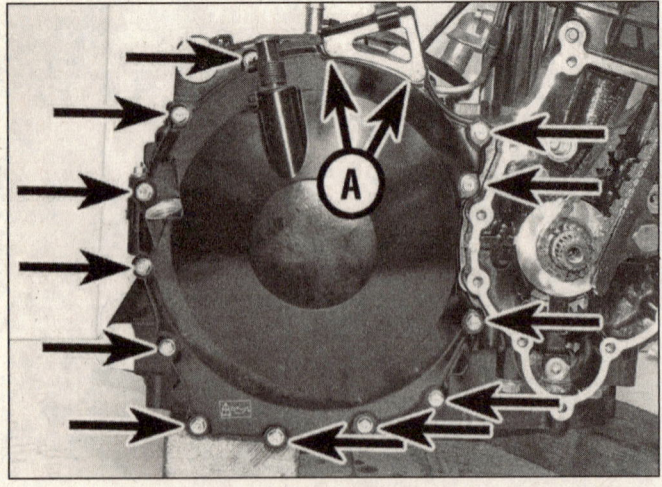

16.5a Undo the clutch cover bolts (arrowed), noting how the two bolts (A) secure the cable bracket . . .

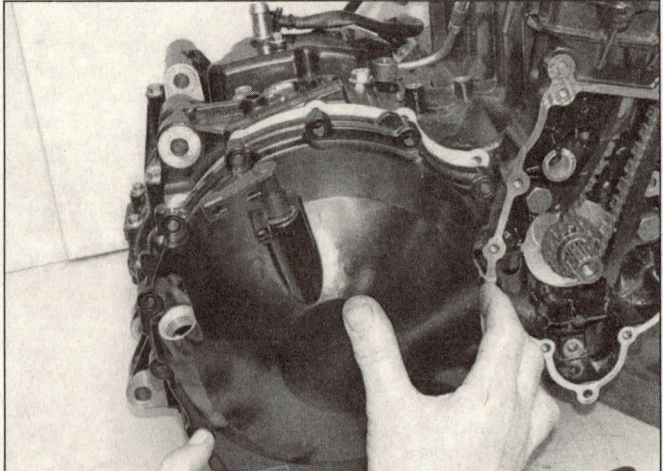

16.5b . . . and draw the cover off

Engine, clutch and transmission 2•35

16.8 Draw the clutch plates out

16.9 Using a commercially available tool to hold the clutch centre while unscrewing the nut

16.11 Draw the bearing sleeve out as described . . .

cover away from the engine, being prepared to catch any residual oil **(see illustration)**.

6 Remove the gasket and discard it. Note the three locating dowels and remove them for safe-keeping if loose **(see illustration 16.32a)**.

7 Working in a criss-cross pattern, gradually slacken the clutch spring retaining bolts until spring pressure is released, then remove the bolts and springs **(see illustration 16.30)**. Lift out the clutch pressure plate and remove the pull-rod **(see illustrations 16.29b and a)**.

8 Grasp the complete set of clutch plates and remove them as a pack – you may have to hook the inner plates out using a piece of wire **(see illustration)**. Unless the plates are being replaced with new ones, keep them in their original order. Note that the outer and inner friction plates are darker in colour to the rest and a bit thicker, and that the tabs on the outer plate locate in the shallow slots in the housing, not in the deep slots with the rest of the plates. Similarly remove the anti-judder spring and spring seat, noting how they fit **(see illustrations 16.27b and a)**.

9 The transmission input shaft must be locked to enable the clutch nut to be slackened. This can be done in several ways. If the engine is in the frame, engage 2nd gear and have an assistant hold the rear brake on hard with the rear tyre in firm contact with the ground. The Triumph service tool (Part No. T3880305) can be located between the clutch centre and clutch housing to lock them together, although you still need to engage 2nd gear and have an assistant hold the rear brake on. If the engine is out of the frame, a commercially available (and not expensive) holding tool can be used to stop the clutch centre from turning whilst the nut is slackened **(see illustration)**. Unscrew the nut and remove the Belleville washer from the input shaft. Discard the washer as a new one must be used on installation. On engines from number 502590 also discard the nut and use a new one.

10 Slide the clutch centre off the input shaft, followed by the large thrust washer **(see illustrations 16.25b and a)**.

11 Jiggle the clutch housing backwards and forwards and draw out the bearing sleeve, using a magnet or a pair of pliers to help, then support

16.12 . . . then slide the clutch housing out

the housing and remove the sleeve, noting which way round it fits **(see illustration)**.

12 Slide the clutch housing off the shaft, noting how the primary driven gear on the back of the housing engages with the primary drive gear on the crankshaft, and manoeuvre it out of the crankcase **(see illustration)**. Note how the oil pump drive pegs locate in the holes in the back of the clutch housing.

Inspection

13 After an extended period of service the clutch friction plates will wear and promote clutch slip. Measure the thickness of each friction plate using a Vernier caliper **(see illustration)**. If any plate has worn to or beyond the service limit given in the Specifications, the friction plates must be replaced with a new set – don't forget there are two different thicknesses of plate.

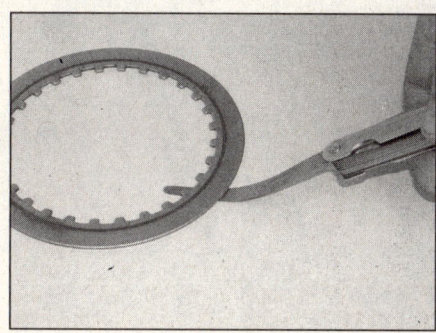

16.15 Check the plain plates for warpage

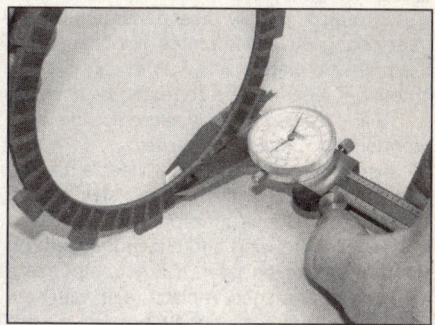

16.13 Measuring clutch friction plate thickness

14 If the plates are good, but the clutch has been slipping, it could be that the springs have sagged. As no specification is available for the spring free length, the only way to check them is to compare them with new ones. If the springs have sagged, replace them as a set.

15 The plain plates should not show any signs of excess heating (bluing). Check for warpage using a flat surface and feeler blades **(see illustration)**. If any plate exceeds the maximum permissible amount of warpage, or shows signs of bluing, all plain plates must be renewed as a set.

16 Inspect the clutch assembly for burrs and indentations on the edges of the protruding tangs of the friction plates and/or slots in the edge of the outer drum with which they engage **(see illustration)**. Similarly check for wear between the inner tongues of the plain plates and the slots in the clutch centre **(see**

16.16a Check for wear of the friction plate tabs and the clutch housing slots . . .

2•36 Engine, clutch and transmission

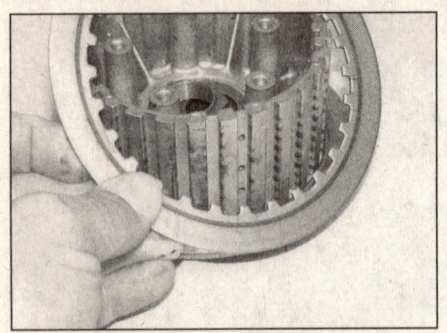

16.16b ... and of the plain plate tongues and clutch centre slots

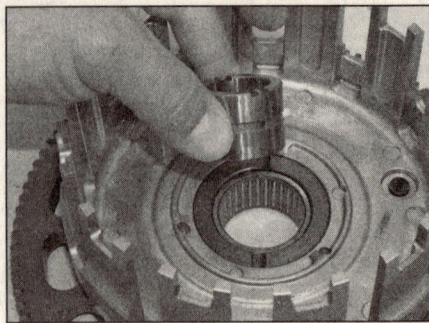

16.17 Inspect the needle bearing and the bearing sleeve

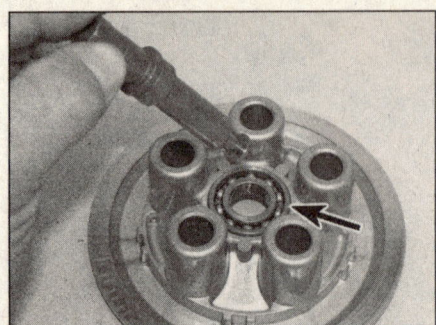

16.19 Check the pull-rod, pressure plate, and bearing (arrowed) for wear

illustration). Wear of this nature will cause clutch drag and slow disengagement during gear changes, as the plates will snag when the pressure plate is lifted. With care a small amount of wear can be corrected by dressing with a fine file, but if this is excessive the worn components should be renewed.

17 Inspect the clutch housing needle bearing and the surface of the bearing sleeve **(see illustration)**. Check the springs in the back of the clutch housing and check the teeth on the primary driven gear. If any components are worn of damaged, replace them with new ones. Note that if the needle bearing is worn or damaged, a new clutch housing must be fitted; the bearing is not available separately.

18 Inspect the anti-judder spring and spring seat for wear. If the spring is flattened, replace the spring and seat as a set **(see illustration 16.27c)**.

19 Check the pull-rod, the pressure plate and the bearing for signs of damage and wear **(see illustration)**. Ensure that the inner race of the bearing spins freely without any sign of notchiness. Push the bearing out of the pressure plate if renewal is required.

20 Check the clutch release mechanism in the clutch cover for smooth operation. Note how the return spring ends locate, then withdraw the shaft from the cover, noting the washer **(see illustration)**. Check the shaft and the bearings for wear **(see illustration)**. The shaft oil seal is available separately, but the bearings are not – if they are worn or damaged a new cover will have to be fitted. If required lever the old seal out and press a new one into place **(see illustrations)**.

21 Check the pull-rod end and its locating cutout in the shaft for signs of wear and damage, and replace them with new ones if necessary **(see illustration)**. Clean all components and lubricate the seal and bearings with grease.

Installation

22 Remove all traces of gasket material from the crankcase and clutch cover mating surfaces.

23 Lubricate the clutch housing bearing sleeve and the needle bearing with clean engine oil **(see illustration 16.17)**.

24 Slide the clutch housing over the input shaft and manoeuvre it into the crankcase so that the inner main section of the primary driven gear engages with the primary drive gear on the crankshaft, then fit the bearing sleeve with the grooved face outwards **(see illustrations 16.12 and 16.11)**. Insert a screwdriver into the holes between the sprung and main sections of the primary drive gear and twist it until the gear teeth align, then push the housing on further so that it is fully engaged with the primary drive gear **(see illustration)**. If necessary, turn the oil pump

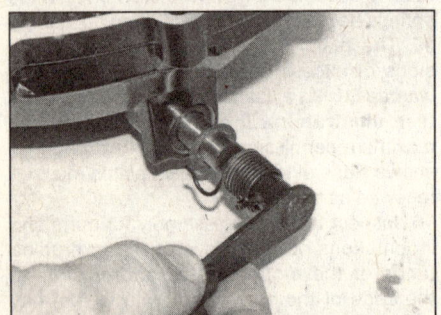

16.20a Withdraw the shaft ...

16.20b ... and check the shaft and the bearings (arrowed) for wear

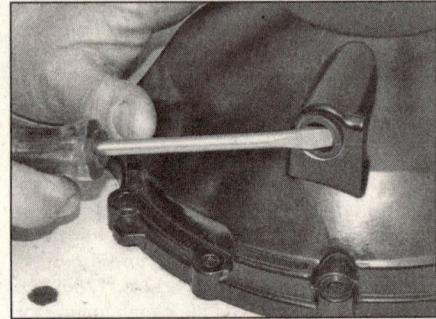

16.20c Lever the grease seal out ...

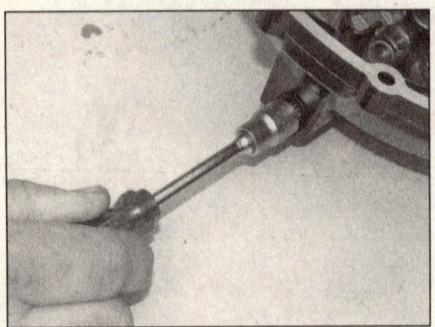

16.20d ... and press in a new one

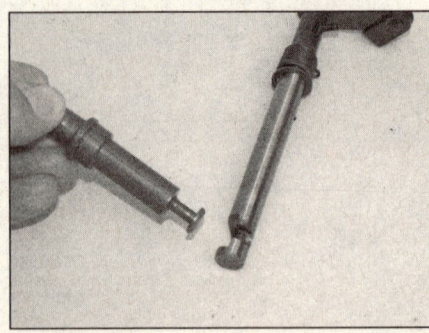

16.21 Check the end of the pull-rod and the cut-out in the shaft for wear and damage

16.24a Align the gear teeth sections as described to allow the driven and drive gears to fully engage

Engine, clutch and transmission 2•37

16.24b Make sure that the oil pump drive sprocket pegs are engaged with the back of the clutch housing by turning the pump driven sprocket

16.25a Fit the large thrust washer . . .

16.25b . . . and slide the clutch centre onto the shaft

16.26a Fit the washer . . .

16.26b . . . and the nut . . .

16.26c . . . and tighten it to the specified torque

driven sprocket until the holes on the clutch housing engage with the pegs on the oil pump drive sprocket **(see illustration)**.

25 Slide the large thrust washer over the input shaft, then slide the clutch centre onto the input shaft splines **(see illustrations)**.

26 Fit the new Belleville washer with its OUT marking facing outwards, then thread the clutch nut on, on engines from number 502590 using a new nut (if a new nut is being fitted on earlier engines it will be the new-spec encapsulated nut and must be tightened to the higher torque setting given at the beginning of the Chapter) **(see illustrations)**. Using the method employed on removal to lock the input shaft, tighten the nut to the specified torque setting **(see illustration)**. *Note: When the nut has been tightened, check that the clutch centre rotates freely with the transmission in neutral.*

27 On 2011-on models, if a new set of clutch plates is being fitted, the height of the new pack must be measured, and if necessary adjusted using the different thicknesses of plain plate supplied as follows: first assemble the pack on a flat surface using five of the 1.6 mm plain plates and four of the 2.0 mm plates arranged as shown, then measure the pack height using a Vernier caliper **(see illustrations)**. If the measured height is greater than 50.37 mm, replace the outermost of the 2.0 mm plain plates with a 1.6 mm plate. Note that a maximum of four 2.0 mm plates can fitted so adjustment can only be made if the measured height of the pack is too high, and there must be a minimum of three 2.0 mm plates and therefore a maximum of six 1.6 mm plates.

28 Fit the anti-judder spring seat into the clutch centre, followed by the anti-judder

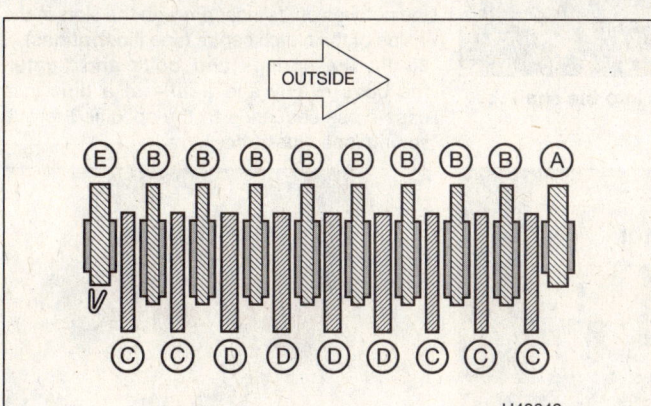

16.27a Arrange the plates as shown

- A Outer friction plate
- B Friction plates
- C 1.6 mm plain plates
- D 2.0 mm plain plates
- E Inner friction plate

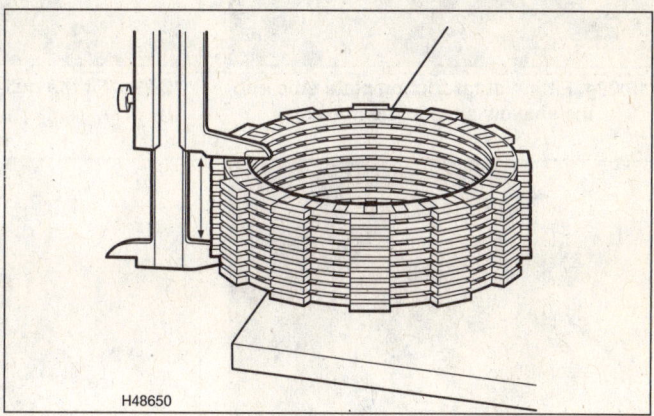

16.27b Measure the height of the pack

2•38 Engine, clutch and transmission

16.28a Fit the spring seat . . .

16.28b . . . and the spring . . .

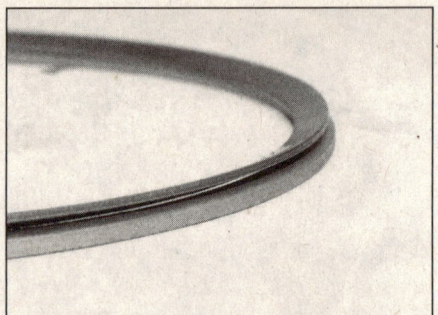
16.28c . . . making sure it is the correct way round

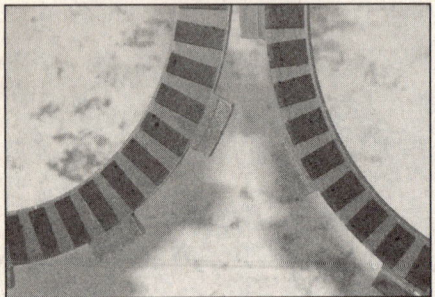
16.28d The inner and outer friction plates, as shown on the right, are narrower than the rest

16.28e Fit the dark inner friction plate . . .

16.28f . . . then a plain plate, and so on

spring, fitting the spring so that its outer edge is raised off the spring seat **(see illustrations)**. Coat each clutch plate with engine oil prior to installation. Identify the inner and outer friction plates – they are thicker, have a larger internal diameter (i.e. the plate is narrower) and have different shaped friction pads **(see illustration)**. Build up the clutch plates, starting with the inner friction plate that is narrower and thicker, then a plain plate and alternating normal friction and plain plates until all but the last friction plate are installed **(see illustrations)** – on 2011-on Speed Triple models (from VIN 461332), Tiger SE and Tiger Sport models make sure the plain plates are fitted in the correct positions according to thickness **(see illustration 16.27a)**. Fit the outer friction plate (narrower and thicker), locating its tabs in the shallow slots, rather than in the deep slots with the other friction plates **(see illustration)**.

29 Insert the pull-rod into the end of the shaft, then fit the pressure plate assembly, engaging the notches on its inner rim with the slots in the inside of the clutch centre **(see illustrations)**.

30 Fit the springs and bolts and tighten the bolts evenly and a little at a time in a criss-cross sequence to the specified torque setting **(see illustration)**.

16.28g Fit the outer friction plate tabs into the shallow slots in the housing

16.29a Fit the pull-rod into the shaft . . .

16.29b . . . then fit the pressure plate . . .

16.29c . . . making sure it engages correctly

16.30 Fit the springs and the bolts then tighten them evenly in a criss-cross sequence

Engine, clutch and transmission 2•39

16.31 Make sure the spring ends (arrowed) locate correctly

16.32a Locate a new gasket over the dowels (arrowed)

16.32b Fit the cover, making sure the shaft and pull-rod engage

31 If removed, make sure the washer is on the shaft then fit it into the cover (see illustration 16.20a). Locate the spring ends as shown (see illustration)
32 Fit the dowels into the crankcase if removed, then fit a new gasket, locating it over the dowels (see illustration). Fit the cover, angling the release shaft arm so it engages with the pull-rod (see illustration).
33 Fit the cover bolts, not forgetting the cable bracket, and tighten them evenly in a criss-cross sequence to the specified torque setting (see illustration 16.5a). Operate the release lever and make sure it picks up the end of the pull-rod correctly – it should come up solid when it is pointing across the engine.
34 Attach the clutch cable to the release lever on the clutch cover and check the operation of the clutch (see Section 17).
35 Install the right-hand crankcase cover and the starter cover (see Section 10).
36 If you drained the engine oil, replenish it (see Chapter 1).
37 On Sprint models, install the right-hand fairing side panel (see Chapter 7). On Tiger models install the belly pan (see Chapter 7).

17 Clutch cable

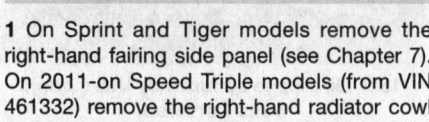

1 On Sprint and Tiger models remove the right-hand fairing side panel (see Chapter 7). On 2011-on Speed Triple models (from VIN 461332) remove the right-hand radiator cowl (See Chapter 7).
2 Slacken the locknuts securing the cable in the bracket on the clutch cover and thread the rear locknut off the adjuster (see illustration).
3 Slip the cable end out of the retainer on the clutch arm, noting how it fits, then draw the cable out of the bracket, collecting the rear locknut as you do.
4 On Sprint and 2005 to 2007 Speed Triple models fully slacken the clutch cable freeplay adjuster lockring (see illustration). On all models thread the adjuster into the lever bracket. Align the slots in the adjuster and lockring (where fitted) with the slot in the bracket.
5 Pull the outer cable end from the socket in the adjuster and release the inner cable from the lever (see illustrations). Remove the cable from the machine, noting its routing and any guides or clips.

> **HAYNES HiNT** Before removing the cable from the bike, tape the lower end of the new cable to the upper end of the old cable. Slowly pull the lower end of the old cable out, guiding the new cable down into position. Using this method will ensure the cable is routed correctly.

6 Installation is the reverse of removal. Apply grease to the cable ends. Make sure the cable is correctly routed. Make sure the cable lower end is properly located in the retainer on the release mechanism arm. Check the clutch release mechanism for smooth operation and any signs of wear or damage. Remove it for inspection if required (see Section 16).
7 Adjust the clutch lever freeplay (see Chapter 1). On Sprint and Tiger models install the fairing side panel (see Chapter 7). On 2011-on Speed Triple models (from VIN 461332) install the right-hand radiator cowl (See Chapter 7).

18 Sump and oil strainer

Note: *The sump can be removed with the engine in the frame. If work is being carried out with the engine removed ignore the steps which don't apply.*

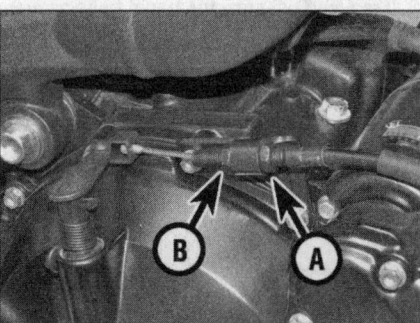

17.2 Slacken the front locknut (A) and thread the rear locknut (B) off the cable

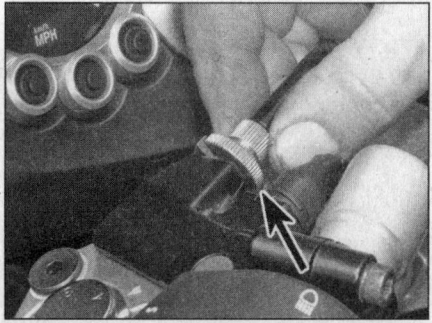

17.4 Slacken the lockring (arrowed) where fitted, then thread the adjuster into the lever bracket

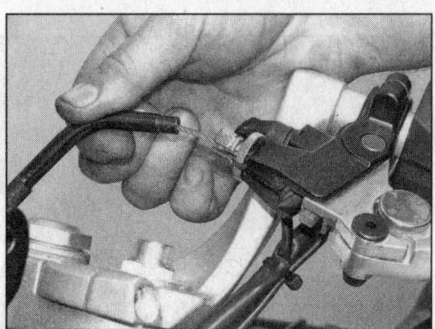

17.5a Draw the outer cable end from the adjuster and slip the inner cable out via the slots . . .

17.5b . . . then detach the inner cable end from the lever

2•40 Engine, clutch and transmission

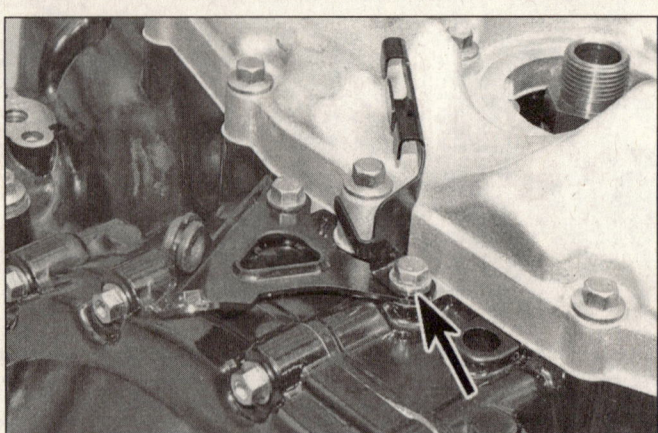

18.5 Unscrew the bolt (arrowed) and remove the guide, noting how it locates

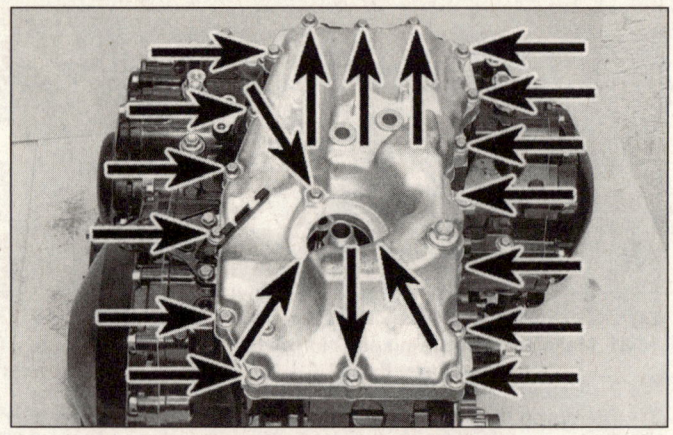

18.6 Sump bolts (arrowed)

Removal

1 On Sprint models remove the fairing side panels (see Chapter 7). On Tigers remove the belly-pan (see Chapter 7).
2 Drain the engine oil and remove the oil filter (see Chapter 1).
3 Remove the exhaust system (see Chapter 4).
4 On early Sprint and Speed Triple models unscrew the bolts securing the oil cooler pipes to the sump and detach the pipes, noting which fits where (see illustration 6.3). Discard the O-rings as new ones must be used.
5 Where fitted remove the oxygen sensor wiring guide (see illustration).
6 Unscrew the sump bolts, slackening them evenly in a criss-cross sequence to prevent distortion (see illustration) – on Speed Triples from VIN 461332 and Tiger SE and Tiger Sport models note the position of the drain hose guide. Remove the sump. Discard the sump gasket – a new one must be used.
7 Draw the oil strainer out of its socket, noting which way round it fits, then remove the rubber seal (see illustrations). Check the condition of the seal and discard it if it is damaged, distorted or deteriorated in any way. Clean the strainer in solvent and remove any debris caught in the gauze. The presence of metal caught in the strainer, or in the bottom of the sump, is indicative of engine wear that should be investigated.
8 If required unscrew the banjo bolts securing the internal oil pipe and remove the pipe (see illustration). Discard the sealing washers as new ones must be used.

Installation

9 Remove all traces of gasket material from the sump and crankcase mating surfaces.
10 If removed fit the internal oil pipe using new sealing washers under the banjo bolt heads, and tighten the bolts to the specified torque setting (see illustration).
11 Lubricate the rubber seal for the strainer with oil and fit it into its socket in the crankcase, using a new one if necessary (see illustration). Fit the strainer into the seal, locating the tabs on each side of the rib (see illustration).

18.7a Pull the strainer out of its socket . . .

18.7b . . . and remove the rubber seal

18.8 Oil pipe is secured by three banjo bolts (arrowed)

18.10 Use new sealing washers between the banjo bolts and the oil pipe unions

18.11a Fit the seal . . .

18.11b . . . then fit the strainer, making sure it locates correctly

Engine, clutch and transmission 2•41

18.12a Fit a new gasket . . .

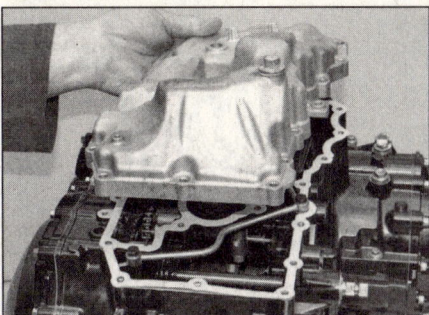

18.12b . . . then fit the sump

19.2 Lock the drive sprocket as described then loosen the driven sprocket bolt (arrowed)

12 Place a new gasket onto the sump if the engine is in the frame, or onto the crankcase if the engine has been removed and is upside down on the bench – use a smear of grease to hold the gasket in place if required. Fit the sump and tighten the bolts evenly in a criss-cross sequence to the specified torque setting, not forgetting the drain hose guide on Speed Triple models from VIN 461332 and Tiger SE and Tiger Sport models, and applying some threadlock to its bolt. After the initial tightening go round all the bolts again as some of the first ones tightened may become a bit loose as the rest are tightened down.

13 Where fitted install the oxygen sensor wiring guide **(see illustration 18.5)**.

14 On early Sprint and Speed Triple models connect the oil cooler pipes using new O-rings, and tighten the bolts to the specified torque setting **(see illustrations 6.7 and 6.3)**.

15 Install the exhaust system (see Chapter 4).

16 Install a new oil filter, then fill the engine with the correct type and quantity of oil (see Chapter 1 and *Pre-ride checks*). Start the engine and check that there are no leaks.

17 On Sprint models install the fairing side panels (see Chapter 7). On Tiger models install the belly-pan (see Chapter 7).

19 Oil pump and oil pressure relief valve

Note: The oil pump can be removed with the engine in the frame, but removal of the pressure relief valve requires removal of the engine and separation of the crankcases.

Oil pump

Removal

1 Remove the clutch (see Section 16).
2 The oil pump drive sprocket must be locked to enable the driven sprocket bolt to be slackened. Triumph provides a service tool to do this (Part No. T3880371). Alternatively, engage a length of bar between the pegs on the drive sprocket and secure it against the crankcase **(see illustration)**. Unscrew the bolt and remove the washer, then draw off the drive and driven sprockets, chain, drive sprocket, needle bearing and sleeve as an assembly **(see illustration 19.11b)**.
3 Unscrew the bolts securing the pump in the crankcase and remove the pump **(see illustration)**.

Inspection

Note: Individual internal parts are not available for the oil pump; if the checks described below indicate that the pump is worn, it must be renewed as a complete unit.

4 Undo the bolt securing the pump cover and remove the cover; remove the dowel for safekeeping if it is loose **(see illustrations)**.
5 Measure the clearance between the inner rotor tip and the outer rotor tip with a feeler gauge **(see illustration)**. Also measure the clearance between the outer rotor and the pump body **(see illustration)**. Finally, lift out the pump shaft, noting the location of the washer and inner rotor drive pin **(see**

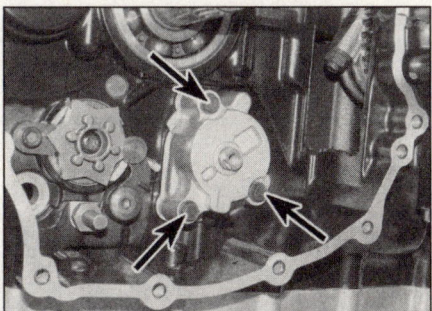

19.3 Unscrew the bolts (arrowed) and remove the pump

19.4a Remove the bolt (arrowed) . . .

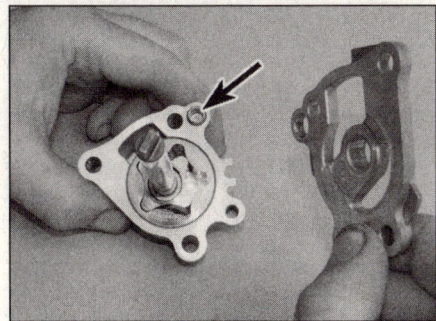

19.4b . . . and lift off the cover, noting the dowel (arrowed)

19.5a Measuring rotor tip clearance

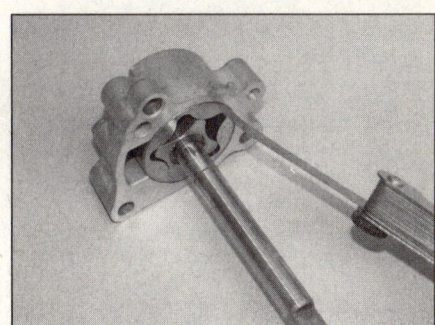

19.5b Measuring outer rotor-to-body clearance

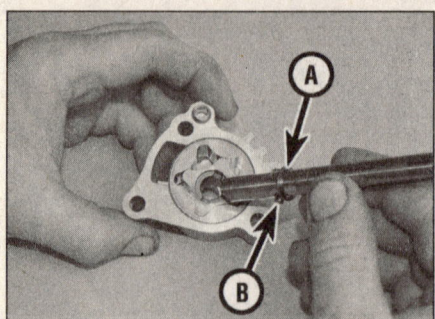

19.5c Note the washer (A) and drive pin (B) on the pump shaft

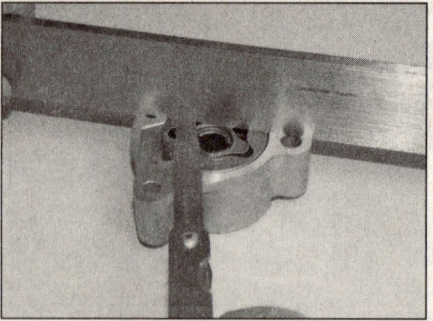

19.5d Measuring rotor end-float

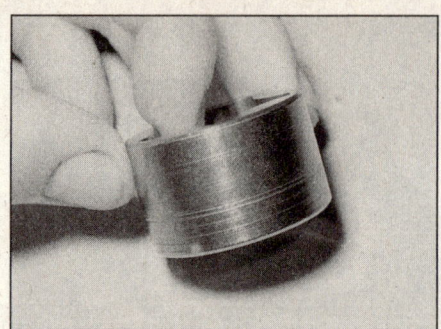

19.6 Look for scoring and wear, such as on this outer rotor

illustration). Lay a straight-edge across the rotors and pump body and measure the rotor end-float (gap between the rotors and straight-edge) with a feeler gauge **(see illustration)**. If any of the results are outside the limits listed in this Chapter's Specifications, replace the pump with a new one.

6 Lift the inner and outer rotors out of the pump, noting which way round they fit. Examine them for scoring and wear **(see illustration)**.

7 Before reassembling the pump, make sure that all parts are clean. Have a supply of the correct grade of engine oil on hand to lubricate the rotors as they are installed. Ensure that the drive pin and washer are assembled on the pump shaft and that the shaft is fitted the right way round **(see illustration 19.5c)**.

8 If removed, fit the dowel into the pump, then fit the cover and tighten the bolt **(see illustrations 19.4b and a)**.

9 Inspect the oil pump drive and driven sprockets and chain for damage and wear and renew them as a set if necessary. Check the needle bearing and sleeve and renew them if they are worn or pitted **(see illustration)**.

Installation

10 Insert the pump shaft into the crankcase and ensure that the tab on its inner end engages with the slot in the water pump drive; temporarily fit the driven sprocket onto the outer end of the shaft and rotate it until the tab is felt to engage and the back of the pump is directly in contact with the crankcase **(see illustration)**. Install the mounting bolts and tighten them to the torque setting specified at the beginning of the Chapter.

11 Fit the sleeve, needle bearing and drive sprocket on the end of the input shaft, then loop the chain over the drive sprocket **(see illustration)**. Fit the driven sprocket into the chain, ensuring the side marked OUT is facing out, then slide the assembly in, ensuring the driven sprocket locates correctly on the oil pump shaft **(see illustration)**.

12 Fit the driven sprocket bolt and washer, then using the method employed on removal to lock the drive sprocket, tighten the bolt to the specified torque setting **(see illustration 19.2)**.

13 Install the clutch (see Section 16).

Oil pressure relief valve

14 The oil pressure relief valve is located in the lower crankcase half. Remove the selector drum forks (see Section 21).

15 Use a socket on the relief valve hex and unscrew it from the crankcase **(see illustration)**.

16 Push the relief valve plunger into the valve body and check that it moves smoothly and freely against the spring pressure **(see illustration)**. If not, remove the circlip, noting

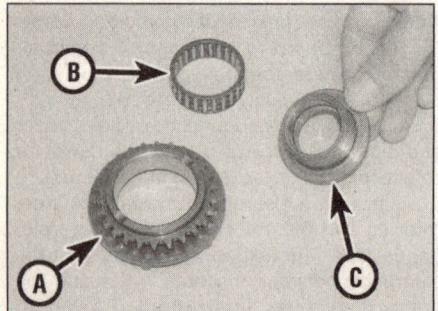

19.9 Check the oil pump drive sprocket (A), needle bearing (B) and sleeve (C)

19.10 Ensure the tab (arrowed) engages with the water pump

19.11a Fit the drive sprocket assembly and chain onto the input shaft . . .

19.11b . . . then install the driven sprocket as described

19.15 Remove the selector drum and forks to access the pressure relief valve (arrowed)

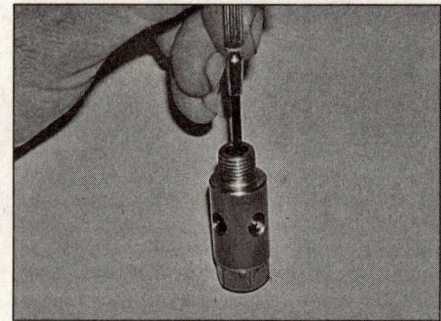

19.16a Push the plunger into the valve and check its action

Engine, clutch and transmission 2•43

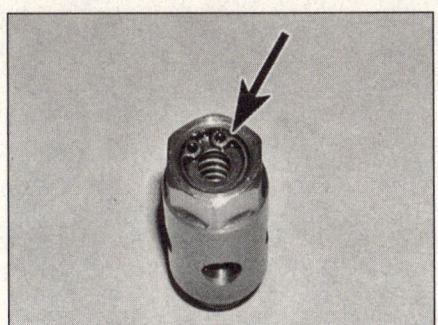

19.16b Remove the circlip (arrowed), noting it is under spring pressure

20.3 Remove the E-clip and washer (arrowed)

20.4 Withdraw the gearchange shaft

that it is under spring pressure, and remove the spring seat, spring and plunger **(see illustration)**. Clean all the components in solvent and check them for scoring, wear or damage. If any is found, fit a new relief valve – individual components are not available. Otherwise, coat the inside of the valve body and the plunger with clean engine oil, then insert the plunger, spring and spring seat and secure them with the circlip. Check the action of the valve plunger again – if it is still suspect, replace the valve with a new one.

17 Apply a drop of non-permanent thread locking compound to the pressure relief valve threads and tighten the valve to the specified torque setting.

18 Install the remaining components and assemblies in a reverse of the removal procedure, referring to the relevant Sections.

20 Gearchange mechanism

Note: *The gearchange mechanism can be removed with the engine in the frame. If the engine has been removed, ignore the steps which don't apply.*

Removal

1 Make sure the transmission is in neutral. Remove the clutch (see Section 16).
2 Note the alignment of the punch mark on the gearchange shaft end with that on the lever or linkage arm clamp (according to model) – if the punch marks are not visible make your own mark where the slot in the lever or arm aligns with the shaft. Unscrew the pinch bolt and slide the lever or arm off the shaft **(see illustration 4.13)**.
3 Remove the E-clip and washer from the shaft **(see illustration)**. Wrap a single layer of thin insulating tape around the gearchange shaft splines to protect the oil seal lips as the shaft is removed.
4 Note how the gearchange shaft centralising spring ends fit on each side of the locating pin in the casing, and how the pawls on the selector arm locate onto the pins on the cam plate end of the selector drum. Grasp the shaft/arm assembly and withdraw it from the crankcase, noting the washer **(see illustration)**.
5 On models up to VIN 340169 and from VIN 562631, note how the stopper arm roller locates in the neutral detent on the selector drum cam, and how the spring ends locate **(see illustration)**. Unscrew the stopper arm

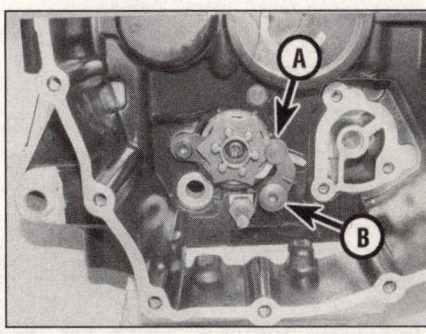

20.5 Note how the roller (A) locates, then unscrew the bolt (B) and remove the arm

bolt and remove the arm, the washer and the spring, noting how they fit.
6 On models from VIN 340170 to VIN 562630, note how the roller locates in the neutral detent on the selector drum cam. Unhook each end of the stopper arm spring and remove it **(see illustration)**. Unscrew the stopper arm bolt and remove the arm and the washer, noting how they fit **(see illustration)**.
7 If the selector drum is being removed later, or if otherwise required, undo the cam plate bolt, locking the selector drum with a holding tool as shown if the sump has been removed, or using a suitable tool wedged between the

20.6a Unhook the spring (arrowed) . . .

20.6b . . . then unscrew the bolt (arrowed) and remove the arm

2•44 Engine, clutch and transmission

20.7a Counter-hold the drum as shown or described . . .

20.7b . . . and unscrew the bolt (arrowed)

20.7c Ease the cam plate off using a screwdriver if necessary

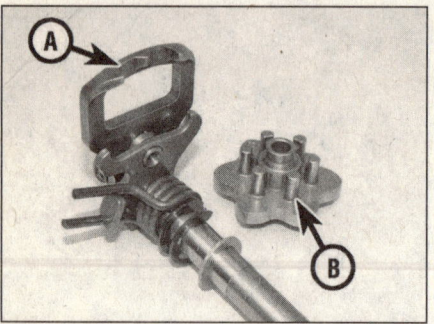

20.8a Check the pawls (A) on the arm and the pins (B) on the plate . . .

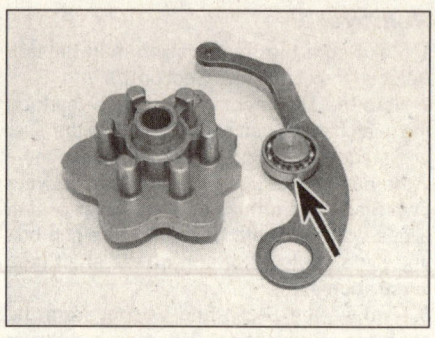

20.8b . . . then check the roller (arrowed) and the cam plate detents

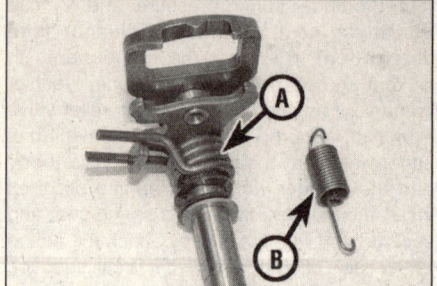

20.9 Check the centralising spring (A) and stopper arm spring (B) – late model type shown

plate and the crankcase **(see illustrations)**. Remove the plate, using a screwdriver to help ease it off if necessary **(see illustration)**. Note that there is a locating pin in the end of the selector drum – it should be tight, but take care as it could drop out. Remove it from the drum for safekeeping if it is loose.

Inspection

8 Check the selector arm for cracks, distortion and wear of its pawls, and check for any corresponding wear on the pins on the selector drum cam plate **(see illustration)**. Also check the stopper arm roller and the detents in the cam plate for any wear or damage, and make sure the roller turns freely **(see illustration)**. Replace any components that are worn or damaged with new ones. If required (and not already done), refer to Step 7 for removal of the cam plate, and to Step 12 for installation.

9 Inspect the shaft centralising spring and the stopper arm return spring for fatigue, wear or damage **(see illustration)**. If any is found, they must be replaced with new ones. To replace the shaft spring on models up to VIN 340169 and from VIN 562631, release the E-clip, then slide it off the end of the shaft. Fit the new spring, locating the ends on each side of the tab, then fit the E-clip, using a new one if necessary. On models from VIN 340170 to VIN 562630 the spring is not listed as being available separately, but check with a Triumph dealer. Make sure the locating pin around which the centralising spring ends locate is tightened to the specified torque setting – if loose, remove it, clean the threads and apply fresh threadlock, then tighten it to the correct torque.

10 Check the gearchange shaft is straight and look for damage to the splines. If the shaft is bent you can attempt to straighten it, but if the splines are damaged the shaft must be replaced with a new one.

11 Check the condition of the shaft oil seal in the left-hand side of the crankcase. If it is damaged, deteriorated or shows signs of leakage it must be replaced with a new one, though it is advisable to fit a new one whatever the apparent condition. Lever out the old seal with a seal hook or screwdriver **(see illustration)**. With the seal removed check the shaft bearing. Press or drive the new seal squarely into place using your fingers, a seal driver or suitable socket **(see illustration)**.

Installation

12 If removed, fit the cam plate locating pin into the end of the selector drum. Locate the cam plate onto the pin, carefully using a drift to tap it into place if necessary **(see illustrations)**. Apply a suitable non-permanent thread locking compound to the cam plate bolt

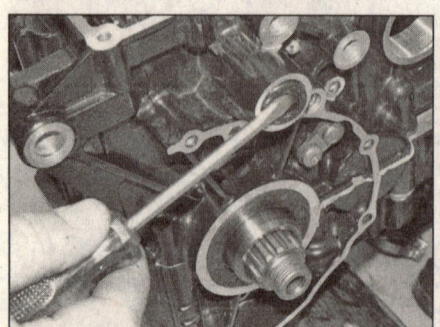

20.11a Lever the seal out . . .

20.11b . . . and press a new one in

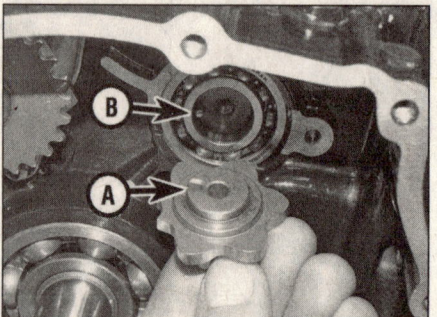

20.12a Align the cut-out (A) with the locating pin (B) and fit the plate . . .

Engine, clutch and transmission 2•45

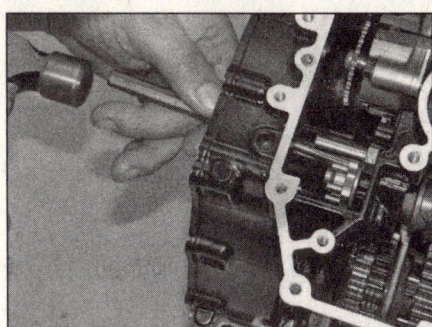
20.12b ... using a drift to tap it into place

20.12c Apply threadlock to the bolt

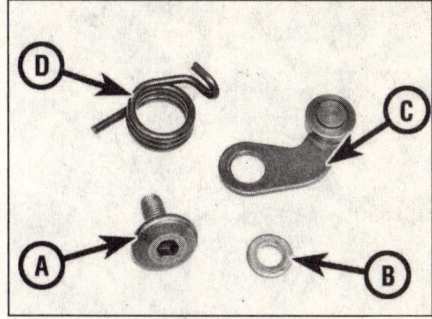
20.13 Pivot bolt (A), washer (B), stopper arm (C) and return spring (D)

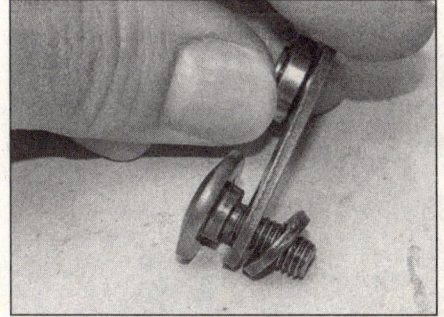
20.14a Assemble the bolt, arm and washer ...

20.14b ... and fit them onto the crankcase

and tighten it to the torque setting specified at the beginning of the Chapter **(see illustration)** – lock the drum with a holding tool as on removal **(see illustration 20.7a)**.

13 On models up to VIN 340169 and from VIN 562631, fit the stopper arm bolt through the arm then fit the washer and spring onto the bolt, positioning the spring ends correctly **(see illustration)**. Apply a suitable non-permanent thread locking compound to the bolt threads. Fit the stopper arm assembly, locating the roller in the neutral detent in the cam plate, and tighten the bolt to the torque setting specified at the beginning of the Chapter **(see illustration 20.5)**.

14 On models from VIN 340170 to VIN 562630, fit the stopper arm bolt through the arm then fit the washer onto the bolt **(see illustration)**. Apply a suitable non-permanent thread locking compound to the bolt threads. Fit the stopper arm assembly and tighten the bolt to the torque setting specified at the beginning of the Chapter **(see illustration)**. Hook the spring onto the end of the arm, locate the roller in the neutral detent in the cam plate, then hook the spring onto the arm on the selector drum bearing retainer **(see illustration 20.6a)**.

15 Check that the shaft centralising spring is properly positioned **(see illustration 20.9)**. Apply some grease to the lips of the gearchange shaft oil seal in the left-hand side of the crankcase. Slide the shaft into place and push it all the way through the case until the splined end comes out the other side, and locate the selector arm pawls onto the pins on the selector drum and the centralising spring ends onto each side of the locating pin in the crankcase **(see illustration 20.4)**. Fit the washer and E-clip onto the left-hand end of the shaft **(see illustration 20.3)**.

16 Check that all components are correctly positioned **(see illustrations)**. Install the clutch (see Section 16).

17 Remove the insulating tape from around the gearchange shaft splines. Slide the gearchange lever or linkage arm (according to model) onto the shaft, aligning the punch marks or the mark made on removal (Step 2) **(see illustration 4.13)**. Fit the pinch bolt and tighten it.

21 Selector drum and forks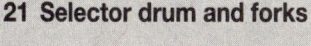

Note: *The selector drum and forks can be removed without separating the crankcases, though the engine must be removed from the frame and the sump removed.*

Removal

1 Remove the engine from the frame and remove the sump, strainer and internal oil pipe (see Section 18), and the gearchange mechanism and cam plate (see Section 20).

2 The selector forks are numbered 00, 01 and 02 from right to left, the numbers facing the left-hand side of the engine **(see illustration)**. If no numbers are visible, mark each fork for identification using paint or a felt pen and note which way round they fit, as an aid to installation. Note how the guide pin on each fork locates in the groove in the selector drum.

3 Where fitted undo the screw securing the selector fork shaft retainer and remove the

20.16a Gearchange mechanism – early models

20.16b Gearchange mechanism – late models

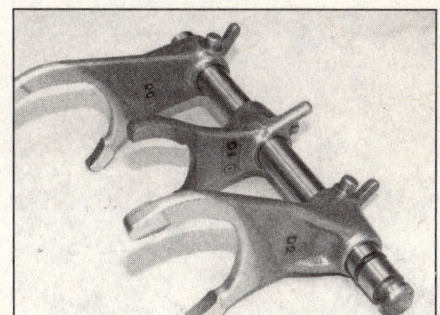
21.2 Note the numbering of the selector forks and which way they face

2•46 Engine, clutch and transmission

21.3a Undo the screw (arrowed) and remove the fork shaft retainer

21.3b Support the forks and withdraw the shaft

21.4a Unscrew the bolt (arrowed) and remove the retainer – late model type shown

21.4b Dislodge the bearing . . .

21.4c . . . and remove the drum

retainer, noting how it fits **(see illustration)**. On engines numbered 563847 and higher remove the two E-clips from the shaft inside the crankcase. Support the selector forks and withdraw the shaft from the left-hand side of the crankcase **(see illustration)**. Where fitted note the O-ring on the shaft and replace it with a new one on assembly.

4 Unscrew the bolt and remove the retainer securing the selector drum bearing **(see illustration)**. Push the bearing out from the inside of the crankcase, using a drift and/or moving the selector drum to dislodge it, then lift the drum out of the crankcase, noting how it fits **(see illustrations)**.

5 Lift the selector forks out of their grooves in the transmission shafts, and slide them back on the shaft in their correct order and way round **(see illustrations 21.12c, b and a, and 21.2)**.

Inspection

6 Check the selector forks and shaft for wear and damage.

7 Locate each selector fork in its corresponding gear pinion groove and measure the fork-to-groove clearance using a feeler gauge **(see illustration)**. If the clearance is outside the service limit, measure the selector fork end widths and the groove in the gear using a Vernier caliper **(see illustrations)**. Replace any component that is worn beyond the service limit with a new one (see Specifications).

8 Check the fit of each fork on the shaft – they should slide freely but with no freeplay

21.7a Measure the fork-to-groove clearance using a feeler gauge

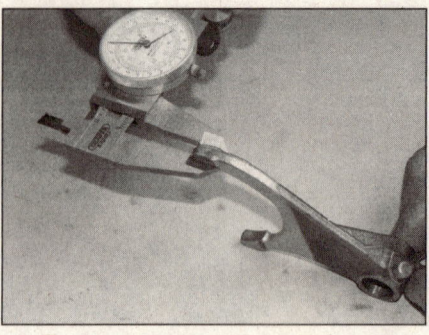

21.7b Measuring the thickness of the fork ends . . .

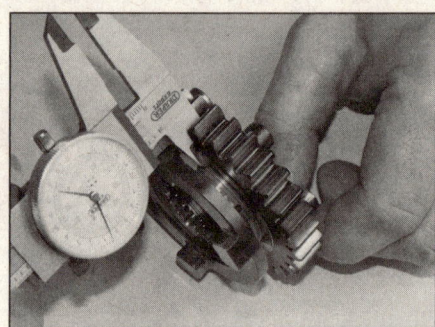

21.7c . . . and the width of the fork groove in the gear pinion

Engine, clutch and transmission 2•47

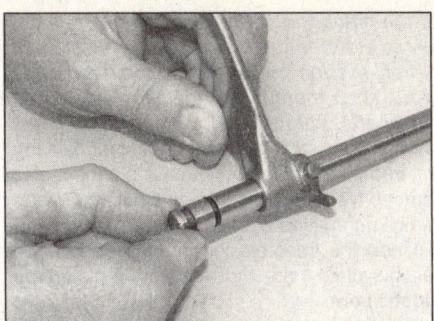
21.8 Check the fit of each fork on the shaft

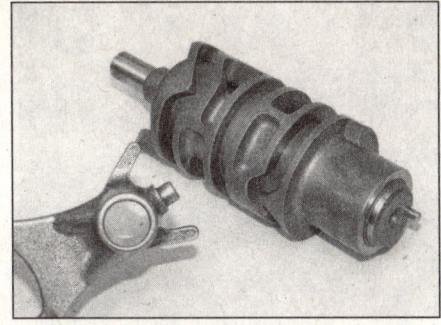
21.9 Check the fork guide pins and the grooves they run in

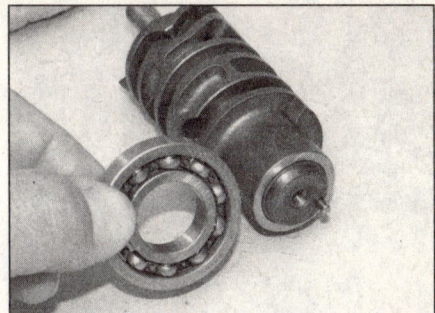
21.10 Check the bearing

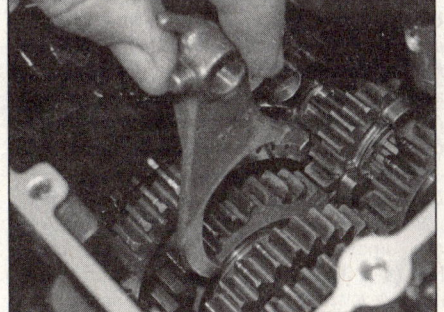
21.12a Fit the right-hand fork (00) ...

21.12b ... the centre fork (0I) ...

21.12c ... and the left-hand fork (02)

between them **(see illustration)**. Check the selector fork shaft for bend by rolling it along a flat surface. A bent shaft will cause difficulty in selecting gears and make the gearchange action heavy. Replace the shaft with a new one if necessary.

9 Inspect the selector drum grooves and selector fork guide pins for wear and damage **(see illustration)**. If they show signs of wear or damage the selector fork(s) and drum must be replaced with new ones.

10 Check that the selector drum bearing rotates freely and has no sign of freeplay between its inner and outer race **(see illustration)**. Fit a new bearing if necessary.

Installation

11 Clean the fork shaft retainer plate screw threads (where fitted) and the selector drum bearing retainer bolt threads to remove all old threadlock.

12 Fit each selector fork into its correct transmission pinion groove, making sure each is the correct way round – see Step 2 **(see illustrations)**.

13 Locate the selector drum in the crankcase **(see illustration 21.4c)** Fit the bearing onto the drum, using a drift on its outer race to drive it in **(see illustrations)**. Apply a suitable non-permanent thread locking compound to the threads of the bearing retainer bolt, then fit the bolt and retainer **(see illustration 21.4a)**. Tighten the bolt to the torque setting specified at the beginning of the Chapter. Rotate the drum so the neutral switch contact point is against the neutral switch plunger (or aligned with its bore if removed) **(see illustration)**.

14 Where removed fit a new O-ring onto the selector fork shaft and smear it with oil **(see illustration)**. Slide the shaft into its bore in the crankcase and through each fork in turn, locating each fork guide pin in its track in the selector drum **(see illustration 21.3b)**. On engines numbered 563847 and higher fit the two E-clips into the grooves in the shaft inside the crankcase.

15 Where removed fit the selector fork shaft

21.13a Fit the bearing onto the drum ...

21.13b ... and tap it into place

21.13c Align the contact point (A) on the drum with the switch plunger (B)

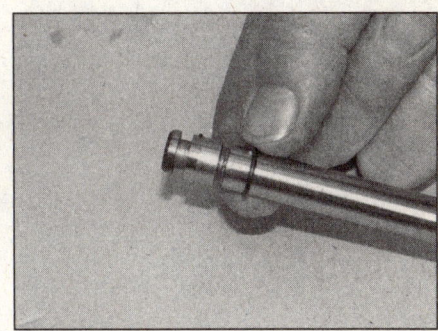
21.14 Fit a new O-ring into the groove

2•48 Engine, clutch and transmission

21.15 Fit the retainer to secure the shaft

22.3 Unscrew the bolts (arrowed) and remove the plate

retainer, locating the cutout in the retainer into the groove in the end of the shaft, then apply a suitable non-permanent thread locking compound to the threads of the retainer bolt and tighten it to the specified torque setting **(see illustration)**.

16 Install the gearchange mechanism and sump and all related assemblies (see Sections 20 and 18).

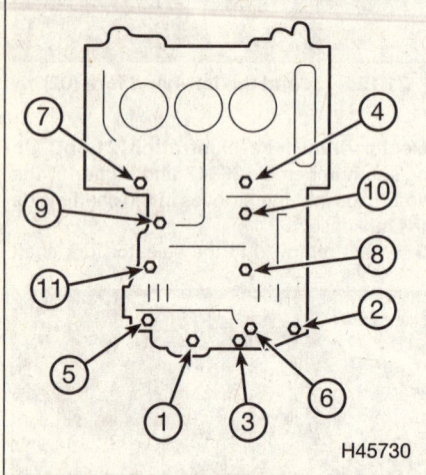

22.4a Upper crankcase bolt slackening sequence

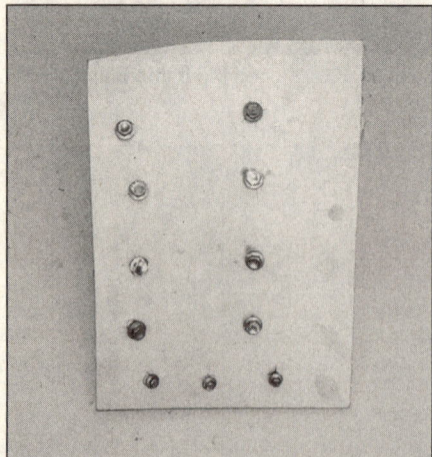

22.4b Store the bolts in holes punched into a piece of card as shown

22 Crankcase separation and reassembly

Separation

1 To access the crankshaft and connecting rods, bearings, balancer shaft, oil pressure relief valve, transmission shafts, gearchange selector drum and forks, the crankcase must be split into two parts.

2 To enable the crankcases to be separated, remove the engine from the frame (see Section 4) and remove the following components with reference to the relevant Sections.

   Camshafts and followers*
   Starter clutch
   Cam chain, tensioner blade and guide blade*
   Cylinder head*
   Cylinder liners and pistons*
   Clutch
   Oil pump drive and driven sprockets and chain
   Gearchange mechanism
   Alternator and starter motor (Chapter 8)
   Sump

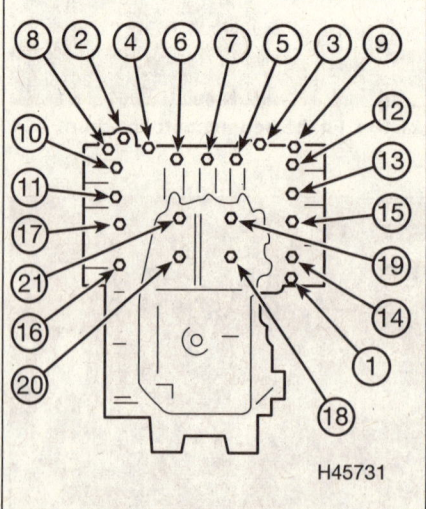

22.5 Lower crankcase bolt slackening sequence

*If the crankcase halves are being separated just to examine the crankshaft, balancer shaft or transmission components without removing them, then there is no need to remove the camshafts, cam chain, cylinder head, liners and pistons, or the gearchange mechanism. If a complete engine overhaul is planned, also remove the water pump (see Chapter 3), and the oil pump (see Section 19).

3 Undo the transmission input shaft bearing retainer plate bolts and remove the plate **(see illustration)**.

4 With the crankcase the right way up, slacken and remove all bolts from the upper crankcase half following the numbered sequence **(see illustration)**. Note: *As each bolt is removed, store it in its relative position in a cardboard template of the crankcase halves* **(see illustration)**. *This will ensure that all bolts are installed in the correct location on reassembly. Also, take note of any brackets on the bolts and store them with the bolts to ensure correct reassembly.*

5 Turn the crankcase upside down. Again, following the numbered sequence, slacken and remove all bolts from the lower crankcase half **(see illustration)**. Note: *As each bolt is removed, store it in its relative position in a cardboard template of the crankcase halves. This will ensure that all bolts are installed in the correct location on reassembly. Also, take note of any brackets and washers on the bolts and store them with the bolts to ensure correct reassembly.*

6 Carefully lift the lower crankcase half off the upper half, leaving the crankshaft, balancer shaft and transmission shafts in the upper half of the crankcase **(see illustration)**. As the lower half is lifted away take care not to dislodge or lose any main bearing shells. If they haven't been removed note how the gear selector forks engage with their respective slots in the transmission gears. Note: *If the halves don't separate easily, make sure all fasteners have been removed. Don't lever between the crankcase mating surfaces or they will leak; initial separation can be achieved by tapping gently around the joint with a soft-faced mallet.*

7 Remove the three locating dowels if they are loose – they could be in either crankcase half **(see illustration 22.11)**. Remove the

22.6 Lift the lower crankcase half off carefully so as not to dislodge components

Engine, clutch and transmission

22.8 Make sure the hose (arrowed) is measured as described and fitted accordingly onto the union

22.11 Make sure the dowels (arrowed) are in place

22.12 Fit a new oil passage O-ring (arrowed)

O-ring from the oil passage joint and discard it as a new one must be fitted (see illustration 22.12). Note the crankcase breather hose that fits to a union on the breather in the upper crankcase and protrudes down through the lower crankcase and into the sump – release the spring clip and remove the hose if required, noting how far on its union it is fitted (see illustration 22.8). Replace the hose with a new one if it is deformed or has deteriorated.

Reassembly

8 Remove all traces of sealant from the crankcase mating surfaces. If the crankcase breather hose was removed, on Sprint and Speed Triple models measure its length before fitting it. If it is 220 mm long fit it half way onto the union. If it is 240 mm long fit it all the way onto the union (see illustration). On Tiger models fit the hose fully onto the union. Secure the hose with the spring clip.

9 Ensure that all components are in place in the upper and lower crankcase halves. If the transmission shafts have not been removed, remove the oil seal from the left-hand end of the output shaft and replace it with a new one (see Section 28). Check the position of the selector drum and forks and transmission shafts – make sure they're in the neutral position (i.e. the transmission shafts rotate independently of each other).

10 Lubricate the transmission shafts and crankshaft journals with clean engine oil, then use a rag soaked in high flash-point solvent to wipe over the mating surfaces of both halves to remove all traces of oil.

11 If removed, fit the three locating dowels into the upper crankcase half (see illustration).

12 Fit a new O-ring onto the oil passage joint (see illustration).

13 Apply a small amount of suitable silicone sealant (Triumph use ThreeBond 1215) to the indicated areas of the mating surface of the lower crankcase half.

Caution: Take care not to apply an excessive amount of sealant, as it will ooze out when the case halves are assembled and may obstruct oil passages and prevent the bearings from seating.

14 Make sure that the main bearing shells are in position, then carefully guide the lower crankcase half onto the upper half (see illustration 22.6). If they haven't been removed make sure the selector forks engage with their respective slots in the transmission gears as the halves are joined.

15 Check that the lower crankcase half is correctly seated and that all shafts are free to rotate. **Note:** *If the casings are not correctly seated, remove the lower crankcase half and investigate the problem. Do not attempt to pull them together using the crankcase bolts as the casing will crack and be ruined.*

16 Clean the threads of the lower crankcase bolts and insert them in their original locations, including any brackets and washers (see illustration). Secure all bolts finger-tight at this stage.

17 Turn the crankcase over so that it is upright. Clean the threads of the upper crankcase bolts and install them in their original locations. Secure all bolts finger-tight at this stage.

Caution: Note that two sizes of bolt are used, 6 mm and 8 mm. Care must be taken to distinguish between them during the tightening sequence, as the larger 8 mm bolts are set tighter, and if a 6 mm bolt is mistaken for an 8 mm bolt, it may shear or strip threads.

18 Tighten the crankcase bolts as follows: turn the crankcase over and tighten all lower crankcase bolts to 12 Nm, tightening them in the correct numbered sequence (see illustration). Now turn the engine over again and tighten all upper crankcase bolts

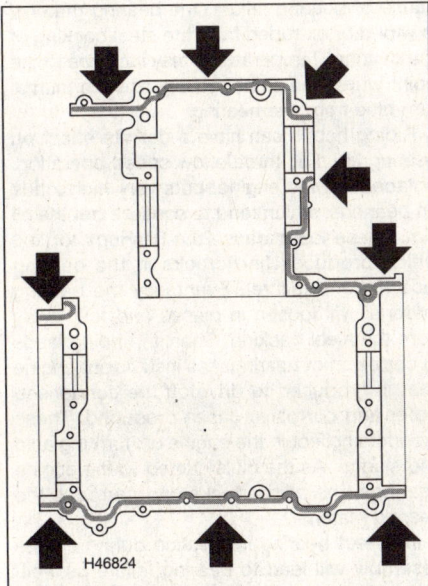

22.13 Apply sealant to the crankcase as shown

22.16 Fit all the lower crankcase bolts with their washers and tighten them finger-tight

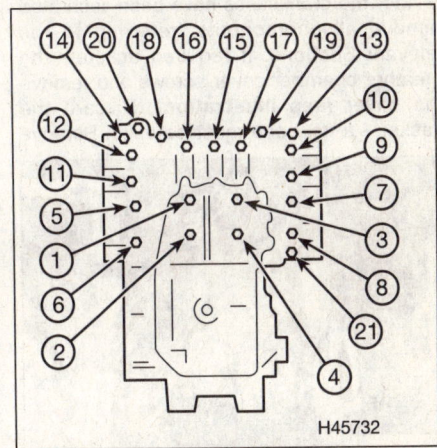

22.18a Lower crankcase bolt tightening sequence

2•50 Engine, clutch and transmission

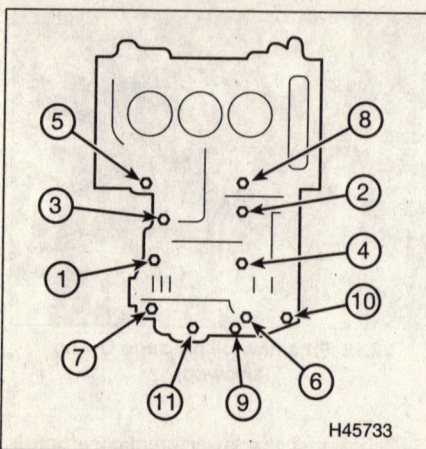

22.18b Upper crankcase bolt tightening sequence

to 12 Nm, tightening them in the correct numbered sequence (see illustration).
19 Now tighten the M8 size upper crankcase bolts (No. 1 to 8) to 32 Nm in the correct sequence (see illustration 22.18b). Turn the engine over. Finally tighten the M8 size lower crankcase bolts (No. 1 to 14) to 32 Nm in the correct sequence (see illustration 22.18a).
20 With all crankcase fasteners tightened, check that the crankshaft and transmission shafts rotate smoothly and easily. If there are any signs of undue stiffness or of any other problem, the fault must be rectified before proceeding further.
21 Clean the transmission input shaft bearing retainer plate bolt threads and apply some fresh threadlock. Fit the plate with the OUT mark facing out and tighten the bolts (see illustration 22.3).
22 Install all other removed assemblies in the reverse of the sequence in Step 2.

23 Crankcase inspection

1 After the crankcases have been separated remove all components, referring to the relevant Sections. If required unscrew the breather chamber cover screws and remove the cover (see illustration). Discard the gasket – a new one must be used. Remove the oil gallery plugs. Where fitted, replace the plug sealing washers with new ones.
2 Clean the crankcases and oil passages thoroughly with new solvent and dry them with compressed air, blowing through all oil passages.
3 Remove all traces of old gasket sealant from the mating surfaces. Minor damage to the surfaces can be cleaned up with a fine sharpening stone or grindstone.
4 Fit the breather chamber using a new gasket, and apply some threadlock to the screws (see illustration 23.1). Fit and tighten the oil gallery plugs, using new sealing washers where fitted.

Caution: Be very careful not to nick or gouge the crankcase mating surfaces or leaks will result. Check both crankcase halves very carefully for cracks and other damage.

5 Small cracks or holes in aluminium castings may be repaired with an epoxy resin adhesive as a temporary measure. Permanent repairs can be effected by argon-arc welding, and only a specialist in this process is in a position to advise on the economy or practical aspect of such a repair. Alternatively you could try one of the low temperature aluminium welding kits available. If any damage is found that can't be repaired, renew the crankcase halves as a set.
6 Damaged threads can be economically reclaimed by using a diamond section wire insert, of the Helicoil type, which is easily fitted after drilling and re-tapping the affected thread.
7 Sheared studs or screws can usually be removed with screw extractors, which consist of a tapered, left thread screws of very hard steel. These are inserted into a pre-drilled hole in the stud, and usually succeed in dislodging the most stubborn stud or screw. If a problem arises which seems beyond your scope, it is worth consulting a professional engineering firm before condemning an otherwise sound casing. Many of these firms advertise regularly in the motorcycle press.

HAYNES HINT *Refer to 'Tools and Workshop Tips' in the Reference section for details of how to install a thread insert and use a screw extractor.*

24 Main and connecting rod bearing information

1 Even though main and connecting rod bearings are generally renewed during the engine overhaul, the old bearings should be retained for close examination as they may reveal valuable information about the condition of the engine.
2 Bearing failure occurs mainly because of lack of lubrication, the presence of dirt or other foreign particles, overloading the engine and/or corrosion. Regardless of the cause of bearing failure, it must be corrected before the engine is reassembled to prevent it from happening again.
3 When examining the bearings, remove the main bearings from the crankcase halves and the rod bearings from the connecting rods and caps and lay them out on a clean surface in the same general position as their location on the crankshaft journals. This will make it possible for you to match any noted bearing problems with the corresponding crankshaft journal.
4 Dirt and other foreign particles get into the engine in a variety of ways. It may be left in the engine during assembly or it may pass through filters or breathers. It may get into the oil and from there into the bearings. Metal chips from machining operations and normal engine wear are often present. Abrasives are sometimes left in engine components after reconditioning operations, especially when parts are not thoroughly cleaned using the proper cleaning methods. Whatever the source, these foreign objects often end up imbedded in the soft bearing material and are easily recognised. Large particles will not imbed in the bearing and will score or gouge the bearing and journal. The best prevention for this cause of bearing failure is to clean all parts thoroughly and keep everything spotlessly clean during engine reassembly. Frequent and regular oil and filter changes are also recommended.
5 Lack of lubrication or lubrication breakdown has a number of interrelated causes. Excessive heat (which thins the oil), overloading (which squeezes the oil from the bearing face) and oil leakage or throw off from excessive bearing clearances, worn oil pump or high engine speeds all contribute to lubrication breakdown. Blocked oil passages will also starve a bearing and destroy it. When lack of lubrication is the cause of bearing failure, the bearing material is wiped or extruded from the steel backing of the bearing. Temperatures may increase to the point where the steel backing and the journal turn blue from overheating.
6 Riding habits can have a definite effect on bearing life. Full throttle low speed operation, or labouring the engine, puts very high loads on bearings, which tend to squeeze out the oil film. These loads cause the bearings to flex, which produces fine cracks in the bearing face (fatigue failure). Eventually the bearing material will loosen in pieces and tear away from the steel backing. Short trip riding leads to corrosion of bearings, as insufficient engine heat is produced to drive off the condensed water and corrosive gases produced. These products collect in the engine oil, forming acid and sludge. As the oil is carried to the engine bearings, the acid attacks and corrodes the bearing material.
7 Incorrect bearing installation during engine assembly will lead to bearing failure as well. Tight fitting bearings which leave insufficient bearing oil clearances result in oil starvation. Dirt or foreign particles trapped behind a

23.1 Breather chamber screws (arrowed)

Engine, clutch and transmission 2•51

25.5 Measure the connecting rod side clearance using a feeler gauge

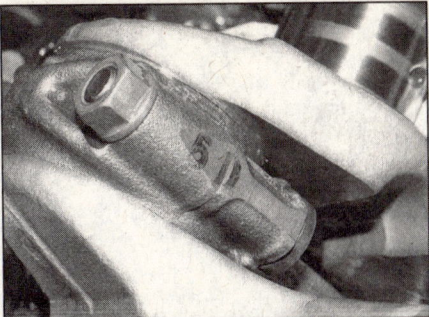

25.6 Note the rod size and weight grade marks across the front of the rod and cap

25.7 Working on one rod at a time, unscrew the cap nuts (arrowed) . . .

bearing insert result in high spots on the bearing which lead to failure.
8 To avoid bearing problems, clean all parts thoroughly before reassembly, double check all bearing clearance measurements and lubricate the new bearings with clean engine oil during installation.

25 Connecting rods

Note 1: *The connecting rod nuts and bolts must be discarded and new ones used on installation – it is best to obtain the new parts in advance. The old bolts can however be used for the oil clearance check.*
Note 2: *There are a number of different ways in which the connecting rods can be removed, and your best approach will depend on what other work, if any, you are doing on the engine.*
- *If the pistons have already been separated from the rods, then you can either remove the crankshaft with the rods still attached, and then separate them afterwards, or you can leave the crankshaft in situ, remove the rod caps and then remove the rods from the top of the crankcase.*
- *If the pistons have not been separated from the rods, they cannot be removed along with the crankshaft as the pistons will not fit through the crankcase main bearing webs. Remove the rod caps first, then remove the rod and piston assemblies from the top of the crankcase.*
Note 3: *If the crankshaft and transmission shafts are left in situ, take great care not to dislodge them when the rods/pistons are being removed.*

Removal

1 Remove the engine from the frame (see Section 4).
2 Remove the cylinder head (see Section 12).
3 If the Triumph special tool or a liner extractor is available, remove the cylinder liners now (see Section 14).
4 Separate the crankcase halves (see Section 22).

5 Before separating the rods from the crankshaft, measure the side clearance on each rod with a feeler gauge **(see illustration)**. If the clearance on any rod is greater than the service limit listed in this Chapter's Specifications, replace that rod with a new one.
6 Using paint or a marker pen, mark the relevant cylinder identity across the join between each connecting rod and cap at the back – these ensure that the cap and rod are fitted correctly on reassembly. Cylinders are numbered 1 to 3, from the left to the right-hand side of the engine. **Note:** *The number and letter already across the rod and cap at the front indicate rod size and weight grade respectively, not cylinder number* **(see illustration)**.
7 Working on one connecting rod at a time, unscrew the connecting rod cap nuts and remove them **(see illustration)**.
8 If the crankshaft and transmission shafts are being left in situ, lift the crankcase and support it with sufficient clearance for the rods or rod and piston assemblies to be removed through the top of the crankcase.
9 Separate the cap, complete with the lower bearing shell, from the crankpin **(see illustration)**. If the cap appears stuck, tap it lightly on one end with a hammer while pulling it.
10 Support the rod to prevent it marking the liner bore or block, and detach it, complete with the upper bearing shell, from the crankpin, then remove the rod or rod and piston assembly **(see illustration)**.

> **HAYNES HINT** *If required, to ease removal of the pistons from the tops of the liners, carefully remove any ridge of carbon built up on the top of each liner bore using a scraper. If there is a pronounced wear ridge, remove it using a ridge reamer.*

Caution: *Do not try to remove the piston/ connecting rod from the bottom of the crankcase. The piston will not pass the crankcase main bearing webs.*

11 Fit the relevant bearing shells (if removed), cap, nuts and bolts on each piston/connecting rod assembly so that they are all kept together as a matched set.
12 If required and not already done, separate the pistons from the connecting rods (see Section 15). If not already done remove the liners (see Section 14).

Inspection

13 Check the connecting rods for cracks and other obvious damage. Refer to Section 15 and check the piston pin and connecting rod small-end bore dimensions for wear. Replace any components that are worn beyond the specified limit with new ones.
14 Refer to Section 24 and examine the connecting rod bearing shells. If they are scored, badly scuffed or appear to have seized, new shells must be installed. Always replace the shells in the connecting rods as a set. If they are badly damaged, check the corresponding crankpin. Evidence of

25.9 . . . and remove the connecting rod cap . . .

25.10 . . . then detach the rod from the crankpin (arrowed)

2•52 Engine, clutch and transmission

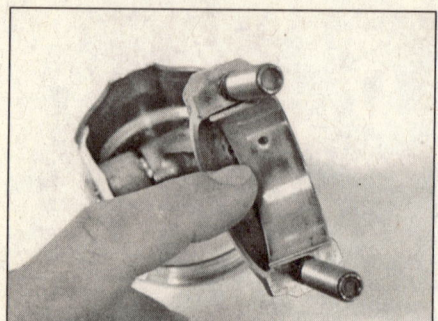

25.18 To remove a big-end bearing shell, push it sideways and lift it out

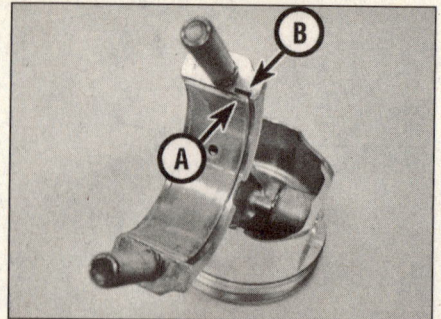

25.19 Make sure the tab (A) locates in the notch (B)

25.21a Tighten the nuts using a torque wrench . . .

extreme heat, such as discoloration, indicates that lubrication failure has occurred. Be sure to thoroughly check the oil pump and pressure relief valve as well as all oil holes and passages before reassembling the engine.

15 Have the rods checked for twist and bending by a Triumph dealer if you are in doubt about their straightness.

Oil clearance check

16 Whether new bearing shells are being fitted or the original ones are being re-used, the connecting rod bearing oil clearance should be checked prior to reassembly. Work on one rod at a time when checking the clearances.

17 If it is in situ, lift the crankshaft out of the upper crankcase half, taking care not to dislodge the main bearing shells. Ensure that the crankshaft is securely supported on the work surface.

18 Remove the bearing shells from the rod and cap, keeping them in order (see illustration). Clean the backs of the shells and the bearing locations in both the connecting rod and cap, and the crankpin journal.

19 Press the bearing shells into their locations, ensuring that the tab on each shell engages the notch in the connecting rod/cap (see illustration). Make sure the bearings are fitted in the correct locations and take care not to touch any shell's bearing surface with your fingers. Apply a smear of grease to each crankpin and a smear of silicone release agent to each bearing shell in the rod and cap.

20 Cut a length of the appropriate size Plastigauge (it should be slightly shorter than the width of the crankpin). Place a strand of Plastigauge on the crankpin journal for the rod being checked. Fit the rod onto its crankpin, then fit the cap, making sure it is fitted the correct way around so the previously made markings align. Note that the accuracy of this check is dependant on the rod not turning on the crankpin while it is installed and tightened – if it does, the Plastigauge will be disturbed and an inaccurate reading will result. Apply a smear of molybdenum disulphide grease to the bolt threads and to the underside of the nuts and install them finger-tight.

21 Tighten the nuts in five stages, using a torque wrench and a degree disc, as follows. First tighten the nuts to 22 Nm, then slacken them by 140°. Now tighten the nuts to 10 Nm, then to 14 Nm, and finally tighten them by 120° (see illustrations and Haynes Hint).

22 Slacken the cap nuts and remove the connecting rod cap, again taking great care not to rotate the crankshaft.

23 Compare the width of the crushed Plastigauge on the crankpin to the scale printed on the Plastigauge envelope to obtain the connecting rod bearing oil clearance (see illustration). Be sure to use the appropriate scale as both imperial and metric scales are shown.

24 On completion carefully scrape away all traces of the Plastigauge material from the crankpin and bearing shells using a fingernail or other object which will not score the bearing surfaces.

25 If the clearance is within the range listed in this Chapter's Specifications and the bearing shells are in perfect condition, they can be reused.

26 If the clearance is beyond the specified service limit, first measure the diameter of the crankpin with a micrometer and compare the result with the Specifications at the beginning of this Chapter. If the journal diameter is larger than the service limit, new bearing shells can be fitted (see Steps 28 to 30). If the journal diameter is smaller than the service limit, the crankshaft must be replaced with a new one.

27 Repeat the procedure for the remaining connecting rods. If the oil clearance is too great on any one, replace all of the shells (on all three rods) at the same time.

Bearing shell selection

28 The connecting rod big-end bearing oil clearance is controlled in production by selecting one of three grades of bearing shell. The grades are indicated by a colour-coding marked on the edge of each shell (see illustration). New bearing shells are selected as follows using the crankpin journal diameter and connecting rod size marking.

29 Measure the crankpin journal diameter using a micrometer and record the result. Inspect the connecting rod for its size marking, either the number 4 or 5 (see illustration 25.6).

30 Match the rod marking with the measured journal diameter and select a set of new bearing shells using the following tables.

25.21b . . . and a degree disc as specified

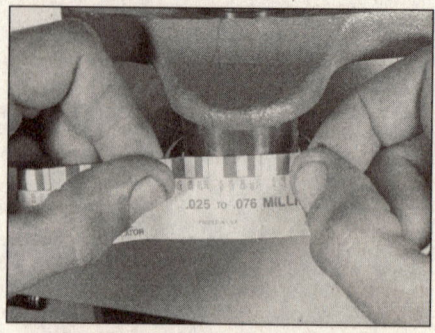

25.23 Measure the crushed Plastigauge using the appropriate scale on the pack

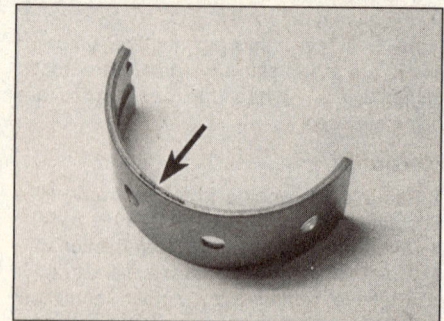

25.28 The colour code is marked on the side of the shell (arrowed)

Engine, clutch and transmission 2•53

Note: *The old condition crankshaft is fitted to all Speed Triples up to engine No. 506365, and on the following later Nos.: 513923, 514367, 514684, 514729, 514746, 514848, 514868, 514956, 514978, 515007, 515069, 515103, 515123, 515177, 515560, 515811, 516237, 516392, 516563, 516951, 516989, 517127, 517135, 517217, 517284, 517300, 517613.*

Con-rod marking	Crankpin journal diameter	Shell colour
5	34.992 to 35.000 mm	White
5	34.984 to 34.991 mm	Red
4	34.992 to 35.000 mm	Red
4	34.984 to 34.991 mm	Blue

'New condition' crankshaft

Con-rod marking	Crankpin journal diameter	Shell colour
5	35.018 to 35.010 mm	White
5	35.009 to 35.002 mm	Red
4	35.018 to 35.010 mm	Red
4	35.009 to 35.002 mm	Blue

Installation

Note 1: *New connecting rod nuts and bolts must be used for final assembly.*
Note 2: *There are a number of different ways in which the connecting rods can be installed, and your best approach will depend on what other work, if any, you are doing on the engine.*

- If the pistons have been separated from the rods and the crankshaft has been removed, then you can either fit the rods onto the crankshaft and then install the crankshaft, or you can install the crankshaft and then install the rods from the top of the crankcase.
- If the pistons have not been separated from the rods, the rod and piston assemblies cannot be installed attached to the crankshaft as the pistons will not fit through the crankcase main bearing webs. Install the rod and piston assemblies from the top of the crankcase then install the crankshaft. You will also have to make a decision regarding installation of the liners, as the rod and piston assemblies can be installed before them, with them or after them – see Section 14 for details.
- If it makes no difference, we advise fitting the pistons onto the rods first, then fitting the rod and piston assemblies into the liners, then installing the liners. At this point the cylinder head can be installed to avoid the risk of disturbing the liner seals when installing the crankshaft.

31 Remove the bearing shells from the rods and caps, keeping them in order **(see illustration 25.18)**. Clean the backs of the shells and the bearing locations in both the connecting rod and cap, and the crankpin journal. If new shells are being fitted, ensure that all traces of the

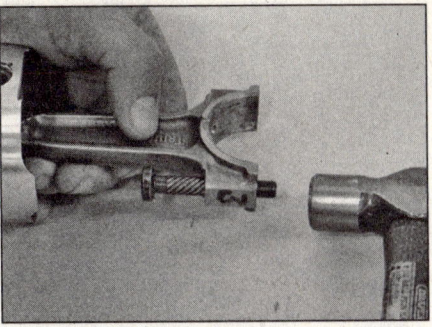

25.32 Tap out the old bolts and install new ones

protective grease are cleaned off using paraffin (kerosene). Wipe the shells, cap and rod dry with a clean lint free cloth.
32 Remove the old bolts from the rods and discard them, then fit the new ones – it will probably be necessary to tap the old bolts out using a hammer **(see illustration)**.
33 Apply a smear of molybdenum disulphide grease to the upper inner surface of the connecting rod big end. Press the bearing shells into their locations, ensuring that the tab on each shell engages the notch in the connecting rod/cap **(see illustration 25.19)**. Make sure the bearings are fitted in the correct locations and take care not to touch any shell's bearing surface with your fingers.
34 Decide upon your installation procedure, then assemble the rods, pistons, cylinder liners and crankshaft as required, referring to the relevant Sections. **Note:** *When installing the connecting rods on the crankshaft, refer to the previously made marks to ensure they are fitted in the correct positions (see Step 6).*
35 Lubricate the shells with new engine oil. Fit the rod onto its crankpin, then fit the cap, making sure it is the correct way around so the previously made markings align. Apply a smear of molybdenum disulphide grease to the bolt threads and to the underside of the nuts **(see illustration)**. Fit the nuts and tighten them finger-tight at this stage. Check to make sure that all components have been returned to their original locations using the marks made on disassembly.
36 Tighten the nuts in five stages, using a torque wrench and a degree disc, as follows.

 **HAYNES HINT** *If a degree disc is not available, the angle can be determined by using the points on the connecting rod cap nut. There are six points on the nut, so the angle between each point is 60°. Select one point as a reference and mark it with paint or a marker. Now select the second point clockwise from it and mark its position on the connecting rod cap. Tighten the nut – when the mark on the first point aligns with the mark made on the connecting rod cap, it will have turned through 120°.*

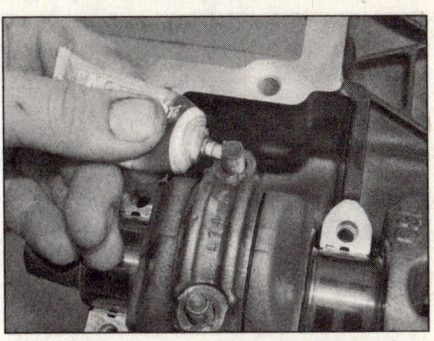

25.35 Lubricate the threads with molybdenum disulphide grease

First tighten the nuts to 22 Nm, then slacken them by 140°. Now tighten the nuts to 10 Nm, then to 14 Nm, and finally tighten them by 120° **(see illustrations 25.21a and b)**.
37 Install the other connecting rods in the same way. Check to make sure that all components have been returned to their original locations using the marks made on disassembly.
38 Check that the crankshaft rotates freely and that the rods rotate smoothly and freely on the crankpins. If there are any signs of roughness or tightness, remove the rods and re-check the bearing clearance. Sometimes tapping the bottom of the connecting rod cap will relieve tightness, but if in doubt, recheck the clearances. **Note:** *If the cylinder liners have been installed, ensure appropriate measures have been taken to prevent them lifting off their seals when the crankshaft is rotated (see Section 14).*
39 Reassemble the crankcase halves and the rest of the engine according to your removal procedure, referring to the relevant Sections.

26 Crankshaft and main bearings

Removal

1 Remove the engine from the frame (see Section 4) and separate the crankcase halves (see Section 22).
2 Refer to Section 25 and separate the connecting rods from the crankshaft (unless the pistons have been removed, in which case the rods can remain attached for now, and removed later if required). **Note:** *If no work is to be carried out on the piston/connecting rod assemblies there is no need to remove them from the bores (unless the liners have been removed), but, making sure the liners are secure (see Section 14), you can push them up to the top of the bores so that the big-ends are clear of the crankshaft.*
3 Before removing the crankshaft, check the amount of end-float using a dial gauge. If it exceeds the limit specified, the crankshaft and/or the crankcases must be replaced with new ones. Lift out the balancer shaft, noting how the shaft driven gear aligns with the gear on the crankshaft (see Section 27). Lift the

26.3 Carefully lift the crankshaft out of the crankcase

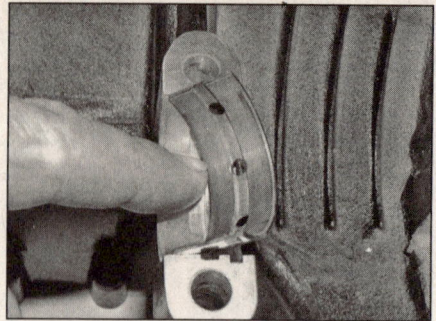

26.4 To remove a main bearing shell, push it sideways and lift it out

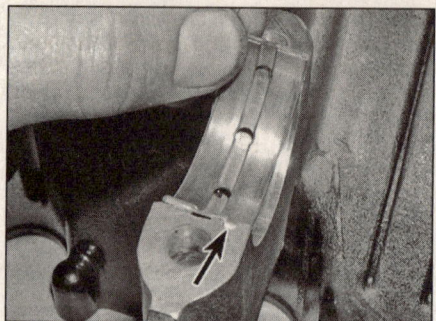

26.10 Press each shell into place, locating the tab in the notch (arrowed)

crankshaft out of the upper crankcase half, taking care not to dislodge the main bearing shells **(see illustration)**.

4 If required, remove the bearing shells from the crankcase halves by pushing their centres to the side, then lifting them out **(see illustration)**. Keep the shells in order. If the shells have been removed also remove the three piston oil jets.

Inspection

5 Clean the crankshaft with solvent, squirting it through all oil passages. If available, blow it through and dry with compressed air.

6 Refer to Section 24 and examine the main bearing shells. If they are scored, badly scuffed or appear to have been seized, new shells must be installed. Always renew the main bearings as a set. If they are badly damaged, check the corresponding crankshaft journals. Evidence of extreme heat, such as discoloration, indicates that lubrication failure has occurred. Be sure to thoroughly check the oil pump and pressure relief valve as well as all oil holes and passages before reassembling the engine.

7 Inspect the crankshaft journals, paying particular attention where damaged bearing shells have been discovered. If the journals are scored or pitted in any way a new crankshaft will be required. Note that oversize shells are not available, precluding the option of re-grinding the crankshaft.

Oil clearance check

8 Whether new bearing shells are being fitted or the original ones are being re-used, the main bearing oil clearance should be checked prior to reassembly.

9 If not already done, remove the bearing shells from the crankcase halves by pushing their centres to the side, then lifting them out **(see illustration 26.4)**. Keep the shells in order. Clean the backs of the shells and their locations in both the crankcase halves.

10 Press the bearing shells back into their locations, ensuring that the tab on each shell engages in the notch **(see illustration)**. Make sure the shells are fitted in the correct locations and take care not to touch any shell's bearing surface with your fingers.

11 Ensure that the shells and crankshaft are clean and dry. Lay the crankshaft in position in the upper crankcase **(see illustration 26.3)**.

12 Cut several lengths of the appropriate size Plastigauge (they should be slightly shorter than the width of the crankshaft journal). Place a strand of Plastigauge on each (cleaned) crankshaft journal.

13 If removed, fit the three locating dowels into the upper crankcase half **(see illustration 22.11)**. Carefully guide the lower crankcase half onto the upper half **(see illustration 22.6)**. Make sure that the selector forks (if fitted) engage with their respective slots in the transmission gears (if fitted) as the halves are joined. Check that the lower crankcase half is correctly seated. **Note:** *If the casings are not correctly seated, remove the lower crankcase half and investigate the problem. Do not attempt to pull them together using the crankcase bolts as the casing will crack and be ruined.* Install the eight 8 mm lower crankcase bolts in their original locations and tighten them in the correct numerical sequence in the two stages and to the torque settings as described in Section 22. Make sure that the crankshaft is not rotated as the bolts are tightened.

14 Slacken and remove the crankcase bolts, working in a criss-cross pattern from the outside in, then carefully lift off the lower crankcase half, making sure the Plastigauge is not disturbed.

15 Compare the width of the crushed Plastigauge on each crankshaft journal to the scale printed on the Plastigauge envelope to obtain the main bearing oil clearance **(see illustration 25.23)**.

16 On completion carefully scrape away all traces of the Plastigauge material from the journals and bearing shells using a fingernail or other object which will not score the bearing surfaces.

17 If the clearance is within the range listed in this Chapter's Specifications and the bearing shells are in perfect condition, they can be reused. If the clearance is beyond the specified service limit, first measure the diameter of the crankshaft journals with a micrometer and compare the results with the Specifications at the beginning of this Chapter. If the journal diameters are larger than the service limit, new bearing shells can be fitted (see Steps 18 and 19). If the journal diameters are smaller than the service limit, the crankshaft must be replaced with a new one.

Bearing shell selection

18 The main bearing oil clearance is controlled in production by selecting one of four grades of bearing shell. The grades are indicated by a colour-coding marked on the edge of each shell **(see illustration 25.28)**. New shells are selected with reference to the following chart, having first measured the crankshaft journal diameter and the crankcase bore diameter.

19 Measure the diameter of each crankshaft journal with a micrometer and record the results. Next, assemble the crankcase halves with the bearing shells and crankshaft removed, and tighten the 8 mm crankshaft journal bolts in the correct numerical sequence in the two stages and to the torque settings as described in Section 22. Measure each crankshaft journal bore diameter using a bore gauge and micrometer and record the results. Refer to *Tools and Workshop Tips* in the Reference Section for details on how to use the measuring equipment.

Crankcase bore dia.	Crankshaft journal dia.	Shell colour
41.101 to 41.109 mm	37.969 to 37.976 mm	White
41.101 to 41.109 mm	37.960 to 37.968 mm	Red
41.110 to 41.118 mm	37.969 to 37.976 mm	Red
41.110 to 41.118 mm	37.960 to 37.968 mm	Blue
41.119 to 41.127 mm	37.969 to 37.976 mm	Blue
41.119 to 41.127 mm	37.960 to 37.968 mm	Green

Installation

20 Clean the backs of the bearing shells and the bearing recesses in both crankcase halves. If new shells are being fitted, ensure that all traces of the protective grease are cleaned off using paraffin (kerosene). Wipe the shells and crankcase halves dry with a lint-free cloth. If removed fit the three piston oil jets into their bores.

21 Press the bearing shells into their

Engine, clutch and transmission 2•55

locations, ensuring that the tab on each shell engages in the notch **(see illustration 26.10)**. Make sure the bearings are fitted in the correct locations and take care not to touch any shell's bearing surface with your fingers. Lubricate all the shells with clean engine oil.

22 Identify the two teeth on the balancer drive gear on the crankshaft marked with a dot – these two teeth must sit on each side of the marked tooth on the balancer shaft driven gear when it is installed **(see illustration 27.2)**. Lower the crankshaft into position in the upper crankcase, with the marked teeth facing forwards **(see illustration 26.3)**. Install the balancer shaft ensuring that it is correctly timed to the crankshaft (see Section 27).

23 If removed, install the connecting rods (see Section 25), then reassemble the crankcase halves and the rest of the engine according to your removal procedure, referring to the relevant Sections.

27 Balancer shaft

Removal

1 Remove the engine from the frame and separate the crankcase halves (see Sections 4 and 22).

2 The balancer shaft is gear driven off the right-hand end of the crankshaft – the crankshaft drive gear and the balancer shaft driven gear are marked so that precise timing of the two shafts can be achieved. The balancer shaft driven gear incorporates an outer spring-loaded backlash eliminator gear – rotate the crankshaft until the tooth marked with a line on the backlash eliminator gear aligns with the two teeth marked with dots on the crankshaft drive gear **(see illustration)**.

3 Note how the circlips on the ends of the balancer shaft locate in the grooves in the crankcase, then lift out the balancer shaft **(see illustrations)**. Note that as the shaft is lifted out, the backlash eliminator gear will spring out of alignment.

Inspection

4 Inspect the teeth of both inner and outer driven gears for signs of wear or damage,

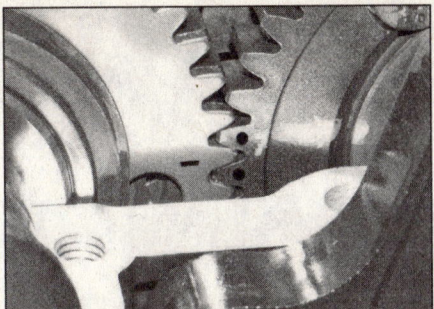

27.2 Balancer shaft driven gear and crankshaft drive gear alignment marks

27.3b . . . and right-hand ends of the balancer shaft (arrowed)

and replace them with new ones if necessary. If damage is found, check the teeth of the drive gear on the crankshaft. Note that when the gears are not under tension (i.e. meshed with the crankshaft drive gear) the tooth on the outer gear marked with a line will not align with the tooth on the inner gear marked with a dot **(see illustration)**.

5 The shaft can be disassembled if required – all components are available individually. Remove the circlip securing the outer gear, then remove the wave washer and lift off the gear, noting how the pin on the inside face locates against one end of the backlash spring **(see illustrations)**. On assembly, ensure that the pins on the inner and outer gears are correctly located between the ends of the backlash spring – the pin on the outer gear must be to the right of the pin on the inner gear.

6 If required, hold the shaft in a soft-jawed vice and unscrew the right-hand end cap. Check the needle bearings on each end of the shaft and

27.5a Remove the circlip . . .

27.5b . . . and the wave washer

27.3a Note the location of the circlip (arrowed) on the left . . .

27.4 Outer gear is marked with a line, inner gear with a dot

replace them with new ones if necessary. The bearings are secured by circlips; fit new circlips if the bearings have been removed. On assembly, apply a suitable non-permanent thread locking compound to the end cap threads and tighten the cap to the torque setting specified at the beginning of this Chapter.

Installation

7 Before installing the balancer shaft, ensure the two teeth on the drive gear on the crankshaft marked with dots are facing forwards **(see illustration 27.2)**.

8 Align the tooth on the balancer shaft inner gear marked with a dot with the tooth on the outer gear marked with a line **(see illustration 27.4)**. To do this, first mark the top edge of the inner gear tooth with paint so that it can be identified when the two gears are aligned, then use two small screwdrivers inserted through the holes in the gears to draw the gears into position against the tension of the backlash

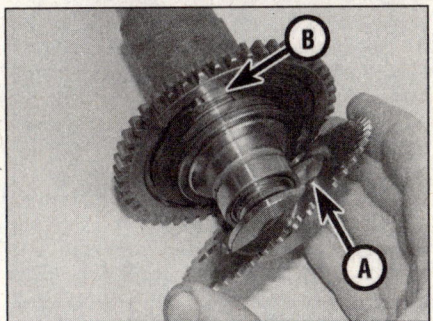

27.5c Note how the pin (A) locates against the end of the backlash spring (B)

2•56 Engine, clutch and transmission

27.8a Align the marked gears (arrowed) as described . . .

27.8b . . . and lock them together

28.2 Lift out the transmission output shaft

spring **(see illustration)**. Lock the gears together; Triumph provides a special tool to do this (Part No. T3880016), or alternatively use a piece of crushed tube or similar between the gear teeth – note that when the balancer shaft is installed in the crankcase the locking tool must not interfere with the meshing of the driven and drive gears **(see illustration)**.

9 Lubricate the needle bearings with clean engine oil, then lay the shaft in the crankcase, ensuring that the tooth marked with a line on the backlash eliminator gear is between the two teeth marked with dots on the crankshaft drive gear **(see illustration 27.2)**. If necessary, rotate the shafts slightly to ensure that the gears are correctly aligned. Check that the circlips on the ends of the shaft are located in their grooves **(see illustrations 27.3a and 3b)**.

10 Remove the locking tool and check that both the inner and outer balancer shaft driven gears are correctly aligned with the crankshaft drive gear – use the painted mark on the top edge of the inner driven gear to check its position.

⚠ **Warning: If the balancer shaft and crankshaft gears are not correctly aligned, severe engine vibration will occur leading to damage to engine components.**

11 Reassemble the crankcase halves and the rest of the engine according to your removal procedure, referring to the relevant Sections.

28 Transmission shaft removal and installation

Removal

1 Remove the engine from the frame and separate the crankcase halves (see Sections 4 and 22).

2 Lift the output shaft out of the crankcase, noting how the ball bearing retaining ring and oil seal lip locate in the grooves and the needle bearing pin locates in the hole **(see illustration)**. Remove the oil seal from the left-hand end and discard it – a new one must be used **(see illustration 28.6b)**. Note the bearing retaining ring that sits between the seal and the bearing and take care not to lose it **(see illustration 28.6a)**.

3 Lift the input shaft out of the crankcase, again noting how the needle bearing pin locates in the hole **(see illustration)**.

4 If necessary, the transmission shafts can be disassembled and inspected for wear or damage as described in Section 29.

Installation

5 Install the input shaft, making sure the needle bearing pin locates in its hole **(see illustration 28.3)**.

6 Make sure the bearing retaining ring is in place on the sleeve on the left-hand end of the output shaft, then fit a new oil seal onto the sleeve **(see illustrations)**. Install the output shaft, making sure the pin locates in its hole **(see illustration 28.2)**, and the retaining ring and oil seal lip locate in their grooves **(see illustration)**.

7 Ensure that the gears of both shafts mesh correctly and that they're in the neutral position i.e. the input shaft can be turned whilst the output shaft is held stationary.

8 Reassemble the crankcase halves and the rest of the engine according to your removal procedure, referring to the relevant Sections.

29 Transmission shaft overhaul

1 Remove the shafts from the crankcase as described in Section 28.

> **HAYNES HiNT** When disassembling the transmission shafts, place the parts on a long rod or thread a wire through them to keep them in order and facing the proper direction.

28.3 Lift out the transmission input shaft

28.6a Fit the retaining ring if removed . . .

28.6b . . . then fit a new oil seal onto the shaft

28.6c Make sure the lip on the oil seal (A) and the bearing retaining ring (B) locate in their grooves

Engine, clutch and transmission 2•57

Input shaft disassembly

2 Slide the needle bearing outer race off the left-hand end of the shaft then slide the bearing off **(see illustrations 29.17d and c)**.
3 Slide the thrust washer off the shaft **(see illustration 29.17b)**. On Sprint ST models, Sprint GT and Tiger models up to engine No. 536532, Speed Triple models up to engine No. 539022, and Speed Triple R models up to engine No. 520031, slide the 2nd gear pinion off the shaft **(see illustration 29.17a)**. On all other models, the 2nd gear pinion is a press fit – to remove it place the shaft in a press with the 2nd gear pinion facing up and with the shaft supported on the 6th gear pinion, then press the shaft down through the pinions until the 2nd gear pinion is free, making sure you support the bottom end of the shaft as it will drop once the gear is released **(see illustration)**.
4 Slide the 6th gear pinion and its splined bush off the shaft, followed by the thrust washer **(see illustrations 29.16c, b and a)**.
5 Remove the circlip securing the combined 3rd/4th gear pinion then slide the pinion off the shaft **(see illustrations 29.15b and a)**.
6 Remove the circlip securing the 5th gear pinion, then slide the thrust washer and the pinion off the shaft **(see illustrations 29.14c, b and a)**. The 1st gear pinion is integral with the shaft **(see illustration)**.

Input shaft inspection

7 Wash all of the components in clean solvent and dry them off.
8 Check the gear teeth for cracking and other

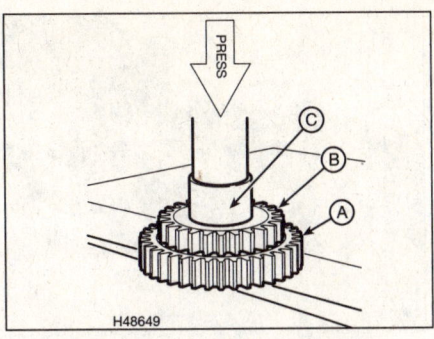

29.3 Removing the 2nd gear pinion

A 6th gear pinion C Input shaft
B 2nd gear pinion

obvious damage. Check the 6th gear bush and the surface in the inner diameter of the gear for scoring or heat discoloration. If the gear or bush is damaged, replace it with a new one. Check the 5th gear bush – if the oil retaining dimples are no longer visible replace the pinion with a new one **(see illustration)**.
9 Inspect the dogs and the dog holes in related gears for excessive wear. Renew the paired gears as a set if necessary.
10 Measure the gearchange fork groove width in the 3rd/4th gear pinion as described in Section 21.
11 The shaft is unlikely to sustain damage unless the engine has seized, placing an unusually high loading on the transmission, or the machine has covered a very high mileage. Check the surface of the shaft, especially where a pinion turns on it, and the edges of the splined sections, and replace the shaft with a

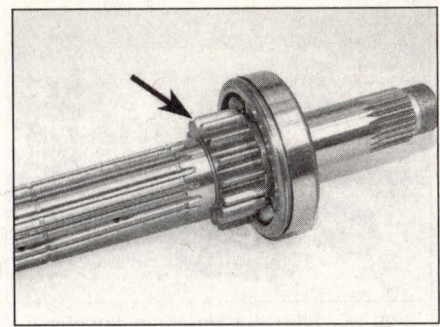

29.6 1st gear pinion (arrowed)

new one if it has scored or picked up. Damage of any kind can only be cured by renewal.
12 The ball bearing on the left-hand end of the shaft is a press fit **(see illustration)**. Refer to *Tools and Workshop Tips* in the Reference Section for more information on bearing checks and removal and installation methods – note which way round the bearing fits. Replace the needle bearing with a new one if it is worn or damaged, or does not run freely.

Input shaft reassembly

13 During reassembly, always use new circlips. Lubricate the components with the correct grade of engine oil before assembling them.
14 Slide on the 5th gear with its dogs facing away from the integral 1st gear pinion, then slide the thrust washer against it **(see illustrations)**. Fit the circlip, making sure it locates in its groove **(see illustrations)**.

29.8 Check the bush (arrowed) for wear

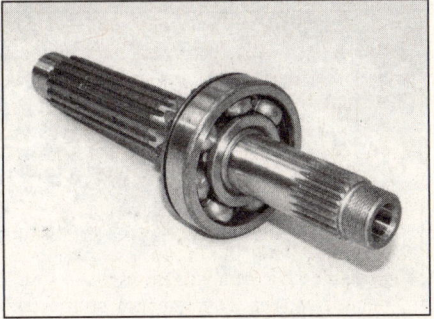

29.12 Check the bearing and replace with a new one if necessary

29.14a Slide the 5th gear pinion on the shaft . . .

29.14b . . . followed by the thrust washer . . .

29.14c . . . then fit the circlip . . .

29.14d . . . making sure it locates in its groove

2•58 Engine, clutch and transmission

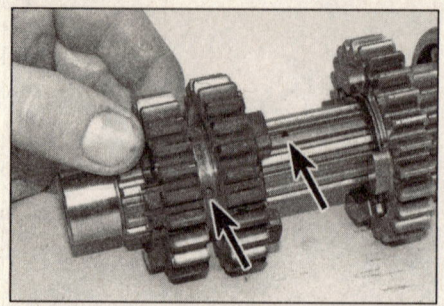

29.15a Slide the 3rd/4th gear pinion onto the shaft, making sure the oil holes (arrowed) do not align, . . .

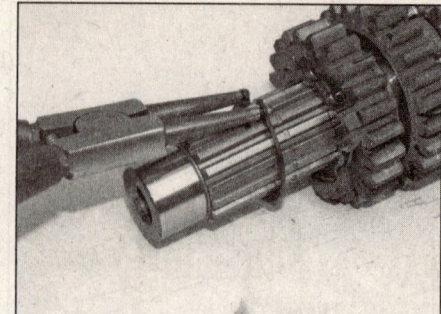

29.15b . . . then fit the circlip . . .

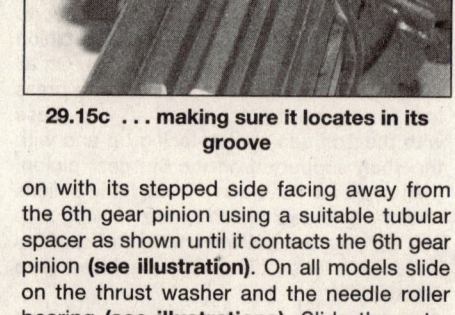

29.15c . . . making sure it locates in its groove

15 Slide the combined 3rd/4th gear pinion with the larger (4th) gear facing the 5th gear pinion, making sure the oil hole does NOT align with the oil hole in the shaft **(see illustration)**. Fit the circlip, making sure it locates in its groove **(see illustrations)**.

16 Slide the thrust washer against the circlip, then fit the 6th gear pinion bush making sure the oil hole does not align with the oil hole in the shaft **(see illustrations)**. Slide on the 6th gear pinion with its dogs facing the 3rd gear **(see illustration)**.

17 On Sprint ST models, Sprint GT and Tiger models up to engine No. 536532, Speed Triple models up to engine No. 539022, and Speed Triple R models up to engine No. 520031, fit the 2nd gear pinion with its stepped side facing away from the 6th gear pinion **(see illustration)**. On all other models, clean the inner face of the 2nd gear pinion and the section of the shaft it fits on with solvent, then apply a drop of Threebond 1375B locking compound to the inner face of the gear and smear it evenly around. Place the shaft in a press with the 6th gear pinion facing up and with the ball bearing supported on its inner race, then press the 2nd gear pinion on with its stepped side facing away from the 6th gear pinion using a suitable tubular spacer as shown until it contacts the 6th gear pinion **(see illustration)**. On all models slide on the thrust washer and the needle roller bearing **(see illustrations)**. Slide the outer

29.16a Slide the thrust washer on . . .

29.16b . . . followed by the bush, offsetting the oil holes (arrowed) . . .

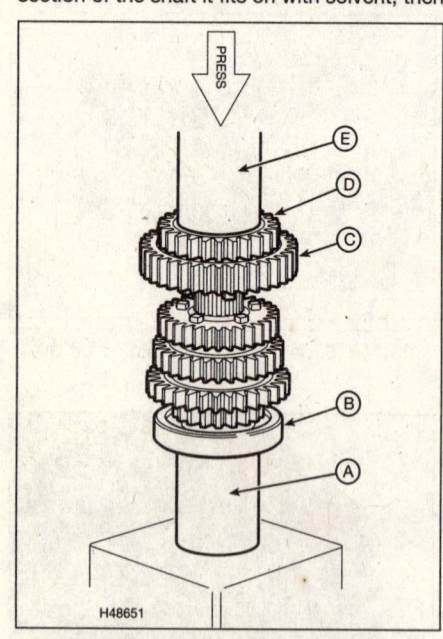

29.17b Mount the shaft in an hydraulic press as shown

- A Support under bearing inner race
- B Bearing
- C 6th gear pinion
- D 2nd gear pinion
- E Spacer between 2nd gear pinion and press

29.16c . . . then fit the 6th gear pinion onto the bush

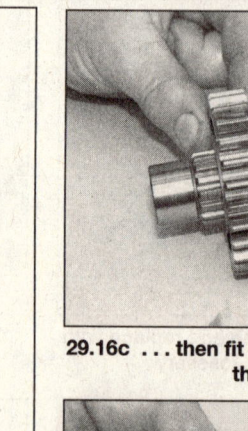

29.17c . . . followed by the thrust washer . . .

29.17a Slide the 2nd gear pinion onto the shaft . . .

29.17d . . . the needle bearing . . .

Engine, clutch and transmission 2•59

29.17e ... and its outer race

29.17f The assembled input shaft should be as shown

race over the bearing **(see illustration)**. The assembled input shaft should be as shown **(see illustration)**.

Output shaft disassembly

18 Slide the needle bearing outer race, bearing and thrust washer off the right-hand end of the shaft **(see illustrations 29.36c, b and a)**.
19 Make a paint mark on the outer face of the 1st gear pinion, then slide it off the shaft, followed its needle bearing, the thrust washer and the 5th gear pinion **(see illustrations 29.35d, c, b and a)**.
20 Remove the circlip, then slide off the thrust washer, and the 4th gear pinion **(see illustrations 29.34c, b and a)**.
21 Slide the 3rd gear pinion and its bush off the shaft, and the thrust washer **(see illustrations 29.33c, b and a)**.
22 Remove the circlip and slide off the 6th gear pinion **(see illustrations 29.32b and a)**.
23 Remove the circlip, then slide off the thrust washer and the 2nd gear pinion **(see illustrations 29.31c, b and a)**.

Output shaft inspection

24 Wash all of the components in clean solvent and dry them off.
25 Check the gear teeth for cracking and other obvious damage. Check the 3rd gear bush and the surface in the inner diameter of the gear for scoring or heat discoloration. If the gear or bush is damaged, replace them both with new ones.

26 Inspect the dogs and the dog holes in related gears for excessive wear. Renew the paired gears as a set if necessary.
27 Measure the gearchange fork groove width in the 5th and 6th gear pinions (see Section 21).
28 The shaft is unlikely to sustain damage unless the engine has seized, placing an unusually high loading on the transmission, or the machine has covered a very high mileage. Check the surface of the shaft, especially where a pinion turns on it, and the edges of the splined sections, and replace the shaft with a new one if it has scored or picked up. Damage of any kind can only be cured by renewal.
29 The ball bearing and sleeve on the left-hand end of the shaft are a press fit **(see illustration)**. Refer to *Tools and Workshop*

Tips in the Reference Section for more information on bearing checks and removal and installation methods – note which way round the bearing fits, and how the sleeve (which must be drawn off with the bearing and pressed back on after it) fits outside it. Replace the needle bearing with a new one if it is worn or damaged, or does not run freely.

Output shaft reassembly

30 During reassembly, always use new circlips. Lubricate the components with engine oil before assembling them.
31 Slide the 2nd gear pinion onto the shaft, with its dished side facing away from the ball bearing, followed by the thrust washer **(see illustrations)**. Fit the circlip, making sure it locates in its groove **(see illustration)**.

29.29 Check the bearing (arrowed) and replace with a new one if necessary

29.31a Slide the 2nd gear pinion onto the shaft ...

29.31b ... followed by the thrust washer ...

29.31c ... then fit the circlip ...

29.31d ... making sure it locates in its groove

2•60 Engine, clutch and transmission

29.32a Slide the 6th gear pinion onto the shaft, making sure the oil holes (arrowed) do not align, . . .

29.32b . . . then fit the circlip . . .

29.32c . . . making sure it locates in its groove

29.33a Slide the thrust washer on . . .

29.33b . . . followed by the bush, aligning the oil holes (arrowed) . . .

29.33c . . . then fit the 3rd gear pinion onto the bush

29.34a Slide the 4th gear pinion onto the shaft . . .

29.34b . . . followed by the thrust washer . . .

29.34c . . . then fit the circlip . . .

29.34d . . . making sure it locates in its groove

29.35a Slide the 5th gear pinion onto the shaft, making sure the oil holes (arrowed) do not align, . . .

29.35b . . . followed by the thrust washer . . .

Engine, clutch and transmission 2•61

29.35c ... the needle bearing ...

29.35d ... then fit the 1st gear pinion onto the bearing

29.36a Fit the thrust washer ...

29.36b ... the needle bearing ...

29.36c ... and its outer race

29.37 The assembled output shaft should be as shown

32 Slide 6th gear pinion onto the shaft with its gearchange fork groove facing away from the 2nd gear pinion, making sure the oil holes in the gear do NOT align with the oil hole in the shaft (see illustration). Secure the gear with the circlip, making sure it locates in the shaft groove (see illustration).

33 Slide the thrust washer onto the shaft, followed by the 3rd gear pinion bush, making sure the oil hole in the bush aligns with the hole in the shaft (see illustrations). Slide the 3rd gear pinion onto the bush with its stepped side facing away from the 6th gear pinion (see illustration).

34 Slide on the 4th gear pinion, with its recessed side facing away from the 3rd gear, followed by the thrust washer (see illustration). Fit the circlip, making sure it locates in its groove (see illustrations).

35 Slide the 5th gear pinion onto the shaft with its gearchange fork groove facing away from the 4th gear pinion, making sure the oil holes in the gear do NOT align with the hole in the shaft (see illustration). Fit the thrust washer (see illustration). Slide the 1st gear pinion needle bearing onto the shaft, then fit the 1st gear pinion onto the bearing, with the paint mark made on removal facing out (see illustrations).

36 Fit the thrust washer, needle roller bearing and its outer race (see illustrations).

37 The assembled output shaft should be as shown (see illustration).

30 Recommended running-in procedure

1 Make sure the engine oil and coolant levels are correct (see Pre-ride checks).
2 Make sure there is fuel in the tank.
3 Start the engine and let it run at a moderately fast idle until it reaches normal operating temperature.

 Warning: If the oil pressure warning light doesn't go off, or it comes on while the engine is running, stop the engine immediately.

4 Check carefully that there are no oil leaks and make sure the transmission and controls, especially the brakes, function properly before road testing the machine.
5 Upon completion of the road test, and after the engine has cooled down completely, recheck the valve clearances and check the engine oil and coolant levels (see Pre-ride checks).
6 Treat the machine gently for the first few miles to make sure oil has circulated throughout the engine and any new parts installed have started to seat.

 *If a lubrication failure is suspected, stop the engine immediately and try to find the cause. If an engine is run without oil, even for a short period of time, severe damage will occur.*

7 Even greater care is necessary if new pistons and liners or a new crankshaft has been installed. In the case of new pistons and liners, the bike will have to be run in as if when new. This means greater use of the transmission and a restraining hand on the throttle. There's no point in keeping to any set road speed limit – it's the engine revs that are important. For the first 500 miles (800 km) the main idea is to keep from labouring the engine and to gradually increase performance – and allow the engine to warm up gently. It is best to vary engine and road speed as much as possible, so use the gearbox. These recommendations can be lessened to an extent when only a new crankshaft is installed. Between 500 and 1000 miles (800 and 1600 km) gradually work engine speeds up to the maximum, again avoiding labouring or straining the engine, or being in the wrong gear. Experience is the best guide, since it's easy to tell when an engine is running freely.

Notes

Chapter 3
Cooling system

Contents

	Section number		Section number
Coolant change	see Chapter 1	Cooling system checks	see Chapter 1
Coolant hoses, pipes and unions	8	General information	1
Coolant level check	see Pre-ride checks	Oil cooler	see Chapter 2
Coolant reservoir	3	Radiator	6
Coolant temperature gauge	see Chapter 8	Radiator pressure cap	2
Coolant temperature sensor	see Chapter 4	Thermostat	5
Cooling fan and relay	4	Water pump	7

Degrees of difficulty

Easy, suitable for novice with little experience	Fairly easy, suitable for beginner with some experience	Fairly difficult, suitable for competent DIY mechanic	Difficult, suitable for experienced DIY mechanic	Very difficult, suitable for expert DIY or professional

Specifications

Coolant
Mixture type and capacity .... see Chapter 1

Radiator
Cap valve opening pressure.................................. 16 psi (1.1 Bar)

Cooling fan
Cooling fan cut-in temperature .... 103°C

Thermostat
Opening temperature... 83 to 92°C

Torque wrench settings
Coolant inlet union bolts
   Speed Triple models from VIN 461332-on, Tiger SE, Tiger Sport ... 8 Nm
   All other models .... 12 Nm
Radiator mounting bolts.. 9 Nm
Thermostat housing bolts
   Speed Triple models from VIN 461332-on, Tiger SE, Tiger Sport ... 8 Nm
   All other models .... 12 Nm
Water pump bolts... 10 Nm

3•2 Cooling system

1 General information

The cooling system uses a water/antifreeze coolant to carry away excess energy in the form of heat. The cylinders are surrounded by a water jacket from which the heated coolant is circulated by thermo-syphonic action in conjunction with a water pump. The water pump is driven by the oil pump. The hot coolant passes upwards to the thermostat and through to the radiator. The coolant then flows across the radiator core, where it is cooled by the passing air, to the water pump and back to the engine where the cycle is repeated.

A thermostat is fitted in the system to prevent the coolant flowing through the radiator when the engine is cold, therefore accelerating the speed at which the engine reaches normal operating temperature. A coolant temperature sensor transmits information to the engine management system. This information is used to help optimise the fuelling of the engine at all temperatures. The engine management system also controls the temperature gauge and the cooling fan, via a relay. Because the control side of these cooling system functions is integral with the engine management system, they are dealt with in Chapter 4. The function side of the cooling fan and relay are in this Chapter, while the function of the temperature gauge is in Chapter 8.

The complete cooling system is partially sealed and pressurised, the pressure being controlled by a valve contained in the spring-loaded radiator cap. By pressurising the coolant the boiling point is raised, preventing premature boiling in adverse conditions. The overflow pipe from the system is connected to a reservoir into which excess coolant is expelled under pressure. The discharged coolant automatically returns to the radiator when the engine cools.

⚠ **Warning: Do not remove the pressure cap from the radiator when the engine is hot. Scalding hot coolant and steam may be blown out under pressure, which could cause serious injury. When the engine has cooled, place a thick rag, like a towel over**

2.2 Remove the pressure cap as described

the pressure cap; slowly rotate the cap anti-clockwise to the first stop. This procedure allows any residual pressure to escape. When the steam has stopped escaping, press down on the cap while turning it anti-clockwise and remove it. Do not allow antifreeze to come into contact with your skin or painted surfaces of the motorcycle. Rinse off any spills immediately with plenty of water. Antifreeze is highly toxic if ingested. Never leave antifreeze lying around in an open container or in puddles on the floor; children and pets are attracted by its sweet smell and may drink it. Check with the local authorities about disposing of used antifreeze. Many communities will have collection centres which will see that antifreeze is disposed of safely.

Caution: At all times use the specified type of antifreeze, and always mix it with distilled water in the correct proportion. The antifreeze contains corrosion inhibitors which are essential to avoid damage to the cooling system. A lack of these inhibitors could lead to a build-up of corrosion which would block the coolant passages, resulting in overheating and severe engine damage. Distilled water must be used as opposed to tap water to avoid a build-up of scale which would also block the passages.

Many of the bolts used on Triumph motorcycles are of the Torx type. Unless you are already equipped with a good range of Torx bits, you are advised to obtain a set. Make sure you get bits that can be used in conjunction with a socket set so that a torque wrench can be applied – a Torx key set will not be adequate on its own, though will be useful in addition to the bits.

2 Radiator pressure cap

1 If problems such as overheating or loss of coolant occur, check the entire system as described in Chapter 1.

2 Remove the pressure cap from the filler neck in the radiator as follows: turn the cap anti-clockwise until it reaches a stop – if you hear a hissing sound (indicating there is still pressure in the system), wait until it stops; now press down on the cap and continue turning it until it can be removed **(see illustration)**. Check the cap seals – if you are in any doubt as to their effectiveness replace the cap with a new one – maintaining a good seal to retain the pressure in the cooling system is essential to the efficient function of the system.

3 If no obvious problems can be found have the radiator cap opening pressure checked by a Triumph dealer equipped with the special tester required for the job. If the cap is defective, replace it with a new one. If you are unable to get the cap tested fit a new one anyway – the cost is minimal.

3 Coolant reservoir

Removal

1 On Sprint models, remove the left-hand fairing side panel (see Chapter 7). Turn the handlebars fully to the right. Unscrew the ECM bracket bolts and displace the ECM to one side, making sure it is adequately supported **(see illustration)**. Detach the hose from the top of the reservoir **(see illustration)**. Place a container suitable to collect the contents of the reservoir below the bottom hose, then detach the hose and allow the coolant to drain. Unscrew the reservoir bolts and manoeuvre it out **(see illustration)**.

2 On 2005 to 2010 Speed Triple models (up

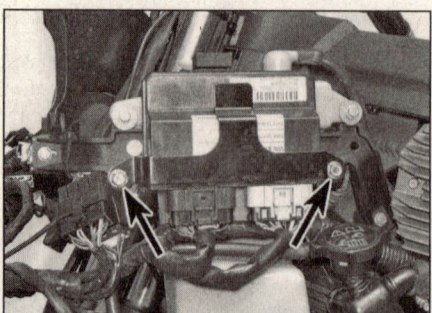

3.1a Unscrew the bolts (arrowed) and displace the ECM

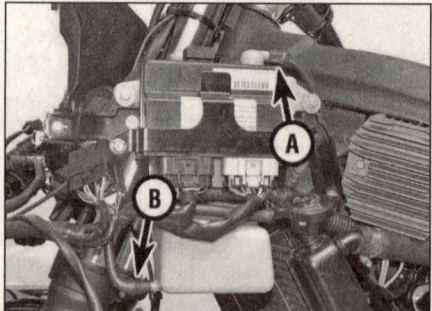

3.1b Detach the top hose (A), then detach the bottom hose (B) and drain the reservoir

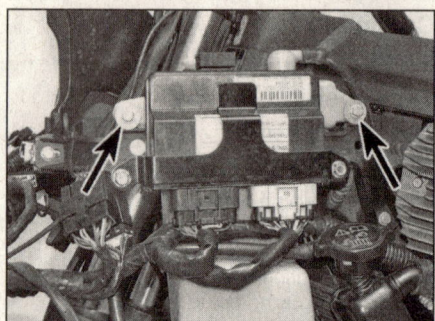

3.1c Reservoir mounting bolts (arrowed)

Cooling system 3•3

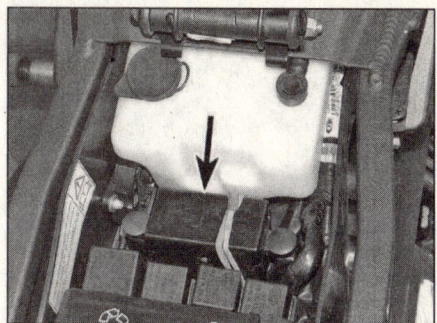

3.2a Displace the fusebox (arrowed)

to VIN 461331) remove the fuel tank (see Chapter 4). Displace the fusebox **(see illustration)**. Release the clamps securing the hoses to the unions on the reservoir and detach them, noting which fits where **(see illustration)**. Unscrew the bolts and remove the reservoir. Remove the filler cap and tip the contents into a suitable container.

3 On 2011-on Speed Triple models (from VIN 461332) remove the fuel tank (see Chapter 4). Remove the harness guide from the front sprocket cover **(see illustration)**. On California models remove the EVAP canister. Release the clamp securing the top hose to the reservoir and detach it **(see illustration)**. Undo the screw and displace the reservoir, noting how it locates. Tilt the reservoir back, release the clamp securing the bottom hose to the reservoir and detach it, then remove the reservoir, take the filler cap off and tip the contents into a suitable container.

4 On Tiger models, remove the left-hand fairing side panel (see Chapter 7). Detach the hose from the top of the reservoir **(see illustration)**. Place a container suitable to collect the contents of the reservoir below the bottom hose, then detach the hose from the radiator filler neck and allow the coolant to drain. Undo the screw, the lift the reservoir to free the locating peg on the bottom from the grommet, and manoeuvre it out.

Installation

5 Installation is the reverse of removal. Make sure the hoses are correctly installed and secured with their clamps. On completion refill the reservoir (see *Pre-ride checks*).

4 Cooling fan and relay

Cooling fan

Check

1 If the engine is overheating and the cooling fan isn't coming on, first check the fan fuse (see Chapter 8). Next check the fan relay as described below.

2 If the fuse and relay are good and the fan still does not come on, the fault could lie in either the cooling fan motor itself, or the relevant wiring and connectors. Test all the wiring and

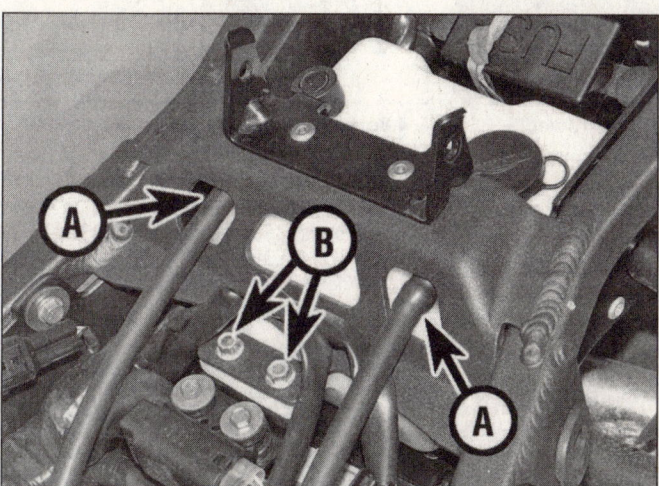

3.2b Detach the hoses (A), then unscrew the bolts (B) and remove the reservoir

3.3a Unscrew the bolts (arrowed) and remove the guide

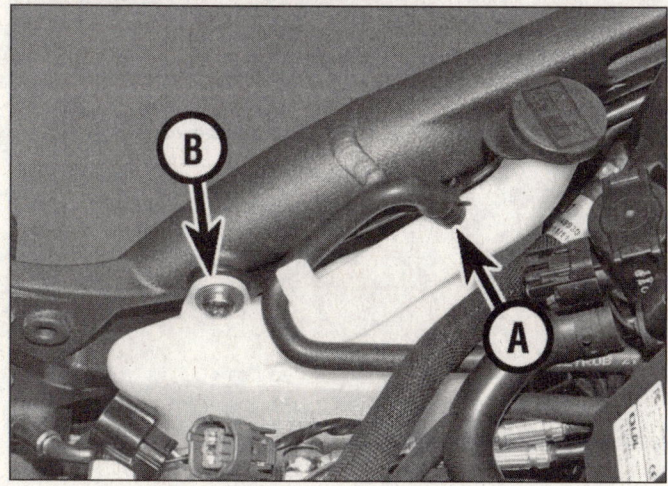

3.3b Detach the hose (A). Reservoir mounting screw (B)

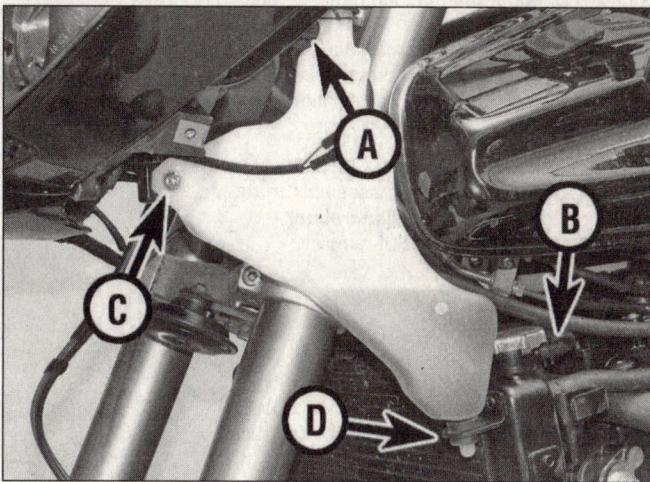

3.4 Top hose (A), bottom hose (B), mounting screw (C) and locating peg (D)

3•4 Cooling system

4.4a Cooling fan wiring connector – Sprint (Speed Triple similar location)

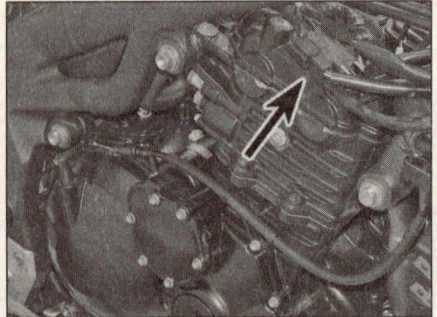

4.4b Cooling fan wiring connector location (arrowed) – Tiger

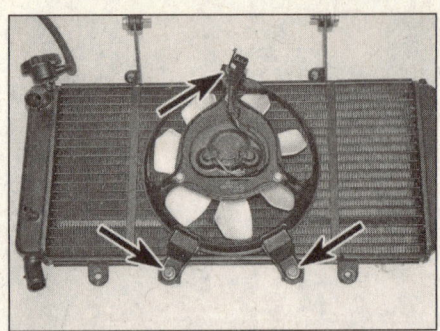

4.5 Fan motor screws (arrowed)

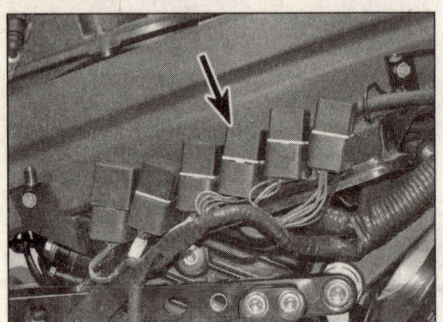

4.8a Cooling fan relay (arrowed) – Sprint ST models

4.8b Cooling fan relay (arrowed) – Sprint GT models

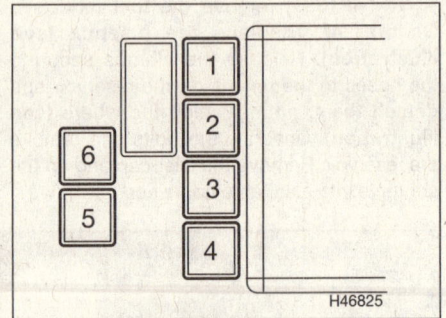

4.8c Relay identification – 2005 to 2007 Speed Triple models

1. Starter relay
2. Headlight relay
3. Engine management system (EMS) relay
4. Turn signal relay
5. Cooling fan relay
6. Fuel pump relay

connections, referring to Electrical system fault finding at the beginning of Chapter 8 and to the Wiring Diagram for your model at the end of it.

3 To access the cooling fan motor, on Sprint and Speed Triple models remove the airbox (see Chapter 4), and on Tiger models remove the right-hand fairing side panel (see Chapter 7).

4 Trace the wiring from the fan motor and disconnect it at the connector **(see illustrations)**. Using a 12 volt battery and two jumper wires, connect the positive (+) battery lead to the brown/pink wire terminal on the fan wiring connector and the negative (-) lead to the black wire terminal. Once connected the fan should operate. If it does not, and the wiring is all good, then the fan motor is faulty. Replace the fan assembly with a new one – individual components are not available. If all tests so far have shown no problems, test the coolant temperature sensor (see Chapter 4).

Renewal

5 Remove the radiator (see Section 6). Undo the screws securing the fan assembly to the radiator and remove it **(see illustration)**.
6 Installation is the reverse of removal.

Cooling fan relay

Check

Note: *Refer to the Wiring Diagrams at the end of Chapter 8 for relay terminal identification.*

7 If the engine is overheating and the cooling fan isn't coming on, first check the fan fuse (see Chapter 8). If the fuse is blown, check the fan circuit for a short to earth (see the wiring diagrams at the end of this book).
8 If the fuse is good, on Sprint models

remove the right-hand fairing side panel, and on Speed Triple and Tiger models remove the seat (see Chapter 7). Disconnect the relay from its connector block **(see illustrations)**. Check the terminals and sockets for damage and corrosion.

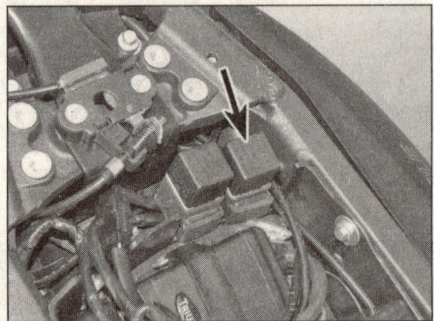

4.8d Cooling fan relay (arrowed) – 2008 to 2010 Speed Triple (up to VIN 461331)

4.8e Cooling fan relay (arrowed) – 2011-on Speed Triple models (from VIN 461332)

4.8f Cooling fan relay (arrowed) – Tiger models (except Sport)

4.8g Cooling fan relay (arrowed) – Tiger Sport

5.3a Unscrew the bolts (arrowed), detach the cover . . .

5.3b . . . and withdraw the thermostat (arrowed)

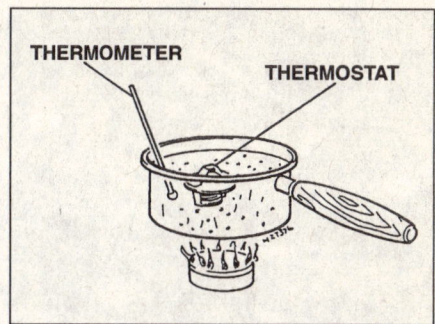

5.5 Thermostat testing set-up

9 Each terminal on the relay has a number, either marked next to the terminal on the underside of the relay, or that can be identified using the relevant wiring diagram at the end of Chapter 8 by matching the wire colours marked on the diagram to the wires themselves in the relay socket and their applicable terminals on the relay, according to model. On some models the terminals are numbered 1, 2, 3 and 5, on others they are numbered 1, 4, 6 and 8. Identify the terminal numbers used, then test the relay as follows: connect a continuity tester or a multimeter set to the ohms x 1 scale between either the No. 3 and No. 5 terminals, or between the No. 1 and No. 8 terminals, according to model – there should be no continuity or infinite resistance. If there is continuity or zero resistance replace the relay with a new one. Leaving the tester or meter connected, connect the positive (+) terminal of a fully-charged 12 volt battery to either the No. 1 or to the No. 6 terminal on the relay, and the negative (–) terminal to either the No. 2 or to the No. 4 terminal on the relay. At this point the relay should be heard to click and there should be continuity or zero resistance shown on the tester or meter. If this is the case the relay is proved good. If the relay does not click when battery voltage is applied and the tester or meter indicates no continuity or infinite resistance, the relay is faulty and must be replaced with a new one. If the relay is good, test the fan motor (see Step 3).

Renewal

10 On Sprint models remove the right-hand fairing side panel, and on Speed Triple and Tiger models remove the seat (see Chapter 7).
11 Disconnect the relay from its connector block (see illustration 4.8a, b, c, d, e, f or g).
12 Plug the new relay into its connector.

5 Thermostat

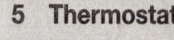

1 The thermostat is automatic in operation and should give many years service without requiring attention. In the event of a failure, the valve will probably jam open, in which case the engine will take much longer than normal to warm up. Conversely, if the valve jams shut, the coolant will be unable to circulate and the engine will overheat. Neither condition is acceptable, and the fault must be investigated promptly.

Removal

2 Drain the cooling system (see Chapter 1).
3 Unscrew the bolts securing the thermostat housing, then detach it from the cylinder head and remove the thermostat, noting how it fits (see illustrations). Discard the O-ring as a new one must be used (see illustration 5.7).

Check

4 Examine the thermostat visually before carrying out the test. If it remains in the open position at room temperature, it should be replaced with a new one.
5 Suspend the thermostat by a piece of wire in a container of cold water. Place a thermometer in the water so that the bulb is close to the thermostat, and not in contact with the container (see illustration). Heat the water, noting the temperature when the thermostat opens, and compare the result with the specified opening temperature given at the beginning of the Chapter. If the thermostat opens at a different temperature, does not open at all, or is permanently open, it is faulty and must be replaced with a new one.
Note: *In the event of thermostat failure, as an emergency measure only, it can be removed and the machine used without it. Take care*

5.6 Install the thermostat with the jiggle-pin at the top

5.7 Fit a new O-ring into the groove

when starting the engine from cold as it will take much longer than usual to warm up. Ensure that a new unit is installed as soon as possible.

Installation

6 Fit the thermostat into the cylinder head with the toggle pin at the top (see illustration).
7 Fit a new O-ring into the groove in the housing, then fit the housing and tighten the bolts to the specified torque setting (see illustration).
8 Refill the cooling system (see Chapter 1 and *Pre-ride checks*).

6 Radiator

Removal

⚠ **Warning: The engine must be completely cool before carrying out this procedure.**

1 Drain the cooling system (see Chapter 1).
2 On Sprint and Speed Triple models remove the airbox (see Chapter 4).
3 Trace the wiring from the fan motor and disconnect it at the connector (see illustration 4.4a or b).
4 On 2005 to 2010 Speed Triple models (up to VIN 461331), disconnect the turn signal wiring connectors, then unscrew the radiator panel and turn signal bolts and remove the panels and turn signals, noting the routing of the

3•6 Cooling system

6.4a Disconnect the wiring connectors (arrowed) . . .

6.4b . . . then undo the screws (arrowed – 2008 to 2010 type shown) and remove the panels/turn signals

6.4c Release the cable from the guide (arrowed)

wiring **(see illustrations)**. On 2011-on Speed Triple models (from VIN 461332) remove the radiator cowls (see Chapter 7), and the horn (see Chapter 8), and release the clutch cable from its guide **(see illustration)**.

5 Displace the oil cooler and support it clear of the radiator (see Chapter 2) – there is no need to detach the hoses.

6 On Sprint models detach the air intake duct and rubber heat shield from the top of the radiator **(see illustrations)**.

7 Slacken or release (according to type) the clamps securing all the radiator hoses and detach them from the radiator, noting which fits where **(see illustrations)**.

8 Unscrew the bolts securing the radiator, noting the arrangement of the collars and rubber grommets, and any hose or cable guide, then lift the radiator off **(see illustration)**. Where fitted note how the bottom mounting lug(s)

6.6a Undo the screws (arrowed) to release the duct . . .

locate(s) in the grommet(s) **(see illustration)**.
9 If necessary, remove the cooling fan from the radiator (see Section 4).
10 Check the radiator for signs of damage and clear any dirt or debris that might obstruct

6.6b . . . then release the heat shield clips (arrowed)

air flow and inhibit cooling. If the radiator fins are badly damaged or broken the radiator must be renewed. Also check the rubber mounting grommets, and replace them with new ones if necessary **(see illustration)**.

6.7a Radiator hoses (arrowed) – Sprint models

6.7b Right-hand side radiator hose (arrowed) – where fitted

6.7c Left-hand side radiator hoses (arrowed) – Speed Triple and Tiger models

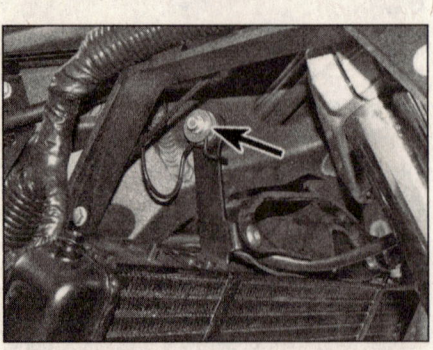

6.8a Radiator mounting bolt (arrowed – there is one on each side) – Sprint models

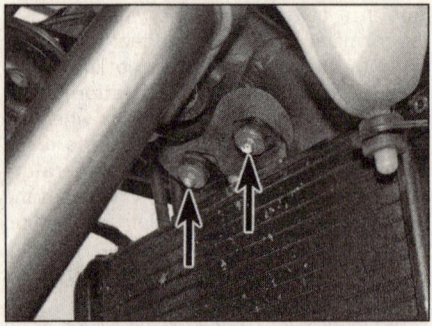

6.8b Radiator mounting bolts (arrowed) – Speed Triple and Tiger models

6.10 Make sure the collars and grommets are in good condition

Cooling system

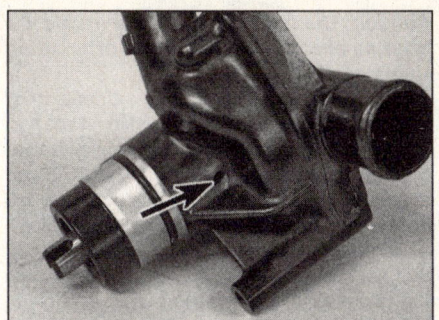

7.2 Water pump drain hole (arrowed)

7.3 Check the impeller (arrowed) as described

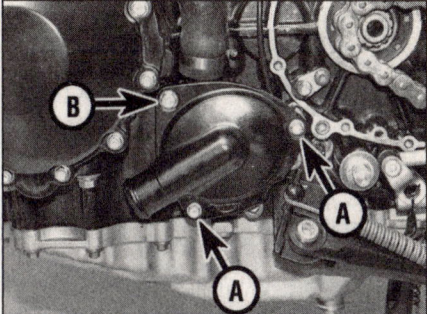

7.6 The bolts (A) secure the pump to the engine as well as the cover, the bolt (B) just secures the cover

Installation

11 Installation is the reverse of removal, noting the following.
- Make sure the collars and grommets and any wiring or hose guide are correctly installed with the mounting bolts **(see illustration 6.10)**. Tighten the bolts to the torque setting specified at the beginning of the Chapter.
- Make sure that the wiring connector is correctly connected **(see illustration 4.4a or b)**.
- Ensure the coolant hoses are in good condition (see Chapter 1), and are retained by their clamps, using new ones if necessary.
- On completion refill the cooling system as described in Chapter 1 and Pre-ride checks.

7 Water pump

Check

1 The water pump is located on the left-hand side of the engine.
2 To prevent leakage of water from the cooling system to the lubrication system and vice versa, two seals are fitted on the pump shaft. The seal on the water pump side is of the mechanical type which bears on the rear face of the impeller. The second seal, which is mounted behind the mechanical seal is of the normal feathered lip type. There is a drain hole between the seals in the seal housing section of the pump **(see illustration)**. If either seal fails, the drain allows the coolant or oil to escape and prevents them mixing. However, neither seal is available as a separate item as the pump is sold as an assembly. Therefore, if on inspection the drainage hole shows signs of leakage, the pump must be removed and replaced with a new one.
3 Drain the cooling system (see Chapter 1). Remove the pump cover (see Step 6). Wiggle the water pump impeller back-and-forth and in-and-out, and spin it by hand **(see illustration)**. If there is excessive movement,

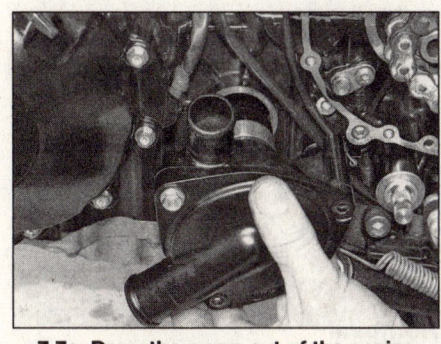

7.7a Draw the pump out of the engine

or the pump is noisy or rough when turned, or if any damage is found, replace the pump with a new one – individual components are not available.
4 Check the pump housing and cover, and the impeller and shaft for cracks, deformation and any other damage. Check that the shaft is straight – if it is bent, replace the pump with a new one. Also check for corrosion or a build-up of scale in the pump body and clean or renew the pump as necessary.

Removal

5 Drain the cooling system (see Chapter 1). If the bike is on its sidestand drain the engine oil as well.
6 If you just want to remove the cover to inspect the pump, unscrew the three bolts, then hold the housing and detach the cover (the hose can stay attached) **(see illustration)**.

7.8a Unscrew the remaining cover bolt (arrowed) . . .

7.7b Discard the O-ring

Note that the cover seal is not listed as being available separately, but check with a dealer – if not it may be the same seal as fitted to earlier models, which is available.
7 To remove the pump, slacken the clamp securing the top coolant hose and detach it **(see illustration 7.6)**. Unscrew the lower and rear bolts only **(see illustration 7.6)** and draw the pump out of the engine **(see illustration)**. Note how the slot in the end of the pump shaft engages with the tab on the end of the oil pump shaft. Discard the O-ring as a new one must be used **(see illustration)**.
8 To remove the cover, unscrew the remaining bolt **(see illustration)**. It is possible that the dowels locating the cover have corroded, in which case the cover could be difficult to remove. Spray some penetrating oil around the joint and tap it with a soft-faced hammer to dislodge it – do not try to lever it off as the

7.8b . . . and remove it, noting the dowels (arrowed)

3•8 Cooling system

7.8c Discard the cover O-ring

8.4 Coolant inlet union bolts (arrowed)

mating surfaces could be damaged, or the cover could crack. Remove the dowels if they are loose and discard the cover O-ring as a new one must be used **(see illustrations)**.

Installation

9 Installation is the reverse of removal, noting the following:
- Fit new O-rings into the grooves in the cover (if removed) and in the pump body **(see illustrations 7.7b and 8c)**. Note that the cover seal is not listed as being available separately, but check with a dealer – if not it may be the same seal as fitted to earlier models, which is available.
- Fit the dowels into the cover if removed **(see illustration 7.8b)**. Clean the dowels and smear them with grease if they were corroded.
- Make sure the slot in the end of the pump shaft engages with the tab on the end of the oil pump shaft.
- Tighten the pump mounting bolts to the torque setting specified at the beginning of the Chapter.
- Make sure the coolant hoses are pushed fully onto their unions and are secured by their clamps.
- Refill the cooling system (see Chapter 1 and Pre-ride checks).

8 Coolant hoses, pipes and unions

Removal

1 Before removing a hose, pipe or union, drain the coolant (see Chapter 1).

2 Use a screwdriver to slacken the larger-bore hose clamps, then slide them back along the hose and clear of the union spigot. The smaller-bore hoses are secured by spring clamps which can be expanded by squeezing their ears together with pliers.

Caution: The radiator unions are fragile. Do not use excessive force when attempting to remove the hoses.

3 If a hose proves stubborn, release it by rotating it on its union before working it off. If all else fails, cut the hose with a sharp knife then slit it at each union so that it can be peeled off in two pieces. Whilst this means renewing the hose, it is preferable to buying a new radiator.

4 Remove the coolant inlet union and the thermostat housing on the engine by detaching the hoses (see above), then unscrewing the bolts **(see illustration and 5.3a)**. Discard the O-rings as new ones must be used.

Installation

5 Slide the clamp onto the hose. Work the hose on to its union, seating it against the spigot where present, and making sure it is correctly aligned at each end so there is no twist.

> **HAYNES HINT** *If the hose is difficult to push on its union, it can be softened by soaking it in very hot water, or alternatively a little soapy water can be used as a lubricant.*

6 Slide the clamp into place, positioning it between 3 and 7 mm from the end of the hose, and tighten it securely.

7 If the inlet union or thermostat housing on the engine have been removed, fit new O-rings into the grooves and tighten the bolts to the torque setting specified at the beginning of the Chapter **(see illustration 5.7)**.

Chapter 4
Engine management system (fuel and ignition)

Contents

	Section number		Section number
Airbox	3	Fuel tank	2
Air filter	see Chapter 1	General information and precautions	1
Catalytic converter	17	Idle air control unit	15
Clutch switch	see Chapter 8	Idle speed adjustment	see Chapter 1
EMS relay	13	Ignition coils	11
Engine management system and electronic control module (ECM)	12	Ignition switch	see Chapter 8
EVAP system – California models	16	Neutral switch	see Chapter 8
Exhaust system	10	Secondary air injection system	see Chapter 1
Fuel hoses	see Chapter 1	Sensors	14
Fuel level sensor	6	Sidestand switch	see Chapter 8
Fuel pressure and pressure regulator	5	Spark plugs	see Chapter 1
Fuel pump and relay	4	Throttle body removal and installation	7
Fuel rail and injectors	8	Throttle body synchronisation	see Chapter 1
Fuel system check	see Chapter 1	Throttle cable check and adjustment	see Chapter 1
		Throttle cable removal and installation	9

Degrees of difficulty

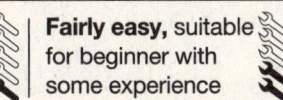

Easy, suitable for novice with little experience   **Fairly easy**, suitable for beginner with some experience   **Fairly difficult**, suitable for competent DIY mechanic   **Difficult**, suitable for experienced DIY mechanic   **Very difficult**, suitable for expert DIY or professional

Specifications

Fuel
Grade
  UK and Europe .... Unleaded, minimum 95 RON (Research Octane Number)
  US .... Unleaded, minimum 89 (R+M)/2 (CLC or AKI Octane rating)
Fuel tank capacity
  Sprint
    Plastic tank .... 21 litres
    Steel tank .... 20 litres
  Speed Triple
    Up to VIN 461331 .... 18 litres
    From VIN 461332-on .... 17.5 litres
  Tiger .... 20 litres
Fuel quantity remaining when low level warning light comes on
  Sprint and Speed Triple .... 4.0 litres
  Tiger .... 3.5 litres

Fuel injection system
Operating pressure (nominal) .... 43.5 psi (3.0 Bar) @
  Sprint and Speed Triple .... 1200 rpm
  Tiger .... 1170 rpm
Idle air control unit stepper motor resistance .... 4 to 12 ohms
Fuel injector resistance .... 12.5 to 14.0 ohms
EVAP system purge valve resistance (California models) ... 24 to 28 ohms

Ignition system
Type .... Digital inductive
Firing order 1–2–3
Cylinder identification .... 1–2–3, from left to right
Spark plugs .... see Chapter 1
Ignition coil resistance .... 0.8 to 1.2 ohms
Crankshaft position sensor (pick-up coil) resistance .... 0.56 K-ohms ± 10% @ 20°C
Crankshaft position sensor (pick-up coil) air gap .... 1.0 mm
Rev limiter cut-in .... 9500 rpm

Engine management system

Type	Electronic
Control sensors	atmospheric pressure, engine coolant temperature, crankshaft position, manifold absolute pressure, intake air temperature, throttle position, oxygen content (lambda), speed (road), tip-over

Coolant temperature sensor resistance
- Warm engine: 200 to 400 ohms
- Cold engine
  - 20°C ambient: 2.35 to 2.65 K-ohms
  - 15°C ambient: 2.9 to 3.3 K-ohms
  - -10°C ambient: 8.5 to 10.25 K-ohms

Intake air temperature sensor resistance
- 80°C ambient: 200 to 400 ohms
- 20°C ambient: 2.35 to 2.65 K-ohms
- -10°C ambient: 8.5 to 10.25 K-ohms

Torque settings

Crankshaft position sensor	10 Nm
Exhaust system	
Sprint ST	
Silencer mounting bolt	15 Nm
Silencer-to-intermediate pipe clamp bolt	22 Nm
Intermediate pipe-to-downpipe assembly clamp bolt	15 Nm
Downpipe assembly rear mounting bolt	15 Nm
Downpipe assembly nuts	23 Nm (see Text)
Sprint GT	
Silencer mounting bolt	28 Nm
Intermediate pipe-to-downpipe assembly clamp bolt	15 Nm
Downpipe assembly rear mounting bolt	22 Nm
Downpipe assembly nuts	23 Nm (see Text)
Speed Triple	
Silencer mounting bolt	15 Nm
Silencer-to-intermediate pipe clamp bolt	10 Nm
Intermediate pipe-to-downpipe assembly clamp bolt	15 Nm
Downpipe assembly rear mounting bolt	
Up to VIN 461331	15 Nm
From VIN 461332	25 Nm
Downpipe assembly nuts	
Up to VIN 461331	19 Nm (see Text)
From VIN 461332	23 Nm (see Text)
Tiger	
Silencer mounting bolt	15 Nm
Silencer-to-downpipe assembly clamp bolt	
Tiger	15 Nm
Tiger SE, Tiger Sport	10 Nm
Downpipe assembly rear mounting bolt	15 Nm
Downpipe assembly nuts	23 Nm (see Text)
Fuel level sensor bolts (Sprint models with plastic tank)	5 Nm
Fuel pump mounting plate bolts	9 Nm
Fuel rail bolts	6 Nm
Fuel tank mountings	
Sprint	9 Nm
Speed Triple	
Front	
Up to VIN 461331	8 Nm
From VIN 461332	4 Nm
Rear	9 Nm
Tiger SE, Tiger Sport	
Front	9 Nm
Rear	7 Nm
Idle air control unit mounting screws	3.5 Nm
Intake stub screws	12 Nm
Oxygen sensor	
Sprint, Speed Triple up to VIN 461331	40 Nm
Tiger, Speed Triple from VIN 461332	25 Nm
Throttle position sensor screws	
Speed Triple models from VIN 461332	2 Nm
All other models	3.5 Nm

Engine management system (fuel and ignition) 4•3

1 General information and precautions

General information

All models are fitted with an electronic engine management system which controls both the fuel and ignition system functions. The system is controlled by an electronic control module, or ECM. The ECM receives information from various sensors around the motorcycle, which it uses to determine the optimum fuel requirements for the fuel injection system and the optimum timing for the ignition system for all engine speeds and loads.

The sensors used are for atmospheric pressure, crankshaft position, engine coolant temperature, manifold absolute pressure, intake air temperature, oxygen (lambda), road speed, throttle position, and tip-over. Information on the function of these sensors is in Section 14.

The fuel system consists of the fuel tank, the fuel pump with integral filter and pressure regulator, the fuel hose, fuel rail and injectors, the throttle bodies and throttle control cable, and the air intake system. The fuel pump is housed inside the tank. There is an injector for each cylinder, housed in the throttle body. The low fuel warning circuit is operated by a level sensor inside the tank. Cold starting and idle speed is controlled by the ECM which reacts to the information sent by the intake air temperature sensor and the coolant temperature sensor, and adjusts the fuel requirements accordingly via a throttle stepper motor on the right-hand end of the throttle bodies – there is no manual method (i.e. a choke) for assisting cold starting, or for adjusting engine idle speed. Many of the fuel system service procedures are considered routine maintenance items and for that reason are included in Chapter 1.

The ignition system type is digital inductive, which due to its lack of mechanical parts is totally maintenance free. The coil for each spark plug is incorporated in the spark plug cap. The system incorporates an electronic advance system controlled by the ECM, which reacts to the information sent to it from the various sensors to provide the spark at the optimum time. A rev limiter prevents the engine exceeding its maximum rpm. The system incorporates a safety interlock circuit which will cut the ignition if the sidestand is put down whilst the engine is running and in gear, or if a gear is selected whilst the engine is running and the sidestand is down. The tip-over sensor will cut the ignition if it detects that the machine has fallen over.

The engine management system has an in-built two-stage diagnostic function. The initial stage is fault detection, whereupon the system notes the fault and counts the occurrences, looking for repetition. If the fault was a temporary glitch that does not reoccur, no DTC (diagnostic trouble code, or fault code) is registered. If the fault continues a DTC is registered, and the ECM records and stores all engine and system data at that moment, and the malfunction indicator lamp (MIL) in the instrument cluster illuminates. Recorded faults can then be checked using Triumph's diagnostic tool, which reads the data and lists a code to indicate the exact fault. If this happens, the management system in most cases switches itself into 'limp home' mode, so that in theory you should not be left stranded, or in some cases switches itself off, in which case you will be left stranded, depending on the severity of the fault – with minor faults it is possible that you will notice no difference in the running of the motorcycle. If after the DTC has been logged and the MIL comes on the fault clears itself, the MIL will remain on until the engine has been through three engine warm-up and system power-down cycles without the fault recurring, and the DTC will self-erase after forty such cycles. If the fault does not clear itself but is repaired the DTC can be erased using Triumph's tool and the MIL will turn itself off.

Because of their nature, the individual system components can be checked but not repaired. If system troubles occur, and the faulty component can be isolated, the only cure for the problem is to replace the part with a new one. Keep in mind that most electrical parts, once purchased, cannot be returned. To avoid unnecessary expense, make very sure the faulty component has been positively identified before buying a new part.

Many of the bolts used on Triumph motorcycles are of the Torx type. Unless you are already equipped with a good range of Torx bits, you are advised to obtain a set. Make sure you get bits that can be used in conjunction with a socket set so that a torque wrench can be applied – a Torx key set will not be adequate on its own, though will be useful in addition to the bits.

Precautions

⚠️ **Warning: Petrol (gasoline) is extremely flammable, so take extra precautions when you work on any part of the fuel system. Don't smoke or allow open flames or bare light bulbs near the work area, and don't work in a garage where a natural gas-type appliance is present. If you spill any fuel on your skin, rinse it off immediately with soap and water. When you perform any kind of work on the fuel system, wear safety glasses and have a fire extinguisher suitable for a class B type fire (flammable liquids) on hand.**

Always perform fuel-related procedures in a well-ventilated area to prevent a build-up of fumes.

Never work in a building containing a gas appliance with a pilot light, or any other form of naked flame. Ensure that there are no naked light bulbs or any sources of flame or sparks nearby.

Do not smoke (or allow anyone else to smoke) while in the vicinity of petrol (gasoline) or of components containing it. Remember the possible presence of vapour from these sources and move well clear before smoking.

Check all electrical equipment belonging to the house, garage or workshop where work is being undertaken (see the Safety first! section of this manual). Remember that certain electrical appliances such as drills, cutters etc. create sparks in the normal course of operation and must not be used near petrol (gasoline) or any component containing it. Again, remember the possible presence of fumes before using electrical equipment.

Always mop up any spilt fuel and safely dispose of the rag used.

Any stored fuel that is drained off during servicing work must be kept in sealed containers that are suitable for holding petrol (gasoline), and clearly marked as such; the containers themselves should be kept in a safe place. Note that this last point applies equally to the fuel tank if it is removed from the machine; also remember to keep its filler cap closed at all times.

Read the Safety first! section of this manual carefully before starting work.

Owners of machines used in the US, particularly California, should note that their machines must comply at all times with Federal or State legislation governing the permissible levels of noise and of pollutants such as unburnt hydrocarbons, carbon monoxide etc. that can be emitted by those machines. All vehicles offered for sale must comply with legislation in force at the date of manufacture and must not subsequently be altered in any way which will affect their emission of noise or of pollutants.

In practice, this means that adjustments may not be made to any part of the fuel, ignition or exhaust systems by anyone who is not authorised or mechanically qualified to do so, or who does not have the tools, equipment and data necessary to properly carry out the task. Also if any part of these systems is to be replaced it must be replaced with only genuine Triumph components or by components which are approved under the relevant legislation. The machine must never be used with any part of these systems removed, modified or damaged.

2 Fuel tank

 Warning: Refer to the precautions given in Section 1 before starting work.

Removal

Sprint models with plastic tank

1 Make sure the fuel cap is secure. Have some rag to hand to catch any residual fuel

4•4 Engine management system (fuel and ignition)

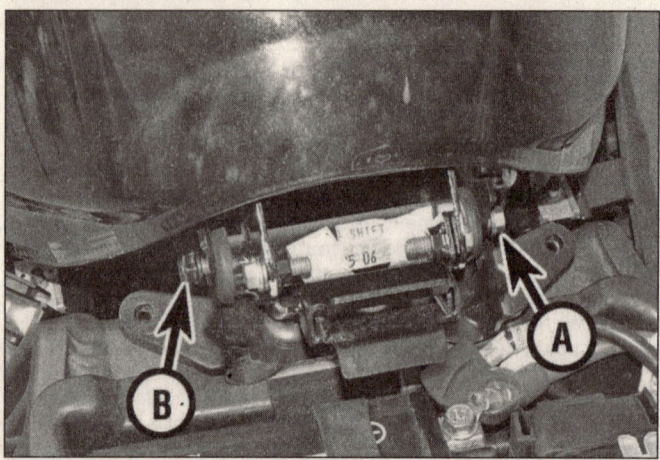

2.13 Unscrew the nut (A) then withdraw the bolt (B)

2.14 Disconnect the hoses (arrowed), noting which fits where

in the connector and its union as the fuel hose is disconnected – the tank and hose are both self-sealing so there won't be much.

2 Remove the seat and the seat cowling (see Chapter 7). Disconnect the battery (see Chapter 8).

3 Unscrew the nut and withdraw the bolt securing the rear of the tank **(see illustration 2.13)**. Raise and support the rear of the tank.

4 Mark or tag the drain and breather hoses on the right-hand side of the tank so they can be installed on the correct union. Detach the hoses from the unions.

5 Trace the wiring from the fuel level sensor on the underside of the tank and disconnect it at the connector.

6 Mark the socket into which the fuel pump wiring connector is fitted – there are two sockets, but only one is used. Disconnect the wiring connector.

7 On models up to VIN 307684 press in the clips on the fuel hose connector and pull the hose off its union.

8 On models from VIN 307685-on slide the orange fuel hose connector cover down to reveal the clips, then press the clips in and pull the hose off its union **(see illustration 2.16)**.

9 Carefully draw the tank back until the locating tab at the front is clear of its bracket then lift the tank off the bike and remove it.

10 Remove the trim panels if required **(see illustration 2.18)**. Inspect the tank support rubbers for signs of damage or deterioration and replace them with new ones if necessary.

Sprint models with steel tank

11 Make sure the fuel cap is secure. Have some rag to hand to catch any residual fuel in the connector and its union as the fuel hose is disconnected – the tank and hose are both self-sealing so there won't be much.

12 Remove the seat, and on ST models the seat cowling, and on GT models the side panels (see Chapter 7). Disconnect the battery (see Chapter 8).

13 Unscrew the nut and withdraw the bolt securing the rear of the tank **(see illustration)**. Raise and support the rear of the tank.

14 Mark or tag the drain and breather hoses so they can be installed on the correct union **(see illustration)**. Detach the hoses from the unions.

15 Mark each of the wiring connectors and the sockets into which they fit with different markings so each can be returned to the same socket. Disconnect the wiring connectors – one is for the fuel pump and the other for the fuel level sensor **(see illustration)**.

16 Slide the orange fuel hose connector cover down to reveal the clips, then press the clips in and pull the hose off its union **(see illustration)**.

17 Carefully draw the tank back until the locating tab at the front is clear of its bracket then lift the tank off the bike and remove it **(see illustration)**.

18 Remove the trim panels if required **(see illustration)**. Inspect the tank support rubbers for signs of damage or deterioration and replace them with new ones if necessary.

Speed Triple models - 2005 to 2010 (up to VIN 461331)

19 Make sure the fuel cap is secure. Have some rag to hand to catch any residual fuel in the connector and its union as the fuel hose is disconnected – the tank and hose are both self-sealing so there won't be much.

20 Remove the seat and the side panels (see Chapter 7). Disconnect the battery (see Chapter 8).

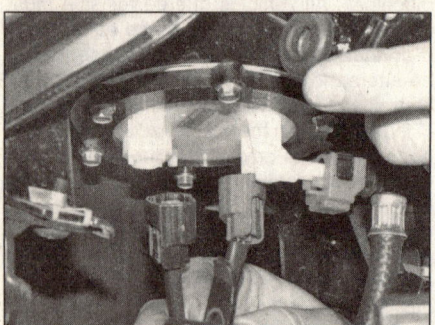

2.15 Disconnect the wiring connectors, noting which fits where

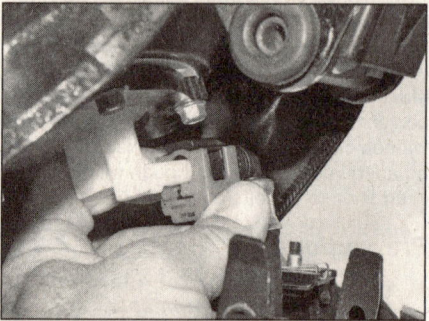

2.16 Release the fuel hose as described

2.17 Carefully lift the tank off the frame and remove it

2.18 Undo the screws (arrowed) and remove the trim panels

Engine management system (fuel and ignition) 4•5

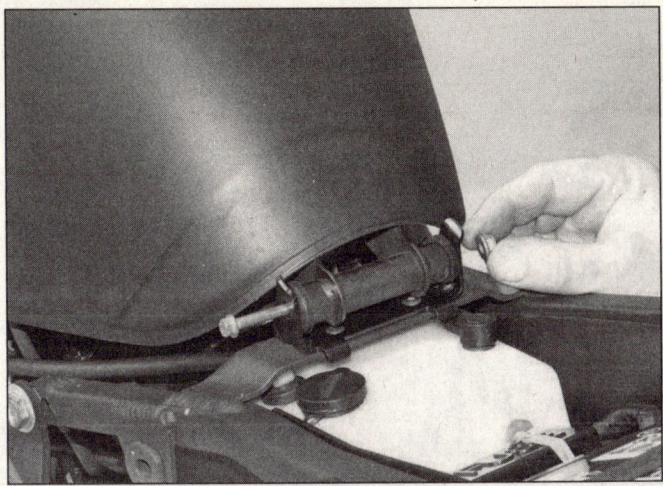

2.21 Unscrew the nut then withdraw the bolt

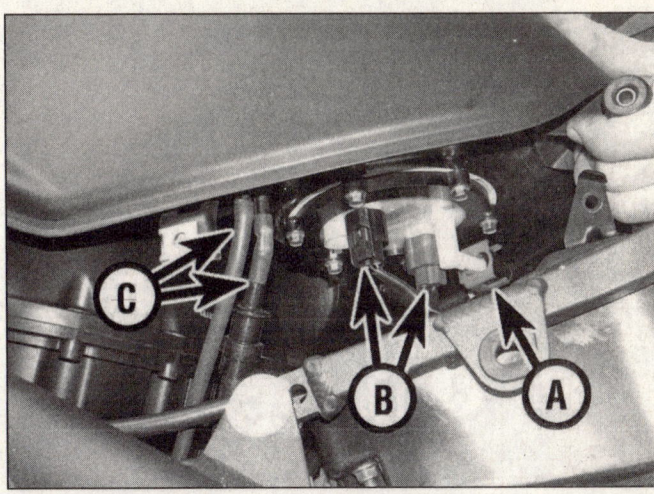

2.22 Fuel hose connector (A), wiring connectors (B – late models), drain and breather hoses (C)

21 Unscrew the nut and withdraw the bolt securing the rear of the tank **(see illustration)**. Raise and support the rear of the tank.

22 Press in the clips on the fuel hose connector and pull the hose off its union **(see illustration)**.

23 On models up to VIN 305059 (Jet black and Neon blue models), VIN 305222 (Roulette green models), or VIN 305251 (Fusion white models), disconnect the fuel pump/level sensor wiring connector. On all later models mark each of the wiring connectors and the sockets into which they fit with different markings so each can be returned to the same socket **(see illustration 2.22)**. Disconnect the wiring connectors – one is for the fuel pump and the other for the fuel level sensor.

24 Mark or tag the drain and breather hoses so they can be installed on the correct union **(see illustration 2.22)**. Detach the hoses from the unions.

25 On models up to VIN 305059 (Jet black and Neon blue models), VIN 305222 (Roulette green models), or VIN 305251 (Fusion white models), unscrew the bolt securing the front of the tank, noting the arrangement of the washers, sleeve and rubber grommet. On all later models note how the front of the tank locates around the post **(see illustration)**.

26 Carefully lift the tank off the bike and remove it.

27 Inspect the tank support rubbers for signs of damage or deterioration and replace them with new ones if necessary.

Speed Triple models – 2011-on (from VIN 461332)

28 Make sure the fuel cap is secure. Have some rag to hand to catch any residual fuel in the connector and its union as the fuel hose is disconnected – the tank and hose are both self-sealing so there won't be much.

29 Remove the seat and the fuel tank front trim panel (see Chapter 7). Remove the tank prop from the underside of the seat **(see illustration)**. Disconnect the battery (see Chapter 8).

30 Unscrew the bolts securing the front of the tank **(see illustration)**. Raise the front of the tank and place the prop between it and the airbox **(see illustration)**.

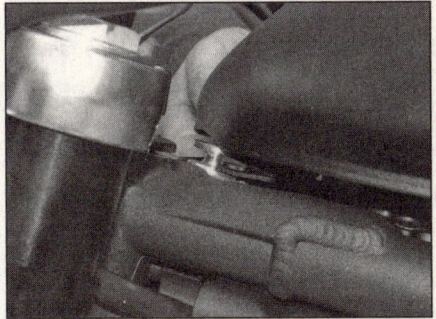

2.25 Note how the tank locates at the front

2.29 Remove the prop

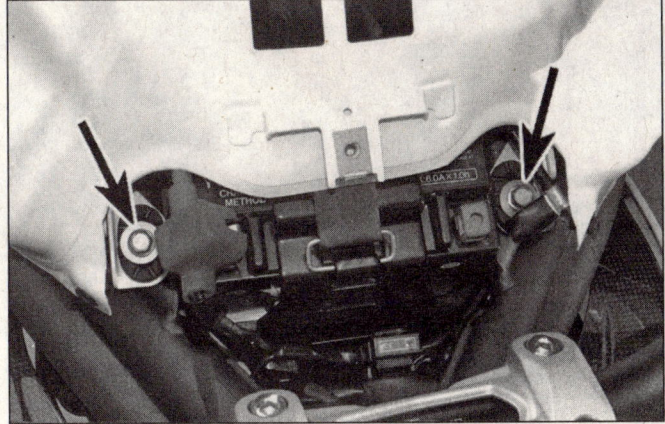

2.30a Unscrew the bolts (arrowed) ...

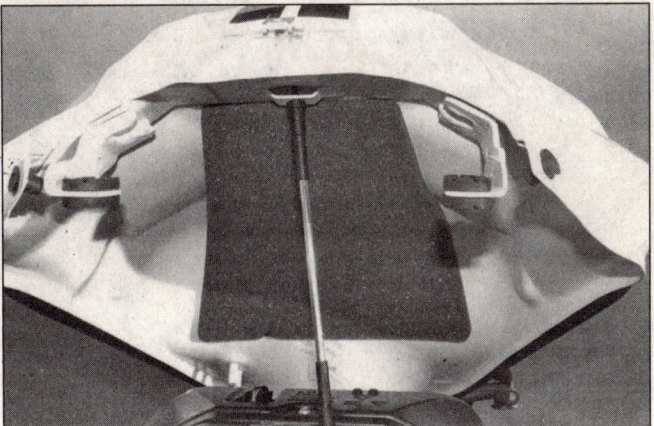

2.30b ... raise the tank and fit the prop

4•6 Engine management system (fuel and ignition)

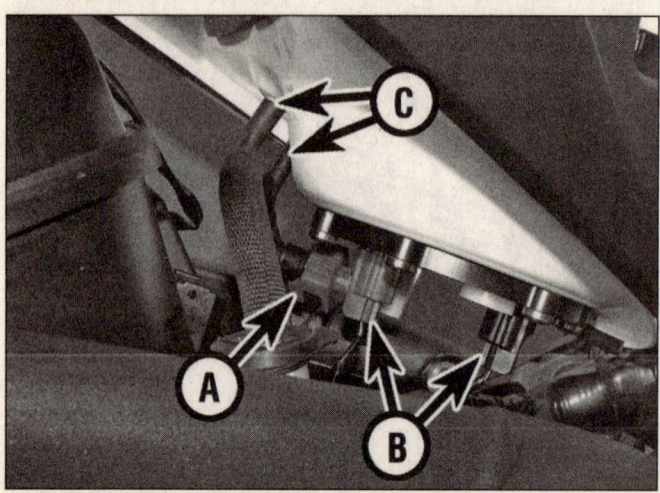

2.31 Fuel hose connector (A), wiring connectors (B), drain and breather hoses (C)

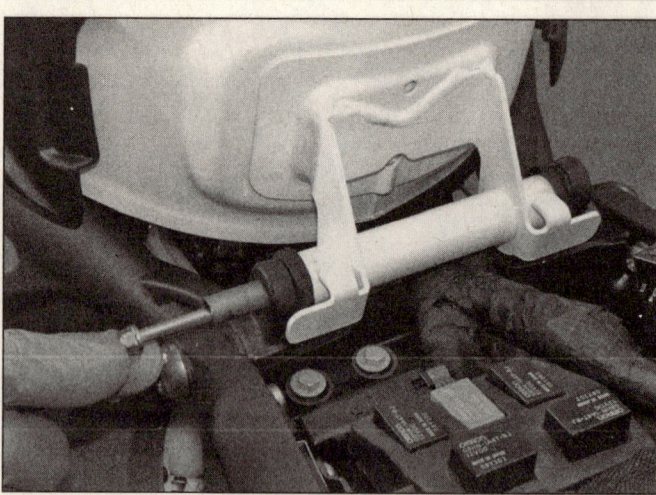

2.34 Remove the rear bolt and its sleeve

31 Slide the fuel hose connector cover down to reveal the clips, then press the clips in and pull the hose off its union **(see illustration)**.

32 Mark each of the wiring connectors and the sockets into which they fit with different markings so each can be returned to the same socket **(see illustration 2.31)**. Disconnect the wiring connectors – one is for the fuel pump and the other for the fuel level sensor.

33 Mark or tag the drain and breather hoses so they can be installed on the correct union **(see illustration 2.31)**. Detach the hoses from the unions.

34 Remove the prop and lower the tank. Unscrew the rear bolt and remove it with its sleeve **(see illustration)**. Carefully lift the tank off the bike and remove it.

35 Inspect the tank support rubbers for signs of damage or deterioration and replace them with new ones if necessary. If required remove the side trim panels (see Chapter 7).

Tiger models

36 Make sure the fuel cap is secure. Have some rag to hand to catch any residual fuel in the connector and its union as the fuel hose is disconnected – the tank and hose are both self-sealing so there won't be much.

37 Remove the seat, the side panels, and the fairing side panels (see Chapter 7). Disconnect the battery (see Chapter 8). Cut the cable-tie securing the wiring to the front of the tank on the right-hand side **(see illustration)**.

38 Unscrew the bolts securing the rear of the tank **(see illustration)**. Unscrew the bolt securing the front of the tank **(see illustration)**. Raise and support the rear of the tank.

39 On models up to VIN 281465 press in the clips on the fuel hose connector and pull the hose off its union **(see illustration)**. On models from VIN 281466 slide the fuel hose connector

2.37 Cut the cable-tie (arrowed) to free the wiring

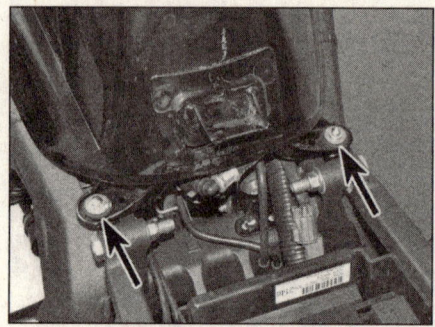

2.38a Unscrew the bolts (arrowed) at the back . . .

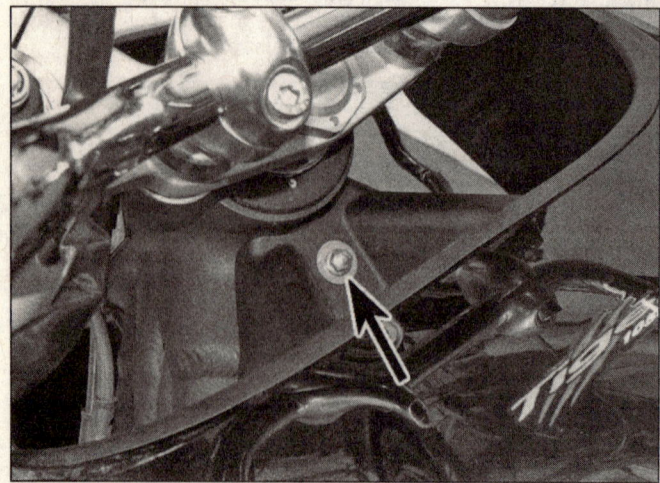

2.38b . . . and the bolt (arrowed) at the front

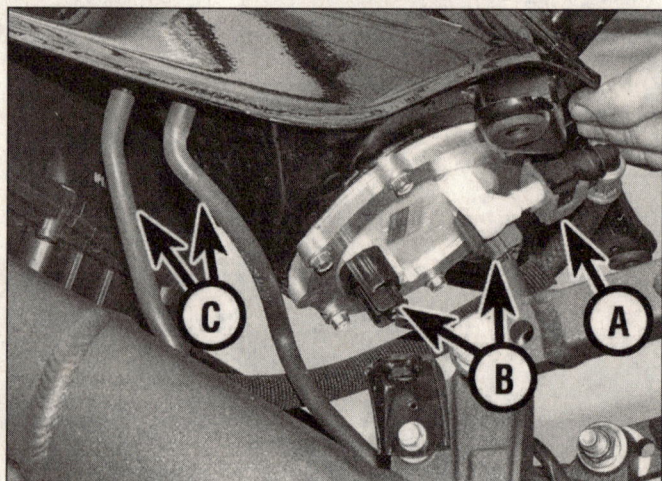

2.39 Fuel hose connector (A), wiring connectors (B – late models), drain and breather hoses (C)

Engine management system (fuel and ignition) 4•7

2.42a Carefully lift the tank off the frame and remove it

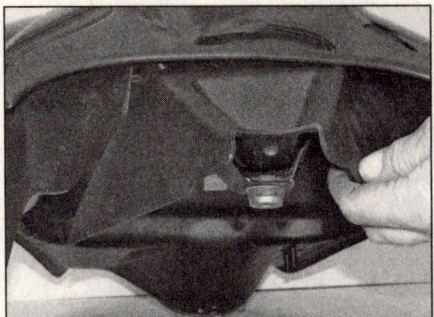

2.42b Remove the trim piece from the front

2.43 Check the tank rubber (arrowed) on each side

cover down to reveal the clips, then press the clips in and pull the hose off its union.

40 Mark each of the wiring connectors and the sockets into which they fit with different markings so each can be returned to the same socket **(see illustration 2.31)**. Disconnect the wiring connectors – one is for the fuel pump and the other for the fuel level sensor.

41 Mark or tag the drain and breather hoses so they can be installed on the correct union **(see illustration 2.31)**. Detach the hoses from the unions.

42 Carefully lift the tank off the bike and remove it **(see illustration)**. Remove the plastic trim piece from the front **(see illustration)**.

43 Inspect the tank support rubbers for signs of damage or deterioration and replace them with new ones if necessary **(see illustration)**.

Installation – all models

44 Installation is the reverse of removal, noting the following:
- Check the condition of all the rubber grommets and supports and replace them with new ones if they are damaged, deformed or deteriorated. Make sure they correctly located before fitting the tank and stay located while fitting it.
- Make sure the fuel hose connector is fully pushed onto the union until the clips locate, then where fitted push the connector cover up.
- Make sure the electrical connectors are secure – on models with two connectors the brown one goes into the right hand socket on the pump on Sprint and Speed Triple models and into the rear socket on Tiger models, the black into the left or front socket accordingly.
- Make sure the drain and breather hoses are secure and fitted to the correct unions. On Speed Triples from VIN 461332 fitted with a belly-pan note that when raising the tank on removal the hoses will have been pulled up – after installing the tank make sure the hoses are correctly re-positioned so the open ends are below the bottom edge of the pan.
- Make sure all collars, sleeves and washers are correctly fitted. Tighten the fuel tank mounting bolt(s) to the torque settings specified at the beginning of the Chapter.
- Before installing the body panels, switch the ignition ON and check that there are no leaks around the hose unions as the pump pressurises.

Cleaning and repair

45 All repairs to the fuel tank should be carried out by a professional who has experience in this critical and potentially dangerous work. Even after cleaning and flushing of the fuel system, explosive fumes can remain and ignite during repair of the tank.

46 If the fuel tank is removed from the bike, it should not be placed in an area where sparks or open flames could ignite the fumes coming out of the tank. Be especially careful inside garages where a natural gas-type appliance is located, because the pilot light could cause an explosion.

3 Airbox

Removal

Sprint, 2005 to 2010 Speed Triple models (up to VIN 461331), Tiger

1 Remove the fuel tank (see Section 2).
2 Release the clip securing the secondary air injection hose to the front of the airbox and detach the hose **(see illustration)** – do this after displacing the airbox to improve access if required.
3 Disconnect the intake air temperature (IAT) sensor wiring connector **(see illustration)**. If required remove the IAT sensor from the airbox (see Section 14). Undo the manifold absolute pressure (MAP) sensor screw, then displace the sensor and free the hose from its guide in the airbox **(see illustrations)**. On

3.2 Release the clip and detach the hose (arrowed)

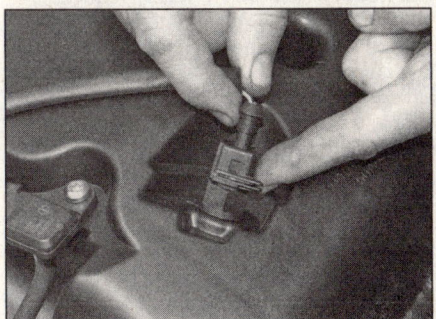

3.3a Push the clip in and disconnect the IAT sensor wiring connector

3.3b Displace the MAP sensor . . .

3.3c . . . and free its hose

3.4 Release the clip and detach the hose (arrowed)

3.5a Unscrew the bolts (arrowed)

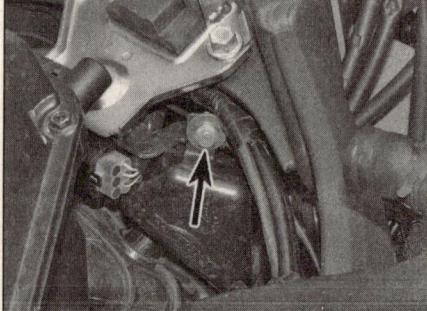

3.5b On Sprint models unscrew the bolt (arrowed)

3.6 Lift the rear of the airbox and detach the hose

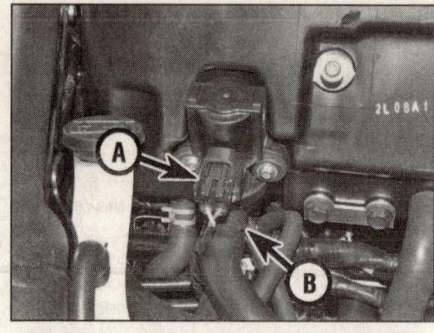

3.9 Disconnect the wiring connector (A) and detach the hose (B)

3.10a IAT sensor wiring connector (arrowed)

Tiger Sport disconnect the immobiliser wiring connector.

4 Release the clip and disconnect the drain hose from the back of the airbox on the left-hand side **(see illustration)**.

5 Unscrew the bolts securing the airbox to

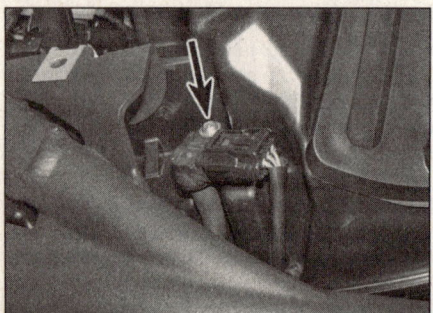

3.10b MAP sensor screw (arrowed)

its bracket at the back **(see illustration)**. On Sprint models unscrew the bolt securing the resonance chamber **(see illustration)**, and the bolt securing the front of the airbox **(see illustration 3.2)**.

6 Self releasing spring clamps are used to

3.11 Immobiliser unit screws (arrowed)

secure the intake ducts to the throttle bodies. Lift up the rear of the box to release it from the throttle bodies, then release the clip and disconnect the crankcase breather hose from the underside of the right-hand rear corner **(see illustration)**. Draw the airbox back and remove it – on Sprint models note how the intake locates in the duct above the radiator, and remove the resonance chamber as well; on Speed Triple and Tiger models note how the peg at the front locates in the grommet on the bracket on the valve cover. Block the throttle bodies with a clean rag to prevent anything falling in.

2011-on Speed Triple models (from VIN 461332)

7 Remove the fuel tank (see Section 2).
8 Remove the battery (see Chapter 8).
9 Disconnect the wiring connector and detach the hose from the secondary air injection control valve on the back of the airbox **(see illustration)**. Remove the valve if required.
10 Disconnect the intake air temperature (IAT) sensor wiring connector **(see illustration)**. If required remove the IAT sensor from the airbox (see Section 14). Undo the manifold absolute pressure (MAP) sensor screw, then displace the sensor and free the hose from its guide in the airbox **(see illustration)**.
11 Undo the immobiliser control unit screws and displace the unit **(see illustration)**.
12 Remove the air filter (see Chapter 1).
13 Release the clips and disconnect the drain hose and crankcase breather hose from the back of the airbox **(see illustration)**.
14 Undo the screws securing the front of the airbox **(see illustration)**.

3.13 Detach the hoses (arrowed)

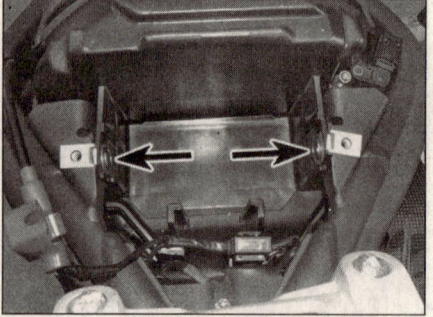

3.14 Undo the front screws (arrowed) . . .

Engine management system (fuel and ignition) 4•9

3.15 . . . and the rear bolts (arrowed) . . .

3.16 . . . and remove the airbox as described

15 Unscrew the bolts securing the rear of the airbox **(see illustration)**.
16 Self releasing spring clamps are used to secure the intake ducts to the throttle bodies. Lift up the rear of the box to release it from the throttle bodies **(see illustration)**. Draw the airbox back and remove it – note how the intake at the front locates in the duct. Block the throttle bodies with a clean rag to prevent anything falling in.

Installation

17 Installation is the reverse of removal, noting the following:
- Do not forget to remove the rag from the throttle bodies.
- Lubricate the inside of each intake adapter lightly with oil or a spray lubricant to ease the fit onto the throttle bodies **(see illustration)**.
- On Sprint models make sure the duct and resonance chamber locate correctly **(see illustration 3.5b)**.
- On Speed Triple models up to VIN 461331 and Tiger models make sure the peg on the front of the box locates correctly in the grommet **(see illustration)**.

- Make sure each duct locates correctly its throttle body all the way round, and that the self gripping spring clamps seat correctly.
- Make sure all hoses and wiring connectors are correctly and securely attached.

4 Fuel pump and relay

⚠ **Warning: Refer to the precautions given in Section 1 before starting work.**

Fuel pump

Check

1 The fuel pump is located inside the fuel tank.
2 The fuel pump runs for a few seconds when the ignition is switched ON, then cuts out when the system is up to operating pressure, and cuts in again when the engine is started. If you can't hear anything, first check the No. 2 fuse on Sprint and Tiger models and the No. 4 fuse on Speed Triple models (see Chapter 8).

Next check the wiring and wiring connectors in the fuel pump and relay circuit, referring to Electrical system fault finding at the beginning of Chapter 8 and to the Wiring Diagram for your model at the end of it. Next, check the relay (see below). If they are all good, remove the pump (see below) and check the internal connections.
3 If the pump still does not work, using a fully charged 12 volt battery and two insulated jumper wires, connect the negative (-) lead to the black wire terminal, then briefly touch the positive (+) lead to the purple/white wire terminal – the pump should operate. If the pump does not operate, replace it with a new one. The pump is controlled by the ECM and its relay, so if the pump, its relay and the wiring are all good, it is possible the ECM or its relay is faulty. Refer to Sections 12 and 13 for further information.
4 If the pump operates but is thought to be delivering an insufficient amount of fuel, first check that the fuel tank breather hose is unobstructed, and that the fuel hose is in good condition and not pinched or trapped.

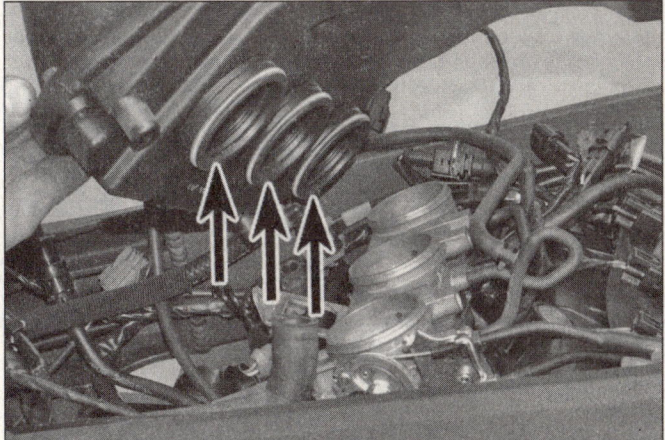

3.17a Lubricate the intake adapters (arrowed) to ease their entry on to the throttle body

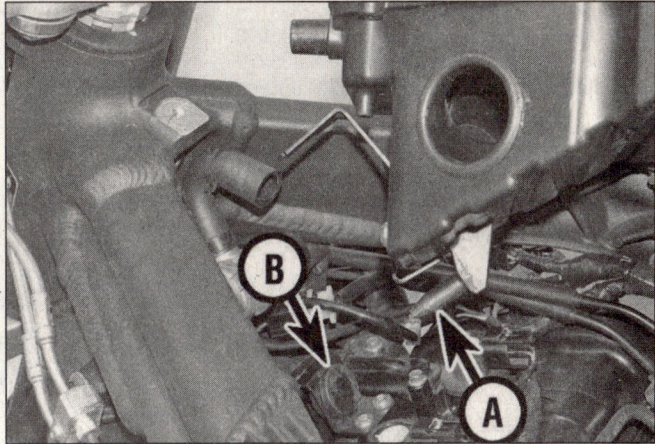

3.17b On Speed Triple and Tiger models locate the peg (A) in the grommet (B)

4•10 Engine management system (fuel and ignition)

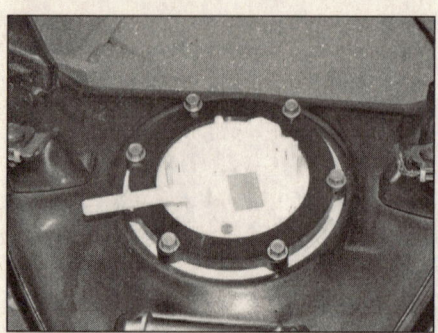

4.6a Fuel pump orientation and mounting bolts – Sprint models

4.6b Fuel pump orientation and mounting bolts – late Speed Triple models

4.6c Fuel pump orientation and mounting bolts – Tiger models

Remove the pump (see below) and check that the fuel strainer and filter are not blocked. Also check the fuel rail and injectors for blockages. If all is good, check the fuel pressure and the pressure regulator (see Section 5).

Removal

5 Make sure the ignition is switched OFF. Using a siphon pump, drain the fuel from the tank into a suitable container. Remove the fuel tank (see Section 2). Turn the tank upside down and rest it on some rag.

6 Note the orientation of the fuel pump and its mounting plate **(see illustrations)**. Unscrew the bolts, then remove the plate and withdraw the pump assembly – on Sprint models with a steel tank, on all Tiger models, and on Speed Triples with a VIN number later than those mentioned in Step 8, disconnect the fuel level sensor wiring connector from the pump when it becomes accessible **(see illustration)**. Remove the pump seal, noting which way round it fits, and discard it as a new one must be used **(see illustration 4.9a)**.

Disassembly

7 On Sprint and Tiger models, and on Speed Triples with a VIN number later than those mentioned in Step 8, the pump assembly comes as a sealed unit for which no individual parts are available. If the pump or one of its components fails the complete unit must be replaced with a new one.

8 On Speed Triple models up to VIN 305059 (Jet black and Neon blue models), VIN 305222 (Roulette green models), or VIN 305251 (Fusion white models) the pump can be disassembled and all individual parts are available for it. How you disassemble the pump depends on which part needs to be replaced: to fit a new level sensor disconnect the wiring connector and undo the screw securing the sensor to the bracket; to fit a new pump disconnect the wiring connector, then undo the fuel pipe bracket screws and release the hose clamps and remove the bracket/pipe and hose together, then remove the pump clamp and remove the pump; to remove the filter undo the fuel pipe bracket screws and release the hose clamps and remove the bracket/pipe/ hoses and filter together, then detach the filter from the hoses; remove the pressure regulator from the union below the fuel filter and discard the O-ring as a new one must be used. Reassemble the pump in reverse order as required, using new parts as required – always use a new O-ring on the pressure regulator. Make sure the filter is installed with the arrow pointing to the mounting base, i.e. in the direction of fuel flow. The blue wiring connector fits into the inner socket.

Installation

9 Installation is the reverse of removal, noting the following:
- Make sure the fuel tank and pump mounting plate mating surfaces are clean.
- On Sprint and Tiger models, and on Speed Triples with a VIN number later than those mentioned in Step 8, fit a new seal onto the pump with the raised lip facing up **(see illustration)**. Manoeuvre the pump into the tank, making sure the seal remains in place and seats correctly – on Sprint models with a steel tank, on all Tiger models, and on Speed Triples with a VIN number later than those mentioned in Step 8, do not forget to reconnect the level sensor wiring connector **(see illustration 4.6d)**. The pump and its mounting plate can only fit one way – the pump has a tab that locates in a cut-out in the plate, and the plate has an offset mounting bolt hole **(see illustration)**. Make sure everything is correctly aligned and seated, then tighten the mounting plate bolts evenly and a little at a time in a criss-cross pattern to the torque setting specified at the beginning of the Chapter **(see illustrations 4.6c, b and a)**.
- On Speed Triple models up to VIN 305059 (Jet black and Neon blue models), VIN 305222 (Roulette green models), or VIN 305251 (Fusion white models) fit a new seal into the groove in the tank. Manoeuvre the pump into the tank with the FRONT arrow facing to the front of the tank, making sure the seal remains in place and the pump seats correctly. Make sure everything is correctly aligned and seated, then tighten the mounting plate bolts evenly and a little at a time in a criss-cross sequence to the torque setting specified at the beginning of the Chapter.
- On completion, start the engine and check carefully that there is no leakage from around the pump mounting plate and from the hose connection.

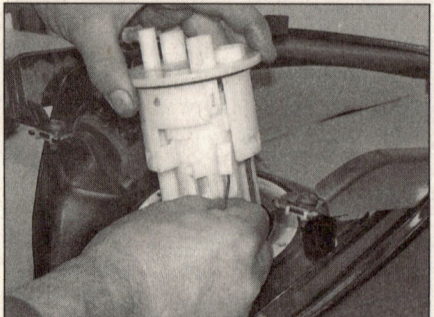

4.6d Disconnect the level sensor wiring connector as you withdraw the pump

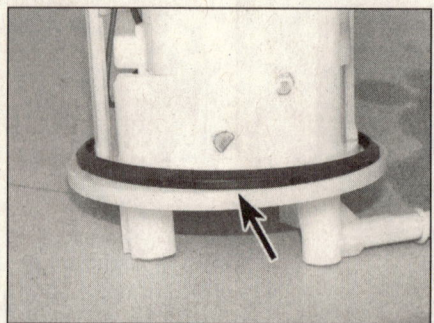

4.9a Fit a new seal (arrowed) and make sure it is the correct way up

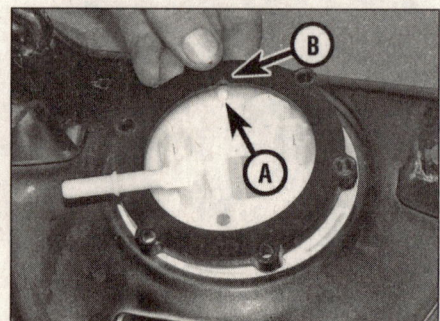

4.9b Locate the tab (A) on the pump in the cut-out (B) in the plate

Engine management system (fuel and ignition) 4•11

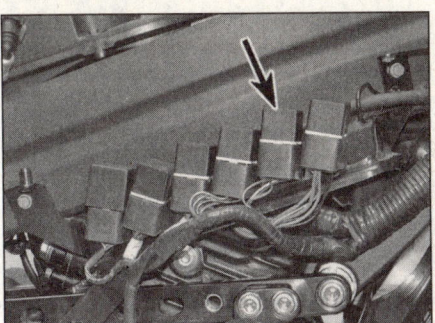

4.10a Fuel pump relay (arrowed) – Sprint ST models

4.10b Fuel pump relay (arrowed) – Sprint GT

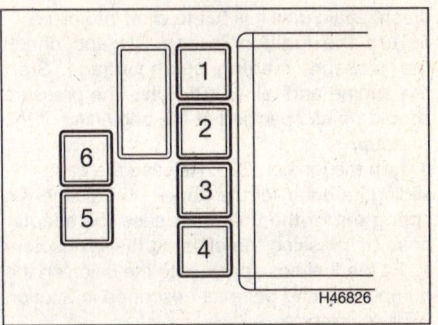

4.10c Relay identification – 2005 to 2007 Speed Triple models

1 Starter relay
2 Headlight relay
3 Engine management system (EMS) relay
4 Turn signal relay
5 Cooling fan relay
6 Fuel pump relay

Fuel pump relay

Check

Note: *Refer to the Wiring Diagrams at the end of Chapter 8 for relay terminal identification.*

10 On Sprint models remove the right-hand fairing side panel, and on Speed Triple and Tiger models remove the seat (see Chapter 7). Disconnect the relay from its connector block **(see illustrations)**. Check the terminals and sockets for damage and corrosion.

11 Each terminal on the relay has a number, either marked next to the terminal on the underside of the relay, or that can be identified using the relevant wiring diagram at the end of Chapter 8 by matching the wire colours marked on the diagram to the wires themselves in the relay socket and their applicable terminals on the relay, according to model. On some models the terminals are numbered 1, 2, 3 and 5, on others they are numbered 1, 4, 6 and 8. Identify the terminal numbers used, then test the relay as follows.

12 Connect a continuity tester or a multimeter set to the ohms x 1 scale between either the No. 3 and No. 5 terminals, or between the No. 1 and No. 8 terminals, according to model – there should be no continuity or infinite resistance. If there is continuity or zero resistance replace the relay with a new one. Leaving the tester or meter connected, connect the positive (+) terminal of a fully-charged 12 volt battery to either the No. 1 or to the No. 6 terminal on the relay, and the negative (–) terminal to either the No. 2 or to the No. 4 terminal on the relay. At this point the relay should be heard to click and there should be continuity or zero resistance shown on the tester or meter. If this is the case the relay is proved good. If the relay does not click when battery voltage is applied and the tester or meter indicates no continuity or infinite resistance, the relay is faulty and must be replaced with a new one. If the relay is good, test the pump (see above).

Removal and installation

13 On Sprint models remove the right-hand fairing side panel, and on Speed Triple and Tiger models remove the seat (see Chapter 7).

14 Disconnect the relay from its connector block **(see illustration 4.10a, b, c, d, e, f or g)**.

15 Plug the new relay into its connector.

5 Fuel pressure and pressure regulator

Warning: *Refer to the precautions given in Section 1 before starting work.*

Fuel pressure check

1 To check the fuel pressure, the Triumph tool (Pt. No. T3880001) is needed. The tool comprises a gauge and two adapter hoses, one marked A, the other marked B. On Speed Triple models up to VIN 305059 (Jet black and Neon blue models), VIN 305222 (Roulette green models), or VIN 305251 (Fusion white models) use the adapter marked A. On Sprint, Tiger and all other Speed Triples use adapter B. A commercial pressure gauge will not be of any use.

2 Make sure the ignition switch is in the OFF position. Raise and support the tank as described for your model in Section 2 so you have access to the underside.

3 Detach the fuel hose from the fuel pump mounting plate as described for your model in Section 2.

4 Fit the union on the gauge joint end of the hose into the fuel hose connector, then fit the connector on the other end onto the union on the pump mounting plate. Press each connector onto its union until it is felt and heard to click into place. Fit the gauge into its

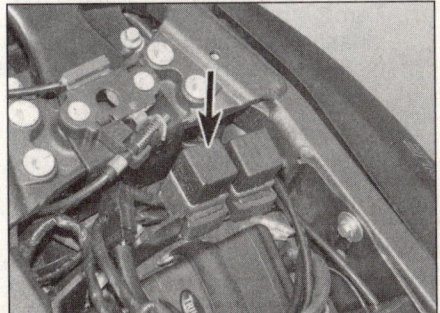

4.10d Fuel pump relay (arrowed) – 2008 to 2010 Speed Triple (up to VIN 461331)

4.10e Fuel pump relay (arrowed) – 2011-on Speed Triple (from VIN 461332)

4.10f Fuel pump relay (arrowed) – Tiger models (except Sport)

4.10g Fuel pump relay (arrowed) – Tiger Sport

union, again until it is felt to click into place.
5 Turn the ignition switch ON and check the pressure reading on the gauge. Start the engine and allow it to idle. The pressure should be as specified at the beginning of the Chapter.
6 Turn the ignition OFF. Release the gauge by sliding its outer ferrule down – the gauge will spring out of the union. Release the adapter hose by pressing the clips on the connectors in. Fit the fuel hose back onto the union on the pump mounting plate as described in Section 2 for your model.
7 If the pressure is too low, either the pressure regulator is stuck open, the fuel pump is faulty, the strainer or filter is blocked, or there is a leak in the system, probably from a hose joint.
8 If the pressure is too high, there could be a blockage, and/or the pressure regulator could be stuck closed, or the fuel pump check valve could be faulty.
9 Refer to the relevant Sections of this Chapter and Chapter 1 and check the possible problems.

Pressure regulator

10 The fuel pressure regulator is incorporated in the fuel pump assembly inside the fuel tank.
11 On Sprint and Tiger models, and on Speed Triples with a VIN number later than those mentioned in Step 12, the pump assembly comes as a sealed unit for which no individual parts are available. If the pressure regulator fails the complete unit must be replaced with a new one.
12 On Speed Triple models up to VIN 305059 (Jet black and Neon blue models), VIN 305222 (Roulette green models), or VIN 305251 (Fusion white models) the pressure regulator can be removed and a new one fitted – refer to Section 4.

6 Fuel level sensor

Warning: Refer to the precautions given in Section 1 before starting work.

Check

1 If the low fuel level warning light fails to come on either when the ignition is first turned on or if the fuel level is low, first check the level sensor and instrument cluster wiring connectors (see Section 6 and Chapter 8 respectively), then check the wiring between the sensor and the instrument cluster for continuity, referring to the Electrical system fault finding at the beginning of Chapter 8 and to the wiring diagrams at the end of it.
2 Triumph provide no test data or procedure for checking the operation of the sensor, but it is safe to assume that if you connect a multimeter set to read resistance (ohms) to the sensor wiring connector, then as the float in the sensor moves up and down the resistance will change – in the case of Sprint and Tiger models with a fuel gauge, the resistance should change gradually as the float moves, while in the case of Speed Triples with only a warning light, there should be infinite resistance when the float is at the top of the sensor, and little or no resistance when it is at the bottom. To perform this test you will have to start with an empty fuel tank, then gradually fill it while watching the reading on the ohmmeter. Remove the appropriate body panels according to your model to gain access to the sensor wiring connector (see Section 2).
3 If the sensor does not behave as described, or if you are in any doubt, remove it from the tank (see below) and check it for damage and wear. Alternatively take it to Triumph dealer for further assessment. If everything appears to be working correctly it is possible the fault lies in the instrument cluster – refer to Chapter 8.

Removal

4 Make sure the ignition is switched OFF. Remove the fuel tank and drain it (see Section 2). Turn the tank upside down and rest it on some clean rag.
5 On Sprint models with a plastic tank unscrew the sensor mounting plate bolts and withdraw the sensor from the tank. Discard the seal as a new one must be used. If required, release the tabs at the top of the sensor tube using a small screwdriver and lift off the cap. Slide out the float, noting how it fits. **Note:** *Be prepared to catch any residual fuel.* Check all components for wear and damage and fit a new sensor if necessary. Slide the float into the tube, ensuring that the small magnet on the bottom of the float faces towards the bottom of the tube. Tilt the sensor tube slowly and check that the float slides freely up and down. Fit the cap and ensure that the tabs lock correctly.
6 On Sprint models with a steel tank, on Speed Triple models with a VIN number later than those mentioned in Step 7, and on all Tiger models, remove the fuel pump from the tank (see Section 4). Press the side locating tangs and release the sensor from its bracket, noting there is also an upper locating tang,

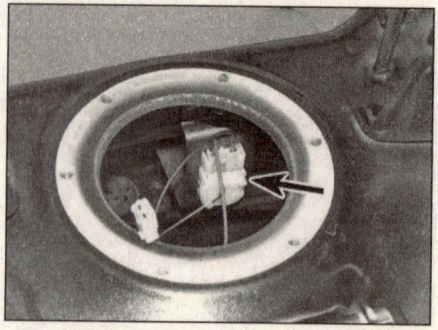

6.6 Fuel level sensor (arrowed)

and carefully draw the sensor out of the tank, taking care not to snag the float arm **(see illustration)**. Check the float for damage, and make sure the arm moves up and down smoothly and freely.
7 On Speed Triple models up to VIN 305059 (Jet black and Neon blue models), VIN 305222 (Roulette green models), or VIN 305251 (Fusion white models) the level sensor is incorporated in the fuel pump assembly inside the fuel tank, but is available separately. Remove the fuel pump assembly from the tank, then remove the sensor from the pump assembly (see Section 4).

Installation

8 Installation is the reverse of removal, noting the following:
● *On Sprint models with a plastic tank make sure the fuel tank and sensor mounting plate mating surfaces are clean. Fit the sensor using a new seal. Tighten the bolts evenly and a little at a time in a criss-cross sequence to the torque setting specified at the beginning of the Chapter.*
● *On Sprint models with a steel tank, on Speed Triple models with a VIN number later than those mentioned in Step 7, and on all Tiger models make sure the three locating tangs all locate correctly to secure the sensor to the bracket.*
● *On all models, after installing the fuel tank, start the engine and check carefully that there is no leakage from around the pump or sensor mounting plate.*

7 Throttle body removal, cleaning, inspection and installation

 Warning: Refer to the precautions given in Section 1 before starting work.

Removal

1 Remove the fuel tank and the airbox (see Sections 2 and 3).
2 On Sprint models remove the fairing side panels (see Chapter 7).
3 Disconnect the throttle position sensor wiring connector **(see illustration)**.

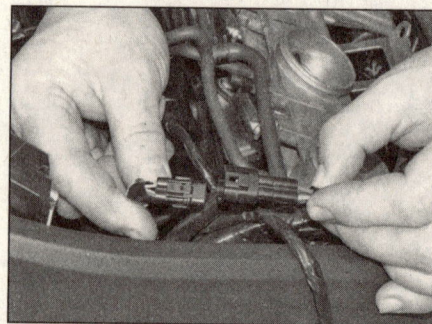

7.3 Disconnect the throttle position sensor wiring connector . . .

Engine management system (fuel and ignition) 4•13

7.4 ... and the idle unit wiring connector (arrowed)

7.5a Slacken the clamps (arrowed) ...

7.5b ... and displace the throttle body

7.6a Undo the screws (arrowed) and detach the bracket ...

7.6b ... then free the cable ends from the cam

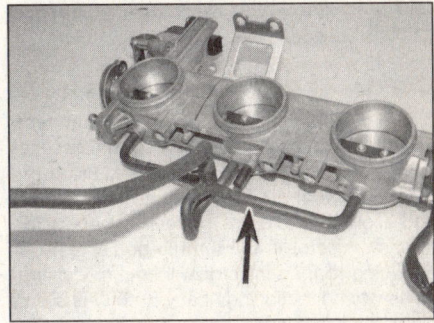

7.8 Remove the MAP sensor hose assembly (arrowed) if required

4 Disconnect the idle air control unit wiring connector **(see illustration)**.

5 Release the clamps securing the throttle body assembly, then ease the assembly out of the intake stubs **(see illustrations)**.

6 Undo the throttle cable bracket screws and detach the cable ends from the cam **(see illustrations)**.

7 Unless you are removing the intake stubs (Step 10) plug them with clean rags to prevent anything dropping inside. Note the location of the clamps on the stubs to aid reassembly.

8 If required, detach and remove the MAP sensor hoses, noting which fits where **(see illustration)**.

9 Do not remove the throttle position sensor or idle air control unit from the throttle bodies unless you know there is a fault and are fitting a new one, or unless you are replacing the throttle bodies with new ones **(see illustrations)**. If you do need to remove either or both, note that correct set-up is essential and can only be done using the Triumph diagnostic tool. There is no alternative, unless you want to run the risk of having the bike running incorrectly. Refer to Section 12 for further information on the engine management section, and to Section 14 for the throttle position sensor and Section 15 for the idle air control valve.

10 If required undo the screws securing each intake stub to the cylinder head and remove them. Discard the O-rings – new ones must be used. Plug the intakes in the cylinder head with clean rag.

Cleaning

Caution: Use only a dedicated spray cleaner (such as a carburettor and injector cleaner) for throttle body cleaning.

11 Spray the cleaner over the throttle bodies to remove any dirt and grime, paying particular attention to the throttle cam assembly and spring. Use a nylon brush if required, but be careful not to embed dirt particles into the cam assembly as this could cause the throttles to stick. Ensure no dirt is lodged in the bores for the throttle body synchronising screws. Take great care not to disturb any screw settings.

12 If you have removed the intake stubs clean them and their mating surfaces on the cylinder head.

Inspection

13 Check the throttle bodies for cracks or any other damage which may result in air getting in.

14 Check that the throttle butterflies move smoothly and freely in the bodies, and make sure that the inside of each body is completely clean.

15 Check that the throttle cable cam moves smoothly and freely, taking into account spring pressure. Clean any grit and dirt from around the cam. Check the spring for signs of damage and distortion.

16 If a body or the butterfly linkage assembly is damaged, the whole assembly must be replaced as individual components are not available.

Installation

17 Installation is the reverse of removal, noting the following:
- *Do not forget to remove the rag from the intakes.*
- *If removed, fit the intake stubs using new O-rings and tighten the screws to the torque setting specified at the beginning of the Chapter.*

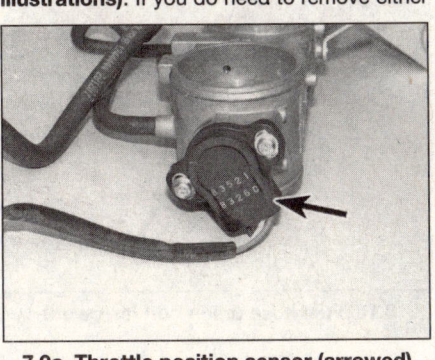

7.9a Throttle position sensor (arrowed)

7.9b Idle air control unit (arrowed)

4•14 Engine management system (fuel and ignition)

- *Connect each MAP sensor hose to its union as noted on removal (see illustration 7.8).*
- *Ensure that the throttle bodies are fully engaged with the intake stubs before tightening the clamps.*
- *Make sure the wiring connectors are reconnected (see illustrations 7.3 and 7.4).*
- *Check the operation of the throttle cables and adjust as necessary (see Chapter 1).*

8 Fuel rail and injectors

 Warning: Refer to the precautions given in Section 1 before proceeding.

Check

1 If the MIL light has come on, and you suspect an injector to be faulty, you can either have a Triumph dealer confirm this using the diagnostic tool, or, if the engine runs, start it and allow it to idle, then check the operation of each injector in the throttle bodies using a sounding rod; an injector will emit a 'clicking' noise when functioning. If any injector is silent, either the injector or its wiring harness is faulty.
2 If the engine does not run, remove the fuel tank (Section 2). Disconnect the wiring connector from each injector (see illustration). Connect an ohmmeter between the terminals of each injector in turn and measure the resistance. Compare the reading for each injector to that given in the Specifications. If the resistance of any injector differs greatly from that specified a new injector should be installed.
3 If the injectors are good check for continuity in the wiring from each injector to the ECM and the EMS (engine management system) relay, referring to electrical system fault finding at the beginning of Chapter 8 and to the wiring diagram for your model at the end of it. If all is good check the EMS fuse (see Chapter 8), the EMS relay (Section 13), then the ECM (Section 12).

Removal

4 Before removing the fuel rail and injectors, disconnect the fuel pump wiring connector (see Section 2), then turn the engine over on the starter for a few seconds – this reduces the pressure in the fuel rail and so prevents the fuel from being sprayed out when the rail is removed or the hose is detached.
5 Remove the fuel tank and the airbox (see Sections 2 and 3). If required, remove the throttle body unit and disconnect the fuel hose from its union on the fuel rail.
6 Release the wiring secured to the fuel rail and disconnect the individual injector wiring connectors (see illustrations).
7 Unscrew the bolts securing the fuel rail to its bracket, then ease the fuel rail and injectors off the cylinder head (see illustration). If required unscrew the bolts and remove the bracket (see illustration).
8 To remove the injectors from the fuel rail, release the clips and carefully pull the injectors out (see illustrations 8.13c and b).
9 Remove and discard the injector O-rings as new ones must be used (see illustration 8.13a).
10 If required undo the screw securing the hose union and remove it from the fuel rail (see illustration 8.10). Discard the O-ring – a new one must be used.
11 Modern fuels contain detergents which should keep the rail injectors clean and free of gum or varnish from residue fuel. Clean the rail in a dedicated cleaner and blow it through with compressed air. If an injector is suspected of being blocked, flush it through with injector cleaner.

Installation

12 If removed, fit the fuel hose union onto the fuel rail using a new O-ring (see illustration 8.10).
13 Fit new O-rings onto each injector (see illustration). Push each injector into the fuel rail, making sure you do not turn it whilst doing so, and that it is properly seated (see illustration). Secure each injector with its clip (see illustration).
14 If removed fit the fuel rail bracket onto the cylinder head (see illustration 8.7b). Fit the fuel rail and injector assembly onto the cylinder head, making sure each injector seats correctly (see illustration). Fit the fuel rail bolts and tighten them to the specified torque setting (see illustration 8.7a).
15 Connect the injector wiring connectors and secure the wiring to the rail as noted on removal (see illustrations 8.6b and a).

8.2 Disconnect the wiring connector and measure the resistance between the terminals (arrowed)

8.6a Cut the cable-ties (arrowed) and free the wiring

8.6b Disconnect the wiring connector from each injector

8.7a Unscrew the bolts (arrowed) and carefully remove the fuel rail with the injectors attached

8.7b Unscrew the bolts (arrowed) and remove the bracket if required

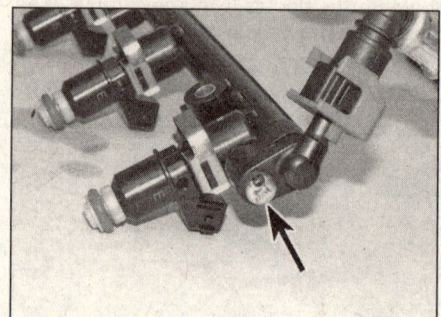

8.10 Fuel hose union bolt (arrowed)

Engine management system (fuel and ignition) 4•15

8.13a Fit new O-rings (arrowed) on each end of the injector

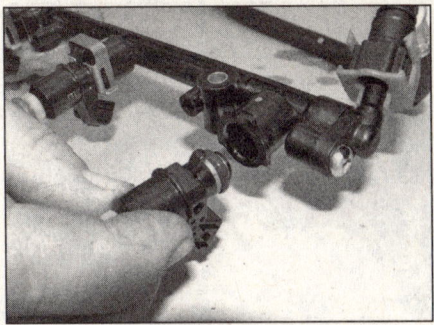
8.13b Fit the injectors into the fuel rail . . .

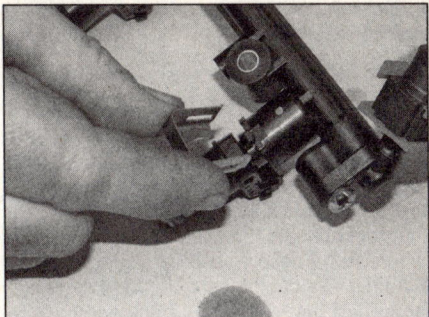
8.13c . . . and secure them with the clips

8.14 Align the fuel injectors and ensure they seat correctly

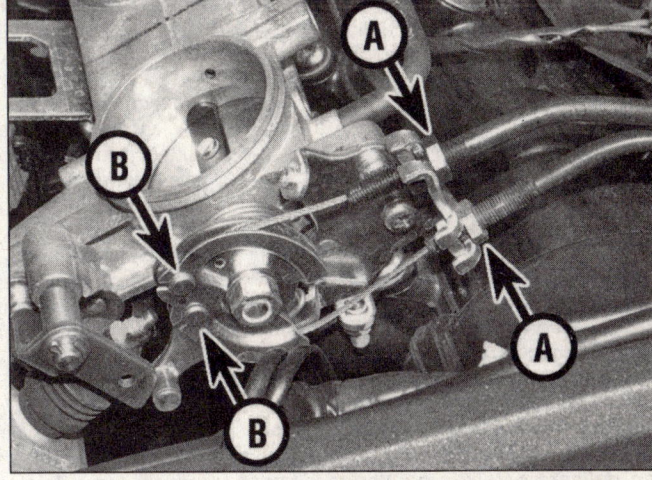
9.2 Fully slacken the locknuts (A), free the cables from the bracket, then detach the ends (B) from the cam

16 If detached connect the fuel hose to its union on the fuel rail.
17 If removed, install the throttle bodies (see Section 7).
18 Install the remaining components in the reverse order of removal.

9 Throttle cable removal and installation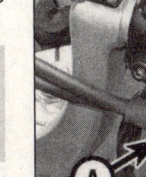

Warning: *Refer to the precautions given in Section 1 before proceeding.*

Removal

1 Remove the fuel tank and the airbox (see Sections 2 and 3). Note the routing of the cables and mark them according to their location at each end.
2 Slacken the locknuts securing the opening and closing cables in the bracket and thread them up **(see illustration)**. Slip the outer cables out of the bracket and detach the inner cable ends from the throttle cam.
3 Pull the rubber boot off the throttle pulley housing on the handlebars, then undo the housing screws **(see illustration)**. Separate the halves, then detach the inner cable ends from the pulley and free the cable elbows, noting how it all fits **(see illustrations)**.

9.3a Pull back the rubber boot (A), then undo the screws (B)

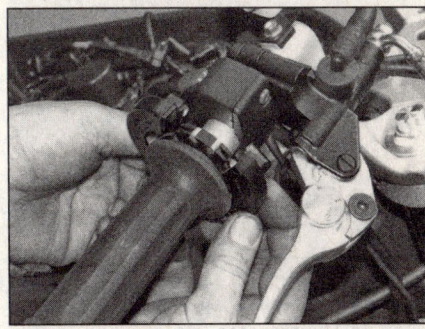
9.3b Separate the housing halves . . .

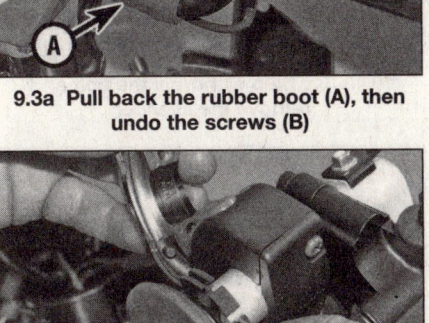
9.3c . . . then free the cable ends from the throttle pulley . . .

9.3d . . . and the elbows from the housings

4•16 Engine management system (fuel and ignition)

4 Remove the cables from the machine noting their correct routing.

Installation

5 Installation is the reverse of removal. If necessary, lubricate the cables (see Chapter 1). Make sure the cables are correctly routed – they must not interfere with any other component and should not be kinked or bent sharply. Lubricate the end of each inner cable with multi-purpose grease.

6 Adjust the cables as described in Chapter 1. Turn the handlebars back and forth to make sure the cables don't cause the steering to bind.

7 Install the airbox and fuel tank (Sections 3 and 2).

8 Start the engine and check that the engine speed does not rise as the handlebars are turned. If it does, correct the problem before riding the motorcycle.

10 Exhaust system

Warning: If the engine has been running the exhaust system will be very hot. Allow the system to cool before carrying out any work.

Caution: The exhaust system incorporates a catalytic converter and oxygen sensor. Take care when handling the downpipe assembly, not to strike or drop it because the delicate catalytic converter element could be damaged.

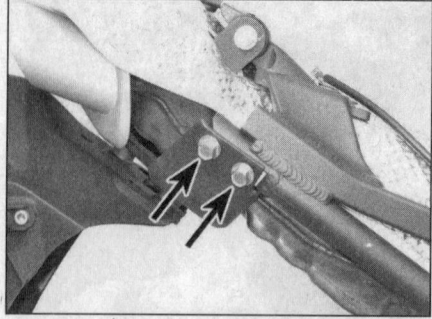

10.2 Unscrew the bolts (arrowed) on each side and detach the rear light assembly

Sprint ST model

Silencer

1 Remove the seat cowling (see Chapter 7).

2 Unscrew the bolts securing the rear light bracket, and with it the pannier slide assembly if fitted, then detach and support the assembly (see illustration).

3 Note the orientation of the clamp securing the silencer to the intermediate pipe and how the tabs locate in the slots, then slacken the bolt (see illustration).

4 Unscrew and remove the nut on the silencer mounting bolt (see illustration). Support the silencer and withdraw the bolt. Draw the silencer out of the intermediate pipe, noting how the front support lugs locate (see illustration). Remove the mounting bolt sleeve and the rubber bushes for safekeeping if required (see illustration).

5 Check the condition of the sealing ring

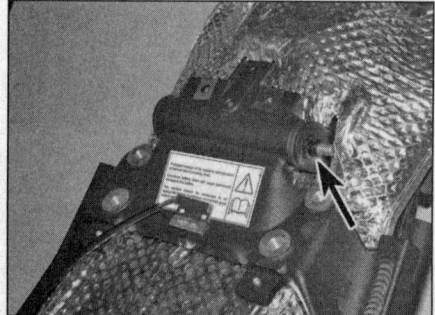

10.4a Unscrew the nut (arrowed) . . .

10.4b . . . then withdraw the bolt and remove the silencer

10.4c Note the rubber bushes (arrowed) and take care not to lose them

10.5 Check the sealing ring (arrowed)

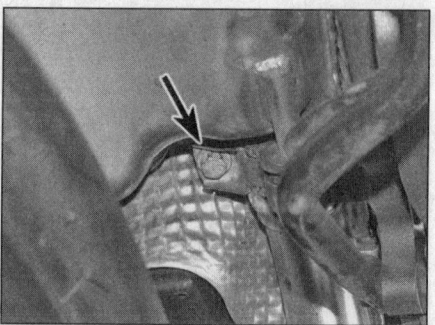

10.3 Slacken the clamp bolt (arrowed)

between the silencer and intermediate pipe and replace it with a new one if necessary (see illustration) – unless it is obviously in need of renewal it is best to leave it in place as it will be ruined when you dig it out.

6 Installation is the reverse of removal. Check the condition of the rubber bushes and replace them with new ones if hardened or cracked (see illustration 10.4c). Fit a new sealing ring into the intermediate pipe if necessary. When inserting the silencer make sure it does not catch on the rim of the sealing ring as it is easily damaged. Make sure the clamp is correctly orientated and located. Tighten the silencer mounting bolt to the torque setting specified at the beginning of the Chapter, then tighten the clamp bolt to the specified torque. Run the engine and check that there are no leaks from the exhaust system.

Intermediate pipe

7 Remove the silencer (see above).

8 Note the orientation of the clamp securing the intermediate pipe to the downpipe assembly, then slacken the bolt (see illustration).

9 Ease the intermediate pipe off the downpipe and manoeuvre it out.

10 Check the condition of the sealing ring between the intermediate pipe and downpipe and replace it with a new one if necessary (see illustration 10.19) – leave it in place if still serviceable.

11 Installation is the reverse of removal. Fit a new sealing ring into the intermediate pipe if necessary. When fitting the pipe make sure the downpipe does catch on the rim of the sealing ring as it is easily damaged. Make sure

10.8 Slacken the clamp bolt (arrowed)

Engine management system (fuel and ignition) 4•17

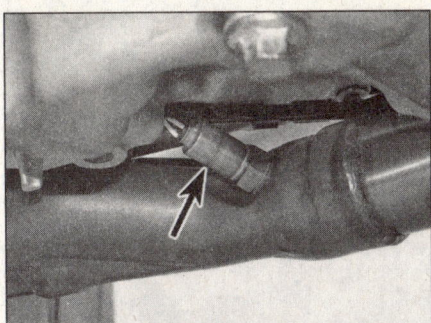
10.14 Oxygen sensor (arrowed)

10.16 Unscrew the bolt (arrowed)

10.17a Unscrew the nuts (arrowed) . . .

10.17b . . . and remove the downpipe assembly

10.18a Remove and discard the gaskets

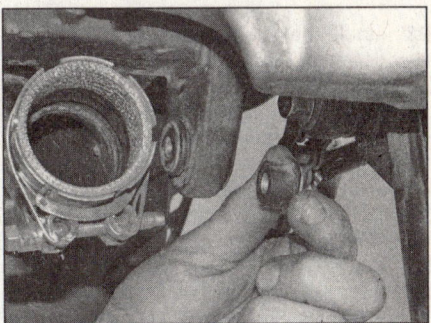
10.18b Remove and check the bushes

the clamp is correctly orientated and located. Tighten the clamp bolt to the specified torque. Run the engine and check that there are no leaks from the exhaust system.

Downpipe assembly

12 Remove the fairing side panels (see Chapter 7). If required remove the silencer and intermediate pipe (see above) – the downpipe assembly can be removed by itself if required, leaving the silencer and intermediate pipe in place, or if you just remove the silencer, the downpipe assembly can be removed with the intermediate pipe attached.
13 Drain the engine oil and coolant (see Chapter 1). Remove the oil cooler (see Chapter 2). Remove the radiator (see Chapter 3).
14 Trace the wiring from the Lambda (oxygen) sensor, freeing it from its guides and any ties, and disconnect it at the wiring connector (see illustration). Feed the wiring back down to the sensor, noting its routing. If required remove the sensor (see Section 14).

15 If required detach the silencer or intermediate pipe, note the orientation of the clamp securing the downpipe assembly to the intermediate pipe, then slacken the bolt (see illustration 10.8).
16 Unscrew the bolt securing the rear of the downpipe assembly, noting the arrangement of the collars and rubber bushes (see illustration).
17 Unscrew the six downpipe assembly nuts from the cylinder head (see illustration). Draw the downpipes out of the cylinder head, and the intermediate pipe if not removed, and remove the assembly (see illustration).
18 Remove the gasket from each port in the cylinder head and discard them as new ones must be fitted (see illustration). Remove the collars and bushes from the rear mounting for safekeeping if required (see illustration). Check the condition of the rubber bushes and replace them with new ones if hardened or cracked.

19 If the silencer or intermediate pipe have been disturbed, check the condition of the joint sealing rings and replace them if necessary (see illustration).
20 Installation is the reverse of removal. Apply a smear of grease to the new gaskets to keep them in place and fit one into each of the cylinder head ports (see illustration). If removed, fit the bushes and collars into the rear mounting (see illustration 10.18b).
21 Manoeuvre the assembly into position so that the head of each downpipe is located in its port in the cylinder head, then locate the rear of the assembly in the intermediate pipe, taking care not to damage the sealing ring, and install the rear mounting bolt, but do not yet tighten it. Fit the downpipe nuts and tighten them in the sequence shown (1 to 6) to the torque setting specified at the beginning of the Chapter (see illustration). Now tighten nuts 1 to 3 again to the same torque setting. Tighten the rear mounting bolt to the specified torque.

10.19 Check the sealing ring (arrowed)

10.20 Smear the gaskets with grease to stop them falling out

10.21 Downpipe nut tightening sequence

4•18 Engine management system (fuel and ignition)

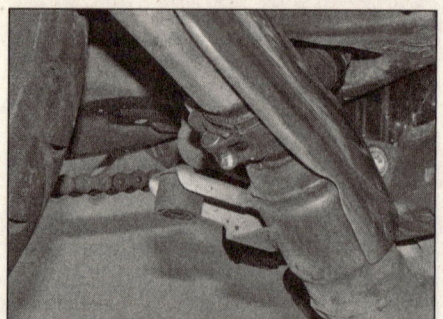

10.27 Slacken the clamp bolt

10.28 Remove the silencer mounting bolt nut then remove the bolt and washer

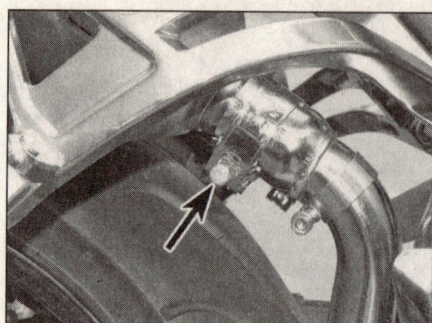

10.33 Slacken the clamp bolt (arrowed) – cover removed

22 Install the oxygen sensor if removed (Section 14). Reconnect the sensor wiring connector.
23 Install the intermediate pipe and the silencer if removed (see above).
24 Install the radiator (see Chapter 3) and the oil cooler (see Chapter 2). Refill the cooling system and replenish the engine oil (see Chapter 1 and *Pre-ride checks*).
25 Run the engine and check that there are no leaks from the exhaust system before installing the fairing side panels.

Sprint GT model

Silencer

26 Remove the right-hand pannier.
27 Note the orientation of the clamp securing the silencer to the downpipe assembly and how the tabs locate in the slots, then slacken the bolt **(see illustration)**.
28 Unscrew and remove the nut on the silencer mounting bolt **(see illustration)**. Support the silencer and withdraw the bolt with its washer. Draw the silencer out of the downpipe assembly. Remove the mounting bolt collar and the rubber bushes for safekeeping if required.
29 Check the condition of the sealing ring between the silencer and downpipe assembly and replace it with a new one if necessary **(see illustration 10.19)**.
30 Installation is the reverse of removal. Check the condition of the rubber bushes and replace them with new ones if hardened or cracked. Fit a new sealing ring into the downpipe if necessary. When inserting the silencer make sure it does not catch on the rim of the sealing ring as it is easily damaged. Make sure the clamp is correctly orientated and located. Tighten the silencer mounting bolt to the torque setting specified at the beginning of the Chapter, then tighten the clamp bolt to the specified torque. Run the engine and check that there are no leaks from the exhaust system.

Downpipe assembly

31 Remove the fairing side panels (see Chapter 7). Remove the silencer (see above). Follow Steps 13 to 25 above, omitting Step 15.

Speed Triple model

Silencers

32 Remove the side panel (see Chapter 7).
33 Note the orientation of the clamp securing the silencer to the intermediate pipe, and on 2005 to 2010 models (up to VIN 461331) how the clamp cover tabs locate, then slacken the bolt, and on 2005 to 2010 models (up to VIN 461331) remove the cover **(see illustration)**.
34 Unscrew the silencer mounting bolt **(see illustration)**. Draw the silencer out of the intermediate pipe. Remove the collars and rubber bushes for safekeeping if required.
35 Check the condition of the sealing ring between the silencer and intermediate pipe and replace it with a new one if necessary – unless it is obviously in need of renewal it is best to leave it in place as it will be ruined when you dig it out.
36 Installation is the reverse of removal. Check the condition of the rubber bushes and replace them with new ones if hardened or cracked. Fit a new sealing ring into the intermediate pipe if necessary. When inserting the silencer make sure it does catch on the rim of the sealing ring as it is easily damaged. Make sure the clamp is correctly orientated and located, and on 2005 to 2010 models (up to VIN 461331) the cover locates correctly. Tighten the silencer mounting bolt to the torque setting specified at the beginning of the Chapter, then tighten the clamp bolt to the specified torque. Run the engine and check that there are no leaks from the exhaust system.

Intermediate pipes

37 Remove the silencers (see above).
38 On 2005 to 2010 models (up to VIN 461331) trace the wiring from the Lambda (oxygen) sensor, freeing it from its guides and any ties, and disconnect it at the wiring connector **(see illustration 10.14)**. Feed the wiring back down to the sensor, noting its routing. If required remove the sensor (see Section 14).
39 Note the orientation of the clamp securing the intermediate pipe to the downpipe assembly, then slacken the bolt **(see illustration)**. On 2011-on models (from VIN 461332), unscrew the bolt securing the intermediate pipe, noting the arrangement of the collars and rubber bushes **(see illustration)**.
40 Ease the intermediate pipe off the downpipe and manoeuvre it out.
41 Check the condition of the sealing ring between the intermediate pipe and downpipe and replace it with a new one if necessary.
42 Installation is the reverse of removal. Fit a

10.34 Silencer mounting bolt (arrowed)

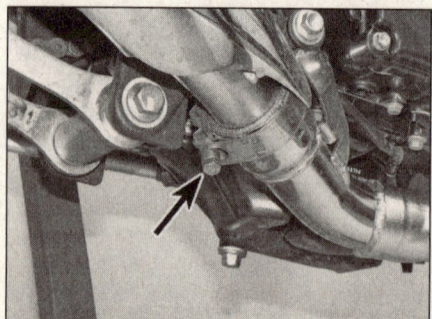

10.39a Slacken the clamp bolt (arrowed)

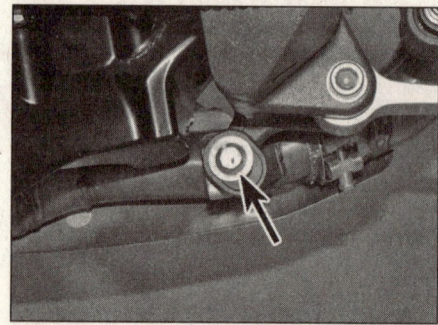

10.39b Intermediate pipe bolt (arrowed)

Engine management system (fuel and ignition) 4•19

10.45a Unscrew the bolts (arrowed) and remove the guide . . .

10.45b . . . and disconnect the connector (arrowed)

new sealing ring into the downpipe assembly if necessary. When fitting the pipe make sure it does not catch on the rim of the sealing ring as it is easily damaged. Make sure the clamp is correctly orientated and located. Tighten the clamp bolt to the specified torque. Run the engine and check that there are no leaks from the exhaust system.

Downpipe assembly

43 If required remove the silencer and intermediate pipe (see above) – the downpipe assembly can be removed by itself if required, leaving the silencer and intermediate pipe in place, or if you just remove the silencer, the downpipe assembly can be removed with the intermediate pipe attached.

44 Drain the engine oil and coolant (see Chapter 1). Remove the oil cooler (see Chapter 2). Remove the radiator (see Chapter 3).

45 On 2011-on models (from VIN 461332), remove the harness guide from the front sprocket cover and disconnect the oxygen sensor wiring connector **(see illustrations)**. Feed the wiring back down to the sensor, noting its routing. On all other models if the intermediate pipe is being removed along with the downpipe assembly, disconnect the Lambda (oxygen) sensor wiring connector (Step 38). On all models, if required remove the sensor (see Section 14).

46 If required and not already done (see Step 39), note the orientation of the clamp securing the downpipe assembly to the intermediate pipe, then slacken the bolt **(see illustration 10.39a)**.

47 Unscrew the bolt securing the rear of the downpipe assembly, noting the arrangement of the collars and rubber bushes **(see illustration)**.

48 Unscrew the six downpipe assembly nuts from the cylinder head **(see illustration 10.17a)**. Draw the downpipes out of the cylinder head, and the intermediate pipe if not removed, and remove the assembly **(see illustration 10.17b)**.

49 Remove the gasket from each port in the cylinder head and discard them as new ones must be fitted **(see illustration 10.18a)**. Remove the collars and bushes from the rear mounting for safekeeping if required. Check the condition of the rubber bushes and replace them with new ones if hardened or cracked.

50 Check the condition of the sealing ring between the silencer and intermediate pipe and replace it with a new one if necessary.

51 Installation is the reverse of removal. Apply a smear of grease to the new gaskets to keep them in place and fit one into each of the cylinder head ports **(see illustration 10.20)**. If removed, fit the bushes and collars into the rear mounting.

52 Manoeuvre the assembly into position so that the head of each downpipe is located in its port in the cylinder head, then locate the rear of the assembly in the intermediate pipe, taking care not to damage the sealing ring, and install the rear mounting bolt, but do not yet tighten it **(see illustration 10.47)**. Fit the downpipe nuts and tighten them in the sequence shown (1 to 6) to the torque setting specified at the beginning of the Chapter **(see illustration 10.21)**. Now tighten nuts 1 to 3 again to the same torque setting. Tighten the rear mounting bolt to the specified torque.

53 Install the oxygen sensor if removed (Section 14). Reconnect the sensor wiring connector.

54 Install the intermediate pipe and the silencer if removed (see above).

55 Install the radiator (see Chapter 3) and the oil cooler (see Chapter 2). Refill the cooling system and replenish the engine oil (see Chapter 1 and *Pre-ride checks*).

56 Run the engine and check that there are no leaks from the exhaust system.

Tiger model

Silencer

57 Remove the seat cowling (see Chapter 7).

58 Note the orientation of the clamp securing the silencer to the downpipe assembly, then slacken the bolt **(see illustration)**.

59 Unscrew and remove the nut on the silencer mounting bolt **(see illustration)** – Triumph specify to discard the nut and use a new one on installation. Support the silencer and withdraw the bolt. Draw the silencer out of the downpipe assembly. Note the arrangement of the collars and the rubber bushes and remove them for safekeeping if required.

60 Check the condition of the sealing ring between the silencer and downpipe and replace it with a new one if necessary.

61 Installation is the reverse of removal. Check the condition of the rubber bushes and replace them with new ones if hardened or cracked. Fit a new sealing ring into the downpipe assembly if necessary. When inserting the silencer make sure it does not catch on the rim of the sealing ring as it is easily damaged. Make sure the clamp is correctly orientated and located. Tighten the new silencer mounting bolt nut to the torque setting specified at the beginning of the Chapter, then tighten the clamp bolt to the specified torque. Run the engine and check that there are no leaks from the exhaust system.

Downpipe assembly

62 If required remove the silencer (see above). Remove the belly pan (see Chapter 7).

63 Drain the engine oil and coolant (see Chapter 1). Remove the oil cooler (see Chapter 2). Remove the radiator (see Chapter 3).

64 Trace the wiring from the Lambda (oxygen) sensor, freeing it from its guides and any ties, and disconnect it at the wiring connector **(see illustration 10.14)**. Feed the wiring back down to the sensor, noting its routing. If required remove the sensor (see Section 14).

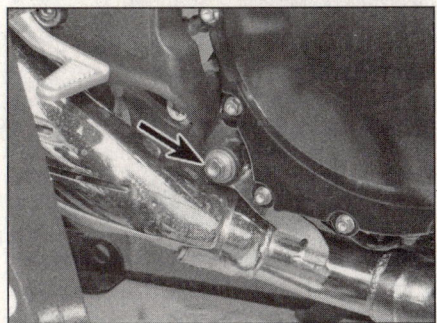

10.47 Unscrew the bolt (arrowed)

10.58 Slacken the clamp bolt (arrowed)

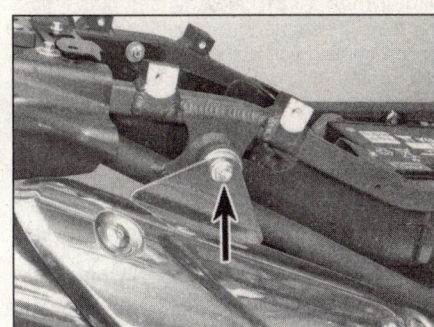

10.59 Silencer mounting bolt (arrowed)

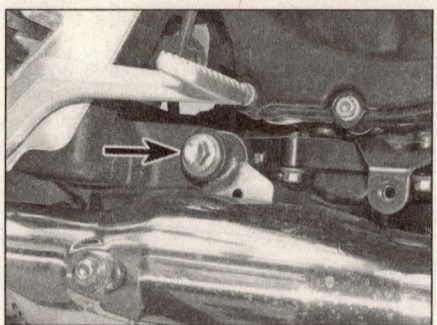

10.66 Unscrew the bolt (arrowed)

11.3 Disconnect the wiring connector . . .

11.4 . . . and pull the coil off the spark plug

65 If the silencer has not been removed, note the orientation of its clamp, then slacken the bolt **(see illustration 10.52)**.

66 Unscrew the bolt securing the rear of the downpipe assembly, noting the arrangement of the collars and rubber bushes **(see illustration)**.

67 Unscrew the six downpipe assembly nuts from the cylinder head **(see illustration 10.17a)**. Draw the downpipes out of the cylinder head, and the silencer if not removed, and remove the assembly **(see illustration 10.17b)**.

68 Remove the gasket from each port in the cylinder head and discard them as new ones must be fitted **(see illustration 10.18a)**. Remove the collars and bushes from the rear mounting for safekeeping if required. Check the condition of the rubber bushes and replace them with new ones if hardened or cracked.

69 Check the condition of the sealing ring between the silencer and downpipe and replace it with a new one if necessary.

70 Installation is the reverse of removal. Apply a smear of grease to the new gaskets to keep them in place and fit one into each of the cylinder head ports **(see illustration 10.20)**. If removed, fit the bushes and collars into the rear mounting.

71 Manoeuvre the assembly into position so that the head of each downpipe is located in its port in the cylinder head, then locate the rear of the assembly in the silencer pipe if it wasn't removed, taking care not to damage the sealing ring, and install the rear mounting bolt, but do not yet tighten it **(see illustration 10.66)**. Fit the downpipe nuts and tighten them in the sequence shown (1 to 6) to the torque setting specified at the beginning of the Chapter **(see illustration 10.21)**. Now tighten nuts 1 to 3 again to the same torque setting. Tighten the rear mounting bolt to the specified torque.

72 Install the oxygen sensor if removed (Section 14). Reconnect the sensor wiring connector.

73 Install the silencer if removed (see above).

74 Install the radiator (see Chapter 3) and the oil cooler (see Chapter 2). Refill the cooling system and replenish the engine oil (see Chapter 1 and *Pre-ride checks*).

75 Run the engine and check that there are no leaks from the exhaust system before installing the seat cowling, fairing side panels and belly pan.

11 Ignition coils

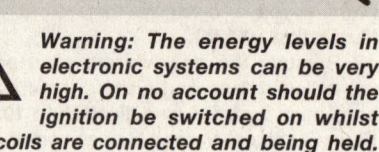

> **Warning:** *The energy levels in electronic systems can be very high. On no account should the ignition be switched on whilst the coils are connected and being held. Shocks from the HT circuit can be most unpleasant. Secondly, it is vital that the plugs are soundly earthed (grounded) when the system is checked for sparking. The ignition system components can be seriously damaged if the HT circuit becomes isolated.*

1 Before testing the coils, check that the spark plugs are in good condition and that the electrode gap is correct (see Chapter 1).

2 If not already done, remove the fuel tank and the airbox (see Sections 2 and 3).

3 Working on one coil at a time, disconnect the wiring connector **(see illustration)**.

4 Pull the coil off the spark plug **(see illustration)**. Reconnect the wiring connector. Fit a new spark plug into the cap and hold the coil so the plug threads are in contact with the engine. Do not hold the plug against an engine cover that is magnesium coated as the coating could be damaged.

> **Warning:** *Do not remove any of the spark plugs from the engine to perform this check – atomised fuel being pumped out of the open spark plug hole could ignite, causing severe injury!*

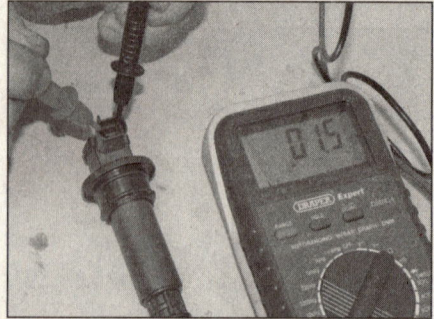

11.8a To test the coil primary resistance, connect the meter as shown

5 Check that the kill switch is in the RUN position and the transmission is in neutral, then turn the ignition switch ON, pull the clutch lever in and turn the engine over on the starter motor. If the system is in good condition a regular, fat blue spark should be evident at the plug electrodes. If the spark appears thin or yellowish, or is non-existent, further investigation will be necessary. Turn the ignition OFF. Repeat the check for the other coils.

6 The ignition system must be able to produce a spark which is capable of jumping a particular size gap. Triumph provide no specification, but a healthy system should produce a spark capable of jumping at least 6 mm. Ignition spark gap testing tools are available from good suppliers – follow the manufacturer's instructions.

7 If the system is in good condition a regular, fat blue spark should be seen to jump the gap on the tool. If the test results are good the entire ignition system can be considered good. If the spark appears thin or yellowish, or is non-existent, further investigation is necessary.

8 Using an ohmmeter or multimeter set to the ohms x 1 scale, measure the primary circuit resistance between the terminals on the coil **(see illustration)**. The resistance should be as specified at the beginning of the Chapter. If not, the coil is faulty and must be replaced with a new one. Set the ohmmeter or multimeter to the K-ohms scale and measure the secondary circuit resistance between one of the terminals on the coil and the plug contact in the base **(see illustration)**. Triumph do not specify a

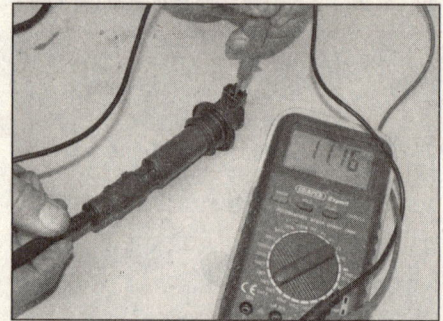

11.8b To test the coil secondary resistance, connect the meter as shown

Engine management system (fuel and ignition) 4•21

resistance but the coil we tested showed just over 11 K-ohms. If the value deviates from this figure by +/- 10%, the coil is faulty and must be replaced with a new one. The coil is a sealed unit and cannot therefore be repaired.

9 If the coils and spark plugs are good, then there is a fault elsewhere in the system. The likely faults are listed below, starting with the most probable source of failure. Work through the list systematically, referring to the subsequent sections for full details of the necessary checks and tests. **Note:** *Before checking the following items ensure that the battery is fully charged and that all fuses are in good condition.*

- Loose, corroded or damaged wiring connections, broken or shorted wiring between any of the component parts of the ignition system – refer to 'Electrical system fault finding' at the beginning of Chapter 8 and to the wiring diagram for your model at the end of it.
- Faulty spark plug, dirty, worn or corroded plug electrodes, or incorrect gap between electrodes (see Chapter 1).
- Blown EMS fuse (see Chapter 8) or faulty EMS relay (see Section 13).
- Faulty ignition switch or engine kill switch (see Chapter 8).
- Faulty clutch, neutral or sidestand switch (see Chapter 8).
- Faulty crankshaft position sensor, incorrect air gap, or damaged triggers.
- Faulty ECM.

10 If the above checks don't reveal the cause of the problem, have the engine management system tested by a Triumph dealer. Triumph produce a diagnostic tool which can perform a complete analysis of the engine management system. Refer to Sections 1 and 12 for more information.

12 Engine management system and electronic control module (ECM)

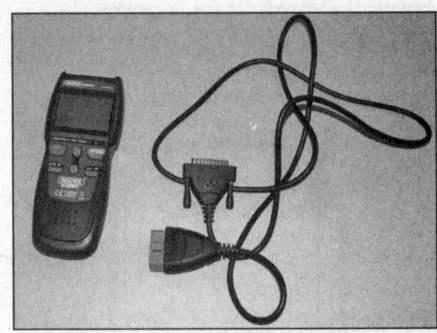

12.1 A typical fault code reader with OBD2 fitting

⚠ **Warning:** *Refer to the precautions given in Section 1 before starting work.*

1 For a general description of the system, see Section 1.

Diagnostic tool and fault codes

2 To diagnose the exact cause of a failure in the system, either the Triumph diagnostic tool or an EOBD (OBD2) fault code reader is essential **(see illustration)**.

3 The ECM has in-built diagnostic functions which record and store all data should a permanent fault occur. Diagnostic trouble codes (DTCs) can then be read using the diagnostic tool, which lists a P-code to indicate the exact fault. Should a fault occur, the malfunction indicator light or symbol (MIL) in the instrument cluster illuminates. If this happens, the management system switches itself into 'limp home' mode, so that in theory you should not be left stranded. Depending on the problem, it is possible that you will notice no difference in the running of the motorcycle.

4 The socket for the diagnostic tool is located under the seat. With the ignition off, plug the code reader into the socket. Turn the ignition on and allow the code reader to process any stored fault codes – these will be displayed as a four digit number prefixed by the letter P. Turn off the ignition and disconnect the code reader once the P-code has been noted. Refer to the accompanying table to link the code with the faulty circuit. Once the fault has been rectified the code reader can be used to delete the stored code from the ECM's memory.

5 If you don't have access to a code reader it is possible to perform certain tests and checks to identify a particular fault, but the difficulty is knowing in which part of the system the fault has occurred, and therefore where to start

P-code	Circuit affected
P0201	Injector cyl 1 circuit fault – misfire = open circuit, flooding = short circuit
P0202	Injector cyl 2 circuit fault – misfire = open circuit, flooding = short circuit
P0203	Injector cyl 3 circuit fault – misfire = open circuit, flooding = short circuit
P0030	Oxygen sensor heater – circuit fault
P0031	Oxygen sensor heater – open circuit to battery/short to earth
P0032	Oxygen sensor heater – short circuit to battery
P0107	MAP sensor low voltage
P0108	MAP sensor high voltage
P0112	Intake air temperature too high
P0113	Intake air temperature too low
P0117	Engine coolant temperature too high – sensor short circuit to earth
P0118	Engine coolant temperature too low – sensor open circuit or short circuit to battery+
P0122	Throttle position sensor low input – short to earth or open circuit
P0123	Throttle position sensor high input – short to sensor supply
P0130	Oxygen sensor cyl 1 circuit fault

P-code	Circuit affected
P0335	Crankshaft position sensor circuit fault
P0351	Ignition coil circuit fault cyl 1
P0352	Ignition coil circuit fault cyl 2
P0353	Ignition coil circuit fault cyl 3
P0413	SAIS solenoid valve short circuit to earth or open circuit
P0414	SAIS solenoid valve short circuit to battery
P0444	EVAP purge control valve short circuit to earth or open circuit
P0445	EVAP purge control valve short circuit to battery
P0460	Fuel level sensor circuit fault
P0500	Speed (speedometer) sensor fault or ABS sensor fault
P0505	Idle speed control system fault
P0560	Motorcycle voltage system fault
P0603	EEPROM fault
P0616	Starter relay coil short circuit to earth or open circuit
P0617	Starter relay short circuit to battery+
P0685	EMS relay fault
P1105	MAP sensor vacuum hose fault
P1107	Ambient air pressure sensor circuit low voltage
P1108	Ambient air pressure sensor circuit high voltage

P-code	Circuit affected
P1231	Fuel pump short circuit to earth or open circuit
P1232	Fuel pump relay short circuit to battery+
P1508	Immobiliser (or tyre pressure sensor system) and ECM unmatched
P1520	ABS modulator ID incompatible
P1521	No signal to ABS modulator
P1552	Cooling fan – short or open circuit
P1553	Cooling fan – short to battery voltage/over temperature
P1614	ECM and instruments incorrect matched
P1631	Tip-over sensor circuit low voltage
P1632	Tip-over sensor circuit high voltage
P1650	No signal between immobiliser (or tyre pressure sensor system) and ECM
P1659	Ignition voltage input circuit fault
P1690	CAN-bus network communication fault between ECM and instruments
P1695	No signal to instrument cluster
P1696	5 volt sensor supply circuit – short circuit to earth
P1697	5 volt sensor supply circuit – short circuit to Vbat (battery voltage)
P1698	5 volt sensor supply circuit fault

4•22 Engine management system (fuel and ignition)

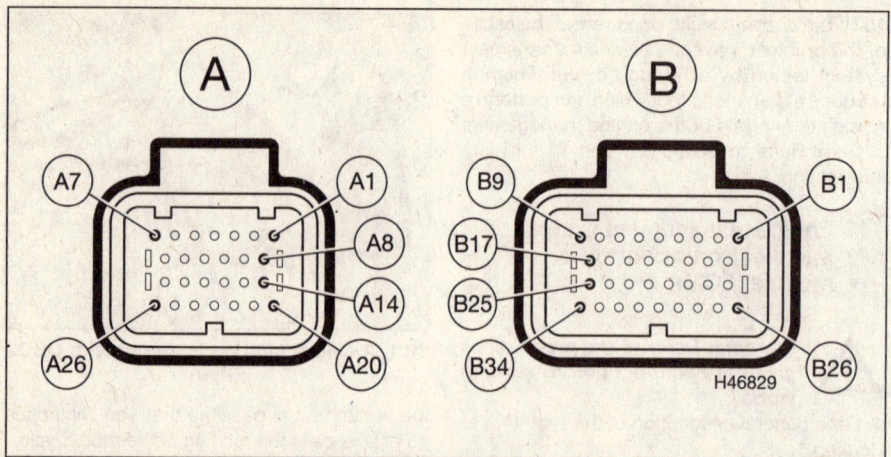

12.8a ECM wiring connector pin identification – Sprint and Speed Triple models up to VIN 281465

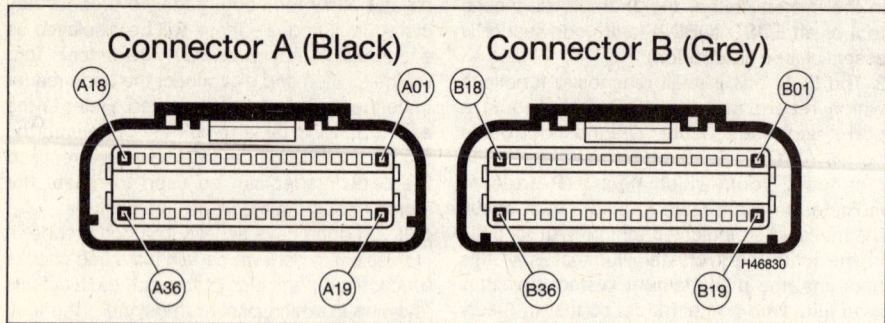

12.8b ECM wiring connector pin identification – Sprint and Speed Triple models from VIN 281466, and all Tiger models

Fault tracing

Note: *Refer to 'Electrical system fault finding' at the beginning of Chapter 8 and to the wiring diagram for your model at the end of it.*

6 Two different electronic control modules (ECM) have been used on the Sprint and Speed Triple models (the early type up to VIN 281465, the later from VIN 281466-on), with the later type also used on all Tiger models, though overall their function is very similar. They are distinguishable by their different connectors **(see illustrations 12.8a and b)**.

7 If a fault is indicated, check the wiring and connectors to and from the ECM (electronic control module) and the various sensors and all their related components – see the relevant Step below according to model for access to the ECM and its connectors. It may be that a connector is dirty or corroded or has come loose – a dirty or corroded terminal or connector will affect the resistance in that circuit, which will upset the information going to the ECM, and therefore affect the decisions it makes in controlling the system. Triumph recommends that the ECM and main wiring loom connector pins are lightly coated with petroleum jelly (e.g. Vaseline) to deter corrosion.

8 A wire could be pinched and is shorting out – a continuity test of all wires from connector to connector will locate this. Albeit a fiddly and laborious task, the only way to determine any wiring faults is to systematically work through the Wiring Diagrams at the end of Chapter 8 and test each individual wire and connector for continuity – all wires are colour-coded. When making continuity checks, isolate the wire being tested by disconnecting the wiring connectors at each end. The Wiring Diagrams show the terminal identification for each wire on the ECM with the letter given on the wiring diagram indicating the relevant ECM connector, and the number referring to the terminal within that connector, as shown **(see illustrations)** – match these to the terminals on the ECM connector(s) when making the tests.

9 If all the wiring and connectors appear good, remove the relevant sensor and make sure its sensing tip or head is clean and undamaged, as this can often be the cause of inaccurate signals being sent to the ECM.

ECM removal and installation

10 Disconnect the battery (see Chapter 8).
11 On Sprint ST models remove the left-hand fairing side panel (see Chapter 7). Unscrew the bolts securing the bracket and remove the bracket, then disconnect the wiring connectors and remove the ECM **(see illustration)**.
12 On Sprint GT models remove the seat (see Chapter 7). Release the battery strap, then lift the ECM and disconnect the wiring connectors **(see illustration)**.
13 On 2005 to 2010 Speed Triple models (up to VIN 416331) remove the coolant reservoir (see Chapter 3). Displace the ECM and disconnect the wiring connectors **(see illustration)**.
14 On 2011-on Speed Triple models (from

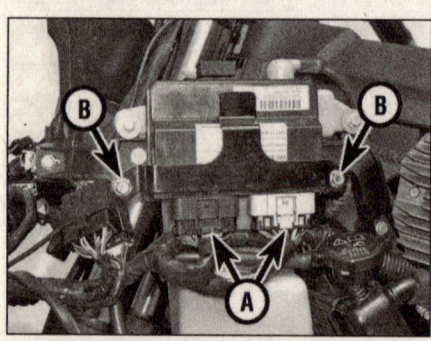

12.11 ECM wiring connectors (A) and bracket bolts (B) – Sprint ST models

12.12 ECM (arrowed) is retained by battery strap – Sprint GT

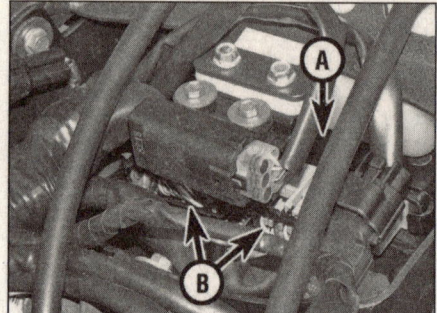

12.13 The ECM (A) is under the reservoir, and the wiring connectors (B) are under the tip-over sensor

Engine management system (fuel and ignition) 4•23

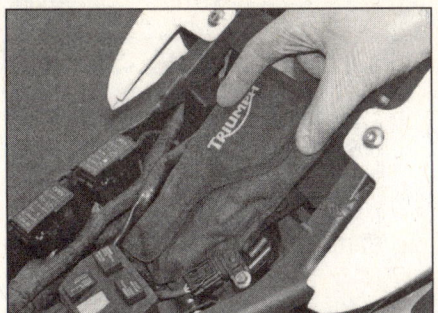

12.14a Remove the toolkit . . .

12.14b . . . and displace the connector . . .

12.14c . . . and the relays . . .

VIN 416332) remove the toolkit **(see illustration)**. Displace the diagnostic connector **(see illustration)**. Displace the relays, noting which fits where **(see illustration)**. If a security clamp is fitted around the ECM black wiring connector carefully drill the head off the shear bolt. Release the trim clips and remove the ECM cover **(see illustration)**. Displace the ECM, remove the security clamp if fitted, and disconnect the wiring connectors.

15 On Tiger models (except Sport) remove the seat (see Chapter 7). Lift the ECM out of its holder and disconnect the wiring connectors **(see illustration)**.

16 On Tiger Sport models remove the seat and seat cowling (see Chapter 7). Undo the atmospheric pressure sensor screw **(see illustration)**. Release the fusebox/relay tray trim clips **(see illustration)**. Displace the starter solenoid and disconnect its wiring connector **(see illustration)**. Lift the right-hand

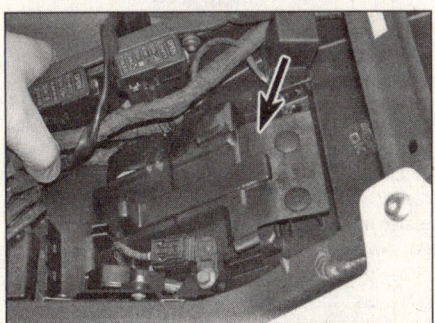

12.14d . . . then remove the ECM cover (arrowed)

side of the tray and release the tabs on the left from the slots, then hold the tray up at the back, lift the ECM out and disconnect the wiring connectors **(see illustrations)**.

17 Installation is the reverse of removal. Check the terminal pins and connectors for

12.15 Lift the ECM out to access the wiring connectors – Tiger (except Sport)

damage and corrosion. On models with a security clamp fit a new shear bolt and tighten it until the head shears off.

13 EMS relay

Note: Before disconnecting the relay, make sure the ignition is switched OFF, then remove the seat(s) (see Chapter 7) and disconnect the battery (see Chapter 8). Refer to the Wiring Diagrams at the end of Chapter 8 for relay terminal identification.

1 The engine management system (EMS) has its own power relay which is designed to provide a steady voltage supply to the ECM. The ECM holds the relay open after the ignition is switched off to enable it perform various power-down functions, such as writing data to the memory, referencing the position of the

12.16a Undo the AP sensor screw (arrowed) . . .

12.16b . . . then release the trim clips (arrowed)

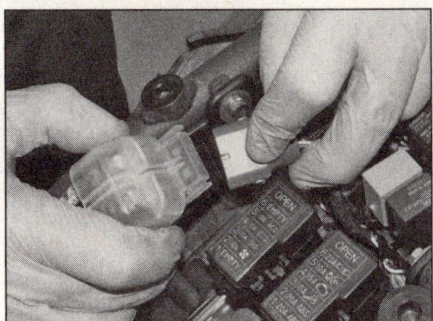

12.16c Displace the solenoid and disconnect the connector

12.16d Lift the tray and release the tabs from the slots (arrowed) . . .

12.16e . . . and hold it up to remove the ECM (arrowed)

4•24 Engine management system (fuel and ignition)

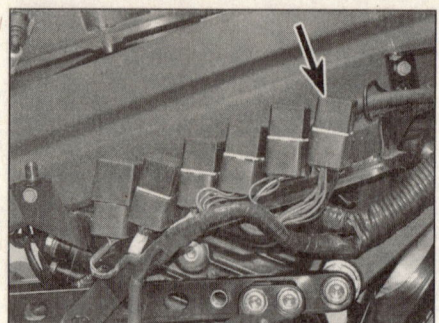

13.2a EMS relay (arrowed) – Sprint ST models

13.2b EMS relay (arrowed) – Sprint GT models

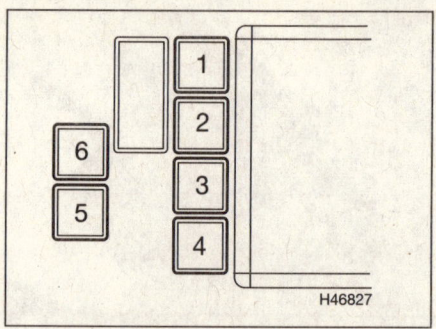

13.2c Relay identification – 2005 to 2007 Speed Triple models

1 Starter relay
2 Headlight relay
3 Engine management system (EMS) relay
4 Turn signal relay
5 Cooling fan relay
6 Fuel pump relay

idle air control valve, and if necessary, running the cooling fan.

Check

2 On Sprint ST models remove the right-hand fairing side panel, and on Sprint GT, Speed Triple and Tiger models remove the seat (see Chapter 7). Disconnect the relay from its connector block **(see illustrations)**. Check the terminals and sockets for damage and corrosion.

3 Each terminal on the relay has a number, either marked next to the terminal on the underside of the relay, or that can be identified using the relevant wiring diagram at the end of Chapter 8 by matching the wire colours marked on the diagram to the wires themselves in the relay socket and their applicable terminals on the relay, according to model. On some models the terminals are numbered 1, 2, 3 and 5, on others they are numbered 1, 4, 6 and 8. Identify the terminal numbers used, then test the relay as follows: connect a continuity tester or a multimeter set to the ohms x 1 scale between either the No. 3 and No. 5 terminals, or between the No. 1 and No. 8 terminals, according to model – there should be no continuity or infinite resistance. If there is continuity or zero resistance replace the relay with a new one. Leaving the tester or meter connected, connect the positive (+) terminal of a fully-charged 12 volt battery to either the No. 1 or to the No. 6 terminal on the relay, and the negative (–) terminal to either the No. 2 or to the No. 4 terminal on the relay. At this point the relay should be heard to click and there should be continuity or zero resistance shown on the tester or meter. If this is the case the relay is proved good. If the relay does not click when battery voltage is applied and the tester or meter indicates no continuity or infinite resistance, the relay is faulty and must be replaced with a new one. If the relay is good, test the fan motor (see Step 3).

Removal and installation

4 On Sprint ST models remove the right-hand fairing side panel, and on Sprint GT, Speed Triple and Tiger models remove the seat (see Chapter 7).

5 Disconnect the relay from its connector block **(see illustration 13.2a, b, c, d, e, f or g)**.

14 Sensors

Note: *Before disconnecting the wiring connector from any sensor, make sure the ignition is switched OFF, then remove the seat (see Chapter 7) and disconnect the battery (see Chapter 8).*

Atmospheric pressure sensor

Function

1 The sensor reads the pressure of the atmospheric (barometric) pressure (i.e. air density). The ECM combines this with other information to determine fuelling requirements.

Removal and installation

2 On Sprint models the sensor is located behind the steering head **(see illustration)** –

13.2d EMS relay (arrowed) – 2008 to 2010 Speed Triple (up to VIN 461331)

13.2e EMS relay (arrowed) – 2011-on Speed Triple models (from VIN 461332)

13.2f EMS relay (arrowed) – Tiger models (except Sport)

13.2g EMS relay (arrowed) – Tiger Sport

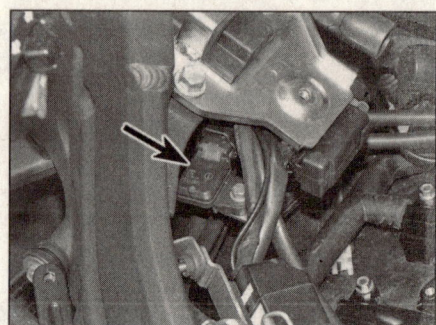

14.2a Atmospheric pressure sensor (arrowed) – Sprint models

remove the fuel tank for access (see Section 2). On Speed Triple and Tiger Sport models the sensor is located under the seat **(see illustrations)** – remove the seat for access (see Chapter 7). On all other Tiger models the sensor is under the battery – remove the battery for access (see Chapter 8).
3 Disconnect the wiring connector from the sensor, then undo the screw securing it. Installation is the reverse of removal.

Crankshaft position sensor

Function

4 The sensor reads the position of the crankshaft and how fast it is turning; this information is used by the ECM to determine which cylinder is on its ignition stroke and when it should fire. The ECM combines engine speed with information from other sensors to determine fuelling and ignition requirements.

Test, removal and installation

5 The crankshaft position sensor is located on the left-hand side of the crankcase **(see illustration)**. On Sprint models remove the left-hand fairing side panel (see Chapter 7).
6 To check the sensor, first make sure the ignition is switched OFF, then trace the wiring from the sensor and disconnect it at the connector. Using an ohmmeter or multimeter set to the K-ohms scale, measure the resistance between the terminals on the sensor side of the connector. If the result is as specified, check that there is no continuity between each terminal and earth (ground).
7 Remove the alternator cover (see Chapter 8). Inspect the sensor and the sensor triggers on the alternator rotor for damage **(see illustration)**. Use a feeler gauge to measure the air gap between the sensor and the triggers and compare the result with the Specifications at the beginning of the Chapter. The air gap is not adjustable. Install the alternator cover (see Chapter 8).
8 If the sensor is faulty, replace it with a new one.
9 Undo the sensor mounting plate screw and remove the sensor, noting how the plate locates **(see illustration 14.5)**. Discard the O-ring as a new one must be fitted.

14.2b Atmospheric pressure sensor (arrowed) – Speed Triple models

10 Fit a new O-ring onto the sensor and smear it with oil. Fit the mounting plate in the slot in the sensor body, then fit the sensor and tighten the bolt to the torque setting specified at the beginning of the chapter. Reconnect the wiring connector.

Engine coolant temperature sensor

Function

11 The sensor reads the temperature of the engine coolant, and the ECM uses the information to determine fuelling requirements, particularly for hot and cold starting.

Test

12 The sensor is located in the left-hand side of the cylinder head **(see illustration)**.
13 Make sure the ignition is switched OFF. Remove the airbox (see Section 3).
14 To test the sensor resistance, trace the wiring from the sensor and disconnect the wiring connector. Measure the resistance between the sensor terminals using an ohmmeter or multimeter set to the relevant scale for the temperature of the engine if warm, or the air if the engine is cold – see Specifications. If the result is not as specified, the sensor is faulty.

Removal and installation

15 The sensor is located in the left-hand side of the cylinder head **(see illustration 14.12)**. Drain the cooling system (see Chapter 1). Remove the airbox (see Section 3). Trace the

14.2c Atmospheric pressure sensor (arrowed) – Tiger Sport

wiring from the sensor and disconnect the wiring connector.
16 Pull the rubber boot back and unscrew the sensor from the cylinder head. Discard the sealing washer as a new one must be used. Fit a new sealing washer onto the sensor, then thread it into the head and tighten it.
17 Reconnect the wiring connector, then fill the cooling system (see Chapter 1).
18 Install the airbox (see Section 3).

Intake air temperature sensor

Function

19 The sensor reads the temperature of the air in the airbox. As changes in temperature affect air density, the ECM uses the information to determine fuelling requirements.

Test, removal and installation

20 The sensor is threaded into the airbox **(see illustration 3.3a or 3.10a)**. Make sure the ignition is switched OFF. Remove the fuel tank (see Section 2).
21 To test the sensor resistance, disconnect the wiring connector and measure the resistance between the sensor terminals using an ohmmeter or multimeter set to the K-ohms scale. If the result is not as specified for the relevant temperature, the sensor is faulty.
22 To remove the sensor, unscrew it from the airbox. Installation is the reverse of removal.

Manifold absolute pressure sensor

Function

23 The sensor reads the pressure of the air

14.5 Crankshaft position sensor (arrowed)

14.7 Check the sensor tip (arrowed) and the triggers, and make sure the air gap between them is correct

14.12 Engine coolant temperature sensor (arrowed)

4•26 Engine management system (fuel and ignition)

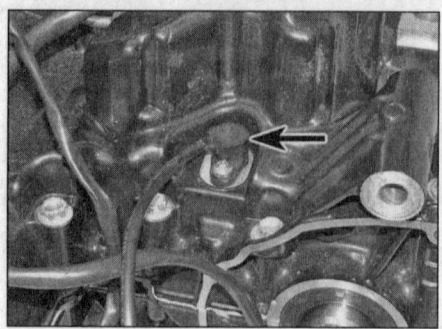

14.29 Speed sensor (arrowed)

in the throttle bodies. The ECM combines this with other information to determine engine load and adjusts fuelling requirements accordingly.

Removal and installation

24 The sensor is mounted on the airbox **(see illustration 3.3b or 3.10b)**. Make sure the ignition is switched OFF. Remove the fuel tank (see Section 2). Disconnect the wiring connector from the sensor, then undo the screw securing it to the airbox and disconnect the hose. Installation is the reverse of removal.

Oxygen (lambda) sensor
Function

25 The sensor measures oxygen left in the unburnt exhaust gases and generates a signal voltage which is fed back to the ECM. In this way the ECM can correct the mixture supplied to the engine to ensure that the oxygen content of the exhaust gases remains within a narrow range and suitable for the operation of the catalytic converter. This type of system is called closed-loop control.

Removal and installation

26 On Sprint and Tiger models, the sensor is located at the 3-into-1 junction in the exhaust downpipe assembly **(see illustration 10.14)**. On Speed Triple models, the sensor is located in the front of the intermediate pipe, just before it divides. Remove the downpipe assembly or intermediate pipe according to model (see Section 10).

27 To remove the sensor, unscrew it from the downpipe or intermediate pipe – the sensor and catalytic converter are fragile so care must be taken not to apply undue force. If the sensor is difficult to unscrew or the area around it is badly corroded, apply a penetrating fluid. When installing the sensor, apply copper grease to the sensor threads and tighten it to the torque setting specified at the beginning of the Chapter – a special tool is required for this because of the wiring.

Speed sensor
Function

28 The sensor reads the road speed of the bike by counting the rate at which the transmission output shaft is turning. This information is used by the ECM in conjunction with engine speed information to determine which gear the bike is in, and controls fuelling and ignition accordingly. The information also helps to determine the idle air control valve setting.

Removal and installation

29 The speed sensor is located in the top of the crankcase at the back on the left-hand side **(see illustration)**. Make sure the ignition is switched OFF. Remove the fuel tank, and if required the airbox, to access the wiring connector (see Sections 2 and 3) – trace the wiring from the sensor to locate it. Disconnect the wiring connector, then undo the screw and remove the sensor. Installation is the reverse of removal – check the condition of the O-ring and replace it with a new one if it is deformed or has deteriorated, or there is evidence of oil leakage from it.

Throttle position sensor
Function

30 The sensor reads the amount of throttle being used, and the ECM uses this in conjunction with the information from other sensors to determine fuelling and ignition requirements.

Removal and installation

31 The sensor is located on the left-hand end of the throttle body **(see illustration 7.9a)**. Do not remove the throttle position sensor unless you know it is faulty and are replacing it with a new one, or unless you are replacing the throttle body with a new one. If you do remove it, it has to be set up using the Triumph diagnostic tool. There is no alternative, unless you want to run the risk of having the bike running incorrectly.

32 Remove the throttle body (see Section 7). Undo the screws and remove the washers securing the sensor, then draw the sensor off the end of the throttle shaft, noting the position of the O-ring.

33 Fit the O-ring onto the sensor, using a new one if necessary. Locate the sensor onto the end of the throttle shaft, making sure the O-ring seats correctly. Tighten the screws to the torque setting specified at the beginning of the Chapter.

34 Install the throttle body (see Section 7). The sensor must now be set up correctly using the Triumph diagnostic tool.

Tip-over sensor
Function

35 The sensor is basically a safety switch that tells the ECM if the bike has fallen over, in which case the ECM will shut down the fuel pump and stop the engine. The switch can be reset by picking the bike up and turning the ignition off, then on again.

Removal and installation

36 On Sprint ST models and on GT models up to VIN 503669 the sensor is located under the front of the airbox **(see illustration)** – remove the airbox for access (see Section 2). On Sprint GT models from VIN 503670-on and on Speed Triple models the sensor is located under the seat **(see illustration)** – remove the seat for access (see Chapter 7). On Tiger

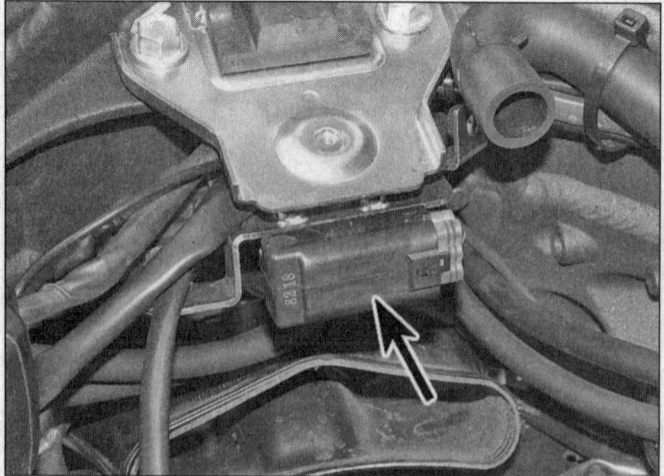

14.36a Tip-over sensor (arrowed) – Sprint models

14.36b Tip-over sensor (arrowed) – Speed Triple models

Engine management system (fuel and ignition) 4•27

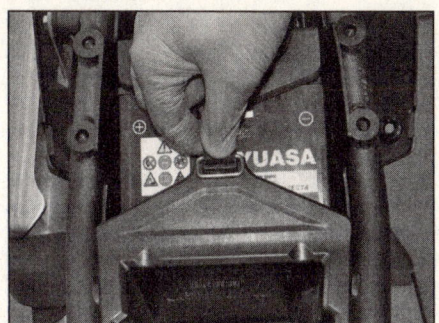

14.36c Release the battery strap . . .

14.36d . . . then unscrew the bolts (arrowed) . . .

14.36e . . . and remove the tray . . .

14.36f . . . to access the sensor (arrowed)

Sport models the sensor is under the storage tray – remove the seat (see Chapter 7), then remove the tray **(see illustrations)**. On all other Tiger models the sensor is under the battery – remove the battery for access (see Chapter 8).

37 Disconnect the wiring connector. Undo the screws and remove the sensor – on Sprint models the screws are on the underside.

38 Install the sensor with the UP mark at the top and apply some threadlock to the threads.

15 Idle air control unit

Check

1 The idle air control unit, located on the right-hand end of the throttle body, is actuated by the ECM and set according to information received by the ECM from the various sensors **(see illustration 7.9b)**. The unit is used to control the engine idle speed, to adjust the air supply on engine overrun, to correct for altitude, and for cold starting. The idle speed cannot be adjusted manually.

2 The ECM actuates a stepper motor which moves an arm connected to a lever that contacts the throttle cam and varies the closed throttle position setting. If a fault in the valve is suspected check the wiring connector for loose, corroded or damaged terminals, and the wiring between the valve and the ECM for continuity, referring to 'Electrical system fault finding' at the beginning of Chapter 8 and the wiring diagrams at the end of it.

3 Remove the fuel tank and the airbox (see Sections 2 and 3).

4 To test the stepper motor resistance, first make sure the ignition is switched OFF. Disconnect the control valve wiring connector. First measure the resistance between the orange/brown and orange/white wire terminals in the sensor side of the connector using an ohmmeter or multimeter set to the ohms x 10 scale. Next, measure the resistance between the orange/blue and orange/pink wire terminals in the sensor side of the connector. If either of the results is not as specified, the stepper motor is faulty.

Renewal

5 The idle air control unit is located on the right-hand end of the throttle bodies **(see illustration 7.9b)**. Do not remove it unless you know it is faulty and are replacing it with a new one, or unless you are replacing the throttle bodies with new ones. If you do remove it, it has to be set up using the Triumph diagnostic tool. There is no alternative, unless you want to run the risk of having the bike running incorrectly.

6 Remove the throttle body (see Section 7). Make a careful note of the how the actuating lever locates in relation to the throttle cam **(see illustration)**.

7 Unscrew the nylon nut securing the arm in the lever and remove the metal and plastic washers

8 Undo the screws securing the valve to its bracket, then draw the sensor down to free the arm from the lever. Note the plastic collar and spring on the arm.

9 Make sure the spring and plastic collar are in place on the arm, then fit the unit, locating the arm in the lever, and tighten the screws to the torque setting specified at the beginning of the Chapter. Fit the plastic and metal washers and the nylon nut to secure the arm in the lever. Make sure everything is correctly positioned **(see illustrations 7.9b and 15.6)**.

10 Install the throttle bodies (see Section 7). The sensor must now be set up correctly using the Triumph diagnostic tool.

16 EVAP system – California market models

1 This system prevents the escape of fuel vapour into the atmosphere by storing it in a charcoal-filled canister located on the frame right-hand side at the rear.

2 When the engine is stopped, fuel vapour from the tank is directed into the canister where it is absorbed and stored whilst the motorcycle is standing. When the engine is started, the purge control valve opens, thus drawing vapours which are stored in the canister into the throttle bodies to be burned during the normal combustion process.

3 The tank vent pipe also incorporates a roll-over valve which closes and prevents any fuel from escaping through it in the event of the bike falling over. The tank filler cap has a one-way valve which allows air into the tank as the volume of fuel decreases, but prevents any fuel vapour from escaping.

4 The system is not adjustable and can be properly tested only by a Triumph dealer, as the diagnostic tool is required. However the owner can check that all the hoses are in good condition and are securely connected at each end. Replace any hoses that are cracked, split or generally deteriorated with new ones.

5 You can also check the purge valve by disconnecting the wiring connector and measuring the resistance of the valve using an ohmmeter. If the result is not as specified at the beginning of the Chapter, in particular if there is infinite or no resistance, replace the valve with a new one.

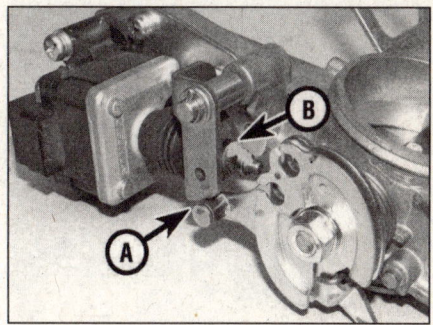

15.6 Note the relative positions of the lever and cam (A), and the lever and arm (B)

17 Catalytic converter

General information

1 The catalytic converter minimises the level of exhaust pollutants released into the atmosphere. It consists of a canister containing a fine mesh impregnated with a catalyst material, over which the hot exhaust gases pass. The catalyst speeds up the oxidation of harmful carbon monoxide, unburned hydrocarbons and soot, effectively reducing the quantity of harmful products released into the atmosphere via the exhaust gases.

2 The catalytic converter is housed in the exhaust downpipe assembly.

3 It operates under closed-loop control with an oxygen (Lambda) sensor feeding back gas oxygen content information to the ECM; information on the sensor can be found in Section 14.

Precautions

4 The catalytic converter is a reliable and simple device which needs no maintenance in itself, but there are some precautions the owner should note if the converter is to function properly for its full service life.

- DO NOT use leaded or lead replacement petrol (gasoline) – the additives will coat the precious metals, reducing their converting efficiency and will eventually destroy the catalytic converter.
- Always keep the ignition and fuel systems well-maintained in accordance with the manufacturer's schedule – if the fuel/air mixture is suspected of being incorrect have it checked on an exhaust gas analyser.
- If the engine develops a misfire, do not ride the bike at all (or at least as little as possible) until the fault is cured.
- DO NOT use fuel or engine oil additives – these may contain substances harmful to the catalytic converter.
- DO NOT continue to use the bike if the engine burns oil to the extent of leaving a visible trail of blue smoke.
- Remember that the catalytic converter is FRAGILE – do not strike it with tools during servicing work.

Chapter 5
Frame and suspension

Contents

	Section number		Section number
Footrests, brake pedal and gearchange lever	3	Sidestand and centrestand	4
Fork oil change	7	Sidestand switch	see Chapter 8
Fork overhaul	8	Stand(s) and safety interlock circuit check	see Chapter 1
Fork removal and installation	6	Steering head bearing check and adjustment	see Chapter 1
Frame	2	Steering head bearing overhaul	10
General information	1	Steering stem	9
Handlebars and levers	5	Suspension adjustment	13
Handlebar switches	see Chapter 8	Suspension check	see Chapter 1
Rear shock absorber	11	Swingarm bearings	15
Rear suspension linkage	12	Swingarm removal and installation	14

Degrees of difficulty

| Easy, suitable for novice with little experience | Fairly easy, suitable for beginner with some experience | Fairly difficult, suitable for competent DIY mechanic | Difficult, suitable for experienced DIY mechanic | Very difficult, suitable for expert DIY or professional |

Specifications

Front forks
Fork oil type
  Speed Triple R .... Öhlins fork oil
  All other models .... Showa SS8 or equivalent SAE 10W fork oil
Fork oil capacity
  Sprint ST .... 469 cc
  Sprint GT .... 486 cc
  Speed Triple up to VIN 419555 .... 469 cc
  Speed Triple from VIN 419556 to 461331 .... 480 cc
  Speed Triple from VIN 461332 .... 552 cc
  Speed Triple R .... 478 cc
  Tiger up to VIN 438380 .... 581 cc
  Tiger from VIN 438381 .... 579 cc
  Tiger Sport .... 599 cc
Fork oil level*
  Sprint ST .... 120 mm
  Sprint GT .... 105 mm
  Speed Triple up to VIN 419555 .... 120 mm
  Speed Triple from VIN 419556 to 461331 .... 114 mm
  Speed Triple from VIN 461332 .... 85 mm
  Speed Triple R .... 130 mm
  Tiger up to VIN 438380 .... 74 mm
  Tiger from VIN 438381 .... 81 mm
  Tiger Sport .... 69 mm

*Oil level is measured from the top of the tube with the fork spring removed and the leg fully compressed.

Torque wrench settings
Clutch lever pivot bolt
  Sprint and Speed Triple .... 3 Nm
  Tiger .... 1 Nm
Clutch lever pivot bolt locknut
  Sprint and Speed Triple .... 3 Nm
  Tiger .... 6 Nm
  Tiger SE, Tiger Sport .... 3.5 Nm
Clutch lever bracket clamp bolts
  Speed Triple models from VIN 461332, Tiger SE, Tiger Sport ... 12 Nm
  All other models .... 15 Nm

Torque wrench settings (continued)

Fork clamp bolts – top yoke	20 Nm
Fork clamp bolts – bottom yoke	
Sprint and Tiger	20 Nm
Speed Triple	25 Nm
Fork damper cartridge Allen bolt	
Sprint	25 Nm
Speed Triple up to VIN 461331	24 Nm
Speed Triple from VIN 461332	35 Nm
Tiger	19 Nm
Fork top bolt	
Sprint	30 Nm
Speed Triple up to VIN 461331	25 Nm
Speed Triple from VIN 461332	35 Nm
Tiger	35 Nm
Front brake lever pivot bolt	1 Nm
Front brake lever pivot bolt locknut	6 Nm
Front brake master cylinder bracket clamp bolts	15 Nm
Front footrest bracket bolts	
Sprint and Speed Triple	24 Nm
Tiger	9 Nm
Gearchange lever pivot bolt	22 Nm
Handlebar bolts	
Sprint	
Mounting bolts	26 Nm
Clamp bolts	26 Nm
Speed Triple up to VIN 461331	
Clamp bolts	26 Nm
Holder bolt nuts	45 Nm
Speed Triple from VIN 461332	
Clamp bolts	26 Nm
Holder bolt nuts	35 Nm
Tiger and Tiger SE	
Clamp bolts	26 Nm
Holder bolt nuts	35 Nm
Tiger Sport	
Clamp bolts	26 Nm
Holder bolts	62 Nm
Rear brake pedal pivot bolt	
Sprint models	19 Nm
Tiger models	22 Nm
Rear shock absorber	
Sprint – upper and lower mountings	48 Nm
Speed Triple up to VIN 461331	
Upper mounting	48 Nm
Lower mounting	90 Nm
Speed Triple from VIN 461332 – upper and lower mountings	48 Nm
Tiger	
Upper and lower mountings	48 Nm
Rear sub-frame upper bolts	60 Nm
Rear sub-frame lower bolts	40 Nm
Silencer mounting bolt	15 Nm
Tiger SE	
Upper and lower mountings	55 Nm
Rear sub-frame upper bolts	60 Nm
Rear sub-frame lower bolts	48 Nm
Silencer mounting bolt	15 Nm
Tiger Sport – upper and lower mountings	55 Nm
Rear suspension linkage	
Sprint – all mountings	48 Nm
Speed Triple up to VIN 461331	
Drop link-to-swingarm	48 Nm
Drag link-to-frame	90 Nm
Drag link-to-drop link	90 Nm
Speed Triple models from VIN 461332 – all mountings	48 Nm
Tiger – all mountings	48 Nm
Tiger SE, Tiger Sport – all mountings	55 Nm
Sidestand bracket bolts	40 Nm

Frame and suspension

Torque wrench settings (continued)

Sidestand pivot bolt	20 Nm
Steering head bearing adjuster nut	
Initial (pre-load) setting	40 Nm
Final setting	15 Nm
Steering head bearing adjuster locknut	40 Nm
Steering stem nut	
Sprint ST 2005 to 2009	65 Nm
Sprint ST 2010-on, Sprint GT, Speed Triple and Tiger	90 Nm
Swingarm	
Sprint and Speed Triple up to VIN 461331	
Adjuster bolt	15 Nm
Adjuster bolt locknut	30 Nm
Pivot bolt	60 Nm
Speed Triple models from VIN 461332 and Tiger	
Adjuster	6 Nm
Pivot bolt nut	110 Nm

1 General information

All models have a twin spar aluminium frame that uses the engine as a stressed member.

Front suspension is by a pair of oil-damped telescopic forks with a cartridge-type damper, conventionally mounted on Sprint models and upside-down on Speed Triple and Tiger models. The forks are adjustable for spring pre-load on all models, and for both rebound and compression damping on Speed Triple and Tiger models.

At the rear, an aluminium alloy swingarm acts on a single shock absorber via a three-way linkage. Sprint and Speed Triple models have a single-sided swingarm. Tiger models have the conventional, twin-sided swingarm. The shock absorber is adjustable for spring pre-load and rebound damping on Sprint and Tiger models, and for rebound and compression damping on Speed Triple models.

Many of the bolts used on Triumph motorcycles are of the Torx type. Unless you are already equipped with a good range of Torx bits, you are advised to obtain a set. Make sure you buy bits that can be used in conjunction with a socket set so that a torque wrench can be applied – a Torx key set will not be adequate on its own, though will be useful in addition to the bits.

2 Frame

1 The frame should not require attention unless accident damage has occurred. In most cases, fitment of a new frame is the only satisfactory remedy for such damage. A few frame specialists have the jigs and other equipment necessary for straightening the frame to the required standard of accuracy, but even then there is no simple way of assessing to what extent the frame may have been over stressed.

2 After the machine has accumulated a lot of miles, the frame should be examined closely for signs of cracking or splitting at the welded joints. Loose engine mounting bolts can cause ovaling or fracturing of the mounts themselves. Minor damage can often be repaired by welding, depending on the extent and nature of the damage, but this is a task for an expert.

3 Remember that a frame which is out of alignment will cause handling problems. If misalignment is suspected as the result of an accident, it will be necessary to strip the machine completely so the frame can be thoroughly checked.

3 Footrests, brake pedal and gearchange lever

Footrests

1 Remove the E-clip from the bottom of the footrest pivot pin, then withdraw the pivot pin and remove the footrest **(see illustrations)**. On the rider's footrests, note the fitting of the return spring **(see illustration)**. On the passenger footrests, note the fitting of the detent plate, detent ball and spring, and take care that they do not spring out when removing the footrest **(see illustration)**.

2 On Sprint and Tiger models, the rider's

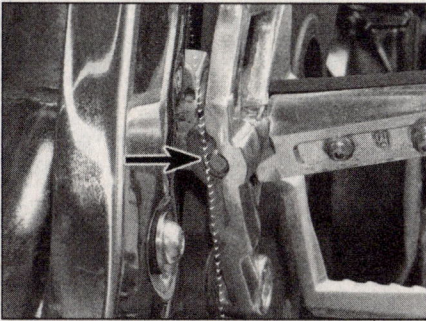

3.1a Rider's footrest E-clip (arrowed)

3.1b Passenger footrest E-clip (arrowed)

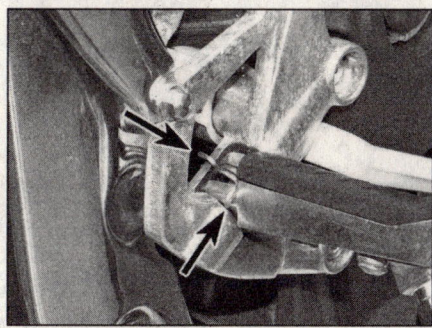

3.1c Note the fitting of the return spring ends (arrowed) on the rider's footrest . . .

3.1d . . . and the detent plate, ball and spring (arrow) on the passenger footrest

5•4 Frame and suspension

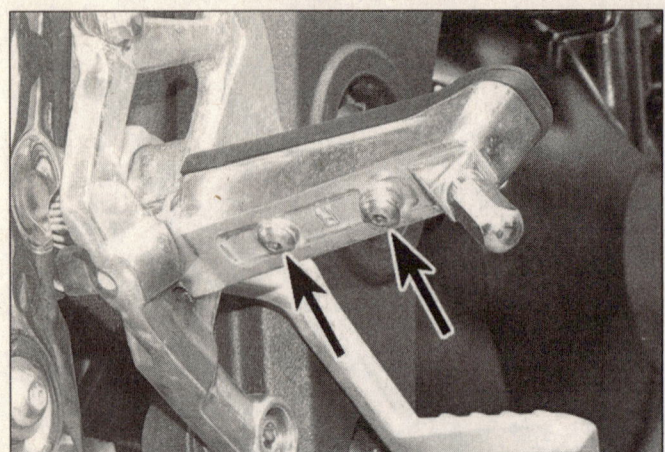

3.2 Footrest rubber screws (arrowed)

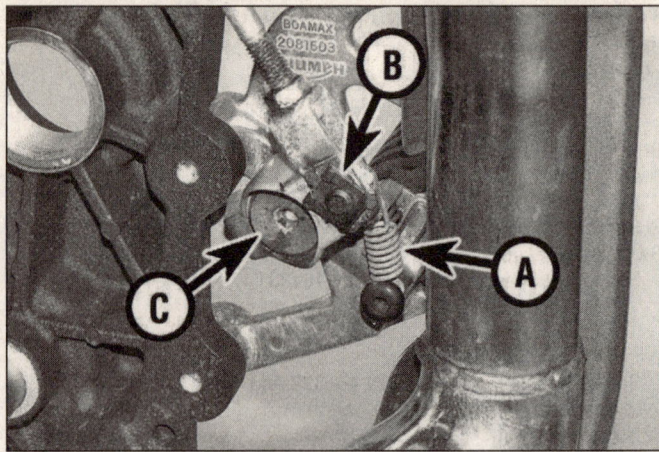

3.4a Brake pedal return spring (A), clevis pin retaining clip (B) and pivot bolt (C) – Sprint models

footrest rubbers, and on Tiger models the passenger footrest rubbers, can be replaced with new ones if required – they are secured to the footrest by two screws or bolts **(see illustration)**.

3 Installation is the reverse of removal.

Brake pedal
Removal

4 Unhook the brake pedal return spring, and on Speed Triple models the brake light switch spring **(see illustrations)**.

5 Remove the retaining clip from the clevis pin securing the brake pedal to the master cylinder pushrod. Remove the clevis pin and separate the pedal from the pushrod.

6 On Sprint and Speed Triple models, the pivot bolt is on the back of the footrest bracket.

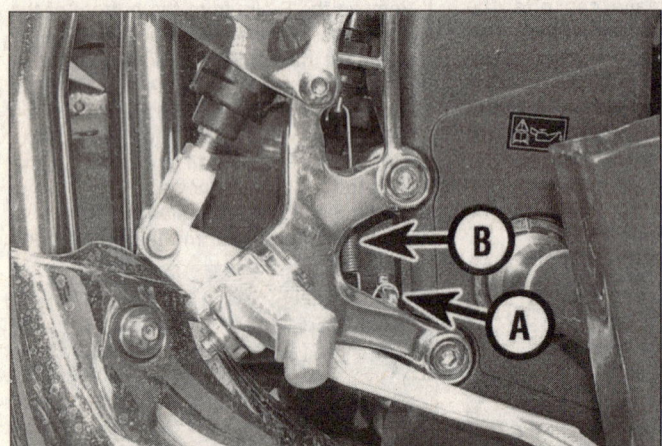

3.4b Brake pedal return spring (A), brake light switch spring (B) . . .

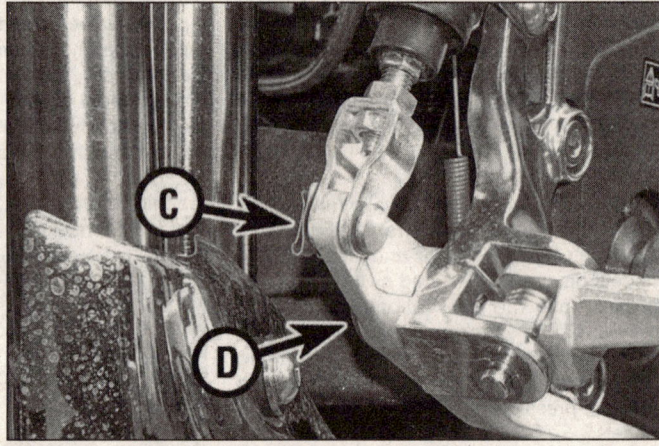

3.4c . . . clevis pin retaining clip (C) and brake pedal pivot bolt (D) – Speed Triple models

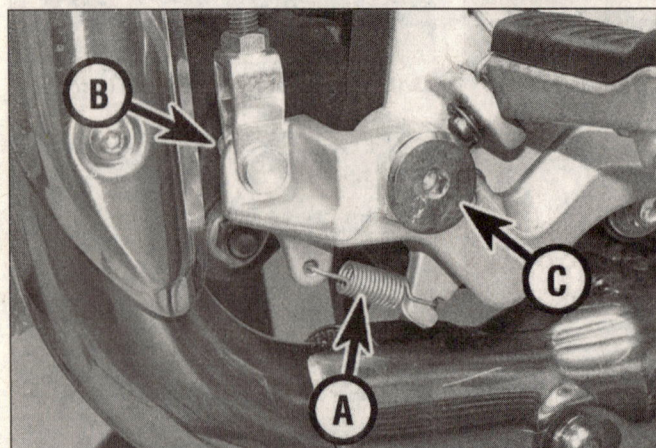

3.4d Brake pedal return spring (A), clevis pin retaining clip (B) and pivot bolt (C) – Tiger models

3.6 Unscrew the bolts (arrowed) and displace the bracket to access the pivot bolt

Unscrew the bolts securing the bracket to the frame **(see illustration)**. Unscrew the pivot bolt and remove the pedal.

7 On Tiger models, unscrew the pivot bolt and remove the pedal.

Installation

8 Installation is the reverse of removal, noting the following:
- Apply grease to the brake pedal pivot, pedal and bush, as required according to model. Tighten the pedal pivot bolt to the torque setting specified at the beginning of the Chapter for your model, where given.
- On Sprint and Speed Triple models clean the threads of the footrest bracket bolts, then apply some fresh threadlock and tighten them to the specified torque.
- If necessary use a new retaining clip on the clevis pin securing the brake pedal to the master cylinder pushrod.
- Check the operation of the rear brake light switch (see Chapter 1, Section 10).

Gearchange lever

Removal

9 On Sprint models release the clip and

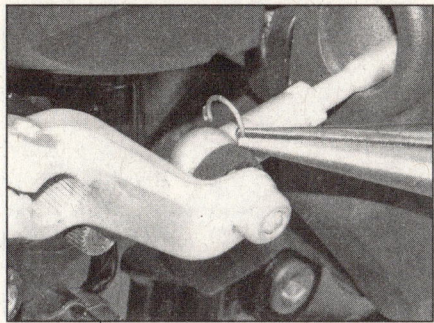
3.9a Release the clip . . .

3.9b . . . and detach the rod from the arm

detach the linkage rod from the linkage arm. Unscrew the bolts securing the footrest bracket to the frame and draw the linkage rod out **(see illustrations)**. Unscrew the lever pivot bolt and remove the lever.

10 On 2005 and 2006 Speed Triple models make an alignment mark across the gearchange shaft end and the gearchange lever as an aid to installation, then unscrew the pinch bolt and slide the lever off the shaft.

11 On 2007-on Speed Triple models, release the clip and detach the linkage rod from the pedal **(see illustration)**. Unscrew the bolts securing the footrest bracket to the frame **(see illustration)**. Unscrew the lever pivot bolt and remove the lever.

12 On Tiger models release the clip and detach the linkage rod from the pedal **(see illustration)**. Unscrew the lever pivot bolt and remove the lever.

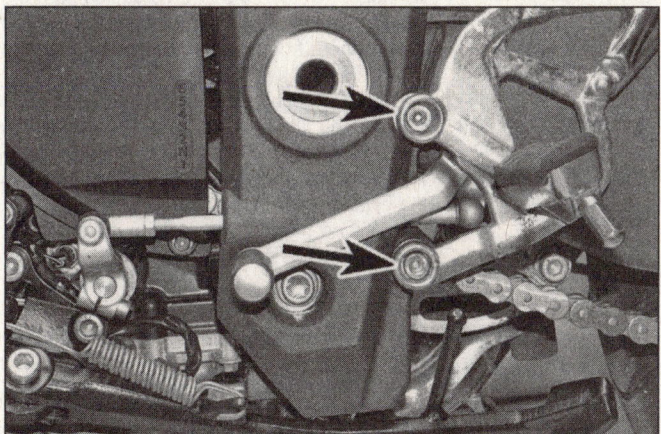
3.9c Unscrew the bolts (arrowed) and remove the footrest/lever assembly

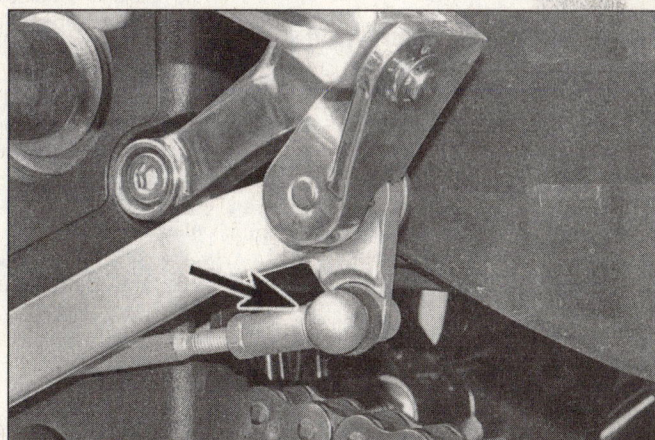
3.11a Release the clip (arrowed) and detach the rod from the lever

3.11b Unscrew the bolts (arrowed) and remove the footrest/lever assembly

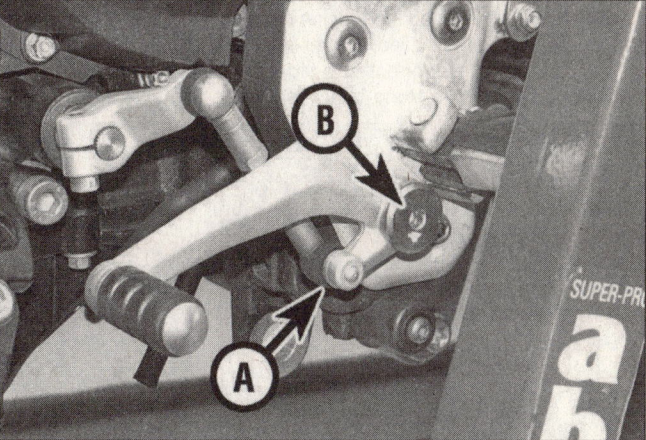
3.12 Release the clip (A) and detach the rod from the lever, then unscrew the pivot bolt (B)

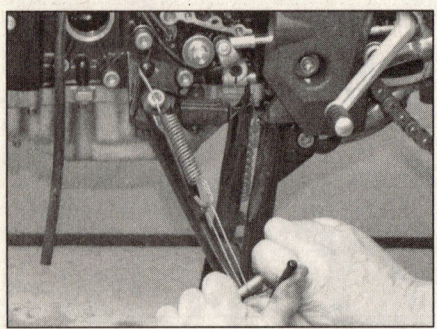
4.2 Unhook the springs . . .

4.3 . . . then unscrew the pivot bolt and remove the stand

4.8 Unhook the springs . . .

Installation

13 Installation is the reverse of removal, noting the following:
- Apply grease to the gear lever pivot and tighten the pivot bolt to the torque setting specified at the beginning of the Chapter.
- On Sprint and 2007-on Speed Triple models clean the threads of the front footrest bracket bolts, then apply some fresh threadlock and tighten them to the specified torque.

4 Sidestand and centrestand

Sidestand

1 Support the motorcycle securely in an upright position using an auxiliary stand, or on Sprint models the centrestand.
2 Unhook the stand springs (see illustration).
3 Unscrew the pivot bolt and remove the stand, noting how it locates against the switch plunger (see illustration).
4 If required refer to Chapter 8, Section 20 and remove the sidestand bracket and switch.
5 On installation apply grease to the pivot section of the bolt and to the contact surfaces of the stand and bracket. Tighten the stand pivot bolt, and if removed the bracket bolts, to the torque settings specified at the beginning of the Chapter. Reconnect the sidestand springs and check the stand is held securely up when not in use – an accident is almost certain to occur if the stand extends while the machine is in motion.
6 Check the operation of the sidestand switch (see Chapter 8).

Centrestand (Sprint models)

7 Support the motorcycle on its sidestand.
8 Unhook the stand springs (see illustration).
9 Counter-hold the pivot bolts then unscrew the nuts on the inside and remove the washers (see illustration). Withdraw the bolts and remove the stand, noting the pivot collars.
10 On installation apply grease to the pivot bolts and collars and to the contact surfaces of the stand and bracket. Reconnect the springs and check the stand is held securely up when not in use – an accident is almost certain to occur if the stand extends while the machine is in motion.

5 Handlebars and levers

Handlebars

Removal

Note: *The handlebars can be displaced from the forks or top yoke without having to remove the lever or switch assemblies.*

1 On Sprint and Tiger models, to prevent the possibility of damage should a tool slip, remove the fairing, fairing side panels and fuel tank as required (see Chapters 7 and 4). On Speed Triple if required, remove the mirrors (see Chapter 7).
2 On the right-hand side, displace the front brake master cylinder and reservoir (see Chapter 6). There is no need to disconnect the hydraulic hose. Keep the reservoir upright to prevent possible fluid leakage and make sure no strain is placed on the hydraulic hose. Displace the handlebar switch housing (see Chapter 8). There is no need to disconnect the loom wiring connector. Detach the throttle cables from the twistgrip (see Chapter 4) – there is no need to detach them from the throttle bodies. Release any ties on the handlebar.
3 On the left-hand side, displace the handlebar switch (see Chapter 8). There is no need to disconnect the loom wiring connector. Unscrew the two bolts securing the clutch lever bracket to the handlebar and displace it (see illustration). There is no need to detach the clutch cable. Release any ties on the handlebar.
4 Remove the handlebar end-weights from the ends of the handlebars, noting how they fit (see illustration). Slide the throttle twistgrip off the right-hand bar. Remove the grip from the left-hand bar – it may be necessary to slit it open using a sharp blade as it may have been glued in place, though a screwdriver between the grip and the handlebar and some aerosol lubricant directed into the grip will usually work (take care to shield your eyes). Depending on your removal method and its success, a new grip may be required on assembly.
5 Where fitted remove the blanking caps from the heads of the handlebar mounting or clamp

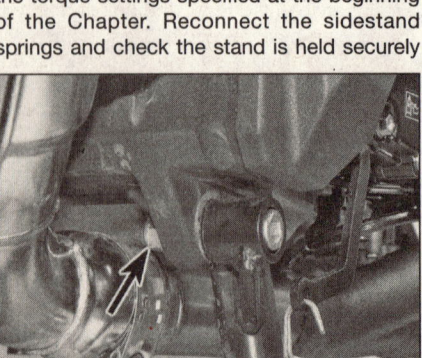
4.9 . . . then unscrew the nut (arrowed) and remove the pivot bolt on each side

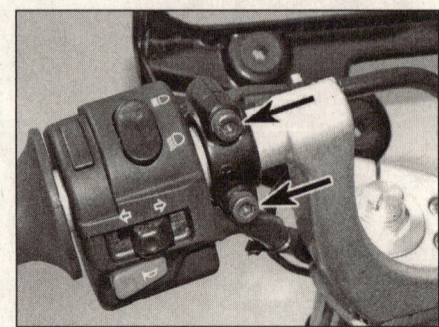
5.3 Clutch lever bracket clamp bolts (arrowed)

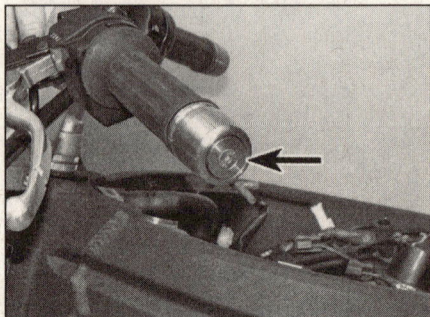
5.4 Remove the end-weight (arrowed) from each side

Frame and suspension

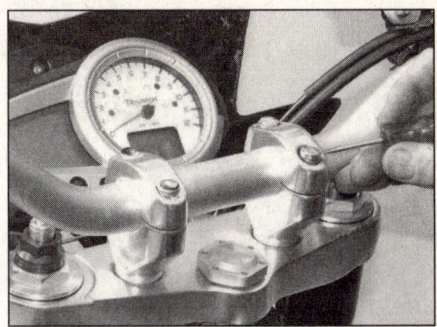

5.5 Carefully prise out the blanking caps – they are easily damaged

5.6a Handlebar mounting bolts (arrowed)

5.6b Slacken the clamp bolt (arrowed) and lift the bar off the fork

bolts using a small flat-bladed screwdriver **(see illustration)**.

6 On Sprint models unscrew the handlebar mounting bolts **(see illustration)**. Slacken the handlebar clamp bolt **(see illustration)**. Ease the handlebar up and off the fork and either remove it, or displace it and lay it aside on some rag.

7 On Speed Triple and Tiger models, unscrew the handlebar holder clamp bolts, then remove the clamps and either remove the handlebars, or displace them and lay them on some rag **(see illustration)**. If required unscrew the handlebar holder bolts (Tiger Sport) or nuts (all other models) on the underside of the top yoke and remove the holders, noting the washers and the arrangement of the caps (where fitted), rubber dampers and sleeves on Speed Triple models from VIN 461332 and Tiger models **(see illustration)**.

Installation

8 Installation is the reverse of removal, noting the following.

- On Sprint models, tighten the handlebar mounting bolts before the clamp bolt, and tighten the bolts to the torque setting specified at the beginning of the Chapter.
- On Speed Triple and Tiger models, if you removed the handlebar holders from *the* top yoke tighten the nuts or bolts on the underside to the torque setting specified at the beginning of the Chapter according to model, on Speed Triple models from VIN 461332 and Tiger models making sure the sleeves and rubber dampers, and where fitted the caps, are correctly fitted – use new dampers if necessary. Make sure the handlebars are central in the holders, and

5.7a Handlebar holder clamp bolts (arrowed)

align the punch mark or + mark in the front of the handlebar with the mating surfaces of the clamp and holder. Tighten the front clamp bolts first, then the rear, to the torque setting specified at the beginning of the Chapter.

- Where removed fit the blanking caps into the tops of the bolts.
- Apply some rubber adhesive to the left-hand bar before fitting the grip. Apply some grease to the right-hand bar before sliding on the throttle twistgrip.
- Refer to the relevant Chapters as directed for the installation of the handlebar mounted assemblies.
- Fit the clutch lever bracket and front brake master cylinder clamps with the UP mark facing up and align the clamp/bracket mating surface with the punch mark or + mark on the handlebar. Tighten the upper clamp bolt first, then the lower bolt, to the specified torque setting.

5.7b Handlebar holder nut (arrowed)

- Adjust throttle and clutch cable freeplay (see Chapter 1).
- Check the operation of the switches, the throttle, the front brake and the clutch before taking the machine on the road.

Clutch lever

9 On Sprint and early 2005 to 2007 Speed triple models slacken the clutch cable adjuster lockring **(see illustration)**. On all models thread the adjuster fully into the bracket to provide maximum freeplay in the cable **(see illustration)**. Unscrew the lever pivot bolt locknut, then withdraw the pivot bolt and remove the lever, detaching the cable nipple as you do so **(see illustration)**.

10 Installation is the reverse of removal. Apply grease to the pivot bolt shaft and the contact areas between the lever and its bracket, and to the clutch cable nipple. Tighten the pivot bolt to the torque setting specified at the

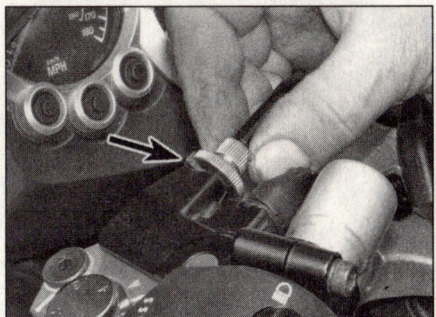

5.9a Slacken the lockring (arrowed) then thread the adjuster fully in

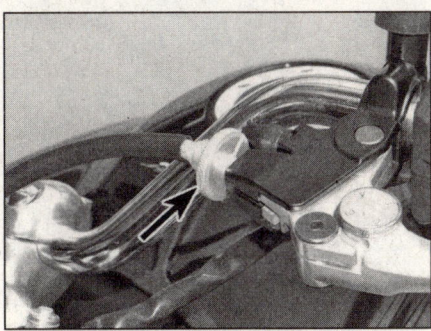

5.9b Clutch cable adjuster (arrowed) – 2008-on Speed Triples and all Tiger models

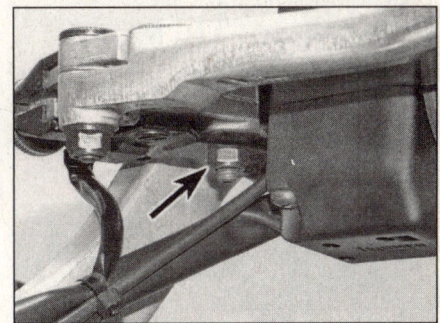

5.9c Clutch lever pivot bolt locknut (arrowed)

5•8 Frame and suspension

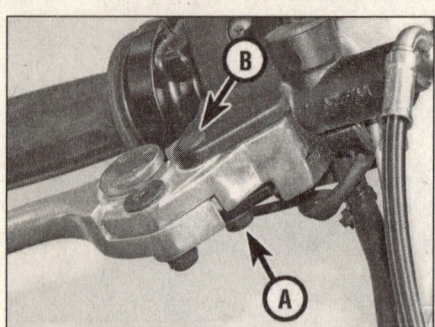

5.11 Brake lever pivot bolt locknut (A), pivot bolt (B)

beginning of the Chapter, then fit the locknut and tighten it to the specified torque. Adjust the clutch cable freeplay (see Chapter 1).

Front brake lever

11 Unscrew the lever pivot bolt locknut, then unscrew the pivot bolt and remove the lever **(see illustration)**.

12 Installation is the reverse of removal. Apply grease to the pivot bolt shaft and the contact areas between the lever and its bracket. Tighten the pivot bolt to the torque setting specified at the beginning of the Chapter, then fit the locknut and tighten it to the specified torque.

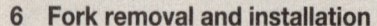
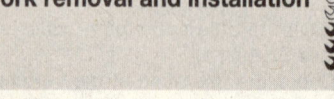

6 Fork removal and installation

Removal

Caution: *Although not strictly necessary, and where applicable, before removing the forks it is recommended that the fairing side panels and/or fairing are removed (see Chapter 7). This will prevent accidental damage to the paintwork should a tool slip.*

1 On Sprint and Tiger models if required, remove the fairing and the fairing side panels (see Chapter 7).
2 Displace the front brake calipers (see Chapter 6). There is no need to disconnect the hydraulic hoses. On models with ABS displace the front wheel sensor (see Chapter 6).
3 Remove the front wheel (see Chapter 6).
4 Remove the front mudguard (see Chapter 7).

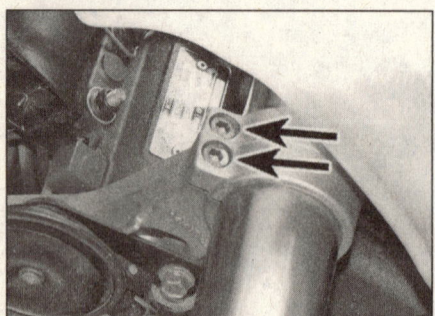

6.9b Bottom yoke fork clamp bolts (arrowed) – Tiger models

6.7a Top yoke fork clamp bolt (arrowed) – Sprint models

5 Work on each fork individually. Mark each fork to denote on which side it fits. Note the routing of the various cables and hoses around the forks, and release any cable-ties that secure them.
6 On Sprint models, slacken the handlebar clamp bolt in the top yoke **(see illustration 5.6b)**.
7 Slacken the fork clamp bolts in the top yoke **(see illustrations)**.
8 If the forks are to be overhauled, or if the fork oil is being changed, slacken the fork top bolt now whilst it is still clamped in the bottom yoke **(see illustration)**.
9 Note the alignment of the tops of the fork tube with the top yoke. Slacken but do not remove the fork clamp bolts in the bottom yoke **(see illustrations)**. Remove the fork by twisting it and pulling it downwards **(see illustration)**. Note which fork fits on which side.

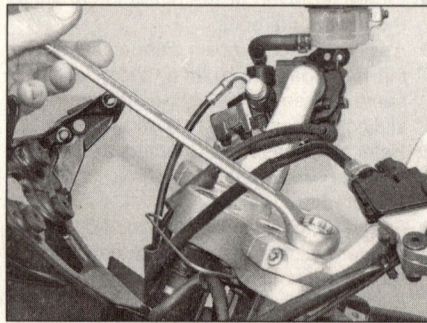

6.8 Slacken the fork top bolt now if required

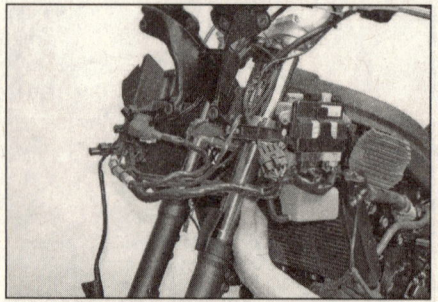

6.9c Slide the fork down and out of the yokes, collecting the handlebar where applicable

6.7b Top yoke fork clamp bolt (arrowed) – Speed Triple models

 *If the fork legs are seized in the yokes, spray the area with penetrating oil and allow time for it to soak in before trying again.*

Installation

10 Remove all traces of corrosion from the fork tubes and the yokes. Make sure you fit the fork to its correct side as noted on removal. Slide the fork up through the bottom yoke, and the handlebar on Sprint models, and up into the top yoke, making sure the wiring, cables and hoses are the correct side of the fork as noted on removal **(see illustration 6.9c)**. Set the fork in the top yoke so the joint between the fork top bolt and the top of the fork tube is flush with the top of the handlebar bracket on Sprint models **(see illustration)**, is flush

6.9a Bottom yoke fork clamp bolts (arrowed) – Sprint models

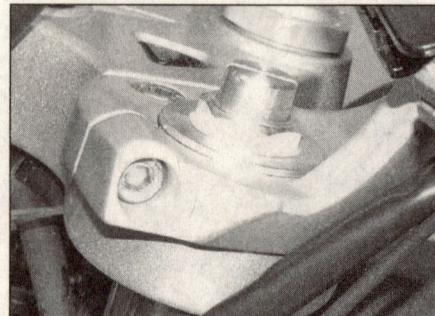

6.10a Fork position in the top yoke/ handlebar bracket – Sprint

Frame and suspension 5•9

6.10b Fork position in the top yoke – Tiger Sport

6.10c Fork position in the top yoke (index line arrowed) – Speed Triple from VIN 461332

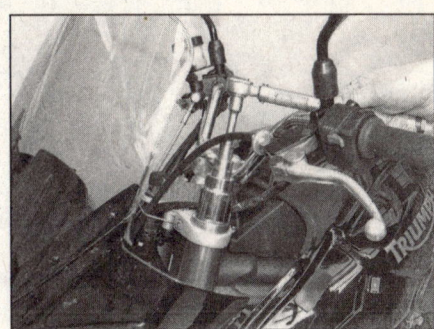

6.11 Tighten the fork top bolt to the specified torque if necessary

with the top surface of the top yoke on Speed Triple models up to VIN 461331 and Tiger and Tiger SE models, is 35.5 mm above the underside of the top yoke on Tiger Sport **(see illustration)**, and on Speed Triple models from VIN 461332 so the index line in the outer tube is 5 mm below the underside of the top yoke **(see illustration)**.

11 Tighten the fork clamp bolts in the bottom yoke to the torque setting specified at the beginning of the Chapter **(see illustration 6.9a or b)**. If the fork leg has been dismantled or if the fork oil has been changed, tighten the fork top bolt to the specified torque setting **(see illustration)**. Now tighten the fork clamp bolt in the top yoke, and the handlebar clamp bolt on Sprint models, to the specified torque settings **(see illustrations 6.7a and 5.6b, or 6.7b)**.

12 Install the front mudguard (see Chapter 7), front wheel (see Chapter 6), the brake calipers (see Chapter 6), and on models with ABS the wheel sensor (see Chapter 6).

13 On Sprint and Tiger models, install the fairing and the fairing side panels (see Chapter 7).

14 Check the operation of the front forks and brakes before taking the machine out on the road.

7 Fork oil change

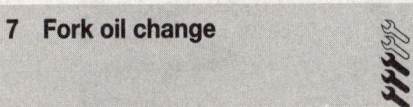

1 After a high mileage the fork oil will deteriorate and its damping and lubrication qualities will be impaired. Always change the oil in both forks. Work on one fork at a time.

2 Remove the fork – make sure the top bolt is loosened while the leg is still clamped in the bottom yoke (see Section 6).

Sprint

3 Support the fork upright and unscrew the top bolt from the top of the inner tube **(see illustration)**. Slide the inner tube down into the outer tube. Counter-hold the locknut above the slotted washer and unscrew the top bolt, threading it off the damper rod **(see illustrations)**.

4 Lift the damper rod and remove the slotted washer from under the locknut **(see illustration)**. Remove the spring, noting which way up it fits **(see illustration)**.

5 Invert the fork leg over a suitable container and pump the inner tube to expel as much oil as possible **(see illustration)**.

6 Support the leg and allow it to drain for several minutes. Wipe any excess oil off the spring. If the fork oil contains metal particles inspect the fork components for signs of wear (see Section 8).

7.3a Unscrew the top bolt

7.3b Hold the locknut (arrowed) . . .

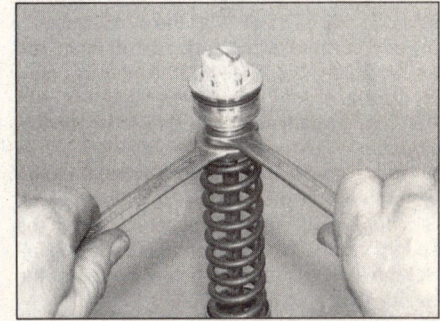

7.3c . . . and thread the top bolt off

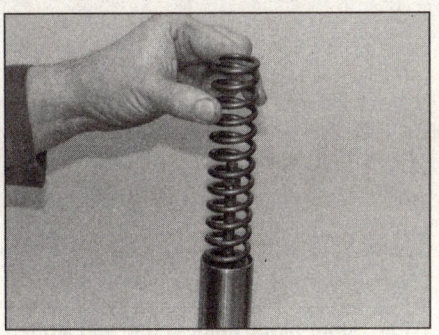

7.4a Remove the slotted washer . . .

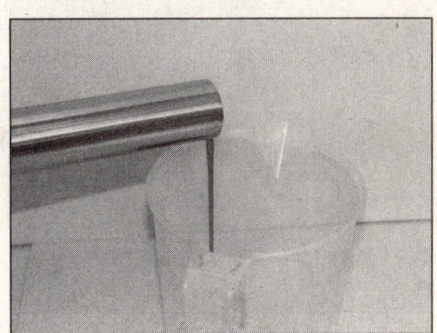

7.4b . . . then lift out the spring

7.5 Drain the oil from the fork

5•10 Frame and suspension

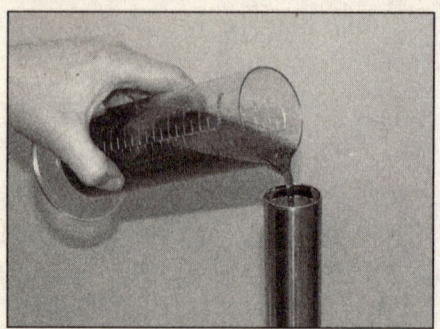

7.7a Pour in the correct type and quantity of oil . . .

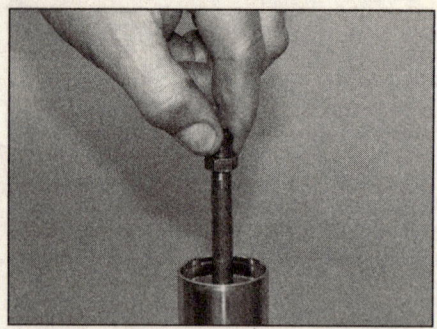

7.7b . . . and pump the damper rod to circulate it

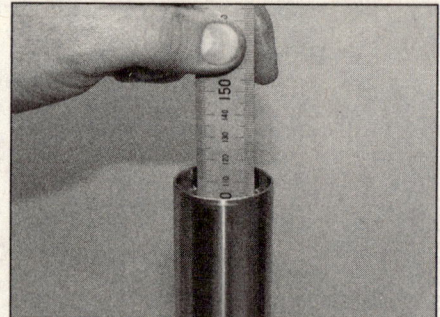

7.8 Measure the oil level and adjust if necessary

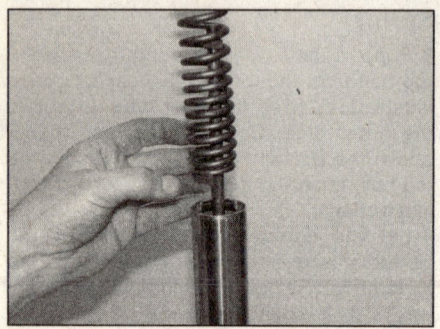

7.9a Make sure the closer-wound coils are at the bottom

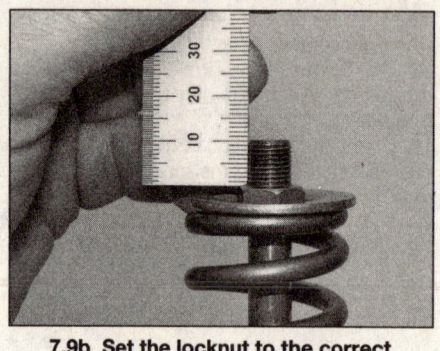

7.9b Set the locknut to the correct position on the rod

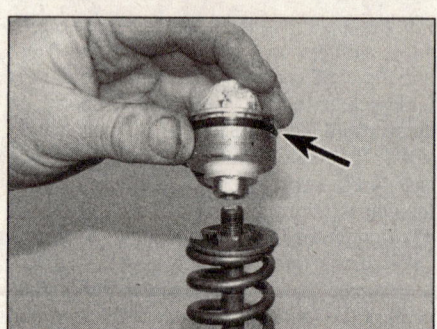

7.10 Check and lubricate the O-ring (arrowed) before fitting the top bolt

7 Slowly pour in the correct quantity and type of fork oil as specified at the beginning of this Chapter **(see illustration)**. Pump the inner tube and damper rod several times to circulate the oil and expel air **(see illustration)**. Secure the fork leg upright and allow it to stand for several minutes to allow all the air to escape.

8 Fully compress the fork and damper rod and measure the oil level from the top **(see illustration)**. Add or subtract oil until it is at the level specified at the beginning of this Chapter.

9 Fit the spring into the fork with its closer wound coils at the bottom **(see illustration)**. Slip the slotted washer between the top of the spring and the locknut **(see illustration 7.4a)**. Set the locknut 10.5 mm below the top of the damper rod **(see illustration)**.

10 Make sure the top bolt O-ring is in good condition then smear some fork oil onto it

(see illustration). Thread the top bolt on to the damper rod and down on to the locknut, then counter-hold the nut and tighten the top bolt against it **(see illustration 7.3c)**. Fit the top bolt into the inner tube and thread it in, making sure it does not cross-thread **(see illustration 7.3a)**. Tighten the bolt to the specified torque setting after the fork leg has been installed and is securely clamped in the bottom yoke.

11 Install the fork (see Section 6).

Speed Triple (except R) and Tiger

Special Tool: *A special holding tool is needed to disassemble the forks – see Step 13.*

12 Support the fork upright and unscrew the top bolt from the top of the outer tube **(see illustration)**. Slide the outer tube down over the inner tube.

13 With the aid of an assistant, pull up on

the fork top bolt, then press down on the spacer to compress the spring and expose the locknut on the bottom of the top bolt. **Note:** *Triumph produces a service tool kit, comprising a spacer holder and stopper plate (Pt. No. TT3880067) to do this. Alternatively, use the set-up shown – the inner end of each handle locates in a hole in the spacer, and the slotted washer locates around the damper rod and under the locknut, so must be sized accordingly.* Insert the stopper plate or slotted washer under the locknut **(see illustration)**. Carefully release the pressure on the spacer and allow the plate or slotted washer to rest against the underside of the locknut under spring pressure.

14 Counter-hold the locknut and loosen the top bolt, then thread the top bolt assembly off the damper rod and remove it, drawing the damping adjuster rod out as you do **(see**

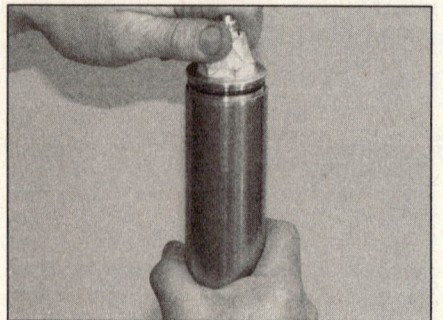

7.12 Unscrew the top bolt

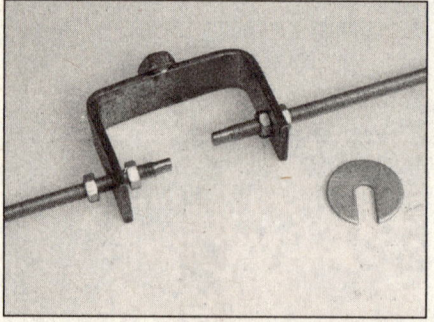

7.13a Home-made holding tool and slotted washer

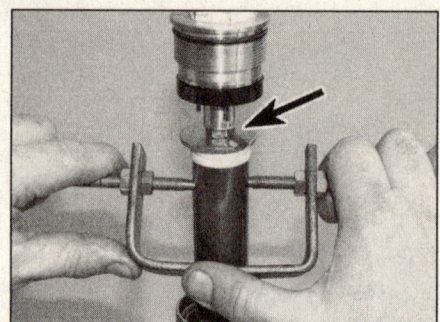

7.13b Fit the tool onto the spacer then use it to compress the spring so the washer (arrowed) can be fitted under the locknut

Frame and suspension 5•11

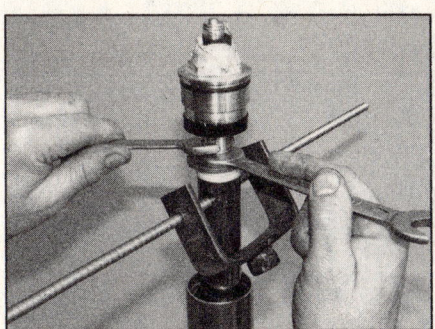

7.14a Counter-hold the locknut then unscrew the top bolt . . .

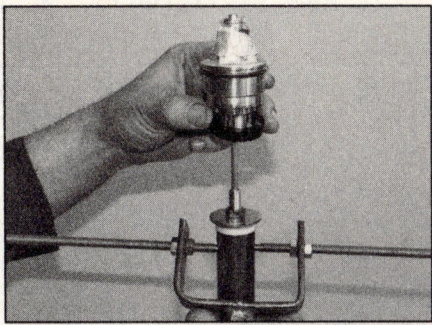

7.14b . . . and draw the adjuster rod out

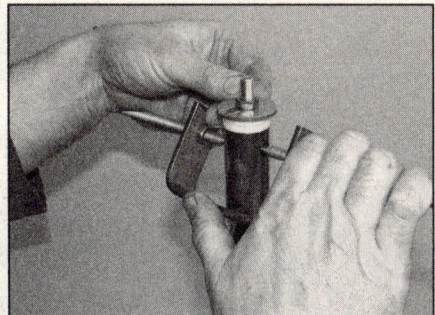

7.15 Compress the spring and remove the washer

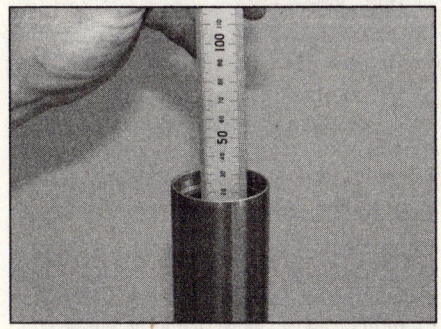

7.19 Measure the oil level and adjust if necessary

7.20 Fit the spring into the fork

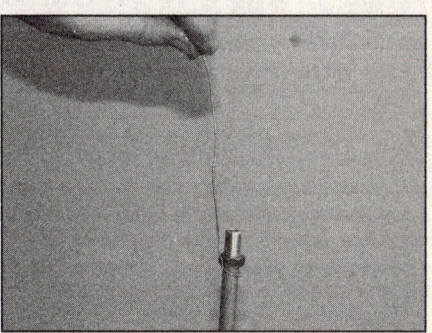

7.21a Fit a piece of wire under the locknut to keep the rod extended

illustrations). Note the rubber damper on the underside of the top bolt. **Note:** *The top bolt assembly should not be disassembled.*

15 Compress the spacer and remove the plate or slotted washer, then carefully allow the spring to relax **(see illustration)**. Remove the washer (where fitted) and the spacer, noting the nylon bush on its top **(see illustration 7.22d)**. Withdraw the spring from the tube, noting which way up it fits **(see illustration 7.19)**.

16 Invert the fork leg over a suitable container and pump the fork and damper rod to expel as much oil as possible **(see illustration 7.5)**.

17 Support the leg and allow it to drain for several minutes, pumping it again. Wipe any excess oil off the spring and spacer. If the fork oil contains metal particles inspect the fork components for signs of wear (see Section 8).

18 Slowly pour in the correct quantity and type of fork oil as specified at the beginning of this Chapter for your model **(see illustration 7.7a)**. Draw the damper rod out of the fork using long-nosed pliers and pump the rod several times to circulate the oil and expel air from the damper cartridge **(see illustration 7.7b)**. Secure the fork leg upright and allow it to stand for several minutes to allow all the air to escape. Now pump the rod several times again – once all the air is expelled you should feel stiff resistance when pumping the rod. Take great care to ensure that all air is expelled from the damper cartridge at this stage.

19 Fully compress the fork and damper rod and measure the oil level from the top of the tube **(see illustration)**. Add or subtract oil until it is at the level specified at the beginning of this Chapter for your model.

20 Fit the spring into the fork with the closer wound coils at the top **(see illustration)**.

21 Draw the rod out and fit a piece of thin wire around the rod under the locknut to help keep it extended **(see illustration)**. Make sure the lower nylon bush is on the bottom of the spacer **(see illustration)**. Fit the spacer, then fit the upper nylon bush, and where fitted the washer, on its top **(see illustrations)**, sliding them over the wire or holding tool if being used.

22 Keeping the damper rod fully extended, press down on the spacer to compress the spring (see Step 13), then remove the wire and insert the stopper plate or slotted washer under the locknut **(see illustration 7.15)**.

23 On 2005 to 2010 Speed Triple models (up to VIN 461331) set the top of the locknut 10.5 mm below the top of the damper rod **(see illustration 7.9b)**. On 2011-on Speed Triple models (from VIN 461332) and on Tiger models, set the locknut at the bottom of the threads, and turn the rebound damping

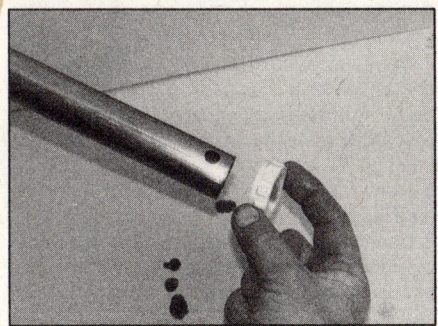

7.21b Fit the lower bush onto the spacer . . .

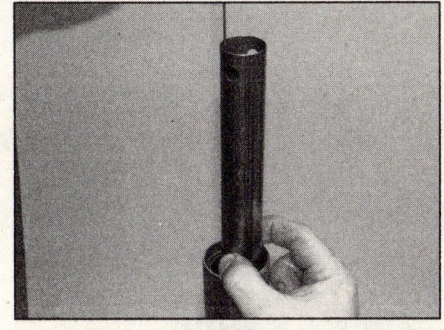

7.21c . . . then fit the spacer . . .

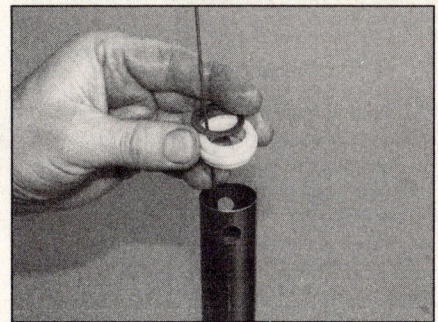

7.21d . . . the upper bush and the washer

5•12 Frame and suspension

7.23 Set the damping adjuster (arrowed) so 1.5 mm is exposed

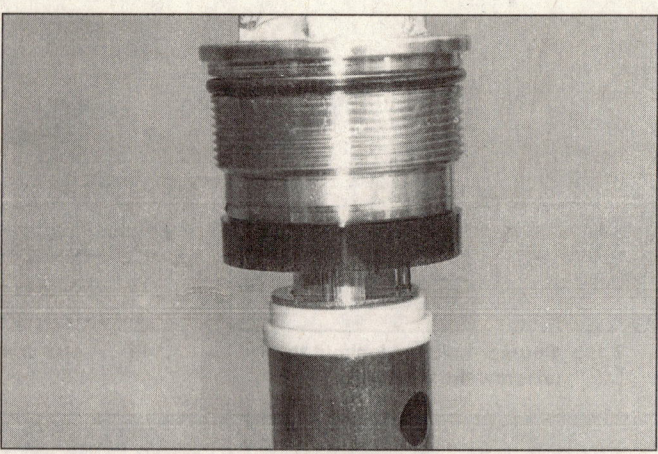

7.26 Make sure that everything is correctly seated under the top bolt as shown

adjuster in the top bolt so there is 1.5 mm exposed at the top **(see illustration)**.

24 Make sure the top bolt O-ring is in good condition then smear some fork oil onto it.

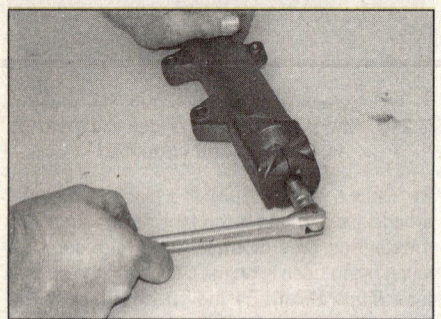

8.2 Slacken the damper rod bolt

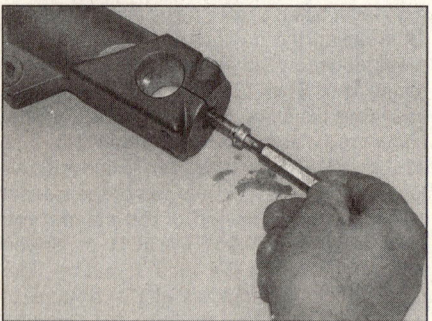

8.4 Remove the damper rod bolt . . .

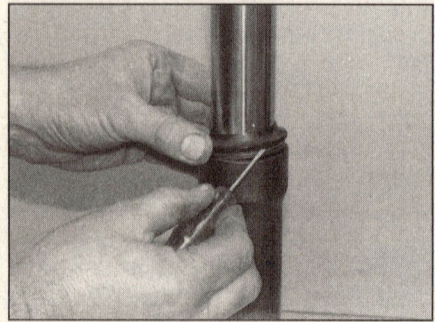

8.6 Prise out the dust seal using a flat-bladed screwdriver . . .

Make sure the rubber damper ring is in place on the underside of the top bolt. Fit the top bolt, sliding the damping adjuster rod into the damper rod, and thread the top bolt all the way down to the locknut **(see illustration 7.14b)**. Counter-hold the locknut and tighten the top bolt against it **(see illustration 7.14a)**.

25 Press down on the spacer to compress the spring and remove the plate or slotted washer, then carefully release the spring pressure, making sure the spacer, upper bush and washer seat correctly **(see illustration)**. Remove the holding tool.

26 Pull the outer tube all the way out of the inner tube and carefully screw the top bolt into the tube making sure it is not cross-threaded **(see illustration 7.12)**. Tighten the top bolt to the specified torque when the fork leg has

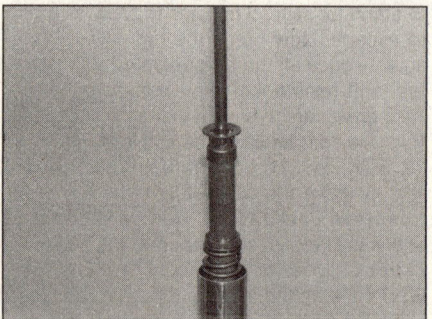

8.5 . . . then withdraw the damper

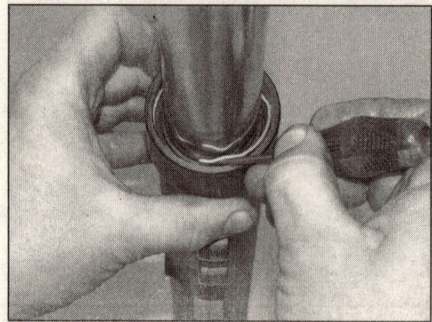

8.7 . . . then remove the retaining clip

been installed and is securely clamped in the bottom yoke.

27 Install the fork (see Section 6).

Speed Triple R models

28 Work on the forks fitted to R models should only be undertaken by an Öhlins service centre. Refer to your Triumph dealer for further details. No procedures are given in this manual for these forks.

8 Fork overhaul

Sprint
Disassembly

1 Remove the fork – make sure that the top bolt is loosened while the leg is still clamped in the bottom yoke (see Section 6). Always dismantle the fork legs separately to avoid interchanging parts. Store all components in separate, clearly marked containers.

2 Slacken the damper cartridge bolt in the bottom of the outer tube, then lightly re-tighten it to prevent oil coming out **(see illustration)**. If the bolt does not loosen, turn the leg upside down and compress the fork so that the spring exerts maximum pressure on the cartridge to prevent it turning, then try to loosen the bolt. If you still have no luck, use an air wrench.

3 Refer to Section 7, Steps 3 to 6, and drain the fork oil.

4 Remove the previously loosened damper cartridge bolt and its sealing washer from the bottom of the outer tube **(see illustration)**. Discard the washer as a new one must be fitted on reassembly.

5 Draw the damper cartridge out of the fork **(see illustration)**.

6 Carefully prise the dust seal from the top of the outer tube to gain access to the oil seal retaining clip **(see illustration)**. Discard the dust seal as a new one must be fitted on reassembly.

7 Carefully remove the retaining clip, taking care not to scratch the surface of the inner tube **(see illustration)**.

Frame and suspension 5•13

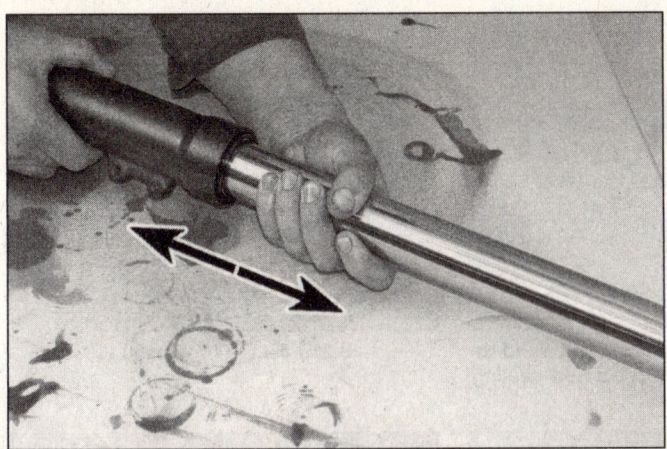

8.8a To separate the inner and outer fork tubes, pull them apart firmly several times – the slide-hammer effect will pull the tubes apart

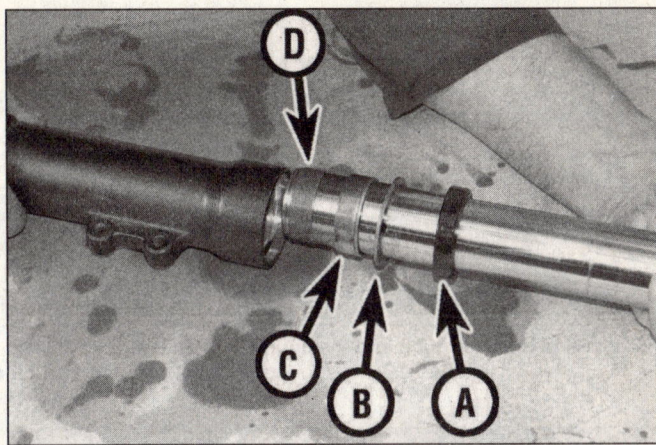

8.8b The oil seal (A), washer (B), and top bush (C) will come out with the fork tube. Bottom bush (D)

8.10 Tip the oil lock piece out

8.13 Check the working surface (arrowed) of each bush

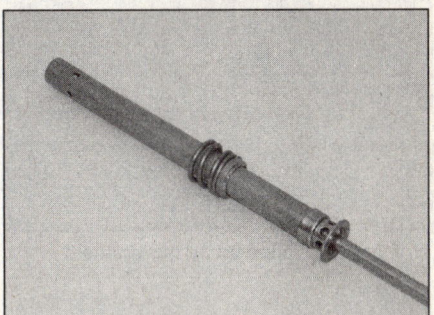

8.16 Check the damper cartridge, rod and rebound spring

8 Grasp the inner tube in one hand and the outer tube in the other, then quickly and repeatedly draw the inner tube out until the oil seal, washer and top bush are displaced from the top of the outer tube by the bottom bush on the bottom of the inner tube **(see illustrations)**. Draw the oil seal, washer and top bush off the inner tube. Discard the oil seal as a new one must be fitted on reassembly.

9 Do not remove the bottom bush unless it is to be replaced with a new one. To remove it, spread its ends using a screwdriver to dislodge it from its seat and slide it off.

10 Tip the oil lock piece out of the bottom of the outer tube **(see illustration)** – you may have to dislodge it by pushing it up off its seat using a rod inserted through the damper cartridge bolt hole. Discard the O-ring – a new one must be used.

Inspection

11 Clean all parts in a suitable solvent and blow them dry with compressed air, if available. Check the surface of the fork inner tube for score marks, scratches, pitting and flaking of the finish, and excessive or abnormal wear. Look for dents in the outer tube and replace the outer tubes in both forks with new ones if any are found.

12 Check the fork inner tube for runout using V-blocks and a dial gauge. If the condition of either inner tube is suspect have it checked by a Triumph dealer or suspension specialist. Triumph provides no specifications for runout.

13 Inspect the inside surface of the outer tube and the working surface of each bush for score marks, scratches and signs of excessive wear (in which case the grey Teflon outer surface will have worn away to reveal the copper inner surface) **(see illustration)**. The bushes are available separately, and should be replaced with new ones if damaged or worn.

14 Check the fork oil seal seat for nicks, gouges and scratches. If damage is evident, leaks will occur. Also check the oil seal washer for damage or distortion and replace it with a new one if necessary.

15 Check the springs (both the main spring and the rebound spring on the damper cartridge) for cracks and other damage. If the spring is defective or has sagged, fit new springs in both forks. Never fit only one new spring.

16 Check the damper cartridge for damage and wear, and replace it with a new one if necessary **(see illustration)**. Hold the cartridge and gently pump the rod in and out. If the rod does not move smoothly the damper must be replaced with a new one.

Reassembly

17 Make sure the bottom bush is correctly located in its recess in the bottom of the inner tube **(see illustration 8.13)**.

18 Insert the damper cartridge into the inner tube so its bottom end protrudes from the bottom of the tube **(see illustration)**. Fit the oil lock piece onto the bottom of the rod **(see illustration)**.

8.18a Insert the damper cartridge . . .

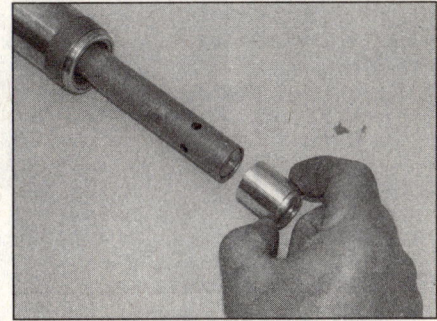

8.18b . . . then fit the oil lock piece

5•14 Frame and suspension

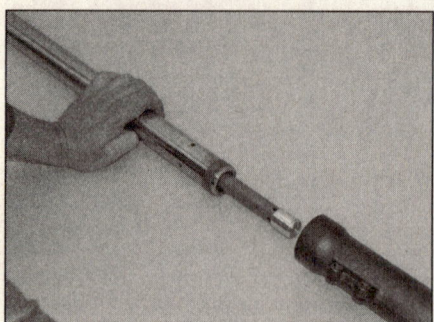

8.19 Slide the inner tube into the outer tube

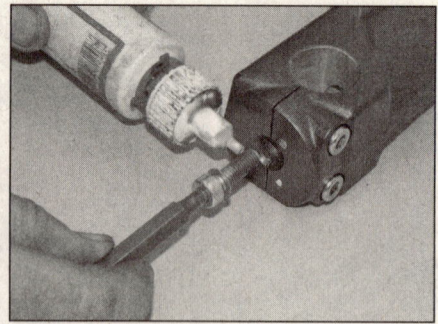

8.20 Apply a thread locking compound to the damper rod bolt and use a new sealing washer

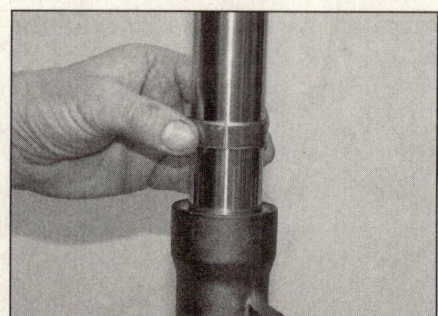

8.21a Fit the top bush . . .

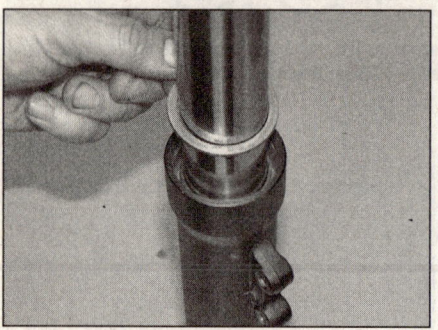

8.21b . . . followed by the washer . . .

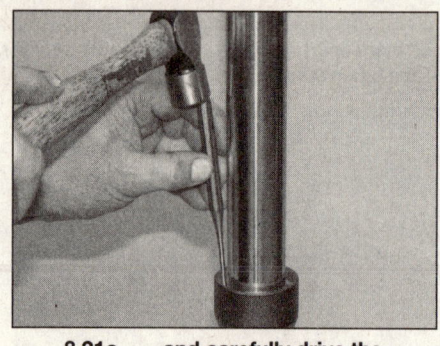

8.21c . . . and carefully drive the bush in . . .

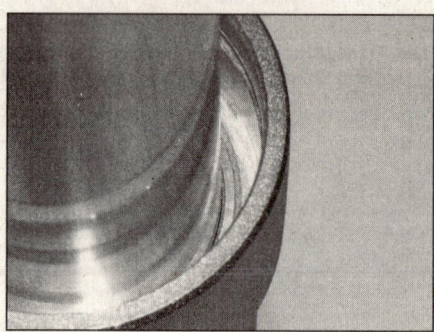

8.21d . . . until it seats

19 Lubricate the bottom bush and the inner surface of the outer tube with the specified fork oil. Slide the inner tube into the outer tube and seat it at the bottom (see illustration).
20 Fit a new sealing washer onto the damper cartridge bolt and apply a few drops of a suitable non-permanent thread locking compound (see illustration). Fit the bolt into the bottom of the outer tube and thread it into the bottom of the damper cartridge and tighten it to the torque setting specified at the beginning of this Chapter. If the damper cartridge rotates inside the tube as you tighten the bolt, wait until the fork is fully reassembled and tighten it then (the pressure of the spring on the cartridge should prevent it from turning, especially if you compress the fork – Step 25).
21 Lubricate the inner and outer surfaces of the top bush with the specified fork oil. Slide the bush down the inner tube and press it as far as possible into the top of the outer tube by hand, making sure it fits squarely (see illustration). Slide the washer onto the top of the bush, then carefully drive the bush into place until it seats using either the special service tool (part No. 3880080-T0301) or a suitable drift or piece of tubing on the washer, using it as an interface to prevent damage to the upper rim of the bush (see illustrations). Take care not to mark the inner tube when driving the bush in. Remove the washer and make sure the bush has fully entered, in which case its upper rim will be flush with the oil seal seat (see illustration). Refit the washer.
22 Lubricate the inner and outer surfaces of the new oil seal with the specified fork oil. Slide the seal, with its marked side facing up, down the inner tube and press it as far as possible into the top of the outer tube by hand, making sure it fits squarely (see illustration). Carefully drive the seal into place until it seats using a suitable drift or piece of tubing, or the special service tool (Pt. No. 57001-1288) – to protect the new seal you can slide the old one on top of it to act as an interface as the new one is

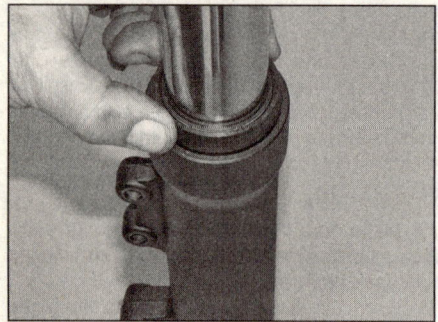

8.22a Fit the new seal . . .

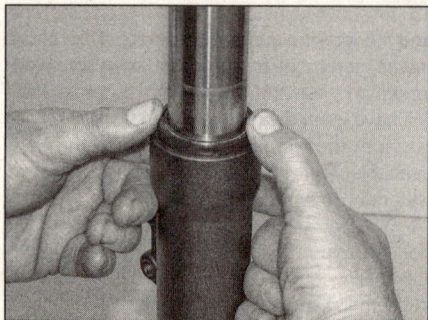

8.22b . . . and press it in

8.22c Fit the old seal on top . . .

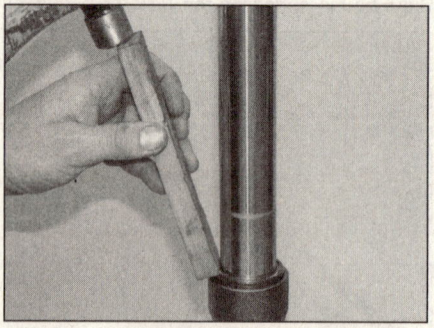

8.22d . . . to protect the new one as you drive it in . . .

Frame and suspension 5•15

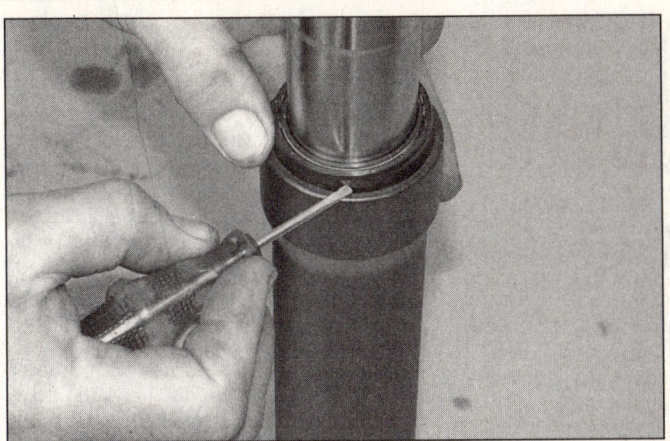

8.22e ... then remove the old seal

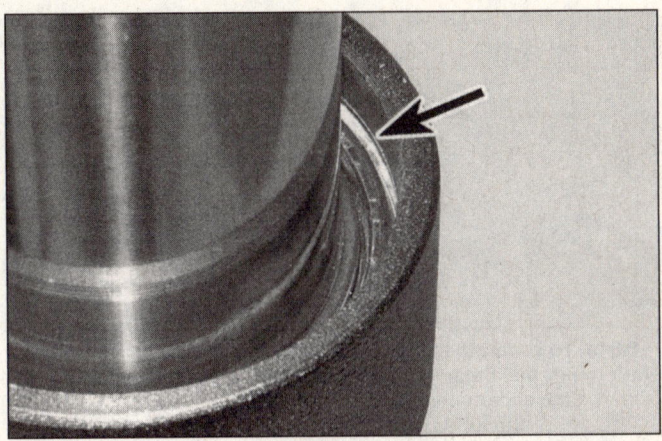

8.22f Check that the retaining clip groove (arrowed) is fully exposed all the way round

driven in **(see illustrations)**. Take care not to mark the inner tube when driving the bush in. Make sure the seal has fully entered, in which case the groove for the retaining ring will be fully exposed.

23 Fit the retaining clip, making sure it is correctly located in its groove **(see illustration)**. Press the new dust seal into place **(see illustration)**.

24 Refer to Section 7, Steps 7 to 10, and put new oil into the fork.

25 If the damper rod bolt requires tightening (see Step 20), place the fork upside down on the floor, using a rag to protect it, then have an assistant compress the fork so that maximum spring pressure is placed on the damper rod head while tightening the bolt to the specified torque setting.

26 If removed thread the axle clamp bolts loosely into the bottom of the right-hand fork.

27 Install the fork (see Section 6). Check and adjust the fork settings as required (see Section 13).

Speed Triple (except R) and Tiger

Disassembly

28 Remove the fork – make sure that the top bolt is loosened while the leg is still clamped in the bottom yoke (see Section 6). Always dismantle the fork legs separately to avoid interchanging parts. Store all components in separate, clearly marked containers. When working on the right-hand fork first remove the axle clamp bolts.

29 If you want to remove the damper cartridge from the fork (this is not necessary if for example you are just fitting new seals or bushes) slacken the damper cartridge bolt in the bottom of the fork, then lightly re-tighten it to prevent oil coming out **(see illustration)**. If the bolt does not loosen, turn the leg upside down and compress the fork so that the spring exerts maximum pressure on the damper cartridge assembly to prevent it turning, then try to loosen the bolt. If you still have no luck, and an air wrench is not available, carry on and obtain a holding tool as described in Step 31.

30 Refer to Section 7, Steps 12 to 17, and drain the fork oil.

31 If required remove the previously loosened damper cartridge bolt and its sealing washer from the bottom of the inner tube **(see illustration 8.48b)**. Discard the washer as a new one must be fitted on reassembly. If the damper cartridge bolt was impossible to slacken as described in Step 29, note that a Triumph service tool (Pt. No. T3880004) is available to hold the damper cartridge in place while the bolt is unscrewed; the tool passes down over the damper rod and engages the top of the cartridge body.

32 Withdraw the damper cartridge assembly from inside the fork tube **(see illustration 8.48a)**.

33 Carefully prise the dust seal from the bottom of the outer tube **(see illustration)**. Remove the retaining clip **(see illustration)**.

8.23a Fit the retaining clip ...

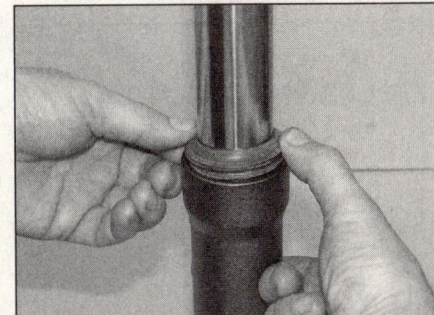

8.23b ... then press the dust seal in

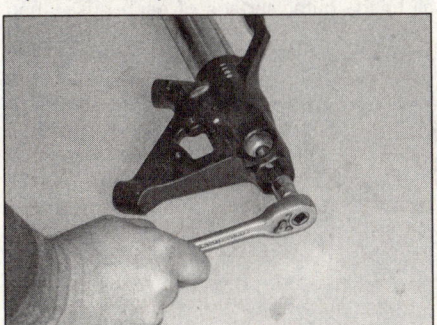

8.29 Slacken the damper rod bolt

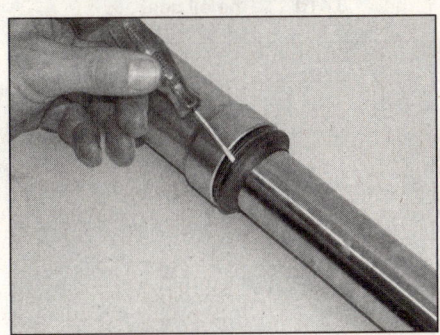

8.33a Prise out the dust seal using a flat-bladed screwdriver ...

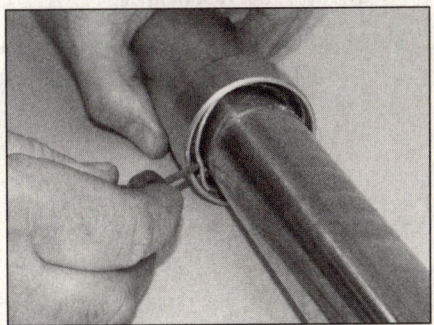

8.33b ... then remove the retaining clip

5•16 Frame and suspension

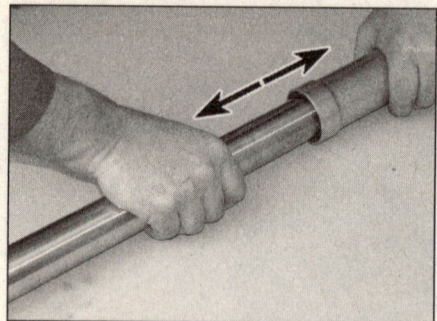

8.34a To separate the inner and outer fork tubes, pull them apart firmly several times – the slide-hammer effect will pull the tubes apart

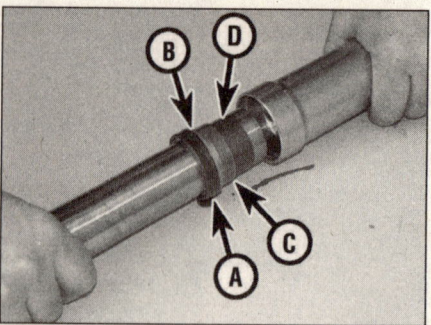

8.34b The oil seal (A), washer (B), and bottom bush (C) will come out with the fork tube. Top bush (D)

Discard the seal as a new one must be fitted on reassembly.

34 Grasp the inner tube in one hand and the outer tube in the other, then quickly and repeatedly draw the inner tube out until the oil seal, washer and bottom bush are displaced from the bottom of the outer tube by the top bush on the top of the inner tube **(see illustrations)**. Remove the top bush by carefully levering its ends apart, then slide the bottom bush, washer, oil seal, retaining clip and dust seal off the inner tube **(see illustrations 8.41g to b)**. Discard the oil and dust seals as new ones must be fitted on reassembly.

Inspection

35 Clean all parts in a suitable solvent and blow them dry with compressed air, if available. Check the surface of the fork inner tube for score marks, scratches, pitting and flaking of the finish, and excessive or abnormal wear. Look for dents in the outer tubes and replace the outer tubes in both forks with new ones if any are found.

36 Check the fork inner tube for runout using V-blocks and a dial gauge. If the condition of either inner tube is suspect have it checked by a Triumph dealer or suspension specialist. Triumph provides no specifications for runout.

37 Inspect the inside surface of the outer tube and the working surface of each bush for score marks, scratches and signs of excessive wear (in which case the grey Teflon outer surface will have worn away to reveal the copper inner surface). The bushes are available separately, and should be replaced with new ones if damaged or worn.

38 Check the fork oil seal seat for nicks, gouges and scratches. If damage is evident, leaks will occur. Also check the oil seal washer for damage or distortion and replace it with a new one if necessary.

39 Check the spring for cracks and other damage. If the spring is defective or has sagged, fit new springs in both forks. Never fit only one new spring.

40 Check the damper cartridge for damage and wear. Hold the cartridge and gently pump the rod in and out. If the rod does not move smoothly the damper must be replaced with a new one.

Reassembly

41 Wrap some insulating tape over the ridges on the top of the fork inner tube to protect the lips of the new oil seal as it is fitted **(see illustration)**. Apply a smear of the specified clean fork oil to the lips of the dust seal, oil seal and the inner surface of each bush, then slide the new dust seal, the retaining clip, the oil seal, and the oil seal washer onto the inner tube, making sure the dust seal is the correct way round and that the marked side of the oil seal faces the dust seal **(see illustrations)**. Remove the insulating tape and slide the bottom bush on, then fit the top bush into its recess **(see illustrations)**.

42 Apply a smear of the specified clean fork oil to the outer surface of each bush, then

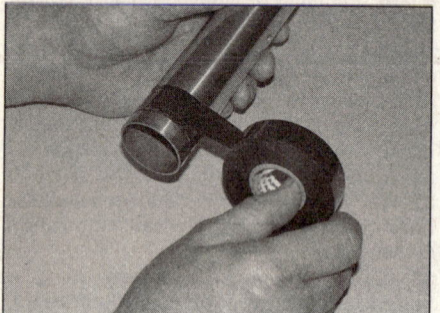

8.41a Wrap some tape over the ridges

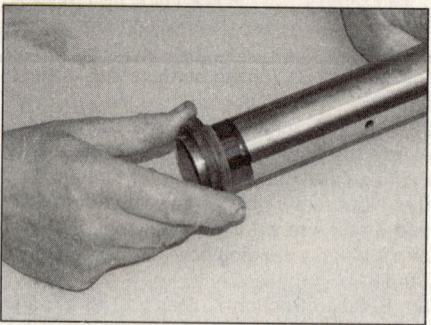

8.41b Slide on the dust seal . . .

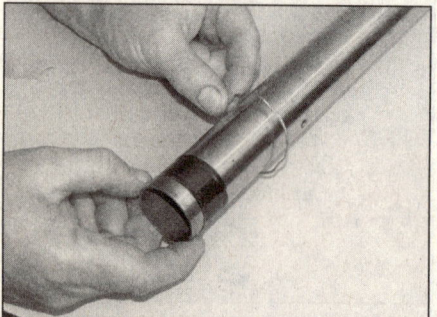

8.41c . . . the retaining clip . . .

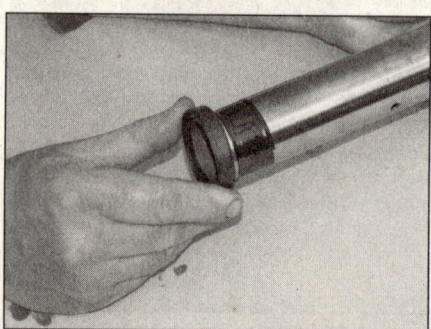

8.41d . . . the oil seal . . .

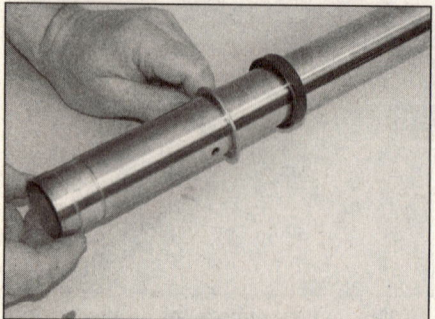

8.41e . . . the washer . . .

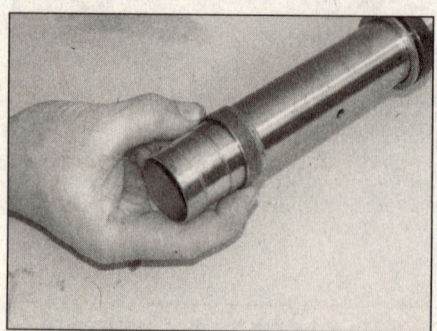

8.41f . . . and the bottom bush . . .

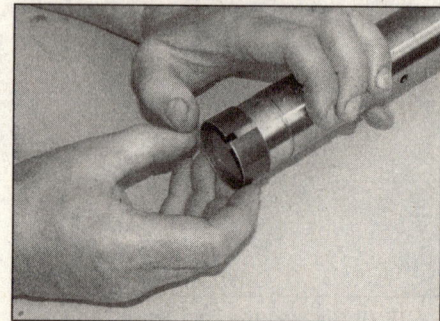

8.41g . . . then fit the top bush into its recess

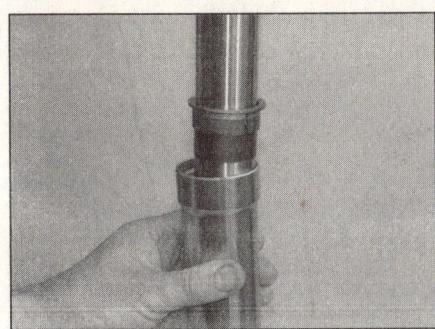

8.42 Slide the inner tube into the outer tube

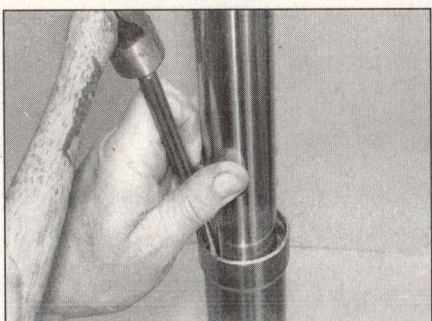

8.44 Carefully drive the bush in until it seats

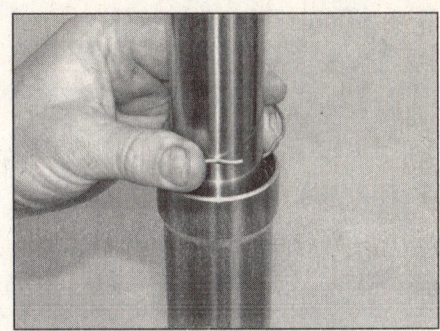

8.47a Fit the retaining clip . . .

carefully insert the inner tube fully into the outer tube **(see illustration)**.

43 Support the fork upside down, then press the bottom bush squarely into its recess in the fork tube as far as possible. Slide the oil seal washer on top of the bush, and keep the oil seal, the retaining clip and the dust seal out of the way by sliding them up the inner tube. If necessary, tape them to the tube to prevent them from falling down and interfering as the bush is drifted into place.

44 Using either the special service tool (part No. T3880003) or a suitable drift, carefully drive the bottom bush fully into its recess – the oil seal washer prevents damaging the edges of the bush **(see illustration)**. If using a drift, wrap tape around it and the fork inner tube to prevent scratches. Make sure the bush enters the recess squarely. It is best to make sure that the inner tube is withdrawn as much as possible from the outer tube so that any accidental scratching is confined to the area that does not affect the oil seal.

45 Lift the washer to check the bush is seated fully and squarely in its recess in the outer tube, then wipe the recess clean and re-seat the washer.

46 Drive the oil seal into place as described in Step 44 until the retaining clip groove is visible.

47 Once the oil seal is correctly seated, fit the retaining clip, making sure it is correctly located in its groove, then press the dust seal into position **(see illustrations)**.

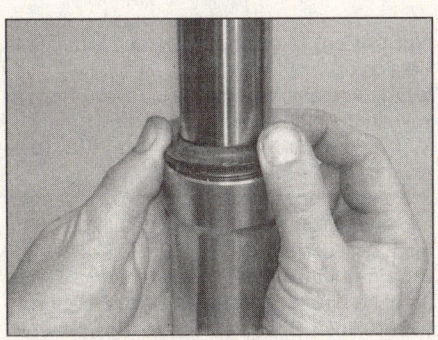

8.47b . . . then press the dust seal in

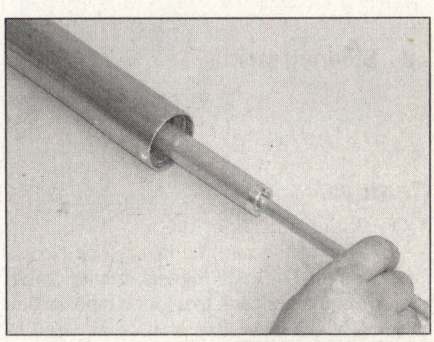

8.48a Insert the damper cartridge

48 If removed insert the damper cartridge into the fork until it contacts the bottom of the inner tube **(see illustration)**. Fit a new sealing washer onto the damper cartridge bolt and apply a few drops of a suitable non-permanent thread locking compound, then fit the bolt into the bottom of the inner tube, thread it into the bottom of the damper cartridge and tighten it to the torque setting specified at the beginning of this Chapter **(see illustrations)**. If the damper cartridge assembly rotates inside the tube, the Triumph service tool described in Step 31 can be used to hold the head of the cartridge body. Alternatively fit the slotted washer under the damper rod locknut and use it to pull up on the rod which should help the bolt to tighten, or wait until the fork is fully reassembled and

tighten it then (the pressure of the spring on the cartridge should prevent it from turning, especially if you compress the fork).

49 Refer to Section 7, Steps 18 to 27, and put new oil into the fork.

50 Loosely fit the axle clamp bolts into the bottom of the right-hand fork.

51 Install the fork (see Section 6). Check and adjust the fork settings as required (see Section 13).

Speed Triple R models

52 Work on the forks fitted to R models should only be undertaken by an Öhlins service centre. Refer to your Triumph dealer for further details. No procedures are given in this manual for these forks.

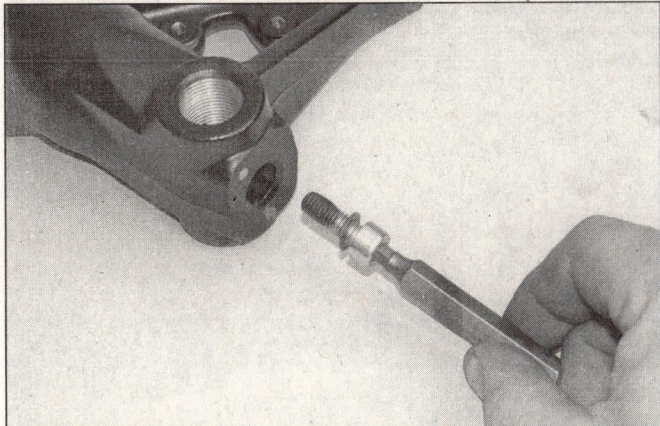

8.48b Apply a thread locking compound to the damper rod bolt and use a new sealing washer . . .

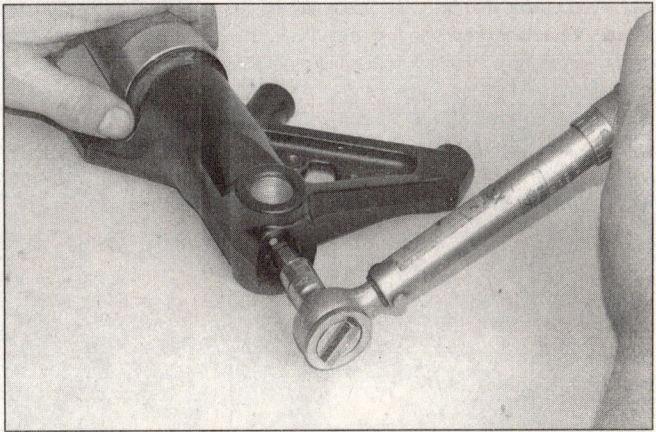

8.48c . . . and tighten the bolt to the specified torque

5•18 Frame and suspension

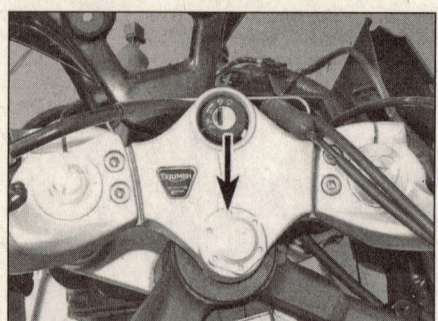

9.4 Slacken the steering stem nut (arrowed)

9.6 Unscrew the steering stem nut . . .

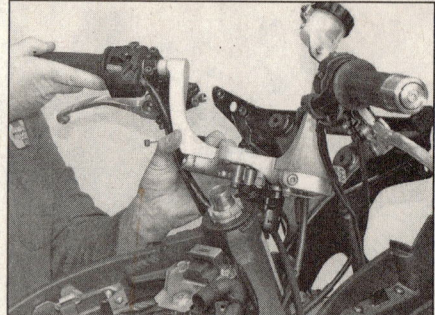

9.7 . . . then displace the top yoke and lay it aside

9 Steering stem

Removal

1 On Sprint and Tiger models if required, remove the fairing and the fairing side panels (see Chapter 7). On all models it is advisable to remove the fuel tank to avoid the possibility of scratching it (see Chapter 4).
2 On Sprint models slacken the handlebar clamp bolts **(see illustration 5.6b)**.
3 On Speed Triple and Tiger models, displace the handlebars from the top yoke (see Chapter 5).
4 Slacken the steering stem nut **(see illustration)**. Remove the front forks (see Section 6).
5 Displace any assemblies from the bottom yoke (horn, brake hose guides, etc).
6 Unscrew the steering stem nut **(see illustration)**.
7 Ease the top yoke assembly up off the forks and lay it clear of the steering stem on some rag **(see illustration)**.
8 Using either the Triumph service tool (Part No. T3880023 for Sprint models and T3880024 for Speed Triple and Tiger models) or a C-spanner, unscrew the locknut, then lift off the tabbed washer **(see illustrations)**.
9 Support the bottom yoke, then unscrew the bearing adjuster nut, noting the plate fitted with it, and gently lower the bottom yoke and steering stem out of the frame **(see illustrations)**.

10 Remove the bearing cover **(see illustration 9.12c)**. Remove the inner race and upper bearing from the top of the steering head **(see illustration)**. Remove the lower bearing from the bottom of the steering stem **(see illustration)**. Remove all traces of old grease from the bearings and races and check them for wear or damage as described in Section 10. **Note:** *Do not attempt to remove the outer races from the steering head or the lower bearing inner race from the steering stem unless they are to be replaced with new ones.*

Installation

11 Smear a liberal quantity of lithium-based grease (see Chapter 1 Specifications) onto the bearing outer races in the steering head. Work

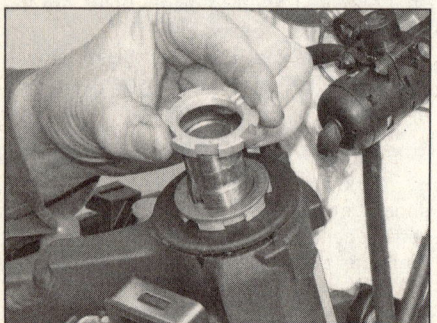

9.8a Unscrew the locknut . . .

9.8b . . . and remove the washer, noting how it locates

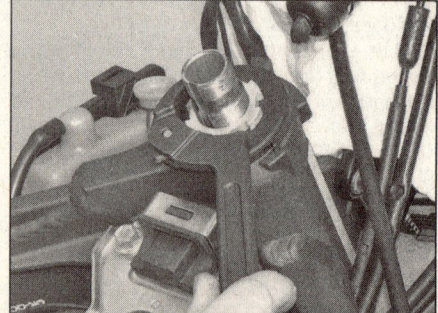

9.9a Unscrew the adjuster nut . . .

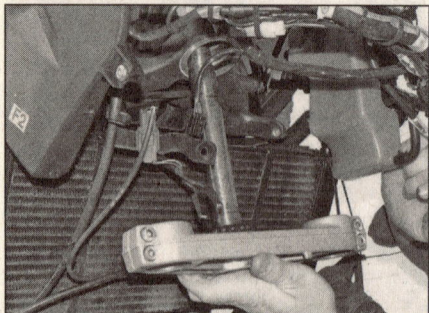

9.9b . . . then lower the bottom yoke to draw the stem out of the head

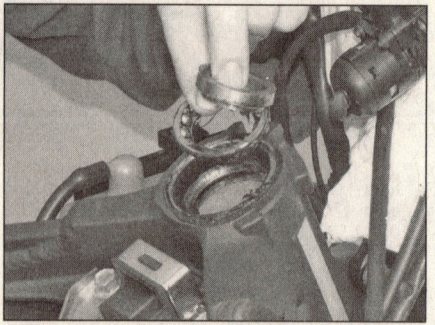

9.10a Remove the inner race and bearing from the top of the head . . .

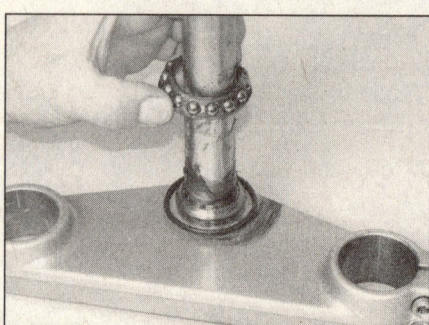

9.10b . . . and the lower bearing from the base of the stem

Frame and suspension 5•19

9.11 Grease the outer races in the head

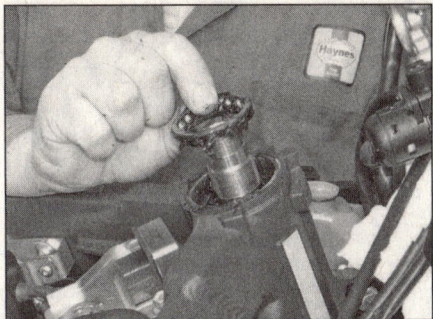
9.12a Fit the upper bearing . . .

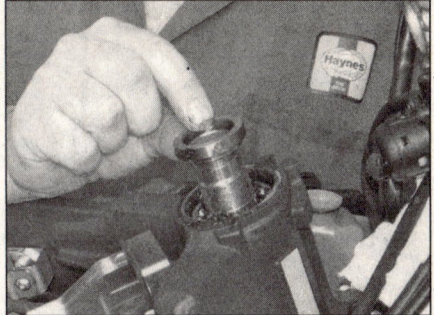
9.12b . . . its inner race . . .

grease well into the upper and lower bearings. Fit the lower bearing onto the steering stem (see illustration 9.10b).

12 Carefully lift the steering stem/bottom yoke up through the steering head and support it (see illustration 9.9b). Fit the upper bearing and its inner race, then fit the bearing cover (see illustrations). Clean any grease off the threads on the steering stem.

13 Make sure the plate is fitted on the underside of the adjuster nut. Thread the adjuster nut onto the steering stem and tighten it finger-tight (see illustration).

14 Triumph specify a torque setting for the adjuster nut, which can only be applied using their service tool (Part No. T3880023 for Sprint models and T3880024 for Speed Triple and Tiger models). With the tool fitted to a torque wrench, apply a torque of 40 Nm to the adjuster nut – this will preload the bearings. Now slacken the nut and tighten it to the final torque setting of 15 Nm.

15 If the service tool isn't available tighten the adjuster nut using a C-spanner until all freeplay is removed, then tighten it a little more (see illustration). This pre-loads the bearings. Now slacken the nut, then tighten it again, setting it so that all freeplay is just removed yet the steering is able to move freely from side to side. To do this tighten the nut only a little at a time, and after each tightening repeat the checks for freeplay and freedom of movement until the bearings are correctly set. The object is to set the adjuster nut so that the bearings are under a very light loading, just enough to remove any freeplay.

16 Fit the tabbed washer, locating the tab in the slot (see illustration 9.8b). Fit the locknut and tighten it to 40 Nm (see illustration 9.8a) – make sure the adjuster does not turn with it, though it shouldn't as the tabbed lockwasher is there to prevent it doing so (if it does you will have to repeat the adjustment procedure).

17 Fit the top yoke onto the steering stem (see illustration 9.7). Fit the steering stem nut and tighten it finger-tight (see illustration 9.6).

18 Install the forks (see Section 6), then tighten the steering stem nut to the specified torque setting.

19 On Sprint tighten the handlebar clamp bolts to the specified torque (see illustration 5.6b).

20 On Speed Triple and Tiger install the handlebars (see Section 5).

21 Carry out a final check of the steering head bearing freeplay as described in Chapter 1, and if necessary re-adjust – this is especially

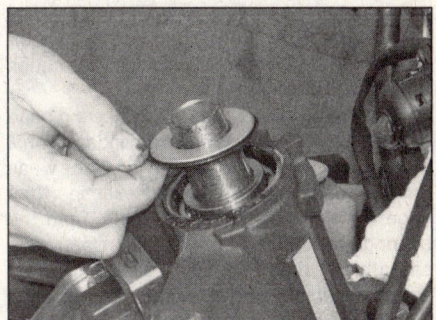
9.12c . . . and the bearing cover

important if the correct torque settings were not applied to the adjuster nut and locknut as the extra weight and inertia of the forks and front wheel will make a difference to the feel of the freeplay and movement checks.

10 Steering head bearing overhaul

Inspection

1 Remove the steering stem (see Section 9).
2 Remove all traces of old grease from the

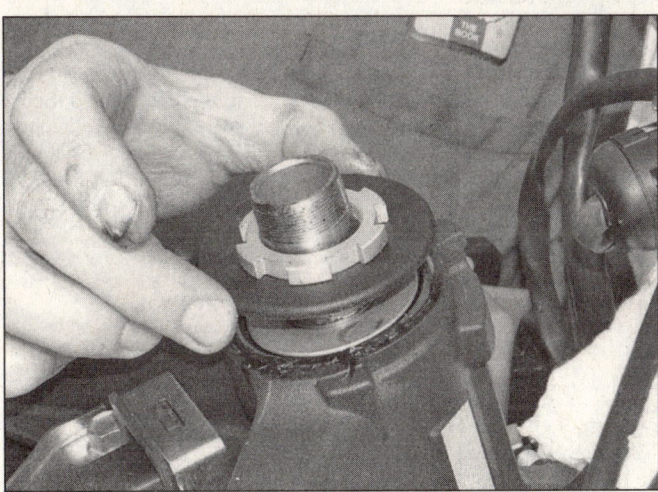
9.13 Fit the adjuster nut – make sure the plate is fitted to its underside

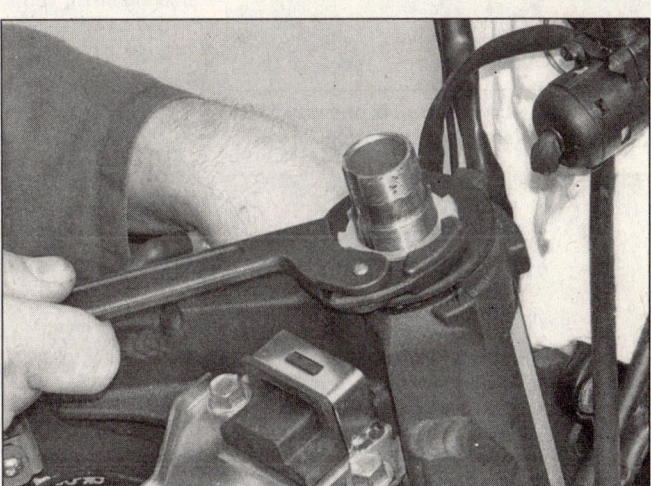
9.15 Tightening the adjuster nut using a C-spanner

5•20 Frame and suspension

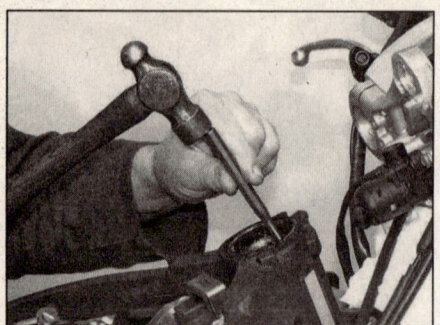

10.5a Drive the outer races from the steering head using a drift . . .

10.5b . . . located in the cut-outs provided

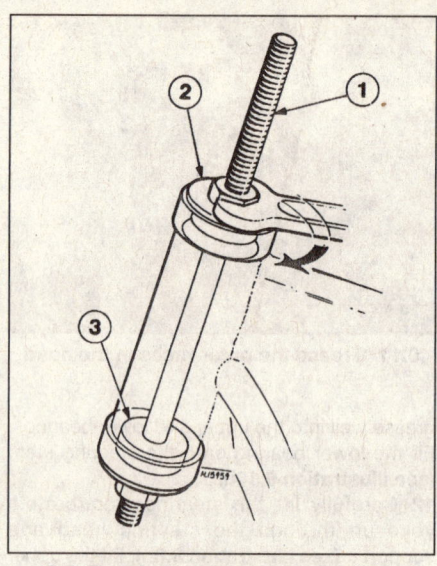

10.7 Drawbolt arrangement for fitting steering stem bearing races

1 Long bolt or threaded bar
2 Thick washer
3 Guide for lower race

bearings and races and check them for wear or damage, referring to *Tools and Workshop Tips* in the Reference Section for information on bearing checks.

3 The bearing outer races in the steering head should be polished and free from indentations. Inspect the bearing rollers for signs of wear, damage or discoloration, and examine their cage for signs of cracks or splits. Spin the bearings by hand. They should spin freely and smoothly. If there are any signs of wear on any of the above components both upper and lower bearing assemblies should be renewed as a set, complete with new outer races. Only remove the outer races in the steering head and the lower bearing from the steering stem if new ones are being fitted – do not re-use them once they have been removed.

Renewal

4 Remove the steering stem (see Section 9).

10.8a Using screwdrivers is one way to try and remove the inner race . . .

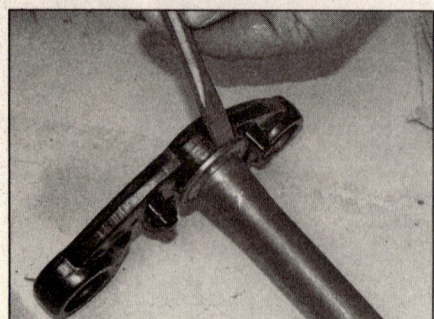

10.8b . . . though a cold chisel is better

5 The bearing outer races are an interference fit in the steering head and can be tapped from position with a suitable drift located on the rim of the race – there are two cut-outs in the race seat to make this easy **(see illustrations)**. Move the drift from one cut-out to the other so that the race is driven out squarely.

6 Alternatively, the races can be removed using a slide-hammer type bearing extractor – these can often be hired from tool shops.

7 The new outer races can be pressed into the steering head using a drawbolt arrangement **(see illustration)**, or by using a large diameter tubular drift. Ensure that the drawbolt washer or drift (as applicable) bears only on the outer edge of the race and does not contact the working surface.

 *Installation of new bearing outer races is made much easier if they are left overnight in the freezer. This causes them to contract slightly making them a looser fit. Alternatively, use a freeze spray.*

8 The lower bearing inner race should only be removed from the steering stem if a new one is being fitted. To remove the race from the steering stem, you can use two screwdrivers placed on opposite sides of the race to work it free, using blocks of wood to improve leverage and protect the yoke **(see illustration)**. Alternatively thread a suitable nut onto the top of the stem to protect the threads, then

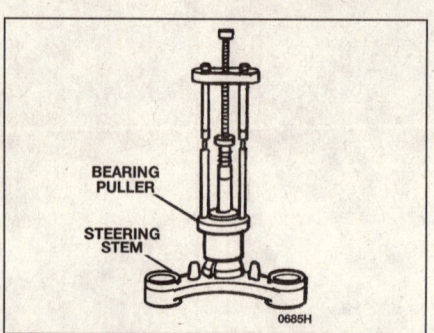

10.8c If necessary remove the inner race using a puller

place the stem on its side and tap under the race using a cold chisel **(see illustration)**. If the race is firmly in place it will be necessary to use a puller **(see illustration)**. Take the steering stem to a Triumph dealer if required. Remove the dust seal and discard it.

9 Fit a new dust seal onto the steering stem. Fit the new race onto the stem and drive it into place using a length of tubing with an internal diameter slightly larger than the steering stem but not so large it contacts the bearing surface **(see illustration)**.

10 Install the steering stem (see Section 9).

11 Rear shock absorber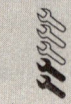

Removal

1 Support the motorcycle securely in an upright position using the centrestand (Sprint only) or an auxiliary stand. Position a support

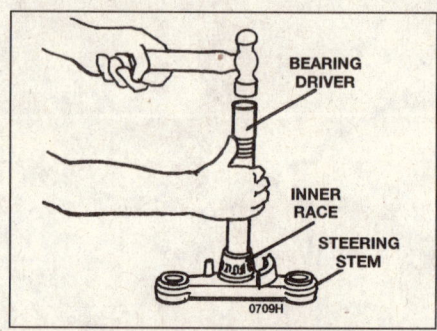

10.9 Drive the new bearing on using a suitable driver or a length of pipe

Frame and suspension 5•21

11.2a Undo the screws (arrowed) and remove the shield – ST models

11.2b Undo the screw (arrowed) and remove the cover . . .

11.2c . . . then unscrew the pre-load adjuster bolt (arrowed)

under the rear wheel so that it does not drop when the shock absorber is removed, but also making sure that the weight of the machine is off the rear suspension so that the shock is not compressed. Note which side the bolts are fitted before removal.

Sprint models

2 Remove the seat (see Chapter 7), and the fuel tank (see Chapter 4). Where fitted remove the splash shield **(see illustration)**. On GT models remove the spring pre-load adjuster cover, then displace the adjuster from its bracket **(see illustrations)**.
3 Unscrew the nut and withdraw the bolt securing the bottom of the shock absorber to the drop link plates **(see illustration)**. Retrieve the spacers.
4 Unscrew the nut on the shock absorber upper mounting bolt, then support the shock absorber and withdraw the bolt **(see illustration)**. Lift the shock out of the frame **(see illustrations)**. Note the sleeve for the upper mounting bolt in the frame **(see illustration 11.8b)**.

2005 to 2010 Speed Triple models (up to VIN 461331)

5 Remove the seat and the side panels (see Chapter 7). Remove the fuel tank (see Chapter 4).
6 Unscrew the nut and withdraw the bolt securing the bottom of the shock absorber to the drop and drag links **(see illustration)**. Pivot the links down and retrieve the collars.
7 Slacken the remote reservoir clamp screw and release the reservoir **(see illustration)**.
8 Unscrew the nut on the shock absorber upper mounting bolt, then support the

11.3 Unscrew the nut and withdraw the bolt securing the shock to the drop link plates, and remove the spacers (arrowed)

shock absorber and withdraw the bolt **(see illustration)**. Lower the shock out of the frame, manoeuvring it as required to feed

11.4a Unscrew the nut and withdraw the bolt . . .

11.4b . . . then twist the shock as shown to avoid snagging the pre-load adjuster . . .

11.4c . . . and lift the shock out

11.6 Unscrew the nut (arrowed), withdraw the bolt, and pivot the links off the shock absorber

11.7 Slacken the clamp screw (arrowed) to release the reservoir

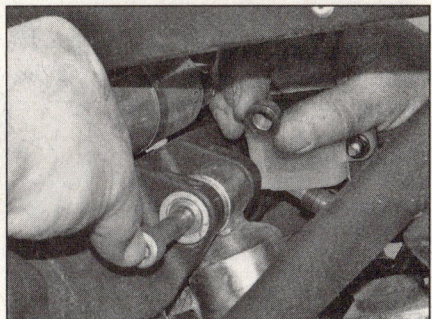

11.8a Unscrew the nut, withdraw the bolt . . .

5•22 Frame and suspension

11.8b ... and lower the shock. Note the sleeve (arrowed) in the frame

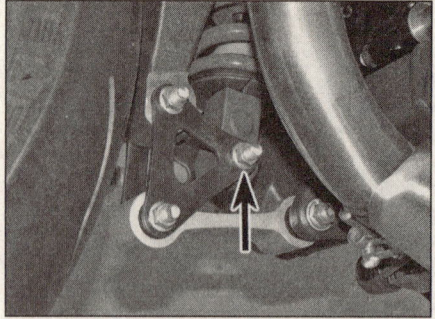

11.10 Unscrew the nut (arrowed) and withdraw the bolt

11.11 Unscrew the nut (arrowed), withdraw the bolt and remove the shock

11.13 Remove the silencer bolt (arrowed)

11.14 Displace the starter relay (arrowed)

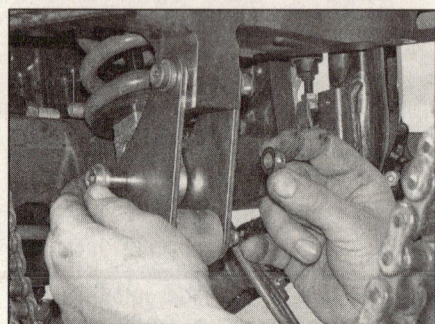

11.15 Unscrew the nut and withdraw the bolt

the reservoir and hose round with it **(see illustration)**. Note the sleeve for the upper mounting bolt in the frame.

2011-on Speed Triple models (from VIN 461332)

9 Remove the exhaust silencers and intermediate pipe (see Chapter 4).
10 Unscrew the nut and withdraw the bolt securing the bottom of the shock absorber to the drop link plates **(see illustration)**. Slacken the nuts on the other two drop link plate bolts.
11 Unscrew the nut on the shock absorber upper mounting bolt, then support the shock absorber and withdraw the bolt **(see illustration)**. Lift the shock out of the swingarm. Note the sleeve for the upper mounting bolt in the frame.

Tiger and Tiger SE models

12 Remove the seat cowling (see Chapter 7), and the battery (see Chapter 8).
13 Unscrew and remove the nut on the silencer mounting bolt **(see illustration)** – Triumph specify to discard the nut and use a new one on installation. Support the silencer and withdraw the bolt.
14 Displace the starter relay from its mount – there is no need to disconnect the wiring or leads **(see illustration)**.
15 Unscrew the nut and withdraw the bolt securing the bottom of the shock absorber to the drop link plates **(see illustration)**. Discard the nut – a new one should be used.
16 Slacken the rear sub-frame lower bolt nuts, then unscrew and remove the upper bolt nuts **(see illustrations)**. Support the sub-frame then withdraw the upper bolts, and

pivot the sub-frame down on the lower bolts. Note that new nuts should be used on all the sub-frame bolts on installation.
17 Unscrew the nut on the shock absorber upper mounting bolt, then support the shock absorber and withdraw the bolt **(see illustration)**. Lift the shock out of the frame. Discard the nut – a new one should be used. Note the sleeve for the upper mounting bolt in the frame **(see illustration 11.8b)**.

Tiger Sport models

18 Remove the rear wheel (see Chapter 6).
19 Unscrew the nut and withdraw the bolt securing the bottom of the shock absorber to the drop link plates **(see illustration 11.15)**. Discard the nut – a new one should be used.
20 Unscrew the nut on the shock absorber upper mounting bolt, then support the shock absorber and withdraw the bolt **(see**

11.16a Slacken the nut on the lower bolt (arrowed) on each side ...

11.16b ... then remove the nuts (arrowed) on the upper bolts

11.17 Shock absorber upper mounting bolt (arrowed)

Frame and suspension 5•23

11.21 Look for cracks, pitting and oil leakage on the damper rod (arrowed)

11.22a Withdraw the sleeve and check the bearing and seals (arrowed)

11.22b Upper mounting bush (arrowed)

illustration 11.17). Lift the shock out of the swingarm. Discard the nut – a new one should be used. Note the sleeve for the upper mounting bolt in the frame.

Inspection – all models

21 Inspect the shock absorber for obvious physical damage and the coil spring for looseness, cracks or signs of fatigue. Inspect the damper rod for signs of bending, pitting and oil leakage **(see illustration)**. On Speed Triple models check the reservoir and its hose for damage, cracks or leakage.

22 Remove the sleeve from the lower mounting bearing **(see illustration)**. Check the condition of the lower mounting seals and the bearing – if necessary lever the old seals out and replace them with new ones. Also check the bush in the upper mounting, and check the mountings themselves for cracks **(see illustration)**. Refer to Section 12 and check the bearings and seals in the drop link.

23 Triumph do not list the upper mounting bushes as being available separately on any models, but on Tiger models the lower mounting bearing and seals are available, on Sprint models the spacers are available, and on Speed Triple models the collars and seals are available. The sleeve in the frame for the upper mounting is available on all models.

24 On Tiger models if the bearing is worn refer to 'Tools and workshop tips' in the Reference section at the end of the book for details of removal and installation methods, noting that once a needle bearing has been removed it cannot be re-used. Also check the remote pre-load adjuster for damage.

25 Replacement parts for the shock absorber itself are not available from Triumph. If it is worn or damaged, it must be replaced with a new one.

Installation – all models

26 Installation is the reverse of removal, noting the following:
- Apply lithium-based grease (see Chapter 1 Specifications) to the shock absorber and linkage pivot points, sleeves, collars and spacers as required according to model.
- Make sure the sleeve for the upper mounting bolt is fitted in the frame **(see illustration 11.8b)**.
- On Sprint models, fit the shock so the pre-load adjuster is on the left-hand side on ST models **(see illustration 11.2)**, and so the pre-load adjuster hose exits the shock to the left on GT models. Fit both bolts loosely before fitting the nuts, not forgetting the spacers with the lower bolt **(see illustration 11.3)**. Tighten the upper mounting bolt nut, then the lower, to the torque setting specified at the beginning of the Chapter.
- On 2005 to 2010 Speed Triple models (up to VIN 461331), fit the shock so the remote reservoir hose union is on the right-hand side. Fit the upper mounting bolt loosely **(see illustration 11.8a)**, then pivot the drop and drag links onto the shock absorber, not forgetting to fit the collars, and insert the lower bolt **(see illustration 11.6)**. Take the bike off the stand so the weight is through the suspension, then tighten the upper mounting bolt nut, then the lower, to the torque settings specified at the beginning of the Chapter.
- On 2011-on Speed Triple models (from VIN 461332), remove the sleeve from the bottom mount and grease the bearing. Fit the both bolts and the new nuts loosely, inserting the bolts from the left. Take the bike off the stand so the weight is through the suspension, then tighten the upper mounting bolt nut, then the lower, to the torque setting specified at the beginning of the Chapter.
- On Tiger and Tiger SE models, use new nuts on both the shock absorber bolts and all of the rear sub-frame bolts. Fit the shock so the pre-load adjuster is on the right-hand side. Fit both bolts loosely from the left before fitting the nuts. Tighten the upper mounting bolt nut, then the lower, to the torque setting specified at the beginning of the Chapter. Tighten the upper sub-frame bolts then the lower bolts to the specified torque settings. Fit a new nut onto the silencer mounting bolt and tighten it to the specified torque **(see illustration 11.13)**.
- On Tiger Sport models, use new nuts on both the shock absorber bolts. Fit the shock so the pre-load adjuster is on the right-hand side. Fit both bolts loosely, upper bolt from the left and lower bolt from the right, before fitting the nuts. Tighten the upper mounting bolt nut, then the lower, to the torque setting specified at the beginning of the Chapter.
- Check the operation of the rear suspension and adjust the shock absorber settings as required before taking the machine on the road.

12 Rear suspension linkage

Removal

1 Support the motorcycle securely in an upright position using the centrestand (Sprint only) or an auxiliary stand. Position a support under the rear wheel so that it does not drop when the shock absorber lower mounting bolt is removed, but also making sure that the weight of the machine is off the rear suspension so that the shock is not compressed. Note which side the bolts are fitted before removal.

Sprint models

2 On ST models remove the exhaust intermediate pipe (see Chapter 4).

3 Unscrew the nut and withdraw the bolt securing the drop link plates to the bottom of the shock absorber **(see illustration 11.3)**. Push the shock forward and remove the spacers.

4 Unscrew the nut and withdraw the bolt securing the drop link plates to the drag link **(see illustration)**. Pivot the drag link down and, where fitted, remove the spacers.

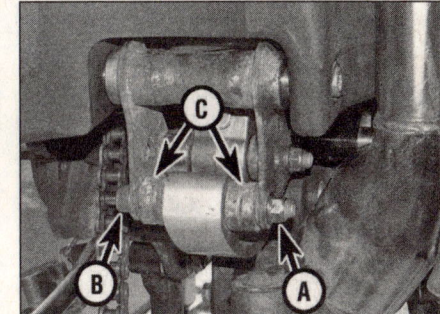

12.4 Unscrew the nut (A), withdraw the bolt (B) and remove the spacers (C)

5•24 Frame and suspension

12.5a Unscrew the bolt (arrowed)

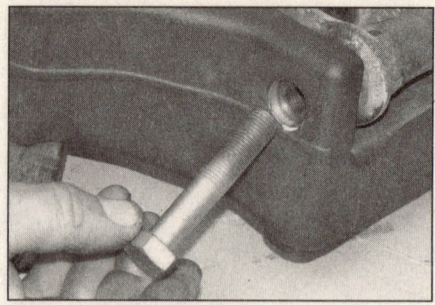

12.5b Thread the specified size bolt into the sleeve to use as a handle to draw the sleeve out

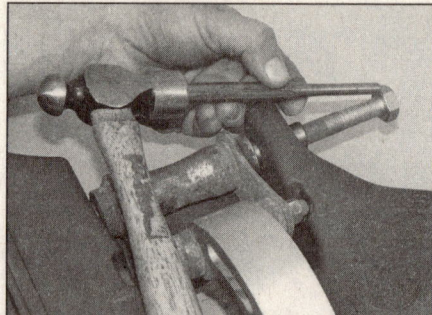

12.5c If necessary use a drift on the bolt head . . .

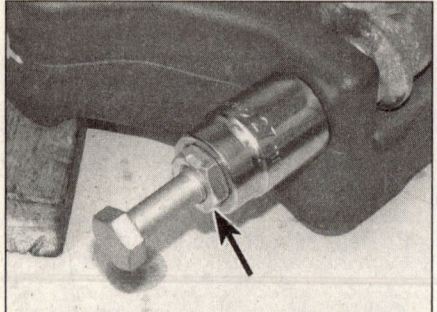

12.5d . . . or create a drawbolt arrangement as shown and turn the nut (arrowed) to extract the sleeve

12.6 Unscrew the nut (arrowed), withdraw the bolt and remove the drag link

12.9 Unscrew the bolt (arrowed)

5 Unscrew the bolt securing the drop link to the swingarm **(see illustration)**. Draw the bearing sleeve out of the swingarm using an M14 bolt with 1.5 mm thread pitch threaded into the sleeve's right-hand end and draw it out by pulling on the bolt head with pliers, and remove the drop link, noting which way round it fits **(see illustration)**. If the sleeve is stuck, remove the swingarm with the drop link still attached (see Section 14) and use a drift under the bolt head, or pull the sleeve out using a socket and nut fitted with the bolt to convert it to a drawbolt tool, or using a slide-hammer attachment **(see illustrations)**.

6 Unscrew the nut and withdraw the bolt securing the drag link to the frame and remove the link and its spacer, noting which way round the link fits **(see illustration)**.

2005 to 2010 Speed Triple models (up to VIN 461331)

7 Remove the exhaust intermediate pipe (see Chapter 4).

8 Unscrew the nut and withdraw the bolt securing the drop and drag links to the bottom of the shock absorber **(see illustration 11.6)**. Pivot the links down and retrieve the collars from the shock absorber.

9 Unscrew the bolt securing the drop link to the swingarm **(see illustration)**. Draw the bearing sleeve out of the swingarm using an M14 bolt with 1.5 mm thread pitch threaded into the sleeve's right-hand end and draw it out by pulling on the bolt head with pliers, and remove the drop link, noting which way round it fits **(see illustration 12.5b)**. If the sleeve is stuck, remove the swingarm (see Section 14) and use a drift under the bolt head, or pull the sleeve out using a socket and nut fitted with the bolt to convert it to a drawbolt tool, or using a slide-hammer attachment **(see illustrations 12.5c and d)**.

10 Unscrew the nut and withdraw bolt securing the drag link to the frame, noting the washer fitted under the head of the bolt **(see illustration)**. Remove the drag link and retrieve the spacers.

2011-on Speed Triple models (from VIN 461332) and Tiger models

11 Unscrew the nut and withdraw the bolt securing the drop link plates to the bottom of the shock absorber **(see illustration 11.12)**.

12 Unscrew the nut and withdraw the bolt securing the drop link plates to the drag link and detach the arm **(see illustration)**.

13 Unscrew the nut and withdraw the bolt securing the drop link plates to the swingarm and remove the plates, noting which way round they fit **(see illustration)**.

12.10 Unscrew the nut (arrowed), withdraw the bolt and remove the drag link

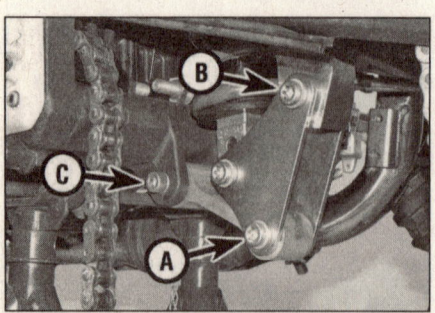

12.12 Drop link plates-to-drag link bolt (A), drop link plates-to-swingarm bolt (B), drag link-to-frame bolt (C)

12.13 Unscrew the nut, withdraw the bolt and remove the plates

Frame and suspension 5•25

12.15a Withdraw the sleeves from the bearings . . .

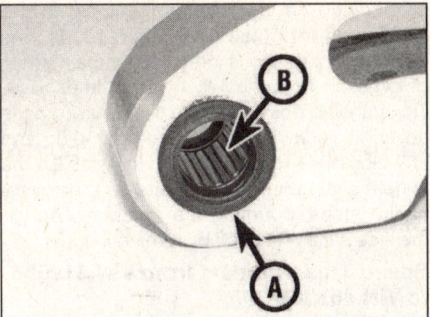

12.15b . . . and inspect the seals (A) and bearings (B) . . .

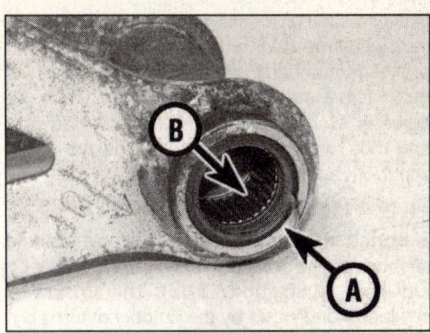

12.15c . . . in all the mounts – Sprint linkage assembly shown

14 Unscrew the nut and withdraw the bolt securing the drag link to the frame and remove the link, noting which way round it fits **(see illustration 12.12)**. Note that Triumph specifies to use new nuts all round.

Inspection

15 Withdraw the bearing sleeves, noting which fits where **(see illustrations)**. Lever the grease seals out. On 2011-on Speed Triple models (from VIN 461332) and Tiger models the drop link sleeve, seals and bearing are in the mount in the swingarm. Thoroughly clean all components, removing all traces of dirt, corrosion and grease.
16 Inspect all components closely, looking for obvious signs of wear such as heavy scoring, or for damage such as cracks or distortion. Slip each sleeve back into its bearing and check that there is not an excessive amount of freeplay between the two components. Renew any components as required.
17 Check the condition of the needle roller bearings. Refer to *Tools and Workshop Tips* (Section 5) in the Reference section for more information on bearings.
18 Worn bearings can be driven out of their bores, but note that removal will destroy them; new bearings should be obtained before work commences. The new bearings should be pressed or drawn into their bores rather than driven into position. In the absence of a press, a suitable drawbolt tool can be made up as described in *Tools and Workshop Tips* (Section 5) in the Reference section.
19 Lubricate the needle roller bearings with grease.

20 Press new grease seals squarely into place. Lubricate the sleeves and fit them into the bearings.

Installation

21 Installation is the reverse of removal, noting the following:
● If not already done clean off old grease and apply new grease to all pivot points, sleeves and spacers, as described in Inspection. Make sure all sleeves and spacers are correctly fitted.
● On Sprint models, the UP mark on the drop link plates must be on the right-hand side – 2010-on models also have a FWD mark on the drop link **(see illustration 12.21a)**. On 2005 to 2009 models make sure the drag link is the correct way up **(see illustration 12.6)**. On 2010-on models the TOP mark on the drag link must be on the top.
● On 2005 to 2010 Speed Triple models (up to VIN 461331) fit the drop link with the cut-away side of the bottom (narrower) end facing to the rear **(see illustration 11.6)**. Fit the bearing sleeve with its threaded end facing to the right-hand side.
● On 2011-on Speed Triple models (from VIN 461332), the outer side of each drop link plate is marked TOP on its upper side so they cannot be installed the wrong way round **(see illustration 12.21b)**. Fit all bolts and the new nuts loosely, inserting the bolts from the left. Take the bike off the stand so the weight is through the suspension, then tighten the bolts to the torque setting specified at the beginning of the Chapter.

● On Tiger models, each drop link plate is marked to show the swingarm mounts (S) and rear shock absorber mounts (R) so they cannot be installed the wrong way round – these marks must face the right-hand side. Fit all bolts loosely from the left on Tiger and Tiger SE models, and the drag link to the frame bolt from the left and all other bolts from the right on Tiger Sport models, before fitting the new nuts.
● Secure the bolts and nuts finger-tight only until all components are in position, then tighten the nuts to the torque settings specified at the beginning of the Chapter.
● Check the operation of the rear suspension before taking the machine on the road.

13 Suspension adjustment

Note: *Refer to the owners handbook supplied with the machine for recommended front and rear suspension settings to suit loading.*

Front forks

1 The forks are adjustable for spring pre-load on all models, and for both rebound and compression damping on Speed Triple and Tiger models.

Sprint models

2 **Spring pre-load** is adjusted using a screwdriver in the slot in the top of the adjuster on the top of each fork **(see illustration)**. The amount of pre-load is indicated by the number

12.21a Make sure the UP and FWD marks are correctly positioned

12.21b Make sure the TOP marks are at the top and facing out

13.2 Spring pre-load adjuster (arrowed) – Sprint

of lines visible on the adjuster above the top bolt hex, or by measuring the amount of protrusion of it. The standard position is with 3 lines (10 mm) visible above the top bolt hex. Turn the adjuster clockwise to increase pre-load and anti-clockwise to decrease it. Always make sure both adjusters are set equally.

Speed Triple models up to VIN 419555

3 Spring pre-load is adjusted using a suitable spanner on the adjuster flats on the top of each fork **(see illustration 13.15)**. The amount of pre-load is indicated by the number of turns out from the fully screwed in (clockwise) position. The standard position is three turns out. Turn the adjuster clockwise to increase pre-load and anti-clockwise to decrease it. To establish the current setting, turn the adjuster in (clockwise) until it stops, counting the number of turns, then reset it as required by turning it out. Note that there are lines on the adjuster which can also be used as a guide. Always make sure both adjusters are set equally.

4 Rebound damping is adjusted using a screwdriver in the slot in the adjuster protruding from the pre-load adjuster **in the left-hand fork** **(see illustration 13.15)**. The amount of damping is indicated by the number of turns out from the fully screwed-in position. The standard position is two turns out. Turn the adjuster clockwise to increase damping and anti-clockwise to decrease it. To establish the current setting, turn the adjuster in (clockwise) until it stops, counting the number of turns, then reset it as required by turning it out.

5 Compression damping is adjusted using a screwdriver in the slot in the adjuster protruding from the pre-load adjuster **in the right-hand fork (see illustration 13.15)**. The amount of damping is indicated by the number of turns out from the fully screwed-in position. The standard position is two turns out. Turn the adjuster clockwise to increase damping and anti-clockwise to decrease it. To establish the current setting, turn the adjuster in (clockwise) until it stops, counting the number of turns, then reset it as required by turning it out.

Speed Triple models from VIN 419556 to VIN 461331

6 Spring pre-load is adjusted using a suitable spanner on the flats of the adjuster on the top of each fork **(see illustration 13.15)**. Turn the adjuster clockwise to increase pre-load and anti-clockwise to decrease it. The amount of pre-load is indicated by the number of lines visible on the adjuster above the top bolt hex. The standard position is with 3 lines visible above the top bolt hex. Always make sure both adjusters are set equally.

7 Rebound damping is adjusted using a screwdriver in the slot in the adjuster protruding from the pre-load adjuster in each fork **(see illustration 13.15)**. Turn the adjuster clockwise to increase damping and anti-clockwise to decrease it. The amount of damping is indicated by the number of turns out from the fully screwed-in position. The standard position is one turn out. To establish the current setting, turn the adjuster in (clockwise) until it stops, counting the number of turns, then reset it as required by turning it out.

8 Compression damping is adjusted using a screwdriver in the slot in the adjuster in the bottom of each fork **(see illustration 13.11)**.

Turn the adjuster clockwise to increase damping and anti-clockwise to decrease it. The amount of damping is indicated by the number of turns out from the fully screwed-in position. The standard position is one turn out. To establish the current setting, turn the adjuster in (clockwise) until it stops, counting the number of turns, then reset it as required by turning it out.

Speed Triple models from VIN 461332

9 Spring pre-load is adjusted using a suitable spanner on the flats of the adjuster on the top of each fork **(see illustration)**. Turn the adjuster clockwise to increase pre-load and anti-clockwise to decrease it. The amount of pre-load is indicated by the number of turns clockwise from the fully screwed out (anti-clockwise) position. The standard position is seven turns clockwise. To establish the current setting, turn the adjuster out (anti-clockwise) until it stops, counting the number of turns, then reset it as required by turning it in. Always make sure both adjusters are set equally.

10 Rebound damping is adjusted using a screwdriver in the slot in the adjuster protruding from the pre-load adjuster in each fork **(see illustration)**. Turn the adjuster clockwise to increase damping and anti-clockwise to decrease it. The amount of damping is indicated by the number of turns out from the fully screwed-in position. The standard position is one and a half turns out. To establish the current setting, turn the adjuster in (clockwise) until it stops, counting the number of turns, then reset it as required by turning it out.

11 Compression damping is adjusted using a screwdriver in the slot in the adjuster in the bottom of each fork **(see illustration)**. Turn the adjuster clockwise to increase damping and anti-clockwise to decrease it. The amount of damping is indicated by the number of turns out from the fully screwed-in position. The standard position is one and a half turns out. To establish the current setting, turn the adjuster in (clockwise) until it stops, counting the number of turns, then reset it as required by turning it out.

Speed Triple R

12 Spring pre-load is adjusted using a suitable spanner on the flats of the adjuster on the top of each fork **(see illustration)**. Turn the adjuster clockwise to increase pre-load and anti-clockwise to decrease it. The amount of pre-load is indicated by the number of turns clockwise from the fully screwed out (anti-clockwise) position. The standard position is seven turns clockwise. To establish the current setting, turn the adjuster out (anti-clockwise) until it stops, counting the number of turns, then reset it as required by turning it in. Always make sure both adjusters are set equally.

13 Rebound damping is adjusted using a 3 mm hex key in the adjuster protruding from the pre-load adjuster **in the right-hand fork (see illustration 13.14)**. Turn the adjuster clockwise to increase damping and anti-clockwise to decrease it. The amount of damping is indicated by the number of clicks when turned out (anti-clockwise) from the fully

13.9 Spring pre-load adjuster (arrowed) – Speed Triple from VIN 461332

13.10 Rebound damping adjuster (arrowed) – Speed Triple from VIN 461332

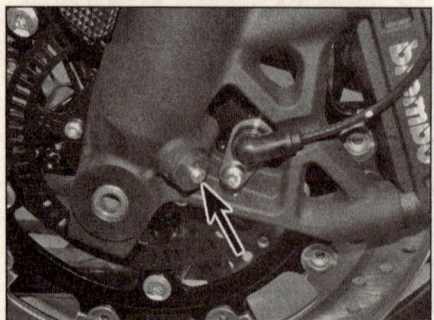

13.11 Compression damping adjuster (arrowed) – Speed Triple from VIN 461332

13.12 Spring pre-load adjuster (arrowed) – Speed Triple R

Frame and suspension 5•27

13.14 Damping adjuster (arrowed) – Speed Triple R

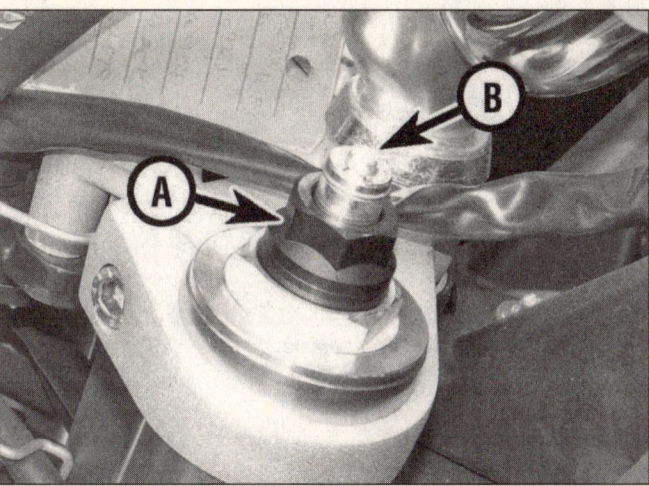

13.15 Spring preload adjuster (A), damping adjuster (B) – Tiger and Speed Triple

turned-in position, noting that the first click is counted as zero, not one. The standard position is ten clicks out out. To establish the current setting, turn the adjuster in (clockwise) until it stops, counting the number of clicks, then reset it as required by turning it out.

14 Compression damping is adjusted using a 3 mm hex key in the adjuster protruding from the pre-load adjuster **in the left-hand fork (see illustration)**. Turn the adjuster clockwise to increase damping and anti-clockwise to decrease it. The amount of damping is indicated by the number of clicks when turned out (anti-clockwise) from the fully turned-in position, noting that the first click is counted as zero, not one. The standard position is fifteen clicks out out. To establish the current setting, turn the adjuster in (clockwise) until it stops, counting the number of clicks, then reset it as required by turning it out.

Tiger models

15 Spring pre-load is adjusted using a suitable spanner on the adjuster flats on the top of each fork **(see illustration)**. The amount of pre-load is indicated by lines on the adjuster. The standard position is with the 3rd line just visible above the top bolt hex. Turn the adjuster clockwise to increase pre-load and anti-clockwise to decrease it. Always make sure both adjusters are set equally.

16 Rebound damping is adjusted using a screwdriver in the slot in the adjuster protruding from the pre-load adjuster **in the left-hand fork (see illustration 13.15)**. The amount of damping is indicated by the number of turns out from the fully screwed-in position. The standard position is one turn out. Turn the adjuster clockwise to increase damping and anti-clockwise to decrease it. To establish the current setting, turn the adjuster in (clockwise) until it stops, counting the number of turns, then reset it as required by turning it out.

17 Compression damping is adjusted using a screwdriver in the slot in the adjuster protruding from the pre-load adjuster **in the right-hand fork (see illustration 13.15)**. The amount of damping is indicated by the number of turns out from the fully screwed-in position. The standard position is one turn out. Turn the adjuster clockwise to increase damping and anti-clockwise to decrease it. To establish the current setting, turn the adjuster in (clockwise) until it stops, counting the number of turns, then reset it as required by turning it out.

Rear shock absorber

18 The shock absorber is adjustable for spring pre-load and rebound damping on Sprint and Tiger models, and for rebound and compression damping on Speed Triple models.

Sprint models

19 Spring pre-load (ST models) is adjusted using a screwdriver in the slot in the adjuster on the top of the shock absorber on the left-hand side, **(see illustration)**. The amount of pre-load is indicated by the number of clicks out from the fully screwed-in position. The standard position is twenty five clicks out. Turn the adjuster clockwise to increase pre-load and anti-clockwise to decrease it. To establish the current setting, turn the adjuster in (clockwise) until it stops, counting the number of clicks, then reset it as required by turning it out.

20 Spring pre-load (GT models) is adjusted by turning the knob on the right-hand side of the bike **(see illustration)**. Turn the adjuster clockwise to increase pre-load and anti-clockwise to decrease it. The amount of pre-load is indicated by the number of clicks when turned anti-clockwise from the fully turned-in position. The standard position is thirty clicks out. To establish the current setting, turn the adjuster in (clockwise) until it stops, counting the number of clicks, then reset it as required by turning it out.

21 Rebound damping is adjusted using a screwdriver in the slot in the adjuster on the base of the shock absorber on the left-hand side **(see illustration)**. The amount of damping

13.19 Spring pre-load adjuster (arrowed) – Sprint ST

13.20 Spring pre-load adjuster (arrowed) – Sprint GT

13.21 Rebound damping adjuster (arrowed) – Sprint

5•28 Frame and suspension

13.22 Rebound damping adjuster (arrowed) – early Speed Triple

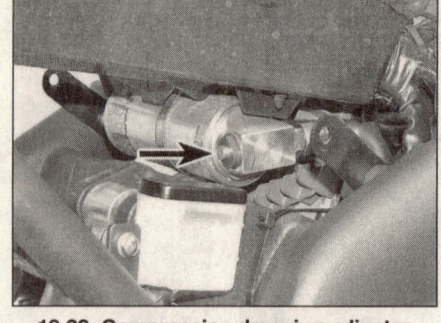

13.23 Compression damping adjuster (arrowed) – early Speed Triple

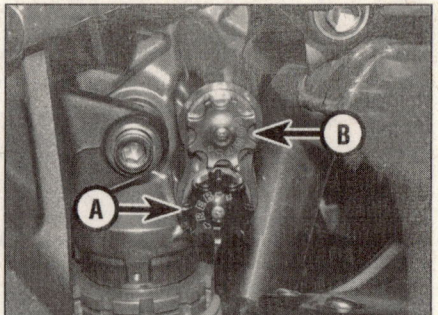

13.24 Rebound damping adjuster (A), compression damping adjuster (B) – Speed Triple R

is indicated by the number of turns out from the fully screwed-in position. The standard position is one and a half turns out. Turn the adjuster clockwise to increase damping and anti-clockwise to decrease it. To establish the current setting, turn the adjuster in (clockwise) until it stops, counting the number of turns, then reset it as required by turning it out.

Speed Triple models

22 Rebound damping is adjusted using a screwdriver in the slot in the adjuster on the base of the shock absorber on the left-hand side **(see illustration)**. The amount of damping is indicated by the number of turns out from the fully screwed-in position. The standard position is two turns out on models up to VIN 419555, one and a half turns out from VIN 419556 to 461331, and one and a quarter turns from VIN 461332. Turn the adjuster clockwise to increase damping and anti-clockwise to decrease it. To establish the current setting, turn the adjuster in (clockwise) until it stops, counting the number of turns, then reset it as required by turning it out.

23 Compression damping is adjusted using a screwdriver in the slot in the adjuster on the reservoir **(see illustration)**. The amount of damping is indicated by the number of turns out from the fully screwed-in position. The standard position is two turns out on models up to VIN 419555, one and a half turns out from VIN 419556 to 461331, and one turn out from VIN 461332. Turn the adjuster clockwise to increase damping and anti-clockwise to decrease it. To establish the current setting, turn the adjuster in (clockwise) until it stops, counting the number of turns, then reset it as required by turning it out.

Speed Triple R

24 Rebound damping is adjusted by turning the black (lower) adjuster dial on the left-hand side of the shock absorber **(see illustration)**. Turn the adjuster clockwise to increase damping and anti-clockwise to decrease it. The amount of damping is indicated by the number of clicks when turned out (anti-clockwise) from the fully turned-in position, noting that the first click is counted as zero, not one. The standard position is ten clicks out out. To establish the current setting, turn the adjuster in (clockwise) until it stops, counting the number of clicks, then reset it as required by turning it out.

25 Compression damping is adjusted by turning the gold (upper) adjuster dial on the left-hand side of the shock absorber **(see illustration 13.24)**. Turn the adjuster clockwise to increase damping and anti-clockwise to decrease it. The amount of damping is indicated by the number of clicks when turned out (anti-clockwise) from the fully turned-in position, noting that the first click is counted as zero, not one. The standard position is seventeen clicks out out. To establish the current setting, turn the adjuster in (clockwise) until it stops, counting the number of clicks, then reset it as required by turning it out.

Tiger models

26 Spring pre-load is adjusted using a screwdriver in the slot in the adjuster on the top of the shock absorber on the right-hand side **(see illustration)**. The amount of pre-load is indicated by the number of clicks out from the fully screwed-in position. The standard position is sixteen clicks out on models up to VIN 438381, and twenty clicks out on all other models including Tiger Sport. Turn the adjuster clockwise to increase pre-load and anti-clockwise to decrease it. To establish the current setting, turn the adjuster in (clockwise) until it stops, counting the number of clicks, then reset it as required by turning it out.

27 Rebound damping is adjusted using a screwdriver in the slot in the adjuster on the base of the shock absorber on the left-hand side **(see illustration)**. The amount of damping is indicated by the number of turns out from the fully screwed-in position. The standard position is one turn out on models up to VIN 438381, and two turns out on all other models including Tiger Sport. Turn the adjuster clockwise to increase damping and anti-clockwise to decrease it. To establish the current setting, turn the adjuster in (clockwise) until it stops, counting the number of turns, then reset it as required by turning it out.

14 Swingarm removal and installation

Removal

Note: *Before removing the swingarm, it is advisable to perform the rear suspension checks described in Chapter 1 to assess the extent of any wear.*

Sprint and 2005 to 2010 Speed Triple models (up to VIN 461331)

Note: *If you want to remove the rear sprocket, disc and axle assembly from the swingarm, do so before removing the swingarm so the rear brake can be used to stop the assembly turning while slackening the hub nut (see Chapter 6).*

1 Remove the rear wheel (see Chapter 6),

13.26 Spring pre-load adjuster (arrowed) – Tiger

13.27 Rebound damping adjuster (arrowed) – Tiger

Frame and suspension 5•29

14.2a Undo the screws (arrowed) and remove the cover to free the hose, and wiring where present

14.2b Undo the screws (arrowed) . . .

14.2c . . . and the screws (arrowed) and remove the chain guards

and on Sprint models the shock absorber (see Section 11).

2 Undo the brake hose cover screws from the chainguard on the swingarm and free the hose, and the wiring on ABS models **(see illustration)**. If required, undo the screws securing the upper and lower chainguards to the swingarm and remove them, noting how they fit **(see illustrations)**.

3 On Speed Triple models release the brake hose guide from the swingarm **(see illustration)**. On both models displace the rear brake caliper from the disc (see Chapter 6) – there is no need to disconnect the hose. Feed the brake caliper over the swingarm and position it clear, making sure no strain is placed on the hose. On Sprint models with ABS displace the rear wheel sensor (see Chapter 6).

4 If the rear sprocket has not been removed, fully slacken the drive chain (see Chapter 1). Disengage the chain from the rear sprocket – if there is not enough slack you will have to remove the front sprocket (see Chapter 6).

5 On Sprint models refer to Section 12, Step 5, and detach the drop link from the swingarm. If the sleeve is stuck, detach the drop link from the drag link instead, remove the swingarm with the drop link attached, and remove it afterwards as described in Section 12.

6 On Speed Triple models refer to Section 11, Steps 7 and 8 and release the reservoir from its clamp and detach the top of the shock absorber from the frame. Place a support under the back of the swingarm. Unscrew

14.3 Unscrew the bolt (arrowed) to free the hose

the bolt securing the rear brake fluid reservoir and position it clear **(see illustration)**. Refer to Section 12, Step 9 and detach the drop link from the swingarm. If the sleeve is stuck, detach the drop link from the drag link instead, remove the swingarm with the drop link attached, and remove it afterwards as described in Section 12.

7 Before removing the swingarm it is advisable to re-check for play in the bearings (see Chapter 1). Any problems which may have been overlooked with the other suspension components attached to the frame are highlighted with them loose.

8 Counter-hold the left-hand end of the swingarm pivot, and unscrew the bolt from the right-hand end **(see illustration)**.

9 Using the Triumph special tool (Pt. No. T3880295) or a suitable peg spanner (which

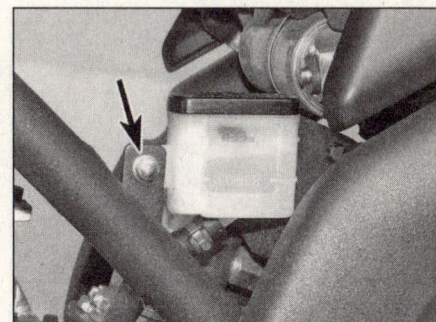

14.6 Unscrew the bolt (arrowed) and move the reservoir clear

can be made by cutting two sections out of an old socket of a suitable size – **(see illustration)**, or by filing two blobs of weld on the flange of a large nut into the correct shape and size as shown), unscrew the locknut on the adjuster bolt on the right-hand side **(see illustration 14.9a)**. Using the Triumph special tool (Pt. No. T3880290) or a suitable peg spanner, now thread the adjuster bolt out of the frame until it no longer protrudes on the inside **(see illustration)**.

10 Support the swingarm, then withdraw the pivot from the left-hand side, using a drift to knock it through if required, and remove the swingarm, on Sprint models tilting it as shown to clear the rear master cylinder, and on Speed Triple models carefully pivoting the back down and the front up until it is clear of the top of the shock absorber, and feeding the reservoir

14.8 Unscrew and remove the pivot bolt (arrowed)

14.9a Unscrew the locknut (arrowed) – our home-made tool is shown here

14.9b Unscrew the adjuster bolt (arrowed) – a peg spanner fabricated from a socket is shown

5•30 Frame and suspension

14.10a Withdraw the pivot...

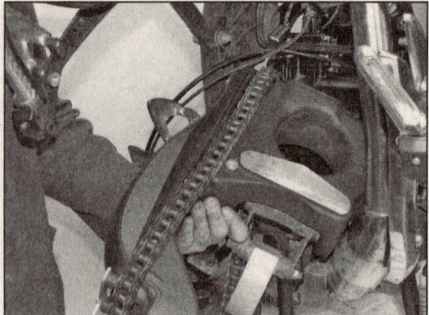
14.10b ...and remove the swingarm

Peg spanners can be made by cutting an old socket as shown – measure the width and depth of the slots in the locknut and adjuster bolt to determine the size of the castellations on the socket. If an old socket is not available, castellations can be welded onto a suitable nut.

14.10c Retrieve the spacer from the frame

through the hole **(see illustrations)**. Remove the spacer from the inside of the frame on the left-hand side **(see illustration)**.

11 Remove the chain slider from the front of the swingarm if necessary, noting how it fits **(see illustration)**. If it is badly worn or damaged, it should be replaced with a new one.

12 Inspect all components for wear or damage as described in Section 15.

2011-on Speed Triple models (from VIN 461332) and Tiger Sport

Note: *If you want to remove the rear sprocket, disc and axle assembly from the swingarm, do so before removing the swingarm so the rear brake can be used to stop the assembly turning while slackening the hub nut (see Chapter 6).*

13 Remove the rear wheel (see Chapter 6).
14 On 2011-on Speed Triple models (from VIN 461332) remove the hugger. Undo the chain slider lower bolt and remove the collar **(see illustration)**. Undo the brake hose cover screws and free the hose, and the wiring on ABS models **(see illustration)**. If required, undo the screws securing the lower chainguard and remove it.
15 On Tiger Sport models remove the hugger/chainguard **(see illustrations)**. Undo the screws securing the lower chainguard and remove it **(see illustration)**. Undo the chain slider screws on the underside, then free the brake hose, and the ABS sensor wire **(see illustration)**.
16 Displace the rear brake caliper from the disc and rest it on some rag (see Chapter 6) – there is no need to disconnect the hose. On models with ABS displace the rear wheel sensor (see Chapter 6).

14.11 Chain slider (arrowed)

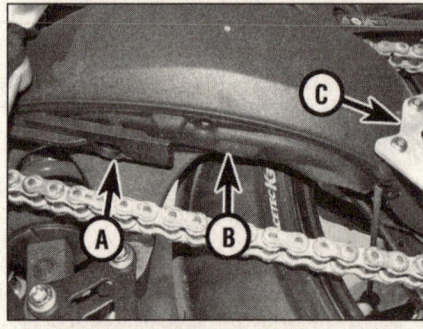
14.14 Displace the slider (A), remove the cover (B), and if required the guard (C)

14.15a Undo the screws (arrowed)...

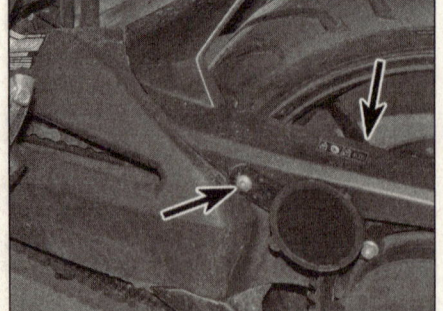
14.15b ...and the screws (arrowed) and remove the hugger/chainguard

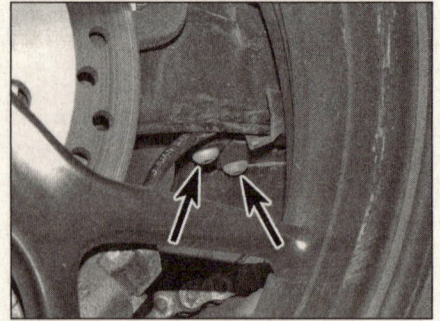
14.15c Lower chainguard screws (arrowed)

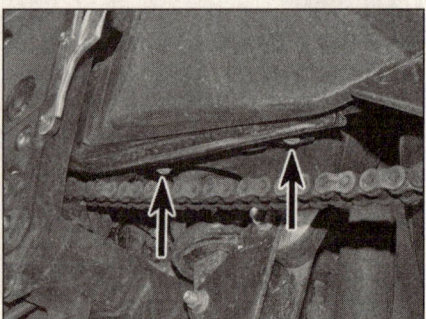
14.15d Undo the screws (arrowed) and release the hose and wire

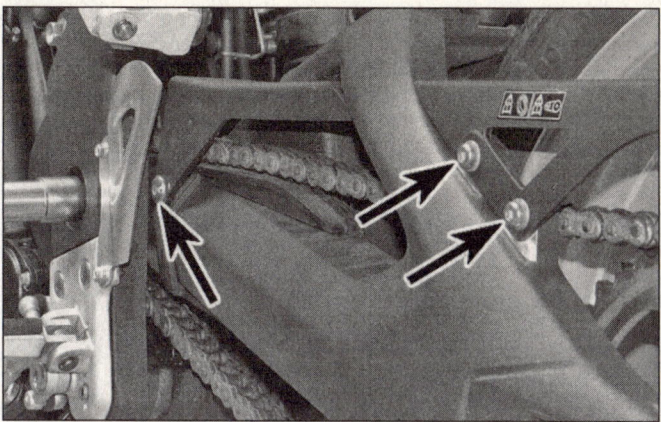

14.26 Undo the screws (arrowed) and remove the chainguard

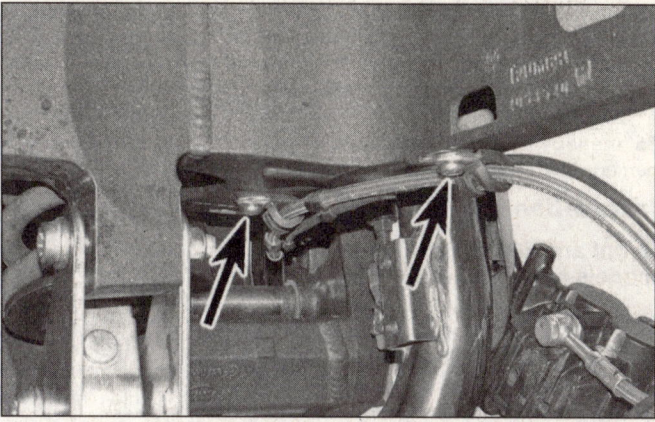

14.27 Undo the screws (arrowed) to release the brake hose

17 Remove the front sprocket cover (see Chapter 6). If the rear sprocket has not been removed, fully slacken the drive chain (see Chapter 1). Disengage the chain from the front sprocket – if there is not enough slack, do this after withdrawing the pivot bolt so there is more slack.

18 Referring to Sections 11 and 12, detach the drop link plates from the swingarm and remove the shock absorber.

19 Before removing the swingarm it is advisable to re-check for play in the bearings (see Chapter 1). Any problems which may have been overlooked with the other suspension components attached to the frame are highlighted with them loose.

20 Remove the swingarm pivot caps. Unscrew the nut and remove the washer from the right-hand end of the pivot bolt. Note that Triumph specifies to use a new nut.

21 Partially withdraw the pivot bolt from the left-hand side, using a drift to knock it through if required. Using the Triumph special tool (Pt. No. T3880104) or a suitable peg spanner (which can be made by cutting two sections out of an old socket of a suitable size – **(see illustration 14.9b)**, or by filing two blobs of weld on the flange of a large nut into the correct shape and size), thread the adjuster out of the frame until it no longer protrudes on the inside.

22 Support the swingarm, then withdraw the pivot from the left-hand side, and remove the swingarm, bringing the drive chain with it **(see illustrations 14.10a and b)**. If a new swingarm is being fitted remove the drive chain.

23 Remove the chain slider from the front of the swingarm if necessary **(see illustration 14.11)**. If the slider is badly worn or damaged, replace it with a new one. Also remove the chainguard if required.

24 Inspect all components for wear or damage as described in Section 15.

Tiger

25 Remove the seat and the side panels (see Chapter 7), the exhaust silencer (see Chapter 4), and the rear wheel (see Chapter 6).

26 If required, undo the screws securing the chainguard to the swingarm and remove it, noting how it fits **(see illustration)**.

27 Release the brake hose guides from the swingarm **(see illustration)**. Position the brake caliper clear, making sure no strain is placed on the hose.

28 Refer to Section 11, Step 12 and detach the bottom of the shock absorber from the drop link plates. Place a support under the back of the swingarm. Refer to Section 12, Step 13 and detach the drop link plates from the swingarm.

29 Remove the front sprocket cover (see Chapter 6). Slip the drive chain off the sprocket.

30 Before removing the swingarm it is advisable to re-check for play in the bearings (see Chapter 1). Any problems which may have been overlooked with the other suspension components attached to the frame are highlighted with them loose.

31 Counter-hold the swingarm pivot bolt head, then unscrew the nut on the right-hand end of the bolt and remove the washer **(see illustration)**. Discard the nut as a new one should be used. Partially withdraw the pivot bolt so it is clear of the adjuster bolt in the right-hand side of the frame.

32 Using the Triumph special tool (Pt. No. T3880104) or a suitable peg spanner (which can be made by cutting two sections out of an old socket of a suitable size – see **Tool Tip** above), thread the adjuster bolt out of the frame until it no longer protrudes on the inside **(see illustration)**.

33 Support the swingarm, then withdraw the pivot bolt from the right-hand side, using a drift to knock it through if required, and remove the swingarm along with the drive chain, lowering it to clear the bottom of the shock **(see illustrations)**.

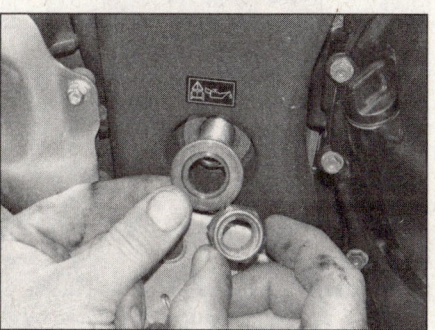

14.31 Unscrew the nut and remove the washer

14.32 Unscrew the adjuster bolt (arrowed) – a peg spanner fabricated from a socket is shown

14.33a Withdraw the pivot bolt . . .

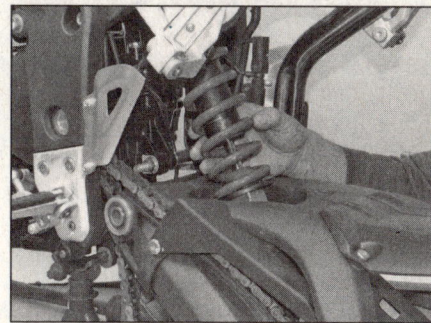

14.33b . . . and manoeuvre the swingarm out

34 Remove the chain slider and hugger from the swingarm if necessary, noting how they fit **(see illustrations)**. If the chain slider is badly worn or damaged, it should be replaced with a new one.

35 Inspect all components for wear or damage as described in Section 15.

Installation

Sprint and 2005 to 2010 Speed Triple models (up to VIN 461331)

36 If not already done, remove the bearing spacer from the right-hand side and the sleeve from the left, and lubricate the bearings, spacer, sleeve and swingarm pivot with grease **(see illustrations)**. Refit the spacer and sleeve. If removed, install the chain slider **(see illustration 14.11)**.

37 Fit the spacer into its recess in the inside of the frame on the left-hand side – a smear of grease will help keep it in place **(see illustration 14.10c)**.

38 Offer up the swingarm, on Sprint models manoeuvring it past the master cylinder as on removal **(see illustration 14.10b)**, and on Speed Triple models feeding the reservoir up through the hole and manoeuvring it down over the shock absorber in a reverse of how it was removed, and have an assistant hold it in place, making sure the chain is looped around it and the spacer remains in place. Slide the pivot through from the left-hand side **(see illustration 14.10a)**.

39 Using the Triumph special tool (Pt. No. T3880290) or a suitable peg spanner **(see illustration 14.9b)**, tighten the adjuster bolt to the torque setting specified at the beginning of the Chapter. Make some reference marks between the adjuster bolt and the frame – these are used to check that the adjuster bolt turns no further when the locknut is tightened. Fit the locknut **(see illustration)**, then tighten it to the specified torque using the Triumph special tool (Pt. No. T3880295) or a suitable peg spanner **(see illustration 14.9a)**. Check that the adjuster bolt hasn't turned – if it has, repeat the tightening procedure.

40 Fit the bolt into the right-hand end of the pivot **(see illustration)**. Counter-hold the pivot and tighten the right-hand bolt to the specified torque.

41 Install all remaining components and assemblies in a reverse of the removal procedure, referring to the relevant Sections and Chapters where necessary. When fitting the brake hose guide on Speed Triple models, position it so the hose is vertical to allow for some forward movement in the caliper bracket, otherwise the end of the bracket could press into the hose and distort or kink it **(see illustration 14.3)**.

42 Check and adjust the drive chain slack (see Chapter 1). Check the operation of the rear suspension and brake before taking the machine on the road. On Sprint models with ABS reset the spring pre-load adjuster.

2011-on Speed Triple models from (VIN 461332) and Tiger Sport

43 If not already done, remove the bearing spacer from the right-hand side and the sleeve from the left, and lubricate the bearings, spacer, sleeve and swingarm pivot with grease **(see illustrations 14.36a and b)**. Refit the spacer and sleeve. If removed, fit the chain slider, but do not yet fit the bottom bolt **(see illustration 14.11)**.

44 Offer up the swingarm and have an assistant hold it in place, and place the chain around the front sprocket. Slide the pivot most of the way through from the left-hand side, leaving it recessed in the adjuster so it can bee tightened **(see illustration 14.10a)**.

45 Using the Triumph special tool (Pt. No. T3880104) or a suitable peg spanner (see **Tool Tip**) **(see illustration 14.9b)**, tighten the adjuster to the torque setting specified at the beginning of the Chapter.

46 Push the pivot bolt all the way in and fit the washer and nut onto the right-hand end. Counter-hold the pivot and tighten the nut to the specified torque.

47 Install all remaining components and assemblies in a reverse of the removal procedure, referring to the relevant Sections and Chapters where necessary. Clean the threads of the brake hose cover bolts and the chain slider bottom bolt and apply some threadlock, fit the cover before fitting the slider bolt, and do not forget the collar.

48 Check and adjust the drive chain slack (see Chapter 1). Check the operation of the rear suspension and brake before taking the machine on the road.

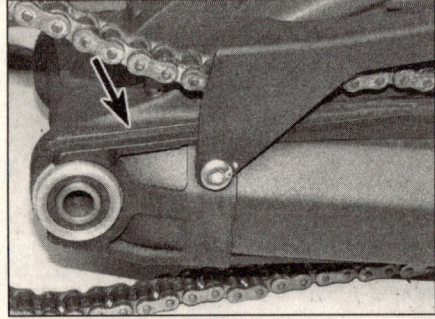

14.34a Remove the chain slider (arrowed) . . .

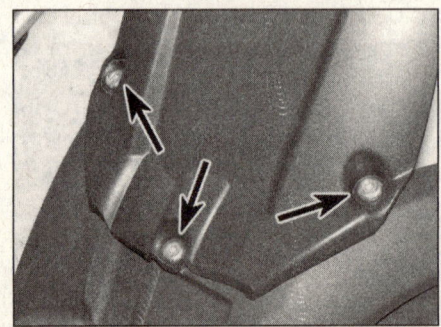

14.34b . . . and the hugger (secured by three screws, arrowed) if required

14.36a Remove the spacer . . .

14.36b . . . and withdraw the sleeve

14.39 Thread the locknut onto the adjuster bolt

14.40 Fit the pivot bolt and tighten to the specified torque

Tiger

49 If not already done, remove the bearing spacer from the right-hand side and the sleeve from the left, and lubricate the bearings, spacer, sleeve and swingarm pivot with grease **(see illustrations)**. Refit the spacer and sleeve. If removed, install the chain slider and hugger.

50 Offer up the swingarm and have an assistant hold it in place, making sure drive chain is looped over the chain slider at the front, and the spacer remains in place **(see illustration 14.21b)**. Slide the pivot bolt through from the left-hand side, leaving it recessed from the head of the adjuster bolt on the right **(see illustration 14.21a)**.

51 Using the Triumph special tool (Pt. No. T3880104) or a suitable peg spanner (see **Tool Tip**), tighten the adjuster bolt to the torque setting specified at the beginning of the Chapter **(see illustration 14.20)**. Push the pivot bolt all the way through.

52 Fit the washer and a new nut onto the right-hand end of the pivot bolt **(see illustration 14.19)**. Counter-hold the bolt on the left-hand end and tighten the nut to the specified torque.

53 Install all remaining components and assemblies in a reverse of the removal procedure, referring to the relevant Sections and Chapters where necessary.

53 Check and adjust the drive chain slack (see Chapter 1). Check the operation of the rear suspension and brake before taking the machine on the road.

15 Swingarm bearings

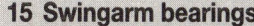

Inspection

1 After removing the swingarm remove the bearing spacer from the right-hand side and the sleeve from the left **(see illustrations 14.36a and b or 14.49a and b, according to model)**. Thoroughly clean the swingarm, removing all traces of dirt, corrosion and grease.

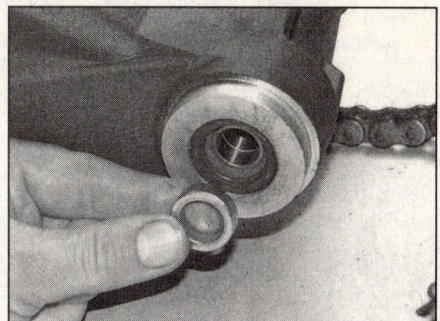

14.49a Remove the spacer . . .

2 Inspect all components closely, looking for obvious signs of wear such as heavy scoring, and cracks or distortion due to accident damage. Check the condition of the grease seals, and check the bearings for roughness, looseness and any other damage, referring to *Tools and Workshop Tips* (Section 5) in the Reference section. Any damaged or worn component must be replaced with a new one.

3 Check the swingarm pivot/pivot bolt is straight by rolling it on a flat surface such as a piece of plate glass (first wipe off all old grease and remove any corrosion using wire wool). If the equipment is available, place the pivot in V-blocks and measure the runout using a dial gauge. If the pivot is bent, replace it with a new one.

Seal and bearing renewal

4 Remove the needle bearing sleeve from the left-hand side, then lever out the grease seal **(see illustration 14.36b or 14.49b)**. Also remove the spacer and seal from the right-hand side **(see illustration 14.36a or 14.49a)**, then remove the circlip securing the ball bearing(s) – Sprint and 2005 to 2010 Speed Triple models (up to VIN 461331) have a single bearing, 2011-on Speed Triple models (from VIN 461332) and Tiger models have two. All models have a single needle bearing in the left-hand side, but on Sprint and Speed Triples there is an inner grease seal as well as an outer. There is an inner sleeve for the pivot bolt. Discard the seals as new ones must be used.

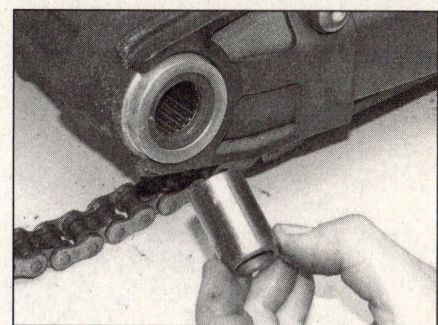

14.49b . . . and withdraw the sleeve

5 Refer to *Tools and Workshop Tips* (Section 5) in the Reference section for more information on bearing checks and removal and installation methods. The needle bearing can be drawn or driven out of its bore, but note that removal will make it unusable; a new bearing should be obtained before work commences. To drive it out pass a long drift with a hooked end through the right-hand side of the swingarm and locate it on the inner edge of the bearing. Tap the drift around the bearing's inner edge to ensure that it leaves its bore squarely. Use the same method to drive out the ball bearing(s), but from the opposite side. Alternatively, and if available, a slide-hammer with knife-edged bearing puller attached can be used, and is better than using a drift, to extract the bearings.

6 Do not forget to fit the central sleeve after fitting the bearing(s) into one side. The new needle bearing should be pressed or drawn into its bore rather than driven into position. In the absence of a press, a suitable drawbolt arrangement can be made up as described in *Tools and Workshop Tips* (Section 5) in the Reference section. The ball bearing(s) can be driven in using a driver or socket that bears only on the outer race, or they can be drawn or pressed in as with the needle bearing. Press the new seals in using your fingers, or tap them in using a suitable socket. Lubricate the bearings, spacer, sleeve and seal lips with the recommended grease (see Chapter 1 Specifications) on installation.

Chapter 6
Brakes, wheels and final drive

Contents

	Section number		Section number
Anti-lock brake system – ABS	11	General information	1
Brake bleeding and fluid change	10	Rear brake caliper	6
Brake fluid level check	see *Pre-ride checks*	Rear brake disc	7
Brake hoses, pipes (ABS models) and fittings	9	Rear brake master cylinder	8
Brake light switches	see Chapter 8	Rear sprocket coupling/rubber dampers	20
Brake pad renewal	2	Rear wheel	15
Brake pad wear check	see Chapter 1	Sprockets	19
Brake system check	see Chapter 1	Tyre information and fitting	17
Drive chain and sprockets check	see Chapter 1	Tyre pressures, tread depth and condition	see *Pre-ride checks*
Drive chain removal, cleaning and installation	18	Wheel alignment check	13
Front brake calipers	3	Wheel bearing check	see Chapter 1
Front brake discs	4	Wheel checks	see Chapter 1
Front brake master cylinder	5	Wheel inspection and repair	12
Front wheel	14	Wheel, sprocket coupling and hub bearings	16

Degrees of difficulty

Easy, suitable for novice with little experience	**Fairly easy,** suitable for beginner with some experience	**Fairly difficult,** suitable for competent DIY mechanic	**Difficult,** suitable for experienced DIY mechanic	**Very difficult,** suitable for expert DIY or professional

Specifications

Brakes
Brake fluid type	DOT 4
Brake pad minimum thickness	1.5 mm
ABS sensor air gap	0.1 to 1.5 mm
Front caliper piston OD	
Speed Triple models from VIN 461332	34 mm
All other models	
Large bore	33.96 mm
Small bore	30.23 mm

Front disc thickness	**Standard**	**Service limit**
Sprint ST without ABS	4.5 mm	4.0 mm
Sprint ST with ABS, Sprint GT, Tiger SE, Tiger Sport	5.0 mm	4.5 mm
Speed Triple up to VIN 461331	4.0 mm	3.5 mm
Speed Triple models from VIN 461332	4.5 mm	4.0 mm
Tiger	4.5 mm	3.5 mm

Front disc maximum runout	
Sprint ST 2010-on, Sprint GT	0.1 mm
All other models	0.3 mm
Front master cylinder bore ID	
Sprint and Tiger	15.8 mm
Speed Triple	14.0 mm
Rear caliper piston OD	27.0 mm
Rear disc thickness	
Standard	6.0 mm
Service limit	5.0 mm
Rear disc maximum runout	
Tiger Sport	0.25 mm
All other models	0.3 mm
Rear master cylinder bore ID	14.0 mm

Wheels
Runout (max)	
Axial (side-to-side)	0.5 mm
Radial (out-of round)	0.5 mm

6•2 Brakes, wheels and final drive

Tyres
Tyre pressures	see *Pre-ride checks*
Tyre sizes*	
Front	120/70-17
Rear	180/55-17

*Refer to the owners handbook, the tyre information label on the swingarm, or your Triumph dealer or a tyre specialist for approved tyre brands and ratings.

Final drive
Chain type	50 (530) X-ring
No. of links	
Sprint ST and Speed Triple up to VIN 461331	106
Sprint GT	116
Speed Triple from VIN 461332	108
Tiger	114
Tiger Sport	120
Drive chain slack and stretch limit	see Chapter 1

Torque wrench settings
Brake caliper bleed valves	
Sprint and Speed Triple	6 Nm
Tiger	5.5 Nm
Brake hose banjo bolts	25 Nm
Brake pipe joint nuts (ABS models)	17 Nm
Front brake caliper joining bolts	24 Nm
Front brake caliper mounting bolts	
Sprint	50 Nm
Speed Triple up to VIN 461331, Tiger	35 Nm
Speed Triple from VIN 461332, Tiger SE, Tiger Sport	55 Nm
Front brake disc bolts	22 Nm
Front brake master cylinder clamp bolts	
Speed Triple from VIN 461332	8 Nm
Tiger SE, Tiger Sport	12 Nm
All other models	15 Nm
Front brake pad retaining pin	
Sprint, Tiger SE, Tiger Sport	18 Nm
Speed Triple	19 Nm
Tiger	17 Nm
Front sprocket nut	132 Nm
Front wheel axle	
Sprint	61 Nm
Speed Triple up to VIN 461331, Tiger	95 Nm
Speed Triple from VIN 461332	65 Nm
Front wheel axle clamp bolts	
Speed Triple from VIN 461332, Tiger SE, Tiger Sport	22 Nm
Speed Triple R	19 Nm
All other models	20 Nm
Front wheel sensor bolts – ABS models	9 Nm
Front wheel pulse ring bolts – ABS models	5 Nm
Rear brake caliper mounting bolts	40 Nm
Rear brake disc bolts	
Speed Triple and Tiger	22 Nm
Sprint	27 Nm
Rear brake light switch – Sprint and Tiger models	15 Nm
Rear brake master cylinder mounting nuts/bolts	
Sprint	20 Nm
Speed Triple	18 Nm
Tiger to VIN 465177	27 Nm
Tiger from VIN 465178 to 565755	24 Nm
Tiger Sport	22 Nm
Rear brake pad retaining pins	18 Nm
Rear sprocket nuts	
Sprint, Speed Triple, Tiger Sport	33 Nm
Tiger, Tiger SE	55 Nm
Rear wheel axle nut – Tiger, Tiger SE	110 Nm
Rear wheel nut – Sprint, Speed Triple, Tiger Sport	146 Nm
Rear wheel sensor bolts – ABS models	9 Nm
Rear wheel pulse ring bolts – ABS models	5 Nm
Sprocket coupling nut – Sprint and Speed Triple	146 Nm

Brakes, wheels and final drive 6•3

1 General information

All models are fitted with cast alloy wheels designed for tubeless tyres only.

Both front and rear brakes are hydraulically operated disc brakes. The front brake has two opposed-piston calipers, each with four pistons. The rear brake has a sliding caliper with two pistons.

The drive to the rear wheel is by chain and sprockets.

Caution: *Disc brake components rarely require disassembly. Do not disassemble components unless absolutely necessary. If an hydraulic brake line is loosened, the system must be thoroughly bled. Do not use solvents on internal brake components. Solvents will cause the seals to swell and distort. Use only clean brake fluid or denatured alcohol for cleaning. Use care when working with brake fluid as it can injure your eyes and it will damage painted surfaces and plastic parts.*

Note: *Before disconnecting any brake hoses or pipes on ABS models, bear in mind that the system must be bled on completion of work, and although this is done initially in the same way as models without ABS, to complete the procedure effectively the Triumph Diagnostic tool must be used to open and close the solenoids within the ABS modulator, and this can only be carried out by a dealer.*

Many of the bolts used on Triumph motorcycles are of the Torx type. Unless you are already

2.1a On Tiger models remove the R-clip, then slacken the pad pin (arrowed)

2.1b Pad retaining pin (arrowed) – Sprint models

equipped with a good range of Torx bits, you are advised to obtain a set. Make sure you get bits that can be used in conjunction with a socket set so that a torque wrench can be applied – a Torx key set will not be adequate on its own, though will be useful in addition to the bits.

2 Brake pad renewal

Warning: *The dust created by the brake system may contain asbestos, which is harmful to your health. Never blow it out with compressed air and don't inhale any of it. An approved filtering mask should be worn when working on the brakes.*

Front

1 On Tiger models remove the R-clip from the inner end of the pad retaining pin (see illustration). On all models except 2008-on Speed Triples with Brembo calipers slacken the pad retaining pin (see illustration). Unscrew the caliper mounting bolts, noting the washers where fitted, and slide the caliper off the disc (see illustrations 3.6a and b or 3.6 c and d). Free the brake hose from its guide(s) and/or clip(s) (according to model and side) to give more freedom of movement if required.

2 On Sprint models, Speed Triple models with Nissin calipers, and Tiger models, unscrew and withdraw the pad pin, noting how it fits through the pad spring, then remove the pad spring (see illustrations). Withdraw the pads from the caliper (see illustration). On Speed Triple models (except R models) with Brembo calipers withdraw the pad pin, noting how it fits through the pad spring, then remove the pad spring (see illustrations). Withdraw the pads from the caliper (see illustration).

2.2a On the Nissin caliper unscrew the pad pin . . .

2.2b . . . remove the pad spring . . .

2.2c . . . and withdraw the pads from the caliper

2.2d On the Brembo caliper withdraw the pad pin . . .

2.2e . . . remove the pad spring . . .

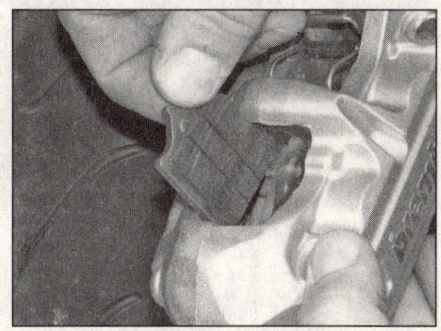

2.2f . . . and withdraw the pads from the caliper

6•4 Brakes, wheels and final drive

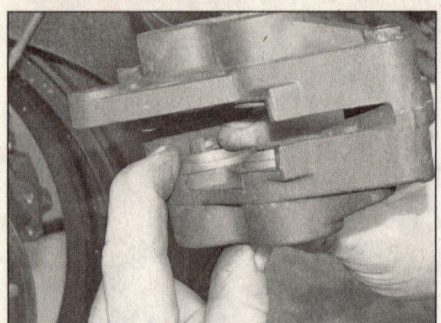

2.7a Push the pistons in using finger pressure . . .

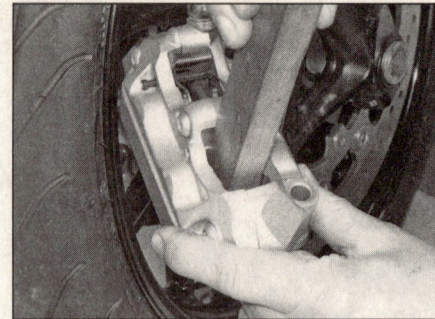

2.7b . . . a piece of wood . . .

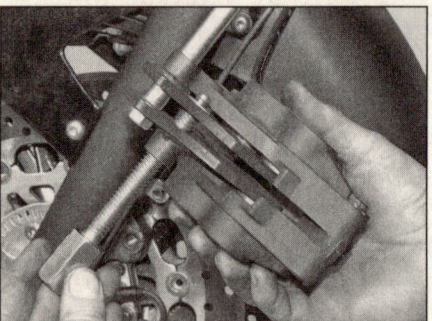

2.7c . . . or a proper tool

Repeat for the other pair of pads. On Speed Triple R models slide one pad to the middle until it is clear of the lugs and remove it from the underside of the caliper, then remove the other in the same way. Remove the pad spring if required, noting how it fits.

3 Inspect the surface of each pad for contamination and check that the friction material has not worn beyond its service limit (see Chapter 1, Section 9). If either pad is worn down to or beyond the service limit wear indicator or the minimum thickness specified, is fouled with oil or grease, or is heavily scored or damaged by dirt and debris, both pads in each caliper must be replaced with new ones. Note that it is not possible to fully degrease the friction material; if the pads are contaminated in any way new ones must be fitted.

4 If the pads are in good condition clean them carefully, using a fine wire brush which is completely free of oil and grease, to remove all traces of road dirt and corrosion. Using a pointed instrument, clean out the groove in the friction material and dig out any embedded particles of foreign matter. Spray with a dedicated brake cleaner to remove any dust.

5 Check the condition of the brake disc (see Section 4).

6 Remove all traces of corrosion from the pad pin(s). Check for signs of damage and wear.

7 Clean around the exposed section of each piston to remove any dirt or debris that could cause the seals to be damaged. If new pads are being fitted, now push the pistons all the way back into the caliper to create room for them; if the old pads are still serviceable push the pistons in a little way. To push the pads back use finger pressure or a piece of wood as leverage, or place the old pads back in the caliper and use a metal bar or a screwdriver inserted between them, or use grips and a piece of wood, rag or card to protect the caliper body **(see illustrations)**. Alternatively obtain a proper piston-pushing tool from a good tool supplier **(see illustration)**. It may be necessary to remove the master cylinder reservoir cap, plate and diaphragm and siphon out some fluid (see Pre-ride checks). If the pistons are difficult to push back, remove the bleed valve cap, then attach a length of clear hose to the bleed valve and place the open end in a suitable container, then open the valve and try again (see Section 10). Take great care not to draw any air into the system. If in doubt, bleed the brakes afterwards.

8 If a piston appears seized, apply the brake lever and check whether the piston in question moves at all – first block or hold the other pistons using wood or cable-ties. If it moves out but can't be pushed back in the chances are there is some hidden corrosion stopping it. If it doesn't move at all, or to fully clean and inspect the pistons, disassemble the caliper and overhaul it (see Section 3).

9 Lightly smear the backs of the pads and the shank of the pad pin with copper-based grease, making sure that none gets on the front or sides of the pads.

10 On Speed Triple R models fit the pad spring if removed, with the arrow in the same direction as that on the caliper. On all models insert the pads into the caliper so that the friction material on each pad faces the other **(see illustration 2.2c or 2.2f)**. On all except Speed Triple R models fit the pad spring onto the pads, making sure it is the correct way up **(see illustration 2.2b or 2.2e)**. Slide the pad retaining pin through the hole in the outer pad, then press down on the pad spring and slide the pin over the spring and through the hole in the inner pad **(see illustration or 2.2d)**. On Sprint models, Speed Triple models with Nissin calipers, and Tiger models tighten the pin finger-tight **(see illustration 2.2a)**. On 2008-on Speed Triple models (except R models) with Brembo calipers make sure the pin is pushed all the way in **(see illustration)**, then repeat for the other pair of pads.

11 Slide the caliper onto the disc making sure the pads locate correctly on each side **(see illustration 3.6b or 3.6d)**. Fit the caliper mounting bolts, with the washers where fitted, and tighten them to the torque setting specified at the beginning of this Chapter. Fit the brake hose into its guide(s) and/or clip(s) if removed.

12 On Sprint models, Speed Triple models

2.10a Make sure the pad pin locates correctly over the spring (Nissin)

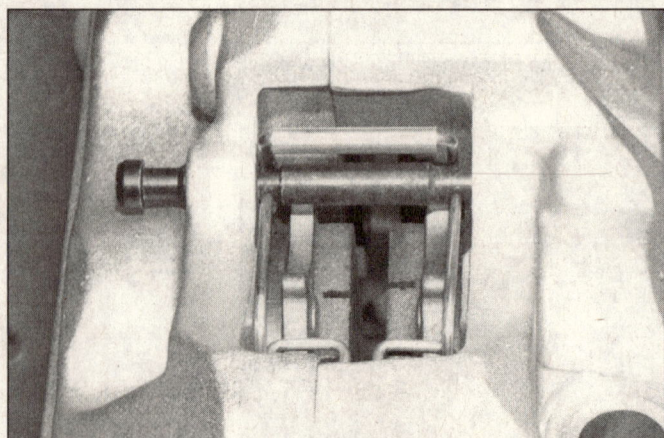

2.10b Make sure the pad pin is all the way in and locates correctly over the spring (Brembo)

Brakes, wheels and final drive

2.16a Slacken the pad retaining pins (arrowed)

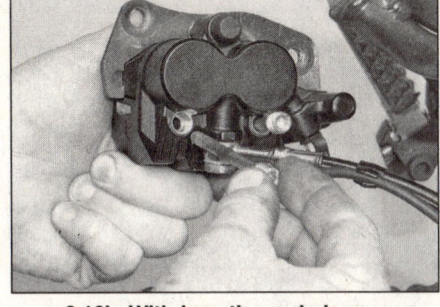

2.16b Withdraw the pad pins . . .

2.16c . . . then remove the outer pad, noting how it locates . . .

with Nissin calipers, and Tiger models tighten the pad pin to the torque setting specified at the beginning of the Chapter. On Tiger models fit the R-clip, using a new one if necessary **(see illustration 2.1a)**.

13 Operate the brake lever until the pads contact the disc. Check the level of fluid in the hydraulic reservoir and top-up if necessary (see *Pre-ride checks*).

14 Check the operation of the brake before riding the motorcycle.

Rear

15 On Sprint, Speed Triple and Tiger Sport models, remove the rear wheel (see Section 15).

16 Slacken the pad retaining pins **(see illustration)**. Unscrew the caliper mounting bolts and slide the caliper off the disc **(see illustrations 6.4a and b)**. Press down on the bottom of the pads and remove the retaining pins **(see illustration)**. Remove the outer pad, noting how it hooks against the pin on the caliper bracket, then remove the inner pad, noting how it fits in the bracket **(see illustrations)**.

17 Refer to Steps 3, 4, 5, and 6 above and inspect the pads and caliper components.

18 Separate the bracket from the caliper by sliding them apart **(see illustration)**. Clean off all traces of corrosion and hardened grease. Check the rubber boots in the caliper **(see illustration)**. If they are damaged or deteriorated, they should be replaced with new ones (but check with a Triumph dealer as they do not list them as being available separately). Note how the pad spring is fitted and remove it if required **(see illustration)**.

19 Clean around the exposed section of the pistons to remove any dirt or debris that could cause the seals to be damaged. If new pads are being fitted, now push the pistons all the way back into the caliper to create room for them; if the old pads are still serviceable push the pistons in a little way. To push the pistons back use finger pressure or a piece of wood as leverage, or place the old pads back in the caliper and use a metal bar or a screwdriver inserted between them, or use grips and a piece of wood, with rag or card to protect the caliper body **(see illustration)**. Alternatively obtain a proper piston-pushing tool from a good tool supplier **(see illustration)**. If there is too much brake fluid in the reservoir it may be necessary to remove the master cylinder reservoir cover, plate and diaphragm and siphon some out (see *Pre-ride) checks*). If a piston is difficult to push back, remove the bleed valve cap, then attach a length of clear hose to the bleed valve and place the open end in a suitable container, then open the valve and try again (see Section 10). Take great care not to draw any air into the system. If in doubt, bleed the brake afterwards.

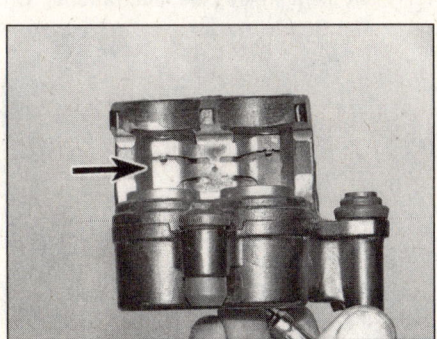

2.16d . . . and the inner pad

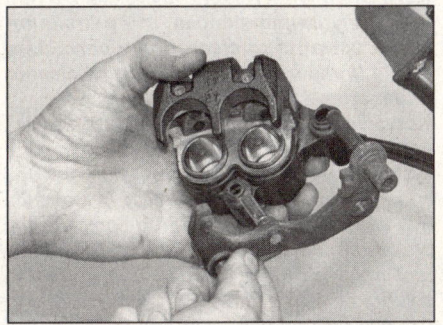

2.18a Slide the bracket out of the caliper

2.18b Check the condition of the boots (arrowed)

2.18c Remove the pad spring (arrowed) if required, noting how it fits

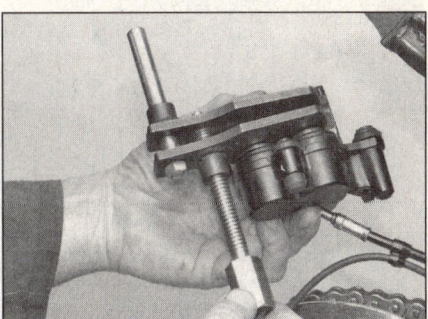

2.19a Push the pistons in using one of the methods described . . .

2.19b . . . or a proper tool

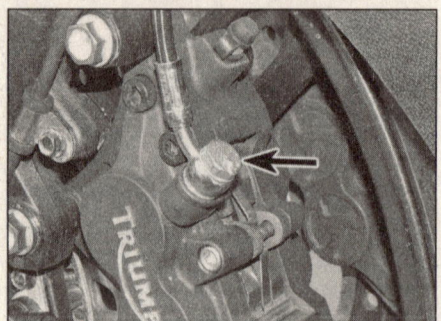

3.3a Brake hose banjo bolt (arrowed) – Sprint

3.3b Brake hose banjo bolt (arrowed) – Tiger and Speed Triple with Nissin calipers

3.3c Brake hose banjo bolt (arrowed – note how the bleed valve threads into it) – Speed Triple with Brembo calipers

20 If a piston appears seized, apply the brake lever and check whether the piston in question moves at all – first block or hold the other piston using wood or cable-ties. If it moves out but can't be pushed back in the chances are there is some hidden corrosion stopping it. If it doesn't move at all, or to fully clean and inspect the pistons, disassemble the caliper and overhaul it (see Section 6).

21 If removed, fit the pad spring into the caliper, making sure it is correctly located (see illustration 2.18c). Apply a smear of copper or silicone based grease to the slider pins. Slide the bracket back onto the caliper (see illustration 2.18a). Check that the caliper body is able to slide freely on the slider pins on the bracket.

22 Fit the inner pad into the caliper and locate its ends against the bracket (see illustration 2.16d). Fit the outer pad, locating the cutout around the pin on the bracket (see illustration 2.16c). Press the pads against the spring and slide the pad retaining pins through (see illustration 2.16b). Make sure the pins pass through the holes in each pad. Tighten the pad retaining pins finger-tight.

23 Slide the caliper onto the brake disc, making sure the pads sit squarely each side of the disc (see illustration 6.4b). Install the caliper mounting bolts and tighten them to the torque setting specified at the beginning of the Chapter. Now tighten the retaining pins to the torque setting specified at the beginning of the Chapter (see illustration 2.16a).

24 On Sprint, Speed Triple and Tiger Sport models, install the rear wheel (see Section 15).

25 Top up the master cylinder reservoir if necessary (see *Pre-ride checks*).

26 Operate the brake pedal several times to bring the pads into contact with the disc. Check the operation of the brake before riding the motorcycle.

3 Front brake calipers

Warning: *If a caliper indicates the need for an overhaul (usually due to leaking fluid or sticky operation), all old brake fluid should be flushed from the system. Also, the dust created by the brake system may contain asbestos, which is harmful to your health. Never blow it out with compressed air and don't inhale any of it. An approved filtering mask should be worn when working on the brakes. Do not, under any circumstances, use petroleum-based solvents to clean brake parts. Use DOT 4 brake fluid, dedicated brake cleaner or denatured alcohol only, as described.*

Note: *Before disconnecting any brake hoses or pipes on ABS models, bear in mind that the system must be bled on completion of work, and although this is done initially in the same way as models without ABS, to complete the procedure effectively the Triumph Diagnostic tool must be used to open and close the solenoids within the ABS modulator, and this can only be carried out by a dealer. The bike should be transported, not ridden, to the dealer.*

Removal

Note: *If the caliper is being overhauled (usually due to sticking pistons or fluid leaks) read through the entire procedure first and make sure that you have obtained all the new parts required, including some new DOT 4 brake fluid.*

1 If the caliper is being overhauled, on Tiger models remove the R-clip from the inner end of the pad retaining pin (see illustration 2.1a). On all models except 2008-on Speed Triples with Brembo calipers slacken the pad retaining pin (see illustration 2.1b). If the caliper is just being displaced from the forks as part of the wheel removal procedure, the brake pads can be left in place.

2 Free the brake hose from its guide(s) and/or clip(s) (according to model and side) to give more freedom of movement if required.

3 If the caliper is being completely removed or overhauled, unscrew the brake hose banjo bolt and detach the banjo union, noting its alignment with the caliper (see illustrations). When working on the right-hand caliper on Sprint models, note the double hose arrangement.

4 Wrap clingfilm around the banjo union and secure the hose in an upright position to minimise fluid loss. Discard the sealing washers, as new ones must be fitted on reassembly.

5 On Nissin calipers if the caliper body is to be split into its halves for overhaul, loosen the caliper body joining bolts at this stage and retighten them lightly (see illustrations). On

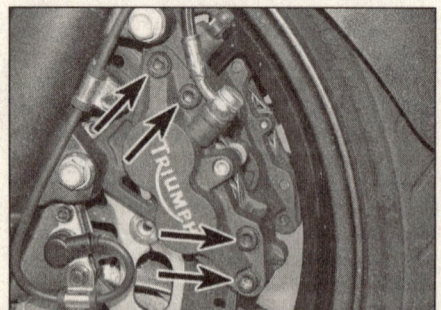

3.5a Caliper body joining bolts (arrowed) – Sprint

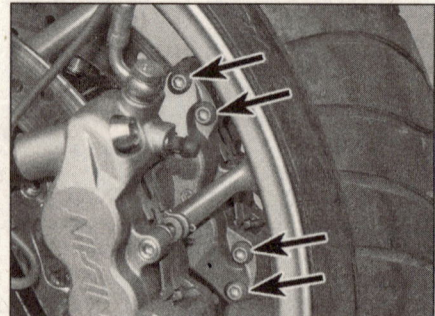

3.5b Caliper body joining bolts (arrowed) – Tiger and Speed Triple with Nissin calipers

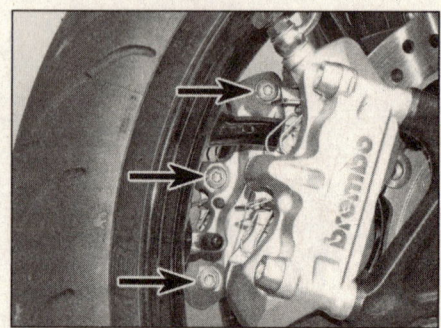

3.5c Caliper body joining bolts (arrowed) – Speed Triple with Brembo calipers

Brakes, wheels and final drive 6•7

3.6a On Sprint models unscrew the bolts (arrowed) . . .

3.6b . . . and slide the caliper off the disc

Speed Triple and Tiger models, if you haven't got the necessary tools to access them you will have to slacken them with the caliper removed so you may need an assistant to hold it, or use a vice with some protective rag.

6 Unscrew the caliper mounting bolts, noting the washers where fitted, and slide the caliper off the disc **(see illustrations)**. If the caliper is just being displaced, secure it to the motorcycle with a cable-tie to avoid straining the brake hose. **Note:** *Do not operate the brake lever while either caliper is off the disc.* If the caliper is being overhauled, remove the brake pads (see Section 2).

Overhaul

7 Clean the exterior of the caliper with denatured alcohol or brake system cleaner. Have some clean rag ready to catch any spilled brake fluid.

8 On Nissin calipers unscrew the caliper body joining bolts and separate the body halves, catching any residual fluid with the rag **(see illustration 3.18b)**. Remove the caliper body O-ring(s) and discard it/them **(see illustration 3.18a)**.

9 Find a suitable bolt and thread it into the banjo bolt bore. Get a wad of rag and hold it against (Nissin calipers) or between (Brembo calipers) the pistons as a protective cushion as

3.6c On Speed Triple and Tiger models unscrew the bolts (arrowed) . . .

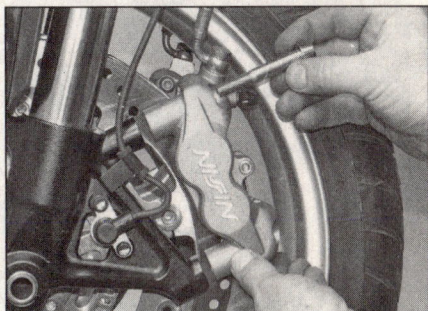

3.6d . . . and slide the caliper off the disc

the pistons are forced out. Apply compressed air gradually and progressively, starting with a fairly low pressure, to the fluid passage on the caliper joint and allow the pistons to ease out of their bores in turn **(see illustrations)**. On Nissin calipers repeat the procedure for the other caliper half.

10 If a piston is stuck in its bore due to corrosion the caliper should be replaced with a new one. Do not try to remove a piston by levering it out or by using pliers or other grips.

11 Mark each piston and the caliper body to ensure that the pistons can be matched to their original bores on reassembly. Note that on many models two sizes of piston are used in each caliper (see Specifications at the beginning of this Chapter).

12 Remove the dust seals and the piston seals from the piston bores taking care to avoid scratching the bores **(see illustration)**. Discard the seals as new ones must be fitted on reassembly.

13 Clean the pistons and bores with DOT 4 brake fluid. If compressed air is available, blow it through the fluid galleries in the caliper to ensure they are clear (make sure it is filtered and unlubricated).

Caution: Do not, under any circumstances, use a petroleum-based solvent to clean brake parts.

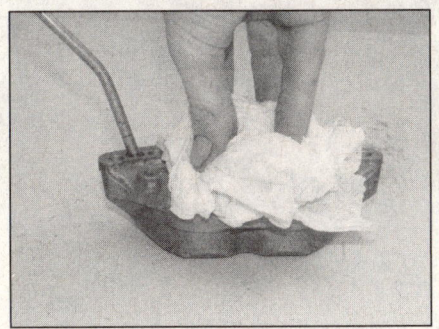

3.9a Apply compressed air to the fluid passage . . .

3.9b . . . until the pistons are displaced

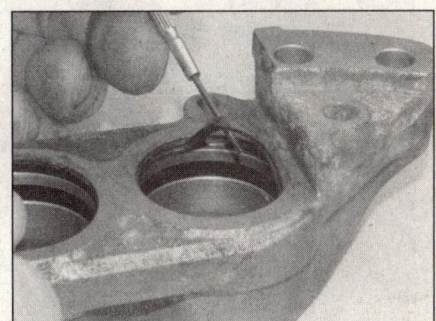

3.12 Remove the seals and discard them

6•8 Brakes, wheels and final drive

3.15a Lubricate the new piston seals with brake fluid . . .

3.15b . . . then fit them into their grooves . . .

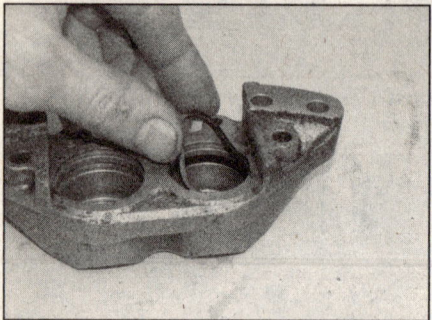

3.16 . . . followed by the new dust seals

3.17 Fit the pistons and push them all the way in

14 Inspect the caliper bores and pistons for signs of corrosion, nicks and burrs and loss of plating. If surface defects are present, the pistons and/or the caliper assembly must be replaced with new ones. If the caliper is in poor condition, the other front caliper and the master cylinder should also be checked.
15 Lubricate the new piston seals with clean brake fluid and fit them in their grooves in the caliper bores – the piston seals are thicker than the dust seals, do not mix them up **(see illustrations)**. Note that on many models there are two sizes of bore in each caliper and care must therefore be taken to ensure that the correct size seals are fitted to the correct bores (see Specifications). The same applies when fitting the new dust seals and pistons.
16 Lubricate the new dust seals with clean brake fluid and install them in their grooves in the caliper bores **(see illustration)**.
17 Lubricate the pistons with clean brake fluid and install them, closed-end first, into the caliper bores, taking care not to displace the seals **(see illustration)**. Using your thumbs, push the pistons all the way in, making sure they enter the bore squarely.
18 On Nissin calipers clean the threads of the caliper body joining bolts. Lubricate the new caliper body O-ring(s) with clean brake fluid and fit it/them into the appropriate half of the caliper body **(see illustration)**. Join the two halves of the caliper body together, ensuring that the O-ring(s) stay(s) in place **(see illustration)**. Apply a threadlock to the joining bolts and tighten them evenly to the torque setting specified at the beginning of this Chapter. If it is not possible to tighten the bolts fully at this stage and you have the necessary tools, tighten them as much as possible now and tighten them fully once the caliper has been installed on the machine.

Installation

19 If removed, install the brake pads (see Section 2).
20 Slide the caliper onto the brake disc, making sure the pads fit on each side of the disc **(see illustration 3.6b or 3.6d)**.
21 Fit the caliper mounting bolts, with the washers where fitted, and tighten them to the torque setting specified at the beginning of this Chapter. If the calipers were overhauled and if not already done, tighten the caliper body joining bolts to the specified torque setting **(see illustration 3.5a, b or c)**.
22 On Sprint models, Speed Triple models with Nissin calipers, and Tiger models tighten the pad pin to the torque setting specified at the beginning of the Chapter. On Tiger models fit the R-clip, using a new one if necessary **(see illustration 2.1a)**.
23 If removed, connect the brake hose(s) to the caliper, using new sealing washers on each side of each banjo fitting. Align the fitting as noted on removal **(see illustration 3.3a, b or c)**. Tighten the banjo bolt to the specified torque setting.
24 Fit the brake hose into its guide(s) and/or clip(s) if removed.
25 Top up the hydraulic reservoir with DOT 4 brake fluid (see *Pre-ride checks*) and bleed the system as described in Section 10. Check that there are no fluid leaks and test the operation of the brake before riding the motorcycle.

3.18a Fit the O-ring into its recess . . .

3.18b . . . then join the caliper halves and tighten the bolts

Brakes, wheels and final drive

4.2a The minimum thickness is marked on the disc

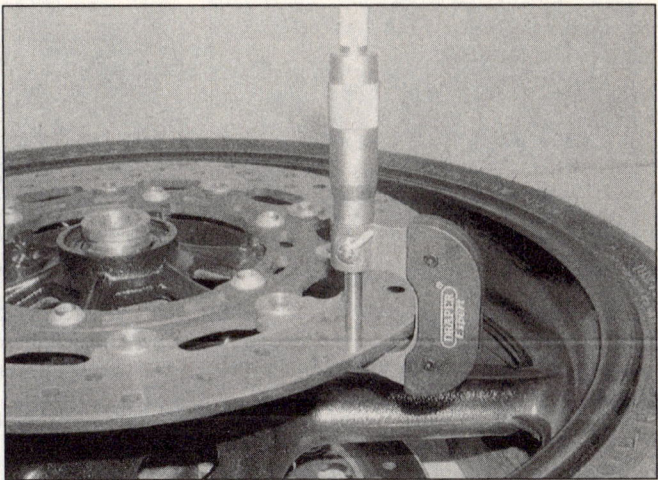
4.2b Using a micrometer to measure disc thickness

4 Front brake discs

Inspection

1 Inspect the surface of the disc for score marks and other damage. Light scratches are normal after use and won't affect brake operation, but deep grooves and heavy score marks will reduce braking efficiency and accelerate pad wear. If a disc is badly grooved replace both discs with new ones – never fit only one new disc.

2 The disc must not be allowed to wear down to a thickness less than the service limit as listed in this Chapter's Specifications. The minimum thickness is also stamped on the disc **(see illustration)**. Check the thickness of the disc with a micrometer and replace both discs with new ones **(see illustration)**.

3 To check if the disc is warped, position the bike on an auxiliary stand with the front wheel raised off the ground. Mount a dial gauge to the fork leg, with the gauge plunger touching the surface of the disc about 10 mm from the outer edge **(see illustration)**. Rotate the wheel and watch the gauge needle, comparing the reading with the limit listed in the Specifications at the beginning of this Chapter. If the runout is greater than the service limit, check the wheel bearings for play (see Chapter 1). If the bearings are worn, install new ones (see Section 16) and repeat this check. If the disc runout is still excessive, a new pair of discs will have to be fitted – never fit only one new disc.

Removal

4 Remove the wheel (see Section 14). On models with ABS, remove the front wheel pulse ring (see Section 11).
Caution: Do not lay the wheel down and allow it to rest on the disc – the disc could become warped. Set the wheel on wood blocks so the disc doesn't support the weight of the wheel.

5 Mark the relationship of the discs to the wheel, so they can be installed in the same position (unless you are fitting new discs). Also mark the discs according to their side as the discs are different. If you are installing new discs, match them to the old ones so they can be installed correctly.

6 Unscrew the disc retaining bolts, loosening them evenly and a little at a time in a criss-cross pattern to avoid distorting the disc, then remove the disc from the wheel **(see illustration)**. Triumph specify that new bolts should be used as they are pre-treated with a threadlock, but if this is not practicable clean the threads of the old bolts and apply some fresh threadlock to them on installation.

Installation

7 Before installing the disc, make sure there is no dirt or corrosion where the disc seats on the hub, particularly right in the angle of the seat, as this will not allow the disc to sit flat when it is bolted down and it will appear to be warped when checked or when using the front brake.

8 Mount the disc on the wheel making sure it is the correct way round, and on the correct side (see Step 5). Align the previously applied matchmarks (if you're reinstalling the original disc).

9 Install new or threadlocked bolts and tighten them evenly and a little at a time in a criss-cross pattern to the torque setting specified at the beginning of the Chapter **(see illustration 4.6)**. Clean off all grease from the brake disc using acetone or brake system cleaner. If a new brake disc has been installed, remove any protective coating from its working surfaces.

10 On models with ABS, install the front wheel pulse ring (see Section 11). Install the front wheel (see Section 14).

11 Operate the brake lever several times to bring the pads into contact with the disc. Check the operation of the brake carefully before riding the bike.

5 Front brake master cylinder

4.3 Set up a dial gauge with the probe contacting the brake disc, then rotate the wheel to check for runout

4.6 Unscrew the bolts (arrowed) and remove the disc

⚠ **Warning: If the brake master cylinder is in need of an overhaul all old brake fluid should be flushed from the system. Overhaul of the brake master cylinder must be done in a spotlessly clean work area to avoid contamination and possible failure of**

6•10 Brakes, wheels and final drive

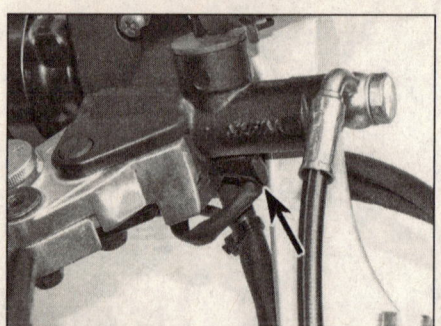

5.1a Brake light switch wiring connectors (arrowed) – Sprint, early Speed Triple, and Tiger

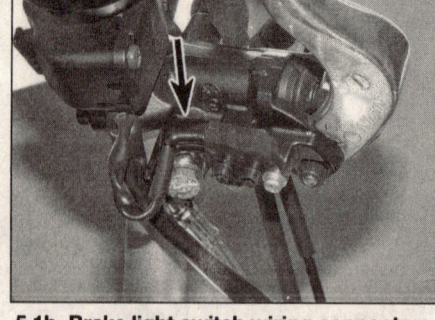

5.1b Brake light switch wiring connectors (arrowed) – 2008-on Speed Triple

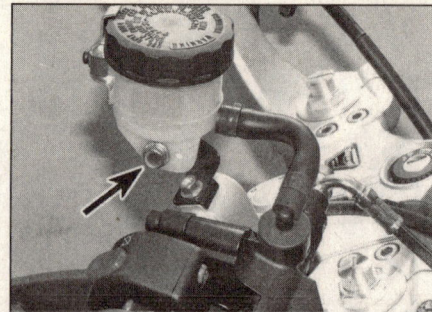

5.2a On Sprint, 2005 to 2007 Speed Triple, and Tiger models unscrew the reservoir bolt (arrowed)

the brake hydraulic system components. Do not, under any circumstances, use petroleum-based solvents to clean brake parts. Use DOT 4 brake fluid, dedicated brake cleaner or denatured alcohol only, as described. To prevent damage from spilled brake fluid, always cover paintwork when working on the braking system.

Note: *Before disconnecting any brake hoses or pipes on ABS models, bear in mind that the system must be bled on completion of work, and although this is done initially in the same way as models without ABS, to complete the procedure effectively the Triumph Diagnostic tool must be used to open and close the solenoids within the ABS modulator, and this can only be carried out by a dealer. The bike should be transported, not ridden, to the dealer.*

Removal

Note: *The master cylinder can be overhauled on all models except 2011-on Speed Triples (from VIN 461332). If the master cylinder is being overhauled (usually due to sticking or poor action, or fluid leaks) read through the entire procedure first and make sure that you have obtained the rebuild kit (which includes the boot, circlip, piston, cup, seal and spring), as the old parts should not be reused once removed. Also get some new DOT 4 brake fluid.*

1 Disconnect the wiring connectors from the brake light switch **(see illustrations)**.

2 If the master cylinder is just being displaced, ensure the fluid reservoir cap is secure. On all except 2008-on Speed Triple models undo the bolt securing the reservoir to the bracket **(see illustration)**. Unscrew the master cylinder clamp bolts and remove the back of the clamp, noting how it fits, then position the master cylinder and reservoir assembly clear of the handlebar **(see illustration)**. Ensure no strain is placed on the hydraulic hose. Keep the reservoir upright to prevent air entering the system.

3 If the master cylinder is being overhauled, remove the brake lever (see Chapter 5).

4 Remove the reservoir cap clamp screw and clamp **(see illustration)**.

5 Unscrew the brake hose banjo bolt and detach the banjo union, noting its alignment with the master cylinder **(see illustrations)**. Wrap clingfilm around the banjo union and secure the hose in an upright position to minimise fluid loss. Discard the sealing washers as new ones must be fitted on reassembly.

6 Undo the bolt securing the reservoir to the bracket **(see illustration 5.2a or 5.2c)**. Unscrew the master cylinder clamp bolts and remove the back of the clamp, noting how it fits, then lift the master cylinder and reservoir away from the handlebar **(see illustration 5.2b or 5.2c)**.

7 Unscrew the reservoir cap and remove the diaphragm plate and the diaphragm. Drain the brake fluid from the master cylinder and reservoir into a suitable container. Release the clip securing the reservoir hose to the union on the master cylinder and detach the hose. Wipe any remaining fluid out of the reservoir with a clean rag.

8 If required, undo the screw securing the brake light switch to the bottom of the

5.2b Master cylinder bolts (arrowed) – Sprint, early Speed Triple, and Tiger

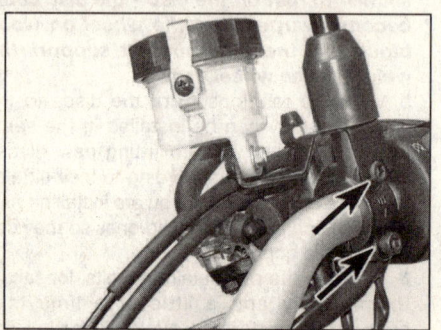

5.2c Master cylinder bolts (arrowed – note how the reservoir bracket locates) – 2008-on Speed Triple

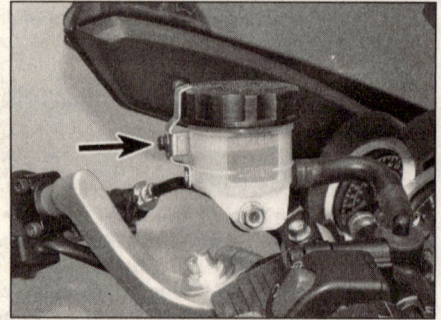

5.4 Undo the screw (arrowed) and remove the clamp

5.5a Brake hose banjo bolt (arrowed) – Sprint, early Speed Triple, and Tiger

5.5b Brake hose banjo bolt (arrowed) – 2008-on Speed Triple

Brakes, wheels and final drive 6•11

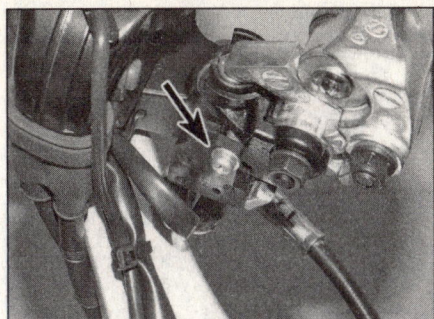

5.8 Brake light switch screw (arrowed) – Sprint, early Speed Triple, and Tiger

master cylinder and remove the switch **(see illustration or 5.1b)**.

Overhaul

9 Carefully remove the dust boot from the master cylinder, noting how it locates.
10 Using circlip pliers, remove the circlip and slide out the piston assembly and the spring, noting how they fit **(see illustration)**. If they are difficult to remove, apply low pressure compressed air to the fluid outlet. Lay the parts out in the proper order to prevent confusion during reassembly.
11 Clean the master cylinder with clean brake fluid. If compressed air is available, use it to dry the cylinder thoroughly (make sure it's filtered and unlubricated).

Caution: Do not, under any circumstances, use a petroleum-based solvent to clean brake parts.

12 Check the master cylinder bore for corrosion, scratches, nicks and score marks. If damage or wear is evident, the master cylinder must be replaced with a new one. If the master cylinder is in poor condition, then the calipers should be checked as well. Check that the fluid inlet and outlet ports are clear.
13 The dust boot, circlip, piston, cup, seal and spring are included in the rebuild kit. Use all of the new parts, regardless of the apparent condition of the old ones. Fit them according to the layout of the old piston assembly. If the seal is not already fitted on the piston, lubricate it with new brake fluid before fitting it, and make sure the wider end will fit into the master cylinder first.
14 Fit the cup onto the narrow end of the spring and lubricate it with new brake fluid. Fit the spring wide-end first into the master cylinder and push the cup in, making sure its lips do not turn inside out.
15 Lubricate the piston with clean brake fluid and slide it into the master cylinder and up against the cup and spring. Make sure the lips on the seal do not turn inside out. Depress the piston and install the new circlip, making sure it locates properly in its groove.
16 Fit the new rubber dust boot, making sure the outer lip is seated correctly in the groove in the piston, and carefully push the inner lip in against the circlip using a blunt tool. Smear silicone grease onto the end of the piston.

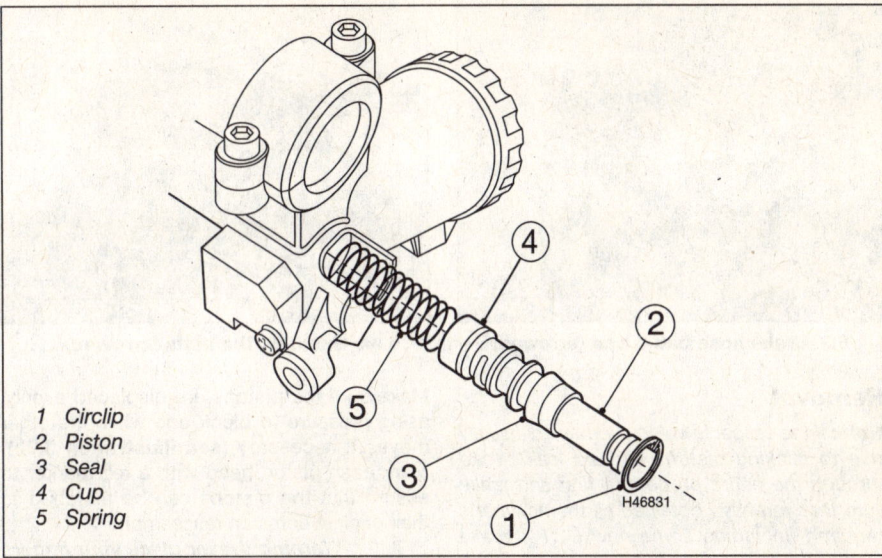

1 Circlip
2 Piston
3 Seal
4 Cup
5 Spring

5.10 Front master cylinder components – Sprint, early Speed Triple, and Tiger

17 Check the reservoir diaphragm and replace it with a new one it if is damaged or deteriorated. Also check the reservoir hose for cracks or splits and fit a new one if necessary.

Installation

18 If removed, fit the brake light switch onto the bottom of the master cylinder and tighten the screw **(see illustration 5.8 or 5.1b)**.
19 Attach the master cylinder to the handlebar, aligning the clamp joint with the punch mark or + mark on the handlebar **(see illustration)**, then fit the back of the clamp with its UP mark facing up **(see illustration 5.2b or c)**. Tighten the upper bolt to the torque setting specified at the beginning of this Chapter, followed by the lower bolt.
20 Locate the fluid reservoir on the bracket and tighten its bolt **(see illustration 5.2a or 5.2c)**. Connect the reservoir hose to the union on the master cylinder and secure it with the clip.
21 Connect the brake hose to the master cylinder, using new sealing washers on each side of the banjo fitting. Align the hose as noted on removal **(see illustration 5.5a or b)**. Tighten the banjo bolt to the torque setting specified at the beginning of this Chapter.

5.19 Align the mating surfaces of the clamp with the punch mark on the handlebar

22 Install the brake lever (see Chapter 5).
23 Connect the brake light switch wiring **(see illustration 5.1a or b)**.
24 Fill the fluid reservoir with new DOT 4 brake fluid (see *Pre-ride* checks). Refer to Section 10 and bleed the air from the system.
25 Check the operation of the brake before riding the motorcycle.

6 Rear brake caliper

Warning: If a caliper is in need of an overhaul all old brake fluid should be flushed from the system. Also, the dust created by the brake system may contain asbestos, which is harmful to your health. Never blow it out with compressed air and do not inhale any of it. An approved filtering mask should be worn when working on the brakes. Overhaul of the brake caliper must be done in a spotlessly clean work area to avoid contamination and possible failure of the brake hydraulic system components. Do not, under any circumstances, use petroleum-based solvents to clean brake parts. Use DOT 4 brake fluid, dedicated brake cleaner or denatured alcohol only, as described. To prevent damage from spilled brake fluid, always cover paintwork when working on the braking system.

Note: *Before disconnecting any brake hoses or pipes on ABS models, bear in mind that the system must be bled on completion of work, and although this is done initially in the same way as models without ABS, to complete the procedure effectively the Triumph Diagnostic tool must be used to open and close the solenoids within the ABS modulator, and this can only be carried out by a dealer. The bike should be transported, not ridden, to the dealer.*

6.3 Brake hose banjo bolt (arrowed)

6.4a Unscrew the bolts (arrowed) . . .

6.4b . . . and slide the caliper off the disc

Removal

Note: *If the caliper is being overhauled (usually due to sticking pistons or fluid leaks) read through the entire procedure first and make sure that you have obtained all the new parts required, including some new DOT 4 brake fluid.*

1 On Sprint, Speed Triple and Tiger Sport models, remove the rear wheel (see Section 15).

2 If the caliper is being overhauled, slacken the pad retaining pins (see illustration 2.16a).

3 If the caliper is being completely removed or overhauled, unscrew the brake hose banjo bolt and detach the banjo union, noting its alignment with the caliper **(see illustration)**. Wrap clingfilm around the banjo union and secure the hose in an upright position to minimise fluid loss. Discard the sealing washers, as new ones must be fitted on reassembly.

4 Unscrew the caliper mounting bolts and slide the caliper off the disc **(see illustrations)**. If the caliper is just being displaced, secure it to the motorcycle with a cable-tie to avoid straining the brake hose – on Sprint and Speed Triple models free the hose from the chainguard **(see illustration 7.3a)**, and on Speed Triple and Tiger models from any guides on the swingarm, as required according to model. **Note:** *Do not operate the brake pedal while the caliper is off the disc.* If the caliper is being overhauled, remove the brake pads (see Section 2).

Overhaul

5 Clean the exterior of the caliper with denatured alcohol or brake system cleaner.

6 Separate the bracket from the caliper by sliding them apart **(see illustration 2.18a)**. If not already done remove the pad spring from the caliper, noting how it fits **(see illustration 2.18c)**.

7 Get a wad of rag and hold it against the pistons as a cushion to protect your hand as the pistons are forced out. Apply compressed air gradually and progressively, starting with a fairly low pressure, to the fluid inlet on the caliper body and allow the pistons to ease out of their bores, controlling them with hand pressure and the rag **(see illustration 3.9a)**.

Make sure the pistons are displaced evenly, using pressure to block one while the other moves if necessary **(see illustration 3.9b)**. Mark each piston head with a felt marker to ensure that the pistons can be matched to their original bores on reassembly.

⚠ **Warning:** *Never place your fingers in front of the pistons in an attempt to catch or protect them when applying compressed air, as serious injury could result.*

8 If a piston is stuck in its bore due to corrosion the caliper should be replaced with a new one. Do not try to remove a piston by levering it out or by using pliers or other grips.

9 Remove the dust seals from the caliper bores, noting which way round they fit **(see illustration 3.12)**. Discard them as new ones must be used on installation. If a metal tool is being used, take great care not to mark the caliper bores.

10 Remove and discard the piston seals in the same way.

11 Clean the pistons and bores with DOT 4 brake fluid. If compressed air is available, use it to dry the parts thoroughly (make sure it's filtered and unlubricated).

Caution: *Do not, under any circumstances, use a petroleum-based solvent to clean brake parts.*

12 Inspect the caliper bores and pistons for signs of corrosion, nicks and burrs and loss of plating. If surface defects are present, the caliper assembly must be renewed. If the caliper is in bad shape the master cylinder should also be checked.

13 Lubricate the new piston seals with clean brake fluid and fit them into the lower grooves in the caliper bores **(see illustrations 3.15a and b)**.

14 Lubricate the new dust seals with clean brake fluid and fit them into the upper grooves in the caliper bores **(see illustration 3.16)**.

15 Lubricate the pistons with clean brake fluid and install them closed-end first into the caliper bores **(see illustration 3.17)**. Using your thumbs, push the pistons all the way in, making sure they enter the bore squarely without dislodging the seals.

16 Clean off all traces of corrosion and hardened grease from the slider pins on the bracket and the rubber boots in the caliper boots. Check the boots **(see illustration 2.18b)** – if they are damaged or deteriorated, they should be replaced with new ones (but check with a Triumph dealer as they do not list them as being available separately). Apply a smear of copper or silicone based grease to the slider pins. Slide the bracket back onto the caliper **(see illustration 2.18a)**. Check that the caliper body is able to slide freely on the slider pins on the bracket.

17 Fit the pad spring back into the caliper, making sure it locates correctly **(see illustration 2.18c)**.

Installation

18 If not already done, carry out the checks in Step 16.

19 If removed, install the brake pads (see Section 2).

20 Slide the caliper onto the brake disc, making sure the pads sit squarely each side of the disc **(see illustration 6.4b)**. Install the caliper mounting bolts and tighten them to the torque setting specified at the beginning of the Chapter. If the pads were removed tighten the retaining pins to the torque setting specified at the beginning of the Chapter **(see illustration 2.16a)**.

21 If removed, connect the brake hose to the caliper, using new sealing washers on each side of the union. Align the hose as noted on removal **(see illustration 6.3)**. Tighten the banjo bolt to the torque setting specified at the beginning of the Chapter. Fit the brake hose back onto the chainguard and/or refit any guides as required according to model.

22 On Sprint, Speed Triple and Tiger Sport models, install the rear wheel (see Section 15).

23 Top up the master cylinder reservoir with DOT 4 brake fluid (see *Pre-ride checks*) and bleed the hydraulic system as described in Section 10. Check that there are no leaks and thoroughly test the operation of the brake before riding the motorcycle.

7 Rear brake disc

Inspection

1 Refer to Section 4 of this Chapter, noting that the dial gauge should be attached to the swingarm.

Brakes, wheels and final drive 6•13

7.3a Undo the screws (arrowed) and remove the cover to free the hose, and wiring where present

7.3b Undo the screws (arrowed) . . .

7.3c . . . and remove the chainguards

7.3d Unstake the nut

7.3e Slacken the clamp bolt (arrowed)

7.3f Remove the nut and the dished washer, noting which way round it fits

Removal

Note: *On Sprint GT models, 2011-on Speed Triple models (from VIN 461332) and Tiger Sport models, Triumph specify to use tool T3880388 to centre the disc and ABS pulse ring on the hub on installation, and warn that failure to do so can affect operation of the ABS. If the tool is not available have the disc installed by a dealer.*

2 Remove the rear wheel (see Section 15).

3 On Sprint, Speed Triple and Tiger Sport models, undo the brake hose cover screws from the chainguard on the swingarm and free the hose **(see illustration)**. Undo the screws securing the upper and lower chainguards to the swingarm and remove them, noting how they fit **(see illustration)**. Unstake the sprocket coupling nut **(see illustration)**. Have an assistant apply the rear brake hard, then slacken the nut. Displace the rear caliper (see Section 6). Slacken the drive chain adjuster clamp bolt **(see illustration)**. Remove the coupling nut and its washer, noting which way round it fits, then slide the sprocket coupling off the axle and disengage it from the chain **(see illustrations)**. Note the shouldered spacer in the outside of the coupling and remove it for safekeeping if required **(see illustration)**. Slide the thrust washer off the end of the axle **(see illustration)**. Draw the axle/disc carrier out of the hub, noting which way round it fits **(see illustration)**. Note that Triumph specify to use a new sprocket coupling nut on installation.

4 On models with ABS remove the rear wheel pulse ring (see Section 11).

5 Mark the relationship of the disc to the carrier or wheel, and note which side of the

7.3g Slide the sprocket coupling off the axle and disengage the chain

carrier the disc sits on, so it can be installed in the same position (unless you are fitting a new disc).

7.3h Remove the spacer for safekeeping if required

7.3i Slide the thrust washer off the end of the axle . . .

7.3j . . . then draw the axle/disc carrier out of the hub

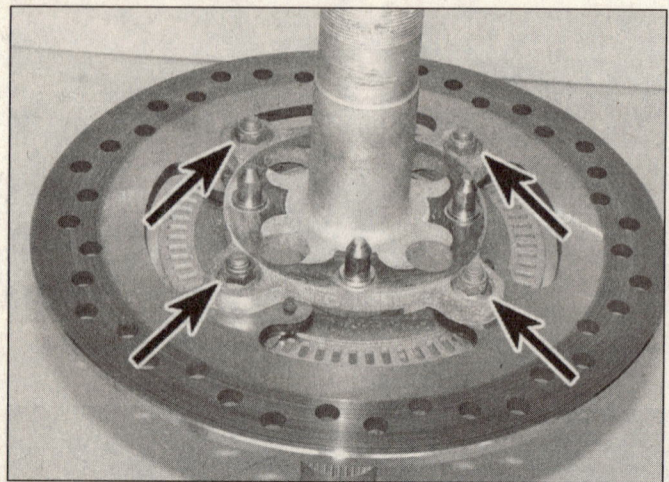

7.6 Rear disc bolt nuts (arrowed) – Sprint and Speed Triple

7.11 Stake the rim of the nut against the detent in the axle

6 Unscrew the disc retaining bolts (on Sprint and Speed Triple models counter-hold the nuts (**see illustration**)), loosening them evenly and a little at a time in a criss-cross pattern to avoid distorting the disc, then remove the disc from the carrier or wheel. Triumph specify that new bolts should be used as they are pre-treated with a threadlock, but if this is not practicable clean the threads of the old bolts and apply some fresh threadlock to them on installation.

Installation

7 Before installing the disc, make sure there is no dirt or corrosion where the disc seats on the hub, particularly right in the angle of the seat, as this will not allow the disc to sit flat when it is bolted down and it will appear to be warped when checked or when using the rear brake.

8 Mount the disc on the carrier or wheel making sure it is the correct way round, and on Sprint and Speed Triple models on the correct side (**see illustration 7.6**). Align the previously applied matchmarks (if you're reinstalling the original disc). On Sprint GT models, 2011-on Speed Triple models (from VIN 461332) and Tiger Sport models, fit the centring tool over the axle with the BRAKE DISC mark facing up (see Note above).

9 Fit the new or threadlocked bolts (on Sprint, Speed Triple and Tiger Sport models the nuts can be reused), then tighten them evenly and a little at a time in a criss-cross pattern to the torque setting specified at the beginning of the Chapter. Clean off all grease from the brake disc using acetone or brake system cleaner. If a new brake disc has been fitted, remove any protective coating from its working surfaces. On Sprint GT models, 2011-on Speed Triple models (from VIN 461332) and Tiger Sport models, remove the centring tool.

10 On models with ABS install the pulse ring (see Section 11).

11 On Sprint and Speed Triple models, slide the axle/disc carrier fully into the hub, making sure it is the correct way round (**see illustration 7.3j**). Slide the thrust washer onto the axle (**see illustration 7.3i**). Fit the shouldered spacer into the outside of the sprocket coupling if removed (**see illustration 7.3h**). Fit the sprocket coupling into the chain and slide it on the axle (**see illustration 7.3g**). Fit the dished washer so that its outer rim is against the spacer and the inner rim is raised off it, then fit the new nut and tighten it finger-tight (**see illustration 7.3f**). Install the brake caliper (see Section 6). Tighten the coupling nut to the torque setting specified at the beginning of the Chapter, applying the rear brake to prevent the coupling turning. Stake the rim of the nut into the cutout in the end of the axle (**see illustration**). Fit the chainguards on the swingarm and the brake hose and its cover on the upper guard (**see illustrations 7.3c, b and a**).

12 Install the rear wheel (see Section 15). Refer to Chapter 1 and adjust the drive chain slack.

13 Operate the brake pedal several times to bring the pads into contact with the disc. Check the operation of the brake carefully before riding the motorcycle.

8 Rear brake master cylinder

> ⚠️ **Warning:** *If the brake master cylinder is in need of an overhaul all old brake fluid should be flushed from the system. Overhaul of the brake master cylinder must be done in a spotlessly clean work area to avoid contamination and possible failure of the brake hydraulic system components. Do not, under any circumstances, use petroleum-based solvents to clean brake parts. Use clean DOT 4 brake fluid, dedicated brake cleaner or denatured alcohol only, as described. To prevent damage from spilled brake fluid, always cover paintwork when working on the braking system.*

Note: *Before disconnecting any brake hoses or pipes on ABS models, bear in mind that the system must be bled on completion of work, and although this is done initially in the same way as models without ABS, to complete the procedure effectively the Triumph Diagnostic tool must be used to open and close the solenoids within the ABS modulator, and this can only be carried out by a dealer. The bike should be transported, not ridden, to the dealer.*

Removal

Note: *If the master cylinder is being overhauled (usually due to sticking or poor action, or fluid leaks) read through the entire procedure first and make sure that you have obtained the rebuild kit (which includes the piston, cup, seal and spring), as the old parts should not be reused once removed. Also get some new DOT 4 brake fluid.*

1 On Sprint models remove the fuel tank (see Chapter 4), and on ST models with ABS remove the splash shield (**see illustration**). On 2005 to 2010 Speed Triple models (up to VIN 461331) remove the right-hand side panel (see Chapter 7).

8.1 Undo the screws (arrowed) and remove the shield

Brakes, wheels and final drive 6•15

8.2a Reservoir mounting bolt (arrowed) – Sprint

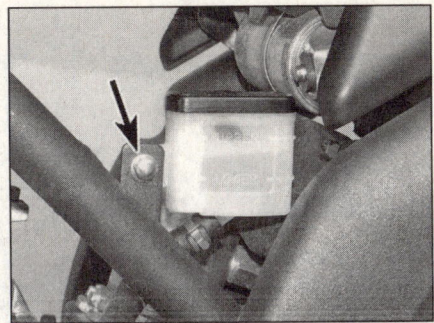
8.2b Reservoir mounting bolt (arrowed) – Speed Triple

8.2c Reservoir mounting bolt (arrowed) – Tiger

8.3 Remove the retaining clip (arrowed) and slide out the clevis pin

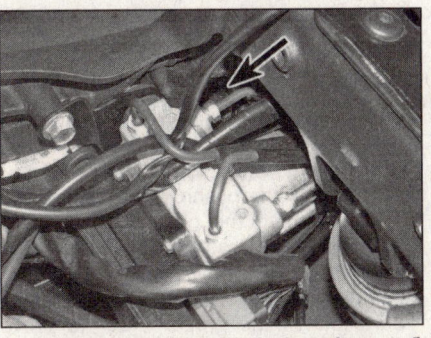
8.4a On Sprint models lift the boot (arrowed) and disconnect the wiring connector

8.4b On Tiger models lift the boot and disconnect the wiring connector (arrowed)

2 Unscrew the bolt securing the reservoir to the frame **(see illustrations)**.

3 Remove the retaining clip from the clevis pin securing the master cylinder pushrod to the brake pedal **(see illustration)**. Withdraw the clevis pin and separate the pushrod from the pedal.

4 On Sprint, Tiger, and 2011-on Speed Triple models (from VIN 461332), displace the rubber boot from the top of the master cylinder and detach the brake light switch wiring connectors **(see illustrations)**.

5 Unscrew the brake hose banjo bolt (Speed Triple) or brake light switch (Sprint models without ABS and Tiger models) and separate the brake hose or pipe from the master cylinder, noting its alignment – on Tiger models with ABS take great care not to bend the pipe **(see illustration)**. Discard the two sealing washers as they must be replaced with new ones. Wrap the end of the hose or pipe in clingfilm to prevent excessive loss of brake fluid, fluid spills and system contamination.

6 On Sprint models with ABS stuff some rag around the back of the ABS modulator, then unscrew the nut securing the brake hose pipe to the modulator and detach the pipe **(see illustration)**. Wrap the end of the pipe in clingfilm to minimise fluid loss.

7 On Tiger models remove the heel guard **(see illustration)**.

8.5 Brake hose banjo bolt (arrowed) – Speed Triple

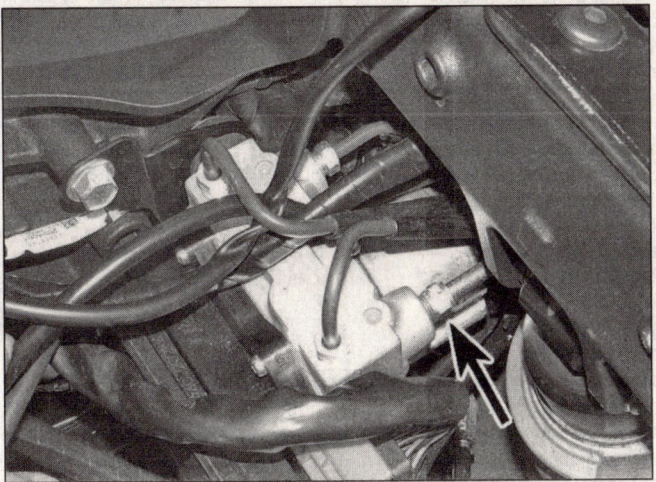
8.6 Unscrew the nut (arrowed) and detach the pipe

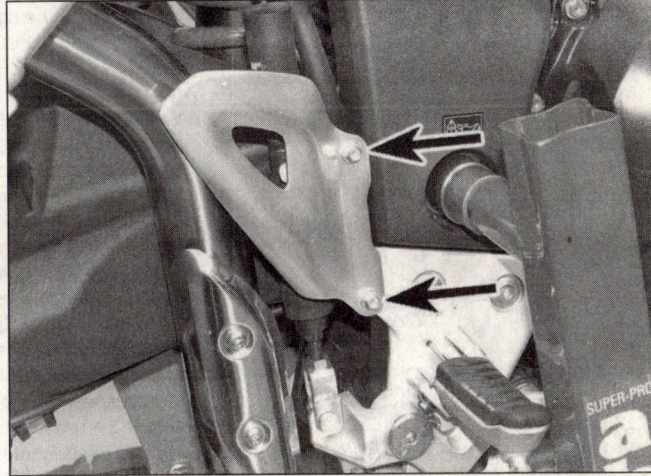
8.7 Unscrew the bolts (arrowed) and remove the guard

6•16 Brakes, wheels and final drive

8.8a Master cylinder nuts (arrowed) – Sprint

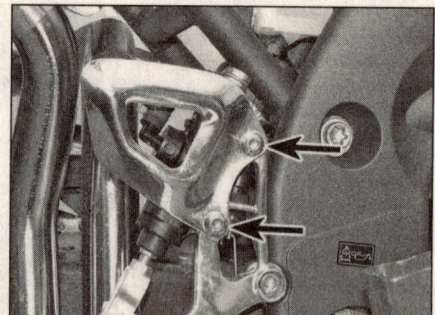

8.8b Master cylinder bolts (arrowed) – Speed Triple

8 Unscrew the two nuts (Sprint models) or bolts (Speed Triple and Tiger) securing the master cylinder and remove it along with the reservoir, on Sprint noting the two washers between it and the frame, and on Speed Triple models noting how the bolts secure the heel guard **(see illustrations)**. If required on Sprint models with ABS, make accurate alignment marks between the brake pipe and the master cylinder (if the pipe is not correctly aligned on installation its other end will not align with its socket on the modulator), then unscrew the brake light switch and detach the pipe. Discard the sealing washers.

9 Remove the reservoir cover or cap, diaphragm plate and diaphragm, and drain the fluid in the reservoir into a suitable container. Release the clamp securing the reservoir hose to the union on the master cylinder and detach the hose.

Overhaul

10 Dislodge the rubber dust boot from the base of the master cylinder to reveal the pushrod retaining circlip **(see illustration)**.
11 Depress the pushrod and, using circlip pliers, remove the circlip. Slide out the pushrod, piston assembly and spring. If they are difficult to remove, apply low pressure compressed air to the fluid outlet. Lay the parts out in the proper order to prevent confusion during reassembly.
12 Clean the master cylinder with clean brake fluid.
Caution: Do not, under any circumstances, use a petroleum-based solvent to clean brake parts. If compressed air is available, use it to dry the parts thoroughly (make sure it's filtered and unlubricated).
13 Check the master cylinder bore for corrosion, scratches, nicks and score marks. If damage is evident, the master cylinder must be replaced with a new one. If the master cylinder is in poor condition, then the caliper should be checked as well.
14 Inspect the reservoir hose for cracks or splits and replace it with a new one if necessary. If required, remove the circlip securing the hose union to the master cylinder and pull the union out. Discard the O-ring as a new one must be used.
15 The piston, cup, seal and spring are included in the rebuild kit. Use all of the new parts, regardless of the apparent condition of the old ones. Fit them according to the layout of the old piston assembly. If the cup and seal are not already fitted onto the piston, lubricate them with new brake fluid before fitting them, and make sure the wider end of each will fit into the master cylinder first.
16 Fit the spring, wide-end first on conical springs, into the master cylinder.
17 Lubricate the piston with clean brake fluid and slide it into the master cylinder and up against the spring. Make sure the lips on the cup and seal do not turn inside out.
18 Fit the rubber boot and circlip on the rod if removed and locate the lower rim of the boot in its groove. Locate the pushrod and push the piston in, then fit the circlip, making sure it is properly seated in the groove. Fit the upper rim of the boot into the groove in the master cylinder.
19 If removed, fit a new reservoir hose union O-ring, then push the union into the master cylinder and secure it with the circlip. Connect the reservoir hose to the union and secure it with the clamp

Installation

20 On Sprint models with ABS fit the brake pipe onto the master cylinder, using new sealing washers on each side of the union, and aligning it exactly as noted on removal. Fit the brake light switch and tighten it to the torque setting specified at the beginning of the Chapter, making sure the pipe does not move.
21 Locate the master cylinder, not forgetting the washers on Sprint models and the heel guard on Speed Triples, and tighten the nuts or bolts to the torque setting specified at the beginning of the Chapter **(see illustration 8.8a or b)**.
22 On Tiger models, fit the heel guard **(see illustration 8.7)**.
23 On all except Sprint models with ABS connect the brake hose or pipe to the master cylinder, using new sealing washers on each side of the union, and aligning it as noted on removal. Tighten the banjo bolt (Speed Triple) or brake light switch (Sprint and Tiger) to the torque setting specified at the beginning of the Chapter. On Sprint and Tiger models, connect the brake light switch wiring connectors, then fit the rubber boot over them **(see illustration 8.4b)**.
24 On Sprint models with ABS connect the brake pipe to the ABS modulator and tighten the nut **(see illustration 8.6)**.
25 Install the reservoir, making sure the hose is correctly routed, and secure it with the bolt **(see illustration 8.2a, b or c)**.
26 Align the brake pedal with the master cylinder pushrod clevis, then slide in the clevis pin, and secure it with the retaining clip **(see illustration 8.3)**.
27 Fill the fluid reservoir with new DOT 4 brake fluid (see Pre-ride checks) and bleed the system following the procedure in Section 10.
28 Fit the rubber diaphragm, making sure it is correctly seated, the diaphragm plate and the cover or cap onto the master cylinder reservoir.
29 On Sprint models install the fuel tank, and on ST models the splash shield, and on Speed Triple models install the right-hand side panel (see Chapter 7).
30 Check the operation of the brake carefully before riding the motorcycle.

9 Brake hoses, pipes (ABS models) and fittings

Inspection

1 Brake hose condition should be checked regularly and the hoses replaced with new ones at the specified interval (see Chapter 1). Twist and flex the hoses while looking for cracks, bulges and seeping hydraulic fluid.

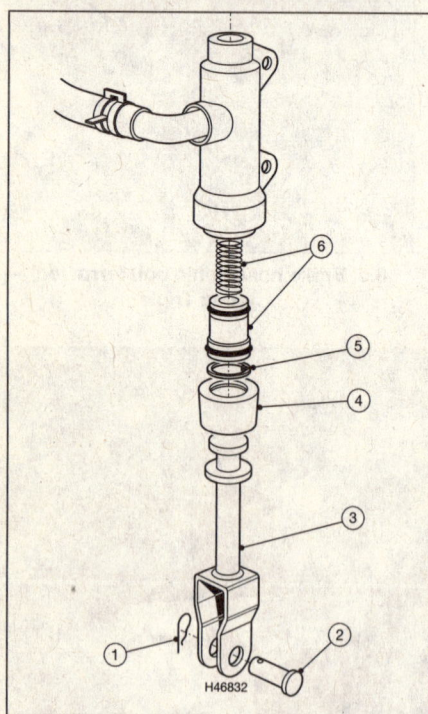

8.10 Rear master cylinder components

1. Retaining clip
2. Clevis pin
3. Pushrod
4. Rubber boot
5. Circlip
6. Piston assembly and spring

Brakes, wheels and final drive 6•17

Check extra carefully around the areas where the hoses connect with the banjo fittings, as these are common areas for hose failure.

2 On models with ABS remove the fuel tank (see Chapter 4) and check the brake pipes, the pipe joints and the ABS hydraulic unit for signs of fluid leakage and for any dents or cracks in the pipes **(see illustration 8.6)**.

3 Inspect the banjo fittings connected to the brake hoses and the pipe joints on ABS models. If the fittings are rusted, scratched or cracked, fit new ones.

Removal and installation

Note: *Before disconnecting any brake hoses or pipes on ABS models, bear in mind that the system must be bled on completion of work, and although this is done initially in the same way as models without ABS, to complete the procedure effectively the Triumph Diagnostic tool must be used to open and close the solenoids within the ABS modulator, and this can only be carried out by a dealer. The bike should be transported, not ridden, to the dealer.*

4 The brake hoses have banjo fittings on each end. Cover the surrounding area with plenty of rags. When working on the rear master cylinder on Sprint and Tiger models lift the rubber boot off the top and disconnect the rear brake light switch wiring connectors **(see illustration 8.4b)**. Unscrew the banjo bolt, or in the case of the rear master cylinder fitting on Sprint models without ABS and Tiger models the rear brake light switch, at each end of the hose, noting the alignment of the fitting with the master cylinder or brake caliper. On Sprint models with ABS it is necessary to remove the rear master cylinder to remove the brake light switch (see Section 8). Free the hose from any clips or guides and remove it, noting its routing. Discard the sealing washers. **Note:** *Do not operate the brake lever or pedal while a brake hose is disconnected.*

5 Position the new hose, making sure it isn't twisted or otherwise strained, and ensure that it is correctly routed through any clips or guides and is clear of all moving components.

6 Check that the fittings align correctly, then install the banjo bolts or brake light switch, using new sealing washers on both sides of the fittings. Tighten the banjo bolts or brake light switch to the torque setting specified at the beginning of this Chapter.

7 On models with ABS the hoses join to pipes that connect the system components to the ABS hydraulic unit. The joints between the hoses and pipes, and where the pipes connect to the hydraulic unit are held by nuts **(see illustration 8.6)**. There are no sealing washers. Unscrew the nuts to separates the hoses from the pipes and to detach the pipes from the hydraulic unit. When refitting them tighten the nuts to the specified torque setting if the correct tools are available.

8 Flush the old brake fluid from the system, refill with new DOT 4 brake fluid (see *Pre-ride checks*) and bleed the air from the system (see Section 10).

9 Check the operation of the brakes before riding the motorcycle.

10 Brake bleeding and fluid change

Note: *If bleeding the system using the conventional method (or one-man kit) described does not work sufficiently well, it is advisable to obtain a vacuum-type brake bleeding tool (see illustration 10.17).*

Note: *Before disconnecting any brake hoses or pipes on ABS models, bear in mind that the system must be bled on completion of work, and although this is done initially in the same way as models without ABS, to complete the procedure effectively the Triumph Diagnostic tool must be used to open and close the solenoids within the ABS modulator, and this can only be carried out by a dealer. The bike should be transported, not ridden, to the dealer.*

Bleeding

1 Bleeding the brakes is simply the process of removing air from the brake fluid reservoir, the hose or pipe, and the brake caliper. Bleeding is necessary whenever a brake system hydraulic connection is loosened, after a component or hose is replaced with a new one, or when the master cylinder or caliper is overhauled. Leaks in the system may also allow air to enter, but leaking brake fluid will reveal their presence and warn you of the need for repair.

2 To bleed the brakes, you will need some new DOT 4 brake fluid, a length of clear vinyl or plastic hose, a small container partially filled with clean brake fluid, some rags, a spanner to fit the brake caliper bleed valve, and help from an assistant **(see illustration)**. Note that 2011-on Speed Triple models (from VIN 461332) have a bleed valve in the front brake master cylinder as well as in each caliper **(see illustration)** – bleed the master cylinder after doing the calipers.

3 Cover painted components to prevent damage in the event that brake fluid is spilled.

4 Refer to 'Pre-ride checks' and remove the reservoir cover or cap, diaphragm plate and diaphragm, and slowly pump the brake lever (front brake) or pedal (rear brake) a few times, until no air bubbles can be seen floating up from the holes in the bottom of the reservoir. This bleeds the air from the master cylinder end of the line. Temporarily refit the reservoir cap or cover.

5 Pull the dust cap off the bleed valve **(see illustrations)**. Attach one end of the clear

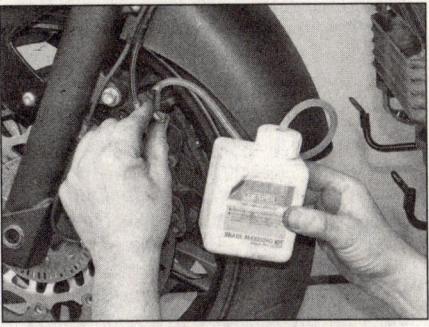

10.2a Bleeding the brakes using a commercially available kit

10.2b Master cylinder bleed valve (arrowed)

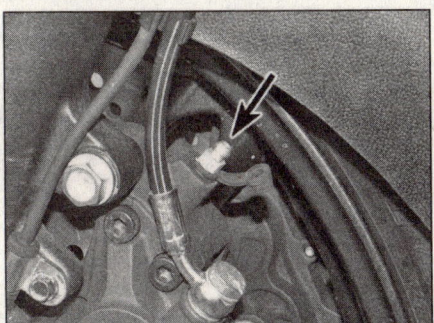

10.5a Front brake caliper bleed valve (arrowed) – Sprint models

10.5b Front brake caliper bleed valve (arrowed) – early Speed Triple and Tiger models

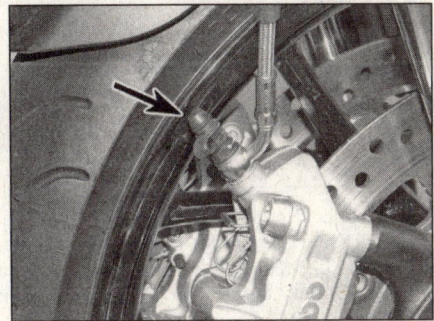

10.5c Front brake caliper bleed valve (arrowed) – 2008-on Speed Triple models

6•18 Brakes, wheels and final drive

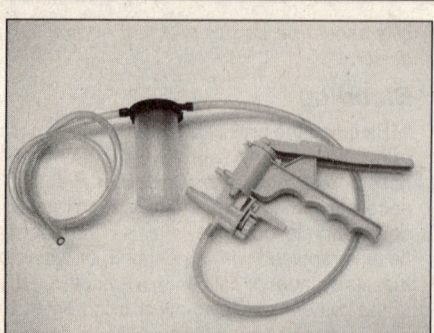

10.17 A commercially available vacuum tool that can be used for drawing brake fluid out

vinyl or plastic hose to the bleed valve and submerge the other end in the clean brake fluid in the container **(see illustration 10.2)**. If you're using a one-man type brake bleeder, there is no need for fluid in the container. **Note:** *To avoid damaging the bleed valve during the procedure, loosen it and then tighten it temporarily with a ring spanner before attaching the hose. With the hose attached, the valve can then be opened and closed either with an open-ended spanner, or by leaving the ring spanner located on the valve and fitting the hose above it.*

6 Check the fluid level in the reservoir. Do not allow the fluid level to drop below the low level mark during the procedure.
7 Carefully pump the brake lever or pedal three or four times, then hold it in (front) or down (rear) and open the bleed valve. When the valve is opened, brake fluid will flow out of the caliper into the clear tubing, and the lever will move toward the handlebar, or the pedal will move down. If there is air in the system there will be air bubbles in the brake fluid coming out of the caliper.
8 Tighten the bleed valve, then release the brake lever or pedal gradually. Top-up the reservoir and repeat the process until no air bubbles are visible in the brake fluid leaving the caliper, and the lever or pedal is firm when applied. On completion, disconnect the hose, then tighten the bleed valve to the torque setting specified at the beginning of this Chapter and install the dust cap.

 If it is not possible to produce a firm feel to the lever or pedal, the fluid may be aerated. Let the brake fluid in the system stabilise for a few hours and then repeat the procedure when the tiny bubbles in the system have settled out.

9 Top-up the reservoir, then install the diaphragm, diaphragm plate and cap (see *Pre-ride checks*). Wipe up any spilled brake fluid. Check the entire system for fluid leaks.
10 Check the operation of the brakes before riding the motorcycle.

Fluid change
11 Changing the brake fluid is a similar process to bleeding the brakes and requires the same materials plus a suitable tool for siphoning the fluid out of the reservoir. Also ensure that the container is large enough to take all the old fluid when it is flushed out of the system.
12 Follow Steps 2, 3 and 5, then remove the reservoir cap, diaphragm plate and diaphragm and siphon the old fluid out of the reservoir. Fill the reservoir with new brake fluid, then carefully pump the brake lever or pedal three or four times and hold it in (front) or down (rear) while opening the caliper bleed valve. When the valve is opened, brake fluid will flow out of the caliper into the clear tubing, and the lever will move toward the handlebar, or the pedal will move down.
13 Tighten the bleed valve, then release the brake lever or pedal gradually. Keep the reservoir topped-up with new fluid to above the LOWER level at all times or air may enter the system and greatly increase the length of the task. Repeat the process until new fluid can be seen emerging from the caliper bleed valve.

 *Old brake fluid is invariably much darker in colour than new fluid, making it easy to see when all old fluid has been expelled from the system.*

14 Disconnect the hose, then make sure the bleed valve is tightened to the specified torque setting and install the dust cap.
15 Top-up the reservoir, then install the diaphragm, diaphragm plate, and cap (see *Pre-ride checks*). Wipe up any spilled brake fluid. Check the entire system for fluid leaks.
16 Check the operation of the brakes before riding the motorcycle.

Draining the system for overhaul
17 Draining the brake fluid is again a similar process to bleeding the brakes. The quickest and easiest way is to use a commercially available vacuum-type brake bleeding tool **(see illustration)** – follow the manufacturer's instructions. Otherwise follow the procedure described above for changing the fluid, but quite simply do not put any new fluid into the reservoir – the system fills itself with air instead.

11 Anti-lock brake system – ABS

General information
> **Warning:** *The ABS system works by comparing the relative speed of the wheels, and is programmed using the wheel and tyre sizes specified and fitted as standard. If non-specified wheels or tyres are fitted the control unit may become confused and the system will not function correctly.*

1 The anti-lock braking system (ABS) prevents the wheels from locking up under hard braking or on uneven road surfaces. A sensor on each wheel picks up information about the speed of wheel rotation from a pulse ring mounted on the wheel and transmits to an electronic control unit in the modulator, and if it senses that a wheel is about to lock, it activates the solenoids in the modulator which releases brake pressure momentarily to that wheel, preventing a skid. When the system is active a pulsing can be felt through the lever or pedal as the fluid pressure is released and reapplied as required. The front and rear systems are entirely independent of each other, even though they function through the same control module and modulator **(see illustrations)**.
2 The ABS system is self-checking, and is automatically switched on with the ignition. ABS will not function at speeds of less than 6 mph (10 km/h), with the ignition off, if a fault is indicated (ABS warning light remains on after start-up or comes on during use), or if the battery is flat.
3 When the ignition switch is turned on, the ABS indicator light on the instrument panel comes on, then goes off when a speed of 6 mph (10 km/h) is reached. If the indicator light stays on, or comes on while riding, then there is probably a fault in the system, in which case it will record a fault code. Stop the motorcycle and switch the ignition switch off. Switch it on again, start the engine and ride the bike – if the light goes off then the system is OK and will work, but the fault code is still stored. Fault codes can only be read and diagnosed using the Triumph special tool.
4 Note that under certain conditions, the

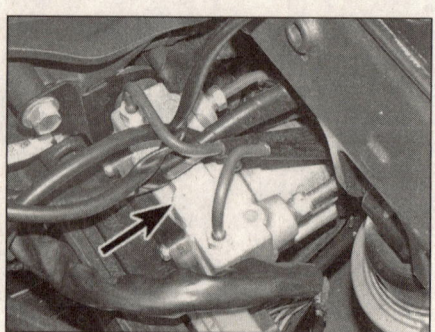

11.1a ABS modulator (arrowed) – Sprint

11.1b ABS modulator (arrowed) – Tiger

Brakes, wheels and final drive

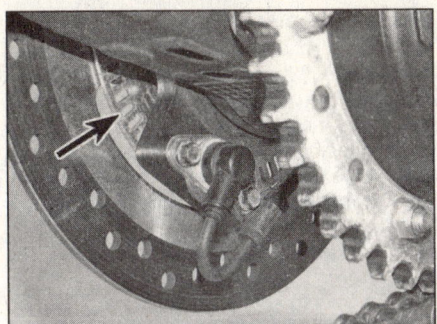

11.5a Make sure the gaps between the poles (arrowed) and the sensor tip are clean

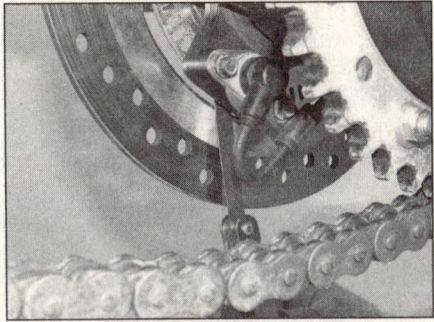

11.5b Measuring the air gap

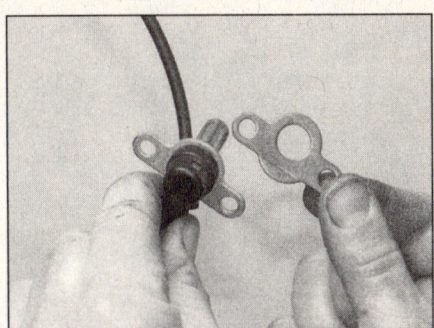

11.5c Different shims are available to adjust the air gap

indicator light could come on and a fault code could be registered, even though there is no actual problem with the system. This is when the effects of the conditions themselves simulate an actual fault. This can occur if the machine is ridden continuously on very bumpy roads, or if the rider does a wheelie, or if the air pressure on one tyre is extremely low, or if the machine is placed on the centrestand or an auxiliary stand with the engine running and the rear wheel is turning when the front is not. If this happens stop the bike and turn the engine off, then restart and ride the bike – the light may not come on again when the system realises everything is OK, but if it does the fault code must be retrieved and then erased before the indicator light will go out.

5 The only actions the owner can take in the case of a fault, and the only maintenance that can be applied, is firstly to make sure there is no dirt or debris on each wheel speed sensor tip or between the poles on the sensor rotor **(see illustration)**. Secondly check the air gap between the sensor tip and one of the poles on the rotor, though once set, this is unlikely to change. Check the gap by inserting a feeler gauge between the sensor and the tip of one of the poles **(see illustration)**. Check the gap in different places by rotating the wheel. If the gap is not as specified at the beginning of the Chapter, remove the sensor (see below) and adjust the air gap by inserting a replacement shim of the required thickness to bring the gap within specifications **(see illustration)**. Shims are available in sizes of 0.5, 1.0, 1.5 and 2.0 mm on Sprint and Tiger models, and 0.8 and 1.6 mm

11.9a Front wheel sensor (arrowed) – Sprint

on Speed Triple models. On completion tighten the bolt(s) to the specified torque setting.

6 Also make a check of all the system wiring and connectors, looking for chafed wires or broken connector pins, damp or corroded terminals, and if required refer to Section 2 at the beginning of Chapter 8 and to the wiring diagrams at the end of it and check all wiring for continuity. Make sure the ignition is OFF before disconnecting any wiring connectors or making any tests.

7 If the indicator light does not come on when the ignition is switched on, check the ABS fuses (see Chapter 8) and the instrument panel and the control module wiring connectors. If all is good, take the machine to a Triumph dealer for testing.

8 Fault diagnosis and any other work on the system, including bleeding it and changing the brake fluid, must be undertaken by a Triumph dealer.

11.9b Front wheel sensor (arrowed) – Tiger

Component removal and installation

Front wheel sensor

9 The sensor is mounted in the bottom of the left-hand fork **(see illustrations)**.

10 Trace the wiring from the sensor and disconnect it at the connector – on Sprint models it is on the underside of the bottom yoke **(see illustration)**; on Speed Triple models remove the airbox (see Chapter 4) – it is above the valve cover **(see illustration)**; on Tiger models remove the right-hand fairing side panel (see Chapter 7) – it is on the right-hand end of the valve cover **(see illustration)**. Free the wiring from any ties or guides and feed it down to the sensor, noting its routing.

11 Unscrew the bolt(s) securing the sensor and withdraw it from the fork.

12 Installation is the reverse of removal. Make sure the sensor tip is clean and undamaged,

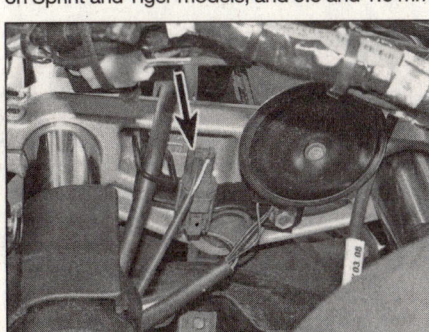

11.10a Front wheel sensor wiring connector (arrowed) – Sprint

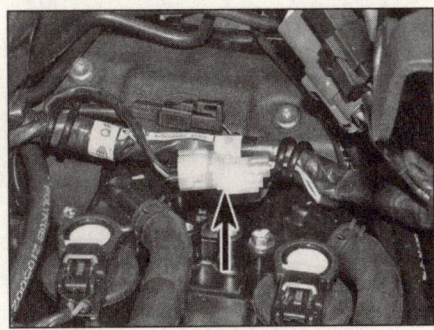

11.10b Front wheel sensor wiring connector (arrowed) – Speed Triple

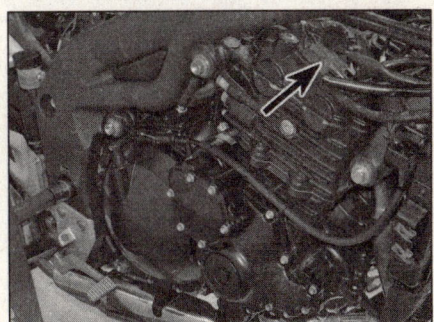

11.10c Front wheel sensor wiring connector (arrowed) – Tiger

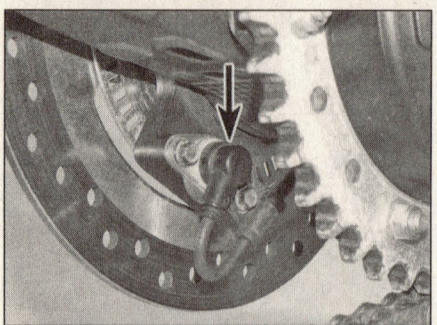

11.13 Rear wheel sensor (arrowed) – Sprint

11.14a On Speed Triple models displace the slider and remove the cover from the underside of the swingarm

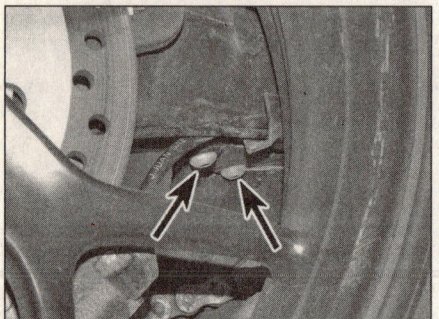

11.14b On Tiger models remove the lower guard (screws arrowed) . . .

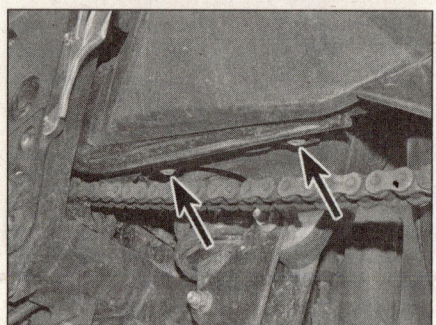

11.14c . . . and the slider (screws arrowed)

and that the mounting lugs are not distorted. Tighten the bolt(s) to the torque setting specified at the beginning of the Chapter. Check the air gap (see Step 5).

Rear wheel sensor
13 The sensor is mounted in the bottom of the rear brake caliper bracket **(see illustration)**.
14 To access the wiring connector remove the fuel tank (see Chapter 4). Trace the wiring from the sensor and disconnect it at the connector. Free the wiring from any ties or guides and feed it down to the sensor, noting its routing – on Speed Triple models undo the chain slider lower bolt and remove the collar, then undo the brake hose cover screws, remove the cover and free the wiring **(see illustration)**, and on Tiger Sport models remove the lower chainguard and the chain slider bolts on the underside, then free the ABS sensor wire **(see illustrations)**.
15 Unscrew the bolt(s) securing the sensor and withdraw it from the bracket.
16 Installation is the reverse of removal. Make sure the sensor tip is clean and undamaged, and that the mounting lugs are not distorted. Tighten the bolt(s) to the torque setting specified at the beginning of the Chapter. Check the air gap (see Step 5).

Front wheel pulse ring
17 Remove the wheel (see Section 14). Support the wheel using wooden blocks so no weight is on the disc.
18 Unscrew the bolts securing the pulse ring and lift it off **(see illustration)**.
19 Before installing the ring, make sure there is no dirt or corrosion between the mating surfaces as this will not allow the ring to sit flat when it is bolted down and it will be warped and could cause the ABS system to indicate a fault. Tighten the bolts evenly in a criss-cross pattern to the torque setting specified at the beginning of the Chapter.

Rear wheel pulse ring
Note: *On Sprint GT, Speed Triple and Tiger Sport models Triumph specify to use tool T3880388 to centre the ABS pulse ring on the hub on installation, and warn that failure to do so can affect operation of the ABS. If the tool is not available have the pulse ring installed by a dealer.*
20 On Sprint models refer to Section 7, Step 3 remove the axle/disc carrier from of the hub.
21 On Tiger models remove the wheel (see Section 15).
22 Unscrew the bolts securing the pulse ring and lift it off, along with the spacer ring on Sprint models.
23 Before installing the ring(s), make sure there is no dirt or corrosion between the mating surfaces as this will not allow the ring to sit flat when it is bolted down and it will be warped and could cause the ABS system to indicate a fault. On Sprint GT, Speed Triple and Tiger Sport models fit the centring tool over the axle with the PULSER RING mark facing up (see **Note** above). Tighten the bolts evenly in a criss-cross pattern to the torque setting specified at the beginning of the Chapter. On Sprint GT, Speed Triple and Tiger Sport models remove the centring tool.

Modulator
Note: *Before disconnecting any brake hoses or pipes, bear in mind that the system must be bled on completion of work, and although this is done initially in the same way as models without ABS, to complete the procedure effectively the Triumph Diagnostic tool must be used to open and close the solenoids within the ABS modulator, and this can only be carried out by a dealer. The bike should be transported, not ridden, to the dealer.*
24 Have some clean rag to hand to catch any spilled brake fluid and some clingfilm to wrap around the end of each pipe as it is disconnected. If required drain the brake fluid from the system (see Section 10).
25 Remove the seat (see Chapter 7). Disconnect the battery (Chapter 8). Remove the fuel tank (see Chapter 4). On Speed Triple models remove the airbox (see Chapter 4), the coolant reservoir (see Chapter 3), and the EVAP canister on California models, and disconnect the regulator/rectifier wiring.
26 Release the security clip and disconnect the wiring connector from the control module **(see illustration)**.

11.18 Front pulse ring bolts (arrowed)

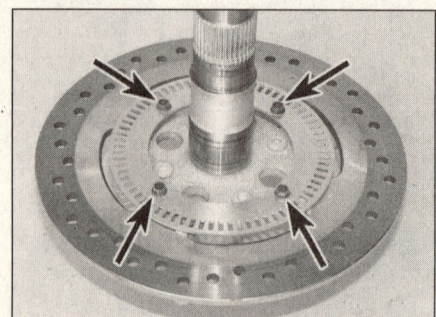

11.22 Rear pulse ring bolts (arrowed) – Sprint

11.26 Release the clip and disconnect the wiring

Brakes, wheels and final drive

11.29 Brake hose bolts (arrowed) – Speed Triple

11.31a Unscrew the bolts (arrowed) . . .

11.31b . . . and the bolt (arrowed)

27 On Sprint models lift the rubber boot off the top of the rear master cylinder and disconnect the rear brake light switch wiring connectors. Remove the retaining clip from the clevis pin securing the master cylinder pushrod to the brake pedal. Withdraw the clevis pin and separate the pushrod from the pedal. Remove the splash shield from the frame. Unscrew the bolt securing the rear brake hose to the control module bracket. Unscrew the nuts securing the master cylinder, then displace it and lay it aside on some rag.

28 On Tiger models remove the heel guard. Lift the rubber boot off the top of the rear master cylinder and disconnect the rear brake light switch wiring connectors. Unscrew the brake light switch and detach the brake pipe from the master cylinder, taking great care not to bend the pipe. Discard the two sealing washers as they must be replaced with new ones. Wrap the end of the pipe in clingfilm. Unscrew the bolt securing the front brake pipe/hose union to the frame on the left-hand side. Unscrew the nut on the upper rear engine mounting bolt on the right-hand side then partially withdraw the bolt so it is clear of the control module bracket. Note that Triumph specify to use a new nut and bolt on installation.

29 Unscrew the input and output pipe nuts (Sprint and Tiger – see illustration 11.1a or b) or hose bolts (Speed Triple – see illustration) and detach the pipes or hoses from the control module, being prepared with some rag to catch any residual fluid, and taking care not to bend the pipes. Wrap the end of each pipe or hose in clingfilm to prevent fluid loss and dirt getting in. On Speed Triple models new sealing washers will be needed on installation.

30 On Sprint models, unscrew the nut securing the bracket on the stud, then carefully manoeuvre the control module out.

31 On Speed Triple models unscrew the bolts, move the brake light switch aside, and carefully manoeuvre the control module/regulator/rectifier assembly out (see illustrations). Remove the regulator/rectifier.

32 On Tiger models unscrew the two bolts, then carefully manoeuvre the control unit out.

33 If required separate the control module from its bracket.

34 Installation is the reverse of removal. Make sure all brake pipes and hoses are connected and their fixings are tightened finger-tight only for correct alignment before tightening any off them fully, and on Tiger models tighten the brake light switch to the specified torque, and tighten the hose/pipe union mounting bolt, before tightening the pipe nuts on the modulator. If the correct tools are available tighten the pipe joint nuts to the specified torque. On Speed Triple models clean the threads of all mounting bolts and apply fresh threadlock, and use new sealing washers on each side of each hose banjo union and tighten the bolts to the specified torque. On Tiger models tighten the new upper rear engine mounting bolt and nut to the torque setting specified at the beginning of Chapter 2.

35 Bleed the hydraulic system following the procedure in Section 10, then transport the bike to a Triumph dealer for bleeding of the control module. Check the operation of both front and rear brakes carefully before riding the motorcycle.

12 Wheel inspection and repair

1 In order to carry out a proper inspection of the wheels, it is necessary to support the bike upright so that the wheel being inspected is raised off the ground. Position the motorcycle on an auxiliary stand (or on the centrestand on Sprint models). Clean the wheels thoroughly to remove mud and dirt that may interfere with the inspection procedure or mask defects. Make a general check of the wheels (see Chapter 1) and tyres (see Pre-ride checks).

2 Attach a dial gauge to the fork or the swingarm and position its tip against the side of the wheel rim. Spin the wheel slowly and check the axial (side-to-side) runout of the rim (see illustration).

3 In order to accurately check radial (out of round) runout with the dial gauge, remove the wheel from the machine, and the tyre from the wheel. With the axle clamped in a vice and the dial gauge positioned on the top of the rim, the wheel can be rotated to check the runout (see illustration 12.2).

4 An easier, though slightly less accurate, method is to attach a stiff wire pointer to the fork or the swingarm and position the end a fraction of an inch from the wheel rim where the wheel and tyre join. If the wheel is true, the distance from the pointer to the rim will be constant as the wheel is rotated. Note: If wheel runout is excessive, check the wheel bearings very carefully before renewing the wheel.

5 The wheels should also be inspected for cracks, flat spots on the rim and other damage. Look very closely for dents in the area where the tyre bead contacts the rim. Dents in this area may prevent complete sealing of the tyre against the rim, which leads to deflation of the tyre over a period of time. If damage is evident, or if runout in either direction is excessive, the wheel will have to be renewed. Never attempt to repair a damaged cast alloy wheel.

13 Wheel alignment check

1 Misalignment of the wheels, which may be due to a cocked rear wheel or a bent frame or fork yokes, can cause strange and possibly serious handling problems. If the frame or yokes are at

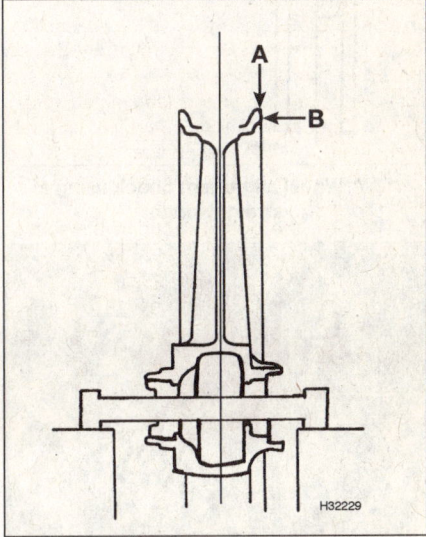

12.2 Check the wheel for radial (out-of-round) runout (A) and axial (side-to-side) runout (B)

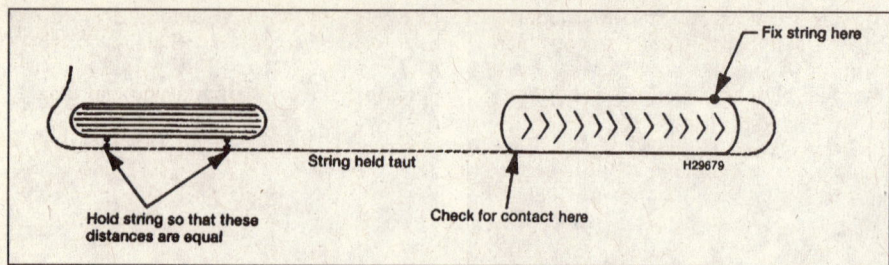

13.5 Wheel alignment check using string

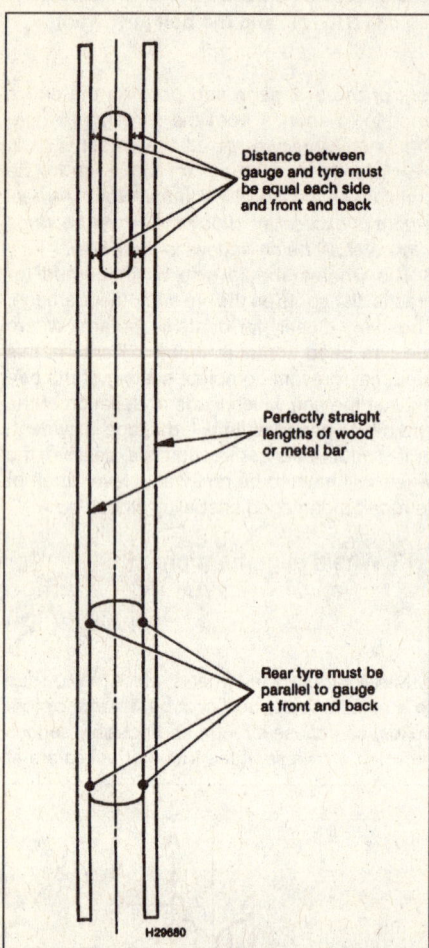

13.7 Wheel alignment check using a straight-edge

fault, repair by a frame specialist or replacement with new parts are the only alternatives.

2 To check the alignment you will need an assistant, a length of string or a perfectly straight piece of wood or metal bar and a ruler. A plumb bob or other suitable weight will also be required.

3 In order to make a proper check of the wheels it is necessary to support the bike in an upright position, using an auxiliary stand (or on its centrestand – Sprint). On Tiger models (except Sport) first ensure that the chain adjuster markings coincide on each side of the swingarm (see Chapter 1, Section 1). Measure the width of both tyres at their widest points. Subtract the smaller measurement from the larger measurement, then divide the difference by two. The result is the amount of offset that should exist between the front and rear tyres on both sides.

4 If a string is used, have your assistant hold one end of it about halfway between the floor and the rear axle, touching the rear sidewall of the tyre.

5 Run the other end of the string forward and pull it tight so that it is roughly parallel to the floor **(see illustration)**. Slowly bring the string into contact with the front sidewall of the rear tyre, then turn the front wheel until it is parallel with the string. Measure the distance from the front tyre sidewall to the string.

6 Repeat the procedure on the other side of the motorcycle. The distance from the front tyre sidewall to the string should be equal on both sides.

7 As previously mentioned, a perfectly straight length of wood or metal bar may be substituted for the string **(see illustration)**. The procedure is the same.

8 If the distance between the string and tyre is greater on one side, or if the rear wheel appears to be out of alignment, have your machine checked by a Triumph dealer or frame specialist.

9 If the front-to-back alignment is correct, the wheels still may be out of alignment vertically.

10 Using a plumb bob, or other suitable weight, and a length of string, check the rear wheel to make sure it is vertical. To do this, hold the string against the tyre upper sidewall and allow the weight to settle just off the floor. When the string touches both the upper and lower tyre sidewalls and is perfectly straight, the wheel is vertical. If it is not, place thin spacers under one leg of the stand until it is.

11 Once the rear wheel is vertical, check the front wheel in the same manner. If both wheels are not perfectly vertical, the frame and/or major suspension components are bent.

14 Front wheel
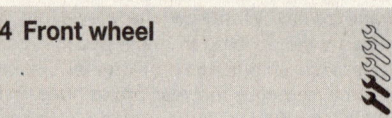

Removal

1 Support the motorcycle securely in an upright position on level ground using an auxiliary stand so the front wheel is off the ground.

2 Displace the front brake calipers (see Section 3). Support the calipers with a piece of wire or a bungee cord so that no strain is placed on the hydraulic hoses. There is no need to disconnect the hoses from the calipers. **Note:** *Do not operate the front brake lever with the calipers removed.*

3 On Sprint and Tiger models with ABS displace the wheel sensor from the fork (see Section 11) – there is no need to disconnect the wiring.

4 On Sprint models remove the front section of the mudguard (see Chapter 7).

5 Slacken the axle clamp bolts on the bottom of the right-hand fork **(see illustration)**. Unscrew the axle **(see illustration)**.

6 Support the wheel, then withdraw the axle from the right-hand side and lower the wheel to the ground **(see illustration)**. Use a drift to drive out the axle if required. Roll the wheel out from between the forks.

14.5a Slacken the clamp bolts (arrowed)

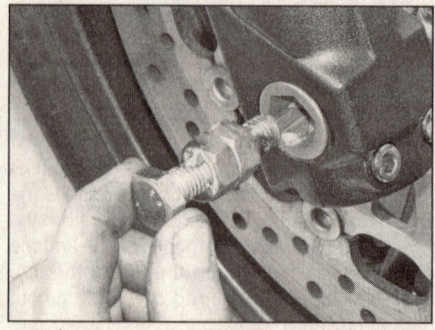

14.5b Unscrew the axle using a large hex bit or a tool made from nuts and bolts as shown

14.6 Withdraw the axle and remove the wheel

Brakes, wheels and final drive 6•23

14.7 Remove the spacer from each side

7 Remove the spacer from each side of the wheel, noting which fits where (see illustration). **Caution: Don't lay the wheel down and allow it to rest on a disc – the disc could become warped. Set the wheel on wood blocks so the disc doesn't support the weight of the wheel, or keep it upright.**

8 Clean off all old grease from the axle and spacers and remove any corrosion using a scouring pad or wire wool. Check the axle is straight by rolling it on a flat surface such as a piece of plate glass If the equipment is available, place the axle in V-blocks and check for runout using a dial gauge. If the axle is bent, replace it with a new one.

9 Check the condition of the wheel bearings (see Section 16).

Installation

10 Apply lithium-based grease to the lips of the bearing seals, to the axle and to the spacers. Fit the spacer into each side of the wheel (see illustration 14.7) – on Sprint models, fit the spacer with the single groove in its outer surface into the right-hand side of the wheel, and that with the twin groove into the left.

11 Manoeuvre the wheel into position.

12 Lift the wheel into place between the forks, making sure the spacers remain in position, and slide the axle in from the right-hand side (see illustration 14.6).

13 Tighten the axle to the torque setting specified at the beginning of the Chapter (see illustration 14.5b). Wipe any excess grease off the axle and around the fork bottoms. Make sure the wheel spins freely.

14 Install the brake calipers, making sure the pads sit squarely on each side of the discs (see Section 3). Apply the front brake a few times to bring the pads back into contact with the discs.

15 On Sprint and Tiger models with ABS install the wheel sensor (see Section 11)

16 Move the bike off its stand, hold the front brake on and pump the forks a few times. Now tighten the axle clamp bolts on the bottom of the right-hand fork to the specified torque setting (see illustration 14.5a).

17 On Sprint models install the front section of the mudguard (see Chapter 7).

18 Check for correct operation of the front brake before riding the motorcycle.

15 Rear wheel

Sprint, Speed Triple and Tiger Sport models

Removal

1 Support the motorcycle securely in an upright position on level ground using an auxiliary stand so the rear wheel is off the ground.

2 Remove the wheel nut retaining clip (see illustration).

3 Unscrew the wheel nut and remove the dished washer, the plain washer and the conical spacer, noting how they fit (see illustrations) – prevent the wheel from turning either by applying the rear brake hard, or by counter-holding the sprocket coupling nut on the other side. Draw the wheel off the axle and remove it, angling it as required to avoid contacting anything (see illustration).

4 Check the hub bearings and sprocket coupling bearing (see Section 16).

Installation

5 Slide the wheel onto the axle, locating the holes on the four studs (see illustration 15.3c). Hold it squarely on and fit the conical spacer, the plain washer and the dished washer (see illustration 15.3b) – fit the dished washer so that its outer rim sits on the plain washer and the inner rim is raised off it. Fit the wheel nut and tighten it to the torque setting specified at the beginning of the Chapter (see illustration 15.3a) – prevent the wheel from turning either by applying the rear brake hard, or by counter-holding the sprocket coupling nut on the other side.

15.2 Remove the retaining clip . . .

15.3a . . . then unscrew the nut . . .

15.3b . . . remove the dished washer, plain washer and conical spacer (arrowed) . . .

15.3c . . . and draw the wheel off the axle

6•24 Brakes, wheels and final drive

15.11a Unscrew the axle nut and remove the washer . . .

15.11b . . . and adjustment position marker

15.12a Withdraw the axle and lower the wheel . . .

6 Fit the wheel nut retaining clip **(see illustration 15.2)**.

Tiger and Tiger SE models

Removal

7 Support the motorcycle securely in an upright position on level ground using an auxiliary stand so the rear wheel is off the ground.
8 Refer to Chapter 1 and slacken the drive chain.
9 Displace the rear brake caliper (see Section 6). Make sure no strain is placed on the hydraulic hose. There is no need to disconnect the hose from the caliper. **Note:** *Do not operate the brake pedal with the caliper removed.*
10 On models with ABS displace the wheel sensor from the caliper bracket (see Section 11) – there is no need to disconnect the wiring.
11 Unscrew the nut from the left-hand end of the axle and remove the washer and the adjustment position marker **(see illustrations)**. Note that Triumph specify to use a new nut.
12 Support the wheel then withdraw the axle along with the right-hand adjustment position marker and lower the wheel to the ground **(see illustration)**. Remove the caliper bracket, noting how it locates between the wheel and the swingarm **(see illustration)**. Disengage the chain from the sprocket and remove the wheel from between the swingarm ends **(see illustration)**.
13 Remove the plain spacer from the left-hand side of the wheel and the shouldered spacer

from the right-hand side for safekeeping if required **(see illustration)**.

 **HAYNES HINT** *If you are working outside or on a dirty floor, tie the chain to the rear sub-frame, or lay some paper or rag on the ground for the chain to rest on, to prevent any dust and grit sticking to it.*

14 Clean off all old grease from the axle and spacers and remove any corrosion using a scouring pad or wire wool. Check the axle is straight by rolling it on a flat surface such as a piece of plate glass If the equipment is available, place the axle in V-blocks and check for runout using a dial gauge. If the axle is bent, replace it with a new one.
15 Check the wheel bearings and sprocket coupling bearings (see Section 16).

Installation

16 Apply a thin coat of lithium-based grease to the lips of each grease seal, and also to the spacers and the axle.
17 Fit the plain spacer into the left-hand side of the wheel and the shouldered spacer into the right-hand side **(see illustration 15.13)**.
18 Manoeuvre the wheel into place between the ends of the swingarm. Fit the drive chain around the sprocket **(see illustration 15.12c)**. Fit the brake caliper bracket onto the swingarm, locating the lug in the groove **(see illustration 15.12b)**.
19 Slide the right-hand adjustment position marker (the one with the raised sections,

15.12b . . . then remove the caliper bracket . . .

which must face out) onto the axle. Lift the wheel into position, making sure the caliper bracket and the spacers remain in place, and slide the axle, with the adjustment marker, through from the right-hand side **(see illustration 15.12a)**. Make sure it passes through the caliper bracket. Align the flats on the axle head between the raised sections on the adjustment marker, and make sure the raised sections are vertical, not horizontal **(see illustration)**.
20 Check that everything is correctly aligned, then fit the left-hand adjustment position marker **(see illustration 15.11b)**. Fit the washer and the new axle nut **(see illustration 15.11a)**. Adjust the chain slack as described in Chapter 1, then tighten the axle nut to the torque setting specified at the beginning of the Chapter, making sure the adjustment

15.12c . . . and slip the chain off the sprocket

15.13 Remove the spacer from each side

15.19 Make sure the axle head and adjustment marker locate correctly

Brakes, wheels and final drive 6•25

15.20 Tighten the axle nut to the specified torque

markers are butted against the adjuster bolt heads **(see illustration)**.
21 Install the brake caliper, making sure the pads sit squarely on each side of the disc (see Section 6).
22 On models with ABS install the wheel sensor (see Section 11)
23 Operate the brake pedal several times to bring the pads into contact with the disc. Check the operation of the rear brake before riding the bike.

16 Wheel, sprocket coupling and hub bearings

Front wheel bearings

Note: *Always renew the wheel bearings in pairs, never individually. Avoid using a high pressure cleaner on the wheel bearing area.*

1 Remove the wheel (see Section 14).
2 On Sprint and Tiger models with ABS remove the pulse ring (see Section 11)
3 Note the set depth of the bearing seal on each side of the hub. Lever out each seal using a flat-bladed screwdriver or a seal hook **(see illustration)**. Take care not to damage the hub. Discard the seals – new ones must be used.

> **HAYNES HiNT** *Position a piece of wood against the wheel to prevent the screwdriver shaft damaging it when levering the grease seal out.*

4 Inspect the bearings – check that the inner race turns smoothly and that the outer race is a tight fit in the hub (see *Tools and Workshop Tips* in the Reference Section). **Note:** *Do not remove the bearings unless they are going to be replaced with new ones.*
5 If the bearings are worn, remove the circlip from the left-hand side of the wheel. Discard the circlip – Triumph specify to use a new one.
6 Using a metal rod (preferably a brass punch) inserted through the centre of the left-hand bearing and located in one of the cut-outs in the bearing spacer, drive the right-hand bearing from the hub, alternating the drift between the cut-outs so it's driven out squarely **(see illustrations)**. The bearing spacer will also come out. Turn the wheel over so that the remaining bearing faces down. Drive the left-hand bearing out of the wheel.
7 Thoroughly clean the hub area of the wheel and inspect the bearing seats for scoring

and wear. If the seats are damaged, consult a Triumph dealer or wheel specialist before reassembling the wheel.
8 Drive the new bearings, marked side facing out, into the hub until they seat using a bearing driver or suitable socket, or draw them in using a drawbolt arrangement (see *Tools and Workshop Tips*) **(see illustration)**. Ensure that the driver or socket bears only on the outer race. Ensure the bearing is fitted squarely and all the way onto its seat.
9 Turn the wheel over then install the bearing spacer and the other new bearing.
10 Fit a new circlip into its groove outside the left-hand bearing.
11 Apply a smear of grease to the new seals, then press them into the hub, setting each to the depth noted before removal **(see illustration)**.
12 On Sprint and Tiger models with ABS install the pulse ring (see Section 11)
13 Clean the brake discs using acetone or brake system cleaner, then install the wheel (see Section 14).

Rear wheel bearings – Tiger and Tiger SE models

14 Remove the wheel (see Section 15). Lift the sprocket coupling out of the wheel, noting how it fits, and the spacer inside it **(see illustrations 16.28a and b)**. A caged ball bearing is fitted in each side of the wheel.
15 Set the wheel on wood blocks with the disc (right-hand side) facing up.
16 Lever out the bearing seal on the right-hand side of the hub using a flat-bladed screwdriver or a seal hook **(see illustration)**.

16.3 Lever out the grease seals

16.6a Knock out the bearings using a drift . . .

16.6b . . . locating it in the notches (arrowed)

16.8 A socket can be used to drive in the bearing

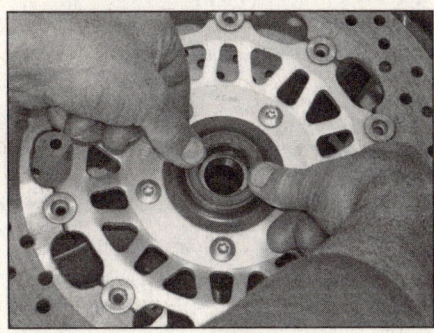

16.11 Fit the grease seal and press or tap it into place

16.16 Lever out the grease seal (arrowed)

6•26 Brakes, wheels and final drive

16.19a Locate the knife edge of the puller in the gap between the bearing and the spacer, then expand it . . .

16.19b . . . and use the slide-hammer to dislodge the bearing

16.22 A socket can be used to drive in the bearing

Take care not to damage the hub. Discard the seals – a new one must be used.

17 Inspect the bearings – check that the inner race turns smoothly and that the outer race is a tight fit in the hub (see *Tools and Workshop Tips* in the Reference Section). **Note:** *Do not remove the bearings unless they are going to be replaced with new ones.*

18 If the bearings are worn, remove the circlip. Discard the circlip – Triumph specify to use a new one.

19 Using an internal expanding puller on a slide-hammer attachment draw the bearing out, holding the wheel securely down as you do **(see illustrations)**.

20 Turn the wheel over – the bearing spacer will drop out. Drive the other bearing out of the wheel using a suitable drift.

21 Thoroughly clean the hub area of the wheel and inspect the bearing seats for scoring and wear. If the seats are damaged, consult a Triumph dealer or wheel specialist before reassembling the wheel.

22 Drive the new bearings, marked side facing out, into the hub until they seat using a bearing driver or suitable socket, or draw them in using a drawbolt arrangement (see *Tools and Workshop Tips*) **(see illustration)**. Ensure that the driver or socket bears only on the outer race. Ensure the bearing is fitted squarely and all the way onto its seat.

23 Turn the wheel over then install the bearing spacer and the other new bearing.

24 Fit a new circlip into its groove.

25 Apply a smear of grease to the new seal, then press it into the right-hand side of the hub.

26 Make sure the spacer is in place, then fit the sprocket coupling into the wheel **(see illustrations 16.28b and a)**. Clean the brake disc using acetone or brake system cleaner, then install the wheel (see Section 15).

Sprocket coupling bearing

27 On Sprint, Speed Triple and Tiger Sport models remove the rear sprocket coupling (see Section 20). Lift the back plate out and remove the spacer from inside the coupling **(see illustrations)**.

28 On Tiger and Tiger SE models remove the rear wheel (see Section 14). Lift the sprocket coupling out of the wheel, noting how it fits, and remove the spacer from inside it **(see illustrations)**.

29 Using a large flat-bladed screwdriver lever out the grease seal from the outside of the coupling, taking care not to damage the rim of the coupling (see *Haynes Hint* on previous page) **(see illustrations)**. Discard the seal – a new one must be used.

16.27a Lift the back plate out . . .

16.27b . . . and remove the spacer from inside the coupling

16.28a Lift the sprocket coupling out of the wheel . . .

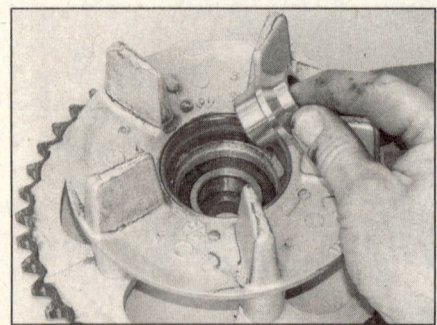

16.28b . . . and remove the spacer from inside it

16.29a Sprocket coupling grease seal (arrowed) – Sprint and Speed Triple

16.29b Levering out the grease seal – Tiger

Brakes, wheels and final drive 6•27

16.31 Drive the bearing out from the inside

16.32 A socket can be used to drive in the bearing

16.33 Press or drive the seal into the coupling

30 Inspect the bearing – check that the inner race turns smoothly and that the outer race is a tight fit in the hub (see *Tools and Workshop Tips* in the Reference Section). **Note:** *Do not remove the bearing unless it is going to be replaced with a new one.*

31 To remove a worn bearing, first check whether a retaining circlip is fitted. If so, remove it and obtain a new one for use with the new bearing. Support the coupling on blocks of wood and drive the bearing out from the inside using a bearing driver or socket **(see illustration)**.

32 Thoroughly clean the bearing recess in the coupling then fit the bearing from the outside of the coupling, with the marked or sealed side facing out. Using the old bearing (if a new one is being fitted), a bearing driver or a socket large enough to contact the outer race of the bearing, drive it in until it is completely seated **(see illustration)**. Secure the bearing with a new circlip (where applicable), making sure it locates in its groove.

33 Apply a smear of grease to the lips of the new seal, and press it into the coupling, using a seal or bearing driver or a suitable socket if necessary **(see illustration)**.

34 Check the sprocket coupling/rubber dampers (see Section 20).

35 On Sprint, Speed Triple and Tiger Sport models, check the condition of the back plate O-ring and replace it with a new one if necessary. Fit the spacer, then fit the back plate into the coupling **(see illus-**

trations 16.27b and a). Install the rear sprocket coupling (see Section 20).

36 On Tiger and Tiger SE models, fit the spacer, then fit the sprocket coupling into the wheel **(see illustrations 16.28b and a)**. Clean the brake disc using acetone or brake system cleaner then install the wheel (see Section 15).

Rear hub assembly bearings – Sprint and Speed Triple models

37 Remove the rear axle/brake disc carrier (see Section 7).

38 Remove the large circlip on the inner (right-hand) end of the hub and slide off the brake caliper carrier, noting how it locates on the swingarm **(see illustrations)**. Draw the hub assembly out of the swingarm **(see illustration)**. Discard the circlip – a new one must be used.

39 The hub assembly houses a caged ball bearing in the left-hand side and a needle roller bearing in the right-hand side. Triumph specify that the bearings are a press-fit, and so require special tools for removal and installation. They advise that if the bearings are worn and need renewing, it is easier to renew the hub assembly as a unit with the bearings already installed. However, the bearings are listed individually – you will have to check on the relative cost, both in money and time.

40 Refer to *Tools and Workshop Tips* in the Reference Section at the back of this manual and check the bearings.

41 On Sprint models up to VIN 388246 and Speed Triple models up to VIN 346970 lever out the grease seal from the right-hand end of the hub using a large flat-bladed screwdriver, taking care not to damage the rim of the hub (see *Haynes Hint on page 6.25*). Discard the seal if it is damaged or deteriorated. On all later models the seal is integral with the bearing. Remove the circlips from the outer ends of the hub and discard them – fit new ones on reassembly.

42 Support the hub on blocks of wood and drive out the left-hand caged ball bearing from the inside, referring to *Tools and Workshop Tips* in the Reference Section for more information on removal methods. Turn the hub over and drive out the needle roller bearing. An inner circlip, and on Sprint models up to VIN 388246 and Speed Triple models up to VIN 346970 a grease seal, are fitted behind the needle bearing.

43 Thoroughly clean the bearing recesses in the hub. Install the new bearings, seals (according to model) and circlips in a reverse of the removal procedure, using a suitable press, such as a large worktop vice, or a drawbolt arrangement. If you do not have the necessary equipment take the hub and the new parts to a dealer – it is not worth damaging the hub by pressing in bearings incorrectly. Apply a smear of grease to the lips of the new seals and to the needle bearing. Make sure the circlips locate in their grooves.

44 Check that the brake caliper carrier peg is tight. Slide the hub assembly into the swingarm **(see illustration 16.38c)**. Fit the

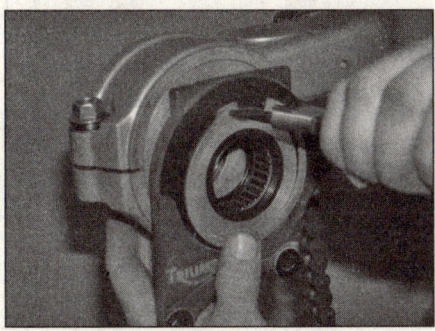

16.38a Remove the circlip . . .

16.38b . . . and the caliper carrier . . .

16.38c . . . then withdraw the hub assembly from the swingarm

6•28 Brakes, wheels and final drive

16.44 Locate the slot in the carrier over the peg (arrowed)

caliper carrier onto the hub, locating its slot over the peg on the swingarm as shown, and secure it with a new circlip **(see illustration)**.
45 Install the rear axle/brake disc carrier (see Section 7).

17 Tyre information and fitting

General information

1 The wheels fitted to all models are designed to take tubeless tyres only. Tyre sizes are given in the Specifications at the beginning of this chapter.

2 Refer to the *Pre-ride checks* listed at the beginning of this manual for tyre maintenance.

Fitting new tyres

3 When selecting new tyres, refer to the tyre information in the Owner's Handbook. Ensure that front and rear tyre types are compatible, the correct size and correct speed rating; if necessary seek advice from a Triumph dealer or tyre fitting specialist **(see illustration)**.
4 It is recommended that tyres are fitted by a motorcycle tyre specialist rather than attempted in the home workshop. This is because the force required to break the seal between the wheel rim and tyre bead is substantial, and is usually beyond the capabilities of an individual working with normal tyre levers. Additionally, the specialist will be able to balance the wheels after tyre fitting.
5 Note that punctured tubeless tyres can in some cases be repaired. Repairs must be carried out by a motorcycle tyre fitting specialist.

18 Drive chain removal, cleaning and installation

Note: *On Sprint models and Speed Triple models up to VIN 461331, if the drive chain fitted is an endless chain, which means it cannot be split, you must remove the swingarm. If the drive chain fitted has a riveted-type soft (joining) link, it can be disassembled using one of several commercially-available chain cutting/staking tools. Such chains can be recognised by the soft link side plate's identification marks (and usually its different colour), as well as by the riveted ends of the link's two pins which look as if they have been deeply centre-punched, instead of peened over as with all the other pins. All Tiger models are fitted with a riveted-type soft (joining) link as it passes through the swingarm brace.*

Endless chain

1 Remove the front sprocket cover (see Section 19). Note that if the front sprocket is being removed, the nut should be slackened before removing the swingarm, so that the rear brake can be used so stop the sprocket turning (see Section 19).
2 Remove the swingarm (see Chapter 5). Slip the chain off the front sprocket and remove it from the bike.
3 If the chain is excessively dirty, soak it in kerosene (paraffin) for approximately five or six minutes, then clean it using a soft brush.
4 Installation is the reverse of removal. On completion adjust and lubricate the chain following the procedures described in Chapter 1.

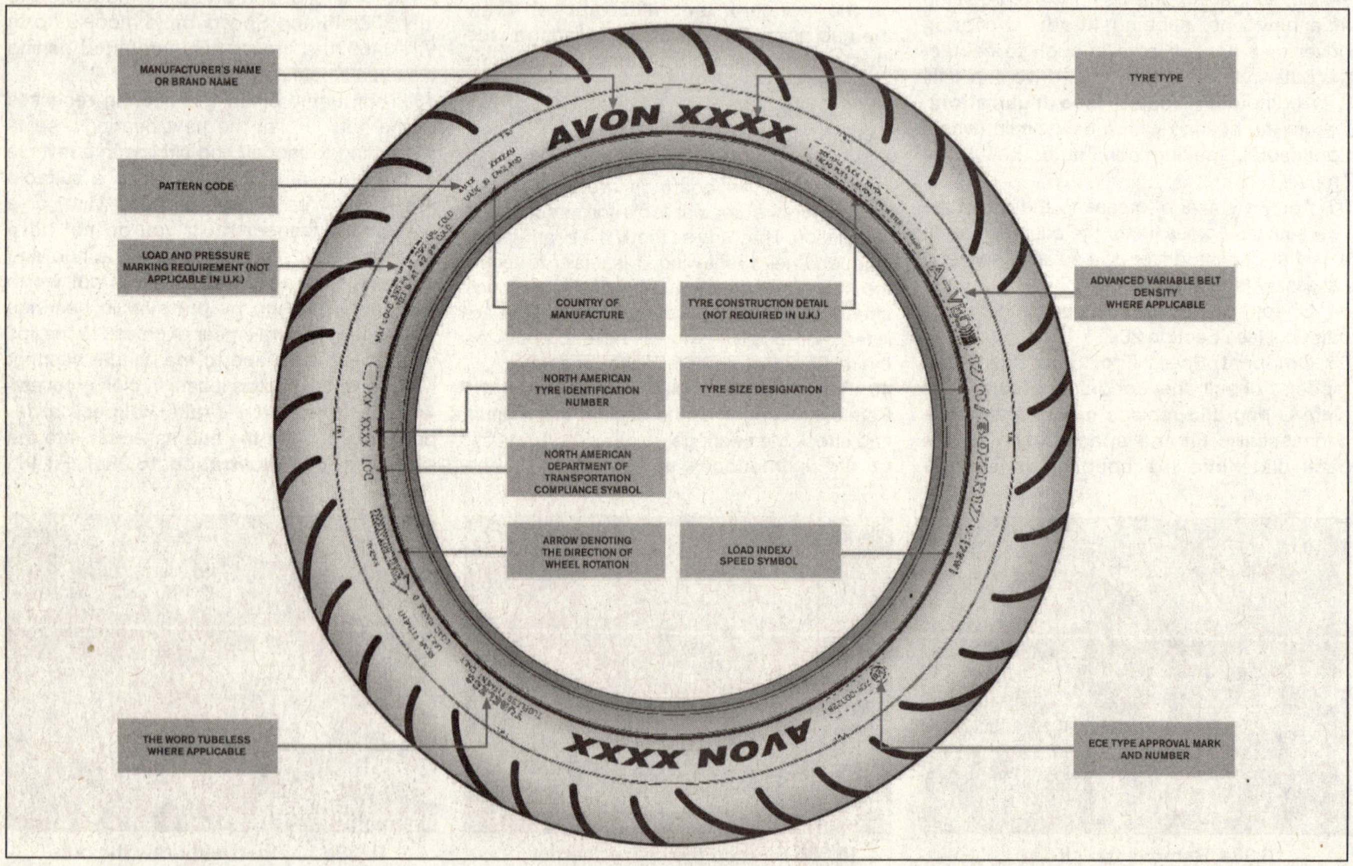

17.3 Common tyre sidewall markings

Brakes, wheels and final drive 6•29

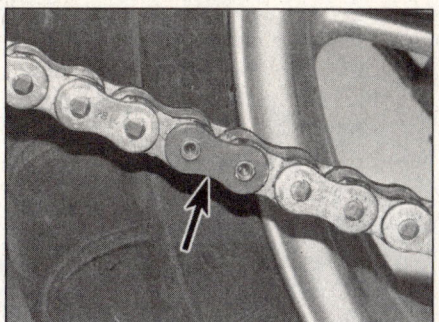

18.6 The soft link (arrowed) should be easy to identify

19.1 Sprocket cover bolts (arrowed)

19.7 Bend back the lockwasher tab(s) then unscrew the nut and remove the washer

Caution: *Don't use gasoline (petrol), solvent or other cleaning fluids which might damage its internal sealing properties. Don't use high-pressure water. Remove the chain, wipe it off, then blow dry it with compressed air immediately. The entire process shouldn't take longer than ten minutes – if it does, the sealing rings in the chain rollers could be damaged.*

Split chain with soft link

5 Remove the front sprocket cover (see Section 19).
6 Identify the soft link and move it to a suitable position to work on by rotating the back wheel **(see illustration)**.
7 Slacken the drive chain as described in Chapter 1.
8 The chain can be separated at the soft link using a chain breaker tool and the soft link withdrawn to split the chain. Refer to Section 8 'Chains' of Tools and Workshop Tips in the Reference section at the end of this manual for details of how to use the tool and how to rivet the new soft link securely. Alternatively follow the tool manufacturer's instructions. Note that it is essential to use a new soft link when re-joining the chain. Never install a clip-type master link.
9 After riveting, check the soft link and pin ends for any signs of cracking. If there is any evidence of cracking, the soft link, O-rings (or X-rings), and side plate must be renewed. Measure the diameter of the riveted pin ends in two directions and check that each pin has been evenly riveted.
10 Install the sprocket cover.
11 On completion, adjust and lubricate the chain following the procedures described in Chapter 1.

19 Sprockets

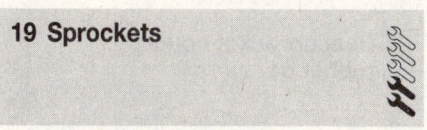

Front sprocket cover

1 Unscrew the bolts securing the front sprocket cover and remove it, along with the hose and wiring cover on Speed Triple models from VIN 461332 **(see illustration)**. If access to the bottom bolt is restricted by the gearchange linkage arm, move the gearchange lever up or down to move the arm out of the way.
2 Installation is the reverse of removal.

Sprocket check

3 Remove the front sprocket cover (Step 1).
4 Check the wear pattern on both sprockets (see Chapter 1, Section 1). If the sprocket teeth are worn excessively, replace the chain and both sprockets as a set. Whenever the sprockets are inspected, the drive chain should be inspected also (see Chapter 1). Always replace the chain and sprockets as a set – worn sprockets can ruin a new drive chain and vice versa.
5 Adjust and lubricate the chain following the procedures described in Chapter 1.

Front sprocket

Note: *Slacken the front sprocket nut before disengaging the chain from the rear sprocket so the rear brake can be used to prevent the front sprocket turning.*

6 Remove the front sprocket cover (Step 1).
7 Bend down the tab(s) on the sprocket nut lockwasher **(see illustration)**. Have an assistant apply the rear brake hard, then unscrew the nut and remove the washer. Discard the washer as a new one should be used. Refer to Chapter 1 and adjust the chain so that it is fully slack.
8 If the sprocket is not being replaced with a new one, mark the outside with a scratch or dab of paint so that it can be installed the same way round. Slide the sprocket and chain off the shaft and slip the sprocket out of the chain **(see illustration)**. If there is not enough slack in the chain to remove the sprocket, disengage the chain from the rear wheel.
9 Engage the new sprocket with the chain and slide it on the shaft **(see illustration)**. Take up the slack in the chain (see Chapter 1).
10 Slide on the new lockwasher, locating it on the splines **(see illustration)**. Fit the nut with its shouldered side facing in and tighten it to the torque setting specified at the beginning of the Chapter, applying the rear brake to prevent

19.8 Slide the sprocket off the shaft and remove it

19.9 Align the splines and slide the sprocket onto the shaft

19.10a Fit the new lockwasher . . .

19.10b ... and the nut, and tighten it to the specified torque

19.10c Bend the tabs up against the nut

19.13 Rear sprocket nuts (arrowed) – Sprint and Speed Triple

the sprocket from turning **(see illustrations)**. Bend up the tabs of the lockwasher against the nut **(see illustration)**.

11 Install the front sprocket cover **(see illustration 19.1)**.

Rear sprocket – Sprint, Speed Triple and Tiger Sport models

12 Refer to Chapter 1 and adjust the chain so that it is fully slack. Disengage the chain from the rear sprocket.

13 Have an assistant apply the rear brake, then unscrew the nuts securing the sprocket to the coupling – counter-hold the bolt heads on the inner side of the coupling if they turn **(see illustration)**. Remove the sprocket, noting which way round it fits.

14 Fit the sprocket on the coupling with the stamped mark facing out, then fit the nuts. Apply the rear brake and tighten the nuts evenly and in a criss-cross sequence to the torque setting specified at the beginning of the Chapter, counter-holding the bolts if required.

15 Fit the chain around the sprocket, then adjust and lubricate the chain following the procedures described in Chapter 1.

Rear sprocket – Tiger and Tiger SE models

16 Remove the rear wheel (see Section 15).
17 Unscrew the nuts securing the sprocket to the coupling **(see illustration)**. Remove the sprocket, noting which way round it fits.
18 Fit the sprocket onto the coupling with the stamped mark facing out, then fit the nuts. Tighten the nuts evenly and in a criss-cross sequence to the torque setting specified at the beginning of the Chapter.
19 Install the rear wheel (see Section 15).

20 Rear sprocket coupling/ rubber dampers

1 On Sprint, Speed Triple and Tiger Sport models, undo the chain slider/brake hose cover/chainguard screws on the swingarm as required according to model to free the brake hose and ABS sensor wire where fitted **(see illustration 7.3a or 11.14a or 11.14c)**. Undo the screws securing the upper and lower chainguards to the swingarm and remove them, noting how they fit **(see illustrations 7.3b and c or 11.14b)**. Unstake the sprocket coupling nut **(see illustration 7.3d)**. Have an assistant apply the rear brake hard, then slacken the nut. Displace the rear caliper (see Section 6). Slacken the drive chain adjuster clamp bolt **(see illustration 7.3e)**. Remove the coupling nut and its washer, noting which way round it fits, then slide the sprocket coupling off the axle and disengage it from the chain **(see illustrations 7.3f and g)**. Note the shouldered spacer in the outside of the coupling and remove it for safekeeping if required **(see illustration 7.3h)**. Note that Triumph specify to use a new sprocket coupling nut on installation. Lift the back plate out and remove the spacer from inside the coupling **(see illustrations 16.27a and b)**.

2 On Tiger and Tiger SE models, remove the rear wheel (see Chapter 6). Lift the sprocket coupling out of the wheel, noting how it fits, and the spacer inside it **(see illustrations 16.28a and b)**.

3 Check the coupling for cracks or any obvious signs of damage.

4 Lift the rubber damper segments from the sprocket coupling or wheel hub as applicable, and check them for cracks, hardening and general deterioration **(see illustrations)**. Replace the rubber dampers with a new set if necessary.

5 On Sprint and Speed Triple models check the condition of the O-ring on the hub and replace it with a new one if necessary. Also check the splines in the hub and on the shaft for signs of wear or damage.

6 Checking and replacement procedures for the sprocket coupling/hub assembly bearings are described in Section 16.

7 Installation is the reverse of removal. On Sprint and Speed Triple models refer to Section 7, Step 11.

19.17 Rear sprocket nuts (arrowed) – Tiger

20.4a Sprocket coupling damper segments – Sprint and Speed Triple

20.4b Sprocket coupling damper segments – Tiger

Chapter 7
Bodywork

Contents

	Section number		Section number
Fairing and body panels	3	Mirrors	4
Front mudguard	6	Seat	2
General information	1	Windshield	5

Degrees of difficulty

| Easy, suitable for novice with little experience | Fairly easy, suitable for beginner with some experience | Fairly difficult, suitable for competent DIY mechanic | Difficult, suitable for experienced DIY mechanic | Very difficult, suitable for expert DIY or professional |

Specifications

Torque wrench settings
Grab-rail mounting bolts – Sprint and Tiger models .... 27 Nm

1 General information

This Chapter covers the procedures necessary to remove and install the body parts. Since many service and repair operations on these motorcycles require the removal of the body parts, the procedures are grouped here and referred to from other Chapters.

In the case of damage to the body parts, it is usually necessary to remove the broken component and replace it with a new (or used) one. The material that the body panels are composed of doesn't lend itself to conventional repair techniques. There are however some shops that specialise in 'plastic welding', so it may be worthwhile seeking the advice of one of these specialists before scrapping an expensive component. There are also DIY kits available for making small repairs.

When attempting to remove any body panel, first study it closely, noting any fasteners and associated fittings, to be sure of returning everything to its correct place on installation. In some cases the aid of an assistant will be required when removing panels, to help avoid the risk of damage to paintwork. Once the evident fasteners have been removed, try to withdraw the panel as described but DO NOT FORCE IT – if it will not release, check that all fasteners have been removed and try again. Where a panel engages another by means of tabs, be careful not to break the tab or its mating slot or to damage the paintwork. Remember that a few moments of patience at this stage will save you a lot of money in replacing broken fairing panels! To undo quick-release fasteners, turn them 90° anti-clockwise.

Many of the bolts used on the motorcycle are of the Torx type. Unless you are already equipped with a good range of Torx bits, you are advised to purchase a set. Make sure you get bits that can be used in conjunction with a socket set so that a torque wrench can be applied – a Torx key set will not be adequate on its own, though will be useful in addition to the bits.

When installing a body panel, first study it closely, noting any fasteners and associated fittings removed with it, to be sure of returning everything to its correct place. Check that all fasteners and damping/rubber mounts are in good condition; any of these must be replaced with new ones if faulty before the panel is reassembled. Check also that all mounting brackets are straight and repair or renew them if necessary before attempting to install the panel. Where assistance was required to remove a panel, make sure your assistant is on hand to install it. To install quick-release fasteners, turn them 90° clockwise.

Tighten the fasteners securely, but be careful not to overtighten any of them or the panel may break (not always immediately) due to the uneven stress.

7•2 Bodywork

2.1a On Sprint ST models, undo the screws . . .

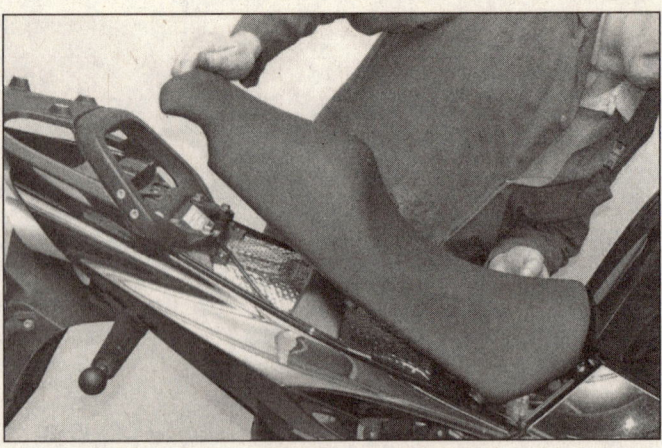

2.1b . . . and lift the seat away . . .

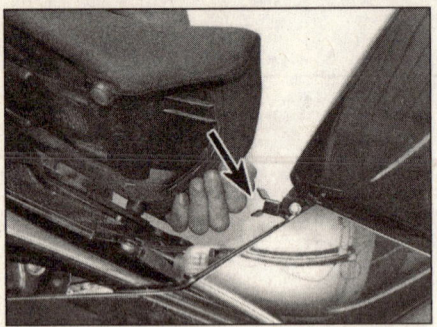

2.1c . . . noting how the tab locates (arrowed)

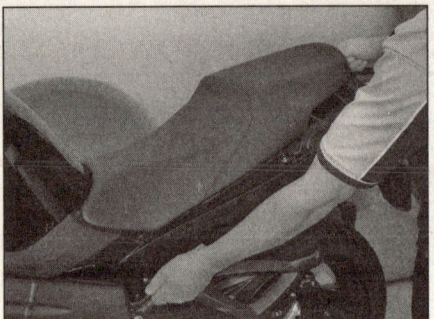

2.2 On Sprint GT models, turn the key, then lift the rear of the seat and remove it, noting where the tabs locate

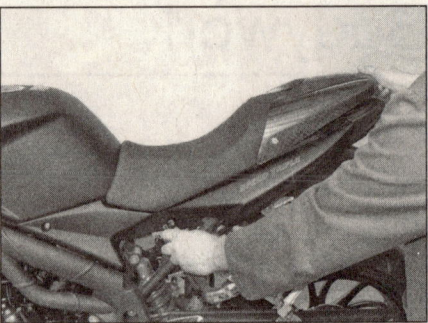

2.3a On the Speed Triple, turn the key, then lift the rear of the seat and remove it . . .

2 Seat

Removal

1 On Sprint ST models, push the rear edge of the seat forwards to expose the two screws, then undo them, and remove the spacers **(see illustration)**. Lift the rear of the seat and draw it back, noting how the tab at the front locates under the tank bracket **(see illustrations)**.
2 On Sprint GT models, insert the ignition key into the seat lock located on the left-hand side of the bike, and turn it anti-clockwise to unlock the seat **(see illustration)**. Lift up the rear of the seat and draw it backwards, noting how the tabs at the front locate.
3 On Speed Triple models, insert the ignition key into the seat lock located on the left-hand side of the bike, and turn it anti-clockwise while pressing down on the rear of the seat **(see illustration)**. Lift up the rear of the seat and draw it backwards, noting how the tab at the front locates **(see illustration)**.
4 On Tiger models, insert the ignition key into the seat lock located on the left-hand side of the bike, and turn it anti-clockwise while pressing down on the rear of the seat **(see illustration)**. Lift up the rear of the seat and draw it backwards, noting how the lip at the front locates against the tank and the hooks in the middle locate under the frame cross-member **(see illustration)**.

Installation

5 Installation is the reverse of removal. On Sprint GT, Speed Triple and Tiger models push down on the seat to engage the latch.

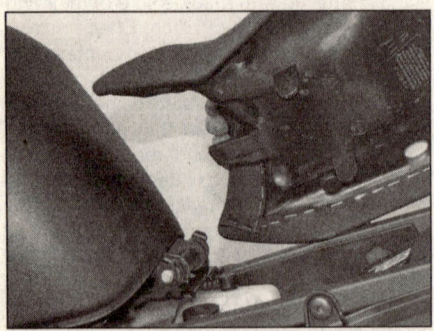

2.3b . . . noting how the tab locates

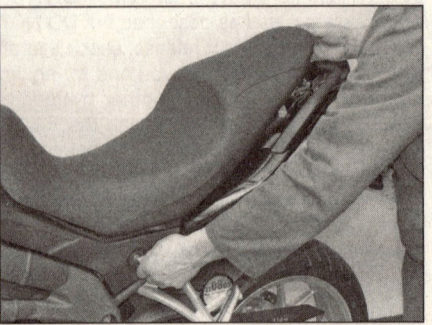

2.4a On the Tiger, turn the key, then lift the rear of the seat and remove it . . .

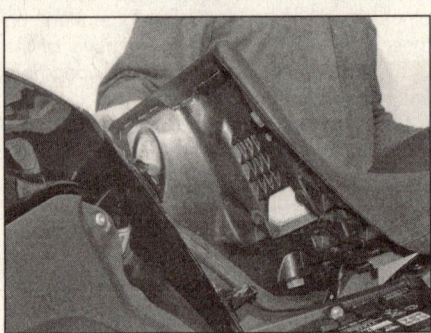

2.4b . . . noting how the tab locates

Bodywork 7•3

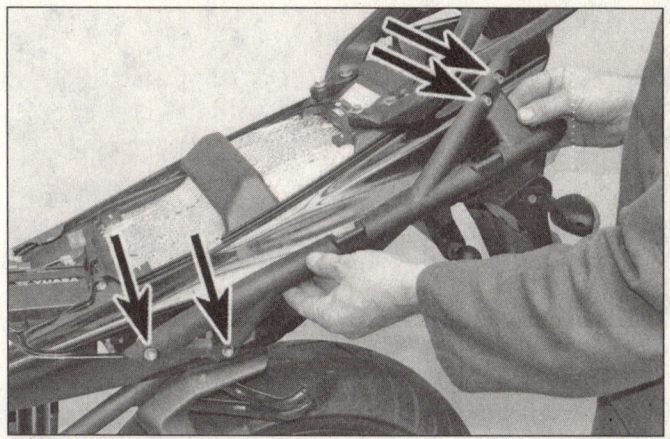

3.2 Unscrew the bolts (arrowed) and remove the pannier rail on each side

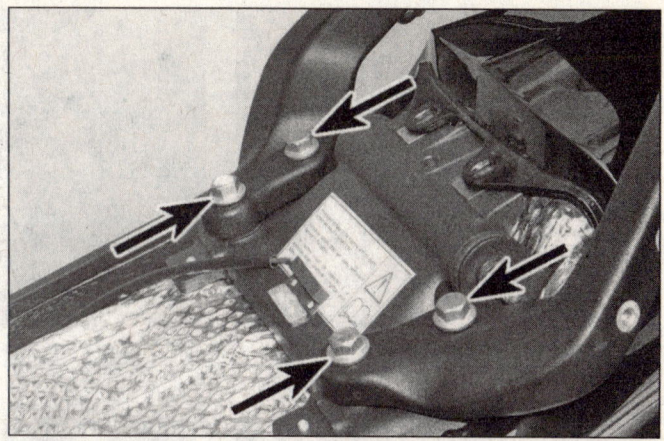

3.3a Unscrew the bolts (arrowed) and remove the grab-rail . . .

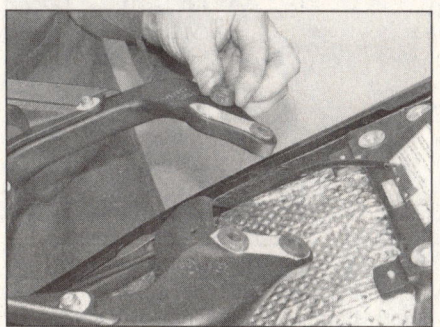

3.3b . . . and collect the spacers on the underside

3.4a Undo the screws (arrowed) . . .

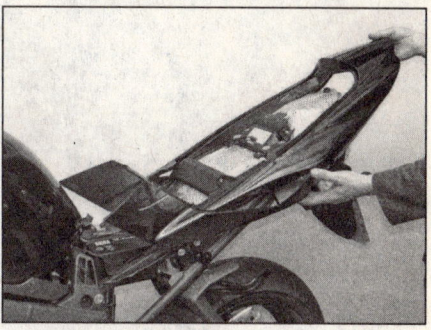

3.4b . . . and carefully draw the cowling back

3 Fairing and body panels

Sprint

Seat cowling – ST models

1 Remove the seat (see Section 2).
2 If fitted remove the panniers, then unscrew the bolts securing each pannier rail to the grab-rail and frame and remove the spacers – there are two plain spacers under the rear bolts and two shouldered spacers for the front bolts fitted into the back of the rail **(see illustration)**.
3 If required unscrew the four bolts securing the grab-rail and remove it, noting there are spacers on the underside **(see illustrations)**.
4 Undo the four screws securing the seat cowling, noting the washers on each side of the panel on the rear screws **(see illustration)**. Carefully pull the sides away at the front and draw the seat cowling back and off the bike **(see illustration)**.
5 Installation is the reverse of removal. If removed, tighten the grab-rail bolts to the torque setting specified at the beginning of the Chapter.

Side panels – GT models

6 Remove the seat (see Section 2).
7 Remove the panniers.

8 Undo the seat lock screws and displace the lock **(see illustration)**. Unscrew the grab-rack bolts, noting there is a nut on the underside of the front right-hand bolt, and there are collars in the top with both front bolts and spacers with the middle bolts **(see illustrations)**.

3.8a Seat lock screws (arrowed)

3.8b Note the nut and collars . . .

3.8c . . . and the spacers

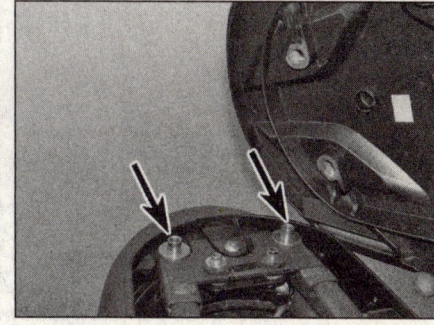

3.8d Rear bolt collars (arrowed)

7•4 Bodywork

3.9a Undo the screw (arrowed) . . .

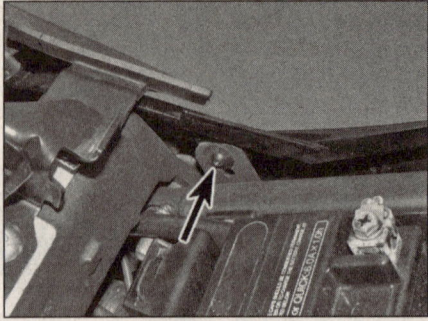

3.9b . . . and release the trim clip (arrowed)

3.9c Release the Velcro . . .

3.9d . . . and pull the peg from the grommet

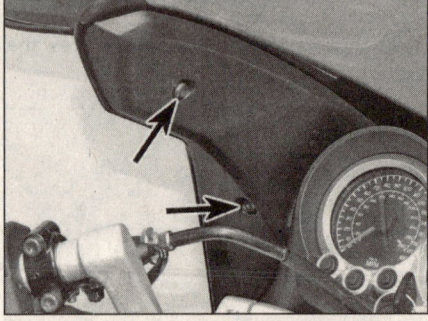

3.11a Undo the screws (arrowed) . . .

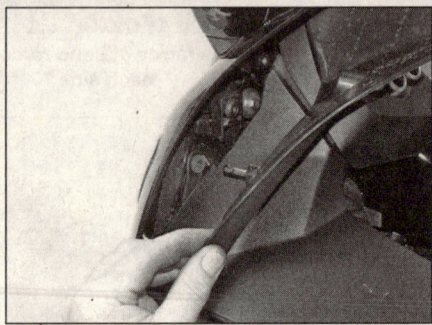

3.11b . . . and release the panel as described

3.12a Remove the lid from the right-hand panel

Remove the rack and retrieve the collars in the underside for the rear bolts **(see illustration)**.
9 Undo the screw and release the trim clip **(see illustrations)**. Carefully release the Velcro patches at the front and back and pull the middle away to release the peg from the grommet **(see illustrations)**.
10 Installation is the reverse of removal. Fit all the grab-rack bolts loosely first to position the rack, then tighten the front two bolts first then the rear four bolts.

Upper and lower cockpit trim panels

11 Undo the two screws securing the upper panel, noting which fits where **(see illustration)**. Ease the panel towards the middle of the bike to free the lip from under the instrument cluster, then draw it back to free the peg from the grommet in the lower panel **(see illustration)**.
12 Remove the storage compartment lid **(see illustration)**. Undo the screw securing the lower panel, then carefully draw it forwards to release the tab from the slot in the fairing side panel **(see illustrations)**.
13 Installation is the reverse of removal.

Fairing side panels

14 Remove the upper and lower cockpit trim panels (Steps 6 and 7).

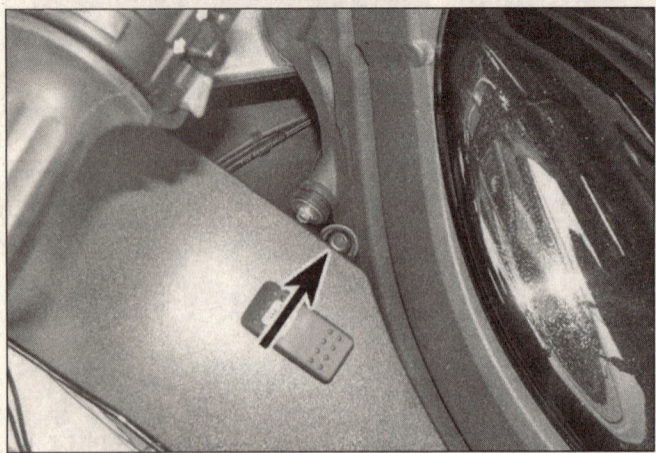

3.12b Undo the screw (arrowed) . . .

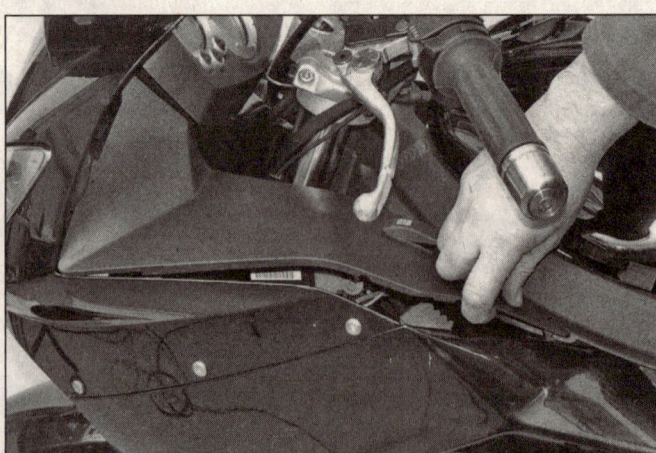

3.12c . . . and release the panel as described

Bodywork 7•5

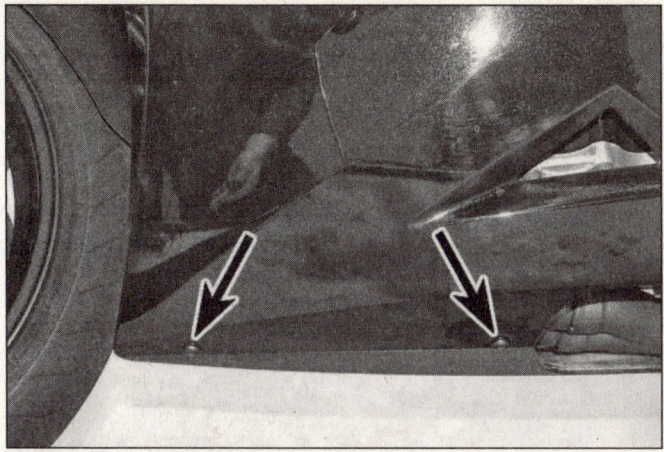

3.15 Undo the screws (arrowed)

3.16a Undo the screw (arrowed) on each side . . .

3.16b . . . and remove the centre panel

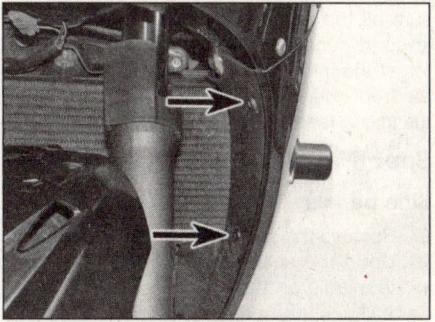

3.17 Undo the screws (arrowed) and remove the inner panel

3.18a Undo the screw (arrowed) . . .

15 Undo the screws securing the panels to each other on the underside **(see illustration)**.

16 Undo the screws securing the centre panel, then lift it out from between the side panels **(see illustrations)**.

17 Undo the screws securing the left-hand inner panel and detach it from the side panel **(see illustration)**.

18 Undo the screws securing the panel to its brackets and to the fairing, then carefully draw it away, noting how it engages with the fairing and locates on the peg **(see illustrations)**.

19 Installation is the reverse of removal. Make sure the panel engages correctly with the fairing and on the peg.

Fairing

20 Remove the upper and lower cockpit trim panels (Steps 6 and 7).

21 Remove the windshield and its trim panel (see Section 5).

22 Remove the instrument cluster (see Chapter 8). Remove the mirrors (see Section 4).

23 Undo the three screws securing the fairing to the fairing side panel on each side **(see illustration)**.

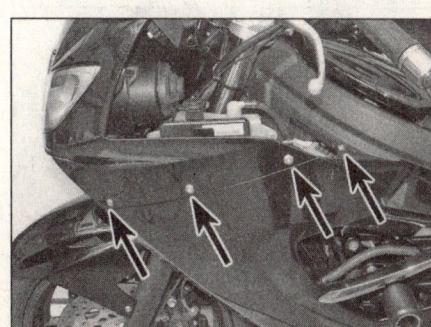

3.18b . . . and the screws (arrowed) . . .

3.18c . . . and remove the panel . . .

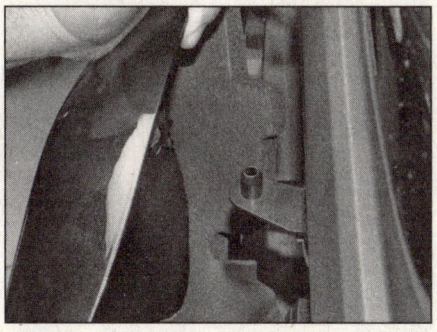

3.18d . . . noting how the grommet locates on the peg

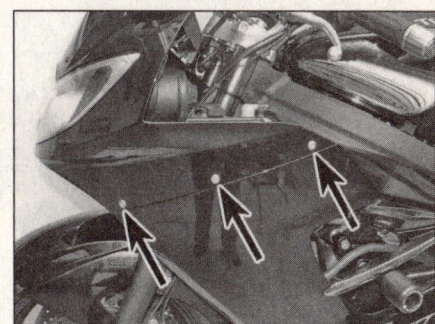

3.23 Undo the three screws (arrowed)

7•6 Bodywork

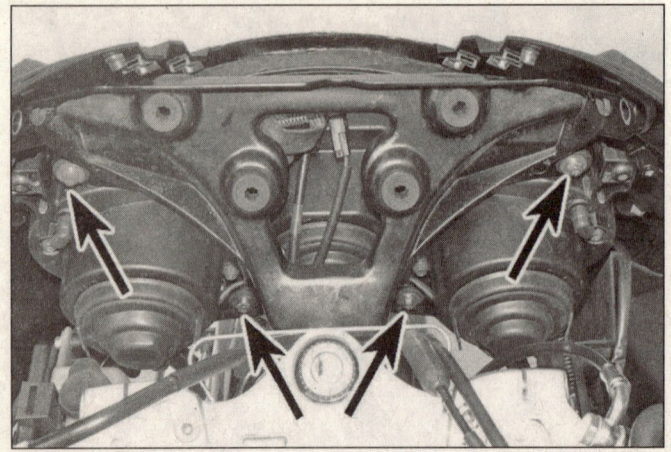

3.24 Undo the four screws (arrowed)

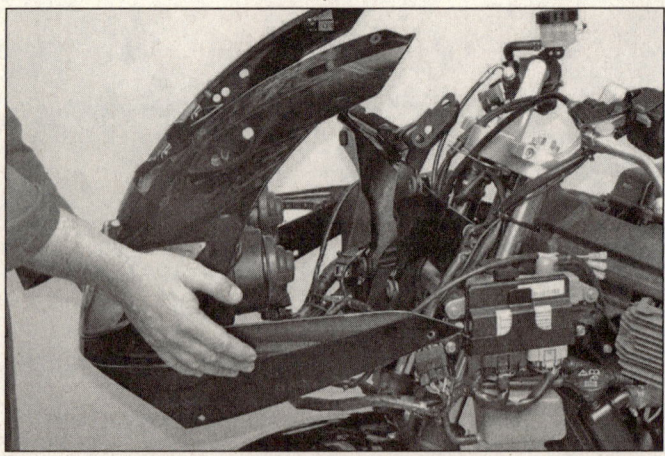

3.25a Draw the fairing forwards ...

24 Undo the four screws securing the fairing and headlight assembly to the fairing stay **(see illustration)**.

25 Ease the fairing/headlight assembly forward, noting how the pegs locate in the grommets, then disconnect the headlight wiring connector **(see illustrations)**. Note the rubber pads for the mirror and remove them for safekeeping if required – they are marked R and L according to side. Note how the front wiring loom locates on top of the lower rim of the fairing.

26 Installation is the reverse of removal. Make sure all the rubber grommets are fitted and in good condition **(see illustration)**. Do not forget the mirror pads, if removed. Make sure the front wiring room locates correctly inside the fairing **(see illustration)**.

Speed Triple

Side panels – 2005 to 2007 models

27 Remove the seat (see Section 2).
28 Undo the screw at the front, the screw in the middle and the two on the underside. Carefully pull the panel away to free the peg from the grommet.

29 Installation is the reverse of removal.

Side panels – 2008 to 2010 models (up to VIN 461331)

30 Remove the seat (see Section 2).
31 To remove the rear (seat) section undo the screw at the front and the trim clip in the middle on the underside **(see illustration)**. Carefully pull the panel away to free the peg from the grommet at the back.
32 To remove the front (tank) section undo the screw at the front **(see illustration)**. Carefully pull the panel away to free the peg from the grommet at the top, then carefully

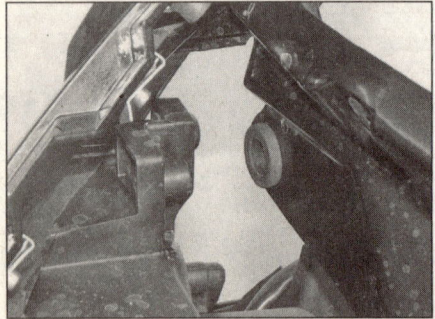

3.25b ... noting how the pegs locate in the grommets ...

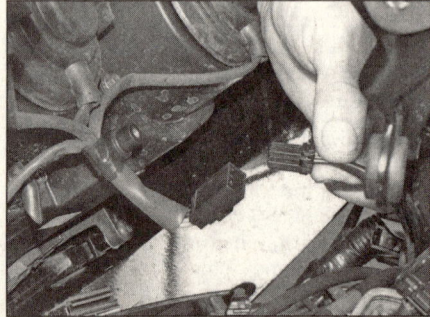

3.25c ... then disconnect the headlight wiring connector

3.26a Make sure all the grommets are in place

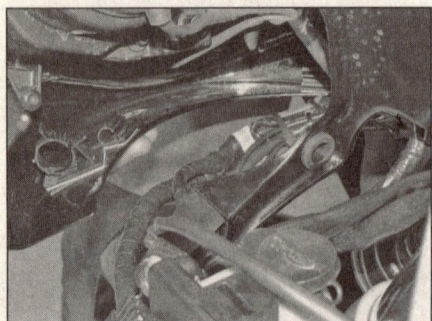

3.26b The wiring loom sits inside the fairing at the bottom

3.31 Undo the screw and the trim clip (arrowed)

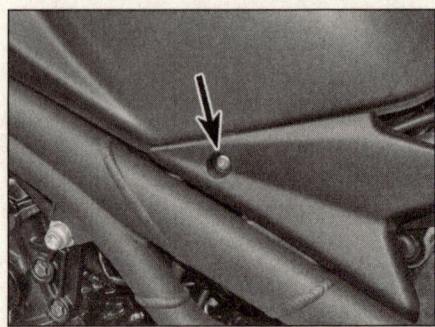

3.32a Undo the screw (arrowed) ...

Bodywork 7•7

3.32b . . . then release the peg from the grommet . . .

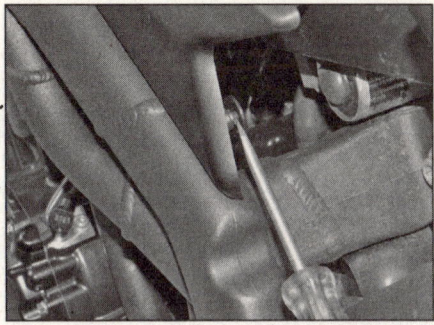

3.32c . . . and lever the trim clip out

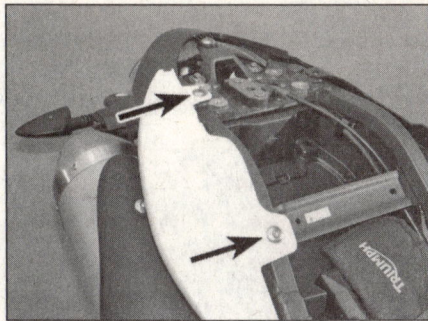

3.35a Undo the screws (arrowed) . . .

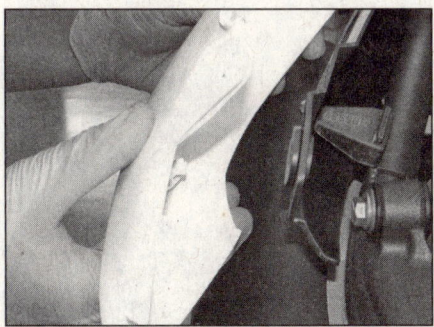

3.35b . . . and free the peg from the grommet

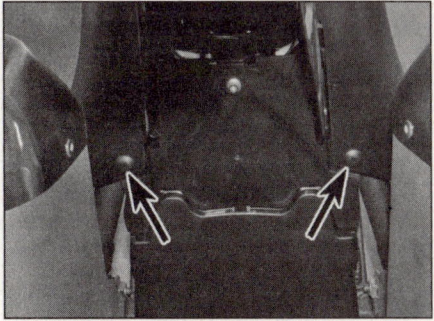

3.38a Release the trim clips (arrowed) on the underside . . .

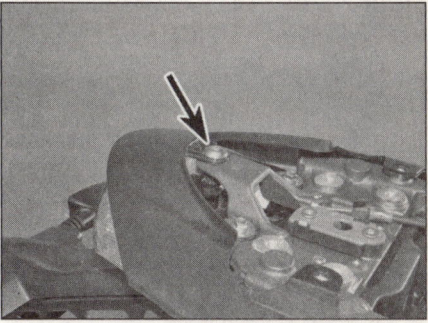

3.38b . . . and the screw (arrowed) on the top . . .

lever the plastic trim clip out from the bottom **(see illustrations)**.

33 Installation is the reverse of removal, except fit the bottom trim clip for the front section last.

Side panels – 2011-on models (from VIN 461332)

34 Remove the seat (see Section 2).
35 Undo the screws **(see illustration)**. Carefully pull the panel away to free the peg from the grommet at the back **(see illustration)**.
36 Installation is the reverse of removal – make sure the grommet is in good condition, and smear it with oil or grease.

Rear cover – 2011-on models (from VIN 461332)

37 Remove the side panels (see above).
38 Release the trim clips and undo the screw **(see illustrations)**. Carefully draw the cover to the rear **(see illustration)**.
39 Installation is the reverse of removal.

Radiator cowls – 2011-on models (from VIN 461332)

40 Undo the three screws **(see illustration)**. Carefully pull the cowl away to release the peg from the grommet, then disconnect the turn signal wiring connector **(see illustrations)**.
41 If required remove the turn signal (see Chapter 8).

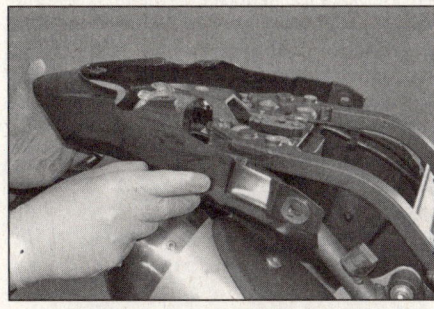

3.38c . . . and remove the cover

42 Installation is the reverse of removal – make sure the grommet is in good condition, and smear it with oil or grease.

Fuel tank trim panels – 2011-on models (from VIN 461332)

43 To remove the front panel undo the screws **(see illustration)**.

3.40a Undo the screws (arrowed) . . .

3.40b . . . free the peg from the grommet

3.40c . . . and disconnect the wiring

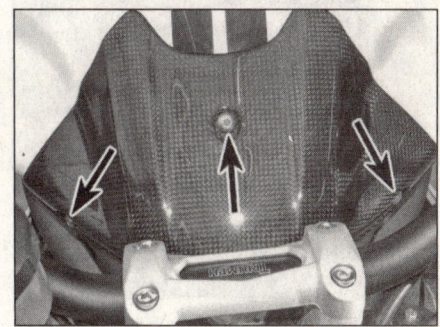

3.43 Front trim panel screws (arrowed)

7•8 Bodywork

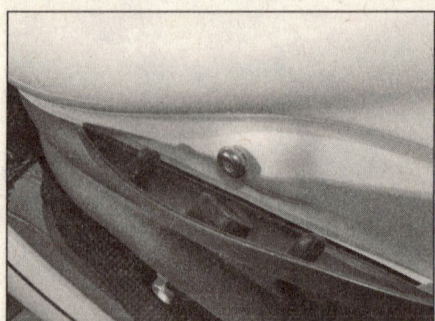

3.44 Note how the slot locates over the screw head on the tank

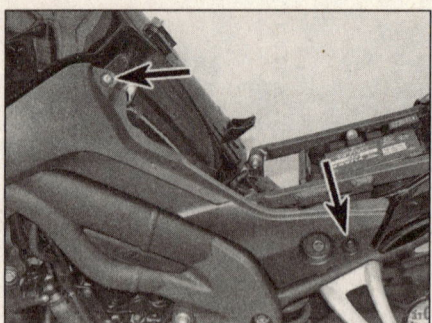

3.47a Undo the screws (arrowed) . . .

3.47b . . . and release the peg from the grommet

3.51 Unscrew the bolts (arrowed) and remove the grab rails

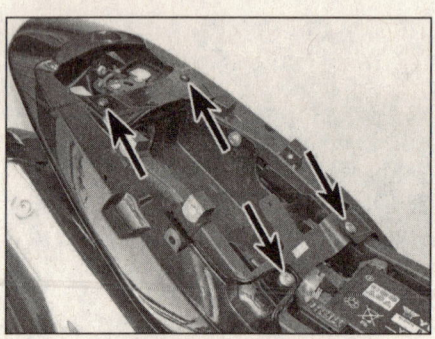

3.52a Undo the screws (arrowed) . . .

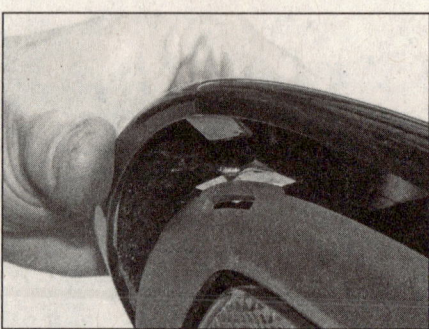

3.52b . . . release the tab at the back . . .

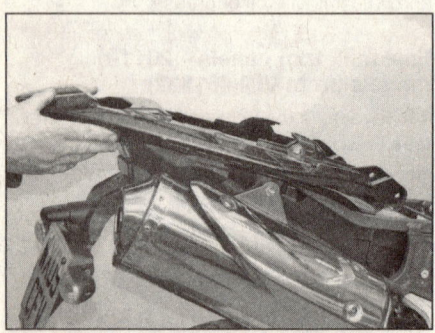

3.52c . . . and remove the panel

44 To remove a side panel remove the seat, then undo the screw. Carefully release the panel from the tank, noting how it locates (see illustration).
45 Installation is the reverse of removal.

Tiger and Tiger SE
Side panels

46 Remove the seat (see Section 2).
47 Undo the two screws securing the side panel to the fuel tank and the seat cowling (see illustration). Carefully pull the front away to release the peg from the grommet and remove the panel (see illustration).
48 Installation is the reverse of removal.

Seat cowling

49 Remove the seat (see Section 2).
50 Remove the side panels (see Step 30).
51 Unscrew the two bolts securing each grab-rail and remove them (see illustration).
52 Undo the four screws securing the seat cowling (see illustration). Carefully draw the seat cowling back, noting how the tab locates, and off the bike (see illustrations).
53 Installation is the reverse of removal. Tighten the grab-rail bolts to the torque setting specified at the beginning of the Chapter.

Upper and lower fairing trim panels

54 Undo the three screws securing the upper panel, then detach the panel, noting how it engages with the fairing, and disconnect the turn signal wiring connector (see illustrations). If required remove the turn signal from the panel (see Chapter 8).
55 Undo the two screws and remove the lower panel (see illustration).
56 Installation is the reverse of removal. When

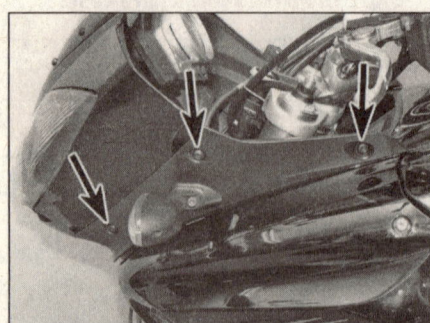

3.54a Undo the screws (arrowed) . . .

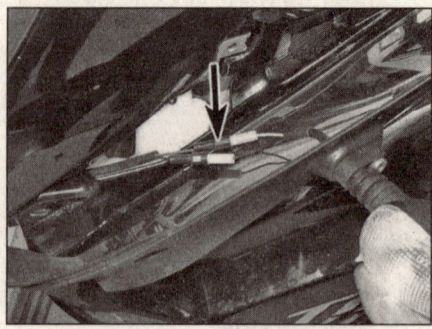

3.54b . . . detach the panel and disconnect the wiring connectors (arrowed)

3.55 Lower panel screws (arrowed)

Bodywork 7•9

3.58 Undo the screw (arrowed) . . .

3.59 . . . and the screws (arrowed) . . .

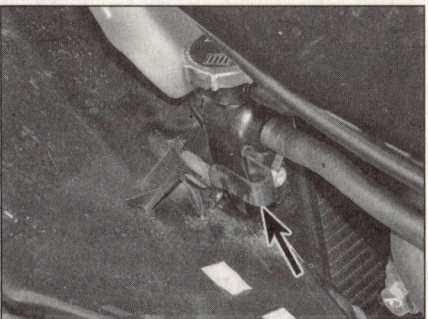
3.60 . . . then release the panel from the hook (arrowed)

3.64 Carefully release the pegs from the grommets

3.67 Undo the screws (arrowed) . . .

fitting the upper panel, engage the panel with the fairing, then tighten the rear screw first, then the middle screw, then the front, all the time making sure the panel alignment with the fairing and fairing side panel is correct.

Fairing side panels
57 Remove the upper and lower fairing trim panels (Steps 37 and 38).
58 Undo the screw securing the panel to the cockpit trim panel **(see illustration)**.
59 Undo the screws securing the panel to the fuel tank **(see illustration)**.
60 Carefully draw the panel forwards to release it from the hook on the radiator and remove it **(see illustration)**.

61 Installation is the reverse of removal. Make sure the panel engages correctly with the radiator.

Cockpit trim panels
62 Remove the upper fairing trim panel (see Step 37).
63 Undo the screw securing the trim panel to the fairing **(see illustration 3.41)**.
64 Carefully draw the panel back to free the pegs from the grommets **(see illustration)**.
65 Installation is the reverse of removal.

Fairing
66 Remove the upper fairing trim panel (see Step 37), and the cockpit trim panels (see Steps 46 and 47).

67 Undo the four screws securing the fairing and headlight assembly to the fairing stay **(see illustration)**.
68 Ease the fairing/headlight assembly forward, noting how the pegs locate in the grommets, then disconnect the headlight wiring connector and free the turn signal relay from its mount **(see illustration)**.
69 Installation is the reverse of removal. Make sure the peg locates in the grommet.

Belly pan
70 Undo the two screws on each side and remove the pan **(see illustration)**.
71 Installation is the reverse of removal.

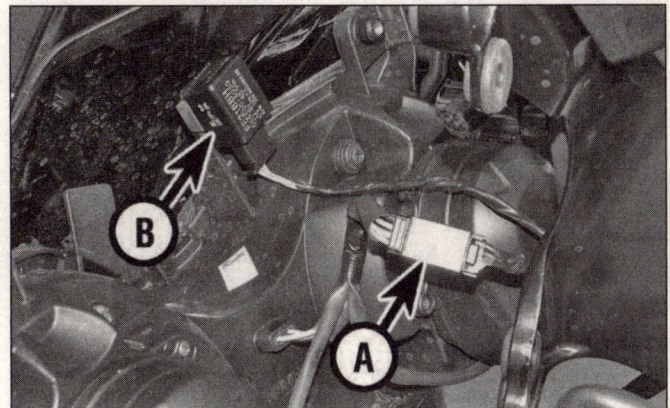
3.68 . . . then displace the fairing, disconnect the wiring connector (A) and release the relay (B)

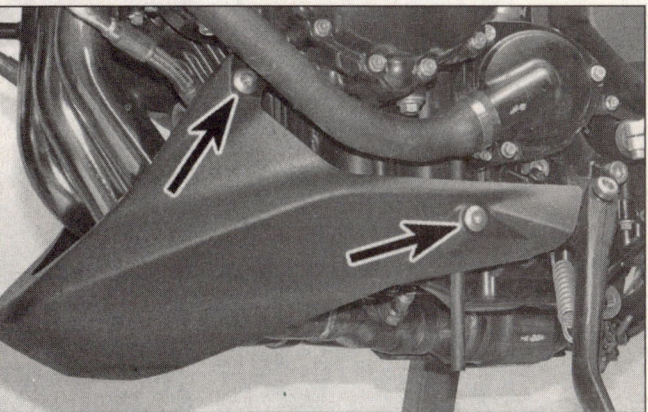
3.70 Undo the screws (arrowed) on each side

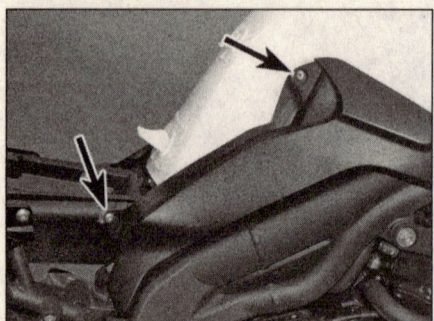

3.73a Undo the screws (arrowed) . . .

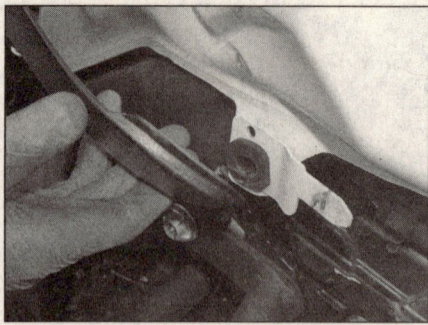

3.73b . . . and free the peg from the grommet

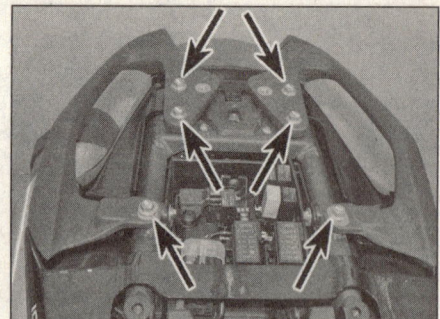

3.76 Grab-rail bolts (arrowed)

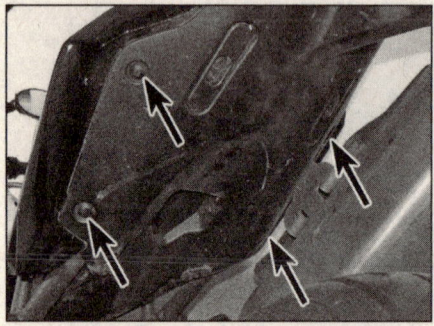

3.77 Release the trim clips (arrowed)

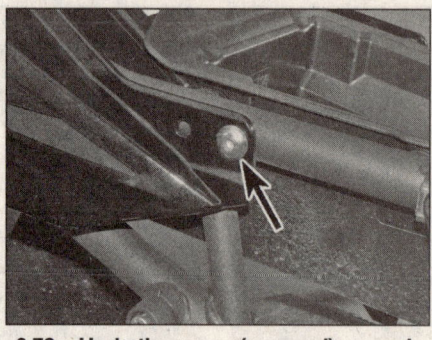

3.78a Undo the screw (arrowed) on each side . . .

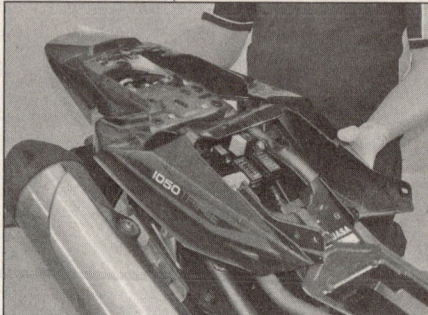

3.78b . . . and remove the cowl

Tiger Sport

Side panels

72 Remove the seat (see Section 2). Remove the fairing side panel (Steps 83 and 84).

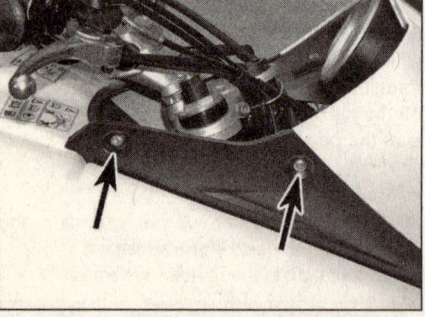

3.81a Undo the screws (arrowed) . . .

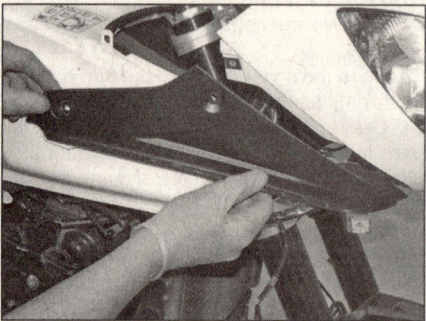

3.81b . . . and remove the trim panel

73 Undo the two screws securing the side panel to the fuel tank and the rear sub-frame **(see illustration)**. Carefully pull the front away to release the peg from the grommet and remove the panel **(see illustration)**.

74 Installation is the reverse of removal.

Seat cowling

75 Remove the seat (see Section 2).
76 Where fitted remove the panniers and the front pannier brackets. Unscrew the bolts securing each grab-rail and remove them **(see illustration)**.
77 Release the four trim clips on the underside **(see illustration)**.
78 Undo the screw on each side at the front **(see illustration)**. Carefully draw the seat cowling back, noting how the tail light tabs locate **(see illustration)**.
79 Installation is the reverse of removal. Tighten the grab-rail bolts to the torque setting specified at the beginning of the Chapter.

Fairing trim panels

80 Remove the fairing side panel (Steps 83 and 84).
81 Undo the two screws and remove the panel, noting how it locates against the fairing **(see illustrations)**.
82 Installation is the reverse of removal.

Fairing side panels

83 Undo the screw at the front and the two screws on the side **(see illustrations)**.
84 Ease the panel forwards to release it from the hooks on the fuel tank and disconnect the turn signal wiring connector **(see illustrations)**.
85 If required remove the turn signal from the panel (see Chapter 8).

3.83a Undo the screw (arrowed) . . .

3.83b . . . and the screws (arrowed)

Bodywork 7•11

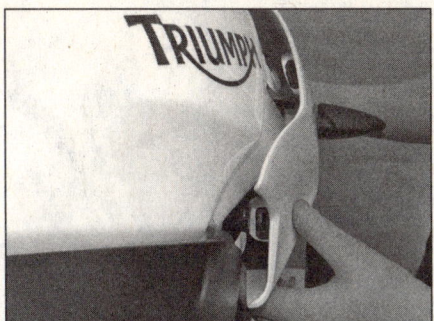
3.84a Draw the panel off the tabs . . .

3.84b . . . and disconnect the wiring

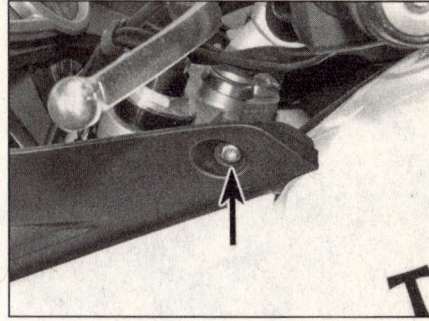
3.87 Undo the screw (arrowed)

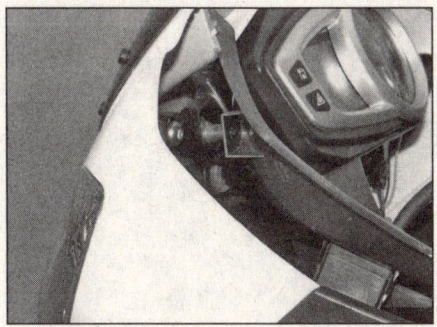
3.88a Release the pegs from the grommets . . .

3.88b . . . and when removing the left panel disconnect the wiring

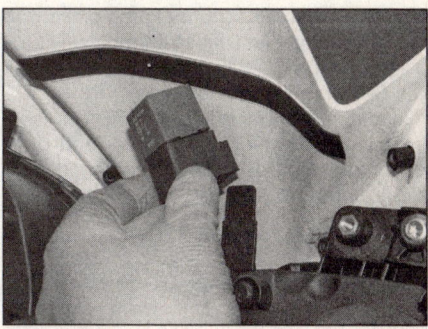
3.92a Displace the relay . . .

86 Installation is the reverse of removal. Make sure the panel engages correctly.

Cockpit trim panels

87 Undo the screw **(see illustration)**.
88 Carefully draw the panel back to free the pegs from the grommets, and on the left-hand panel disconnect the heated grip switch wiring, noting which wire fits where **(see illustrations)**.
89 Installation is the reverse of removal.

Fairing

90 Remove the fairing trim panels (Steps 80 and 81), and the cockpit trim panels (Steps 87 and 88).
91 Unscrew the four bolts securing the fairing and headlight assembly to the fairing stay **(see illustration 3.67)**.
92 Ease the fairing/headlight assembly forward, then displace the relay and disconnect the headlight wiring **(see illustrations)**.
93 Installation is the reverse of removal.

Belly pan

94 Undo the two screws on each side and remove the pan **(see illustration 3.70)**.
95 Installation is the reverse of removal.

4 Mirrors

1 On Sprint models remove the windshield and its trim panel (see Section 5). Remove the instrument cluster (see Chapter 8). Disconnect the turn signal wiring connector **(see illustration)**. Unscrew the two nuts on the inside of the fairing and remove the mirror, along with its rubber insulator pad **(see illustrations)**.

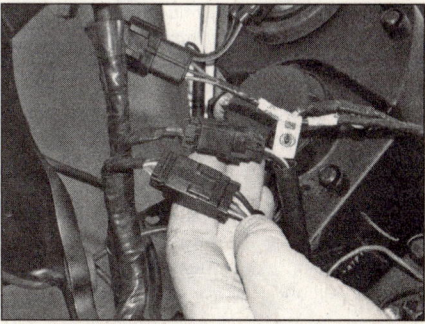
3.92b . . . and disconnect the connectors

2 On Speed Triple models up to VIN 461331, and Tiger models, lift the rubber cover off the base of the mirror, then unscrew it from its mount. On Speed Triple models from VIN 461332-on unscrew the mirror bolt and

4.1a Disconnect the wiring connector (arrowed) . . .

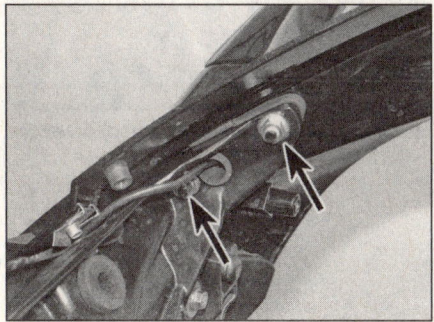
4.1b . . . then unscrew the nuts (arrowed) . . .

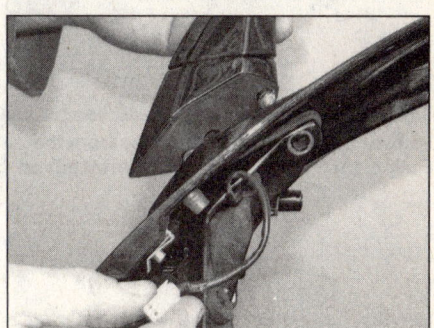
4.1c . . . and remove the mirror

7•12 Bodywork

4.2 Mirror bolt (arrowed) – Speed Triple from VIN 461332

4.3 Make sure the bracket (arrowed) locates correctly

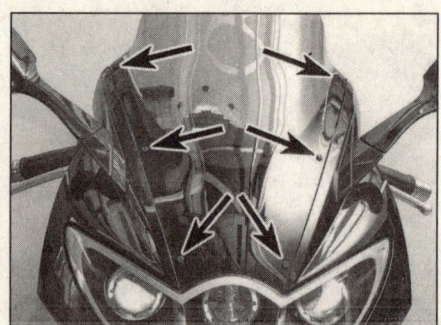

5.1a Windshield screws (arrowed)

remove the mirror, supporting the brake fluid reservoir upright **(see illustration)**.

3 Installation is the reverse of removal. On Speed Triple models from VIN 461332 make sure the brake fluid reservoir bracket is correctly seated and aligned, and does not move as the mirror is tightened **(see illustration)**.

5 Windshield

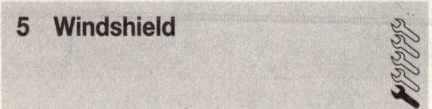

1 On Sprint models, undo the screws securing the windshield to the fairing then draw it up and back, noting how it fits **(see illustration)**. If required undo the screws securing the trim panel and remove it **(see illustration)**. Make sure none of the rubber wellnuts drop out of the fairing, and check that they are all in good condition.

2 On Tiger models, undo the screws securing the windshield to the fairing and remove it. Make sure none of the rubber wellnuts drop out of the fairing, and check that they are all in good condition.

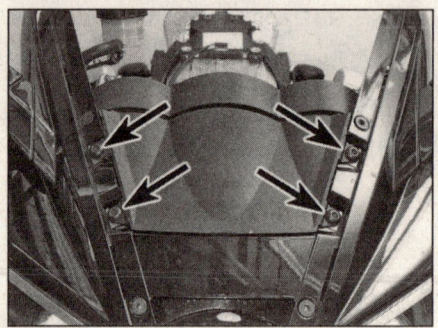

5.1b Trim panel screws (arrowed)

3 Installation is the reverse of removal. Do not overtighten the screws.

6 Front mudguard

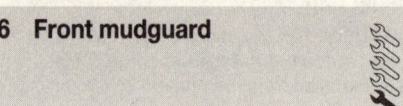

1 On Sprint models, undo the four screws securing the front section of the mudguard, noting which fit where, and draw it forwards **(see illustration)**. Release the brake hose

6.1a Undo the two screws (arrowed) on each side and remove the front section

from its clips on the top of the mudguard **(see illustration)**. Undo the screws securing the rear section of the mudguard and draw it back **(see illustration)**.

2 On Speed Triple and Tiger models, release the brake hoses from the clips on the mudguard. Undo the two screws on each side and draw the mudguard forwards, noting how the fork protectors locate between the mudguard and bracket **(see illustrations)**.

3 Installation is the reverse of removal.

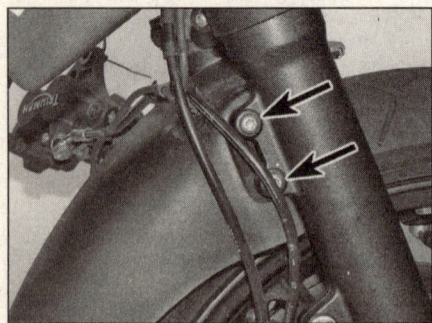

6.1b Release the brake hose from the clips, then undo the screws (arrowed) on each side

6.2a Undo the screws (arrowed) on each side . . .

6.2b . . . and note how the fork protectors locate

Chapter 8
Electrical system

Contents

	Section number
Alternator	28
Battery charging	4
Battery removal and installation	3
Brake light switches	14
Brake/tail and licence plate bulbs	10
Charging system testing	27
Clutch switch	21
Electrical system fault finding	2
Fuel pump and relay	see Chapter 4
Fuses	5
General information	1
Handlebar switches	18
Headlight aim	9
Headlight assembly	8
Headlight and sidelight bulbs	7
Horn	23

	Section number
Ignition switch	17
Ignition system components	see Chapter 4
Instrument cluster	15
Lighting system check	6
Neutral switch	19
Oil pressure switch	22
Regulator/rectifier	29
Relays	16
Sidestand switch	20
Starter motor overhaul	26
Starter motor removal and installation	25
Starter solenoid	24
Tail light assembly	11
Turn signal bulbs	13
Turn signal circuit check and relay	12

Degrees of difficulty

Easy, suitable for novice with little experience	Fairly easy, suitable for beginner with some experience	Fairly difficult, suitable for competent DIY mechanic 	Difficult, suitable for experienced DIY mechanic 	Very difficult, suitable for expert DIY or professional 

Specifications

Battery
Type
- Sprint GT, Speed Triple models from VIN 461332, Tiger Sport ..... Yuasa YTX14-BS
- All other models ..... Yuasa YTX12-BS

Capacity
- Sprint GT, Speed Triple models from VIN 461332, Tiger Sport 12V, 12Ah
- All other models 12V, 10Ah

Current leakage ..... 1 mA (max)
Charging rate ..... 1.0A (max)
Charging time (flat battery) ..... see Section 4

Alternator
Nominal output
- Tiger Sport 50A
- All other models 35A

Regulated output ..... 13.5 to 15 volts DC
Unregulated output ..... 35 to 40 volts AC @ 4000 to 5000 rpm
Stator coil resistance ..... 0.4 to 0.6 ohms

8•2 Electrical system

Fuses
Fuses are also listed on the inside of the fusebox lid

Sprint ST
- Fuse 1 .... 20A (starter circuit, headlights)
- Fuse 2 .... 10A (ignition, tail light, sidelight, fuel pump)
- Fuse 3 .... 10A (turn signals, horn, brake lights)
- Fuse 4 .... 20A (ABS)
- Fuse 5 .... 20A (ABS)
- Fuse 6 .... 10A (heated grips, accessories)
- Fuse 7 .... 15A (fan)
- Fuse 8 .... 10A (engine management)
- Fuse 9 .... 10A (alarm, instruments, diagnostic plug)
- Fuse 10 .... 2A (satellite navigation)
- Main fuse (in starter relay) 30A

Sprint GT
- Main fuse 30A
- Left-hand fusebox
  - Fuse 1 .... 20A (starter circuit, headlights)
  - Fuse 2 .... 20A (engine management)
  - Fuse 3 .... 15A (fan)
  - Fuse 4 .... 10A (fuel pump)
  - Fuse 5 .... 10A (alarm, instruments, ECM)
  - Fuse 6 .... not used
- Right-hand fusebox
  - Fuse 1 .... 20A (ABS)
  - Fuse 2 .... 20A (ABS)
  - Fuse 3 .... not used
  - Fuse 4 .... 10A (heated grips, accessories)
  - Fuse 5 .... 10A (alarm, instruments, diagnostics)
  - Fuse 6 .... 20A (turn signals, brake lights, horn)

Speed Triple 2005 to 2010 (up to VIN 461331)
- Fuse 1 .... 5A (instruments, alarm)
- Fuse 2 .... 30A (ignition)
- Fuse 3 .... 10A (turn signals, horn, brake lights)
- Fuse 4 .... 10A (alarm, diagnostic plug, fuel pump, instruments)
- Fuse 6 .... 20A (engine management)
- Fuse 7 .... 15A (fan)
- Fuse 8 .... 20A (starter circuit)
- Fuse 9 .... 5A (tail light, sidelight)
- Fuse 11 .... 30A (main)

Speed Triple 2011-on models (from VIN 461332)
- Main fuse 30A
- Front fusebox
  - Fuse 1 .... 20A (ABS)
  - Fuse 2 .... 20A (ABS)
  - Fuse 3
    - Non-ABS models to VIN 485952 and ABS models to VIN 490000 .... 10A (tail light, licence plate light, sidelights)
    - All other models .... 5A (licence plate light)
  - Fuse 4
    - Non-ABS models to VIN 485952 and ABS models to VIN 490000 .... 10A (turn signals)
    - All other models .... 10A (turn signals, tail light, licence plate light, sidelights)
  - Fuse 5 .... 5A (alarm, instrument lights)
  - Fuse 6 .... not used
- Rear fusebox
  - Fuse 1 .... 20A (headlights)
  - Fuse 2 .... 20A (engine management)
  - Fuse 3 .... 15A (fan)
  - Fuse 4 .... 10A (fuel pump)
  - Fuse 5 .... 10A (ignition switch)
  - Fuse 6 .... not used

Tiger main fusebox
- Fuse 1 .... 15A (starter circuit, headlight)
- Fuse 2 .... 10A (ignition, fuel pump)
- Fuse 3 .... 10A (heated grips, accessories, satellite navigation)
- Fuse 4 .... 10A (turn signals, alarm, horn, tail light, sidelight diagnostic plug)
- Fuse 5 .... 15A (fan)
- Fuse 6 .... 20A (engine management)
- Main fuse (in starter relay) 30A

Electrical system

Fuses (continued)

Tiger ABS fusebox
- Fuse 1 .... 20A
- Fuse 2 .... 20A

Tiger Sport
- Main fuse 30A
- Left-hand fusebox
  - Fuse 1 .... not used
  - Fuse 2 .... 10A (fan)
  - Fuse 3 .... 10A (tail light, brake light, horn)
  - Fuse 4 .... 10A (heated grips)
  - Fuse 5 .... 10A (accessories)
  - Fuse 6 .... not used
- Right-hand fusebox
  - Fuse 1 .... 20A (ABS)
  - Fuse 2 .... 20A (ABS)
  - Fuse 3 .... 10A (ignition switch)
  - Fuse 4 .... 15A (engine management)
  - Fuse 5 .... 10A (alarm, instrument lights)
  - Fuse 6 .... 20A (headlights)

Bulbs

Headlight
- Sprint .... 12V 55W H7 x 3
- Speed Triple .... 12V 60/55W H4 x 2
- Tiger and Tiger SE
  - Right-hand bulb 12V 65W H9
  - Left-hand bulb 12V 55W H7
- Tiger Sport
  - Main beam bulb .... 12V 55W H11 x 2
  - Dipped beam bulb .... 12V 55W H7 x 2

Brake/tail light .... LED
Turn signal light 12V 10W
Instrument lights .... LED

Torque wrench settings

- Alternator cover bolts .... 9 Nm
- Alternator rotor bolt .... 105 Nm
- Alternator stator and wiring clamp bolts .... 12 Nm
- Neutral switch .... 10 Nm
- Oil pressure switch .... 13 Nm
- Rear brake light switch – hydraulic type .... 15 Nm
- Sidestand bracket bolts .... 40 Nm
- Starter motor mounting bolts .... 10 Nm

1 General information

All models have a 12 volt electrical system charged by a three-phase alternator, with the rotor mounted on the left-hand end of the crankshaft and the stator located in the alternator cover.

The system incorporates a combined regulator/rectifier. The regulator maintains the charging system output within the specified range to prevent overcharging, and the rectifier converts the ac (alternating current) output of the alternator to dc (direct current) to power the lights and other components and to charge the battery.

The starter motor is mounted on the top of the crankcase. The starting system includes the motor, the battery, the relay and the various wires and switches.

Note: *Keep in mind that electrical parts, once purchased, cannot be returned. To avoid unnecessary expense, make very sure the faulty component has been positively identified before buying a replacement part.*

Many of the bolts used on Triumph motorcycles are of the Torx type. Unless you are already equipped with a good range of Torx bits, you are advised to obtain a set. Make sure you get bits that can be used in conjunction with a socket set so that a torque wrench can be applied – a Torx key set will not be adequate on its own, though will be useful in addition to the bits.

2 Electrical system fault finding

1 A typical electrical circuit consists of an electrical component, the switches, relays, etc, related to that component and the wiring and connectors that link the component to the battery and the frame.

2 Before tackling any troublesome electrical circuit, first study the wiring diagram thoroughly to get a complete picture of what makes up that individual circuit. Trouble spots, for instance, can often be narrowed down by noting if other components related to that circuit are operating properly or not. If several components or circuits fail at one time, chances are the fault lies either in the fuse or in the common earth (ground) connection, as several circuits are often routed through the same fuse and earth (ground) connections.

3 Electrical problems often stem from simple causes, such as loose or corroded connections or a blown fuse. Prior to any electrical fault finding, always visually check the condition of the fuse, wires and connections in the problem circuit. Intermittent failures can be especially frustrating, since you can't always duplicate

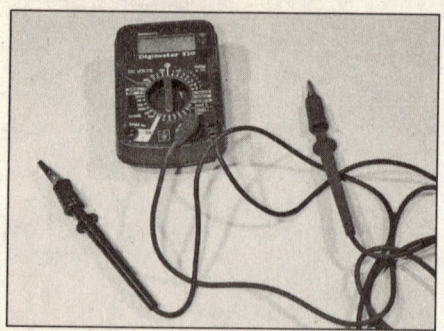

2.4a A digital multimeter can be used for all electrical tests

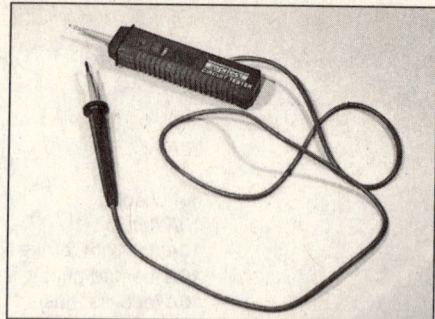

2.4b A battery-powered continuity tester

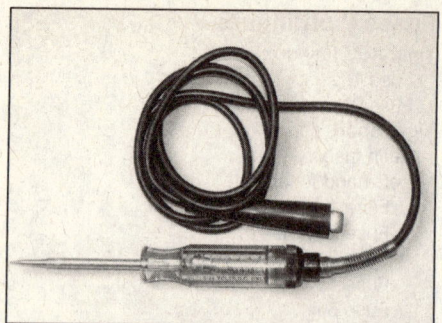

2.4c A simple test light is useful for voltage tests

the failure when it's convenient to test. In such situations, a good practice is to clean all connections in the affected circuit, whether or not they appear to be good – where possible use a dedicated electrical cleaning spray along with sandpaper, wire wool or other abrasive material to remove corrosion, and a dedicated electrical protection spray to prevent further problems. All of the connections and wires should also be wiggled to check for looseness which can cause intermittent failure.

4 If you don't have a multimeter it is highly advisable to obtain one – they are not expensive and will enable a full range of electrical tests to be made. Go for a modern digital one with LCD display as they are easier to use. A continuity tester and/or test light are useful for certain electrical checks as an alternative, though are limited in their usefulness compared to a multimeter **(see illustrations)**.

Continuity checks

5 The term continuity describes the uninterrupted flow of electricity through an electrical circuit. Continuity can be checked with a multimeter set either to its continuity function (a beep is emitted when continuity is found), or to the resistance (ohms / Ω) function, or with a dedicated continuity tester. Both instruments are powered by an internal battery, therefore the checks are made with the ignition OFF. As a safety precaution, always disconnect the battery negative (-) lead before making continuity checks, particularly if ignition switch checks are being made.

6 If using a multimeter, select the continuity function if it has one, or the resistance (ohms) function. Touch the meter probes together and check that a beep is emitted or the meter reads zero, which indicates continuity. If there is no continuity there will be no beep or the meter will show infinite resistance. After using the meter, always switch it OFF to conserve its battery.

7 A continuity tester can be used in the same way – its light should come on or it should beep to indicate continuity in the switch ON position, but should be off or silent in the OFF position.

8 Note that the polarity of the test probes doesn't matter for continuity checks, although care should be taken to follow specific test procedures if a diode or solid-state component is being checked.

Switch continuity checks

9 If a switch is at fault, trace its wiring to the wiring connectors. Separate the connectors and inspect them for security and condition. A build-up of dirt or corrosion here will most likely be the cause of the problem – clean up and apply a water dispersant such as WD40, or alternatively use a dedicated contact cleaner and protection spray.

10 If using a multimeter, select the continuity function if it has one, or the resistance (ohms) function, and connect its probes to the terminals in the connector **(see illustration)**. Simple ON/OFF type switches, such as brake light switches, only have two wires whereas combination switches, like the handlebar switches, have many wires. Study the wiring diagram to ensure that you are connecting to the correct pair of wires. Continuity should be indicated with the switch ON and no continuity with it OFF.

Wiring continuity checks

11 Many electrical faults are caused by damaged wiring, often due to incorrect routing or chaffing on frame components. Loose, wet or corroded wire connectors can also be the cause of electrical problems.

12 A continuity check can be made on a single length of wire by disconnecting it at each end and connecting the meter or continuity tester probes to each end of the wire **(see illustration)**. Continuity (low or no resistance – 0 ohms) should be indicated if the wire is good. If no continuity (high resistance) is shown, suspect a broken wire.

13 To check for continuity to earth in any earth wire connect one probe of your meter or tester to the earth wire terminal in the connector and the other to the frame, engine, or battery earth (-) terminal. Continuity (low or no resistance – 0 ohms) should be indicated if the wire is good. If no continuity (high resistance) is shown, suspect a broken wire or corroded or loose earth point (see below).

Voltage checks

14 A voltage check can determine whether power is reaching a component. Use a multimeter set to the dc voltage scale, or a test light. The test light is the cheaper component, but the meter has the advantage of being able to give a voltage reading.

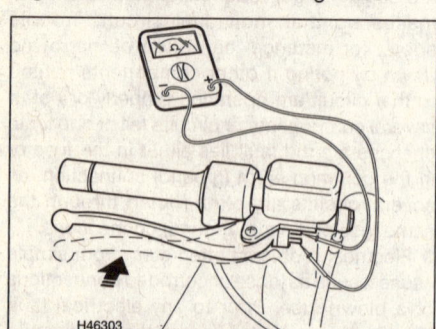

2.10 Continuity should be indicated across switch terminals when lever is operated

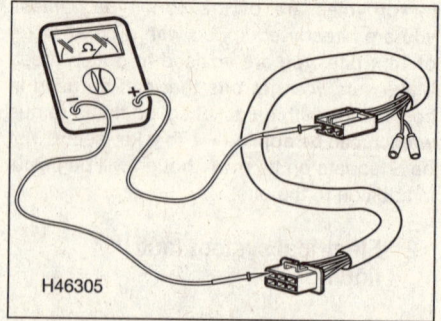

2.12 Wiring continuity check. Connect the meter probes across each end of the same wire

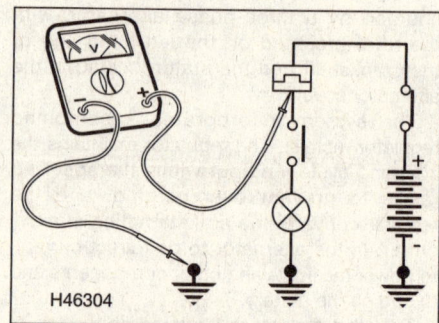

2.15 Voltage check. Connect the meter positive probe to the component and the negative probe to earth

Electrical system 8•5

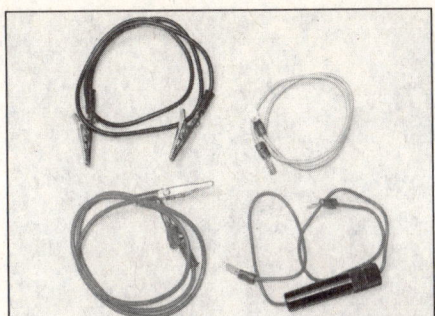

2.23 A selection of insulated jumper wires

15 Connect the meter or test light in parallel, i.e. across the load **(see illustration)**.
16 First identify the relevant wiring circuit by referring to the wiring diagram at the end of this manual. If other electrical components share the same power supply (i.e. are fed from the same fuse), take note whether they are working correctly – this is useful information in deciding where to start checking the circuit.
17 If using a meter, check first that the meter leads are plugged into the correct terminals on the meter (red to positive (+), black to negative (-). Set the meter to the dc volts function, where necessary at a range suitable for the battery voltage – 0 to 20 vdc. Connect the meter red probe (+) to the power supply wire and the black probe to a good metal earth (ground) on the motorcycle's frame or directly to the battery negative terminal. Battery voltage should be shown on the meter with the ignition switch, and if necessary any other relevant switch, ON.
18 If using a test light, connect its positive (+) probe to the power supply terminal and its negative (-) probe to a good earth (ground) on the motorcycle's frame. With the switch, and if necessary any other relevant switch, ON, the test light should illuminate.
19 If no voltage is indicated, work back towards the fuse continuing to check for voltage. When you reach a point where there is voltage, you know the problem lies between that point and your last check point.

Earth (ground) checks

20 Earth connections are made either directly to the engine or frame (such as neutral switch, oil pressure switch etc. which only have a positive feed) or by a separate wire into the earth circuit of the wiring harness. Alternatively a short earth wire is sometimes run from the component directly to the motorcycle's frame.
21 Corrosion is a common cause of a poor earth connection, as is a loose earth terminal fastener.
22 If total or multiple component failure is experienced, check the security of the main earth lead from the negative (-) terminal of the battery, the earth lead bolted to the engine, and the main earth point(s) on the frame. If corroded, dismantle the connection and clean all surfaces back to bare metal. Remake the connection and prevent further corrosion from forming by smearing battery terminal grease over the connection.
23 To check the earth of a component, use an insulated jumper wire to temporarily bypass its earth connection **(see illustration)** – connect one end of the jumper wire to the earth terminal or metal body of the component and the other end to the motorcycle's frame. If the circuit works with the jumper wire installed, the earth circuit is faulty.
24 To check an earth wire first check for corroded or loose connections, then check the wiring for continuity (Step 13) between each connector in the circuit in turn, and then to its earth point, to locate the break.

3 Battery removal and installation

Caution: Be extremely careful when handling or working around the battery. The electrolyte is very caustic and an explosive gas (hydrogen) is given off when the battery is charging.

Removal and installation

1 Remove the seat (see Chapter 7). On Sprint ST models remove the seat cowling (see Chapter 7) and the seat locating bracket **(see illustration)**. On 2011-on Speed Triple models (from VIN 461332) raise the fuel tank (see Chapter 4).
2 Unscrew the negative (–) terminal bolt first and disconnect the lead from the battery **(see illustrations)**. Lift up the insulating cover to access the positive (+) terminal, then unscrew the bolt and disconnect the lead.

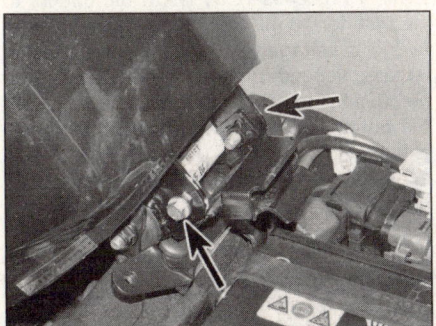

3.1 Unscrew the bolts (arrowed) and remove the bracket

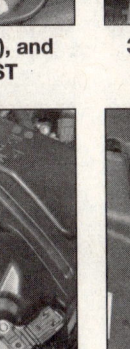

3.2a Battery negative terminal (A), and positive terminal (B) – Sprint ST

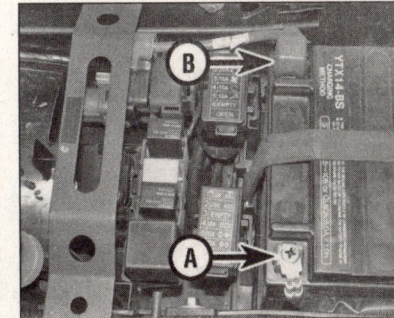

3.2b Battery negative terminal (A), and positive terminal (B) – Sprint GT

3.2c Battery negative terminal (A), and positive terminal (B) – Speed Triple – up to VIN 461331

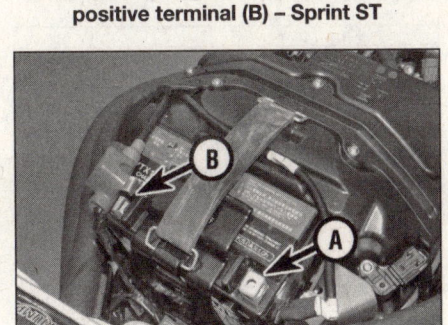

3.2d Battery negative terminal (A), and positive terminal (B) – Speed Triple from VIN 461332

3.2e Battery negative terminal (A), and positive terminal (B) – Tiger

3.3a Unhook the strap

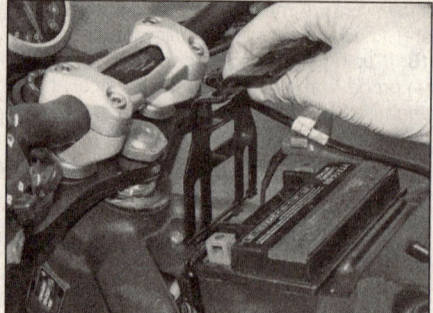

3.3b Remove the holder

3.4 Carefully lift the battery out – it is quite heavy

3 On Sprint, Speed Triple and Tiger Sport models release the battery strap **(see illustration)**. On 2011-on Speed Triple models (from VIN 461332) remove the battery holder **(see illustration)**.
4 Carefully lift the battery from the bike **(see illustration)**.
5 On installation, clean the battery terminals and lead ends with a wire brush, fine sandpaper or steel wool. Reconnect the leads, connecting the positive (+) terminal first.

HAYNES HiNT *Battery corrosion can be kept to a minimum by applying a layer of petroleum jelly (Vaseline) or dielectric grease (available as a spray) to the terminals after the cables have been connected. DO NOT use a mineral based grease.*

Inspection and maintenance

6 The battery fitted on all models is of the maintenance-free (sealed) type, therefore requiring no specific maintenance. However, the following checks should still be regularly performed.
7 Check the battery terminals and leads for tightness and corrosion. If corrosion is evident, unscrew the terminal bolts and disconnect the leads from the battery, disconnecting the negative (–) terminal first, and clean the terminals and lead ends with a wire brush or knife and emery paper. Reconnect the leads, connecting the negative (+) terminal first, and apply a thin coat of petroleum jelly or battery terminal (dielectric) grease to the connections to slow further corrosion. DO NOT use a standard mineral based grease.
8 Keep the battery case clean to prevent current leakage, which can discharge the battery over a period of time (especially when it sits unused). Wash the outside of the case with a solution of baking soda and water. Rinse the battery thoroughly, then dry it.
9 Look for cracks in the case and renew the battery if any are found. If acid has been spilled on the frame or battery box, neutralise it with a baking soda and water solution, dry it thoroughly, then touch up any damaged paint.
10 If the motorcycle sits unused for long periods of time, disconnect the leads from the battery terminals, negative (–) terminal first. Refer to Section 4 and charge the battery once every month to six weeks.
11 The condition of the battery can be assessed by measuring the voltage present at the battery terminals **(see illustration)**. Connect the voltmeter positive (+) probe to the battery positive (+) terminal, and the negative (–) probe to the battery negative (–) terminal. When fully charged there should be 12.8 volts (or more) present. If the voltage falls below 12.3 volts the battery must be removed, disconnecting the negative (–) terminal first, and recharged as described in Section 4.

4 Battery charging

Caution: Be extremely careful when handling or working around the battery. The electrolyte is very caustic and an explosive gas (hydrogen) is given off when the battery is charging.

1 Remove the battery (see Section 3).
2 Connect the charger to the battery, making sure that the positive (+) lead on the charger is connected to the positive (+) terminal on the battery, and the negative (–) lead is connected to the negative (–) terminal **(see illustration)**.
3 The battery should be charged at the specified rate for up to 12 hours if it is completely flat, or until the voltage across the terminals reaches 12.8V (allow the battery to stabilise for 30 minutes after charging before taking a voltage reading). The actual time required depends on the initial voltage present (Section 3, Step 11). Exceeding this can cause the battery to overheat, buckling the plates and rendering it useless. Few owners will have access to an expensive current controlled charger, so if a normal domestic charger is used check that after a possible initial peak, the charge rate falls to a safe level **(see illustration)**. If the battery becomes hot during charging **stop**. Further charging will cause damage. Note that there are many bike-specific

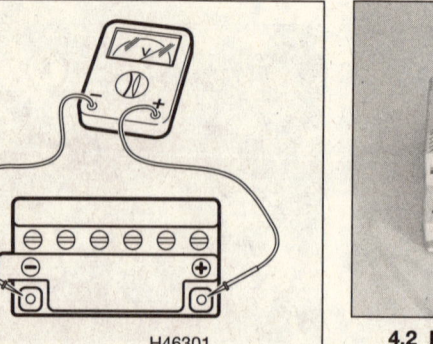

3.11 Checking battery voltage – connect the meter as shown

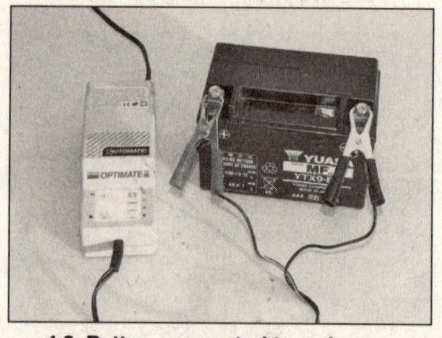

4.2 Battery connected to a charger

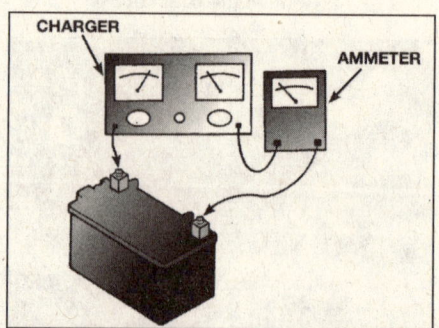

4.3 If the charger doesn't have an ammeter built in, connect one in series as shown. **DO NOT** connect the ammeter between the battery terminals or it will be ruined

chargers available from good suppliers that are designed for the maintenance and recovery of motorcycle batteries, in particular catering for the requirements of heavily discharged MF batteries. They are not too expensive, and are a worthwhile investment, especially if the bike is not used over winter. Follow the manufacturer's instructions.

4 If the recharged battery discharges rapidly when left disconnected it is likely that an internal short caused by physical damage or sulphation has occurred. A new battery will be required. A sound battery will tend to lose its charge at about 1% per day.

5 Install the battery (see Section 3).

6 If the motorcycle sits unused for long periods of time, charge the battery once every month to six weeks and leave it disconnected.

5 Fuses

1 The electrical system is protected by fuses of different ratings. On Sprint and Tiger models the main fuse is housed in the starter solenoid – remove the seat (see Chapter 7), then displace the solenoid and remove the plastic cover for access **(see illustrations)**. On 2011-on Speed Triple models (from VIN 461332) the main fuse is housed in a holder in front of the battery **(see illustration)** – remove the front fuel tank trim panel for access (see Chapter 7). All other fuses on Sprint and 2011-on Speed Triple models (from VIN 461332) models, all fuses on Speed Triples up to VIN 461331, all others except the ABS fuses (where fitted) on Tiger and Tiger SE models, and all others on Tiger Sport, are housed in a fusebox or boxes, which on Sprint ST models is inside the storage compartment on the right-hand side of the fairing, and on Sprint GT, Speed Triple and Tiger models is/are under the seat **(see illustrations)**. On Tiger and Tiger SE models fitted with ABS, the ABS fuses are housed in a separate box, still under the

5.1a Displace the solenoid . . .

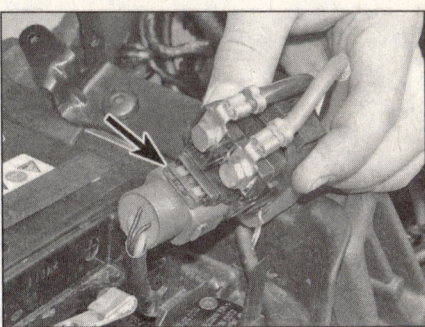
5.1b . . . then remove the cover to access the fuse (arrowed) – Sprint

5.1c Starter solenoid (arrowed) – Tiger

5.1d Main fuse (arrowed) – Speed Triple from VIN 461332

5.1e Fusebox (arrowed) – Sprint ST models

5.1f Fuseboxes (arrowed) – Sprint GT models

5.1g Fusebox (arrowed) – Speed Triple models up to VIN 461331

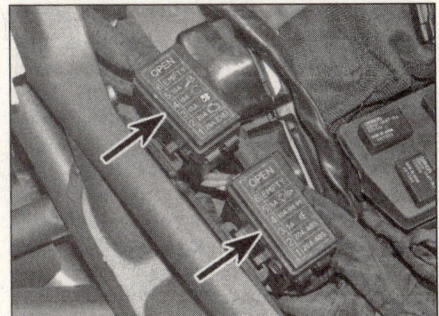
5.1h Fuseboxes (arrowed) – Speed Triple from VIN 461332

5.1i Fusebox (arrowed) – Tiger models

5.1j Main fuse (A), fuseboxes (B) – Tiger Sport

8•8 Electrical system

5.1k ABS fusebox (arrowed) – Tiger

5.2a Unlock and remove the lid

5.2b Unclip the lid to access the fusebox fuses – the identity, location and rating of each fuse is marked on or in the lid

seat, but at the front of the storage tray **(see illustration)**.

2 To access the fuses, on Sprint ST models remove the storage compartment lid **(see illustration)**. On Sprint GT, Speed Triple and Tiger remove the seat (see Chapter 7). Unclip the fusebox lid **(see illustration)**. The identity, location and rating of each fuse is marked either on the inside or on the top of the lid, depending on model.

3 The fuses can be removed and checked visually. If you can't pull the fuse out with your fingertips, use the tool provided in the fusebox, or a suitable pair of pliers **(see illustration)**. A blown fuse is easily identified by a break in the element **(see illustration)**, or can be tested for continuity using an ohmmeter or continuity tester – if there is no continuity, it has blown. Each fuse is clearly marked with its rating and must only be replaced by a fuse of the same rating. If a spare fuse is used, always replace it with a new one so that a spare of each rating is carried on the bike at all times.

⚠ **Warning:** *Never put in a fuse of a higher rating or bridge the terminals with any other substitute, however temporary it may be. Serious damage may be done to the circuit, or a fire may start.*

4 If a fuse blows, be sure to check the wiring circuit very carefully for evidence of a short-circuit. Look for bare wires and chafed, melted or burned insulation. If the fuse is renewed before the cause is located, the new fuse will blow immediately.

5 Occasionally a fuse will blow or cause an open-circuit for no obvious reason. Corrosion of the fuse ends and fusebox terminals may occur and cause poor fuse contact. If this happens, remove the corrosion with a wire brush or emery paper, then spray the fuse end and terminals with electrical contact cleaner.

6 Lighting system check

Note: *Refer to Electrical system fault finding (Section 2) and to the Wiring Diagrams at the end of the Chapter when making electrical tests on any part of the system.*

1 If none of the lights work, check battery voltage (see Section 3) – low voltage indicates either a faulty battery or a defective charging system. Refer to Sections 3 and 4 for battery checks and Section 27 for charging system tests. If there is a problem with more than one circuit at the same time, or with all circuits, it is likely to be a fault relating to a multi-function component, such as the fuse or the ignition switch. When checking for a blown filament in a bulb, it is advisable to back up a visual check with a continuity test of the filament as it is not always apparent that a bulb has blown. When testing for continuity, remember that on single terminal bulbs it is the metal body of the bulb that is the earth (ground).

Headlight

2 If a headlight fails to work, check the bulb(s) and the bulb terminals and wiring connectors first (see Section 7), then the circuit fuse (see Section 5). If they are all good, check for battery voltage at the blue/white (high beam) or blue/red (low beam) supply wire terminal in the headlight wiring connector, with the ignition switch ON, and the dip beam/main beam switch set appropriately. If voltage is present, check for continuity between the black (earth or ground) wire terminal and the battery negative (-) terminal. If there is no continuity, check the earth (ground) circuit for an open or poor connection.

3 If no voltage is indicated, check the wiring and connectors between the headlight, relay, dimmer switch, fusebox, and the ignition switch, and check the switches themselves (see Section 18).

4 If no problem can be found refer to Section 16 and first check the headlight relay(s) on Sprint, Speed Triple and Tiger Sport models, and then the starter relay. On Tiger and Tiger SE models check the starter relay (no headlight relay is fitted). Make sure the relay is secure in its connector and that the terminals are corrosion free and not bent or broken. Then check the function of the relay itself as described.

Tail light

Note: *The tail and brake lights consist of a number of LEDs. If an individual LED fails it cannot be replaced with a new one (the only solution is to fit a complete new tail light unit), but the rest should continue to function. If none of them work, it is more likely to be a circuit problem – follow Steps 5 and 6.*

5 If the tail light fails to work, check the wiring connector first (see Section 10), then the circuit fuse (see Section 5). If they are all good, check for battery voltage at the yellow wire terminal in the loom side of the tail light wiring connector, with the ignition switch ON. If voltage is present, check for continuity between the black (earth or ground) wire terminal and the battery negative (-) terminal. If there is no continuity, check the earth (ground) circuit for an open or poor connection.

6 If no voltage is indicated, check the wiring and connectors between the tail light and the ignition switch, then check the switch (see Section 17).

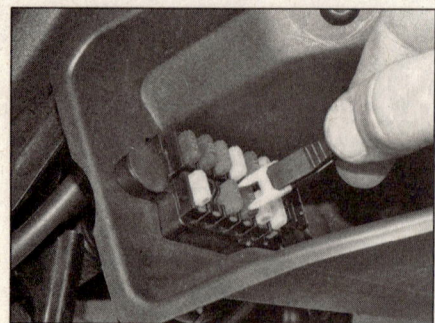

5.3a A fuse removal tool is provided in the fusebox

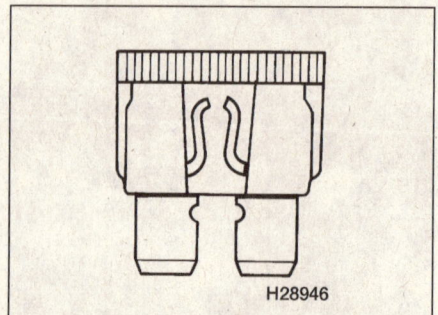

5.3b A blown fuse can be identified by a break in its element

Sidelight and licence plate light

7 If the sidelight and/or licence plate light fails to work, check the bulb and the bulb terminals and wiring connectors first (see Section 7 or 10), then the circuit fuse. If they are all good, check for battery voltage at the yellow wire terminal in the loom side of the wiring connector, with the ignition switch ON. If voltage and continuity are present, check for continuity between the black (earth or ground) wire terminal and the battery negative (-) terminal. If there is no continuity, check the earth (ground) circuit for an open or poor connection.

8 If no voltage is indicated, check the wiring and connectors between the sidelight and the ignition switch, then check the switch (see Section 17).

Brake light

Note: *The tail and brake lights consist of a number of LEDs. If an individual LED fails it cannot be replaced with a new one (the only solution is to fit a complete new tail light unit), but the rest should continue to function. If none of them work, it is more likely to be a circuit or switch problem – follow Steps 9 and 10.*

9 If the brake light fails to work, check the wiring connector first (see Section 10), then the circuit fuse (see Section 5). If they are all good, check for battery voltage at the green/purple wire terminal in the loom side of the tail light wiring connector, with the ignition switch ON, and the brake lever or pedal applied. If voltage is present, check for continuity between the black (earth or ground) wire terminal and the battery negative (-) terminal. If there is no continuity, check the earth (ground) circuit for an open or poor connection.

10 If no voltage is indicated, check the brake light switches (see Section 14), then the wiring and connectors between the tail light and the switches.

Turn signal lights

11 If one light fails to work, check the bulb and the bulb terminals first, then the wiring connectors (see Section 13). If none of the turn signals work, first check the signal circuit fuse (see Section 5).

12 If the fuse is good, see Section 12 for the turn signal circuit check.

7 Headlight and sidelight bulbs

Note: *The headlight bulbs are of the quartz-halogen type. Do not touch the bulb glass as skin acids will shorten the bulb's service life. If the bulb is accidentally touched, it should be wiped carefully when cold with a rag soaked in methylated spirit and dried before fitting.*

⚠ **Warning: Allow the bulb time to cool before removing it if the headlight has just been on.**

Sprint

Headlight

1 To access either of the dipped beam bulbs, remove the upper and lower cockpit trim panels on the relevant side (see Chapter 7). For the left-hand bulb displace and support the coolant reservoir (see Chapter 3) – there is no need to drain it. To access the main beam bulb in the centre you have to remove the fairing (see Section 7).

2 Remove the rubber dust cover, noting how it fits **(see illustration)**.

3 Disconnect the wiring connector from the bulb **(see illustration)**.

4 Release the bulb retaining clip, noting how it fits, then remove the bulb **(see illustrations)**.

5 Fit the new bulb, bearing in mind the information in the **Note** above. Make sure the tabs on the bulb fit correctly in the slots in the bulb housing, and secure it in position with the retaining clip.

6 Connect the wiring connector then fit the dust cover.

7 Install the headlight unit or coolant reservoir and trim panels as required. Check the operation of the headlight.

Sidelight

8 On ST models up to VIN 440391 the sidelight bulbholder is in the underside of the headlight assembly at the front **(see illustration)**. Reaching up under the front of the fairing carefully pull the rubber bulbholder out – do not pull it out by the wires.

9 On later ST models and GT models the sidelight bulb holders are accessed by removing both cockpit trim panels on the relevant side (see Chapter 7). Carefully pull the rubber bulbholder out **(see illustration)** – do not pull it out by the wires.

7.2 Remove the cover . . .

7.3 . . . and disconnect the wiring connector

7.4a Release the clip . . .

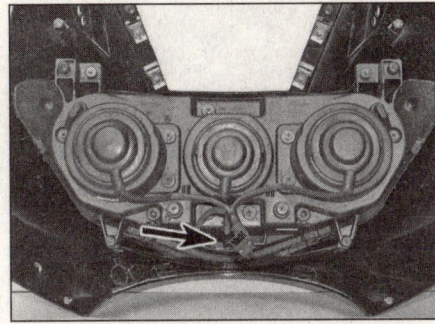

7.4b . . . and remove the bulb

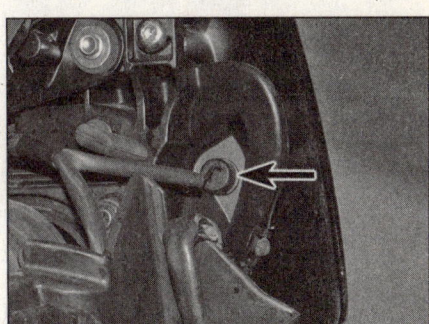

7.8 Sidelight (arrowed)

7.9 Sidelight bulbholder (arrowed)

7.13a Undo the screw and collect the nut . . .

7.13b . . . then remove the rim . . .

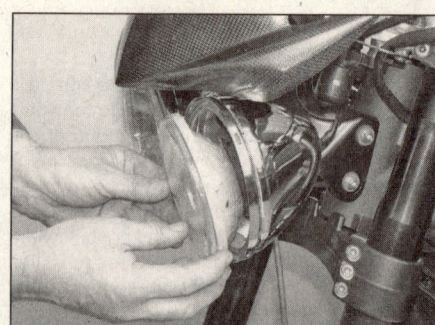

7.13c . . . and displace the light unit

10 Carefully pull the bulb out of the holder.
11 Fit the new bulb in reverse order.
12 Check the operation of the sidelight.

2005 to 2010 Speed Triple (up to VIN 461331)

Headlight

13 Undo the headlight rim clamp screw, taking care not to lose the nut, then support the headlight and remove the rim **(see illustrations)**. Carefully draw the light unit out of the shell, noting how it fits **(see illustration)**. Note the seat for the light unit in the housing **(see illustration 7.19)**.
14 Carefully pull the rubber sidelight bulbholder out – do not pull it out by the wires **(see illustration)**. Disconnect the wiring connector from the headlight bulb **(see illustration)** – place the headlight on a bench.
15 Remove the rubber dust cover, noting how it fits **(see illustration)**.

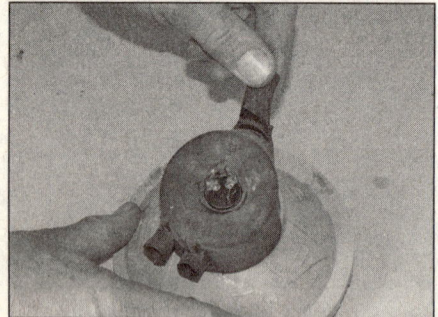

7.15 Remove the cover

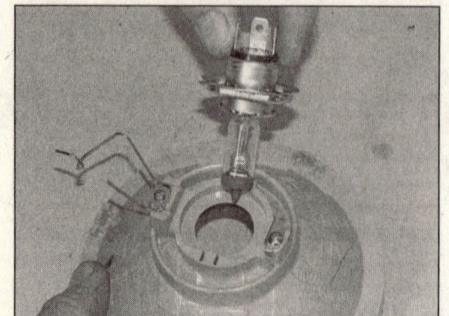

7.16b . . . and remove the bulb

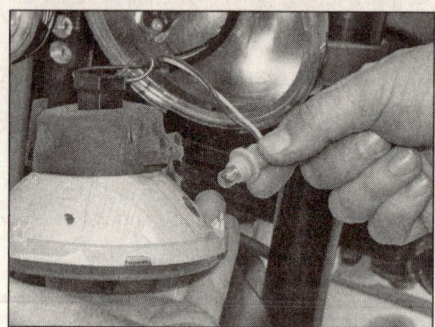

7.14a Pull the sidelight out . . .

16 Release the bulb retaining clip, noting how it fits, then remove the bulb **(see illustrations)**.
17 Fit the new bulb, bearing in mind the information in the **Note** above. Make sure the tabs on the bulb fit correctly in the slots in the bulb housing, and secure it in position with the retaining clip.

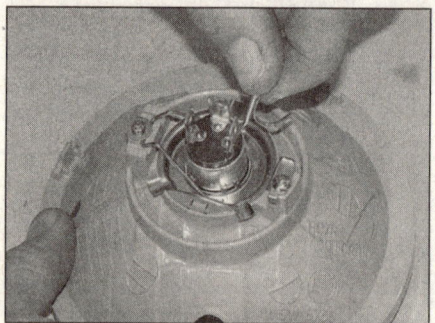

7.16a Release the clip . . .

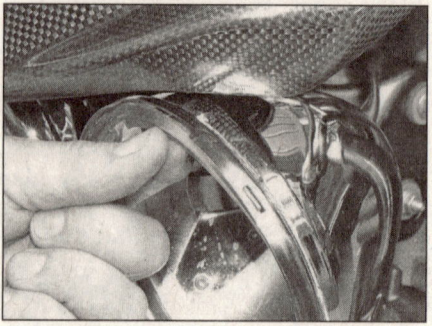

7.19 Make sure the seat is correctly in place

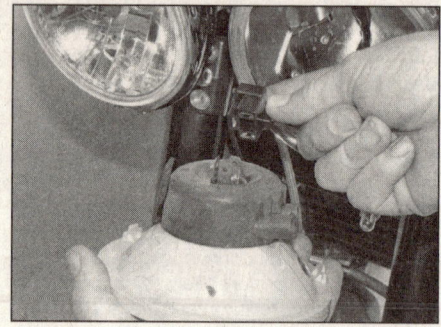

7.14b . . . and disconnect the headlight wiring connector

18 Fit the dust cover then connect the wiring connector.
19 Make sure the light unit seat is correctly fitted in the housing **(see illustration)**, and the unit locates correctly, then fit the rim and tighten the clamp **(see illustrations 7.13c, b and a)**.
20 Check the operation of the headlight.

Sidelight

21 Undo the headlight rim clamp screw, taking care not to lose the nut, then support the headlight and remove the rim **(see illustrations 7.13a and b)**. Carefully draw the light unit out of the shell, noting how it fits **(see illustration 7.13c)**. Note the seat for the light unit in the housing **(see illustration 7.19)**.
22 Carefully pull the rubber bulbholder out **(see illustration 7.14a)** – do not pull it out by the wires.
23 Carefully pull the bulb out of the holder **(see illustration)**.
24 Fit the new bulb in reverse order.
25 Check the operation of the sidelight.

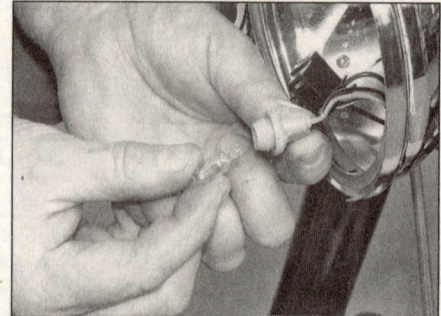

7.23 Carefully pull the bulb out of the holder

Electrical system 8•11

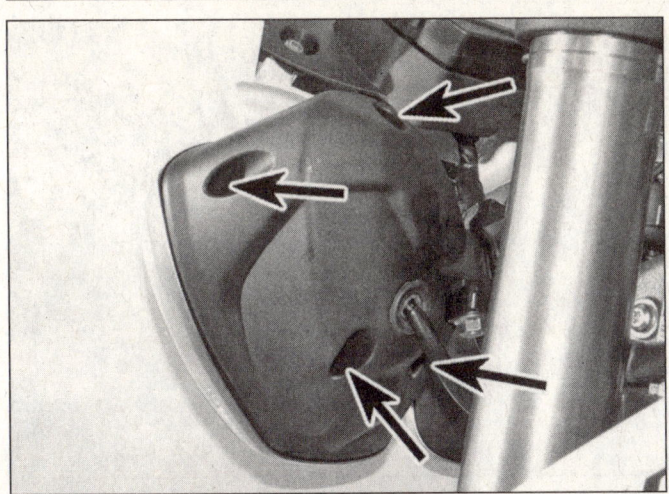
7.26a Undo the screws (arrowed)...

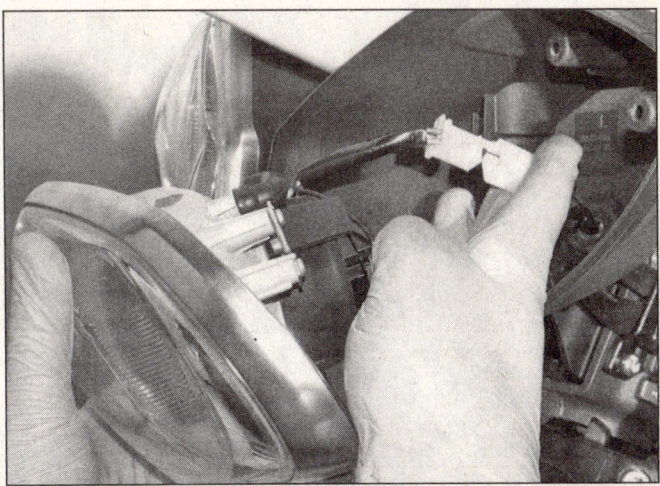
7.26b ...displace the beam unit and disconnect the connector

2011-on Speed Triple models (from VIN 461332)

Headlight

26 Undo the screws on the back of the headlight, draw the beam unit out the front and disconnect the wiring (see illustrations).
27 Disconnect the wiring connector and remove the rubber dust cover (see illustrations).
28 Release the bulb retaining clip, noting how it fits, then remove the bulb (see illustrations).
29 Fit the new bulb, bearing in mind the information in the Note above. Make sure the tabs on the bulb fit correctly in the slots in the bulb housing, and secure it in position with the retaining clip (see illustrations 7.28b and a).
30 Fit the dust cover and connect the wiring (see illustrations 7.27b and a).
31 Connect the wiring connector, fit the beam unit into the housing and tighten the screws (see illustrations 7.26b and a).
32 Check the operation of the headlight.

Sidelight

33 Undo the screws on the back of the headlight, draw the beam unit out the front and disconnect the wiring (see illustrations 7.26a and b).
34 Carefully pull the rubber bulbholder out (see illustration) – do not pull it out by the wires.
35 Carefully pull the bulb out of the holder (see illustration).
36 Fit the new bulb in reverse order.
37 Check the operation of the sidelight.

Tiger and Tiger SE

Headlight

38 Remove the relevant cockpit trim panel

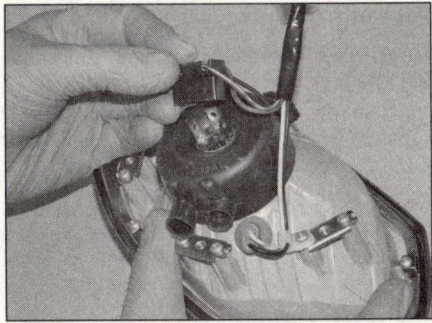
7.27a Pull the connector off...

7.27b ...and remove the cover

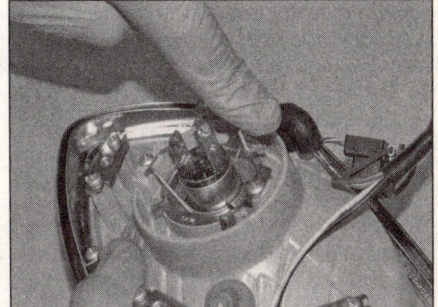
7.28a Release the clip...

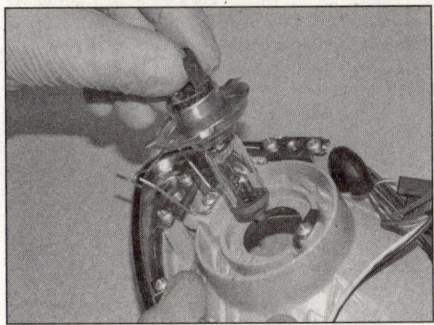
7.28b ...and remove the bulb

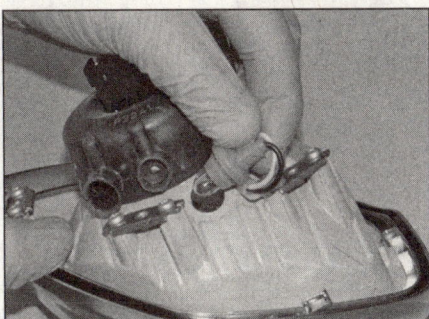
7.34 Pull the bulbholder out of the headlight...

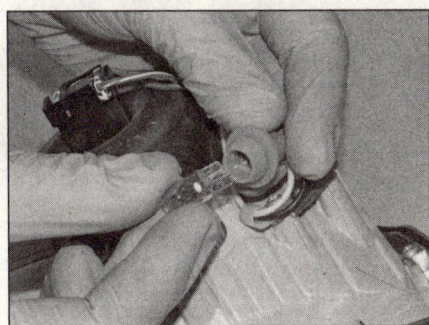
7.35 ...and the bulb out of the holder

8•12 Electrical system

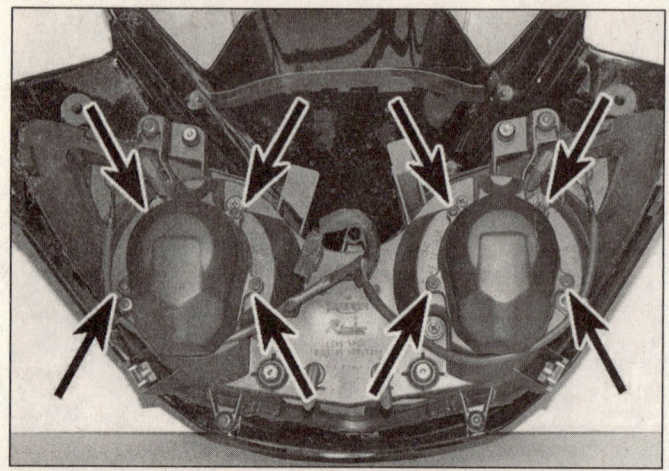
7.38a Undo the relevant screws (arrowed)

7.38b Remove the cover . . .

7.39 . . . and disconnect the wiring connector

7.40a Release the clip . . .

7.40b . . . and remove the bulb

(see Chapter 7). Undo the headlight cover screws on the relevant side and remove the cover **(see illustrations)**.

39 Disconnect the wiring connector from the bulb **(see illustration)**.

40 Release the bulb retaining clip, noting how it fits, then remove the bulb **(see illustrations)**.

41 Fit the new bulb, bearing in mind the information in the **Note** above. Make sure the tabs on the bulb fit correctly in the slots in the bulb housing, and secure it in position with the retaining clip.

42 Connect the wiring connector.

43 Fit the headlight cover. Check the operation of the headlight.

 **HAYNES HiNT** *Always use a paper towel or dry cloth when handling new bulbs to prevent injury if the bulb should break and to increase bulb life.*

Sidelight

44 Remove the relevant cockpit trim panel (see Chapter 7).

45 Carefully pull the rubber bulbholder out – do not pull it out by the wires **(see illustration)**.

46 Carefully pull the bulb out of the holder **(see illustration)**.

47 Fit the new bulb in reverse order.

48 Check the operation of the sidelight.

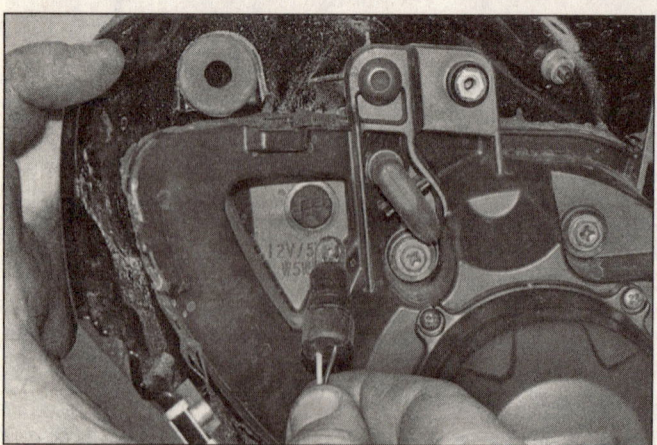
7.45 Pull the bulbholder out of the headlight . . .

7.46 . . . and the bulb out of the holder

Electrical system 8•13

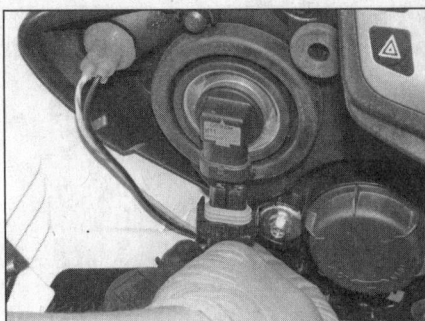
7.49a Disconnect the connector...

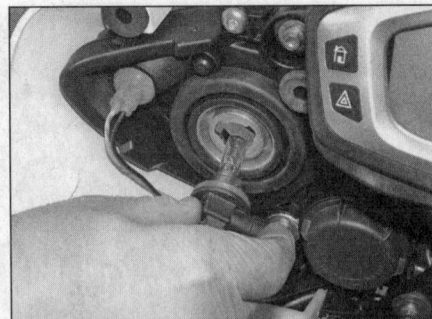
7.49b ...then release and remove the bulb unit

7.50a Remove the cover...

7.50b ...and pull the connector off

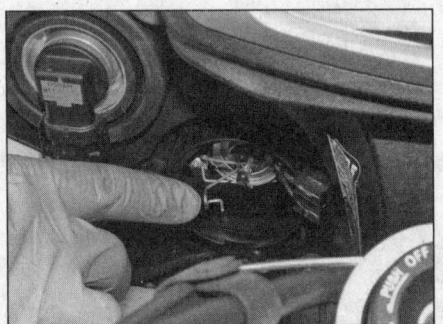
7.50c Release the clip...

7.50d ...and remove the bulb

Tiger Sport

Headlight

49 To replace a main beam bulb remove the relevant cockpit trim panel (see Chapter 7). Disconnect the wiring connector (see illustration). Turn the bulbholder anti-clockwise to release it and draw it out (see illustration) – the bulb is an integral part of the holder.

50 To replace a dipped beam bulb remove the cover by turning it anti-clockwise (see illustration). Disconnect the wiring connector (see illustration). Release the bulb retaining clip, noting how it fits, then remove the bulb (see illustrations).

51 Fit the new bulb, bearing in mind the information in the **Note** above.

52 Connect the wiring connector. Check the operation of the headlight.

53 Fit the cover or trim panel as required.

Sidelight

54 Remove the relevant cockpit trim panel (see Chapter 7).

55 Turn the bulbholder anti-clockwise to release it and draw it out (see illustration).

56 Carefully pull the bulb out of the holder (see illustration).

57 Fit the new bulb in reverse order.

58 Check the operation of the sidelight.

8 Headlight assembly

Removal

Sprint and Tiger

1 Remove the fairing (see Chapter 7).

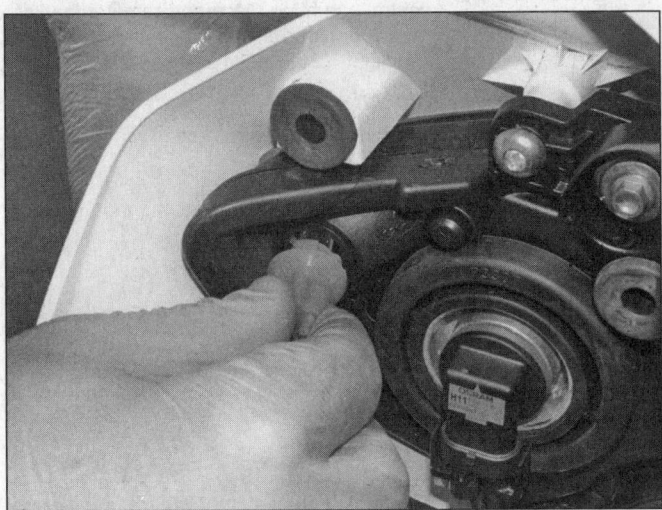
7.55 Release the bulbholder...

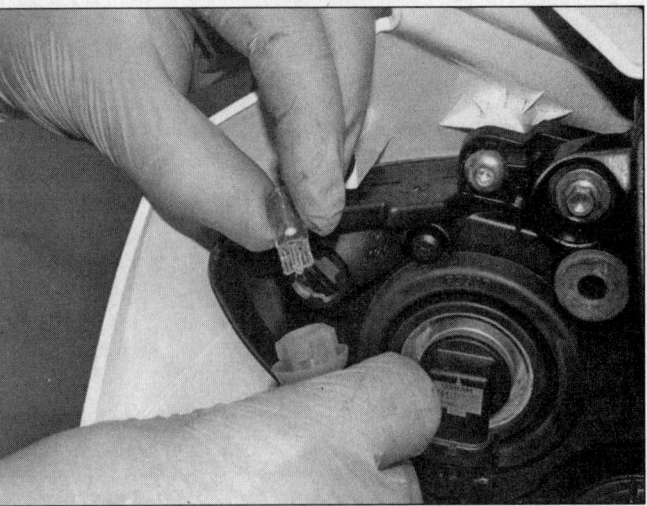
7.56 ...and pull the bulb out

8•14 Electrical system

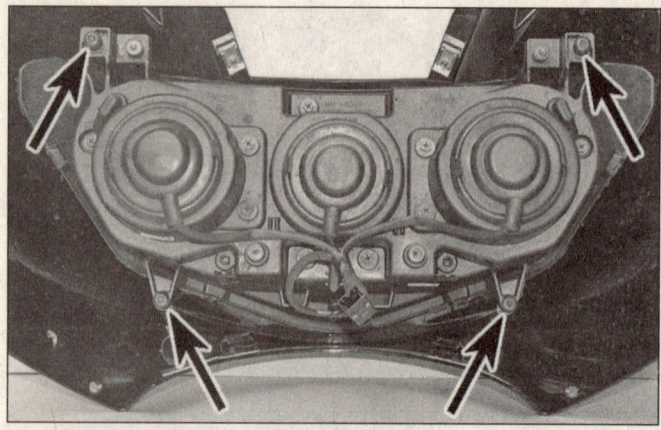

8.2a Headlight mounting bolts (arrowed) – Sprint models

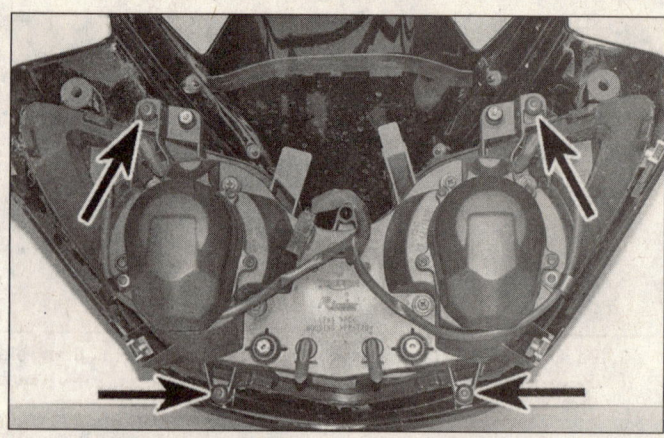

8.2b Headlight mounting bolts (arrowed) – Tiger models (except Sport)

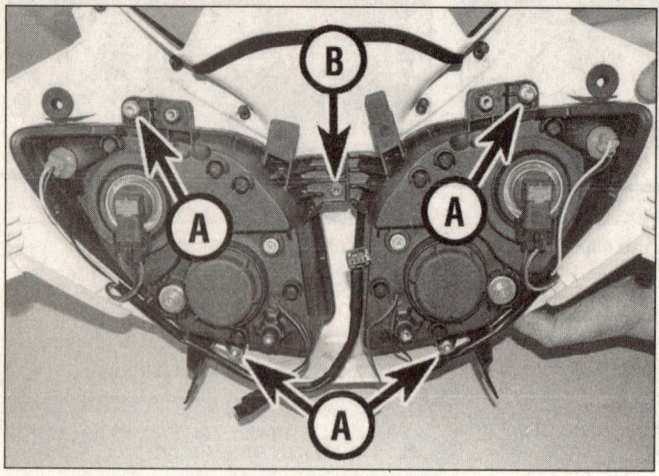

8.2c Headlight mounting bolts (A) and joining bolt (B) – Tiger Sport

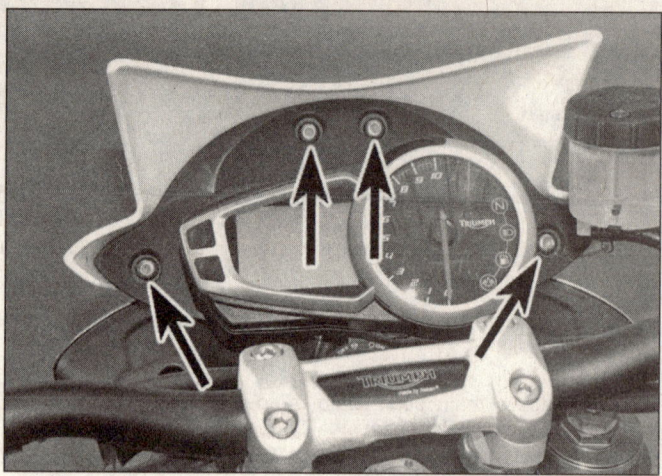

8.5a Cowling bolts (arrowed)

2 Unscrew the bolts securing the headlight assembly and remove it from the fairing **(see illustrations)**. On Tiger Sport the headlight assembly can be split into its left- and right-hand units if required by undoing the centre screw.

3 If required, remove the headlight and sidelight bulbs (see Section 7).

Speed Triple

4 On 2005 to 2010 models (up to VIN 461331) remove the airbox (see Chapter 4). Trace the wiring from the headlight(s) and disconnect it at the connector(s).

5 On 2011-on models (from VIN 461332), pull the cover off or remove the cowling from the back of the instrument cluster **(see illustration)**. Disconnect the headlight wiring connector **(see illustration)**.

6 To remove the complete headlight assembly, support it, then unscrew the two clamp bolts and remove the clamp and the headlights **(see illustration)**.

7 To remove an individual light on 2005 to 2010 models (up to VIN 461331), unscrew the nut and withdraw the bolt securing it to the central mounting piece and remove the light **(see illustration)**. On all other models the headlights come as an assembly.

Installation

8 Installation is the reverse of removal. Make

8.5b Headlight wiring connector (arrowed)

8.6 Headlight assembly clamp bolts (arrowed) – Speed Triple models

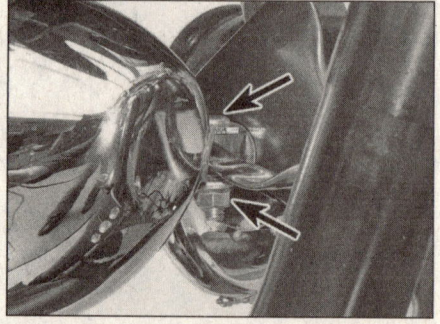

8.7 Individual headlight mounting bolt and nut (arrowed)

Electrical system 8•15

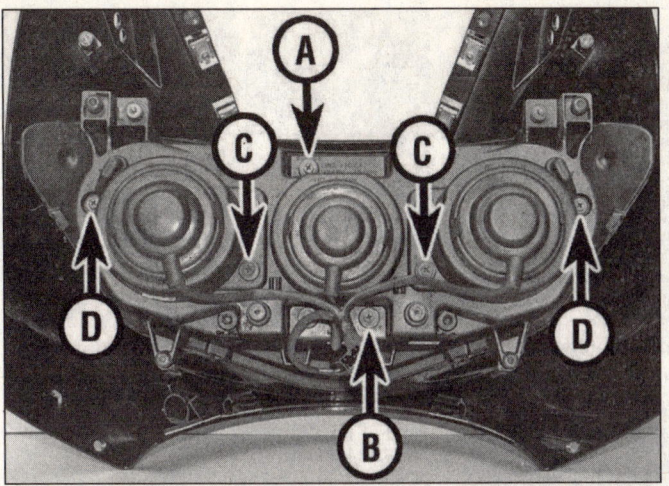

9.2 Main beam vertical adjuster (A), main beam horizontal adjuster (B); dipped beam vertical adjusters (C), dipped beam horizontal adjusters (D) – Sprint

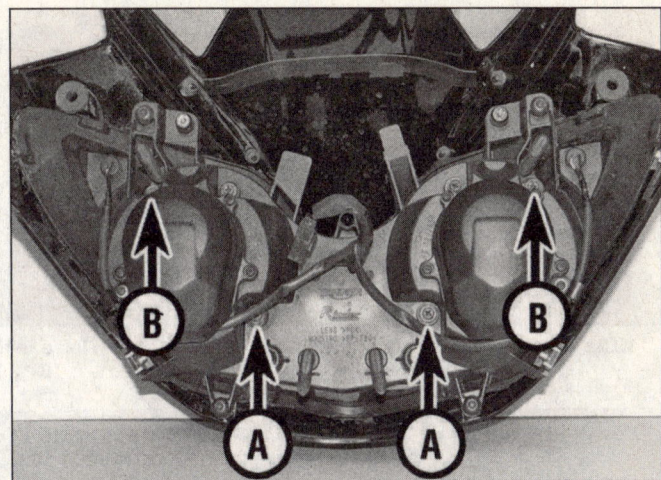

9.10 Vertical adjusters (A), horizontal adjusters (B) – Tiger

sure all the wiring is correctly connected and secured. Check the operation of the headlight and sidelight. Check the headlight aim (see Section 9).

9 Headlight aim

Note: *An improperly adjusted headlight may cause problems for oncoming traffic or provide poor, unsafe illumination of the road ahead. Before adjusting the headlight aim, be sure to consult with local traffic laws and regulations – for UK models refer to MOT Test Checks in the Reference section.*

1 The headlight beam can be adjusted both horizontally and vertically. Before making any adjustment, check that the tyre pressures are correct and the suspension is adjusted as required. Make any adjustments to the headlight aim with machine on level ground, with the fuel tank half full, with an assistant sitting on the seat, and with the headlight on and shining against a dark vertical surface such as a garage wall, and set to main or dipped beam as required. If the bike is usually ridden with a passenger on the back, have a second assistant to do this.

Sprint models

2 To access the main beam vertical adjustment screw remove the windshield and its trim panel (see Chapter 7) **(see illustration)**. To access the dipped beam horizontal adjustment screws remove the upper lower cockpit trim panels for the side being adjusted (see Chapter 7). The main beam horizontal adjustment screw and dipped beam vertical adjustment screws are accessible by reaching up under the fairing, turning the handlebars as required for best access.

3 To raise the main beam turn the adjuster screw clockwise, and to lower it turn it anti-clockwise.
4 To raise a dipped beam turn the adjuster screw anti-clockwise, and to lower it turn it clockwise.
5 To move the main beam to the right turn the adjuster screw anti-clockwise, and to move it to the left turn it clockwise.
6 To move the right-hand dipped beam to the right turn the adjuster screw clockwise, and to move it to the left turn it anti-clockwise.
7 To move the left-hand dipped beam to the right turn the adjuster screw anti-clockwise, and to move it to the left turn it clockwise.

Speed Triple models

8 Vertical adjustment of the headlight is made by slackening the clamp bolts on the headlight mounting and by pivoting the lights up or down as required – the beams can only be moved as a pair and are not individually adjustable **(see illustration 8.5)**. Tighten the bolts on completion.
9 Horizontal adjustment is made by slackening the nut on the bottom of the pivot bolt on each individual headlight mounting and by pivoting the light to the right or left as required – each beam can be adjusted independently of the other **(see illustration 8.6)**. Tighten the bolt securely on completion.

Tiger and Tiger SE models

10 To access the horizontal adjustment screw for each beam remove the cockpit trim panel for the side being adjusted (see Chapter 7) **(see illustration)**. The vertical adjustment screws are accessible by reaching up under the fairing, turning the handlebars as required for best access.
11 Vertical adjustment is made by turning the adjuster screw on the bottom inner corner of each beam unit.

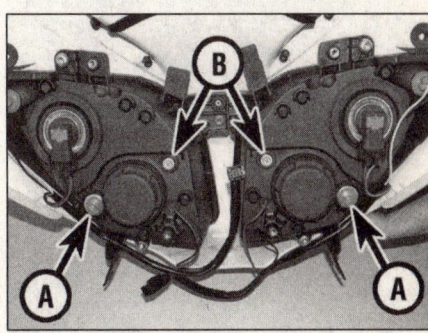

9.14 Vertical adjusters (A), horizontal adjusters (B) – Tiger Sport

12 Horizontal adjustment is made by turning the adjuster screw on the top outer corner of each headlight unit.

Tiger Sport

13 The adjustment screws are accessible from the cockpit, turning the handlebars as required for best access.
14 Vertical adjustment is made by turning the adjuster screw on the bottom outer corner of the dipped beam unit **(see illustration)**.
15 Horizontal adjustment is made by turning the adjuster screw on the top inner corner of the dipped beam unit.

10 Brake/tail and licence plate bulbs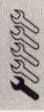

Brake/tail lights

1 The brake and tail lights consist of a number of LEDs. If an individual LED fails it cannot be replaced with a new one (the only solution is to fit a complete new tail light unit), but the rest should continue to function. If none of them

8•16 Electrical system

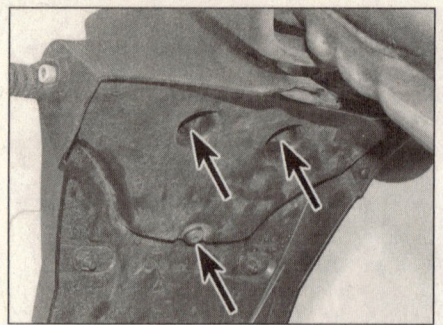

10.2a Undo the screws (arrowed) and remove the cover

10.2b Release the bulbholder . . .

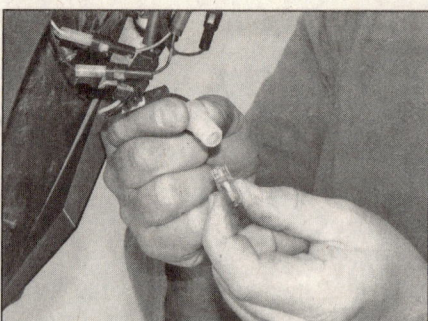

10.2c . . . then pull the bulb out of the holder

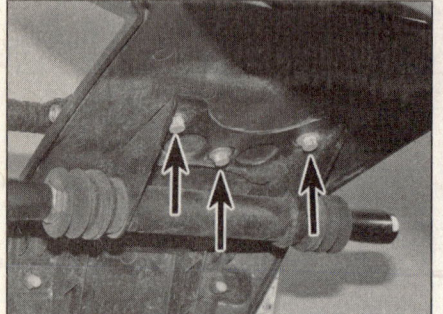

10.3a Link bar bracket bolts (arrowed)

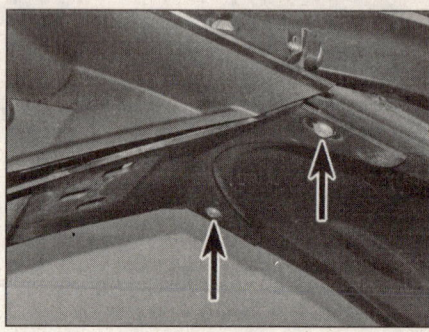

10.3b Undo the screws (arrowed) and remove the guard

work, it is more likely to be a circuit problem (see Section 6).

Licence plate light

2 On Sprint ST models remove the inner cover from the rear mudguard **(see illustration)**. Ease the bulbholder out of the back of the licence plate light, and pull the bulb out of the holder **(see illustrations)**.

3 On Sprint GT models remove the seat (see Chapter 7). Unscrew the pannier link bar bracket bolts and remove the link bar assembly **(see illustration)**. Remove the splashguard **(see illustration)**. Ease the bulbholder out of the back of the licence plate light, and pull the bulb out of the holder **(see illustrations)**.

4 On 2005 to 2010 Speed Triple models (up to VIN 461331) undo the four rearmost screws securing the inner cover to the rear mudguard, then carefully pull it away until you can reach the bulbholder – take care to release the tabs from the side panels or they could break **(see illustration)**. Ease the bulbholder out of the back of the licence plate light, and pull the bulb out of the holder **(see illustrations)**.

5 On 2011-on Speed Triple models (from VIN 461332), undo the turn signal bolts

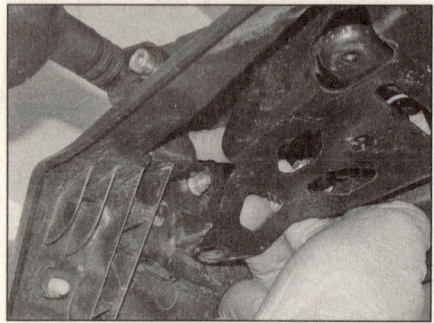

10.3c Remove the bulbholder . . .

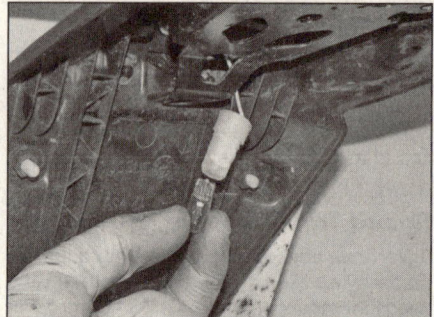

10.3d . . . and pull the bulb out

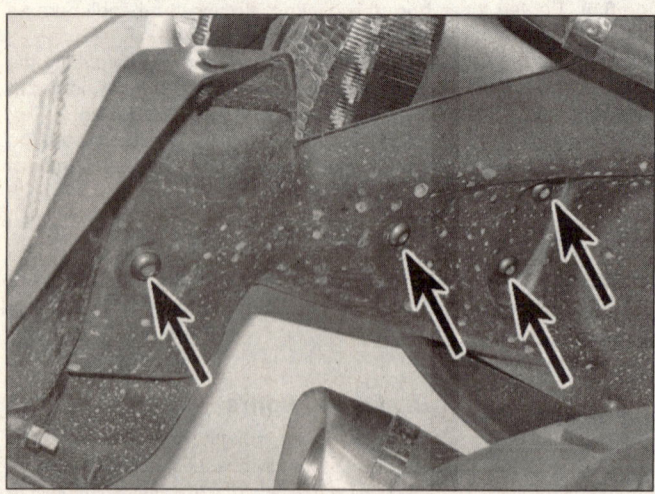

10.4a Undo the screws (arrowed) and release the cover . . .

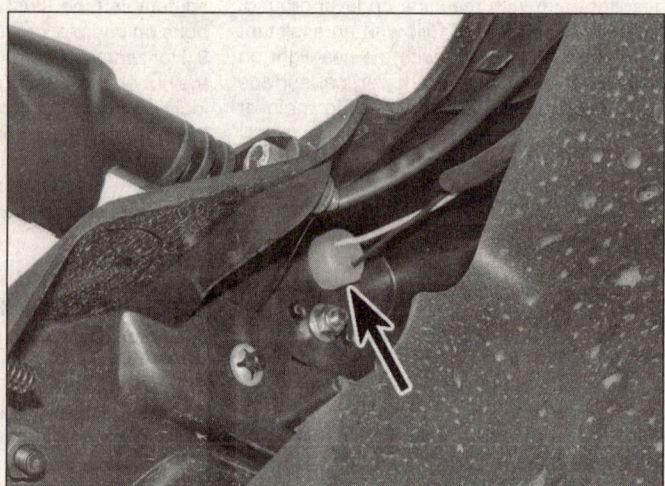

10.4b . . . to access the bulbholder (arrowed)

Electrical system 8•17

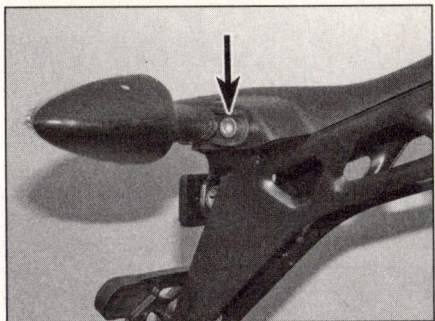

10.5a Unscrew the bolt (arrowed) on each side

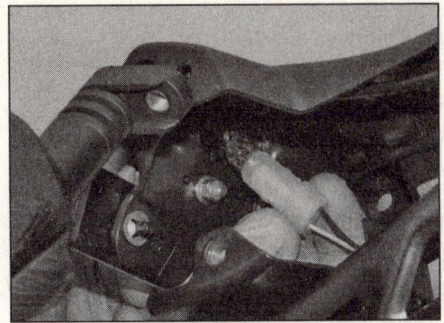

10.5b Raise the bracket and remove the bulbholder . . .

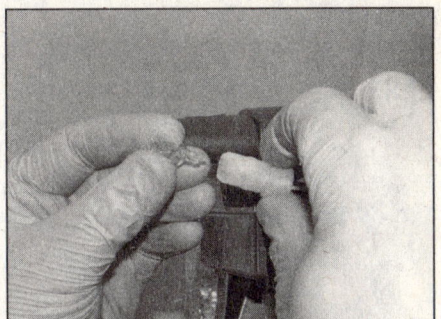

10.5c . . . and pull the bulb out

(see illustration). Slightly raise the licence plate light/turn signal holder, then ease the bulbholder out of the back of the licence plate light, and pull the bulb out of the holder **(see illustrations)**.

6 On Tiger models (except Sport) remove the licence plate, then undo the screws securing the inner cover to the rear mudguard, then carefully pull it away **(see illustrations)**. Counter-hold the nut on the licence plate light bolt, then unscrew the bolt and detach the light. Ease the bulbholder out of the back of the light, and pull the bulb out of the holder.

7 On Tiger Sport models undo the screws on the rear mudguard **(see illustration)**. Carefully lift the licence plate holder up and ease the bulbholder out of the back of the light **(see illustration)**. Pull the bulb out of the holder.

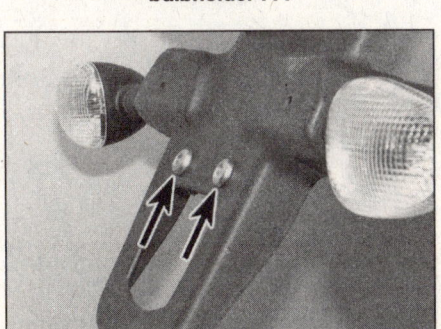

10.6a Undo the screws (arrowed) . . .

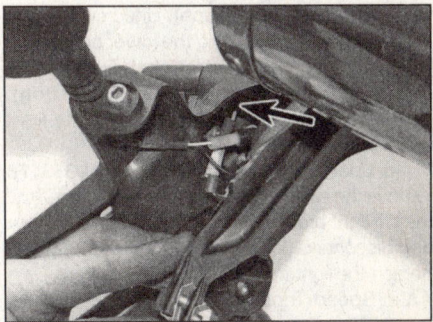

10.6b . . . and release the cover to access the bulbholder (arrowed)

11 Tail light assembly

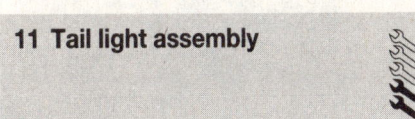

Removal

1 On Sprint ST models remove the inner cover from the rear mudguard **(see illustration 10.2a)**. Disconnect the tail light wiring connector **(see illustration)**. Unscrew the tail light bolts and draw the light out.
2 On Sprint GT models remove the side panels (see Chapter 7). Unscrew the pannier

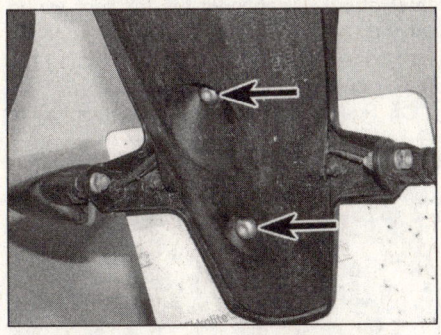

10.7a Undo the screws (arrowed)

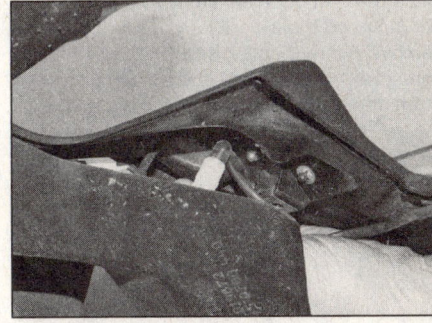

10.7b Lift the holder and remove the bulbholder

link bar bracket bolts and remove the link bar assembly **(see illustration 10.3a)**. Remove the splashguard **(see illustration 10.3b)**. Disconnect the tail light, licence

plate light and turn signal wiring connectors **(see illustration)**. Unscrew the tail light bolts and remove the nut plate **(see illustration)**. Unscrew the bolt on the underside of the

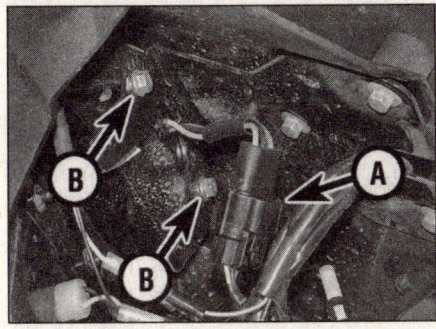

11.1 Disconnect the wiring connector (A), then unscrew the bolts (B)

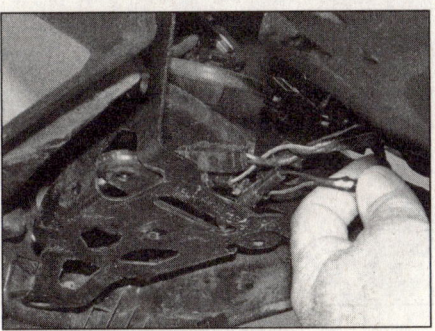

11.2a Disconnect the wiring connectors

11.2b Unscrew the bolts (arrowed)

8•18 Electrical system

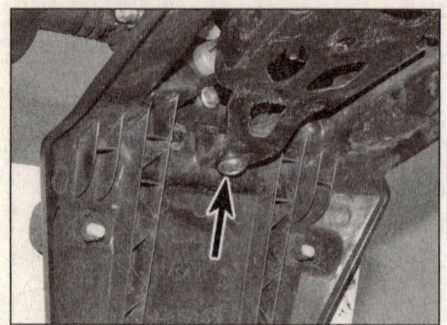

11.2c Unscrew the bolt (arrowed)

11.2d Unscrew the bolts (arrowed) on the right . . .

11.2e . . . and on the left

mudguard **(see illustration)**. Unscrew the two bolts on each side, noting the lower bolt on the right is longer **(see illustrations)**. Remove the rear mudguard assembly **(see illustration)**. Unscrew the tail light bolt and draw the light out **(see illustration)**.

3 On Speed Triple models up to VIN 333178 remove the side panels (see Chapter 7). Unscrew the tail light bracket bolts then draw the light out and disconnect the wiring connector. If required detach the light from the bracket.

4 On Speed Triple models from VIN 333179 to 461331 remove the seat (see Chapter 7). Disconnect the tail light wiring connector **(see illustration)**. Unscrew the tail light bolts and draw the light out **(see illustration)**.

5 On Speed Triple models from VIN 461332-on remove the rear cover (see Chapter 7). Undo the splash guard screw and detach the guard from the underside of the mudguard (see

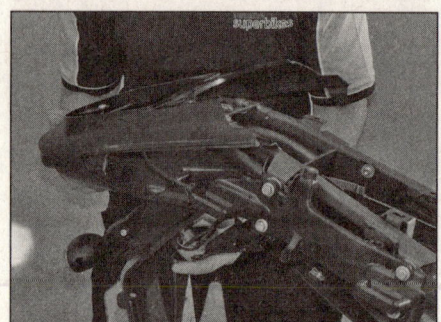

11.2f Draw the mudguard assembly off

illustration). Disconnect the tail light wiring connector **(see illustration)**. Unscrew the tail light bolts and draw the light out, noting the routing of the wiring **(see illustration)**.

6 On Tiger and Tiger SE models remove the

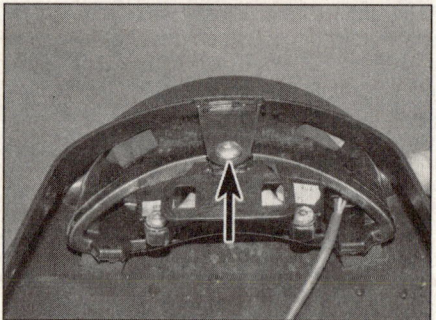

11.2g Tail light bolt (arrowed)

seat cowling (see Chapter 7). Disconnect the tail light wiring connector. Undo the seat lock screws and move the lock aside **(see illustration)**. Undo the tail light screws and draw the light out.

11.4a Disconnect the wiring connector (arrowed) . . .

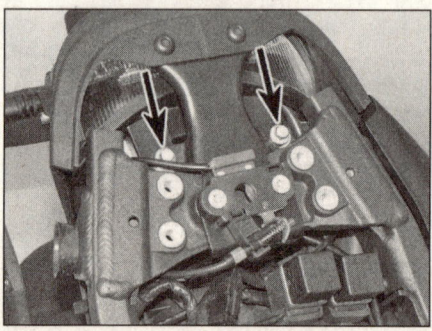

11.4b . . . then unscrew the bolts (arrowed)

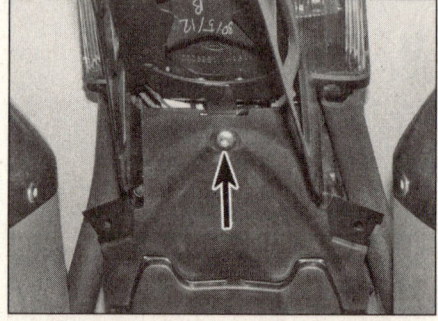

11.5a Splash guard screw (arrowed)

11.5b Disconnect the wiring connector

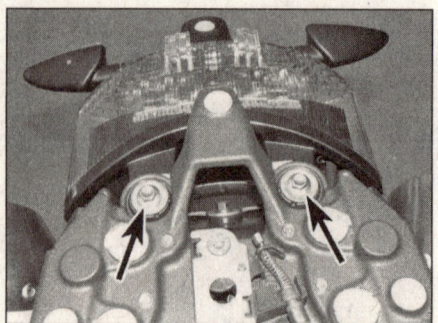

11.5c Tail light bolts (arrowed)

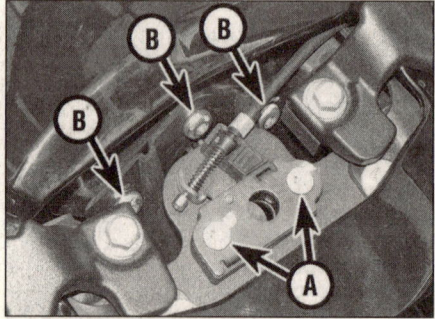

11.6 Undo the screws (A) and displace the lock, then undo the screws (B) and remove the light

Electrical system 8•19

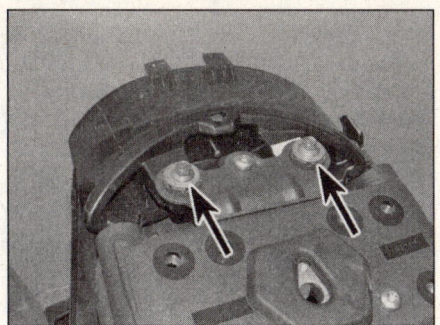

11.7a Unscrew the bolts (arrowed) . . .

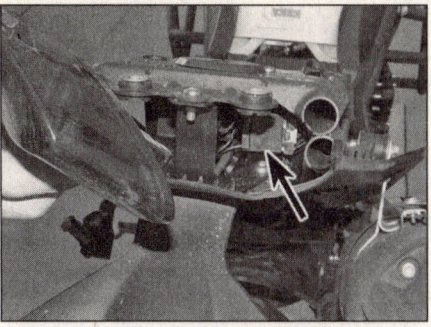

11.7b . . . displace the light and disconnect the connector (arrowed)

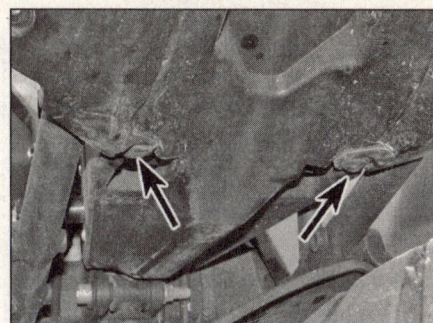

11.7c Release the trim clips (arrowed) . . .

7 On Tiger Sport models remove the seat cowling (see Chapter 7). Unscrew the tail light bolts, draw the light out and disconnect the tail light wiring connector **(see illustrations)** – if the connector is not easily accessible (depending on how the wiring has been routed), release the two trim clips on the underside of the undertray and undo the three screws on top, allowing it to be displaced, giving easy access to the connector **(see illustrations)**.

Installation

8 Installation is the reverse of removal. Check the operation of the tail light and the brake light.

12 Turn signal circuit check and relay

1 Most turn signal problems are the result of a burned out bulb or corroded socket. This is especially true when the turn signals function properly in one direction, but fail to flash in the other direction. Check the bulbs and the sockets (see Section 13) and the wiring connectors. Also, check the signal circuit fuse (see Section 5) and the switch (see Section 18).
2 If the bulbs, sockets, connectors, fuse, switch and battery are good, on all except Tiger Sport models check the turn signal relay – for access to it refer to Chapter 7, and on Sprint ST models remove the right-hand fairing side panel, on Sprint GT and Speed Triple

11.7d . . . undo the screws (arrowed) . . .

models remove the seat, and on Tiger models remove the fairing. On Tiger Sport models the relay is incorporated in the instrument cluster and no test procedures are given.
3 Disconnect the relay from its connector block **(see illustrations 16.1a to j)**. Triumph do not provide any specific test data for the relay itself, so the easiest way to test it is by substituting the suspect one with a known good one. You can however test the wiring to and from the relay as follows.
4 Check for voltage at the orange/green wire on Sprint and Speed Triple models and the yellow wire on Tiger models in the relay wiring connector with the ignition ON. Turn the ignition OFF when the check is complete. If no voltage is present, using the appropriate wiring diagram at the end of this Chapter check the wiring between the relay and the ignition switch and the fusebox. If voltage was

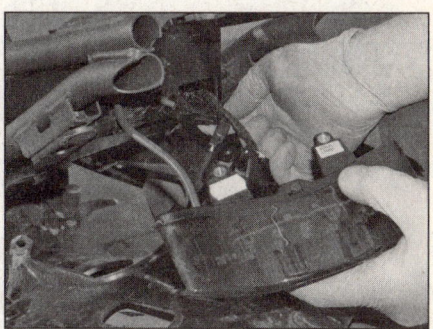

11.7e . . . and displace the undertray to get to the connector

present, on Sprint and Speed Triple models check for continuity to earth in the black wire, then on all models check for continuity in the wiring between the relay, turn signal switch and turn signal lights for continuity. If all the wiring and connectors are good, replace the relay with a new one.

13 Turn signal bulbs

Front turn signal bulbs – Sprint models

1 Undo the screws on the underside of the mirror and carefully remove the glass **(see illustrations)**.
2 Release the bulbholder by turning it anti-clockwise and withdraw it **(see illustration)**.

13.1a Undo the screws . . .

13.1b . . . and remove the mirror glass

13.2 Release the bulbholder . . .

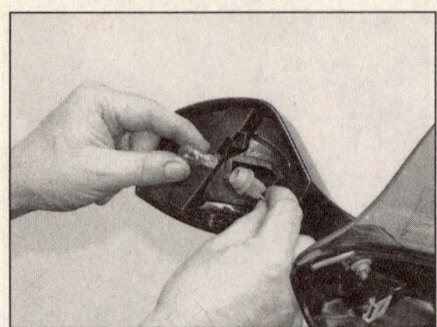

13.3 ... and remove the bulb

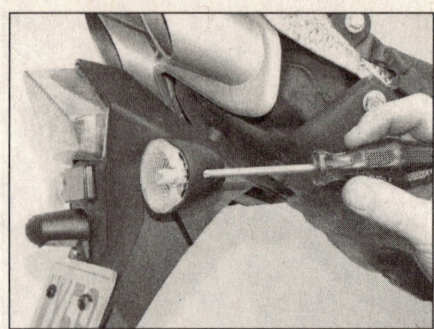

13.5 Undo the screw (which on some models is in the lens side of the turn signal) and detach the lens ...

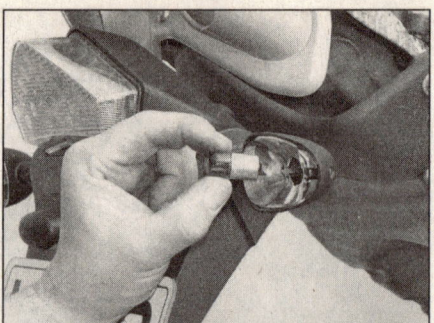

13.6 ... and remove the bulb

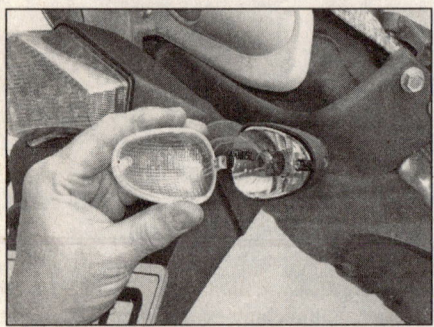

13.7 Make sure the tab locates correctly when fitting the lens

13.9a Disconnect the relevant wiring connectors (arrowed)

13.9b Left-hand turn signal bolt (arrowed)

3 Carefully pull the bulb out of the holder (see illustration). Check the socket terminals for corrosion and clean them if necessary.
4 Push the bulb in, then fit the bulbholder and turn it clockwise to lock it. Fit the mirror glass and secure it with the screws. Do not overtighten the screws as the threads could be damaged.

All other turn signal bulbs

5 Undo the turn signal lens screw and remove the lens, noting how it fits (see illustration).
6 Push the bulb into the holder and twist it anti-clockwise to remove it (see illustration). Check the socket terminals for corrosion and clean them if necessary. Line up the pins of the new bulb with the slots in the socket, then push the bulb in and turn it clockwise until it locks into place.
7 Fit the lens, making sure the tab locates correctly (see illustration). Do not overtighten the screw as the lens or threads could be damaged.

Front turn signals

8 On Sprint models, remove the mirror (see Chapter 7) – the turn signal is an integral part of it and is not available separately.
9 On 2005 to 2010 Speed Triple models (up to VIN 461331) remove the airbox (see Chapter 4). Disconnect the turn signal wiring connectors (see illustration). Unscrew the bolt and remove the turn signal, taking care not to snag the wiring (see illustration).
10 On 2011-on Speed Triple models (from VIN 461332) remove the radiator cowl (see Chapter 7). Unscrew the nut on the inside, counter holding the bolt on the outside, and remove the turn signal, taking care not to snag the wiring (see illustration).
11 On Tiger and Tiger SE models, remove the upper fairing trim panel (see Chapter 7). Unscrew the nut on the inside, counter holding the bolt on the outside, then withdraw the bolt and remove the turn signal, taking care not to snag the wiring (see illustration).
12 On Tiger Sport models, remove the fairing side panel (see Chapter 7). Slacken the panel screw on the inside to release the wire (see illustration). Unscrew the turn

13.10 Turn signal nut/bolt (arrowed)

13.11 Unscrew the nut (arrowed), withdraw the bolt and remove the turn signal

13.12a Slacken the screw (arrowed) ...

Electrical system 8•21

13.12b ... then unscrew the bolt (arrowed)

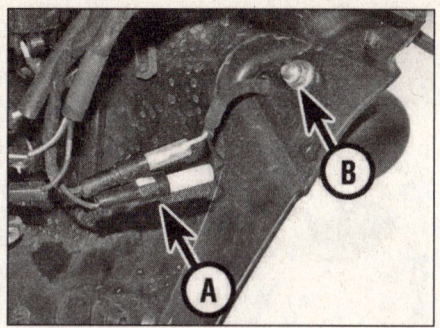
13.14 Disconnect the relevant wiring connectors (A), then unscrew the nut (B), withdraw the bolt and remove the turn signal

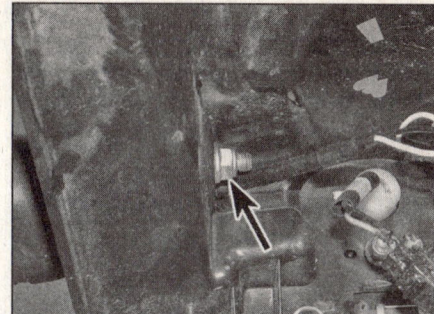
13.15 Turn signal nut (arrowed)

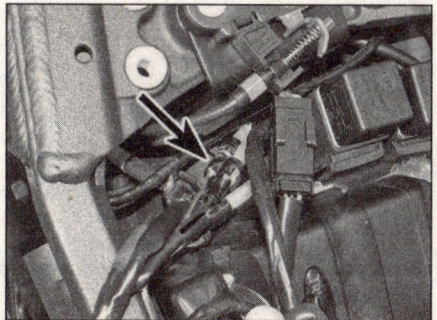
13.16a Disconnect the relevant wiring connectors (arrowed)

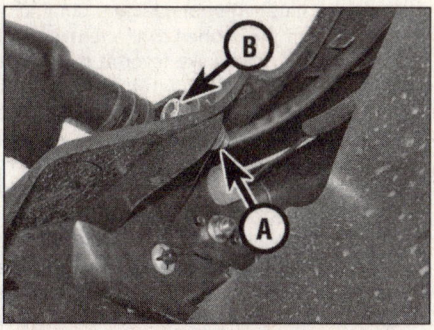
13.16b Unscrew the nut (A), withdraw the bolt (B) and remove the turn signal

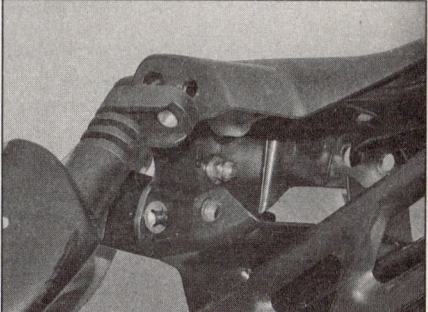
13.17 Lift the holder, feed the wiring down and remove the turn signal

signal bolt, then remove the turn signal, taking care not to snag the wiring **(see illustration)**.

13 Installation is the reverse of removal. Make sure the wiring is correctly routed and securely connected. Check the operation of the turn signals.

Rear turn signals

14 On Sprint ST models remove the inner cover from the rear mudguard **(see illustration 10.2a)**. Disconnect the turn signal wiring connectors **(see illustration)**. Unscrew the nut on the inside, counter holding the bolt on the outside, then withdraw the bolt and remove the turn signal, taking care not to snag the wiring.

15 On Sprint GT models unscrew the pannier link bar bracket bolts and remove the link bar assembly **(see illustration 10.3a)**. Remove the splash guard **(see illustration 10.3b)**. Disconnect the turn signal wiring connectors **(see illustration 11.2a)**. Unscrew the nut on the inside, counter holding the bolt on the outside, then withdraw the bolt and remove the turn signal, taking care not to snag the wiring.

16 On 2005 to 2010 Speed Triple models (up to VIN 461331) remove the seat (see Chapter 7). Disconnect the turn signal wiring connectors **(see illustration)**. Undo the four rearmost screws securing the inner cover to the rear mudguard, then carefully pull it

away – take care to release the tabs from the side panels or they could break **(see illustration 10.4a)**. Unscrew the nut on the inside, counter holding the bolt on the outside, then withdraw the bolt and remove the turn signal, taking care not to snag the wiring **(see illustration)**.

17 On 2011-on Speed Triple models (from VIN 461332) undo the splash guard screw and detach it from the underside of the mudguard **(see illustration 11.5a)**. Disconnect the turn signal wiring connectors **(see illustration 11.5b)**. Unscrew both turn signal bolts **(see illustration 10.5a)**. Lift the license plate light/turn signal holder so you can feed the wiring down, then remove the turn signal, taking care not to snag the wiring **(see illustration)**.

18 On Tiger models except Sport remove the licence plate, then undo the screws securing the inner cover to the rear mudguard, then carefully pull it away **(see illustration 10.6a)**. Disconnect the turn signal wiring connectors. Unscrew the nut on the inside, counter holding the bolt on the outside, then withdraw the bolt and remove the turn signal, taking care not to snag the wiring **(see illustration)**.

19 On Tiger Sport models undo the screws on the rear mudguard **(see illustration 10.7a)**. Carefully lift the licence plate holder up off the mudguard and disconnect the turn signal wiring connectors **(see illustration)**. Unscrew the turn signal nut, counter holding the bolt on the outside, then remove the turn

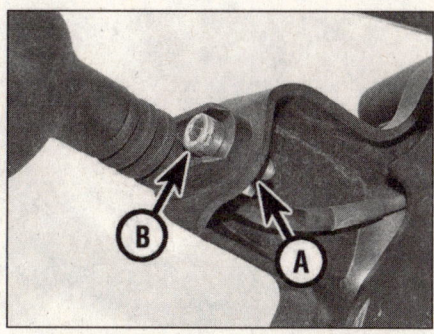
13.18 Unscrew the nut (A), withdraw the bolt (B) and remove the turn signal

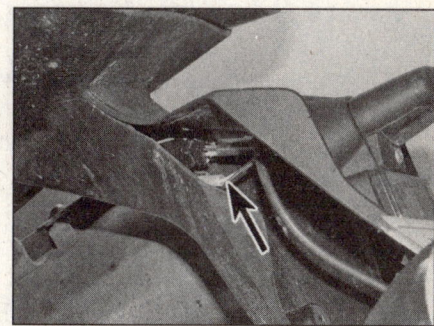
13.19a Disconnect the wiring connectors (arrowed) ...

13.19b ... then unscrew the nut (arrowed)

14.2a Front brake light switch wiring connectors (arrowed) – Sprint, 2005 to 2007 Speed Triple, and Tiger

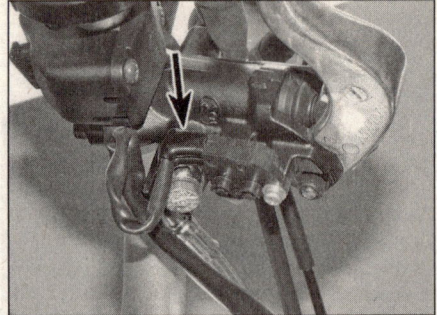

14.2b Front brake light switch wiring connectors (arrowed) – 2008-on Speed Triple

signal, taking care not to snag the wiring **(see illustration)**.

20 Installation is the reverse of removal. Make sure the wiring is correctly routed and securely connected. Check the operation of the turn signals.

14 Brake light switches

Circuit check

1 Before checking the switches, check the brake light circuit (see Section 6).
2 The front brake light switch is mounted on the underside of the brake master cylinder. Disconnect the wiring connectors from the switch **(see illustrations)**. Using a continuity tester, connect the probes to the terminals of the switch. With the brake lever at rest, there should be no continuity. With the brake lever applied, there should be continuity. If the switch does not behave as described, replace it with a new one.
3 The rear brake light switch is mounted on the right-hand side, above the brake pedal. On Sprint models remove the fuel tank (see Chapter 4). On Sprint, 2011-on Speed Triple (from VIN 461332) and Tiger models, pull the rubber boot off the switch and disconnect the wiring connectors **(see illustrations)**. On Speed Triple models up to VIN 461331, trace the wiring from the switch and disconnect it at the connector. Using a continuity tester, connect the probes to the terminals on the switch or the wiring connector, according to model. With the brake pedal at rest, there should be no continuity. With the brake pedal applied, there should be continuity. If the switch does not behave as described, replace it with a new one.
4 If the switches are good, check for voltage at one of the connectors (it could be either one) for the front brake switch, and at the orange/green wire terminal in the connector for the rear brake switch, with the ignition switch ON – there should be battery voltage. If there's no voltage present, check the wiring between the switch and the ignition switch (refer to Section 2 at the beginning of this chapter and the *Wiring Diagrams* at the end of it).

Switch renewal

Front brake light switch

5 The switch is mounted on the underside of the brake master cylinder. Disconnect the wiring connectors from the switch **(see illustration 14.2a or b)**.
6 Remove the single screw securing the switch to the bottom of the master cylinder and remove the switch **(see illustration)**.
7 Installation is the reverse of removal. The switch isn't adjustable.

Rear brake light switch – Sprint, Tiger, 2011-on Speed Triple models from VIN 461332-on

Note: *On models with ABS, before removing the brake light switch, which involves detaching the brake pipe from the master cylinder, bear in mind that the system must be bled on completion of work, and although this is done initially in the same way as models without ABS, to complete the procedure effectively the Triumph Diagnostic tool must be used to open and close the solenoids within the ABS modulator, and this can only be carried out by a dealer. The bike should be transported, not ridden, to the dealer.*

8 On Sprint and Tiger models the rear brake light switch is mounted on the top of the rear master cylinder. On Speed Triple models the switch is in a block in the brake hose – remove the seat for best access. Pull the rubber boot off the switch and disconnect the wiring connectors **(see illustration 14.3a, b or c)**.

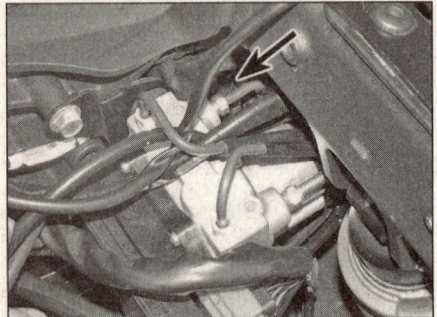

14.3a On Sprint models lift the boot (arrowed) and disconnect the wiring connector

14.3b Rear brake light switch (arrowed) – Speed Triple

14.3c On Tiger models lift the boot and disconnect the wiring connector (arrowed)

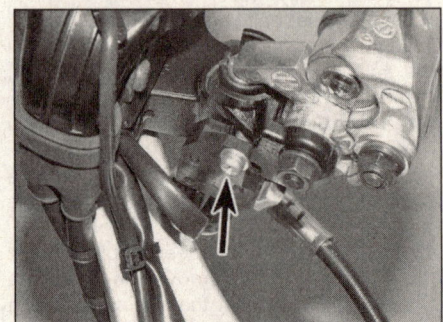

14.6 Front brake light switch screw (arrowed)

Electrical system 8•23

9 On Sprint and Tiger models without ABS, have some rag handy to catch any fluid spills, then unscrew the brake light switch from the master cylinder. Discard the two brake pipe sealing washers as they must be replaced with new ones. Wrap the end of the pipe in clingfilm to prevent excessive loss of brake fluid, fluid spills and system contamination.

10 On Sprint and Tiger models with ABS refer to Chapter 6 and remove the master cylinder, then remove the brake light switch from it as described.

11 On Speed Triple models unscrew the brake light switch from the block.

12 Installation is the reverse of removal. On Sprint and Tiger models use new sealing washers on each side of the brake pipe union and tighten the switch to the torque setting specified at the beginning of the Chapter. On Speed Triple models use a new sealing washer and tighten the switch to the specified torque. Connect the wiring connector, then fit the rubber boot. Bleed the rear brake system as described in Chapter 6.

Rear brake light switch – 2005 to 2010 Speed Triple (up to VIN 461331)

13 The rear brake light switch is mounted on the inside of the right-hand footrest bracket. Trace the wiring from the switch and disconnect it at the connector. Free the wiring from any clips or ties and feed it through to the switch. Detach the lower end of the switch spring from the brake pedal **(see illustration)**. Unscrew and remove the switch from the adjuster nut in the bracket **(see illustration)**.

14 Installation is the reverse of removal. Make sure the brake light is activated just before the rear brake pedal takes effect. If adjustment is necessary, hold the switch and turn the adjuster nut on the switch body until the brake light is activated when required **(see illustration 14.13b)**.

15 Instrument cluster removal and installation

Check

1 Specific test data for the instruments is not available. Refer below for access to the wiring connector and check that it is securely connected to the instrument cluster, and also refer to the relevant Section of this Chapter or to other Chapters and check that the other end of the wiring is securely connected to its source (i.e. neutral switch, oil pressure switch, fuel level sender, coolant temperature sender etc). Check all wires for continuity from pin to pin, referring to electrical system fault finding at the beginning of the Chapter and to the wiring diagrams at the end of it.

2 Check that all earth wires have a good connection. If all the wiring is good, it is possible that there are faults in the switches or sensors or the electronic control module (ECM) of the engine management system which provide much of the information to the instruments. Refer to Chapter 4 for details. If all checks point at faulty instruments rather than wiring or the engine management system, take the instrument cluster to a Triumph dealer for further assessment.

3 All of the warning and instrument lights are LEDs. If the cause of any problem (i.e. neutral light not coming on) cannot be traced it is possible the LED has failed, in which case a new instrument cluster must be fitted.

Removal

4 On Sprint models remove the windshield and its trim panel (see Chapter 7). Remove the clips securing the instrument cluster and lift it off the bracket, noting how the pegs locate in the grommets, then pull the rubber boot back and disconnect the wiring connector **(see illustrations)**.

5 On Speed Triple models, either remove the cover from the back of the instrument cluster, or remove the cowling, according to model **(see illustration)**. Pull back the rubber boot and disconnect the wiring connector **(see illustration)**. Unscrew the bolt securing the cluster to the bracket and lift it off, noting how the pegs locate in the grommets.

6 On Tiger models remove the fairing (see Chapter 7). Pull the rubber boot back and disconnect the wiring connector(s) **(see**

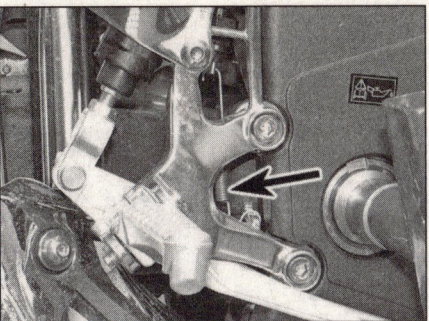

14.13a Unhook the spring (arrowed) . . .

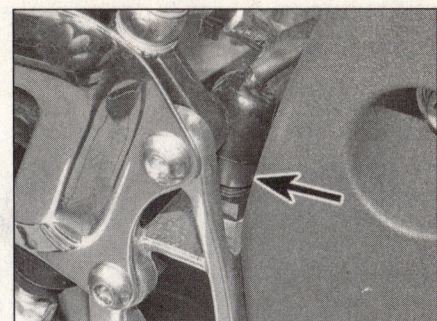

14.13b . . . then unscrew the switch (arrowed)

15.4a Remove the clips . . .

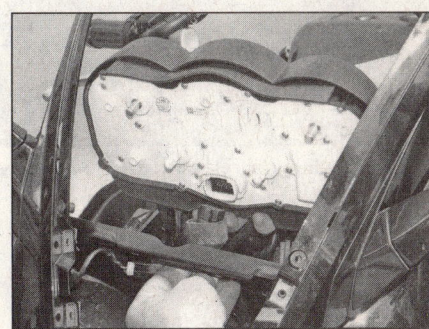

15.4b . . . displace the instruments and disconnect the wiring connector

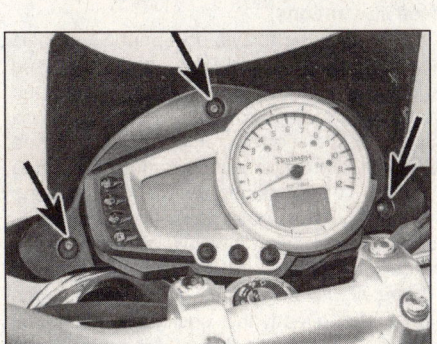

15.5a Where fitted undo the screws (arrowed – later models have 4) and remove the cowling . . .

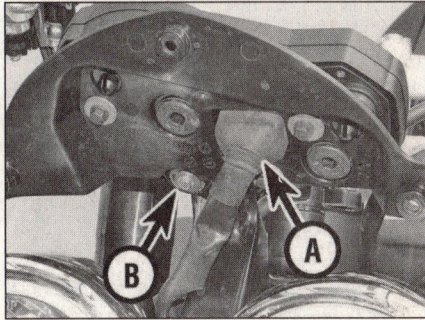

15.5b . . . disconnect the wiring connector (A) then unscrew the bolt (B) and remove the instruments

8•24 Electrical system

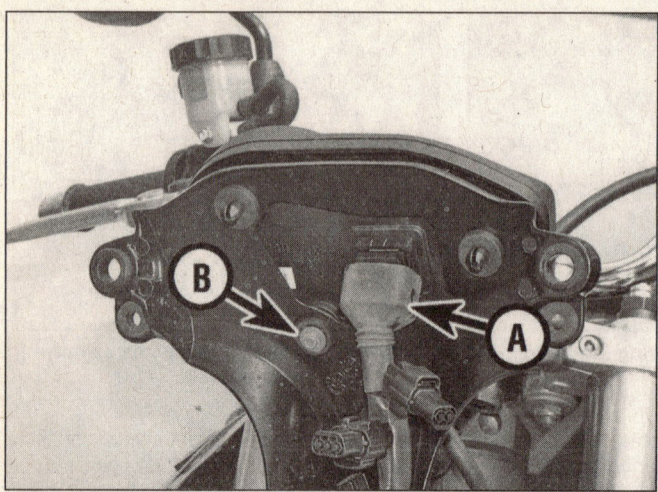

15.6 Disconnect the wiring connector (A) then unscrew the bolt (B) and remove the instruments

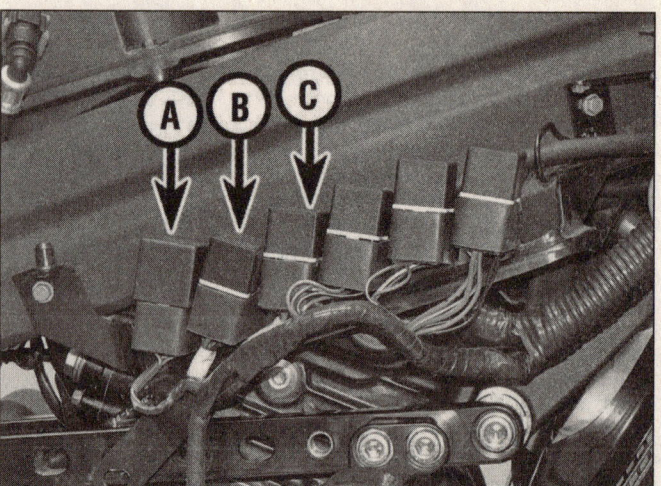

16.1a Turn signal relay (A), headlight relay (B), starter relay (C) – Sprint ST models

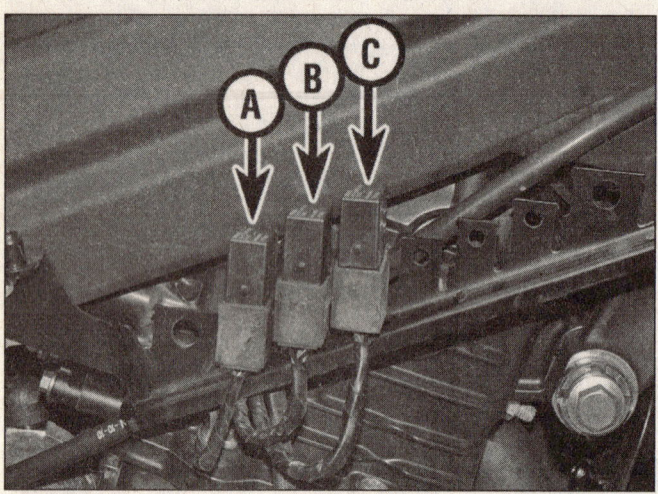

16.1b Cooling fan relay (A), fuel pump relay (B), headlight relay (C) – Sprint GT

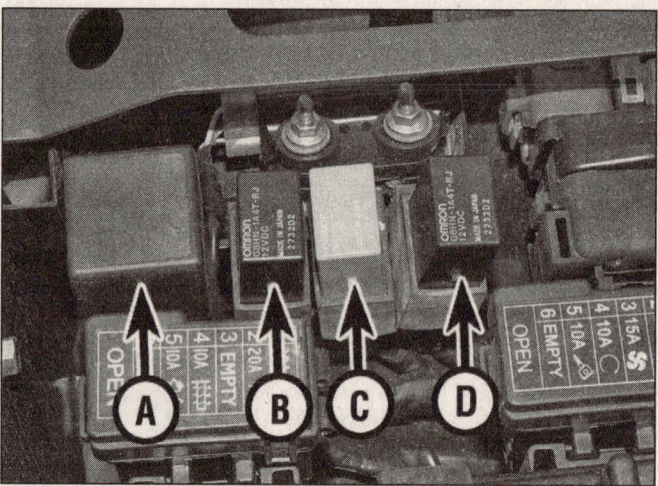

16.1c Turn signal relay (A), starter relay (B), fuel pump relay (C), EMS relay (D) – Sprint GT

illustration). Unscrew the bolt and lift the instrument cluster off the bracket, noting how the pegs locate in the grommets.

Installation

7 Installation is the reverse of removal. Check the rubber grommets for cracks and deterioration and replace them with new ones if necessary. Make sure the wiring connector is secure.

16 Relays

Note: *Refer to the Wiring Diagrams at the end of the Chapter for relay terminal identification.*
1 The following relays are fitted: turn signal relay (see Section 12), headlight relay (Sprint, Speed Triple and Tiger Sport models only – see Step 4), main beam relay (Sprint GT only – see Step 4), starter relay (see Step 5), cooling fan relay (see Chapter 3), engine management system (EMS) relay (see Chapter 4), fuel pump relay (see Chapter 4) **(see illustrations)**.
2 To access the relays, on Sprint ST models remove the right-hand fairing side panel (see Chapter 7), on Sprint GT models remove the right-hand fairing side panel or the seat, on Speed Triple models remove the seat (see Chapter 7), on Tiger models remove the fairing to access the turn signal relay, and remove the seat to access all other relays (see Chapter 7).
3 Before removing a relay disconnect the battery negative (-) terminal (see Section 3). The relays have terminals on their underside which plug directly into sockets – simply pull the relay out of its socket, and fit the new one in its place.
4 Each terminal on a headlight relay has a number, either marked next to the terminal

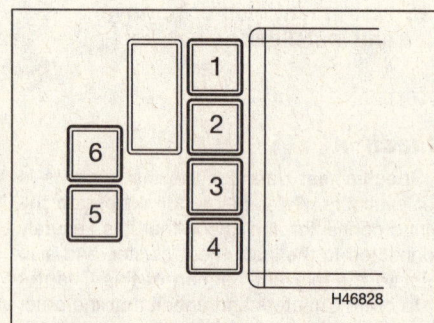

16.1d Relay identification – 2005 to 2007 Speed Triple models

1 Starter relay
2 Headlight relay
3 Engine management system (EMS) relay
4 Turn signal relay
5 Cooling fan relay
6 Fuel pump relay

Electrical system 8•25

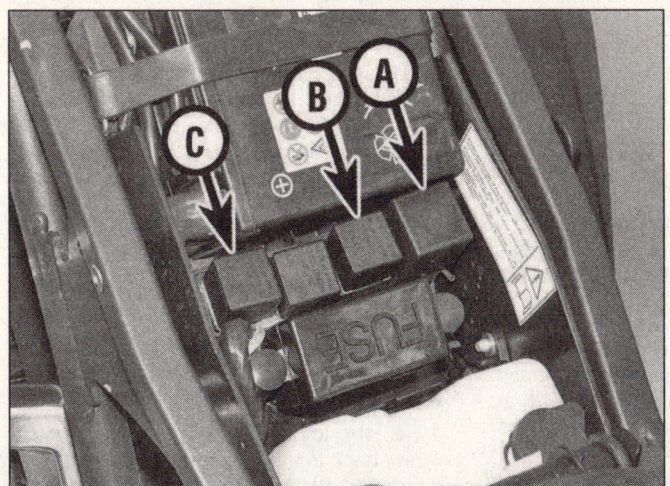

16.1e Starter relay (A), headlight relay (B), turn signal relay (C) – 2008 to 2010 Speed Triple (up to VIN 461331)

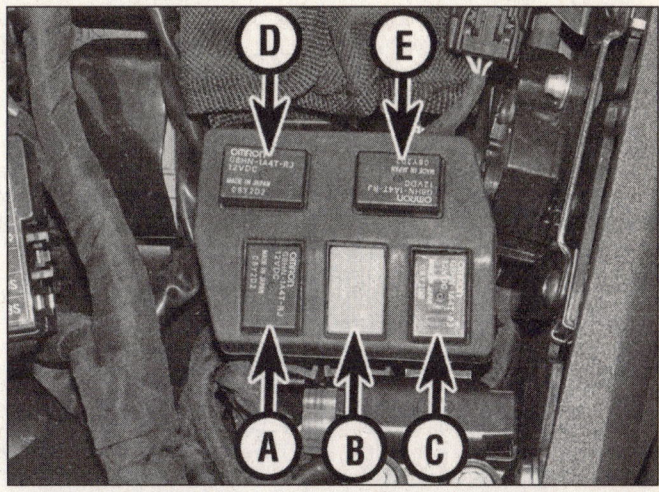

16.1f Headlight relay (A), starter relay (B), EMS relay (C), fuel pump relay (D), cooling fan relay (E) – Speed Triple from VIN 461332

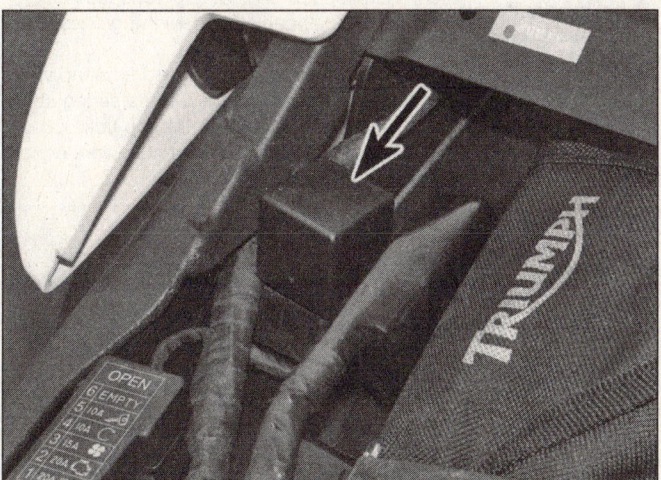

16.1g Turn signal relay (arrowed) – Speed Triple from VIN 461332

16.1h Starter relay (arrowed) – Tiger models

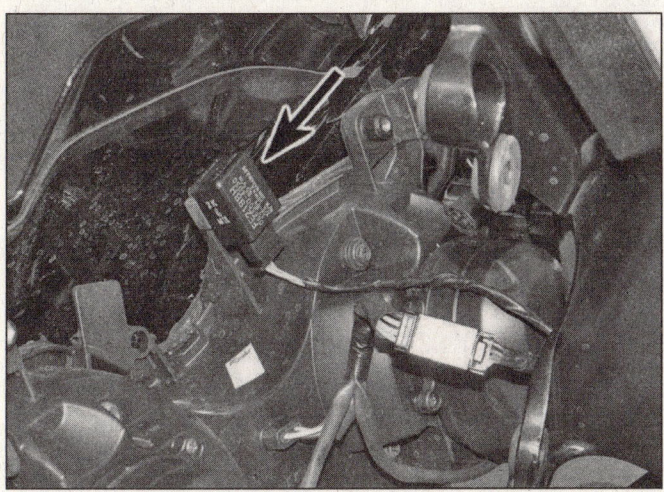

16.1i Turn signal relay (arrowed) – Tiger models

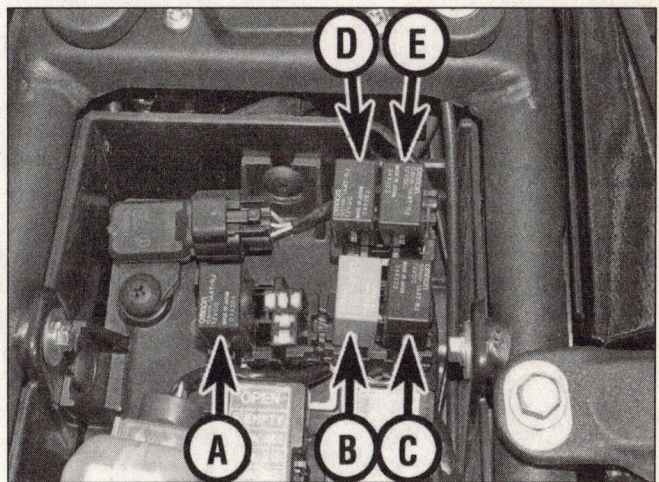

16.1j Headlight relay (A), starter relay (B), fuel pump relay (C), cooling fan relay (D), EMS relay (E) – Tiger Sport

on the underside of the relay, or that can be identified using the relevant wiring diagram at the end of this Chapter by matching the wire colours marked on the diagram to the wires themselves in the relay socket and their applicable terminals on the relay, according to model. On some models the terminals are numbered 1, 2, 3 and 5, on others they are numbered 1, 4, 6 and 8. Identify the terminal numbers used, then test the relay as follows: connect a continuity tester or a multimeter set to the ohms x 1 scale between either the No. 3 and No. 5 terminals, or between the No. 1 and No. 8 terminals, according to model – there should be no continuity or infinite resistance. If there is continuity or zero resistance replace the relay with a new one. Leaving the tester or meter connected, connect the positive (+) terminal of a fully-charged 12 volt battery to either the No. 1 or to the No. 6 terminal on the relay, and the negative (–) terminal to either the No. 2 or to the No. 4 terminal on the relay. At this point the relay should be heard to click and there should be continuity or zero resistance shown on the tester or meter. If this is the case the relay is proved good. If the relay does not click when battery voltage is applied and the tester or meter indicates no continuity or infinite resistance, the relay is faulty and must be replaced with a new one.

5 The starter relay performs a load relief function for the headlight circuit. In its normal position, the relay completes the power supply circuit to the headlight relay on Sprint and Speed Triple models and to the headlight and heated grips on Tiger models. When the starter button is pressed, the relay switches its supply from the headlight circuit to the starter relay circuit, thus enabling full battery power to be available for operation of the starter motor. Testing of the starter relay can be carried out as follows. Each terminal on the starter relay has a number, either marked next to the terminal on the underside of the relay, or that can be identified using the relevant wiring diagram at the end of this Chapter by matching the wire colours marked on the diagram to the wires themselves in the relay socket and their applicable terminals on the relay, according to model. On some models the terminals are numbered 1, 2, 3, 4 and 5, on others they are numbered 1, 4, 5, 6 and 8. Identify the terminal numbers used, then test the relay as follows: connect a continuity tester or a multimeter set to the ohms x 1 scale between either the No. 3 and No. 4 terminals, or between the No. 1 and No. 5 terminals, according to model – there should be no continuity or infinite resistance. If there is continuity or zero resistance replace the relay with a new one. Now transfer the tester or meter to the No. 3 and 5 or 1 and 8 terminals – there should be no continuity. Leave the tester or meter connected, then connect the positive (+) terminal of a fully-charged 12 volt battery to either the No. 1 or to the No. 6 terminal on the relay, and the negative (–) terminal to either the No. 2 or to the No. 4 terminal on the relay. At this point the relay should be heard to click and there should be continuity or zero resistance shown on the tester or meter. If this is the case the relay is proved good. If the relay does not click when battery voltage is applied and the tester or meter indicates no continuity or infinite resistance, the relay is faulty and must be replaced with a new one.

17 Ignition switch

Warning: *To prevent the risk of short circuits, remove the seat(s) and disconnect the battery negative (–ve) lead before making any ignition switch checks.*

Check

1 Trace the ignition switch wiring back from the base of the switch and disconnect it at the connector – on Sprint models remove the fairing (see Chapter 7), on Speed Triple models remove the airbox (see Chapter 4), and on Tiger models remove the fairing side panel (see Chapter 7) and airbox if required (see Chapter 4), for access. Make the checks on the switch side of the connector.

2 Using an ohmmeter or a continuity tester, check the continuity of the connector terminal pairs (see the *Wiring Diagrams* at the end of this Chapter). Continuity should exist between the terminals connected by a solid line on the diagram when the switch key is turned to the indicated position.

3 If the switch fails any of the tests, replace it with a new one.

Removal

4 Referring to Step 1, trace the ignition switch wiring back from the base of the switch and disconnect it at the connector. Feed the wiring back to the switch, freeing it from all clips and ties and noting its correct routing.

5 On Speed Triple and Tiger models displace the handlebars from the top yoke (see Chapter 5). Free all cables and wiring guides from the top yoke.

6 Slacken the fork clamp bolts in the top yoke **(see illustration)**. Unscrew the steering stem nut **(see illustration)**. Lift the top yoke up off the steering stem and move it to a work bench **(see illustration)**.

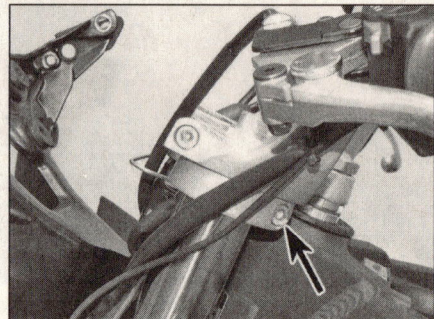

17.6a Slacken the fork clamp bolt (arrowed) on each side – Sprint shown

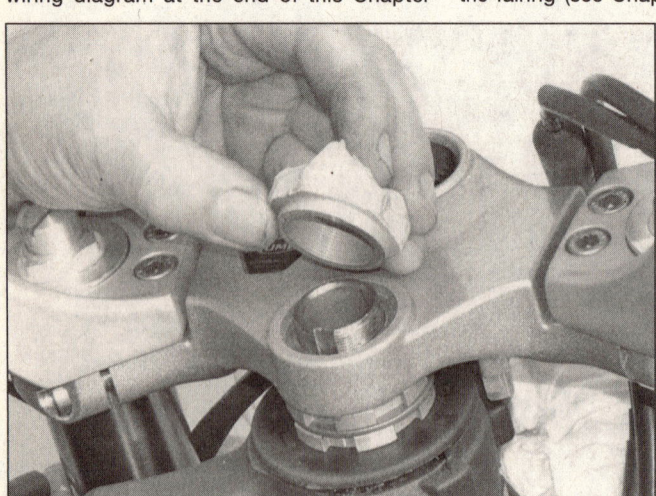

17.6b Unscrew the steering stem nut . . .

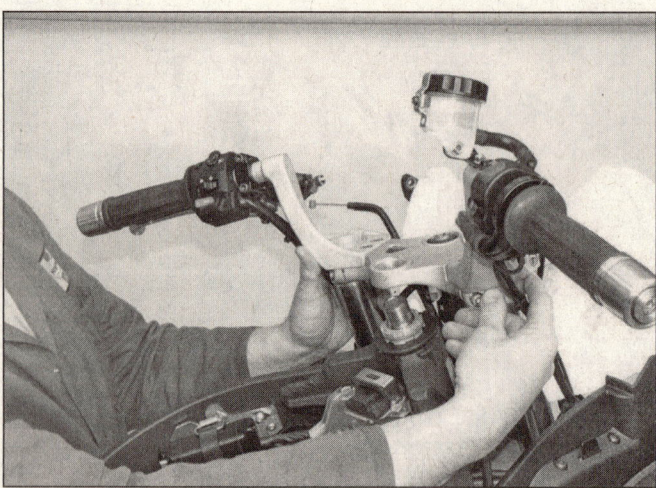

17.6c . . . and draw the yoke up off the forks

Electrical system 8•27

17.7 Ignition switch bolts (arrowed)

18.8a Right-hand switch housing screws (arrowed)

7 Two shear-head bolts mount the ignition switch to the underside of the top yoke **(see illustration)**. The heads of the bolts must be driven round using a suitable punch or drift, or drilled off, before the switch can be removed. Mount the yoke in a vice equipped with soft jaws and padded out with rags to do this. Remove the bolts and withdraw the switch from the top yoke.

Installation

8 Installation is the reverse of removal. Obtain new shear-head bolts and tighten them until their heads shear off. Tighten the steering stem nut, the fork clamp bolts and the handlebar bolts to the torque settings specified at the beginning of Chapter 5, and refer to Sections 5 and 9 in that Chapter for procedural details and illustrations. Make sure all wiring and cables are correctly routed.

18 Handlebar switches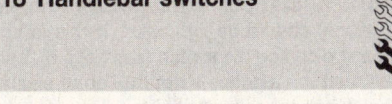

1 Most problems are caused by dirty or corroded contacts, but wear and breakage of internal parts is a possibility that should not be overlooked. If breakage does occur, the entire switch and related wiring harness will have to be replaced with a new one, as individual parts are not available.
2 The switches can be checked for continuity using an ohmmeter or a continuity test light (see Section 2).
3 Trace the wiring back from the switch and disconnect it at the connector – on Sprint models remove the fairing (see Chapter 7), on Speed Triple models remove the airbox (see Chapter 4), and on Tiger models remove the fairing side panel (see Chapter 7) and

airbox if required (see Chapter 4), for access. Make the checks on the switch side of the connector.
4 Check for continuity between the terminals of the switch harness with the switch in the various positions (i.e. switch off – no continuity, switch on – continuity) – see the *Wiring Diagrams* at the end of this Chapter.
5 If the continuity check indicates a problem exists, split the switch housing (see Step 8) and spray the switch contacts with electrical contact cleaner. If they are accessible, the contacts can be scraped clean with a knife or polished with crocus cloth. If switch components are damaged or broken, it should be obvious when the switch is disassembled.

Removal

6 If the switch is to be removed from the bike, rather than just displaced from the handlebar, trace the wiring back from the switch and disconnect it at the connector – on Sprint models remove the fairing (see Chapter 7), on Speed Triple models remove the airbox (see Chapter 4), and on Tiger models remove the fairing side panel (see Chapter 7) and airbox if required (see Chapter 4), for access. Feed the wiring back to the switch, freeing it from all clips and ties and noting its correct routing.
7 When removing the right-hand switch disconnect the wiring connectors from the front brake light switch **(see illustration 14.2a or b)**.
8 Unscrew the handlebar switch screws (either on the back or the underside of the switch) and free the switch from the handlebar by separating the halves **(see illustrations)**.

Installation

9 Installation is the reverse of removal. Where present make sure the locating pin in the switch housing locates in the hole in the

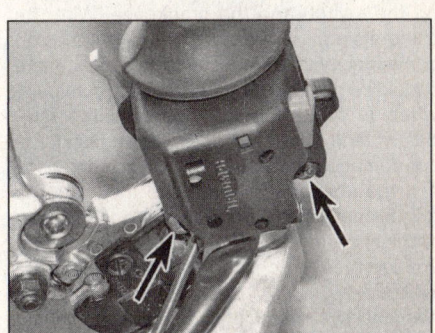

18.8b Left-hand switch housing screws (arrowed)

handlebar. Make sure the wiring connectors are correctly routed and securely connected.

19 Neutral switch

Check

1 The switch is located on the left-hand side of the engine just below the front sprocket cover. Disconnect the wiring connector from the switch **(see illustration)**.

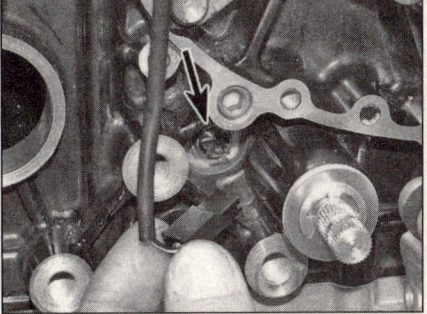

19.1 Disconnect the wiring connector from the switch (arrowed)

8•28 Electrical system

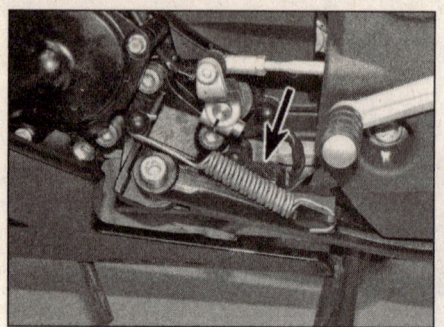

20.1 Sidestand switch (arrowed)

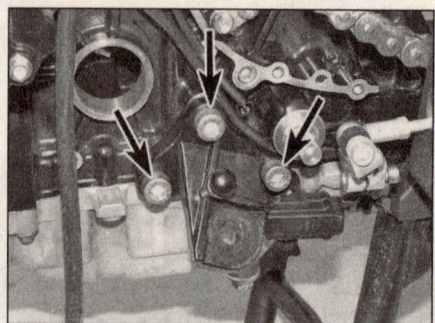

20.8 Unscrew the bolts (arrowed) and remove the bracket . . .

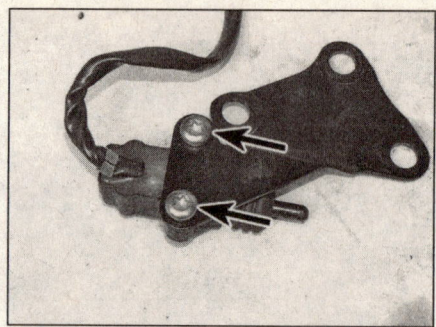

20.9 . . . then undo the screws (arrowed) and remove the switch

2 With the connector disconnected and the ignition switched ON, the neutral light should be out. If not, the wire between the connector and instrument cluster must be earthed (grounded) at some point.

3 Check for continuity between the terminal on the switch and the crankcase. With the transmission in neutral, there should be continuity. With the transmission in gear, there should be no continuity. If there is no continuity when in neutral, remove the switch (see below), and check that the contact plunger is not damaged or seized in the switch body.

4 If the continuity tests prove the switch is good, check for voltage (ignition ON) at the terminal on the wiring connector. If there's no voltage present, check the wire between the switch and the ECM for continuity, referring to electrical system fault finding at the beginning of the Chapter and to the wiring diagrams at the end of it.

Removal

5 The switch is on the left-hand side of the engine just below the front sprocket cover. Drain the engine oil (see Chapter 1).

6 Disconnect the wiring connector from the switch **(see illustration 19.1)**.

7 Unscrew the switch and withdraw it from the casing. Discard the sealing washer as a new one should be used.

Installation

8 Install the switch using a new sealing washer and tighten it to the torque setting specified at the beginning of the Chapter.

9 Connect the wiring connector. Check the operation of the neutral light. Fill the engine with the correct quantity of oil (see Chapter 1 and *Pre-ride checks*).

20 Sidestand switch

Check

1 The sidestand switch is mounted on the sidestand bracket **(see illustration)**. The switch is part of the safety circuit which stops the engine running if the transmission is put into gear whilst the sidestand is down. Before checking the electrical circuit, check the starter circuit fuse (see Section 5).

2 Trace the wiring from the switch and disconnect it at the connector, removing the fairing side panel or fuel tank as required according to model.

3 Check the operation of the switch using an ohmmeter or continuity test light. Connect the meter probes to the terminals on the switch side of the connector. With the sidestand up there should be continuity (zero resistance) between the terminals, and with the stand down there should be no continuity (infinite resistance).

4 If the switch does not perform as expected, it is defective and must be replaced with a new one.

5 If the switch is good, check the other components in the starter circuit as described in the relevant sections of this Chapter. If all components are good, check the wiring between the various components, referring to Section 2 at the beginning of this Chapter and to the wiring diagrams at the end of it.

Removal and installation

6 Refer to Chapter 3 and unscrew the water pump mounting bolts, then draw the pump out of the engine far enough to get access to the sidestand bracket bolts – there is no need to drain the cooling system or disconnect any hoses, but if the bike is on its sidestand you must drain the engine oil (see Chapter 1). If preferred, drain the cooling system and remove the pump (see Chapters 1 and 3).

7 Trace the wiring from the switch and disconnect it at the connector, removing the fairing side panel or fuel tank as required according to model. Feed the wiring down, freeing it from any clips and ties and noting its routing.

8 Unscrew the bolts securing the sidestand bracket and remove the bracket and switch plate, taking care not to snag the wiring connector as you draw it through **(see illustration)**.

9 Undo the screws securing the switch and remove it, noting how it fits **(see illustration)**.

10 Fit the new switch and tighten the screws. Install the switch plate and sidestand assembly and tighten the bracket bolts to the torque setting specified at the beginning of the Chapter.

11 Feed the wiring up to the connector and reconnect it. Check the operation of the switch.

12 Install the water pump and refill the cooling system and engine oil as required according to removal procedure, referring to Chapters 3 and 1.

21 Clutch switch

Check

1 The clutch switch is mounted in the clutch lever bracket. The switch is part of the safety circuit which prevents or stops the engine running if the transmission is in gear whilst the sidestand is down, and prevents the engine from starting unless the transmission is in neutral, the sidestand is up and the clutch lever is pulled in.

2 To check the switch, trace the wiring from it and disconnect it at the connector. Connect the probes of an ohmmeter or a continuity tester to the two terminals on the switch side of the connector. With the clutch lever pulled in, continuity should be indicated. With the clutch lever out, no continuity (infinite resistance) should be indicated. If this is not the case displace the switch (see Step 6), and check that the plunger is not broken or seized in the switch **(see illustration)**.

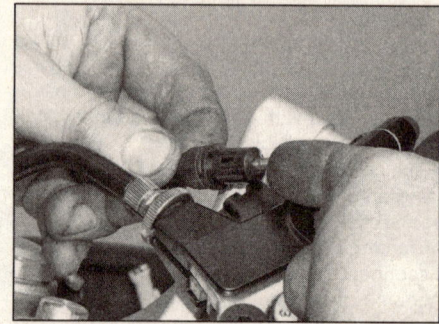

21.2 Make sure the plunger is not seized or broken

Electrical system 8•29

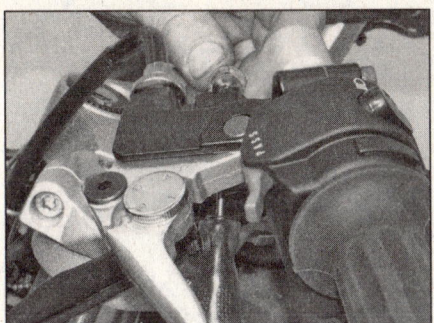

21.6 Release the clip and withdraw the switch

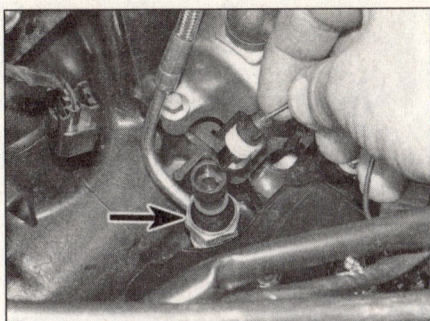

22.2 Oil pressure switch (arrowed)

22.7 Unscrew the switch and remove the sealing washers (arrowed)

3 If the switch is good, turn the ignition on and check that there is voltage at the black wire terminal on the loom side of the connector, and check that there is continuity to earth (ground) in the black/yellow wire. If not check the wiring. Otherwise, check the other components in the starter circuit as described in the relevant sections of this Chapter, and check the wiring between the various components (see the *Wiring Diagrams* at the end of this Chapter).

Renewal

4 The clutch switch is mounted in the clutch lever bracket.
5 Trace the wiring from the switch and disconnect it at the connector. Feed the wiring back to the switch, releasing it from any clips or ties and noting its routing.
6 Use a small screwdriver to release the clip on the underside of the switch and pull it out of the clutch lever bracket **(see illustration)**.
7 Installation is the reverse of removal.

22 Oil pressure switch

Check

1 The oil pressure warning light should come on when the ignition switch is turned ON and extinguish a few seconds after the engine is started. If the oil pressure warning light comes on whilst the engine is running, stop the engine immediately and carry out an oil level check (see *Pre-ride checks*), and if the level is correct, an oil pressure check (see Chapter 2).
2 The oil pressure switch is screwed into the top of the crankcase on the right-hand side **(see illustration)**. Disconnect the wiring connector from the switch – remove the right-hand fairing side panel (see Chapter 7) and/or the fuel tank (see Chapter 4) as required to access the wiring connector according to model. With the ignition switched ON, and using an auxiliary piece of wire fitted against the connector terminal, earth (ground) the wire on the crankcase and check that the warning light comes on. If the light comes on, the switch is proven defective and must be replaced with a new one.

3 If the light still does not come on, check for voltage at the wire terminal. If there is no voltage present, check the wiring between the switch and the instrument cluster for continuity, referring to Section 2 at the beginning of the Chapter and to the wiring diagrams at the end of it.
4 If the warning light comes on whilst the engine is running, yet the oil pressure is satisfactory, remove the wire from the oil pressure switch. With the wire detached and the ignition switched ON the light should be out. If it is illuminated, the wire between the switch and instrument cluster must be earthed (grounded) at some point. If the wiring is good, the switch must be assumed faulty and be replaced with a new one.

Removal

5 The oil pressure switch is screwed into the top of the crankcase on the right-hand side **(see illustration 22.2)**. Remove the right-hand fairing side panel (see Chapter 7) and/or the fuel tank (see Chapter 4) as required to access the switch according to model.
6 Disconnect the wiring connector from the switch **(see illustration 22.2)**.
7 Unscrew the switch, noting how it also secures the oil pipe, and withdraw it from the crankcase **(see illustration)**. Be prepared to catch any residual oil from the pipe. Discard the two sealing washers as new ones should be used.

Installation

8 Install the switch using new sealing washers on each side of the oil pipe union and tighten it to the torque setting specified at the beginning of the Chapter **(see illustration 22.7)**. Connect the wiring connector **(see illustration 22.2)**.
9 Run the engine and check that the switch operates correctly without leakage.
10 Install the right-hand fairing side panel and/or fuel tank as required (see Chapters 7 and 4).

23 Horn

Check

1 If the horn doesn't work, first check the fuse (see Section 5) and the battery (see Section 3).
2 The horn is mounted on the underside of the bottom yoke on Sprint and Tiger models and on the left-hand end of the radiator on Speed Triple models **(see illustrations)**. On Sprint and Tiger models remove the fairing for best access if required (see Chapter 7).
3 Disconnect the wiring connectors from the horn. Using two jumper wires, apply battery voltage directly to the terminals on the horn. If the horn doesn't sound, replace it with a new one.
4 If the horn sounds, check for voltage at the black/blue wire terminal with the ignition switch on. If there is voltage check for continuity in the pink/black wire to the horn button, then in the black/yellow wire from the horn button to earth, referring to Section 2 at the beginning of this Chapter and to the wiring diagrams at

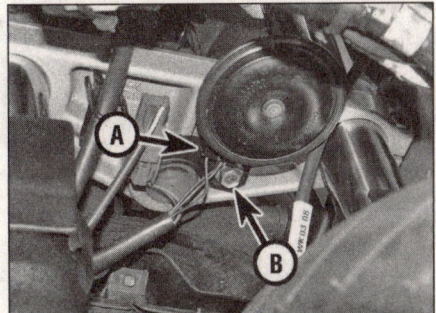

23.2a Horn wiring connectors (A) and mounting bolt (B) – Sprint and Tiger models

23.2b Horn wiring connectors (A) and mounting bolt (B) – Speed Triple models

8•30 Electrical system

24.2a Starter solenoid – Sprint models

24.2b Starter solenoid (arrowed) – Tiger models

24.2c Starter solenoid (arrowed) – Speed Triple models . . .

the end of it, and check the horn button itself in the switch housing (see Section 18). If there was no voltage at the black/blue wire terminal check it for continuity between the connector and the ignition switch.

Renewal

5 The horn is mounted on the underside of the bottom yoke on Sprint and Tiger models and on the left-hand end of the radiator on Speed Triple models **(see illustrations 23.2a or b)**. On Sprint and Tiger models remove the fairing for best access if required (see Chapter 7).

6 Disconnect the wiring connectors, then unscrew the bolt and remove the horn.

7 Install the horn and securely tighten the bolt. Connect the wiring connectors. On Sprint and Tiger models install the fairing if removed (see Chapter 7).

24 Starter solenoid

Check

1 If the starter circuit is faulty, first check the main and starter circuit fuses (see Section 5) and the starter circuit relay (see Section 16).

24.2d . . . release the rubber shroud (arrowed) to access the terminals

24.3a Remove the cover . . .

2 On Sprint and Tiger models remove the seat (see Chapter 7) **(see illustrations)**. On Speed Triple models remove the fuel tank (see Chapter 4), and the right-hand side panel (see Chapter 7), then release the rubber shroud covering the solenoid **(see illustrations)**.

3 Remove the terminal cover and unscrew the nut securing the thick starter motor lead (the black lead) to the solenoid; position the lead away from the terminal **(see illustrations)**. With the ignition switch ON, the engine kill switch in the RUN position, the transmission in neutral, and the clutch lever pulled in, press the starter switch. The solenoid should be heard to click. If the solenoid doesn't click, switch the ignition OFF and remove the solenoid as described below; then test it as follows.

4 Set a multimeter to the ohms x 1 scale and connect it across the solenoid's starter motor and battery lead terminals **(see illustration 24.3b or c)**. Using a fully-charged 12 volt battery and two insulated jumper wires, connect the battery across the two coil terminals of the solenoid (i.e. those which the white/red and black wires connect to on Speed Triple and Tiger models, and those which the two black wires connect to on Sprint models). At this point the solenoid should be heard to click and the multimeter read 0 ohms (continuity). If this is the case the solenoid is

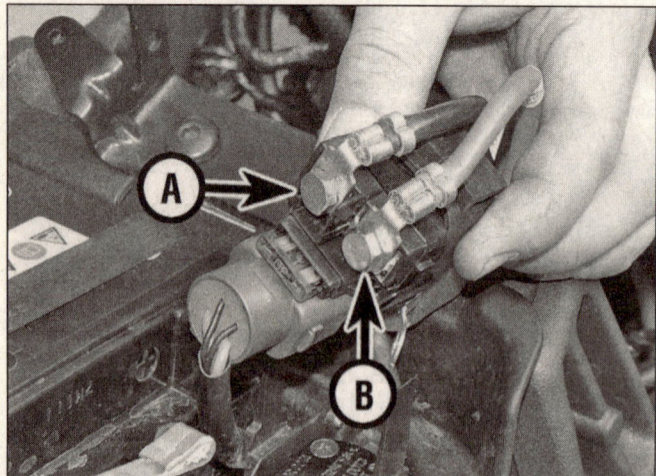

24.3b . . . to access the black starter motor lead (A) and red battery lead (B) – Sprint and Tiger type shown

24.3c Black starter motor lead (A) and red battery lead (B) – Speed Triple type shown

Electrical system 8•31

24.7 Disconnect the wiring connector

25.3 Lift the rubber cover, then unscrew the nut and detach the lead

proved good. If the solenoid does not click when battery voltage is applied and indicates no continuity (infinite resistance) across its terminals, it is faulty and must be replaced with a new one.

5 If the solenoid is good, check for battery voltage at the white/red or black wire terminal on the loom side of the wiring connector when the starter button is pressed. If voltage is present, check the other components in the starter circuit as described in the relevant sections of this Chapter. If no voltage was present, check the wiring between the various components (see *Wiring Diagrams* at the end of this Chapter).

Renewal

6 On Sprint and Tiger models remove the seat (see Chapter 7). On Speed Triple models remove the right-hand side panel (see Chapter 7). Disconnect the battery negative (–) lead before removing the solenoid (see Section 3).
7 Displace the solenoid from its mount **(see illustration 24.2a or b or c and d)**. Remove the terminal cover and detach the starter motor and battery leads, noting which fits where **(see illustration 24.3)**. Disconnect the wiring connector **(see illustration)**. Remove the solenoid. Remove the fuse from the solenoid on Sprint and Tiger models.

8 Installation is the reverse of removal. Make sure the starter motor and battery terminal nuts are securely tightened. Connect the negative (–) lead to the battery.

25 Starter motor removal and installation

Removal

1 The starter motor is mounted on the crankcase, behind the cylinder block. Disconnect the battery negative (–) lead (see Section 3). Remove the fuel tank (see Chapter 4).
2 Remove the oil pressure switch (see Section 22).
3 Peel back the rubber terminal cover and unscrew the nut securing the lead to the starter motor **(see illustration)**. Detach the lead.
4 Unscrew the two bolts securing the starter motor **(see illustration)**. Move the oil pipe aside and draw the starter motor out of the crankcase **(see illustration)**.
5 Remove the O-ring on the end of the starter motor and discard it as a new one must be used **(see illustration 25.6)**.

Installation

6 Fit a new O-ring on the end of the starter motor, making sure it is seated in its groove, and smear it with grease **(see illustration)**.
7 Move the oil pipe aside and manoeuvre the motor into position and slide it into the crankcase **(see illustration 25.4b)**. Ensure that the starter motor teeth mesh correctly with those of the starter idle/reduction gear. Install the mounting bolts and tighten them to the torque setting specified at the beginning of the Chapter **(see illustration 25.4a)**.
8 Connect the lead to the starter motor and secure it with the nut **(see illustration 25.3)**. Fit the rubber cover over the terminal.
9 Install the oil pressure switch (see Section 22).
10 Install the fuel tank (see Chapter 4). Connect the battery negative (–) lead (see Section 3).

26 Starter motor overhaul

Disassembly

1 Remove the starter motor (see Section 25).
2 Make some alignment marks between

25.4a Unscrew the bolts . . .

25.4b . . . and remove the starter motor

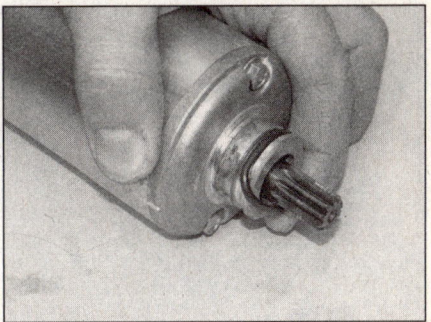

25.6 Fit a new O-ring and smear it with grease

8•32 Electrical system

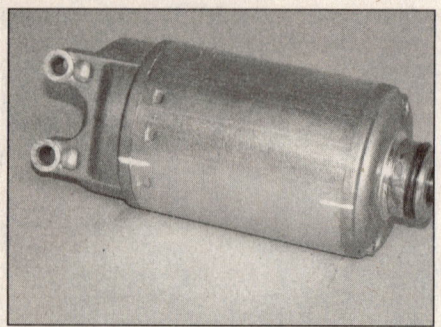

26.2 Make some alignment marks between the housing and the end covers

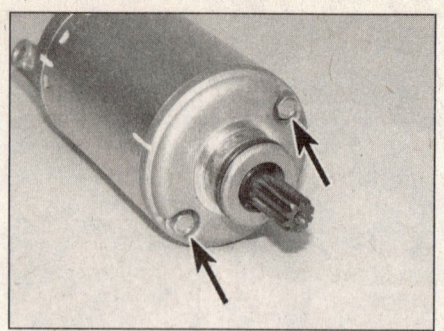

26.3a Unscrew the two long bolts (arrowed), noting the O-rings . . .

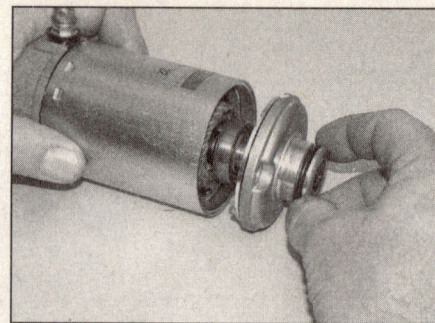

26.3b . . . and remove the front cover

the housing and both end covers **(see illustration)**.
3 Unscrew the two long bolts, then remove the front cover from the motor **(see illustrations)**.
4 Hold the armature in place and draw the main housing off, noting that the attraction of the magnets will hold it in place **(see illustration)**.
5 Draw the armature out of the rear cover **(see illustration)**.
6 Draw the positive brush out of its housing and remove the brushplate **(see illustration 26.15b)**. Unscrew the nut from the terminal bolt and remove the insulating washer and the O-ring **(see illustrations 26.14d and c)**. Withdraw the terminal bolt from the housing **(see illustration 26.14b)**. Note the insulating seat on the bolt **(see illustration 26.14a)**.
7 Slide the negative brush out of its housing.

Inspection

Note: *No replacement parts are available from Triumph for the starter motor. If the following checks indicate a worn or faulty internal component, seek the advice of a Triumph dealer or auto electrical specialist before buying a new starter motor.*

8 The parts of the starter motor that are most likely to wear are the brushes. No specification is given for the minimum length, but anything over 5 mm should be serviceable. If the brushes are not worn excessively, nor cracked, chipped, or otherwise damaged, they may be re-used. Make sure each brush is securely connected to its wire, and the wire is securely connected to the terminal bolt or brushplate.
9 Inspect the commutator bars for scoring, scratches and discoloration **(see illustrations)**. The bars can be cleaned and polished with crocus cloth – do not use sandpaper or emery paper. After cleaning, wipe away any residue with a cloth soaked in electrical system cleaner or denatured alcohol. Make sure the insulation material between each of the bars is below the bars themselves – if necessary carefully scrape some away.
10 Using an ohmmeter or a continuity test light, check for continuity between the commutator bars **(see illustration)**. Continuity should exist between each bar and all of the others. Also, check for continuity between the commutator bars and the armature shaft **(see illustration)**. There should be no continuity (infinite resistance) between the commutator and the shaft. If the checks indicate otherwise, the armature is defective.
11 Check the oil seal in the front cover **(see illustration)**. Inspect the covers for signs of

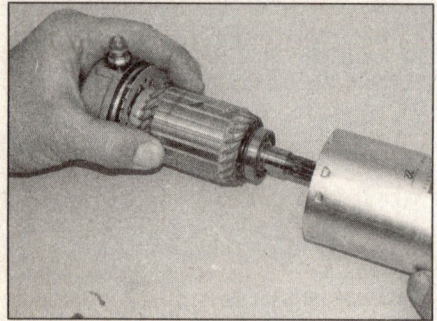

26.4 Draw the main housing off

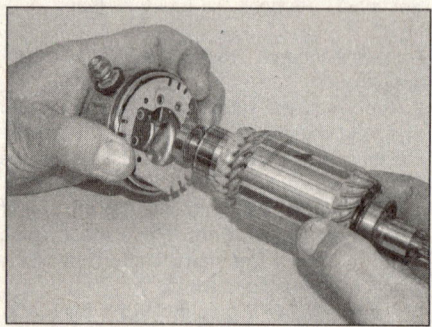

26.5 Draw the armature out of the cover

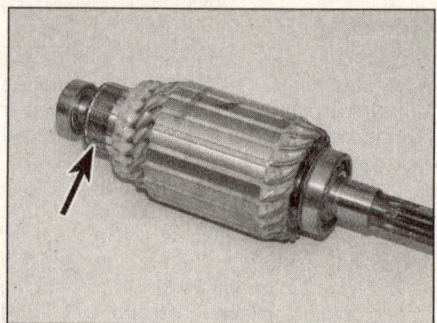

26.9a Check the commutator bars (arrowed) . . .

26.9b . . . and make sure the mica (1) is below the bars (2)

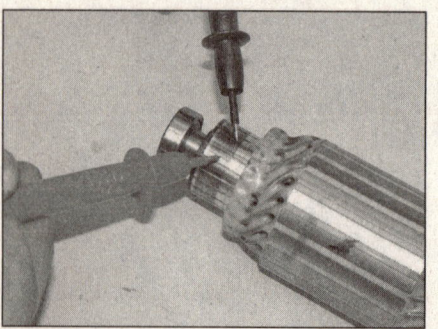

26.10a There should be continuity between the bars . . .

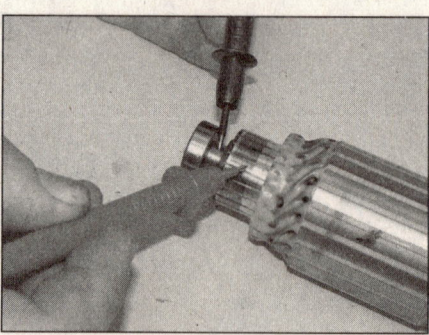

26.10b . . . and no continuity between the bars and the shaft

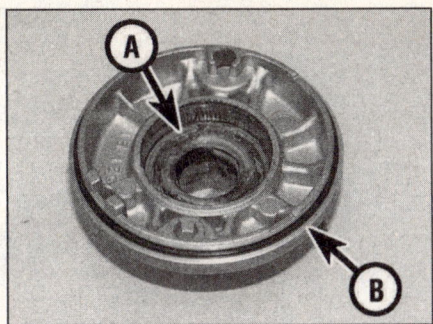

26.11a Check the front cover oil seal (A) and sealing ring (B) ...

26.11b ... and the rear cover sealing ring (arrowed)

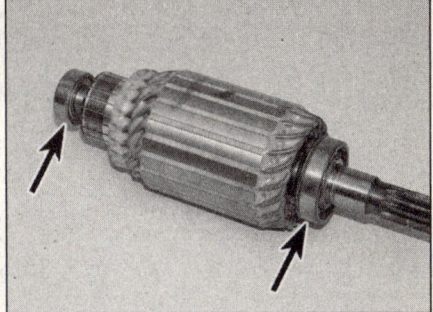

26.11c Check the bearings (arrowed)

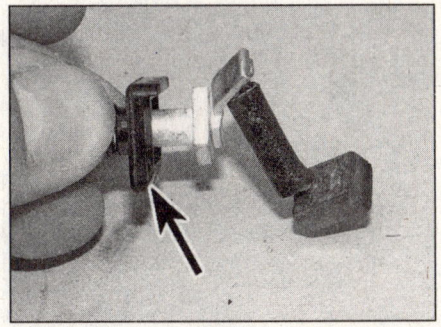

26.14a Fit the insulating seat (arrowed) if removed ...

26.14b ... then fit the terminal into the cover

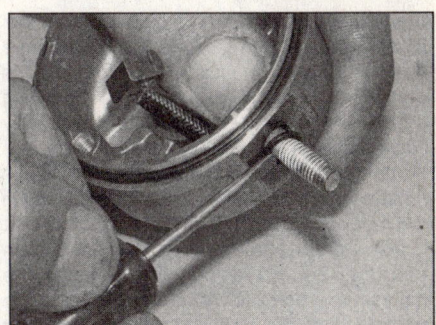

26.14c Fit the O-ring ...

cracks or wear, and make sure the sealing rings are in good condition **(see illustration)**. Check the bearings on the armature shaft **(see illustration)**.

12 Check the starter shaft teeth and the idle gear in the engine for worn, cracked, chipped and broken teeth.

13 Inspect the magnets in the main housing and the housing itself for cracks.

Reassembly

14 Make sure the sealing ring is in place on the rim of the rear cover **(see illustration 26.11b)**. Make sure the rubber insulating seat is in place on the terminal bolt, then insert the bolt through the rear cover **(see illustrations)**. Fit the O-ring, feeding it carefully into the gap between the housing and the bolt **(see illustration)**. Fit the insulating washer with its wider side uppermost, then tighten the nut down onto it **(see illustrations)**.

15 Slide the brushplate brush into its housing then lift its spring and rest it on the outer

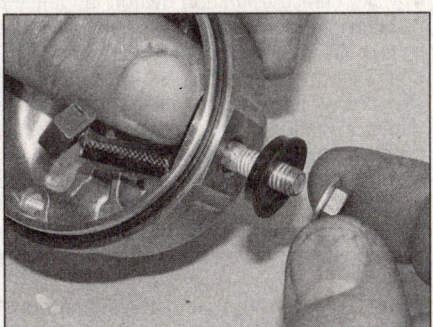

26.14d ... the insulating washer and the nut

end of the brush so it is held retracted in the housing **(see illustration)**. Repeat for the terminal bolt brush **(see illustration)**. Fit the brushplate assembly onto the commutator,

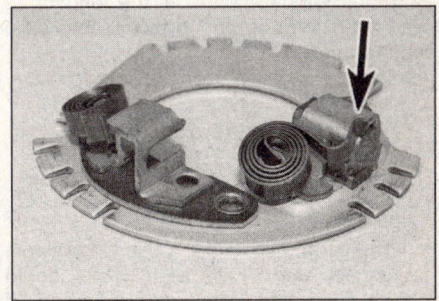

26.15a Fit the brush into the housing and secure it by locating the spring end on its outer end as shown (arrowed)

26.15b Fit the terminal bolt brush and secure it in the same way

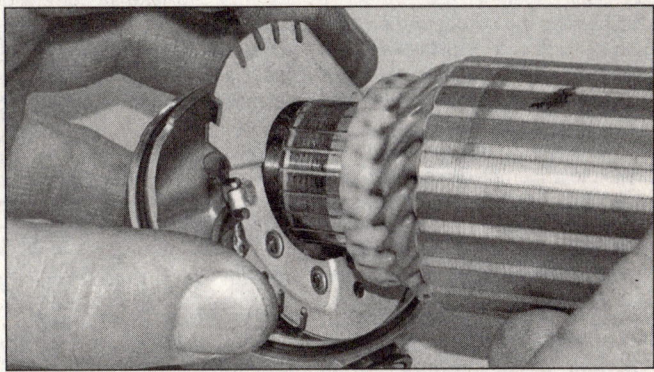

26.15c Slide the plate onto the commutator ...

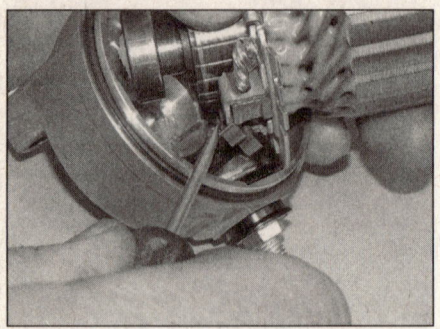

26.15d ... then relocate the spring ends

26.15e Fit the assembly into the rear cover

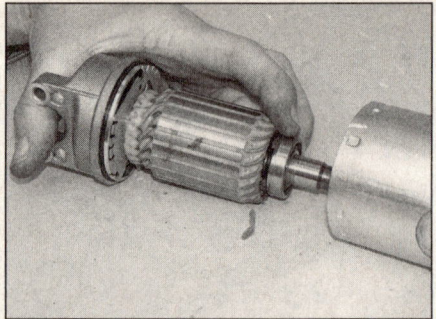

26.16a Carefully fit the housing over the armature ...

then move the brush springs back onto the brushes so they are pressed against the bars **(see illustrations)**. Fit the armature into the rear cover, seating the bearing in its housing and making sure the brushplate is correctly aligned and seated **(see illustration)**.

16 Identify the rear end of the main housing – it has a locating tab that locates into a notch in the rear cover. Grasp the armature to prevent it being draw out and carefully fit the main housing over it, rear end first, aligning the marks made on removal, and making sure the tab locates in the notch – each has alignment marks on the outside **(see illustrations)**.

17 Make sure the sealing ring is in place on the rim of the front cover **(see illustration 26.11a)**. Fit the cover over the shaft and onto the housing, aligning the marks made on removal **(see illustration 26.3b)**.

18 Check the marks made on removal are correctly aligned, then fit the long bolts with their O-rings and tighten them **(see illustration)**.

19 Install the starter motor (see Section 25).

27 Charging system testing

1 If the performance of the charging system is suspect, the system as a whole should be checked first, followed by testing of the individual components. **Note:** *Before beginning the checks, make sure the battery is fully charged and that all system connections are clean and tight.*

2 Checking the output of the charging system and the performance of the various components within the charging system requires the use of a multimeter (with voltage, current and resistance checking facilities). If a multimeter is not available, the job of checking the system should be left to a Triumph dealer or specialist.

3 When making the checks, follow the procedures carefully to prevent incorrect connections or short circuits resulting in irreparable damage to electrical system components.

Leakage test

Caution: Always connect an ammeter in series, never in parallel with the battery,

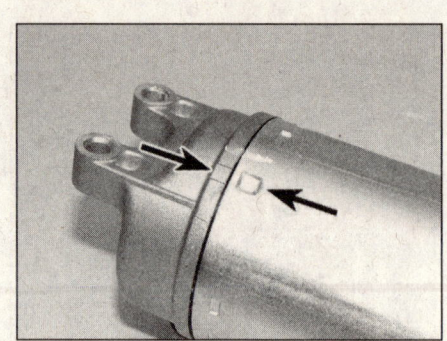

26.16b ... aligning the marks and making sure it locates correctly (arrowed)

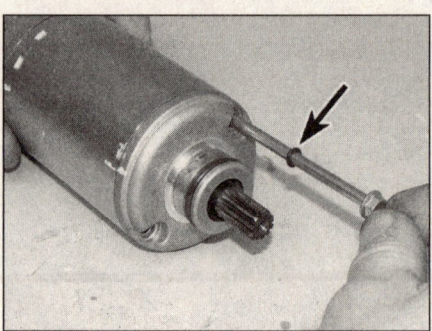

26.18 Make sure the O-ring (arrowed) is fitted under the head of each bolt

otherwise it will be damaged. Do not turn the ignition ON or operate the starter motor when the ammeter is connected – a sudden surge in current will blow the meter's fuse.

4 Make sure the ignition switch is OFF the disconnect the lead from the battery negative (–) terminal (see Section 3).

5 Set the multimeter to the Amps function and connect its negative (–) probe to the battery negative (–) terminal, and positive (+) probe to the disconnected negative (–) lead **(see illustration)**. Always set the meter to a high amps range initially and then bring it down to the mA (milli Amps) range; if there is a high current flow in the circuit it may blow the meter's fuse.

6 No current flow should be indicated. If current leakage is indicated (generally greater than 1 mA), there is a short circuit in the wiring, although if an alarm is fitted remember to take its current draw into account. Using the wiring diagrams at the end of this Chapter, systematically disconnect individual electrical components, checking the meter each time until the source is identified.

7 If no leakage is indicated, disconnect the meter and connect the negative (–) lead to the battery.

Output test

8 Start the engine and warm it up to normal operating temperature. Remove the seat (see Chapter 7).

9 To check the regulated voltage output, allow the engine to idle and connect a multimeter set to the 0 to 20 volts DC scale (voltmeter) across the terminals of the battery (positive (+) lead to battery positive (+) terminal, negative (–) lead to battery negative (–) terminal) **(see illustration)**. Increase engine speed to 2000 rpm and note the reading obtained. The regulated voltage should be around 13.5 to

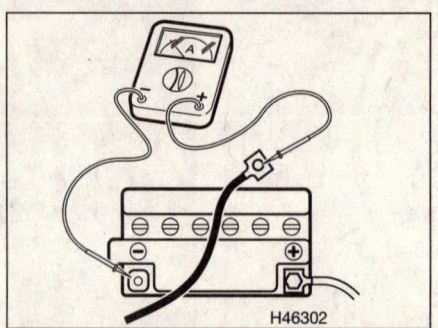

27.5 Checking the charging system leakage rate – connect the ammeter as shown

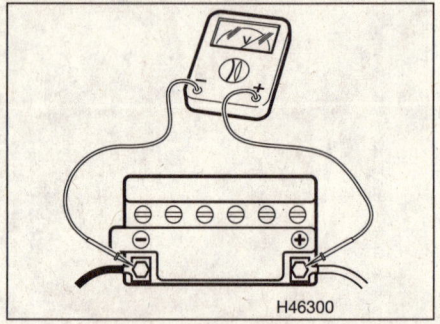

27.9 Checking the charging system output – connect the voltmeter as shown

Electrical system 8•35

15.0V. If the voltage is zero or below the limit, check the alternator first (Section 28), then the regulator/rectifier if necessary (Section 29), if the reading is above the limit check the regulator/rectifier (see Section 29).

 **Clues to a faulty regulator are constantly blowing bulbs, with brightness varying considerably with engine speed, and battery overheating.**

28 Alternator

1 The alternator rotor is mounted on the left-hand end of the crankshaft and the stator is located inside the left-hand engine cover. Disconnect the battery negative (-) lead (see Section 3). On Sprint models remove the left-hand fairing side panel (see Chapter 7). To access the wiring connector, on Sprint models remove the airbox and on Speed Triple models remove the fuel tank (see Chapter 4). On Tiger models (except Sport) you may be able to access the wiring connector from the left-hand side by reaching under the frame above the front sprocket cover, but if required remove the fuel tank (see Chapter 4). On Tiger Sport models remove the engine cover from the left-hand side **(see illustration)**.

Testing

2 Disconnect the battery negative (–) lead. Refer to Step 1, then trace the alternator wiring from the left-hand engine cover and disconnect it at the connector with the three yellow wires **(see illustrations)**.

3 Using a multimeter set to the ohms scale, connect the meter probes to one pair of terminals at a time on the alternator side of the wiring connector and measure the resistance between the terminals. Make a note of the three readings obtained. Now check for continuity between each terminal and ground (earth).

4 If the stator coil windings are in good condition the three readings should be as specified at the beginning of the Chapter, and there should be no continuity (infinite resistance) between any of the terminals and ground (earth). If not, the alternator stator coil assembly is probably faulty and should be taken to a Triumph dealer for further assessment. **Note:** *Before condemning the stator coils, check the fault is not due to a loose wire in the connector or damaged wiring between the connector and coils.*

Removal

5 If the bike is on its sidestand drain the engine oil (see Chapter 1). Disconnect the battery negative (–) lead. Refer to Step 1, then trace the alternator wiring from the left-hand engine cover and disconnect it at

28.1 Pull the cover away to free the pegs from the grommets

28.2b Alternator and regulator/rectifier wiring connectors (arrowed) – Speed Triple

the connector **(see illustration 28.2a, b or c)**. Free the wiring from any clips or ties and feed it through to the cover.

6 Working in a criss-cross pattern, evenly slacken the engine cover bolts then remove them **(see illustration)**.

7 Draw the cover off, noting that it will be held by the attraction of the magnets, and be prepared to catch any residual oil **(see illustration 28.15b)**. Discard the gasket as a new one must be used **(see illustration 28.15a)**. Note the three locating pins and remove them for safekeeping if loose.

8 To remove the rotor bolt it is necessary to stop the crankshaft from turning. Triumph produces a Service Tool (Part No. T3880375) to do this, or alternatively a number of different rotor straps are commercially available, one type of which is shown **(see illustration)**. When fitting the strap

28.6 Unscrew the bolts and remove the cover

28.2a Alternator and regulator/rectifier wiring connectors (arrowed) – Sprint

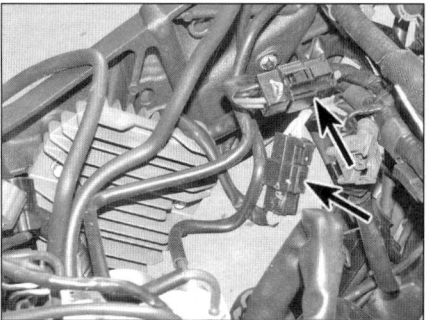

28.2c Alternator and regulator/rectifier wiring connectors (arrowed) – Tiger (except Sport)

make sure it is clear of the crankshaft position (CKP) sensor triggers. If a rotor holding strap or tool is not available, and the engine is in the frame, place the transmission in gear and have an assistant apply the rear brake. Alternatively, a large spanner can be applied to the two flats machined into the boss in the rotor, but note that as the boss is recessed the angle at which the spanner must sit is not ideal and as the bolt is tight there is a danger of the spanner slipping off, which could cause damage – a 'crow's foot' wrench with small extension gets round this problem. Unscrew the bolt and remove the washer.

9 To remove the rotor from the crankshaft taper it is necessary to use a rotor puller. Triumph produces a service tool (Part No. T3880203) to do this, or alternatively a number of rotor pullers are commercially available,

28.8 Using a rotor holder while unscrewing the bolt

28.9 Hold the rotor and displace it using a rotor puller

28.10 Remove the key from its slot if loose

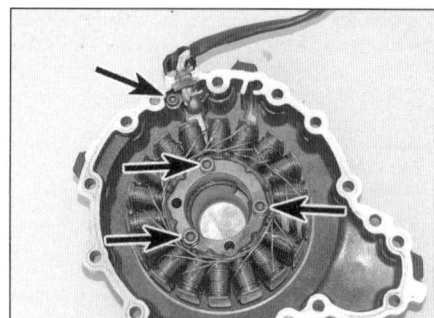
28.11 Alternator stator and wiring clamp bolts (arrowed)

28.13 Slide the rotor onto the shaft, locating its cut-out over the key

28.14a Fit the bolt and washer . . .

28.14b . . . and tighten the bolt to the specified torque

one type of which is shown **(see illustration)**. Fit the puller, then hold the rotor as before to prevent it turning and turn the puller clockwise until the rotor is displaced.

10 Draw off the rotor, noting the location of the Woodruff key in the crankshaft – remove the key for safekeeping if it is loose **(see illustration)**. Note the CKP sensor triggers on the rotor and take care not to damage them.

11 To remove the stator, unscrew the bolts securing it to the cover, and the bolt securing the wiring clamp, then remove the assembly, noting how the wiring grommet fits **(see illustration)**.

Installation

12 Apply a suitable sealant to the stator wiring grommet, then fit the stator into the cover, aligning the grommet with the cut-out **(see illustration 28.11)**. Fit the stator and wiring clamp bolts and tighten them to the specified torque setting.

13 Clean the tapered end of the crankshaft and the corresponding mating surface on the inside of the rotor with a suitable solvent. If removed, fit the Woodruff key in its slot in the crankshaft **(see illustration 28.10)**. Make sure that no metal objects have attached themselves to the magnet on the inside of the rotor, then align the slot on the inside of the rotor boss with the Woodruff key and slide the rotor onto the shaft **(see illustration)**.

14 Fit the rotor bolt with its washer and tighten it to the torque setting specified at the beginning of this Chapter, holding the rotor as on removal to prevent it turning **(see illustrations)**.

15 If removed, fit the cover locating pins into the crankcase, then seat the new gasket onto them **(see illustration)**. Carefully fit the cover, noting that it will be forcibly drawn on by the magnets, making sure it locates correctly onto the pins **(see illustration)**. Tighten the bolts

28.15a Fit the gasket onto the pins (arrowed) . . .

28.15b . . . then carefully fit the cover

evenly in a criss-cross pattern to the torque setting specified at the beginning of the Chapter **(see illustration 28.6)**.

16 Feed the alternator wiring back to its connector, making sure it is correctly routed and secured by any clips or ties, and reconnect it **(see illustration 28.2a, b or c)**.

17 Replenish the engine oil if drained (see Chapter 1).

18 Install the airbox and/or fuel tank as required (see Chapter 4). Connect the battery negative (–) lead and install the seat, and on Sprint models the fairing side panel (see Chapter 7).

29.6a Regulator/rectifier mounting bolts (arrowed) – Sprint

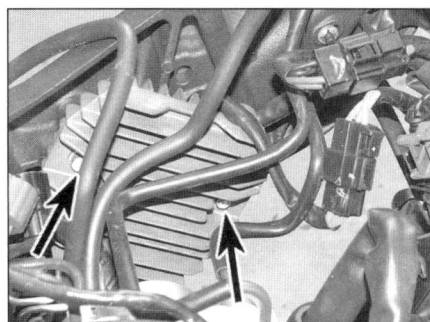

29.6b Regulator/rectifier mounting bolts (arrowed) – Tiger

29 Regulator/rectifier

Testing

1 Triumph provides no test data for the regulator. If the output test in Section 27 indicates a fault, take the unit to a Triumph dealer for further assessment.

2 The rectifier consists of a number of diodes which can be individually tested using a multimeter with a diode testing function. Refer to Section 28, Step 1, and disconnect the regulator/rectifier wiring connectors **(see illustration 28.2a, b or c)**. Set the meter to its diode test function and connect the positive (+) probe to the number 1 terminal (black wire) on the regulator/rectifier side of the 4-pin connector. Connect the negative (–) probe to each of the three yellow wires in the other connector in turn. In each case there should be 0.4 to 0.7 volts. Now reverse the probes and repeat the tests. In each case there should be no reading (open circuit on meter). If any of the results are not as specified one or more of the diodes is faulty and the regulator/rectifier must be replaced with a new one.

3 Now repeat the test, this time with the negative (–) probe connected to the number 4 terminal (red wire) on the regulator/rectifier side of the 4-pin connector, and the positive (+) probe connected to each of the three yellow wires in turn. In each case there should

29.6c Regulator/rectifier upper mounting bolt (arrowed) . . .

be 0.4 to 0.7 volts. Now reverse the probes and repeat the tests. In each case there should be no reading (open circuit on meter). If any of the results are not as specified one or more of the diodes is faulty and the regulator/rectifier must be replaced with a new one.

4 If the tests prove the regulator/rectifier is good, check for constant battery voltage at each of the brown wire terminals in the loom side of the 4-pin connector. If there is none check for continuity in each wire, referring to the wiring diagrams at the end of the chapter for its circuit. Also check for continuity to earth in each of the black wires.

Removal and installation

5 On Sprint models, the regulator/rectifier is mounted on the outside of the left-hand frame beam – remove the left-hand side panel to

29.6d . . . and lower mounting bolt – Speed Triple

access it (see Chapter 7), and the airbox to access the wiring connectors (see Chapter 4). On Speed Triple models, the regulator/rectifier is mounted on the frame cross-piece under the rear of the fuel tank – remove the tank for access (see Chapter 4). On Tiger models, the regulator/rectifier is mounted on the inside of the left-hand frame beam above the gearbox – remove the fuel tank for access (see Chapter 4).

6 On Sprint, Speed Triple and Tiger models (except Sport) trace the wiring to the connectors and disconnect them **(see illustration 28.2a, b or c)**. On Tiger Sport models disconnect the connectors from the regulator/rectifier. Undo the two bolts securing the regulator/rectifier to the frame and remove it **(see illustrations)**.

7 Installation is the reverse of removal.

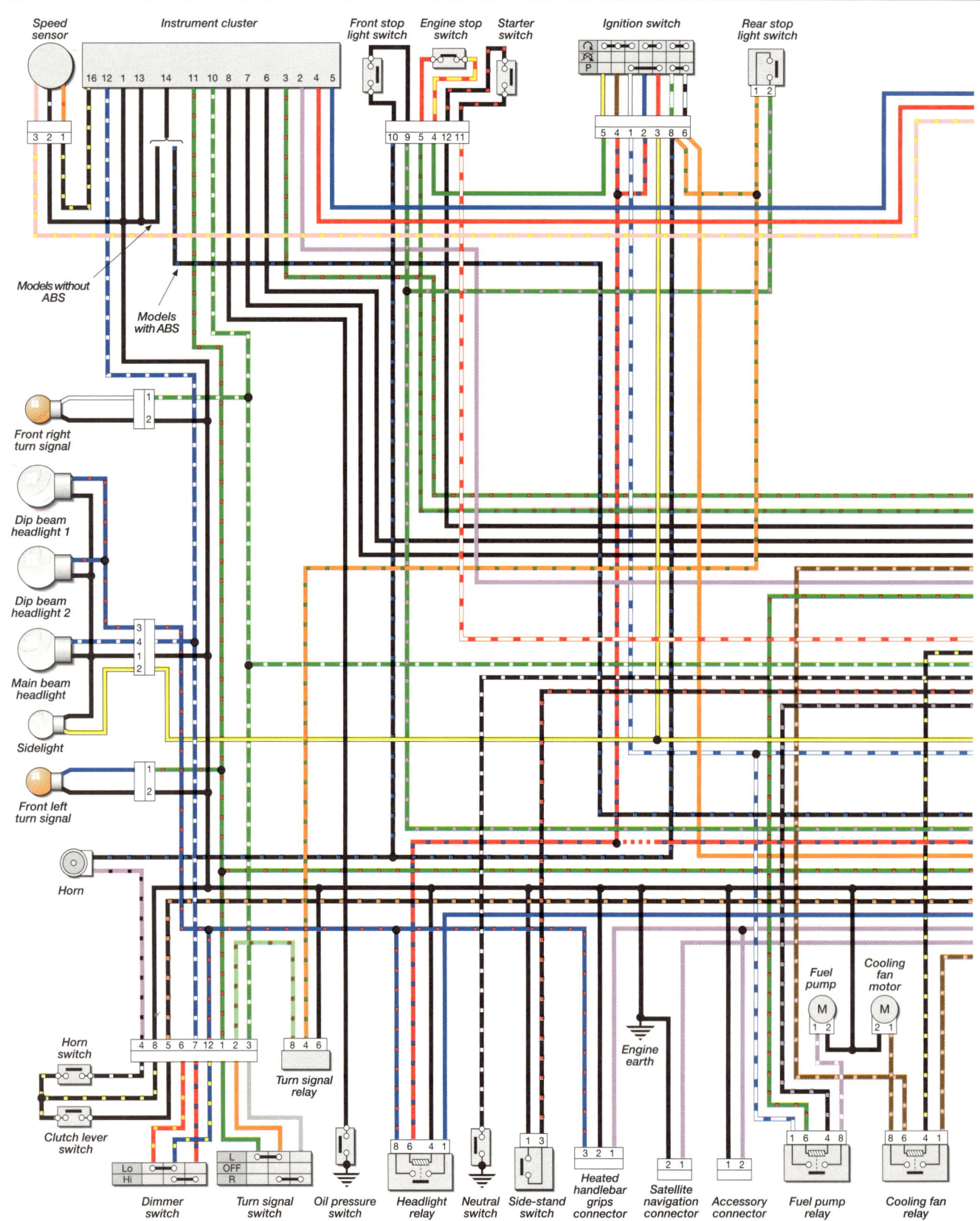

Sprint ST (up to VIN 281465)

Wiring diagrams

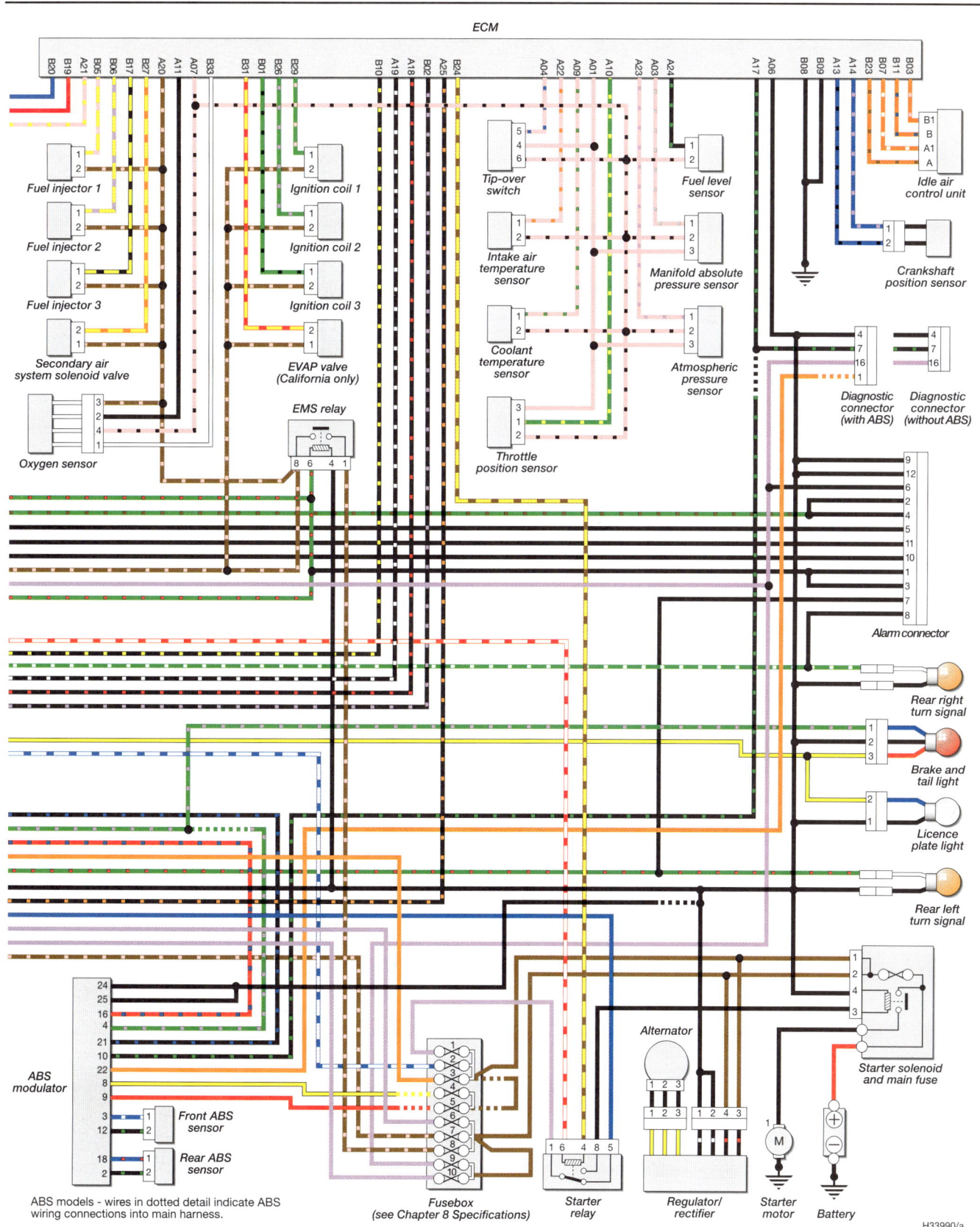

Sprint ST (up to VIN 281465)

8•40 Wiring diagrams

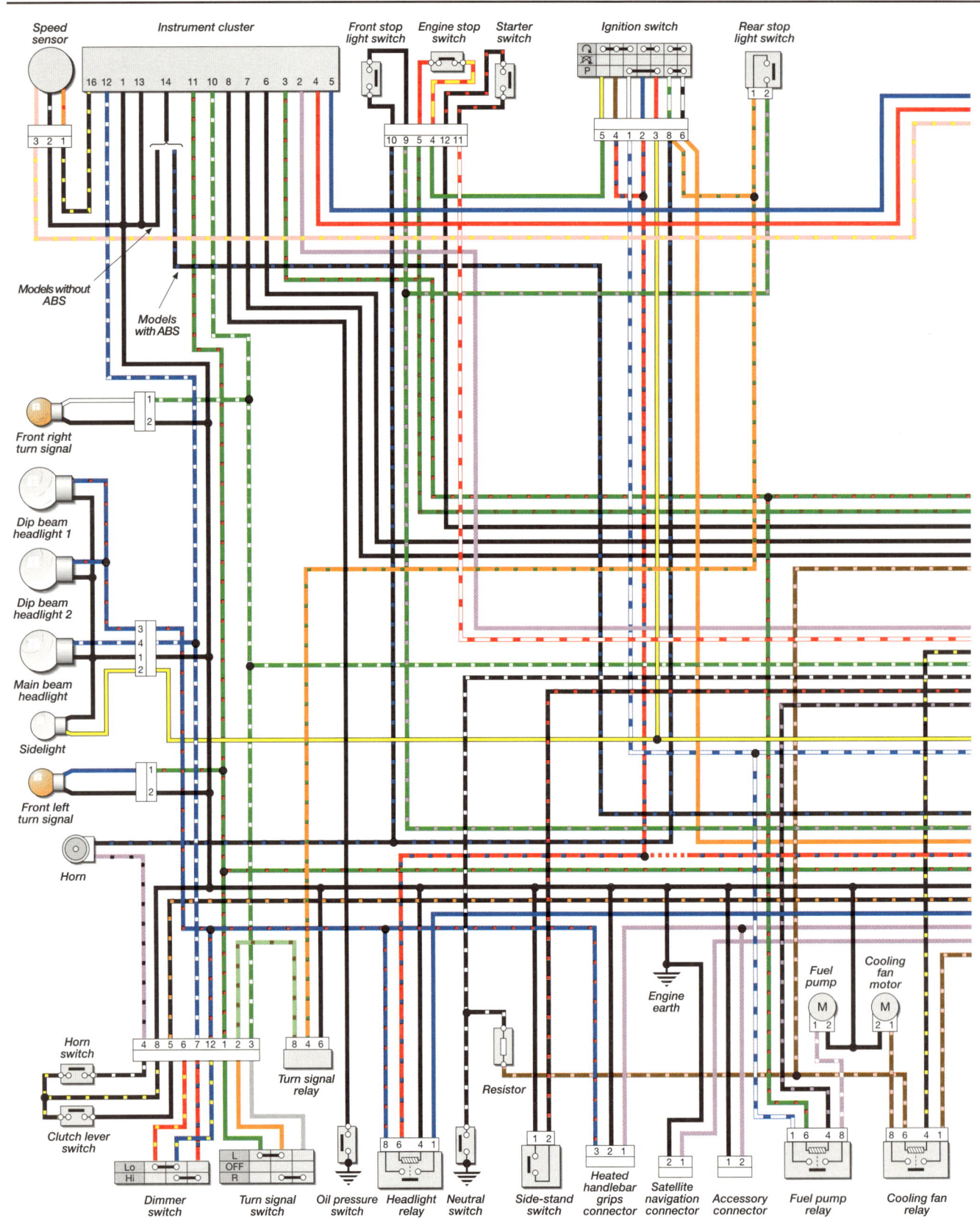

Sprint ST (from VIN 281466)

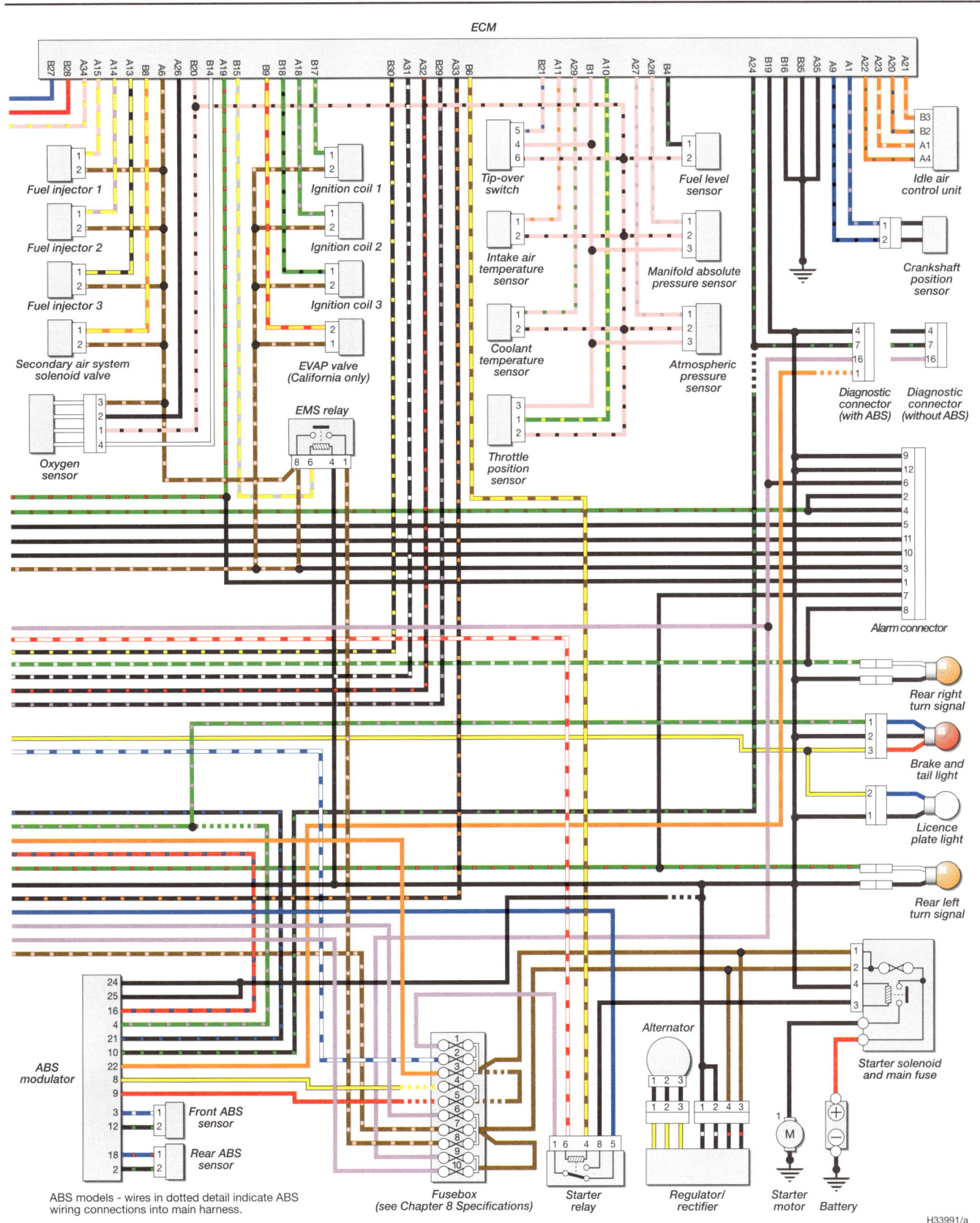

Sprint ST (from VIN 281466)

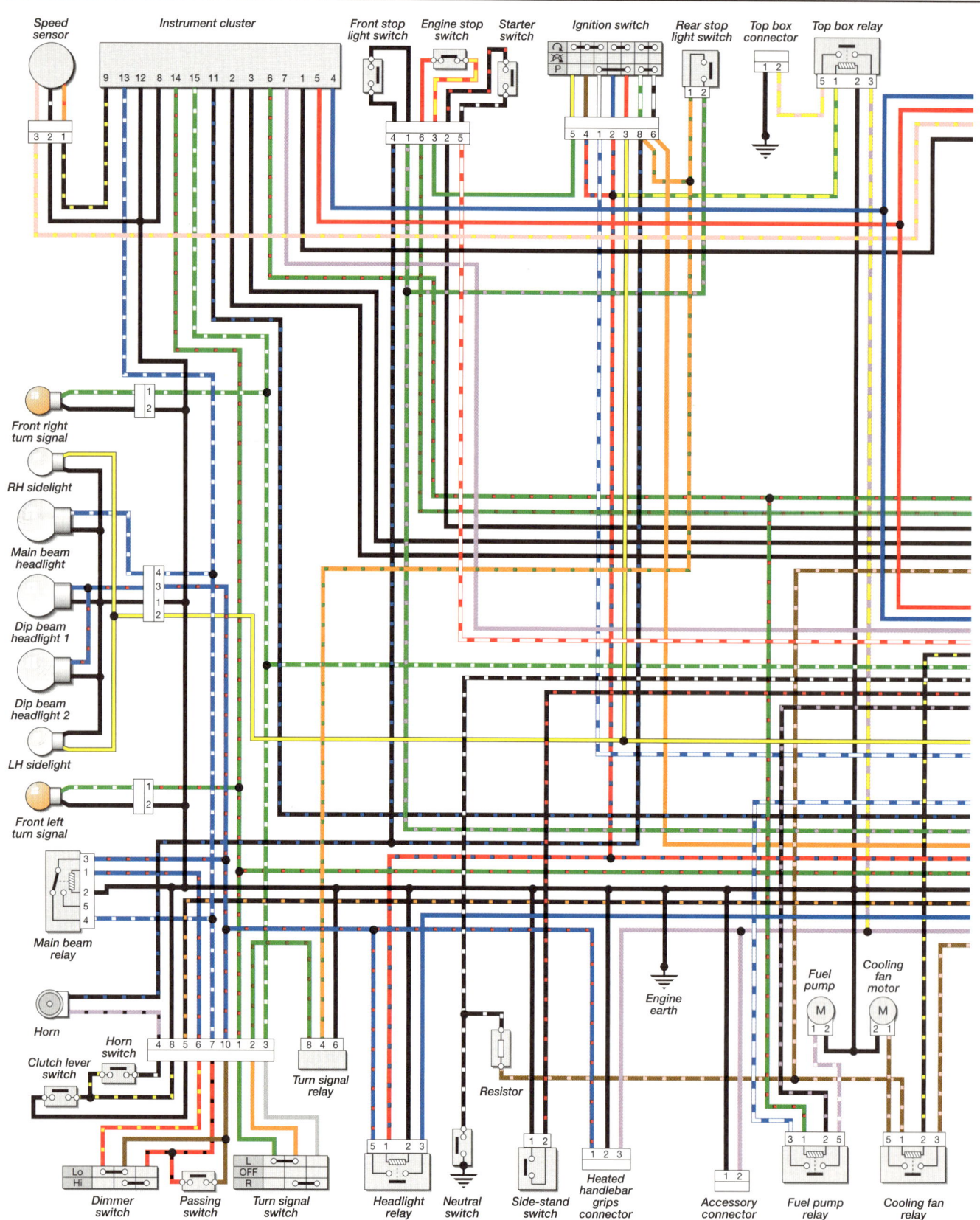

Wiring diagrams 8•43

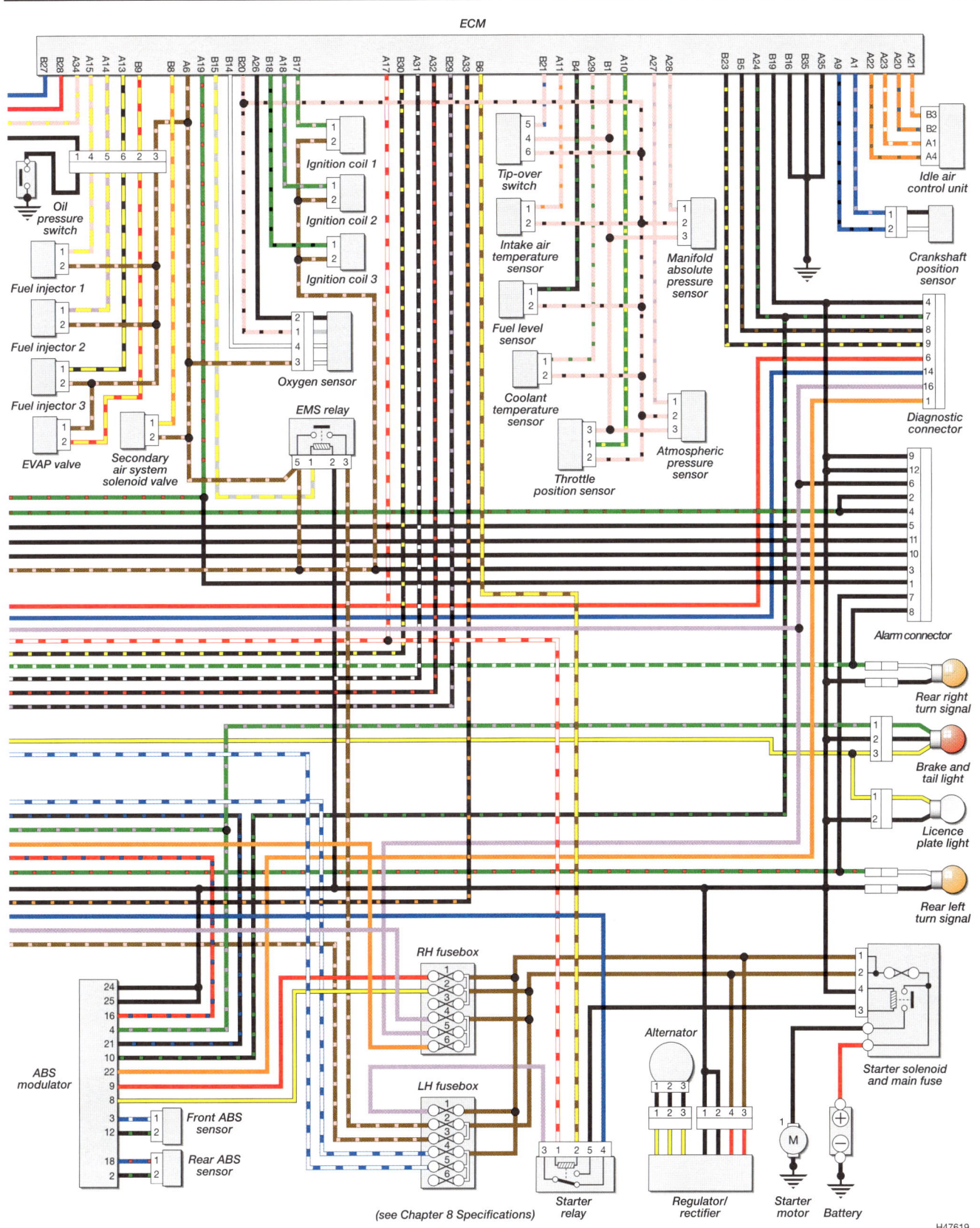

Sprint GT

8•44 Wiring diagrams

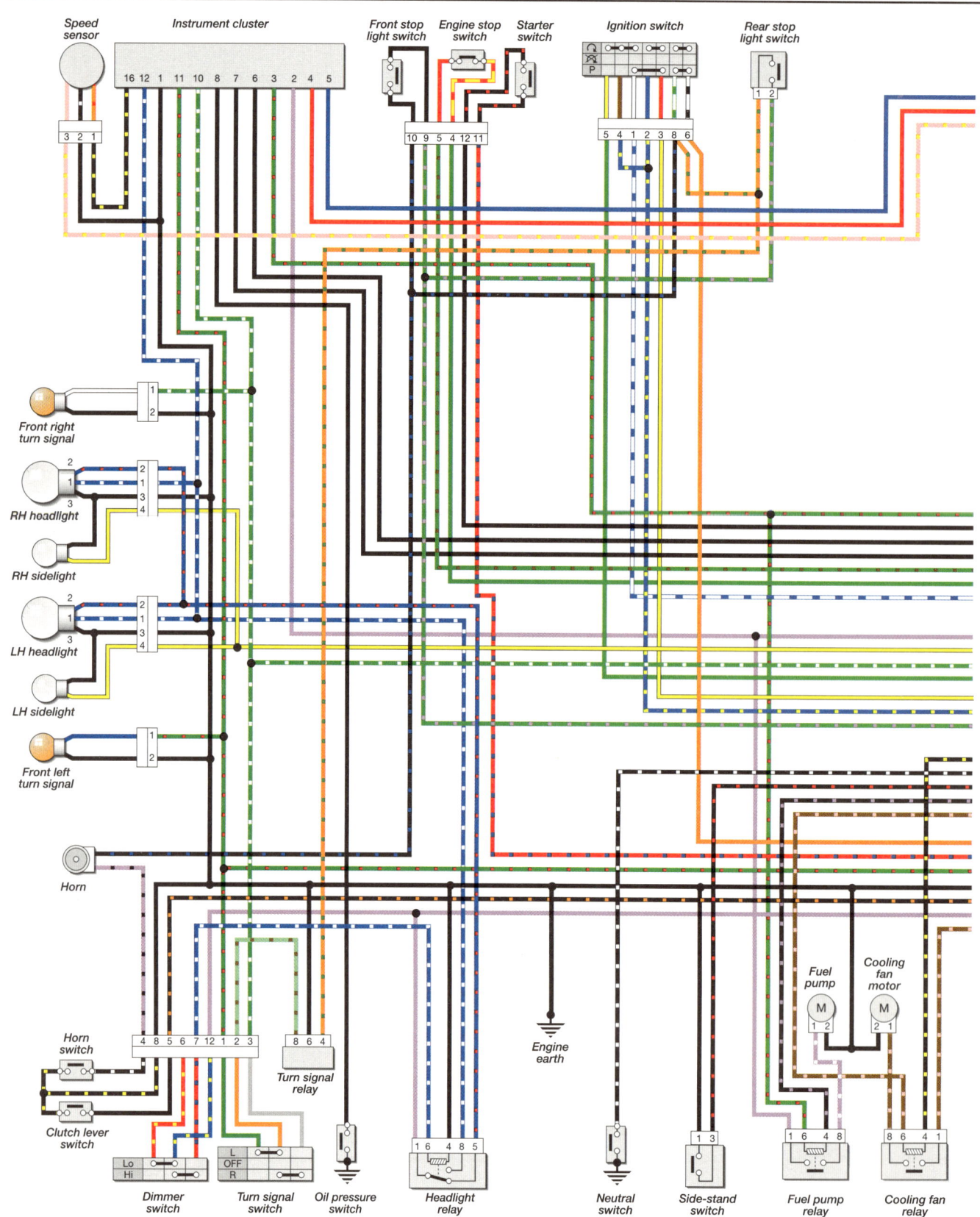

Speed Triple (up to VIN 281465)

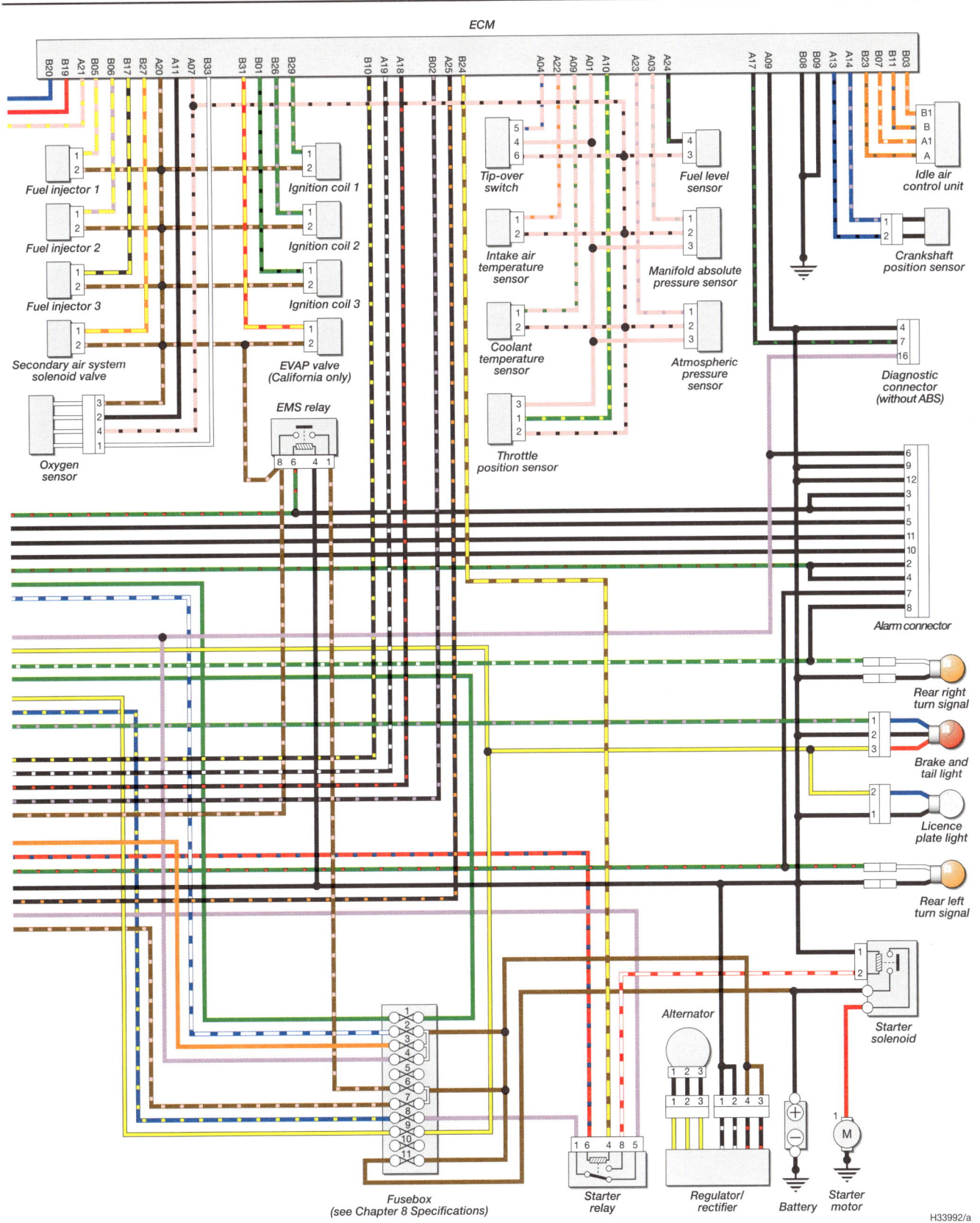

Speed Triple (up to VIN 281465)

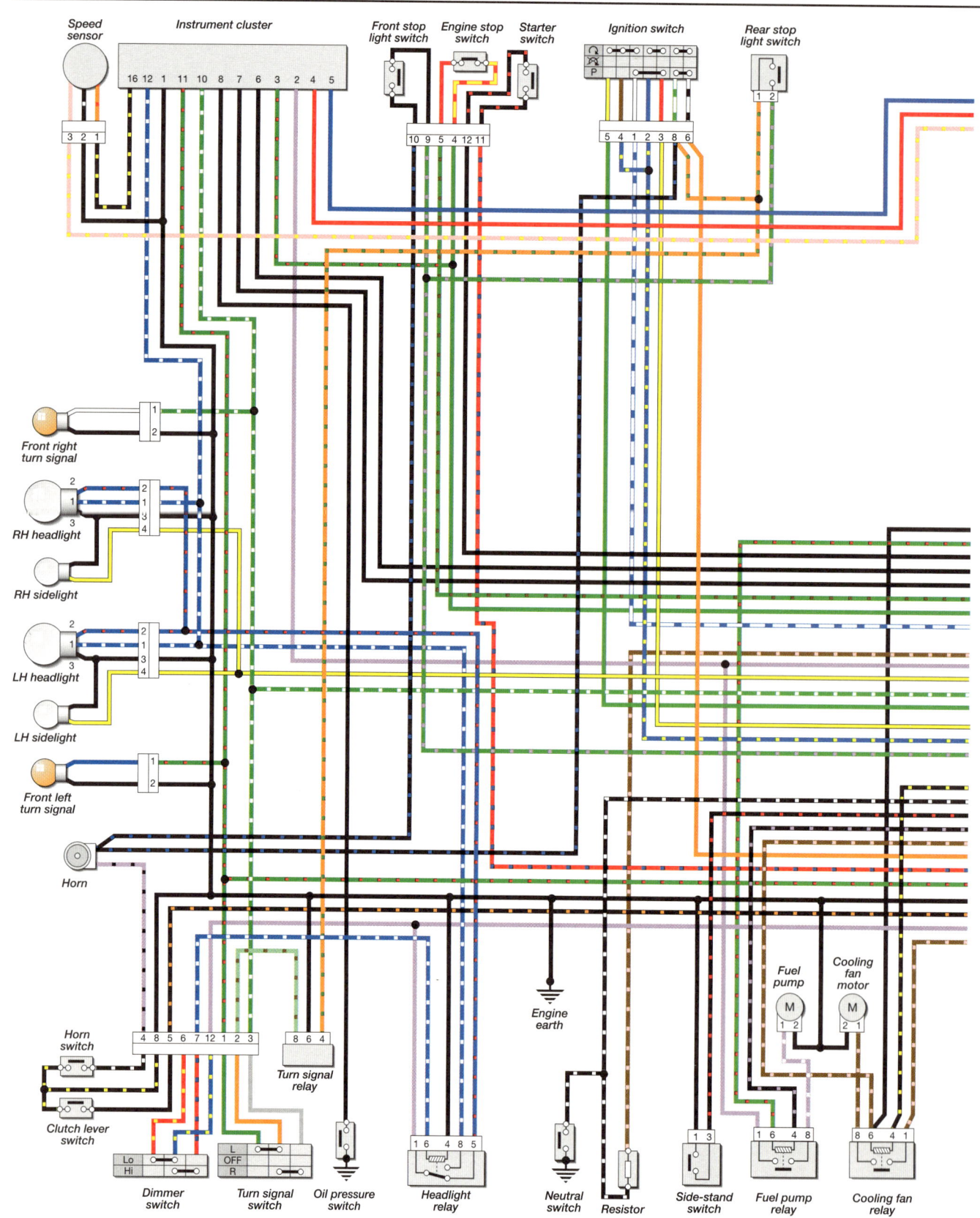

Speed Triple (from VIN 281466 to 461331)

Wiring diagrams 8•47

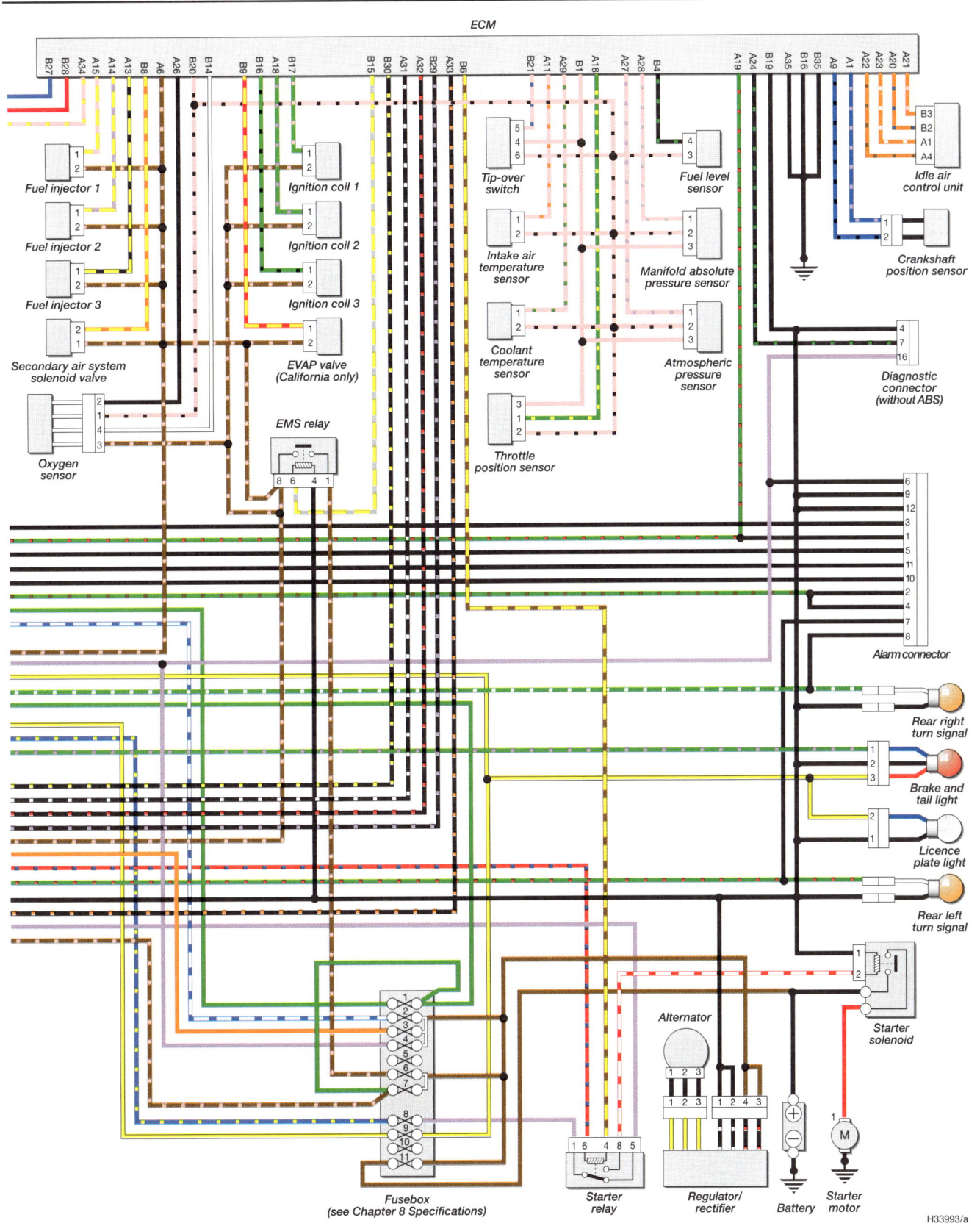

Speed Triple (from VIN 281466 to 461331)

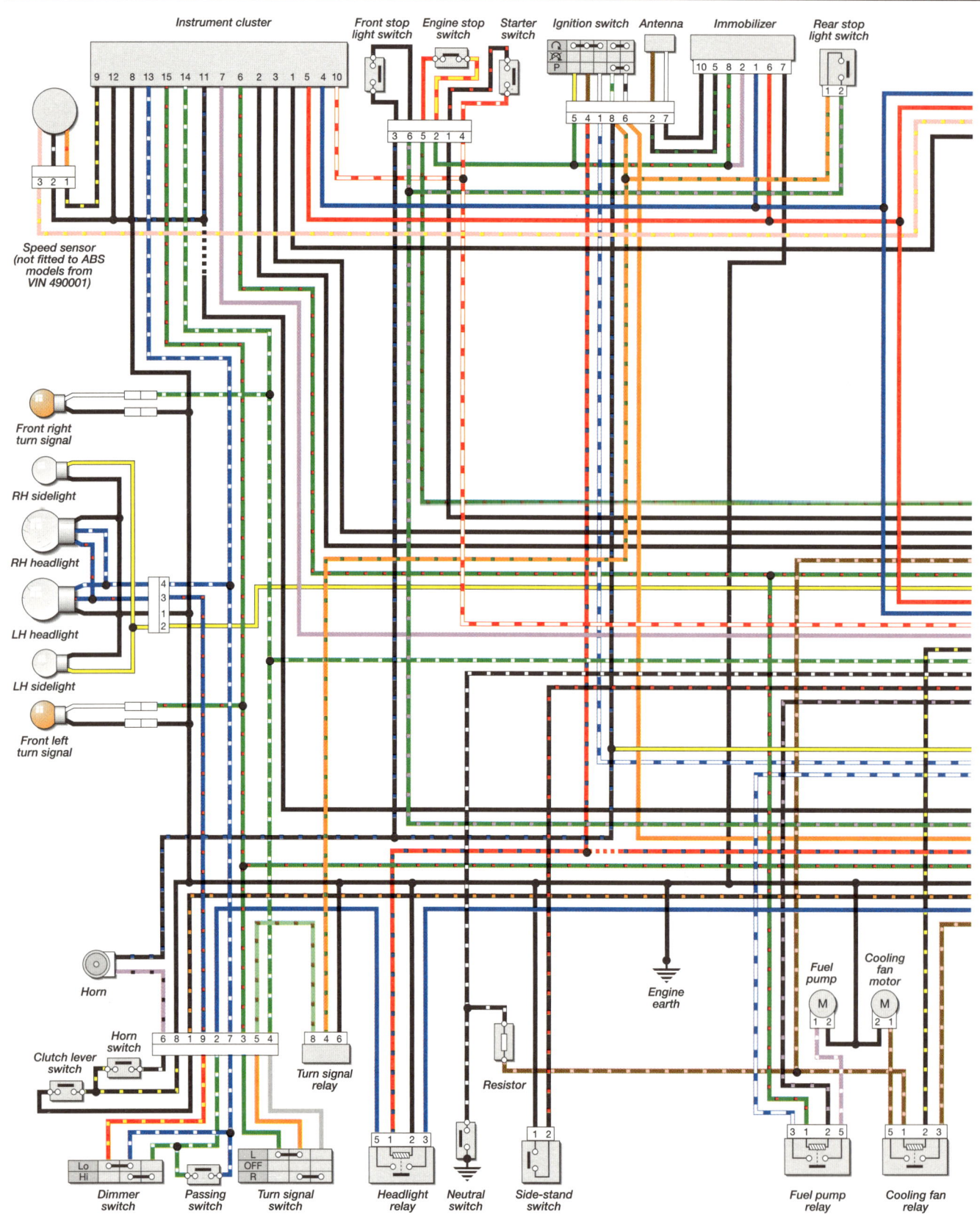

Speed Triple (from VIN 461332)

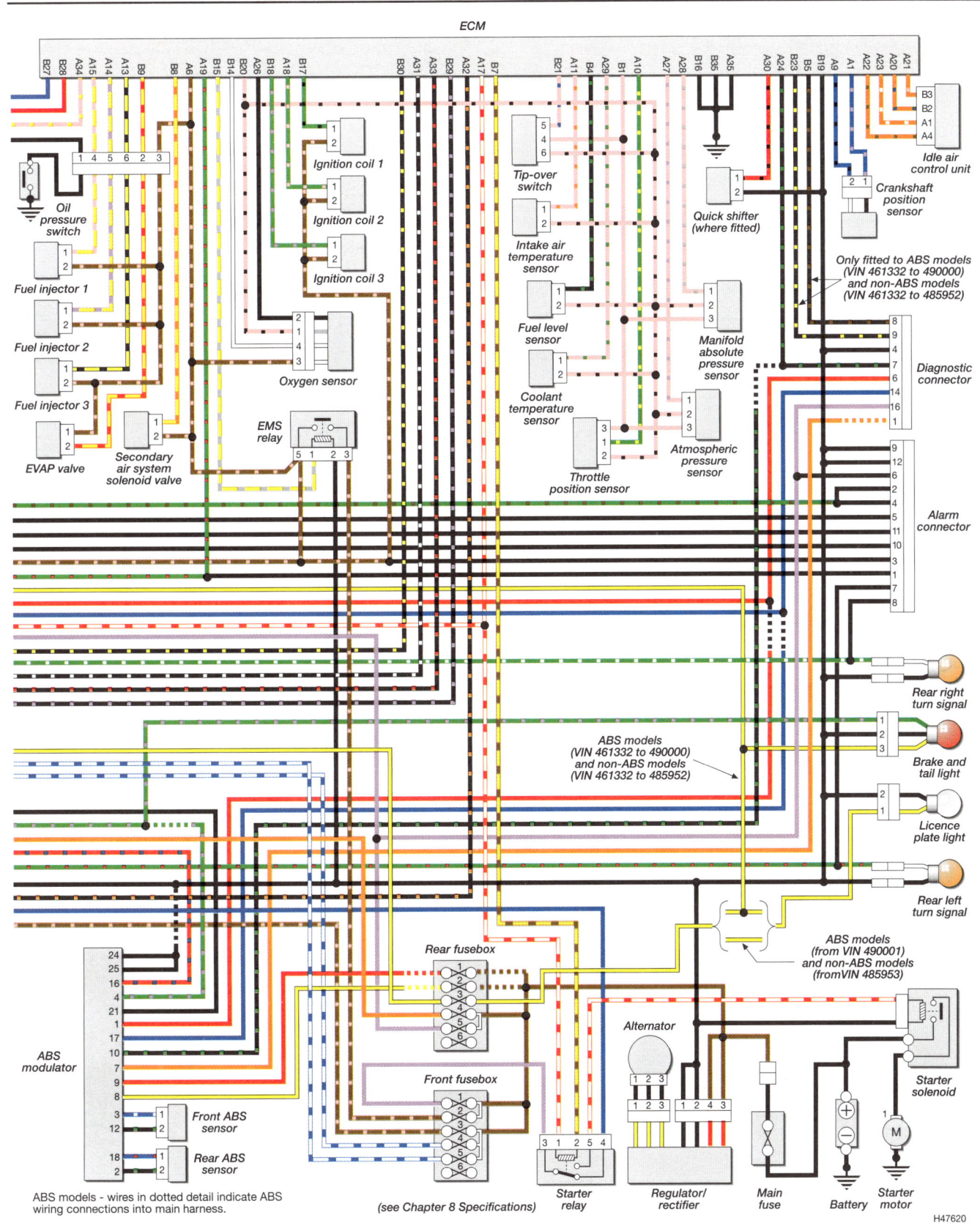

Wiring diagrams 8•49

Speed Triple (from VIN 461332)

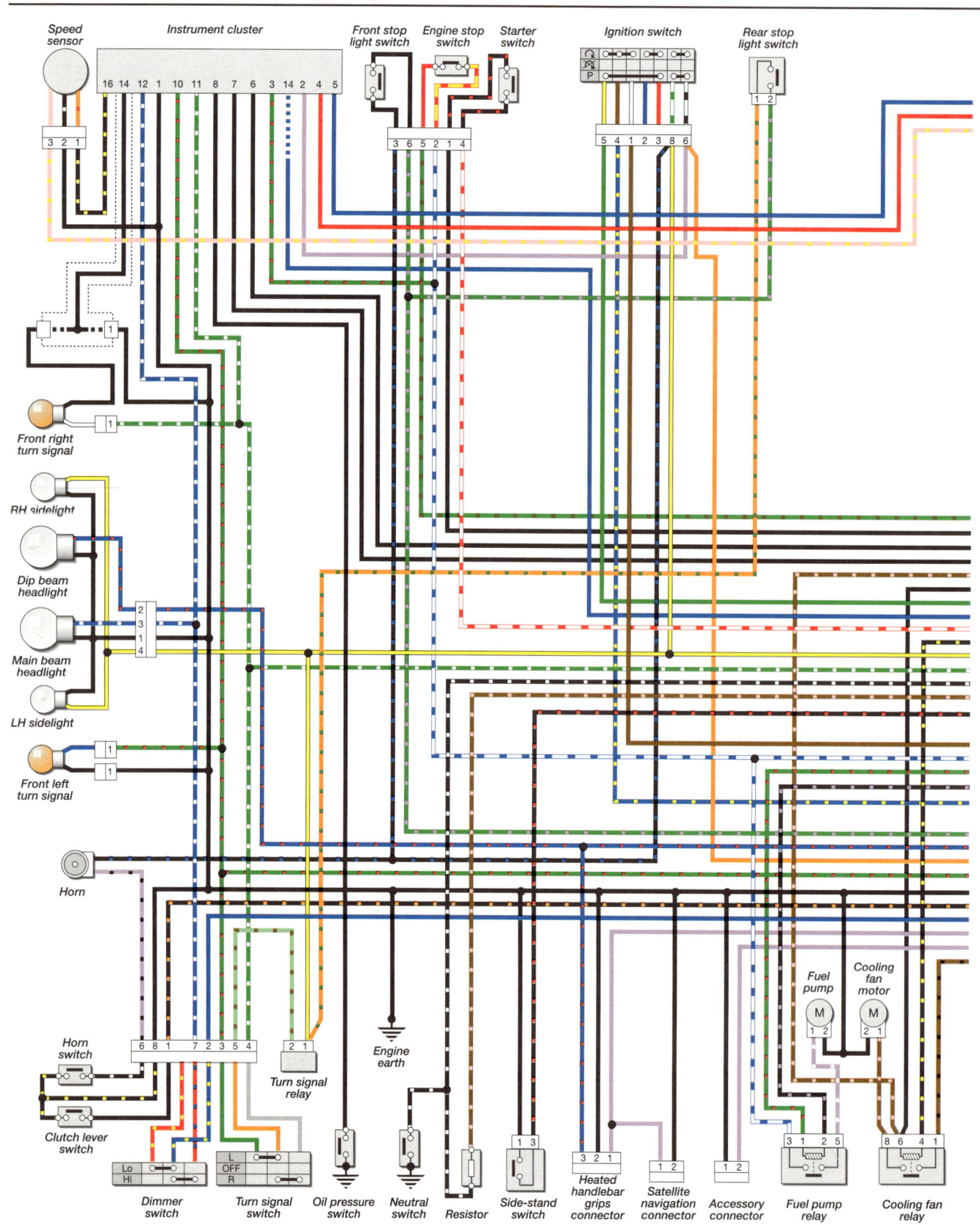
Tiger

Wiring diagrams 8•51

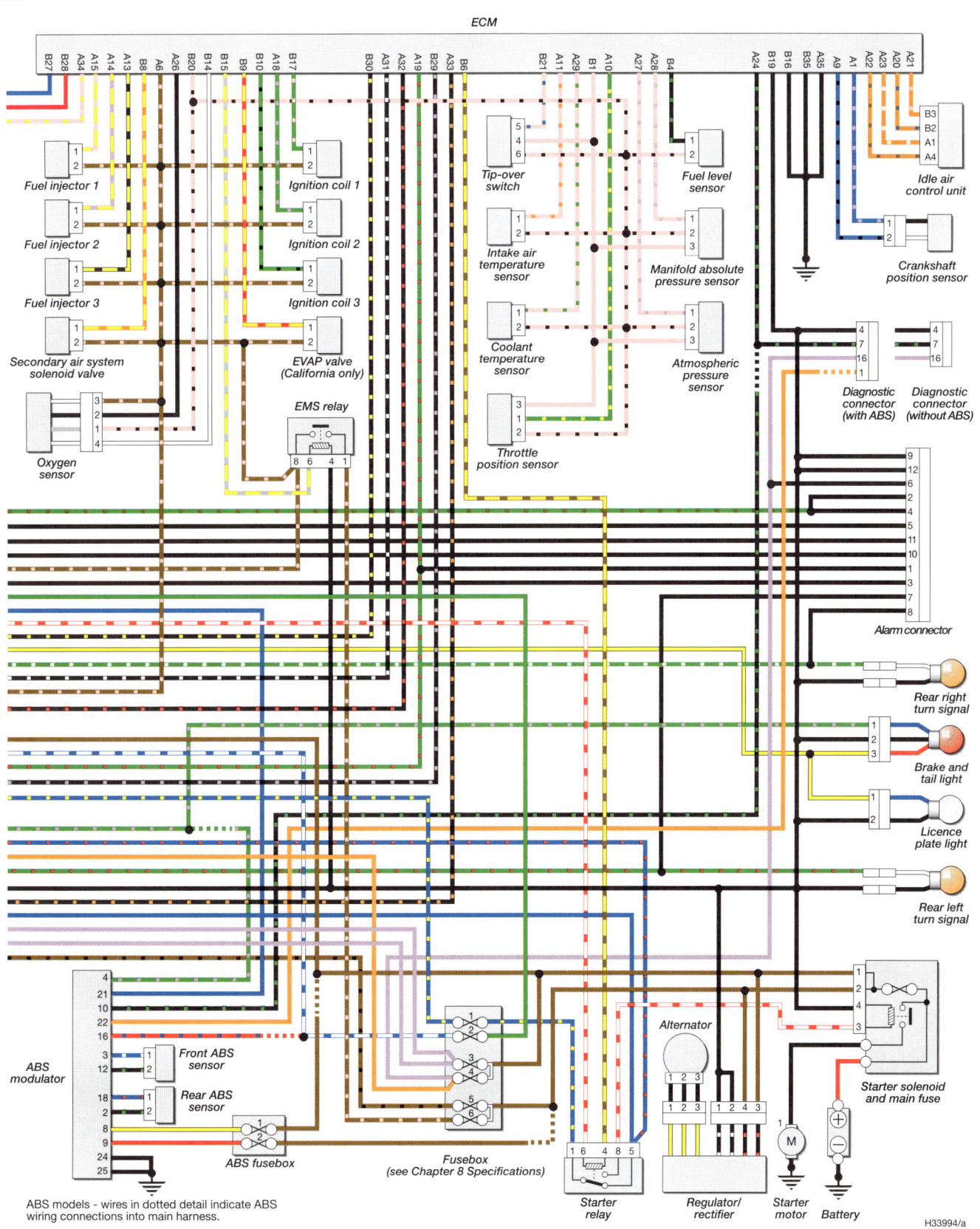

Tiger

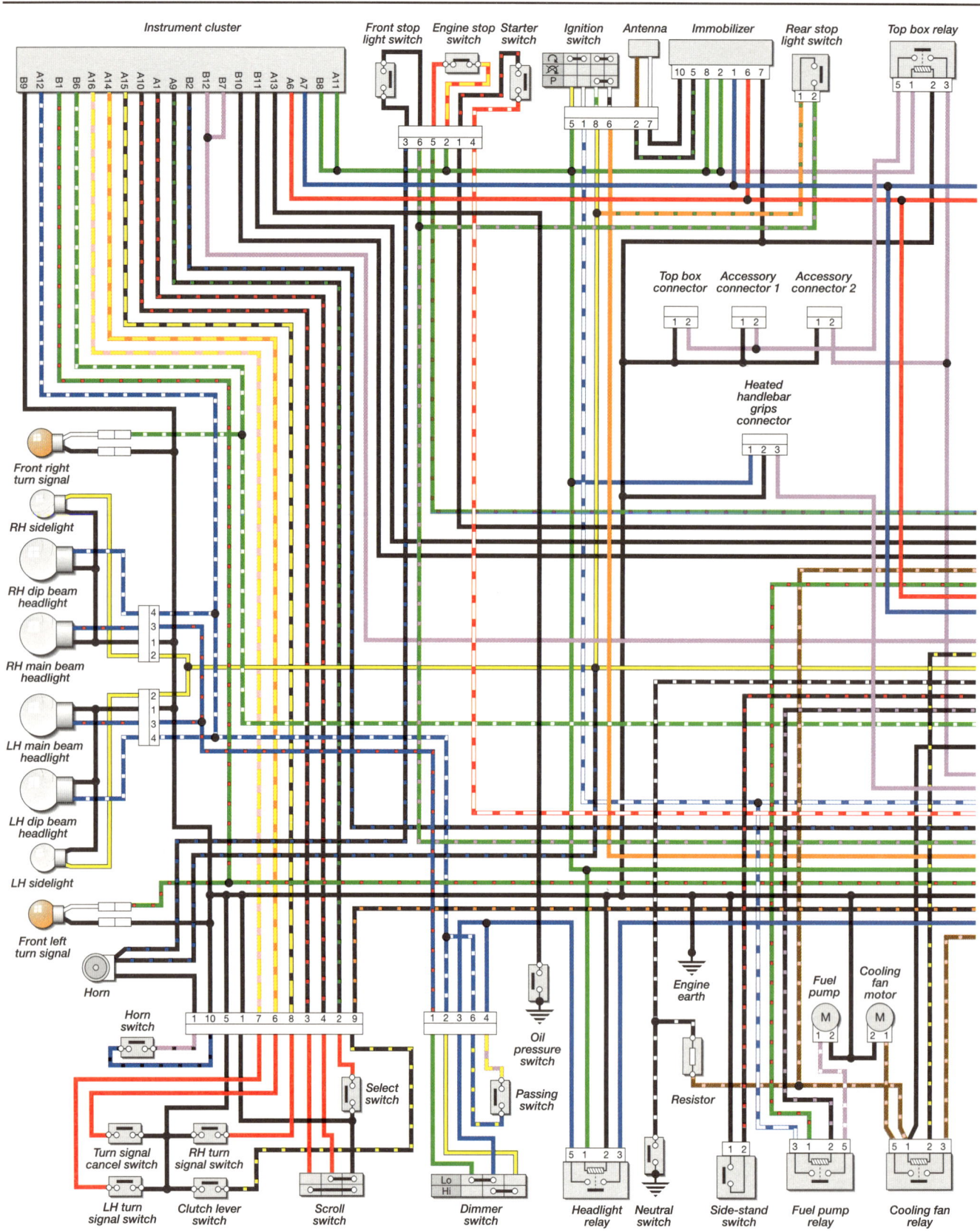

Wiring diagrams 8•53

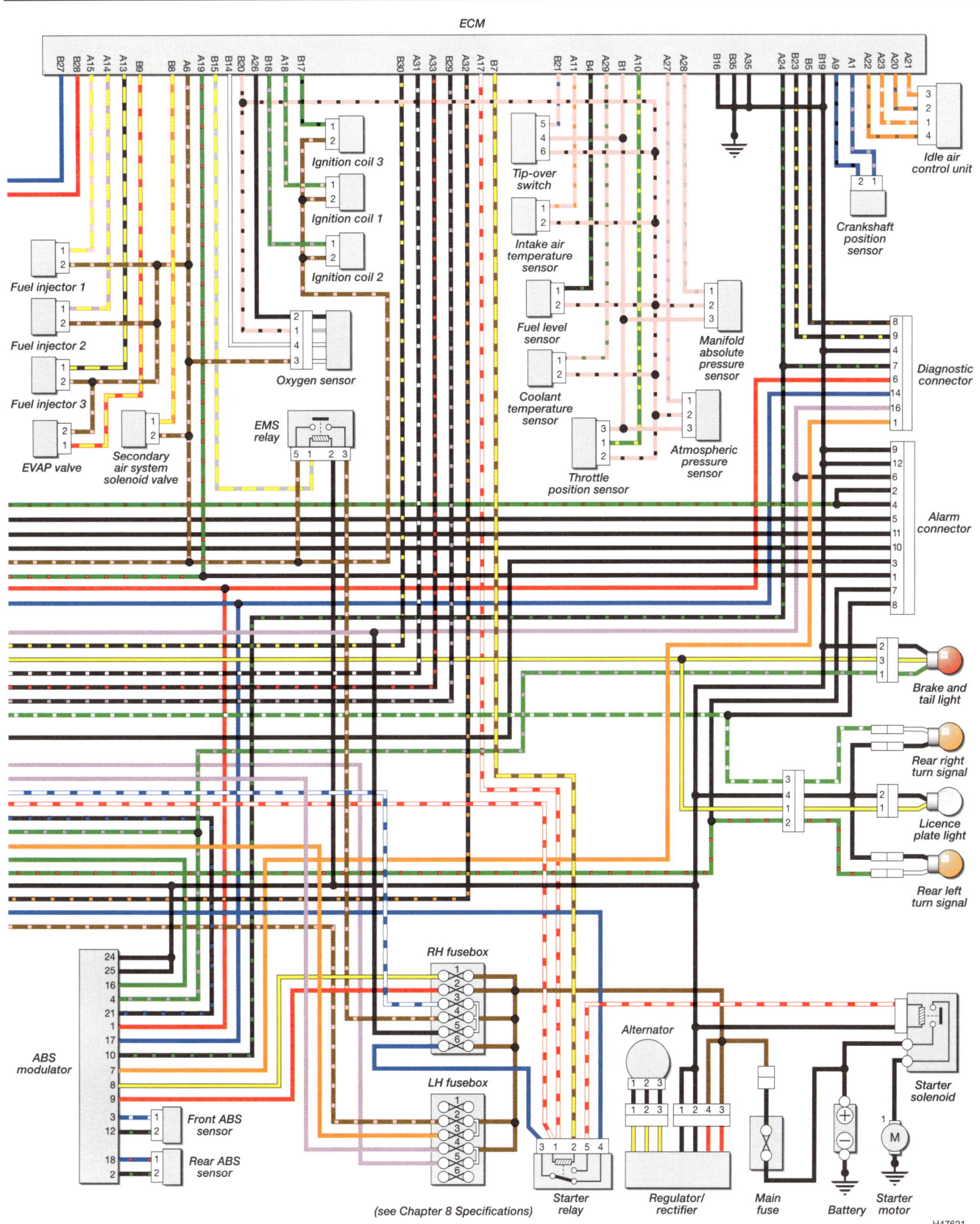

Tiger Sport

Notes

Reference REF•1

Reference

Security   REF•2

- Locks and chains
- U-locks ● Disc locks
- Alarms and immobilisers
- Security marking systems ● Tips on how to prevent bike theft

Lubricants and fluids   REF•5

- Engine oils
- Transmission (gear) oils
- Coolant/anti-freeze
- Fork oils and suspension fluids ● Brake/clutch fluids
- Spray lubes, degreasers and solvents

MOT Test Checks   REF•8

- A guide to the UK MOT test ● Which items are tested ● How to prepare your motorcycle for the test and perform a pre-test check

Conversion Factors   REF•13

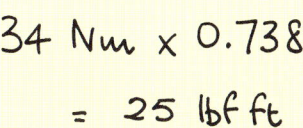

- Formulae for conversion of the metric (SI) units used throughout the manual into Imperial measures

Tools and Workshop Tips   REF•14

- Building up a tool kit and equipping your workshop ● Using tools
- Understanding bearing, seal, fastener and chain sizes and markings
- Repair techniques

Storage   REF•33

- How to prepare your motorcycle for going into storage and protect essential systems ● How to get the motorcycle back on the road

Fault Finding   REF•37

- Common faults and their likely causes ● Links to main chapters for testing or repair procedures

Technical Terms Explained   REF•48

- Component names, technical terms and common abbreviations explained

Index   REF•53

Security

Introduction

In less time than it takes to read this introduction, a thief could steal your motorcycle. Returning only to find your bike has gone is one of the worst feelings in the world. Even if the motorcycle is insured against theft, once you've got over the initial shock, you will have the inconvenience of dealing with the police and your insurance company.

The motorcycle is an easy target for the professional thief and the joyrider alike and the official figures on motorcycle theft make for depressing reading; on average a motor-cycle is stolen every 16 minutes in the UK!

Motorcycle thefts fall into two categories, those stolen 'to order' and those taken by opportunists. The thief stealing to order will be on the look out for a specific make and model and will go to extraordinary lengths to obtain that motorcycle. The opportunist thief on the other hand will look for easy targets which can be stolen with the minimum of effort and risk.

Whilst it is never going to be possible to make your machine 100% secure, it is estimated that around half of all stolen motorcycles are taken by opportunist thieves. Remember that the opportunist thief is always on the look out for the easy option: if there are two similar motorcycles parked side-by-side, they will target the one with the lowest level of security. By taking a few precautions, you can reduce the chances of your motorcycle being stolen.

Security equipment

There are many specialised motorcycle security devices available and the following text summarises their applications and their good and bad points.

Once you have decided on the type of security equipment which best suits your needs, we recommended that you read one of the many equipment tests regularly carried out by the motorcycle press. These tests compare the products from all the major manufacturers and give impartial ratings on their effectiveness, value-for-money and ease of use.

No one item of security equipment can provide complete protection. It is highly recommended that two or more of the items described below are combined to increase the security of your motorcycle (a lock and chain plus an alarm system is just about ideal). The more security measures fitted to the bike, the less likely it is to be stolen.

Lock and chain

Ensure the lock and chain you buy is of good quality and long enough to shackle your bike to a solid object

Pros: *Very flexible to use; can be used to secure the motorcycle to almost any immovable object. On some locks and chains, the lock can be used on its own as a disc lock (see below).*

Cons: *Can be very heavy and awkward to carry on the motorcycle, although some types will be supplied with a carry bag which can be strapped to the pillion seat.*

● Heavy-duty chains and locks are an excellent security measure **(see illustration 1)**. Whenever the motorcycle is parked, use the lock and chain to secure the machine to a solid, immovable object such as a post or railings. This will prevent the machine from being ridden away or being lifted into the back of a van.

● When fitting the chain, always ensure the chain is routed around the motorcycle frame or swingarm **(see illustrations 2 and 3)**. Never merely pass the chain around one of the wheel rims; a thief may unbolt the wheel and lift the rest of the machine into a van, leaving you with just the wheel! Try to avoid having excess chain free, thus making it difficult to use cutting tools, and keep the chain and lock off the ground to prevent thieves attacking it with a cold chisel. Position the lock so that its lock barrel is facing downwards; this will make it harder for the thief to attack the lock mechanism.

Pass the chain through the bike's frame, rather than just through a wheel . . .

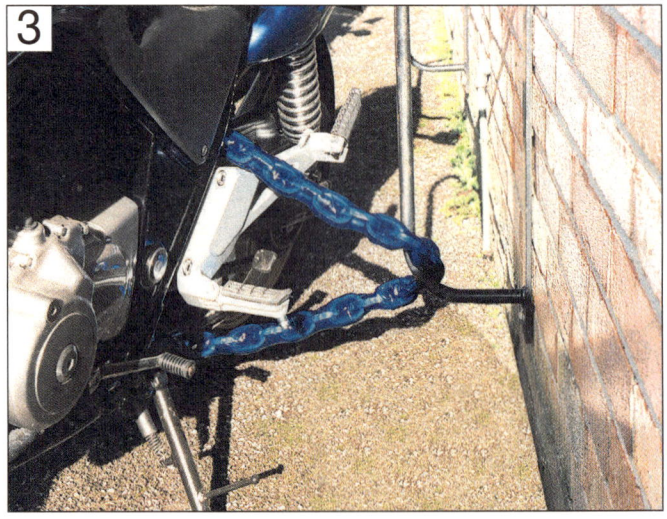

. . . and loop it around a solid object

Security REF•3

U-locks

Pros: *Highly effective deterrent which can be used to secure the bike to a post or railings. Most U-locks come with a carrier which allows the lock to be easily carried on the bike.*

Cons: *Not as flexible to use as a lock and chain.*

● These are solid locks which are similar in use to a lock and chain. U-locks are lighter than a lock and chain but not so flexible to use. The length and shape of the lock shackle limit the objects to which the bike can be secured **(see illustration 4)**.

Disc locks

Pros: *Small, light and very easy to carry; most can be stored underneath the seat.*

Cons: *Does not prevent the motorcycle being lifted into a van. Can be very embarrassing if*

U-locks can be used to secure the bike to a solid object – ensure you purchase one which is long enough

you forget to remove the lock before attempting to ride off!

● Disc locks are designed to be attached to the front brake disc. The lock passes through one of the holes in the disc and prevents the wheel rotating by jamming against the fork/brake caliper **(see illustration 5)**. Some are equipped with an alarm siren which sounds if the disc lock is moved; this not only acts as a theft deterrent but also as a handy reminder if you try to move the bike with the lock still fitted.

● Combining the disc lock with a length of cable which can be looped around a post or railings provides an additional measure of security **(see illustration 6)**.

Alarms and immobilisers

Pros: *Once installed it is completely hassle-free to use. If the system is 'Thatcham' or 'Sold Secure-approved', insurance companies may give you a discount.*

Cons: *Can be expensive to buy and complex to install. No system will prevent the motorcycle from being lifted into a van and taken away.*

● Electronic alarms and immobilisers are available to suit a variety of budgets. There are three different types of system available: pure alarms, pure immobilisers, and the more expensive systems which are combined alarm/immobilisers **(see illustration 7)**.

● An alarm system is designed to emit an audible warning if the motorcycle is being tampered with.

● An immobiliser prevents the motorcycle being started and ridden away by disabling its electrical systems.

● When purchasing an alarm/immobiliser system, check the cost of installing the system unless you are able to do it yourself. If the motorcycle is not used regularly, another consideration is the current drain of the system. All alarm/immobiliser systems are powered by the motorcycle's battery; purchasing a system with a very low current drain could prevent the battery losing its charge whilst the motorcycle is not being used.

A typical disc lock attached through one of the holes in the disc

A disc lock combined with a security cable provides additional protection

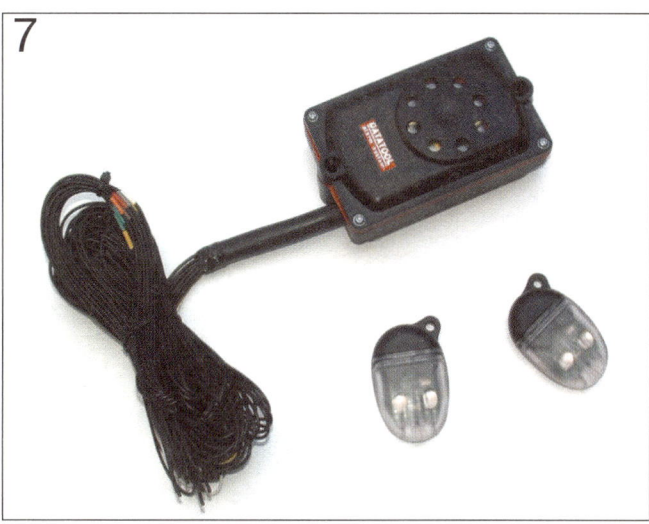

A typical alarm/immobiliser system

REF•4 Security

Indelible markings can be applied to most areas of the bike – always apply the manufacturer's sticker to warn off thieves

Chemically-etched code numbers can be applied to main body panels . . .

. . . again, always ensure that the kit manufacturer's sticker is applied in a prominent position

Security marking kits

Pros: Very cheap and effective deterrent. Many insurance companies will give you a discount on your insurance premium if a recognised security marking kit is used on your motorcycle.

Cons: Does not prevent the motorcycle being stolen by joyriders.

● There are many different types of security marking kits available. The idea is to mark as many parts of the motorcycle as possible with a unique security number **(see illustrations 8, 9 and 10)**. A form will be included with the kit to register your personal details and those of the motorcycle with the kit manufacturer. This register is made available to the police to help them trace the rightful owner of any motorcycle or components which they recover should all other forms of identification have been removed. Always apply the warning stickers provided with the kit to deter thieves.

Ground anchors, wheel clamps and security posts

Pros: An excellent form of security which will deter all but the most determined of thieves.

Cons: Awkward to install and can be expensive.

● Whilst the motorcycle is at home, it is a good idea to attach it securely to the floor or a solid wall, even if it is kept in a securely locked garage. Various types of ground anchors, security posts and wheel clamps are available for this purpose **(see illustration 11)**. These security devices are either bolted to a solid concrete or brick structure or can be cemented into the ground.

Permanent ground anchors provide an excellent level of security when the bike is at home

Security at home

A high percentage of motorcycle thefts are from the owner's home. Here are some things to consider whenever your motorcycle is at home:

● Where possible, always keep the motorcycle in a securely locked garage. Never rely solely on the standard lock on the garage door, these are usual hopelessly inadequate. Fit an additional locking mechanism to the door and consider having the garage alarmed. A security light, activated by a movement sensor, is also a good investment.

● Always secure the motorcycle to the ground or a wall, even if it is inside a securely locked garage.

● Do not regularly leave the motorcycle outside your home, try to keep it out of sight wherever possible. If a garage is not available, fit a motorcycle cover over the bike to disguise its true identity.

● It is not uncommon for thieves to follow a motorcyclist home to find out where the bike is kept. They will then return at a later date. Be aware of this whenever you are returning home on your motorcycle. If you suspect you are being followed, do not return home, instead ride to a garage or shop and stop as a precaution.

● When selling a motorcycle, do not provide your home address or the location where the bike is normally kept. Arrange to meet the buyer at a location away from your home. Thieves have been known to pose as potential buyers to find out where motorcycles are kept and then return later to steal them.

Security away from the home

As well as fitting security equipment to your motorcycle here are a few general rules to follow whenever you park your motorcycle.
● Park in a busy, public place.
● Use car parks which incorporate security features, such as CCTV.
● At night, park in a well-lit area, preferably directly underneath a street light.
● Engage the steering lock.
● Secure the motorcycle to a solid, immovable object such as a post or railings with an additional lock. If this is not possible, secure the bike to a friend's motorcycle. Some public parking places provide security loops for motorcycles.
● Never leave your helmet or luggage attached to the motorcycle. Take them with you at all times.

Lubricants and fluids

A wide range of lubricants, fluids and cleaning agents is available for motor-cycles. This is a guide as to what is available, its applications and properties.

Four-stroke engine oil

● Engine oil is without doubt the most important component of any four-stroke engine. Modern motorcycle engines place a lot of demands on their oil and choosing the right type is essential. Using an unsuitable oil will lead to an increased rate of engine wear and could result in serious engine damage. Before purchasing oil, always check the recommended oil specification given by the manufacturer. The manufacturer will state a recommended 'type or classification' and also a specific 'viscosity' range for engine oil.

● The oil 'type or classification' is identified by its API (American Petroleum Institute) rating. The API rating will be in the form of two letters, e.g. SG. The S identifies the oil as being suitable for use in a petrol (gasoline) engine (S stands for spark ignition) and the second letter, ranging from A to J, identifies the oil's performance rating. The later this letter, the higher the specification of the oil; for example API SG oil exceeds the requirements of API SF oil. **Note:** *On some oils there may also be a second rating consisting of another two letters, the first letter being C, e.g. API SF/CD. This rating indicates the oil is also suitable for use in a diesel engines (the C stands for compression ignition) and is thus of no relevance for motorcycle use.*

● The 'viscosity' of the oil is identified by its SAE (Society of Automotive Engineers) rating. All modern engines require multigrade oils and the SAE rating will consist of two numbers, the first followed by a W, e.g. 10W/40. The first number indicates the viscosity rating of the oil at low temperatures (W stands for winter – tested at –20°C) and the second number represents the viscosity of the oil at high temperatures (tested at 100°C). The lower the number, the thinner the oil. For example an oil with an SAE 10W/40 rating will give better cold starting and running than an SAE 15W/40 oil.

● As well as ensuring the 'type' and 'viscosity' of the oil match the recommendations, another consideration to make when buying engine oil is whether to purchase a standard mineral-based oil, a semi-synthetic oil (also known as a synthetic blend or synthetic-based oil) or a fully-synthetic oil. Although all oils will have a similar rating and viscosity, their cost will vary considerably; mineral-based oils are the cheapest, the fully-synthetic oils the most expensive with the semi-synthetic oils falling somewhere in-between. This decision is very much up to the owner, but it should be noted that modern synthetic oils have far better lubricating and cleaning qualities than traditional mineral-based oils and tend to retain these properties for far longer. Bearing in mind the operating conditions inside a modern, high-revving motorcycle engine it is highly recommended that a fully synthetic oil is used. The extra expense at each service could save you money in the long term by preventing premature engine wear.

● As a final note always ensure that the oil is specifically designed for use in motorcycle engines. Engine oils designed primarily for use in car engines sometimes contain additives or friction modifiers which could cause clutch slip on a motorcycle fitted with a wet-clutch.

Two-stroke engine oil

● Modern two-stroke engines, with their high power outputs, place high demands on their oil. If engine seizure is to be avoided it is essential that a high-quality oil is used. Two-stroke oils differ hugely from four-stroke oils. The oil lubricates only the crankshaft and piston(s) (the transmission has its own lubricating oil) and is used on a total-loss basis where it is burnt completely during the combustion process.

● The Japanese have recently introduced a classification system for two-stroke oils, the JASO rating. This rating is in the form of two letters, either FA, FB or FC – FA is the lowest classification and FC the highest. Ensure the oil being used meets or exceeds the recommended rating specified by the manufacturer.

● As well as ensuring the oil rating matches the recommendation, another consideration to make when buying engine oil is whether to purchase a standard mineral-based oil, a semi-synthetic oil (also known as a synthetic blend or synthetic-based oil) or a fully-synthetic oil. The cost of each type of oil varies considerably; mineral-based oils are the cheapest, the fully-synthetic oils the most expensive with the semi-synthetic oils falling somewhere in-between. This decision is very much up to the owner, but it should be noted that modern synthetic oils have far better lubricating properties and burn cleaner than traditional mineral-based oils. It is therefore recommended that a fully synthetic oil is used. The extra expense could save you money in the long term by preventing premature engine wear, engine performance will be improved, carbon deposits and exhaust smoke will be reduced.

REF•6 Lubricants and fluids

● Always ensure that the oil is specifically designed for use in an injector system. Many high quality two-stroke oils are designed for competition use and need to be pre-mixed with fuel. These oils are of a much higher viscosity and are not designed to flow through the injector pumps used on road-going two-stroke motorcycles.

Transmission (gear) oil

● On a two-stroke engine, the transmission and clutch are lubricated by their own separate oil bath which must be changed in accordance with the Maintenance Schedule.
● Although the engine and transmission units of most four-strokes use a common lubrication supply, there are some exceptions where the engine and gearbox have separate oil reservoirs and a dry clutch is used.
● Motorcycle manufacturers will either recommend a monograde transmission oil or a four-stroke multigrade engine oil to lubricate the transmission.
● Transmission oils, or gear oils as they are often called, are designed specifically for use in transmission systems. The viscosity of these oils is represented by an SAE number, but the scale of measurement applied is different to that used to grade engine oils. As a rough guide a SAE90 gear oil will be of the same viscosity as an SAE50 engine oil.

Shaft drive oil

● On models equipped with shaft final drive, the shaft drive gears are will have their own oil supply. The manufacturer will state a recommended 'type or classification' and also a specific 'viscosity' range in the same manner as for four-stroke engine oil.
● Gear oil classification is given by the number which follows the API GL (GL standing for gear lubricant) rating, the higher the number, the higher the specification of the oil, e.g. API GL5 oil is a higher specification than API GL4 oil. Ensure the oil meets or exceeds the classification specified and is of the correct viscosity. The viscosity of gear oils is also represented by an SAE number but the scale of measurement used is different to that used to grade engine oils. As a rough guide an SAE90 gear oil will be of the same viscosity as an SAE50 engine oil.
● If the use of an EP (Extreme Pressure) gear oil is specified, ensure the oil purchased is suitable.

Fork oil and suspension fluid

● Conventional telescopic front forks are hydraulic and require fork oil to work. To ensure the forks function correctly, the fork oil must be changed in accordance with the Maintenance Schedule.
● Fork oil is available in a variety of viscosities, identified by their SAE rating; fork oil ratings vary from light (SAE 5) to heavy (SAE 30). When purchasing fork oil, ensure the viscosity rating matches that specified by the manufacturer.
● Some lubricant manufacturers also produce a range of high-quality suspension fluids which are very similar to fork oil but are designed mainly for competition use. These fluids may have a different viscosity rating system which is not to be confused with the SAE rating of normal fork oil. Refer to the manufacturer's instructions if in any doubt.

Brake and clutch fluid

● All disc brake systems and some clutch systems are hydraulically operated. To ensure correct operation, the hydraulic fluid must be changed in accordance with the Maintenance Schedule.
● Brake and clutch fluid is classified by its DOT rating with most motorcycle manufacturers specifying DOT 3 or 4 fluid. Both fluid types are glycol-based and can be mixed together without adverse effect; DOT 4 fluid exceeds the requirements of DOT 3 fluid. Although it is safe to use DOT 4 fluid in a system designed for use with DOT 3 fluid, never use DOT 3 fluid in a system which specifies the use of DOT 4 as this will adversely affect the system's performance. The type required for the system will be marked on the fluid reservoir cap.
● Some manufacturers also produce a DOT 5 hydraulic fluid. DOT 5 hydraulic fluid is silicone-based and is not compatible with the glycol-based DOT 3 and 4 fluids. Never mix DOT 5 fluid with DOT 3 or 4 fluid as this will seriously affect the performance of the hydraulic system.

Coolant/antifreeze

● When purchasing coolant/antifreeze, always ensure it is suitable for use in an aluminium engine and contains corrosion inhibitors to prevent possible blockages of the internal coolant passages of the system. As a general rule, most coolants are designed to be used neat and should not be diluted whereas antifreeze can be mixed with distilled water to provide a coolant solution of the required strength. Refer to the manufacturer's instructions on the bottle.
● Ensure the coolant is changed in accordance with the Maintenance Schedule.

Chain lube

● Chain lube is an aerosol-type spray lubricant specifically designed for use on motorcycle final drive chains. Chain lube has two functions, to minimise friction between the final drive chain and sprockets and to prevent corrosion of the chain. Regular use of a good-quality chain lube will extend the life of the drive chain and sprockets and thus maximise the power being transmitted from the transmission to the rear wheel.
● When using chain lube, always allow some time for the solvents in the lube to evaporate before riding the motorcycle. This will minimise the amount of lube which will

Lubricants and fluids

'fling' off from the chain when the motorcycle is used. If the motorcycle is equipped with an 'O-ring' chain, ensure the chain lube is labelled as being suitable for use on 'O-ring' chains.

Degreasers and solvents

● There are many different types of solvents and degreasers available to remove the grime and grease which accumulate around the motorcycle during normal use. Degreasers and solvents are usually available as an aerosol-type spray or as a liquid which you apply with a brush. Always closely follow the manufacturer's instructions and wear eye protection during use. Be aware that many solvents are flammable and may give off noxious fumes; take adequate precautions when using them (see Safety First!).

● For general cleaning, use one of the many solvents or degreasers available from most motorcycle accessory shops. These solvents are usually applied then left for a certain time before being washed off with water.

Brake cleaner is a solvent specifically designed to remove all traces of oil, grease and dust from braking system components. Brake cleaner is designed to evaporate quickly and leaves behind no residue.

Carburettor cleaner is an aerosol-type solvent specifically designed to clear carburettor blockages and break down the hard deposits and gum often found inside carburettors during overhaul.

Contact cleaner is an aerosol-type solvent designed for cleaning electrical components. The cleaner will remove all traces of oil and dirt from components such as switch contacts or fouled spark plugs and then dry, leaving behind no residue.

Gasket remover is an aerosol-type solvent designed for removing stubborn gaskets from engine components during overhaul. Gasket remover will minimise the amount of scraping required to remove the gasket and therefore reduce the risk of damage to the mating surface.

Spray lubricants

● Aerosol-based spray lubricants are widely available and are excellent for lubricating lever pivots and exposed cables and switches. Try to use a lubricant which is of the dry-film type as the fluid evaporates, leaving behind a dry-film of lubricant. Lubricants which leave behind an oily residue will attract dust and dirt which will increase the rate of wear of the cable/lever.

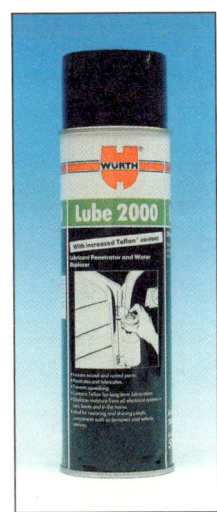

● Most lubricants also act as a moisture dispersant and a penetrating fluid. This means they can also be used to 'dry out' electrical components such as wiring connectors or switches as well as helping to free seized fasteners.

Greases

● Grease is used to lubricate many of the pivot-points. A good-quality multi-purpose grease is suitable for most applications but some manufacturers will specify the use of specialist greases for use on components such as swingarm and suspension linkage bushes. These specialist greases can be purchased from most motorcycle (or car) accessory shops; commonly specified types include molybdenum disulphide grease, lithium-based grease, graphite-based grease, silicone-based grease and high-temperature copper-based grease.

Gasket sealing compounds

● Gasket sealing compounds can be used in conjunction with gaskets, to improve their sealing capabilities, or on their own to seal metal-to-metal joints. Depending on their type, sealing compounds either set hard or stay relatively soft and pliable.

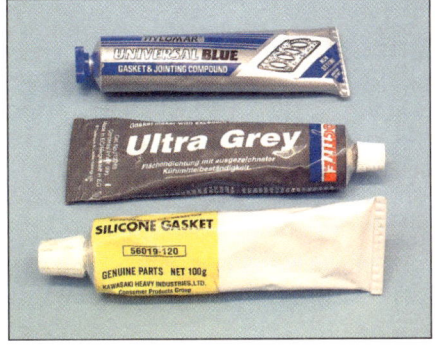

● When purchasing a gasket sealing compound, ensure that it is designed specifically for use on an internal combustion engine. General multi-purpose sealants available from DIY stores may appear visibly similar but they are not designed to withstand the extreme heat or contact with fuel and oil encountered when used on an engine (see 'Tools and Workshop Tips' for further information).

Thread locking compound

● Thread locking compounds are used to secure certain threaded fasteners in position to prevent them from loosening due to vibration. Thread locking compounds can be purchased from most motorcycle (and car) accessory shops. Ensure the threads of the both components are completely clean and dry before sparingly applying the locking compound (see 'Tools and Workshop Tips' for further information).

Fuel additives

● Fuel additives which protect and clean the fuel system components are widely available. These additives are designed to remove all traces of deposits that build up on the carburettors/injectors and prevent wear, helping the fuel system to operate more efficiently. If a fuel additive is being used, check that it is suitable for use with your motorcycle, especially if your motorcycle is equipped with a catalytic converter.

● Octane boosters are also available. These additives are designed to improve the performance of highly-tuned engines being run on normal pump-fuel and are of no real use on standard motorcycles.

REF•8 MOT Test Checks

About the MOT Test

In the UK, all vehicles more than three years old are subject to an annual test to ensure that they meet minimum safety requirements. A current test certificate must be issued before a machine can be used on public roads, and is required before a road fund licence can be issued. Riding without a current test certificate will also invalidate your insurance.

For most owners, the MOT test is an annual cause for anxiety, and this is largely due to owners not being sure what needs to be checked prior to submitting the motorcycle for testing. The simple answer is that a fully roadworthy motorcycle will have no difficulty in passing the test.

This is a guide to getting your motorcycle through the MOT test. Obviously it will not be possible to examine the motorcycle to the same standard as the professional MOT tester, particularly in view of the equipment required for some of the checks. However, working through the following procedures will enable you to identify any problem areas before submitting the motorcycle for the test.

It has only been possible to summarise the test requirements here, based on the regulations in force at the time of printing. Test standards are becoming increasingly stringent, although there are some exemptions for older vehicles. More information about the MOT test can be obtained from the TSO publications, *How Safe is your Motorcycle* and *The MOT Inspection Manual for Motorcycle Testing*.

Many of the checks require that one of the wheels is raised off the ground. If the motorcycle doesn't have a centre stand, note that an auxiliary stand will be required. Additionally, the help of an assistant may prove useful.

Certain exceptions apply to machines under 50 cc, machines without a lighting system, and Classic bikes - if in doubt about any of the requirements listed below seek confirmation from an MOT tester prior to submitting the motorcycle for the test.

Check that the frame number is clearly visible.

Electrical System

Lights, turn signals, horn and reflector

● With the ignition on, check the operation of the following electrical components. **Note:** *The electrical components on certain small-capacity machines are powered by the generator, requiring that the engine is run for this check.*

  a) *Headlight and tail light. Check that both illuminate in the low and high beam switch positions.*
  b) *Position lights. Check that the front position (or sidelight) and tail light illuminate in this switch position.*
  c) *Turn signals. Check that all flash at the correct rate, and that the warning light(s) function correctly. Check that the turn signal switch works correctly.*
  d) *Hazard warning system (where fitted). Check that all four turn signals flash in this switch position.*
  e) *Brake stop light. Check that the light comes on when the front and rear brakes are independently applied. Models first used on or after 1st April 1986 must have a brake light switch on each brake.*
  f) *Horn. Check that the sound is continuous and of reasonable volume.*

● Check that there is a red reflector on the rear of the machine, either mounted separately or as part of the tail light lens.
● Check the condition of the headlight, tail light and turn signal lenses.

Headlight beam height

● The MOT tester will perform a headlight beam height check using specialised beam setting equipment **(see illustration 1)**. This equipment will not be available to the home mechanic, but if you suspect that the headlight is incorrectly set or may have been maladjusted in the past, you can perform a rough test as follows.
● Position the bike in a straight line facing a brick wall. The bike must be off its stand, upright and with a rider seated. Measure the height from the ground to the centre of the headlight and mark a horizontal line on the wall at this height. Position the motorcycle 3.8 metres from the wall and draw a vertical line up the wall central to the centreline of the motorcycle. Switch to dipped beam and check that the beam pattern falls slightly lower than the horizontal line and to the left of the vertical line **(see illustration 2)**.

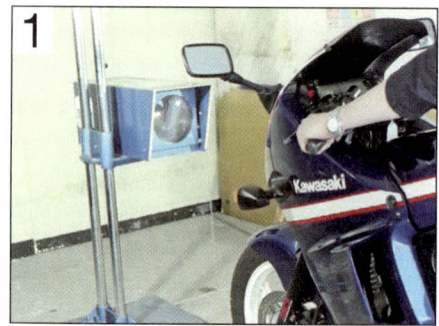

Headlight beam height checking equipment

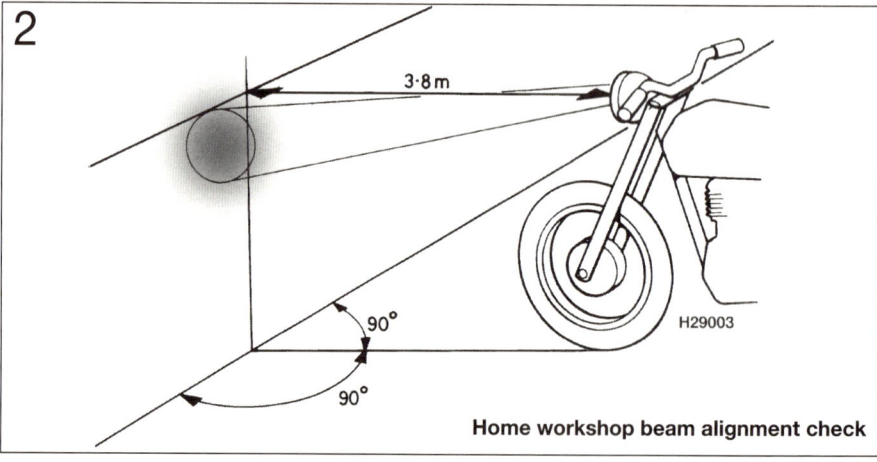

Home workshop beam alignment check

MOT Test Checks

Exhaust System and Final Drive

Exhaust

● Check that the exhaust mountings are secure and that the system does not foul any of the rear suspension components.
● Start the motorcycle. When the revs are increased, check that the exhaust is neither holed nor leaking from any of its joints. On a linked system, check that the collector box is not leaking due to corrosion.
● Note that the exhaust decibel level ("loudness" of the exhaust) is assessed at the discretion of the tester. If the motorcycle was first used on or after 1st January 1985 the silencer must carry the BSAU 193 stamp, or a marking relating to its make and model, or be of OE (original equipment) manufacture. If the silencer is marked NOT FOR ROAD USE, RACING USE ONLY or similar, it will fail the MOT.

Final drive

● On chain or belt drive machines, check that the chain/belt is in good condition and does not have excessive slack. Also check that the sprocket is securely mounted on the rear wheel hub. Check that the chain/belt guard is in place.
● On shaft drive bikes, check for oil leaking from the drive unit and fouling the rear tyre.

Steering and Suspension

Steering

● With the front wheel raised off the ground, rotate the steering from lock to lock. The handlebar or switches must not contact the fuel tank or be close enough to trap the rider's hand. Problems can be caused by damaged lock stops on the lower yoke and frame, or by the fitting of non-standard handlebars.
● When performing the lock to lock check, also ensure that the steering moves freely without drag or notchiness. Steering movement can be impaired by poorly routed cables, or by overtight head bearings or worn bvearings. The tester will perform a check of the steering head bearing lower race by mounting the front wheel on a surface plate, then performing a lock to lock check with the weight of the machine on the lower bearing (see illustration 3).
● Grasp the fork sliders (lower legs) and attempt to push and pull on the forks

Front wheel mounted on a surface plate for steering head bearing lower race check

(see illustration 4). Any play in the steering head bearings will be felt. Note that in extreme cases, wear of the front fork bushes can be misinterpreted for head bearing play.
● Check that the handlebars are securely mounted.
● Check that the handlebar grip rubbers are secure. They should by bonded to the bar left end and to the throttle cable pulley on the right end.

Front suspension

● With the motorcycle off the stand, hold the front brake on and pump the front forks up and down (see illustration 5). Check that they are adequately damped.

Checking the steering head bearings for freeplay

Hold the front brake on and pump the front forks up and down to check operation

REF•10 MOT Test Checks

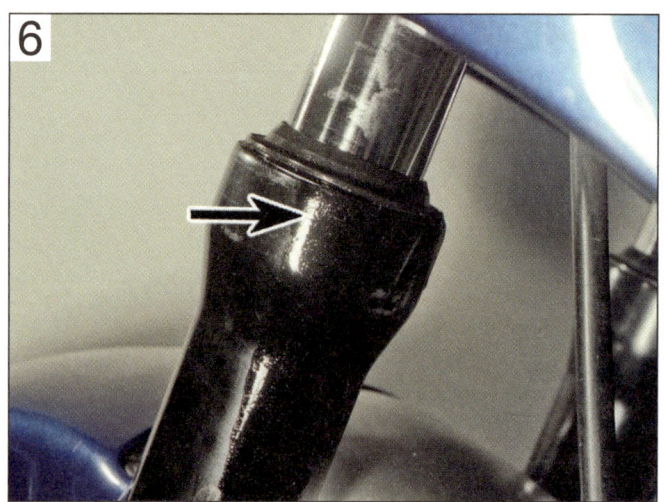

Inspect the area around the fork dust seal for oil leakage (arrow)

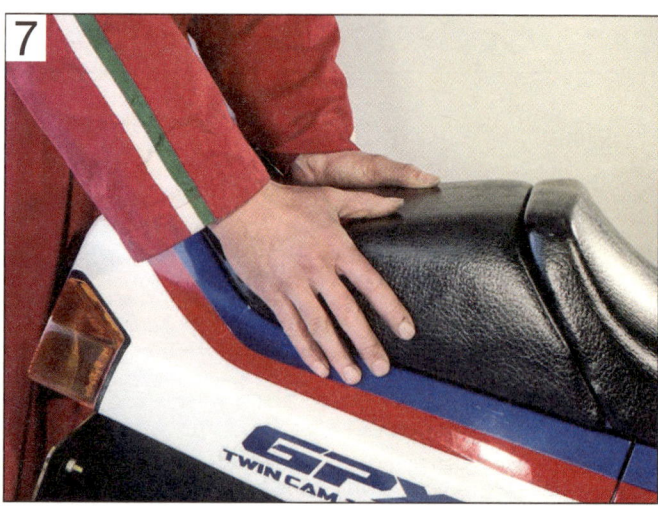

Bounce the rear of the motorcycle to check rear suspension operation

Checking for rear suspension linkage play

● Inspect the area above and around the front fork oil seals **(see illustration 6)**. There should be no sign of oil on the fork tube (stanchion) nor leaking down the slider (lower leg). On models so equipped, check that there is no oil leaking from the anti-dive units.
● On models with swingarm front suspension, check that there is no freeplay in the linkage when moved from side to side.

Rear suspension

● With the motorcycle off the stand and an assistant supporting the motorcycle by its handlebars, bounce the rear suspension **(see illustration 7)**. Check that the suspension components do not foul on any of the cycle parts and check that the shock absorber(s) provide adequate damping.
● Visually inspect the shock absorber(s) and check that there is no sign of oil leakage from its damper. This is somewhat restricted on certain single shock models due to the location of the shock absorber.
● With the rear wheel raised off the ground, grasp the wheel at the highest point and attempt to pull it up **(see illustration 8)**. Any play in the swingarm pivot or suspension linkage bearings will be felt as movement. **Note:** *Do not confuse play with actual suspension movement.* Failure to lubricate suspension linkage bearings can lead to bearing failure **(see illustration 9)**.
● With the rear wheel raised off the ground, grasp the swingarm ends and attempt to move the swingarm from side to side and forwards and backwards - any play indicates wear of the swingarm pivot bearings **(see illustration 10)**.

Worn suspension linkage pivots (arrows) are usually the cause of play in the rear suspension

Grasp the swingarm at the ends to check for play in its pivot bearings

MOT Test Checks

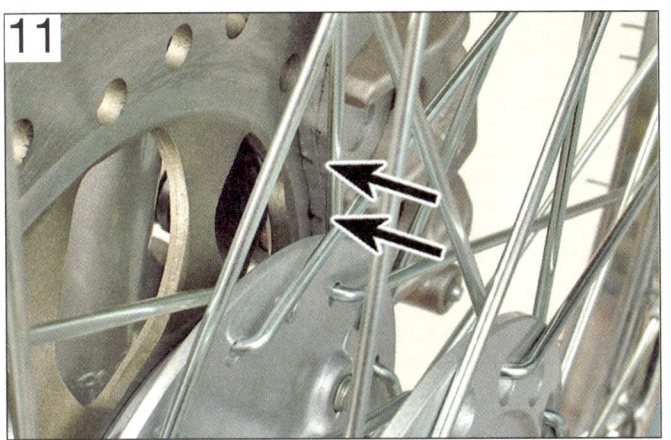

Brake pad wear can usually be viewed without removing the caliper. Most pads have wear indicator grooves (arrowed) and some also have indicator tangs or cut-outs.

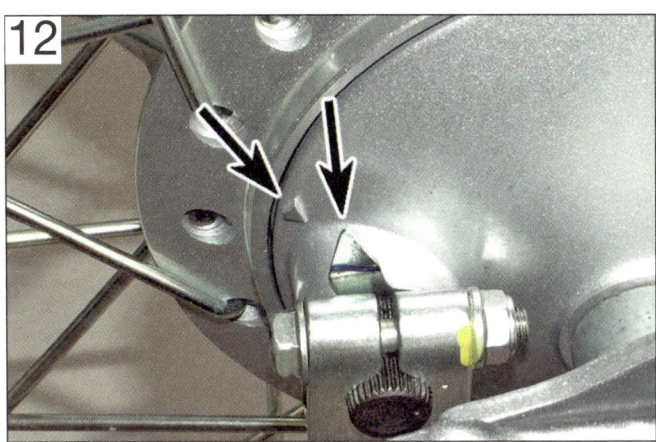

On drum brakes, check the angle of the operating lever with the brake fully applied. Most drum brakes have a wear indicator pointer or scale.

Brakes, Wheels and Tyres

Brakes

- With the wheel raised off the ground, apply the brake then free it off, and check that the wheel is about to revolve freely without brake drag.
- On disc brakes, examine the disc itself. Check that it is securely mounted and not cracked.
- On disc brakes, view the pad material through the caliper mouth and check that the pads are not worn down beyond the limit **(see illustration 11)**.
- On drum brakes, check that when the brake is applied the angle between the operating lever and cable or rod is not too great **(see illustration 12)**. Check also that the operating lever doesn't foul any other components.
- On disc brakes, examine the flexible hoses from top to bottom. Have an assistant hold the brake on so that the fluid in the hose is under pressure, and check that there is no sign of fluid leakage, bulges or cracking. If there are any metal brake pipes or unions, check that these are free from corrosion and damage. Where a brake-linked anti-dive system is fitted, check the hoses to the anti-dive in a similar manner.
- Check that the rear brake torque arm is secure and that its fasteners are secured by self-locking nuts or castellated nuts with split-pins or R-pins **(see illustration 13)**.
- On models with ABS, check that the self-check warning light in the instrument panel works.
- The MOT tester will perform a test of the motorcycle's braking efficiency based on a calculation of rider and motorcycle weight. Although this cannot be carried out at home, you can at least ensure that the braking systems are properly maintained. For hydraulic disc brakes, check the fluid level, lever/pedal feel (bleed of air if its spongy) and pad material. For drum brakes, check adjustment, cable or rod operation and shoe lining thickness.

Wheels and tyres

- Check the wheel condition. Cast wheels should be free from cracks and if of the built-up design, all fasteners should be secure. Spoked wheels should be checked for broken, corroded, loose or bent spokes.
- With the wheel raised off the ground, spin the wheel and visually check that the tyre and wheel run true. Check that the tyre does not foul the suspension or mudguards.
- With the wheel raised off the ground, grasp the wheel and attempt to move it about the axle (spindle) **(see illustration 14)**. Any play felt here indicates wheel bearing failure.

Brake torque arm must be properly secured at both ends

Check for wheel bearing play by trying to move the wheel about the axle (spindle)

REF•12 MOT Test Checks

Checking the tyre tread depth

Tyre direction of rotation arrow can be found on tyre sidewall

Castellated type wheel axle (spindle) nut must be secured by a split pin or R-pin

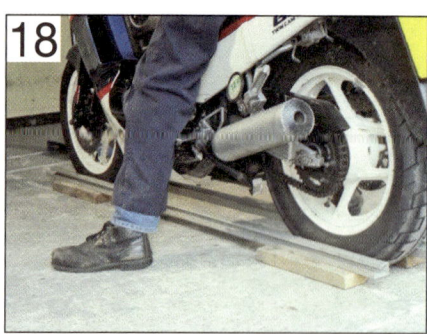

Two straightedges are used to check wheel alignment

- Check the tyre tread depth, tread condition and sidewall condition **(see illustration 15)**.
- Check the tyre type. Front and rear tyre types must be compatible and be suitable for road use. Tyres marked NOT FOR ROAD USE, COMPETITION USE ONLY or similar, will fail the MOT.
- If the tyre sidewall carries a direction of rotation arrow, this must be pointing in the direction of normal wheel rotation **(see illustration 16)**.
- Check that the wheel axle (spindle) nuts (where applicable) are properly secured. A self-locking nut or castellated nut with a split-pin or R-pin can be used **(see illustration 17)**.
- Wheel alignment is checked with the motorcycle off the stand and a rider seated. With the front wheel pointing straight ahead, two perfectly straight lengths of metal or wood and placed against the sidewalls of both tyres **(see illustration 18)**. The gap each side of the front tyre must be equidistant on both sides. Incorrect wheel alignment may be due to a cocked rear wheel (often as the result of poor chain adjustment) or in extreme cases, a bent frame.

General checks and condition

- Check the security of all major fasteners, bodypanels, seat, fairings (where fitted) and mudguards.
- Check that the rider and pillion footrests, handlebar levers and brake pedal are securely mounted.
- Check for corrosion on the frame or any load-bearing components. If severe, this may affect the structure, particularly under stress.

Sidecars

A motorcycle fitted with a sidecar requires additional checks relating to the stability of the machine and security of attachment and swivel joints, plus specific wheel alignment (toe-in) requirements. Additionally, tyre and lighting requirements differ from conventional motorcycle use. Owners are advised to check MOT test requirements with an official test centre.

Conversion factors

Length (distance)
Inches (in)	x 25.4 = Millimetres (mm)	x 0.0394 =	Inches (in)
Feet (ft)	x 0.305 = Metres (m)	x 3.281 =	Feet (ft)
Miles	x 1.609 = Kilometres (km)	x 0.621 =	Miles

Volume (capacity)
Cubic inches (cu in; in^3)	x 16.387 = Cubic centimetres (cc; cm^3)	x 0.061 =	Cubic inches (cu in; in^3)
Imperial pints (Imp pt)	x 0.568 = Litres (l)	x 1.76 =	Imperial pints (Imp pt)
Imperial quarts (Imp qt)	x 1.137 = Litres (l)	x 0.88 =	Imperial quarts (Imp qt)
Imperial quarts (Imp qt)	x 1.201 = US quarts (US qt)	x 0.833 =	Imperial quarts (Imp qt)
US quarts (US qt)	x 0.946 = Litres (l)	x 1.057 =	US quarts (US qt)
Imperial gallons (Imp gal)	x 4.546 = Litres (l)	x 0.22 =	Imperial gallons (Imp gal)
Imperial gallons (Imp gal)	x 1.201 = US gallons (US gal)	x 0.833 =	Imperial gallons (Imp gal)
US gallons (US gal)	x 3.785 = Litres (l)	x 0.264 =	US gallons (US gal)

Mass (weight)
Ounces (oz)	x 28.35 = Grams (g)	x 0.035 =	Ounces (oz)
Pounds (lb)	x 0.454 = Kilograms (kg)	x 2.205 =	Pounds (lb)

Force
Ounces-force (ozf; oz)	x 0.278 = Newtons (N)	x 3.6 =	Ounces-force (ozf; oz)
Pounds-force (lbf; lb)	x 4.448 = Newtons (N)	x 0.225 =	Pounds-force (lbf; lb)
Newtons (N)	x 0.1 = Kilograms-force (kgf; kg)	x 9.81 =	Newtons (N)

Pressure
Pounds-force per square inch (psi; lbf/in^2; lb/in^2)	x 0.070 = Kilograms-force per square centimetre (kgf/cm^2; kg/cm^2)	x 14.223 =	Pounds-force per square inch (psi; lbf/in^2; lb/in^2)
Pounds-force per square inch (psi; lbf/in^2; lb/in^2)	x 0.068 = Atmospheres (atm)	x 14.696 =	Pounds-force per square inch (psi; lbf/in^2; lb/in^2)
Pounds-force per square inch (psi; lbf/in^2; lb/in^2)	x 0.069 = Bars	x 14.5 =	Pounds-force per square inch (psi; lbf/in^2; lb/in^2)
Pounds-force per square inch (psi; lbf/in^2; lb/in^2)	x 6.895 = Kilopascals (kPa)	x 0.145 =	Pounds-force per square inch (psi; lbf/in^2; lb/in^2)
Kilopascals (kPa)	x 0.01 = Kilograms-force per square centimetre (kgf/cm^2; kg/cm^2)	x 98.1 =	Kilopascals (kPa)
Millibar (mbar)	x 100 = Pascals (Pa)	x 0.01 =	Millibar (mbar)
Millibar (mbar)	x 0.0145 = Pounds-force per square inch (psi; lbf/in^2; lb/in^2)	x 68.947 =	Millibar (mbar)
Millibar (mbar)	x 0.75 = Millimetres of mercury (mmHg)	x 1.333 =	Millibar (mbar)
Millibar (mbar)	x 0.401 = Inches of water (inH$_2$O)	x 2.491 =	Millibar (mbar)
Millimetres of mercury (mmHg)	x 0.535 = Inches of water (inH$_2$O)	x 1.868 =	Millimetres of mercury (mmHg)
Inches of water (inH$_2$O)	x 0.036 = Pounds-force per square inch (psi; lbf/in^2; lb/in^2)	x 27.68 =	Inches of water (inH$_2$O)

Torque (moment of force)
Pounds-force inches (lbf in; lb in)	x 1.152 = Kilograms-force centimetre (kgf cm; kg cm)	x 0.868 =	Pounds-force inches (lbf in; lb in)
Pounds-force inches (lbf in; lb in)	x 0.113 = Newton metres (Nm)	x 8.85 =	Pounds-force inches (lbf in; lb in)
Pounds-force inches (lbf in; lb in)	x 0.083 = Pounds-force feet (lbf ft; lb ft)	x 12 =	Pounds-force inches (lbf in; lb in)
Pounds-force feet (lbf ft; lb ft)	x 0.138 = Kilograms-force metres (kgf m; kg m)	x 7.233 =	Pounds-force feet (lbf ft; lb ft)
Pounds-force feet (lbf ft; lb ft)	x 1.356 = Newton metres (Nm)	x 0.738 =	Pounds-force feet (lbf ft; lb ft)
Newton metres (Nm)	x 0.102 = Kilograms-force metres (kgf m; kg m)	x 9.804 =	Newton metres (Nm)

Power
Horsepower (hp)	x 745.7 = Watts (W)	x 0.0013 =	Horsepower (hp)

Velocity (speed)
Miles per hour (miles/hr; mph)	x 1.609 = Kilometres per hour (km/hr; kph)	x 0.621 =	Miles per hour (miles/hr; mph)

Fuel consumption*
Miles per gallon, Imperial (mpg)	x 0.354 = Kilometres per litre (km/l)	x 2.825 =	Miles per gallon, Imperial (mpg)
Miles per gallon, US (mpg)	x 0.425 = Kilometres per litre (km/l)	x 2.352 =	Miles per gallon, US (mpg)

Temperature

Degrees Fahrenheit = (°C x 1.8) + 32   Degrees Celsius (Degrees Centigrade; °C) = (°F - 32) x 0.56

* It is common practice to convert from miles per gallon (mpg) to litres/100 kilometres (l/100km), where mpg x l/100 km = 282

REF•14 Tools and Workshop Tips

Buying tools

A toolkit is a fundamental requirement for servicing and repairing a motorcycle. Although there will be an initial expense in building up enough tools for servicing, this will soon be offset by the savings made by doing the job yourself. As experience and confidence grow, additional tools can be added to enable the repair and overhaul of the motorcycle. Many of the specialist tools are expensive and not often used so it may be preferable to hire them, or for a group of friends or motorcycle club to join in the purchase.

As a rule, it is better to buy more expensive, good quality tools. Cheaper tools are likely to wear out faster and need to be renewed more often, nullifying the original saving.

> **Warning:** To avoid the risk of a poor quality tool breaking in use, causing injury or damage to the component being worked on, always aim to purchase tools which meet the relevant national safety standards.

The following lists of tools do not represent the manufacturer's service tools, but serve as a guide to help the owner decide which tools are needed for this level of work. In addition, items such as an electric drill, hacksaw, files, soldering iron and a workbench equipped with a vice, may be needed. Although not classed as tools, a selection of bolts, screws, nuts, washers and pieces of tubing always come in useful.

For more information about tools, refer to the Haynes *Motorcycle Workshop Practice Techbook* (Bk. No. 3470).

Manufacturer's service tools

Inevitably certain tasks require the use of a service tool. Where possible an alternative tool or method of approach is recommended, but sometimes there is no option if personal injury or damage to the component is to be avoided. Where required, service tools are referred to in the relevant procedure.

Service tools can usually only be purchased from a motorcycle dealer and are identified by a part number. Some of the commonly-used tools, such as rotor pullers, are available in aftermarket form from mail-order motorcycle tool and accessory suppliers.

Maintenance and minor repair tools

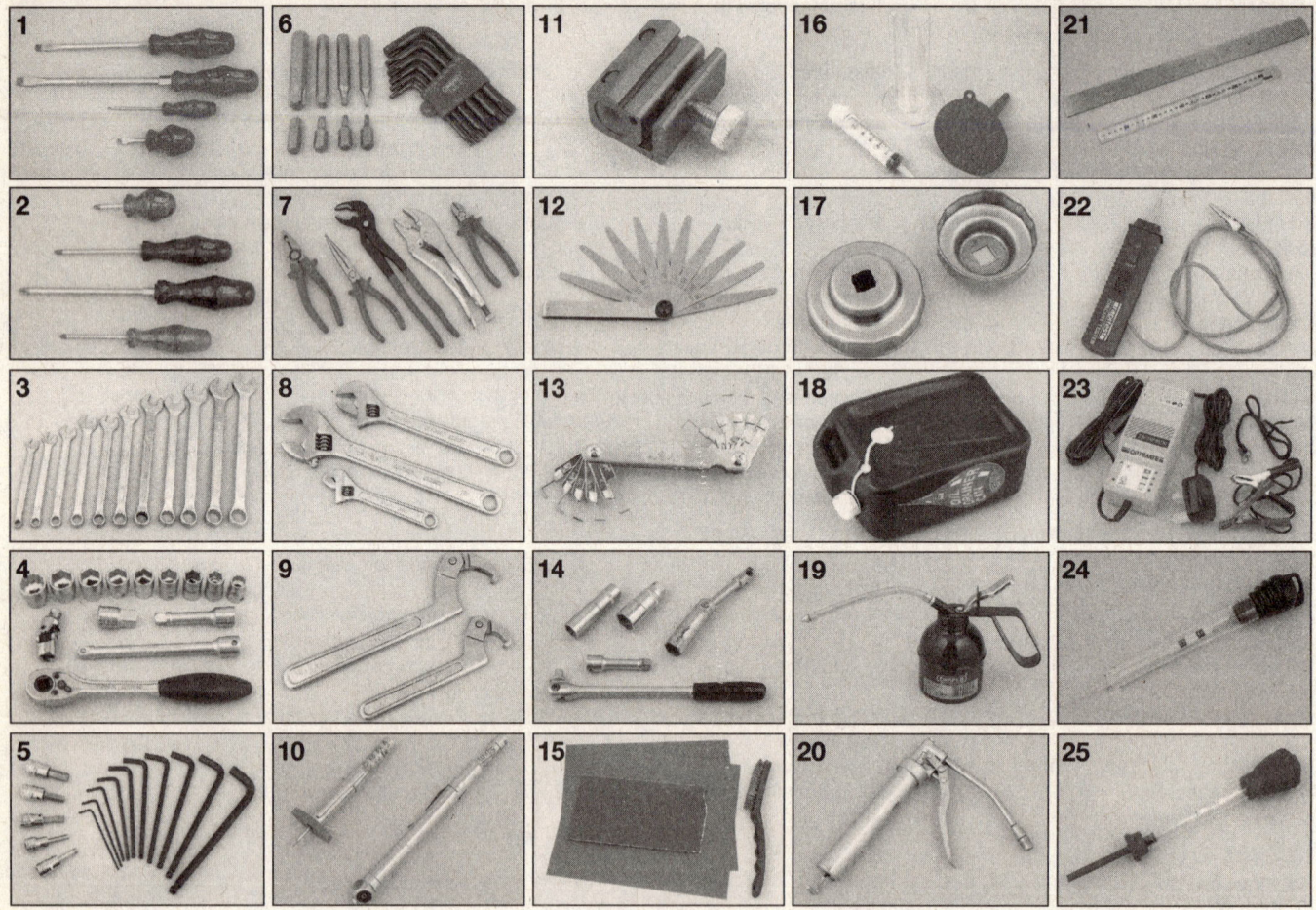

1. Set of flat-bladed screwdrivers
2. Set of Phillips head screwdrivers
3. Combination open-end and ring spanners
4. Socket set (3/8 inch or 1/2 inch drive)
5. Set of Allen keys or bits
6. Set of Torx keys or bits
7. Pliers, cutters and self-locking grips (Mole grips)
8. Adjustable spanners
9. C-spanners
10. Tread depth gauge and tyre pressure gauge
11. Cable oiler clamp
12. Feeler gauges
13. Spark plug gap measuring tool
14. Spark plug spanner or deep plug sockets
15. Wire brush and emery paper
16. Calibrated syringe, measuring vessel and funnel
17. Oil filter adapters
18. Oil drainer can or tray
19. Pump type oil can
20. Grease gun
21. Straight-edge and steel rule
22. Continuity tester
23. Battery charger
24. Hydrometer (for battery specific gravity check)
25. Anti-freeze tester (for liquid-cooled engines)

Tools and Workshop Tips

Repair and overhaul tools

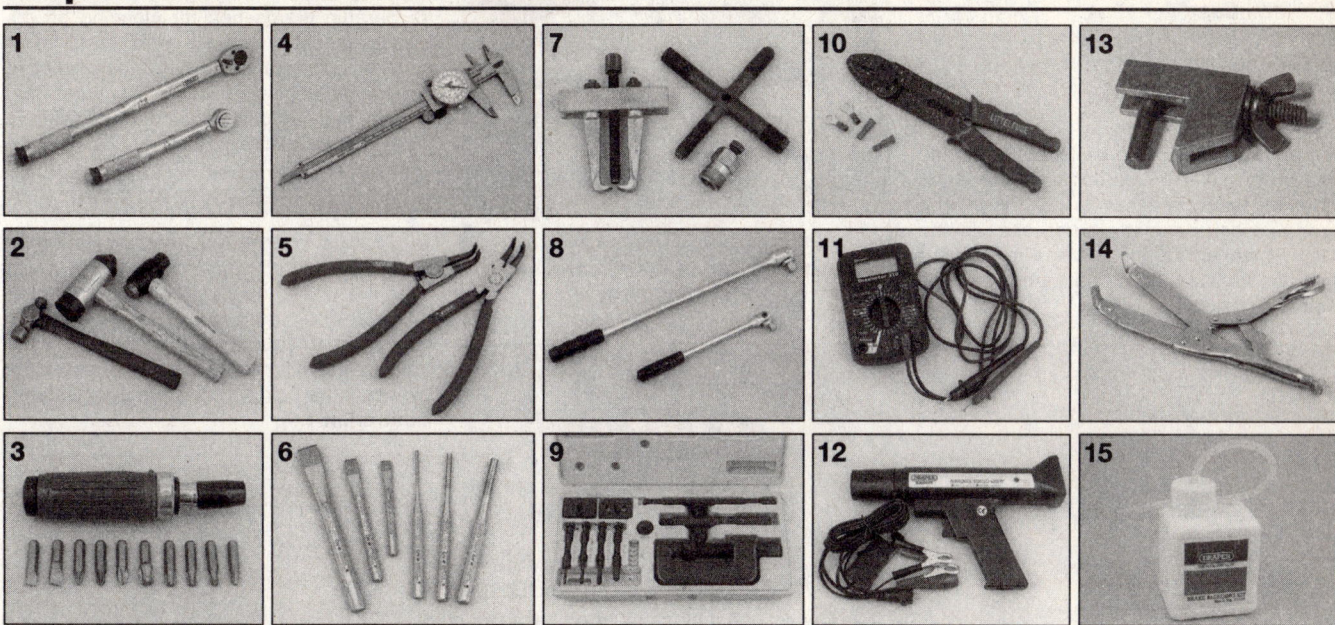

1 Torque wrench (small and mid-ranges)
2 Conventional, plastic or soft-faced hammers
3 Impact driver set
4 Vernier gauge
5 Circlip pliers (internal and external, or combination)
6 Set of cold chisels and punches
7 Selection of pullers
8 Breaker bars
9 Chain breaking/riveting tool set
10 Wire stripper and crimper tool
11 Multimeter (measures amps, volts and ohms)
12 Stroboscope (for dynamic timing checks)
13 Hose clamp (wingnut type shown)
14 Clutch holding tool
15 One-man brake/clutch bleeder kit

Specialist tools

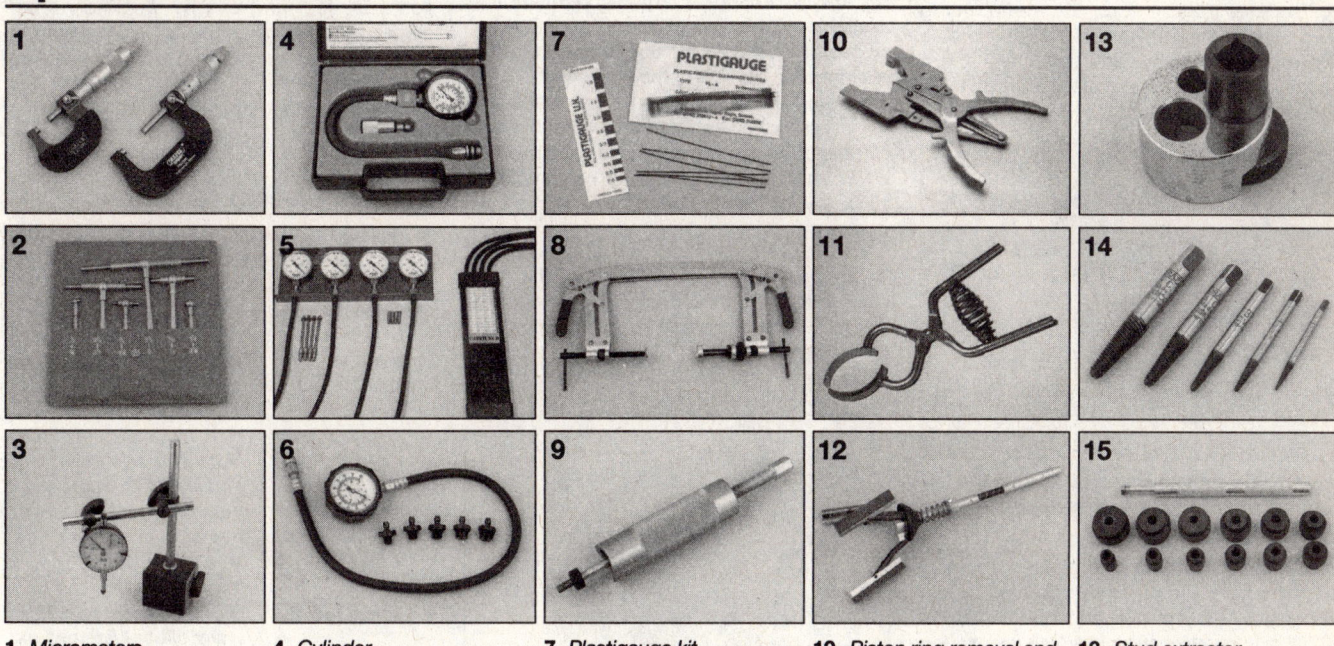

1 Micrometers (external type)
2 Telescoping gauges
3 Dial gauge
4 Cylinder compression gauge
5 Vacuum gauges (left) or manometer (right)
6 Oil pressure gauge
7 Plastigauge kit
8 Valve spring compressor (4-stroke engines)
9 Piston pin drawbolt tool
10 Piston ring removal and installation tool
11 Piston ring clamp
12 Cylinder bore hone (stone type shown)
13 Stud extractor
14 Screw extractor set
15 Bearing driver set

REF•16 Tools and Workshop Tips

1 Workshop equipment and facilities

The workbench

● Work is made much easier by raising the bike up on a ramp - components are much more accessible if raised to waist level. The hydraulic or pneumatic types seen in the dealer's workshop are a sound investment if you undertake a lot of repairs or overhauls **(see illustration 1.1)**.

1.1 Hydraulic motorcycle ramp

● If raised off ground level, the bike must be supported on the ramp to avoid it falling. Most ramps incorporate a front wheel locating clamp which can be adjusted to suit different diameter wheels. When tightening the clamp, take care not to mark the wheel rim or damage the tyre - use wood blocks on each side to prevent this.
● Secure the bike to the ramp using tie-downs **(see illustration 1.2)**. If the bike has only a sidestand, and hence leans at a dangerous angle when raised, support the bike on an auxiliary stand.

1.2 Tie-downs are used around the passenger footrests to secure the bike

● Auxiliary (paddock) stands are widely available from mail order companies or motorcycle dealers and attach either to the wheel axle or swingarm pivot **(see illustration 1.3)**. If the motorcycle has a centrestand, you can support it under the crankcase to prevent it toppling whilst either wheel is removed **(see illustration 1.4)**.

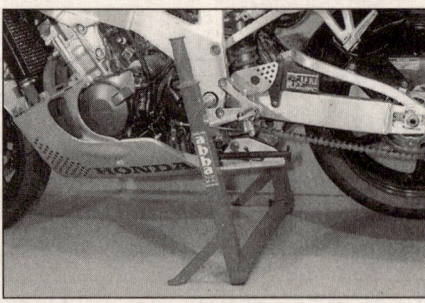

1.3 This auxiliary stand attaches to the swingarm pivot

1.4 Always use a block of wood between the engine and jack head when supporting the engine in this way

Fumes and fire

● Refer to the Safety first! page at the beginning of the manual for full details. Make sure your workshop is equipped with a fire extinguisher suitable for fuel-related fires (Class B fire - flammable liquids) - it is not sufficient to have a water-filled extinguisher.
● Always ensure adequate ventilation is available. Unless an exhaust gas extraction system is available for use, ensure that the engine is run outside of the workshop.
● If working on the fuel system, make sure the workshop is ventilated to avoid a build-up of fumes. This applies equally to fume build-up when charging a battery. Do not smoke or allow anyone else to smoke in the workshop.

Fluids

● If you need to drain fuel from the tank, store it in an approved container marked as suitable for the storage of petrol (gasoline) **(see illustration 1.5)**. Do not store fuel in glass jars or bottles.

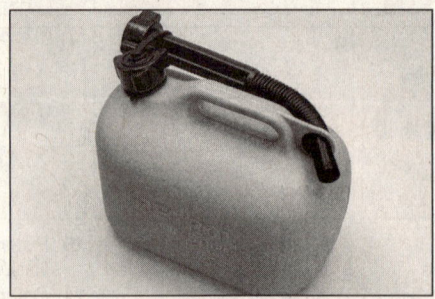

1.5 Use an approved can only for storing petrol (gasoline)

● Use proprietary engine degreasers or solvents which have a high flash-point, such as paraffin (kerosene), for cleaning off oil, grease and dirt - never use petrol (gasoline) for cleaning. Wear rubber gloves when handling solvent and engine degreaser. The fumes from certain solvents can be dangerous - always work in a well-ventilated area.

Dust, eye and hand protection

● Protect your lungs from inhalation of dust particles by wearing a filtering mask over the nose and mouth. Many frictional materials still contain asbestos which is dangerous to your health. Protect your eyes from spouts of liquid and sprung components by wearing a pair of protective goggles **(see illustration 1.6)**.

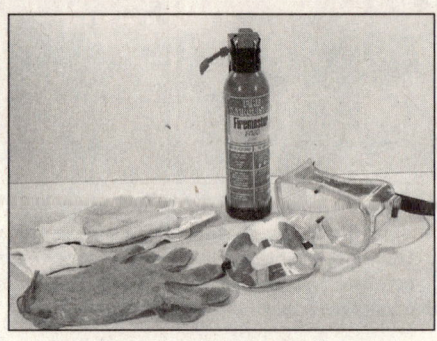

1.6 A fire extinguisher, goggles, mask and protective gloves should be at hand in the workshop

● Protect your hands from contact with solvents, fuel and oils by wearing rubber gloves. Alternatively apply a barrier cream to your hands before starting work. If handling hot components or fluids, wear suitable gloves to protect your hands from scalding and burns.

What to do with old fluids

● Old cleaning solvent, fuel, coolant and oils should not be poured down domestic drains or onto the ground. Package the fluid up in old oil containers, label it accordingly, and take it to a garage or disposal facility. Contact your local authority for location of such sites or ring the oil care hotline.

Note: It is antisocial and illegal to dump oil down the drain. To find the location of your local oil recycling bank in the UK, call 08708 506 506 or visit www.oilbankline.org.uk

In the USA, note that any oil supplier must accept used oil for recycling.

Tools and Workshop Tips REF•17

2 Fasteners - screws, bolts and nuts

Fastener types and applications

Bolts and screws

● Fastener head types are either of hexagonal, Torx or splined design, with internal and external versions of each type **(see illustrations 2.1 and 2.2)**; splined head fasteners are not in common use on motorcycles. The conventional slotted or Phillips head design is used for certain screws. Bolt or screw length is always measured from the underside of the head to the end of the item **(see illustration 2.11)**.

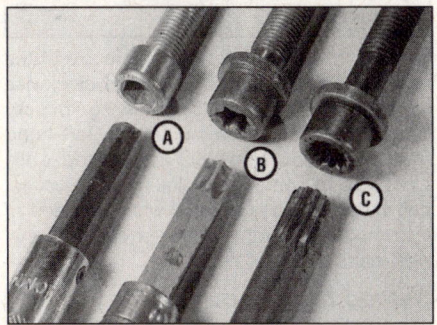

2.1 Internal hexagon/Allen (A), Torx (B) and splined (C) fasteners, with corresponding bits

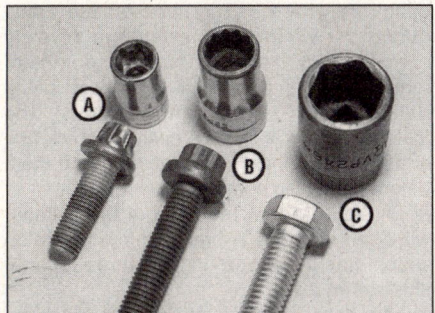

2.2 External Torx (A), splined (B) and hexagon (C) fasteners, with corresponding sockets

● Certain fasteners on the motorcycle have a tensile marking on their heads, the higher the marking the stronger the fastener. High tensile fasteners generally carry a 10 or higher marking. Never replace a high tensile fastener with one of a lower tensile strength.

Washers (see illustration 2.3)

● Plain washers are used between a fastener head and a component to prevent damage to the component or to spread the load when torque is applied. Plain washers can also be used as spacers or shims in certain assemblies. Copper or aluminium plain washers are often used as sealing washers on drain plugs.

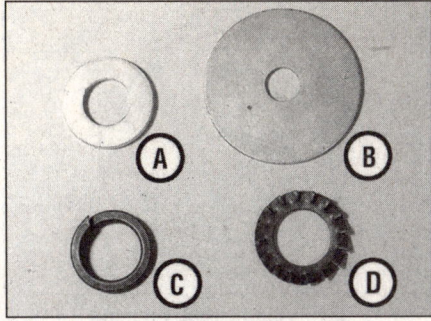

2.3 Plain washer (A), penny washer (B), spring washer (C) and serrated washer (D)

● The split-ring spring washer works by applying axial tension between the fastener head and component. If flattened, it is fatigued and must be renewed. If a plain (flat) washer is used on the fastener, position the spring washer between the fastener and the plain washer.

● Serrated star type washers dig into the fastener and component faces, preventing loosening. They are often used on electrical earth (ground) connections to the frame.

● Cone type washers (sometimes called Belleville) are conical and when tightened apply axial tension between the fastener head and component. They must be installed with the dished side against the component and often carry an OUTSIDE marking on their outer face. If flattened, they are fatigued and must be renewed.

● Tab washers are used to lock plain nuts or bolts on a shaft. A portion of the tab washer is bent up hard against one flat of the nut or bolt to prevent it loosening. Due to the tab washer being deformed in use, a new tab washer should be used every time it is disturbed.

● Wave washers are used to take up endfloat on a shaft. They provide light springing and prevent excessive side-to-side play of a component. Can be found on rocker arm shafts.

Nuts and split pins

● Conventional plain nuts are usually six-sided **(see illustration 2.4)**. They are sized by thread diameter and pitch. High tensile nuts carry a number on one end to denote their tensile strength.

2.4 Plain nut (A), shouldered locknut (B), nylon insert nut (C) and castellated nut (D)

● Self-locking nuts either have a nylon insert, or two spring metal tabs, or a shoulder which is staked into a groove in the shaft - their advantage over conventional plain nuts is a resistance to loosening due to vibration. The nylon insert type can be used a number of times, but must be renewed when the friction of the nylon insert is reduced, ie when the nut spins freely on the shaft. The spring tab type can be reused unless the tabs are damaged. The shouldered type must be renewed every time it is disturbed.

● Split pins (cotter pins) are used to lock a castellated nut to a shaft or to prevent slackening of a plain nut. Common applications are wheel axles and brake torque arms. Because the split pin arms are deformed to lock around the nut a new split pin must always be used on installation - always fit the correct size split pin which will fit snugly in the shaft hole. Make sure the split pin arms are correctly located around the nut **(see illustrations 2.5 and 2.6)**.

2.5 Bend split pin (cotter pin) arms as shown (arrows) to secure a castellated nut

2.6 Bend split pin (cotter pin) arms as shown to secure a plain nut

Caution: *If the castellated nut slots do not align with the shaft hole after tightening to the torque setting, tighten the nut until the next slot aligns with the hole - never slacken the nut to align its slot.*

● R-pins (shaped like the letter R), or slip pins as they are sometimes called, are sprung and can be reused if they are otherwise in good condition. Always install R-pins with their closed end facing forwards **(see illustration 2.7)**.

Tools and Workshop Tips

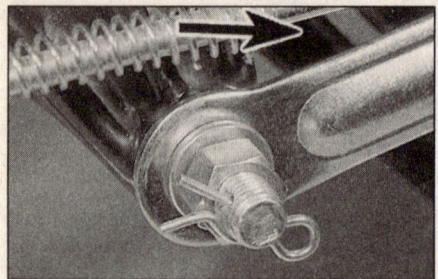

2.7 Correct fitting of R-pin. Arrow indicates forward direction

Circlips (see illustration 2.8)

● Circlips (sometimes called snap-rings) are used to retain components on a shaft or in a housing and have corresponding external or internal ears to permit removal. Parallel-sided (machined) circlips can be installed either way round in their groove, whereas stamped circlips (which have a chamfered edge on one face) must be installed with the chamfer facing away from the direction of thrust load **(see illustration 2.9)**.

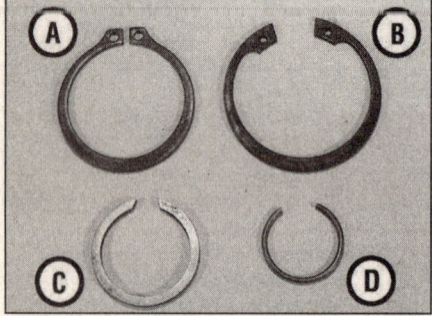

2.8 External stamped circlip (A), internal stamped circlip (B), machined circlip (C) and wire circlip (D)

● Always use circlip pliers to remove and install circlips; expand or compress them just enough to remove them. After installation, rotate the circlip in its groove to ensure it is securely seated. If installing a circlip on a splined shaft, always align its opening with a shaft channel to ensure the circlip ends are well supported and unlikely to catch **(see illustration 2.10)**.

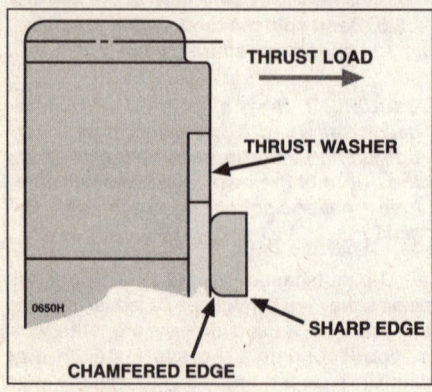

2.9 Correct fitting of a stamped circlip

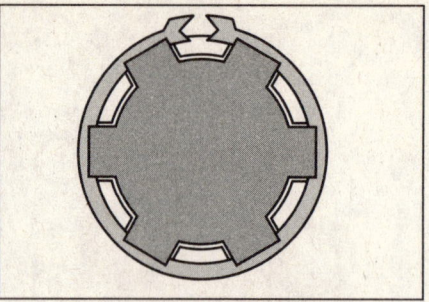

2.10 Align circlip opening with shaft channel

● Circlips can wear due to the thrust of components and become loose in their grooves, with the subsequent danger of becoming dislodged in operation. For this reason, renewal is advised every time a circlip is disturbed.

● Wire circlips are commonly used as piston pin retaining clips. If a removal tang is provided, long-nosed pliers can be used to dislodge them, otherwise careful use of a small flat-bladed screwdriver is necessary. Wire circlips should be renewed every time they are disturbed.

Thread diameter and pitch

● Diameter of a male thread (screw, bolt or stud) is the outside diameter of the threaded portion **(see illustration 2.11)**. Most motorcycle manufacturers use the ISO (International Standards Organisation) metric system expressed in millimetres, eg M6 refers to a 6 mm diameter thread. Sizing is the same for nuts, except that the thread diameter is measured across the valleys of the nut.

● Pitch is the distance between the peaks of the thread **(see illustration 2.11)**. It is expressed in millimetres, thus a common bolt size may be expressed as 6.0 x 1.0 mm (6 mm thread diameter and 1 mm pitch). Generally pitch increases in proportion to thread diameter, although there are always exceptions.

● Thread diameter and pitch are related for conventional fastener applications and the accompanying table can be used as a guide. Additionally, the AF (Across Flats), spanner or socket size dimension of the bolt or nut **(see illustration 2.11)** is linked to thread and pitch specification. Thread pitch can be measured with a thread gauge **(see illustration 2.12)**.

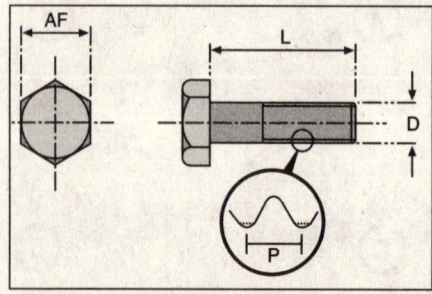

2.11 Fastener length (L), thread diameter (D), thread pitch (P) and head size (AF)

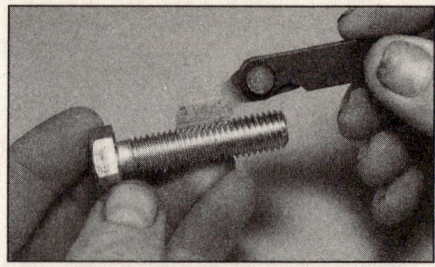

2.12 Using a thread gauge to measure pitch

AF size	Thread diameter x pitch (mm)
8 mm	M5 x 0.8
8 mm	M6 x 1.0
10 mm	M6 x 1.0
12 mm	M8 x 1.25
14 mm	M10 x 1.25
17 mm	M12 x 1.25

● The threads of most fasteners are of the right-hand type, ie they are turned clockwise to tighten and anti-clockwise to loosen. The reverse situation applies to left-hand thread fasteners, which are turned anti-clockwise to tighten and clockwise to loosen. Left-hand threads are used where rotation of a component might loosen a conventional right-hand thread fastener.

Seized fasteners

● Corrosion of external fasteners due to water or reaction between two dissimilar metals can occur over a period of time. It will build up sooner in wet conditions or in countries where salt is used on the roads during the winter. If a fastener is severely corroded it is likely that normal methods of removal will fail and result in its head being ruined. When you attempt removal, the fastener thread should be heard to crack free and unscrew easily - if it doesn't, stop there before damaging something.

● A smart tap on the head of the fastener will often succeed in breaking free corrosion which has occurred in the threads **(see illustration 2.13)**.

● An aerosol penetrating fluid (such as WD-40) applied the night beforehand may work its way down into the thread and ease removal. Depending on the location, you may be able to make up a Plasticine well around the fastener head and fill it with penetrating fluid.

2.13 A sharp tap on the head of a fastener will often break free a corroded thread

Tools and Workshop Tips

- If you are working on an engine internal component, corrosion will most likely not be a problem due to the well lubricated environment. However, components can be very tight and an impact driver is a useful tool in freeing them **(see illustration 2.14)**.

2.14 Using an impact driver to free a fastener

- Where corrosion has occurred between dissimilar metals (eg steel and aluminium alloy), the application of heat to the fastener head will create a disproportionate expansion rate between the two metals and break the seizure caused by the corrosion. Whether heat can be applied depends on the location of the fastener - any surrounding components likely to be damaged must first be removed **(see illustration 2.15)**. Heat can be applied using a paint stripper heat gun or clothes iron, or by immersing the component in boiling water - wear protective gloves to prevent scalding or burns to the hands.

2.15 Using heat to free a seized fastener

- As a last resort, it is possible to use a hammer and cold chisel to work the fastener head unscrewed **(see illustration 2.16)**. This will damage the fastener, but more importantly extreme care must be taken not to damage the surrounding component.

Caution: Remember that the component being secured is generally of more value than the bolt, nut or screw - when the fastener is freed, do not unscrew it with force, instead work the fastener back and forth when resistance is felt to prevent thread damage.

2.16 Using a hammer and chisel to free a seized fastener

Broken fasteners and damaged heads

- If the shank of a broken bolt or screw is accessible you can grip it with self-locking grips. The knurled wheel type stud extractor tool or self-gripping stud puller tool is particularly useful for removing the long studs which screw into the cylinder mouth surface of the crankcase or bolts and screws from which the head has broken off **(see illustration 2.17)**. Studs can also be removed by locking two nuts together on the threaded end of the stud and using a spanner on the lower nut **(see illustration 2.18)**.

2.17 Using a stud extractor tool to remove a broken crankcase stud

2.18 Two nuts can be locked together to unscrew a stud from a component

- A bolt or screw which has broken off below or level with the casing must be extracted using a screw extractor set. Centre punch the fastener to centralise the drill bit, then drill a hole in the fastener **(see illustration 2.19)**. Select a drill bit which is approximately half to three-quarters the diameter of the fastener

2.19 When using a screw extractor, first drill a hole in the fastener . . .

and drill to a depth which will accommodate the extractor. Use the largest size extractor possible, but avoid leaving too small a wall thickness otherwise the extractor will merely force the fastener walls outwards wedging it in the casing thread.

- If a spiral type extractor is used, thread it anti-clockwise into the fastener. As it is screwed in, it will grip the fastener and unscrew it from the casing **(see illustration 2.20)**.

2.20 . . . then thread the extractor anti-clockwise into the fastener

- If a taper type extractor is used, tap it into the fastener so that it is firmly wedged in place. Unscrew the extractor (anti-clockwise) to draw the fastener out.

 *Warning: Stud extractors are very hard and may break off in the fastener if care is not taken - ask an engineer about spark erosion if this happens.*

- Alternatively, the broken bolt/screw can be drilled out and the hole retapped for an oversize bolt/screw or a diamond-section thread insert. It is essential that the drilling is carried out squarely and to the correct depth, otherwise the casing may be ruined - if in doubt, entrust the work to an engineer.
- Bolts and nuts with rounded corners cause the correct size spanner or socket to slip when force is applied. Of the types of spanner/socket available always use a six-point type rather than an eight or twelve-point type - better grip

REF•20 Tools and Workshop Tips

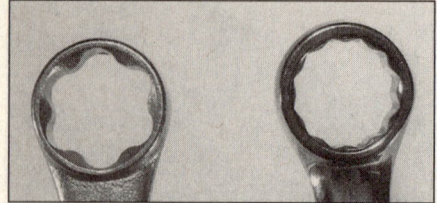

2.21 Comparison of surface drive ring spanner (left) with 12-point type (right)

is obtained. Surface drive spanners grip the middle of the hex flats, rather than the corners, and are thus good in cases of damaged heads **(see illustration 2.21)**.

- Slotted-head or Phillips-head screws are often damaged by the use of the wrong size screwdriver. Allen-head and Torx-head screws are much less likely to sustain damage. If enough of the screw head is exposed you can use a hacksaw to cut a slot in its head and then use a conventional flat-bladed screwdriver to remove it. Alternatively use a hammer and cold chisel to tap the head of the fastener around to slacken it. Always replace damaged fasteners with new ones, preferably Torx or Allen-head type.

A dab of valve grinding compound between the screw head and screwdriver tip will often give a good grip.

Thread repair

- Threads (particularly those in aluminium alloy components) can be damaged by overtightening, being assembled with dirt in the threads, or from a component working loose and vibrating. Eventually the thread will fail completely, and it will be impossible to tighten the fastener.
- If a thread is damaged or clogged with old locking compound it can be renovated with a thread repair tool (thread chaser) **(see illustrations 2.22 and 2.23)**; special thread

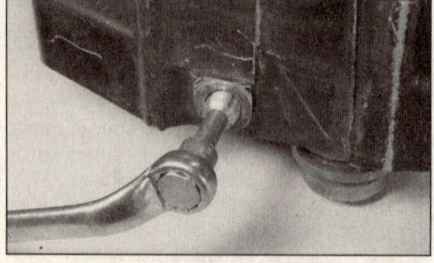

2.22 A thread repair tool being used to correct an internal thread

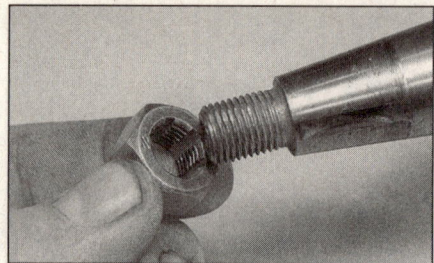

2.23 A thread repair tool being used to correct an external thread

chasers are available for spark plug hole threads. The tool will not cut a new thread, but clean and true the original thread. Make sure that you use the correct diameter and pitch tool. Similarly, external threads can be cleaned up with a die or a thread restorer file **(see illustration 2.24)**.

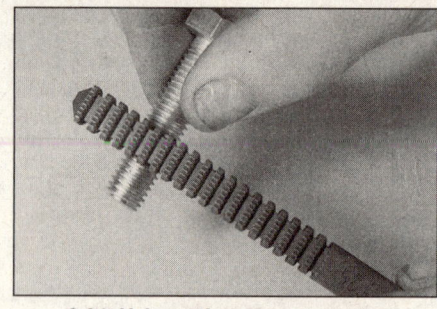

2.24 Using a thread restorer file

- It is possible to drill out the old thread and retap the component to the next thread size. This will work where there is enough surrounding material and a new bolt or screw can be obtained. Sometimes, however, this is not possible - such as where the bolt/screw passes through another component which must also be suitably modified, also in cases where a spark plug or oil drain plug cannot be obtained in a larger diameter thread size.
- The diamond-section thread insert (often known by its popular trade name of Heli-Coil) is a simple and effective method of renewing the thread and retaining the original size. A kit can be purchased which contains the tap, insert and installing tool **(see illustration 2.25)**. Drill out the damaged thread with the size drill specified **(see illustration 2.26)**. Carefully retap the thread **(see illustration 2.27)**. Install the

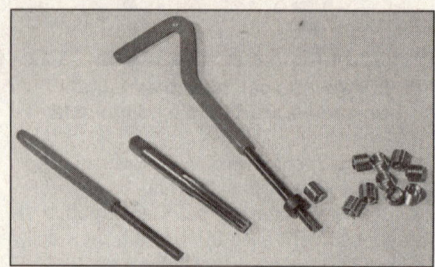

2.25 Obtain a thread insert kit to suit the thread diameter and pitch required

2.26 To install a thread insert, first drill out the original thread . . .

2.27 . . . tap a new thread . . .

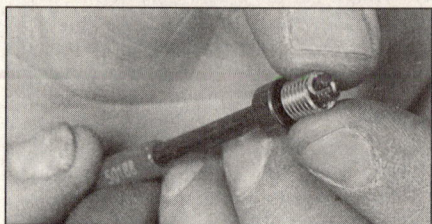

2.28 . . . fit insert on the installing tool . . .

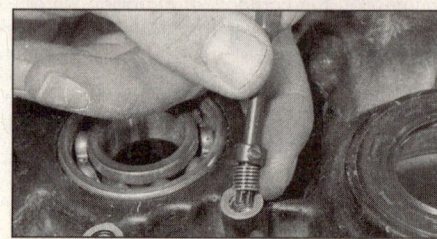

2.29 . . . and thread into the component . . .

2.30 . . . break off the tang when complete

insert on the installing tool and thread it slowly into place using a light downward pressure **(see illustrations 2.28 and 2.29)**. When positioned between a 1/4 and 1/2 turn below the surface withdraw the installing tool and use the break-off tool to press down on the tang, breaking it off **(see illustration 2.30)**.

- There are epoxy thread repair kits on the market which can rebuild stripped internal threads, although this repair should not be used on high load-bearing components.

Tools and Workshop Tips

Thread locking and sealing compounds

● Locking compounds are used in locations where the fastener is prone to loosening due to vibration or on important safety-related items which might cause loss of control of the motorcycle if they fail. It is also used where important fasteners cannot be secured by other means such as lockwashers or split pins.

● Before applying locking compound, make sure that the threads (internal and external) are clean and dry with all old compound removed. Select a compound to suit the component being secured - a non-permanent general locking and sealing type is suitable for most applications, but a high strength type is needed for permanent fixing of studs in castings. Apply a drop or two of the compound to the first few threads of the fastener, then thread it into place and tighten to the specified torque. Do not apply excessive thread locking compound otherwise the thread may be damaged on subsequent removal.

● Certain fasteners are impregnated with a dry film type coating of locking compound on their threads. Always renew this type of fastener if disturbed.

● Anti-seize compounds, such as copper-based greases, can be applied to protect threads from seizure due to extreme heat and corrosion. A common instance is spark plug threads and exhaust system fasteners.

3 Measuring tools and gauges

Feeler gauges

● Feeler gauges (or blades) are used for measuring small gaps and clearances **(see illustration 3.1)**. They can also be used to measure endfloat (sideplay) of a component on a shaft where access is not possible with a dial gauge.

● Feeler gauge sets should be treated with care and not bent or damaged. They are etched with their size on one face. Keep them clean and very lightly oiled to prevent corrosion build-up.

3.1 Feeler gauges are used for measuring small gaps and clearances - thickness is marked on one face of gauge

● When measuring a clearance, select a gauge which is a light sliding fit between the two components. You may need to use two gauges together to measure the clearance accurately.

Micrometers

● A micrometer is a precision tool capable of measuring to 0.01 or 0.001 of a millimetre. It should always be stored in its case and not in the general toolbox. It must be kept clean and never dropped, otherwise its frame or measuring anvils could be distorted resulting in inaccurate readings.

● External micrometers are used for measuring outside diameters of components and have many more applications than internal micrometers. Micrometers are available in different size ranges, eg 0 to 25 mm, 25 to 50 mm, and upwards in 25 mm steps; some large micrometers have interchangeable anvils to allow a range of measurements to be taken. Generally the largest precision measurement you are likely to take on a motorcycle is the piston diameter.

● Internal micrometers (or bore micrometers) are used for measuring inside diameters, such as valve guides and cylinder bores. Telescoping gauges and small hole gauges are used in conjunction with an external micrometer, whereas the more expensive internal micrometers have their own measuring device.

External micrometer

Note: *The conventional analogue type instrument is described. Although much easier to read, digital micrometers are considerably more expensive.*

● Always check the calibration of the micrometer before use. With the anvils closed (0 to 25 mm type) or set over a test gauge

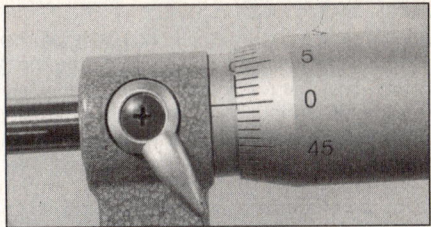

3.2 Check micrometer calibration before use

(for the larger types) the scale should read zero **(see illustration 3.2)**; make sure that the anvils (and test piece) are clean first. Any discrepancy can be adjusted by referring to the instructions supplied with the tool. Remember that the micrometer is a precision measuring tool - don't force the anvils closed, use the ratchet (4) on the end of the micrometer to close it. In this way, a measured force is always applied.

● To use, first make sure that the item being measured is clean. Place the anvil (1) of the micrometer against the item and use the thimble (2) to bring the spindle (3) lightly into contact with the other side of the item **(see illustration 3.3)**. Don't tighten the thimble down because this will damage the micrometer - instead use the ratchet (4) on the end of the micrometer. The ratchet mechanism applies a measured force preventing damage to the instrument.

● The micrometer is read by referring to the linear scale on the sleeve and the annular scale on the thimble. Read off the sleeve first to obtain the base measurement, then add the fine measurement from the thimble to obtain the overall reading. The linear scale on the sleeve represents the measuring range of the micrometer (eg 0 to 25 mm). The annular scale

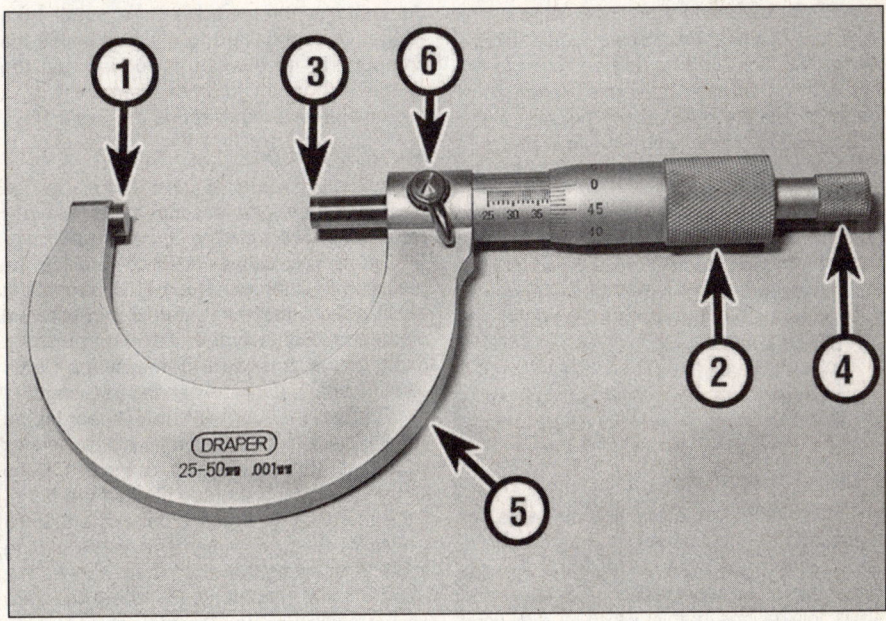

3.3 Micrometer component parts

1 Anvil
2 Thimble
3 Spindle
4 Ratchet
5 Frame
6 Locking lever

Tools and Workshop Tips

on the thimble will be in graduations of 0.01 mm (or as marked on the frame) - one full revolution of the thimble will move 0.5 mm on the linear scale. Take the reading where the datum line on the sleeve intersects the thimble's scale. Always position the eye directly above the scale otherwise an inaccurate reading will result.

In the example shown the item measures 2.95 mm **(see illustration 3.4)**:

Linear scale	2.00 mm
Linear scale	0.50 mm
Annular scale	0.45 mm
Total figure	2.95 mm

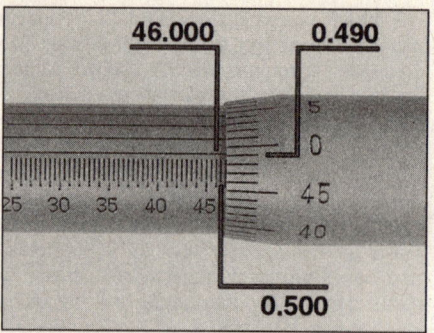

3.5 Micrometer reading of 46.99 mm on linear and annular scales . . .

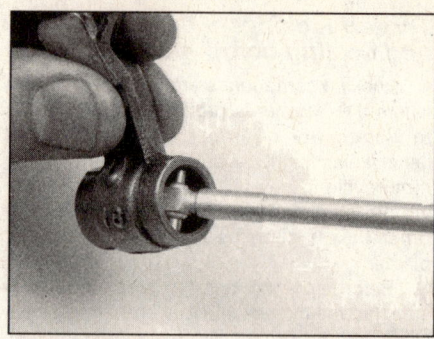

3.7 Expand the telescoping gauge in the bore, lock its position . . .

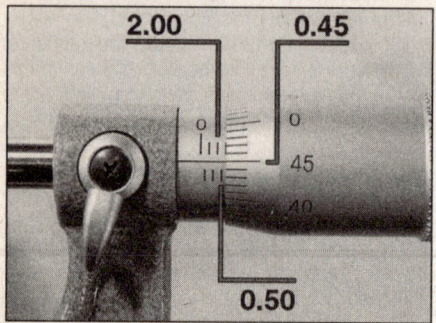

3.4 Micrometer reading of 2.95 mm

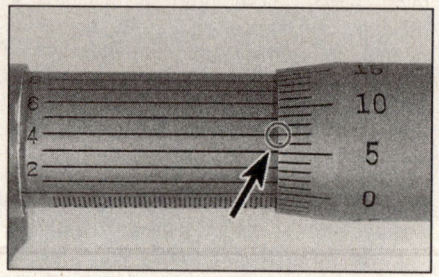

3.6 . . . and 0.004 mm on vernier scale

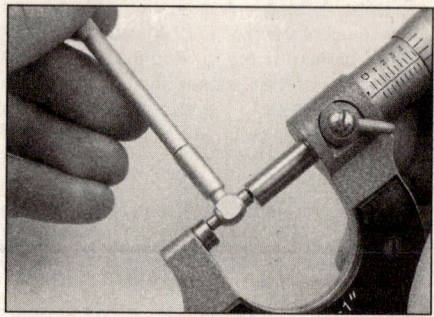

3.8 . . . then measure the gauge with a micrometer

Most micrometers have a locking lever (6) on the frame to hold the setting in place, allowing the item to be removed from the micrometer.
● Some micrometers have a vernier scale on their sleeve, providing an even finer measurement to be taken, in 0.001 increments of a millimetre. Take the sleeve and thimble measurement as described above, then check which graduation on the vernier scale aligns with that of the annular scale on the thimble **Note:** *The eye must be perpendicular to the scale when taking the vernier reading - if necessary rotate the body of the micrometer to ensure this.* Multiply the vernier scale figure by 0.001 and add it to the base and fine measurement figures.

In the example shown the item measures 46.994 mm **(see illustrations 3.5 and 3.6)**:

Linear scale (base)	46.000 mm
Linear scale (base)	00.500 mm
Annular scale (fine)	00.490 mm
Vernier scale	00.004 mm
Total figure	46.994 mm

Internal micrometer

● Internal micrometers are available for measuring bore diameters, but are expensive and unlikely to be available for home use. It is suggested that a set of telescoping gauges and small hole gauges, both of which must be used with an external micrometer, will suffice for taking internal measurements on a motorcycle.
● Telescoping gauges can be used to measure internal diameters of components. Select a gauge with the correct size range, make sure its ends are clean and insert it into the bore. Expand the gauge, then lock its position and withdraw it from the bore **(see illustration 3.7)**. Measure across the gauge ends with a micrometer **(see illustration 3.8)**.
● Very small diameter bores (such as valve guides) are measured with a small hole gauge. Once adjusted to a slip-fit inside the component, its position is locked and the gauge withdrawn for measurement with a micrometer **(see illustrations 3.9 and 3.10)**.

Vernier caliper

Note: *The conventional linear and dial gauge type instruments are described. Digital types are easier to read, but are far more expensive.*
● The vernier caliper does not provide the precision of a micrometer, but is versatile in being able to measure internal and external diameters. Some types also incorporate a depth gauge. It is ideal for measuring clutch plate friction material and spring free lengths.
● To use the conventional linear scale vernier, slacken off the vernier clamp screws (1) and set its jaws over (2), or inside (3), the item to be measured **(see illustration 3.11)**. Slide the jaw into contact, using the thumbwheel (4) for fine movement of the sliding scale (5) then tighten the clamp screws (1). Read off the main scale (6) where the zero on the sliding scale (5) intersects it, taking the whole number to the left of the zero; this provides the base measurement. View along the sliding scale and select the division which

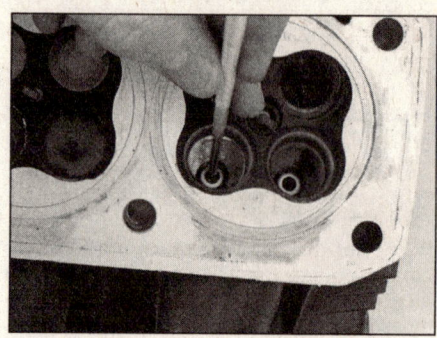

3.9 Expand the small hole gauge in the bore, lock its position . . .

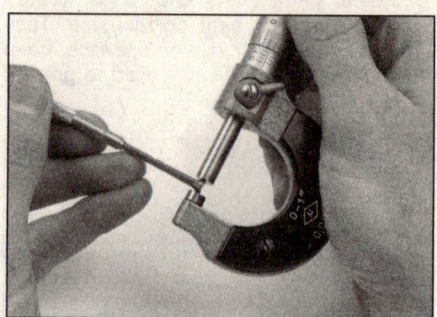

3.10 . . . then measure the gauge with a micrometer

lines up exactly with any of the divisions on the main scale, noting that the divisions usually represents 0.02 of a millimetre. Add this fine measurement to the base measurement to obtain the total reading.

Tools and Workshop Tips REF•23

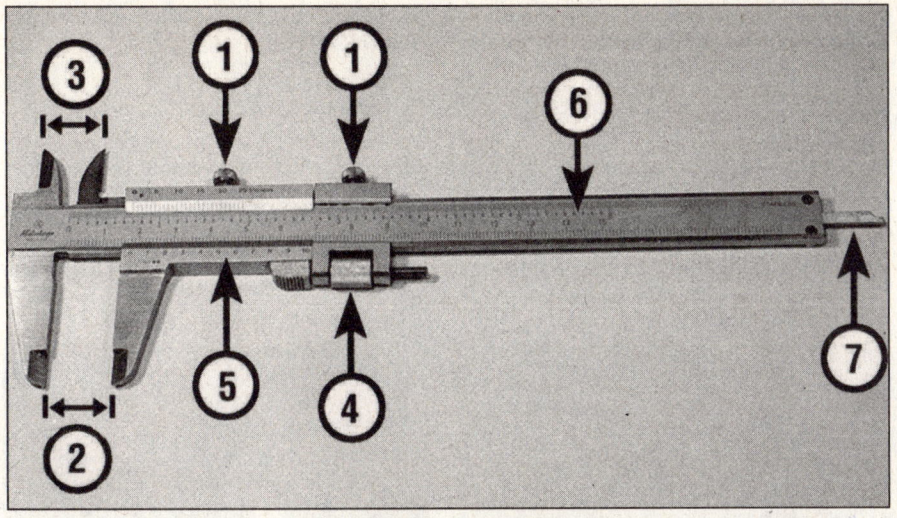

3.11 Vernier component parts (linear gauge)

1 Clamp screws
2 External jaws
3 Internal jaws
4 Thumbwheel
5 Sliding scale
6 Main scale
7 Depth gauge

In the example shown the item measures 55.92 mm **(see illustration 3.12)**:

Base measurement	55.00 mm
Fine measurement	00.92 mm
Total figure	55.92 mm

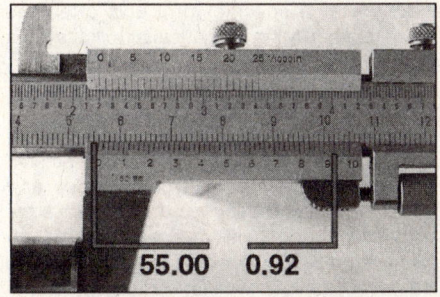

3.12 Vernier gauge reading of 55.92 mm

● Some vernier calipers are equipped with a dial gauge for fine measurement. Before use, check that the jaws are clean, then close them fully and check that the dial gauge reads zero. If necessary adjust the gauge ring accordingly. Slacken the vernier clamp screw (1) and set its jaws over (2), or inside (3), the item to be measured **(see illustration 3.13)**. Slide the jaws into contact, using the thumbwheel (4) for fine movement. Read off the main scale (5) where the edge of the sliding scale (6) intersects it, taking the whole number to the left of the zero; this provides the base measurement. Read off the needle position on the dial gauge (7) scale to provide the fine measurement; each division represents 0.05 of a millimetre. Add this fine measurement to the base measurement to obtain the total reading.

In the example shown the item measures 55.95 mm **(see illustration 3.14)**:

Base measurement	55.00 mm
Fine measurement	00.95 mm
Total figure	55.95 mm

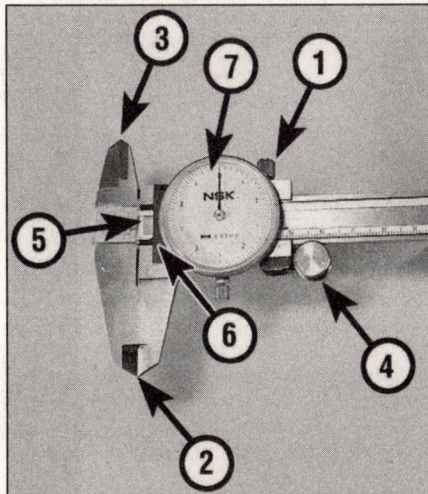

3.13 Vernier component parts (dial gauge)

1 Clamp screw
2 External jaws
3 Internal jaws
4 Thumbwheel
5 Main scale
6 Sliding scale
7 Dial gauge

3.14 Vernier gauge reading of 55.95 mm

Plastigauge

● Plastigauge is a plastic material which can be compressed between two surfaces to measure the oil clearance between them. The width of the compressed Plastigauge is measured against a calibrated scale to determine the clearance.

● Common uses of Plastigauge are for measuring the clearance between crankshaft journal and main bearing inserts, between crankshaft journal and big-end bearing inserts, and between camshaft and bearing surfaces. The following example describes big-end oil clearance measurement.

● Handle the Plastigauge material carefully to prevent distortion. Using a sharp knife, cut a length which corresponds with the width of the bearing being measured and place it carefully across the journal so that it is parallel with the shaft **(see illustration 3.15)**. Carefully install both bearing shells and the connecting rod. Without rotating the rod on the journal tighten its bolts or nuts (as applicable) to the specified torque. The connecting rod and bearings are then disassembled and the crushed Plastigauge examined.

3.15 Plastigauge placed across shaft journal

● Using the scale provided in the Plastigauge kit, measure the width of the material to determine the oil clearance **(see illustration 3.16)**. Always remove all traces of Plastigauge after use using your fingernails.

Caution: Arriving at the correct clearance demands that the assembly is torqued correctly, according to the settings and sequence (where applicable) provided by the motorcycle manufacturer.

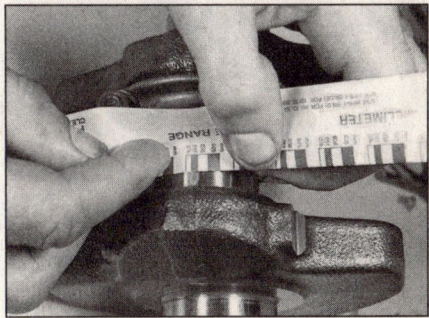

3.16 Measuring the width of the crushed Plastigauge

Tools and Workshop Tips

Dial gauge or DTI (Dial Test Indicator)

● A dial gauge can be used to accurately measure small amounts of movement. Typical uses are measuring shaft runout or shaft endfloat (sideplay) and setting piston position for ignition timing on two-strokes. A dial gauge set usually comes with a range of different probes and adapters and mounting equipment.

● The gauge needle must point to zero when at rest. Rotate the ring around its periphery to zero the gauge.

● Check that the gauge is capable of reading the extent of movement in the work. Most gauges have a small dial set in the face which records whole millimetres of movement as well as the fine scale around the face periphery which is calibrated in 0.01 mm divisions. Read off the small dial first to obtain the base measurement, then add the measurement from the fine scale to obtain the total reading.

In the example shown the gauge reads 1.48 mm (see illustration 3.17):

Base measurement	1.00 mm
Fine measurement	0.48 mm
Total figure	1.48 mm

3.17 Dial gauge reading of 1.48 mm

● If measuring shaft runout, the shaft must be supported in vee-blocks and the gauge mounted on a stand perpendicular to the shaft. Rest the tip of the gauge against the centre of the shaft and rotate the shaft slowly whilst watching the gauge reading (see illustration 3.18). Take several measurements along the length of the shaft and record the maximum gauge reading as the amount of runout in the shaft. **Note:** *The reading obtained will be total runout at that point - some manufacturers specify that the runout figure is halved to compare with their specified runout limit.*

● Endfloat (sideplay) measurement requires that the gauge is mounted securely to the surrounding component with its probe touching the end of the shaft. Using hand pressure, push and pull on the shaft noting the maximum endfloat recorded on the gauge (see illustration 3.19).

3.19 Using a dial gauge to measure shaft endfloat

● A dial gauge with suitable adapters can be used to determine piston position BTDC on two-stroke engines for the purposes of ignition timing. The gauge, adapter and suitable length probe are installed in the place of the spark plug and the gauge zeroed at TDC. If the piston position is specified as 1.14 mm BTDC, rotate the engine back to 2.00 mm BTDC, then slowly forwards to 1.14 mm BTDC.

Cylinder compression gauges

● A compression gauge is used for measuring cylinder compression. Either the rubber-cone type or the threaded adapter type can be used. The latter is preferred to ensure a perfect seal against the cylinder head. A 0 to 300 psi (0 to 20 Bar) type gauge (for petrol/gasoline engines) will be suitable for motorcycles.

● The spark plug is removed and the gauge either held hard against the cylinder head (cone type) or the gauge adapter screwed into the cylinder head (threaded type) (see illustration 3.20). Cylinder compression is measured with the engine turning over, but not running. The gauge will hold the reading until manually released.

Oil pressure gauge

● An oil pressure gauge is used for measuring engine oil pressure. Most gauges come with a set of adapters to fit the thread of the take-off point (see illustration 3.21). If the take-off point specified by the motorcycle manufacturer is an external oil pipe union, make sure that the specified replacement union is used to prevent oil starvation.

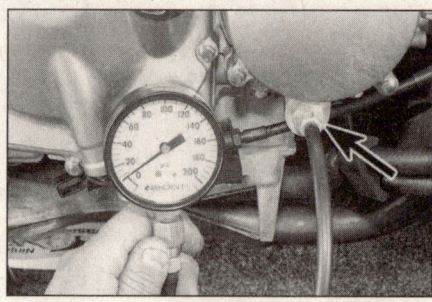

3.21 Oil pressure gauge and take-off point adapter (arrow)

● Oil pressure is measured with the engine running (at a specific rpm) and often the manufacturer will specify pressure limits for a cold and hot engine.

Straight-edge and surface plate

● If checking the gasket face of a component for warpage, place a steel rule or precision straight-edge across the gasket face and measure any gap between the straight-edge and component with feeler gauges (see illustration 3.22). Check diagonally across the component and between mounting holes (see illustration 3.23).

3.22 Use a straight-edge and feeler gauges to check for warpage

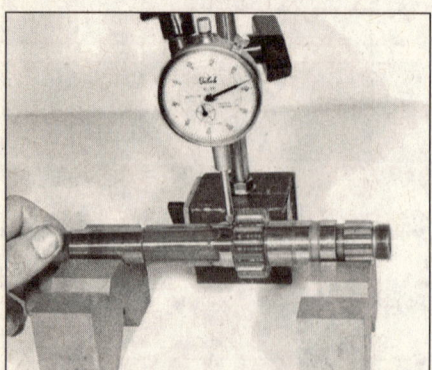

3.18 Using a dial gauge to measure shaft runout

3.20 Using a rubber-cone type cylinder compression gauge

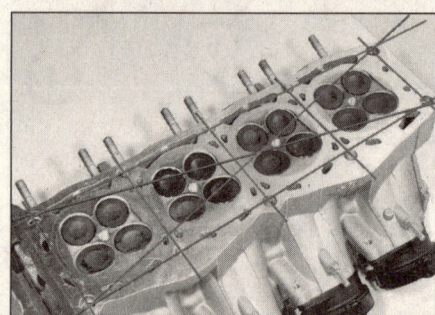

3.23 Check for warpage in these directions

Tools and Workshop Tips

- Checking individual components for warpage, such as clutch plain (metal) plates, requires a perfectly flat plate or piece or plate glass and feeler gauges.

4 Torque and leverage

What is torque?

- Torque describes the twisting force about a shaft. The amount of torque applied is determined by the distance from the centre of the shaft to the end of the lever and the amount of force being applied to the end of the lever; distance multiplied by force equals torque.
- The manufacturer applies a measured torque to a bolt or nut to ensure that it will not slacken in use and to hold two components securely together without movement in the joint. The actual torque setting depends on the thread size, bolt or nut material and the composition of the components being held.
- Too little torque may cause the fastener to loosen due to vibration, whereas too much torque will distort the joint faces of the component or cause the fastener to shear off. Always stick to the specified torque setting.

Using a torque wrench

- Check the calibration of the torque wrench and make sure it has a suitable range for the job. Torque wrenches are available in Nm (Newton-metres), kgf m (kilograms-force metre), lbf ft (pounds-feet), lbf in (inch-pounds). Do not confuse lbf ft with lbf in.
- Adjust the tool to the desired torque on the scale (see illustration 4.1). If your torque wrench is not calibrated in the units specified, carefully convert the figure (see Conversion Factors). A manufacturer sometimes gives a torque setting as a range (8 to 10 Nm) rather than a single figure - in this case set the tool midway between the two settings. The same torque may be expressed as 9 Nm ± 1 Nm. Some torque wrenches have a method of locking the setting so that it isn't inadvertently altered during use.

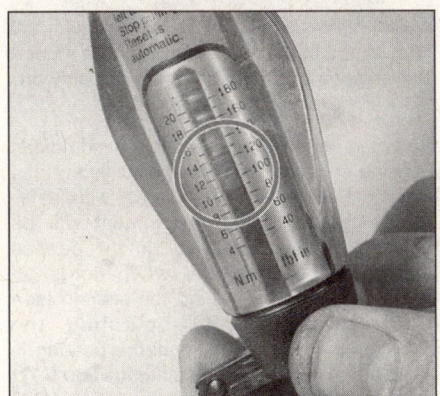

4.1 Set the torque wrench index mark to the setting required, in this case 12 Nm

- Install the bolts/nuts in their correct location and secure them lightly. Their threads must be clean and free of any old locking compound. Unless specified the threads and flange should be dry - oiled threads are necessary in certain circumstances and the manufacturer will take this into account in the specified torque figure. Similarly, the manufacturer may also specify the application of thread-locking compound.
- Tighten the fasteners in the specified sequence until the torque wrench clicks, indicating that the torque setting has been reached. Apply the torque again to double-check the setting. Where different thread diameter fasteners secure the component, as a rule tighten the larger diameter ones first.
- When the torque wrench has been finished with, release the lock (where applicable) and fully back off its setting to zero - do not leave the torque wrench tensioned. Also, do not use a torque wrench for slackening a fastener.

Angle-tightening

- Manufacturers often specify a figure in degrees for final tightening of a fastener. This usually follows tightening to a specific torque setting.
- A degree disc can be set and attached to the socket (see illustration 4.2) or a protractor can be used to mark the angle of movement on the bolt/nut head and the surrounding casting (see illustration 4.3).

4.2 Angle tightening can be accomplished with a torque-angle gauge . . .

4.3 . . . or by marking the angle on the surrounding component

Loosening sequences

- Where more than one bolt/nut secures a component, loosen each fastener evenly a little at a time. In this way, not all the stress of the joint is held by one fastener and the components are not likely to distort.
- If a tightening sequence is provided, work in the REVERSE of this, but if not, work from the outside in, in a criss-cross sequence (see illustration 4.4).

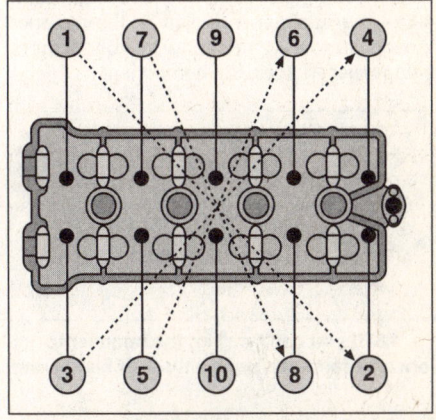

4.4 When slackening, work from the outside inwards

Tightening sequences

- If a component is held by more than one fastener it is important that the retaining bolts/nuts are tightened evenly to prevent uneven stress build-up and distortion of sealing faces. This is especially important on high-compression joints such as the cylinder head.
- A sequence is usually provided by the manufacturer, either in a diagram or actually marked in the casting. If not, always start in the centre and work outwards in a criss-cross pattern (see illustration 4.5). Start off by securing all bolts/nuts finger-tight, then set the torque wrench and tighten each fastener by a small amount in sequence until the final torque is reached. By following this practice,

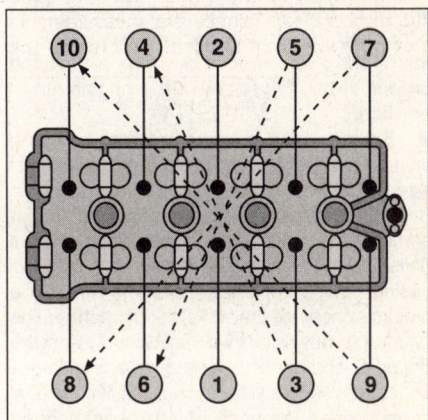

4.5 When tightening, work from the inside outwards

the joint will be held evenly and will not be distorted. Important joints, such as the cylinder head and big-end fasteners often have two- or three-stage torque settings.

Applying leverage

● Use tools at the correct angle. Position a socket wrench or spanner on the bolt/nut so that you pull it towards you when loosening. If this can't be done, push the spanner without curling your fingers around it **(see illustration 4.6)** - the spanner may slip or the fastener loosen suddenly, resulting in your fingers being crushed against a component.

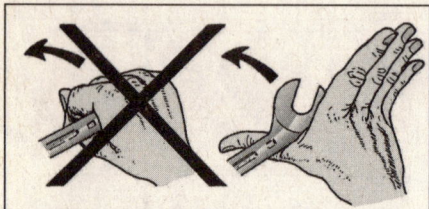

4.6 If you can't pull on the spanner to loosen a fastener, push with your hand open

● Additional leverage is gained by extending the length of the lever. The best way to do this is to use a breaker bar instead of the regular length tool, or to slip a length of tubing over the end of the spanner or socket wrench.
● If additional leverage will not work, the fastener head is either damaged or firmly corroded in place (see Fasteners).

5 Bearings

Bearing removal and installation

Drivers and sockets

● Before removing a bearing, always inspect the casing to see which way it must be driven out - some casings will have retaining plates or a cast step. Also check for any identifying markings on the bearing and if installed to a certain depth, measure this at this stage. Some roller bearings are sealed on one side - take note of the original fitted position.
● Bearings can be driven out of a casing using a bearing driver tool (with the correct size head) or a socket of the correct diameter. Select the driver head or socket so that it contacts the outer race of the bearing, not the balls/rollers or inner race. Always support the casing around the bearing housing with wood blocks, otherwise there is a risk of fracture. The bearing is driven out with a few blows on the driver or socket from a heavy mallet. Unless access is severely restricted (as with wheel bearings), a pin-punch is not recommended unless it is moved around the bearing to keep it square in its housing.

● The same equipment can be used to install bearings. Make sure the bearing housing is supported on wood blocks and line up the bearing in its housing. Fit the bearing as noted on removal - generally they are installed with their marked side facing outwards. Tap the bearing squarely into its housing using a driver or socket which bears only on the bearing's outer race - contact with the bearing balls/rollers or inner race will destroy it **(see illustrations 5.1 and 5.2)**.
● Check that the bearing inner race and balls/rollers rotate freely.

5.1 Using a bearing driver against the bearing's outer race

5.2 Using a large socket against the bearing's outer race

Pullers and slide-hammers

● Where a bearing is pressed on a shaft a puller will be required to extract it **(see illustration 5.3)**. Make sure that the puller clamp or legs fit securely behind the bearing and are unlikely to slip out. If pulling a bearing

5.3 This bearing puller clamps behind the bearing and pressure is applied to the shaft end to draw the bearing off

off a gear shaft for example, you may have to locate the puller behind a gear pinion if there is no access to the race and draw the gear pinion off the shaft as well **(see illustration 5.4)**.

> **Caution:** Ensure that the puller's centre bolt locates securely against the end of the shaft and will not slip when pressure is applied. Also ensure that puller does not damage the shaft end.

5.4 Where no access is available to the rear of the bearing, it is sometimes possible to draw off the adjacent component

● Operate the puller so that its centre bolt exerts pressure on the shaft end and draws the bearing off the shaft.
● When installing the bearing on the shaft, tap only on the bearing's inner race - contact with the balls/rollers or outer race with destroy the bearing. Use a socket or length of tubing as a drift which fits over the shaft end **(see illustration 5.5)**.

5.5 When installing a bearing on a shaft use a piece of tubing which bears only on the bearing's inner race

● Where a bearing locates in a blind hole in a casing, it cannot be driven or pulled out as described above. A slide-hammer with knife-edged bearing puller attachment will be required. The puller attachment passes through the bearing and when tightened expands to fit firmly behind the bearing **(see illustration 5.6)**. By operating the slide-hammer part of the tool the bearing is jarred out of its housing **(see illustration 5.7)**.
● It is possible, if the bearing is of reasonable weight, for it to drop out of its housing if the casing is heated as described opposite.

Tools and Workshop Tips

5.6 Expand the bearing puller so that it locks behind the bearing . . .

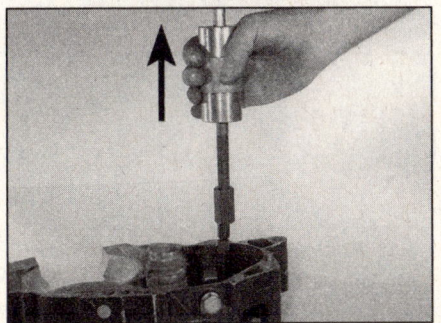

5.7 . . . attach the slide hammer to the bearing puller

If this method is attempted, first prepare a work surface which will enable the casing to be tapped face down to help dislodge the bearing - a wood surface is ideal since it will not damage the casing's gasket surface. Wearing protective gloves, tap the heated casing several times against the work surface to dislodge the bearing under its own weight **(see illustration 5.8)**.

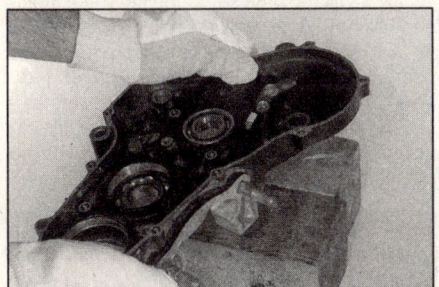

5.8 Tapping a casing face down on wood blocks can often dislodge a bearing

● Bearings can be installed in blind holes using the driver or socket method described above.

Drawbolts

● Where a bearing or bush is set in the eye of a component, such as a suspension linkage arm or connecting rod small-end, removal by drift may damage the component. Furthermore, a rubber bushing in a shock absorber eye cannot successfully be driven out of position. If access is available to a engineering press, the task is straightforward. If not, a drawbolt can be fabricated to extract the bearing or bush.

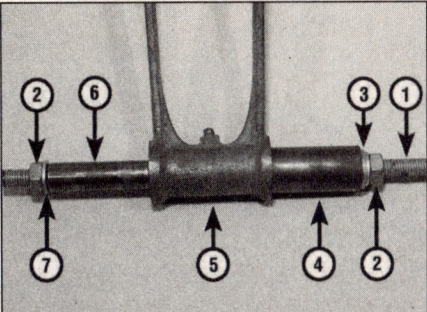

5.9 Drawbolt component parts assembled on a suspension arm

1 Bolt or length of threaded bar
2 Nuts
3 Washer (external diameter greater than tubing internal diameter)
4 Tubing (internal diameter sufficient to accommodate bearing)
5 Suspension arm with bearing
6 Tubing (external diameter slightly smaller than bearing)
7 Washer (external diameter slightly smaller than bearing)

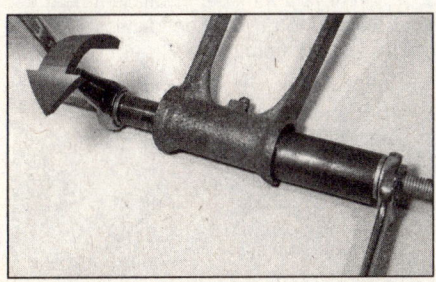

5.10 Drawing the bearing out of the suspension arm

● To extract the bearing/bush you will need a long bolt with nut (or piece of threaded bar with two nuts), a piece of tubing which has an internal diameter larger than the bearing/bush, another piece of tubing which has an external diameter slightly smaller than the bearing/bush, and a selection of washers **(see illustrations 5.9 and 5.10)**. Note that the pieces of tubing must be of the same length, or longer, than the bearing/bush.

● The same kit (without the pieces of tubing) can be used to draw the new bearing/bush back into place **(see illustration 5.11)**.

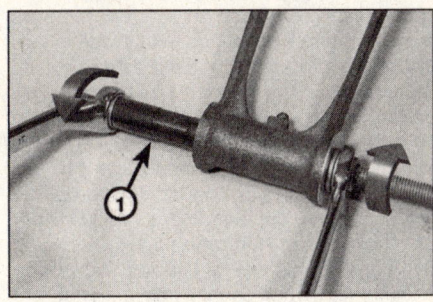

5.11 Installing a new bearing (1) in the suspension arm

Temperature change

● If the bearing's outer race is a tight fit in the casing, the aluminium casing can be heated to release its grip on the bearing. Aluminium will expand at a greater rate than the steel bearing outer race. There are several ways to do this, but avoid any localised extreme heat (such as a blow torch) - aluminium alloy has a low melting point.

● Approved methods of heating a casing are using a domestic oven (heated to 100°C) or immersing the casing in boiling water **(see illustration 5.12)**. Low temperature range localised heat sources such as a paint stripper heat gun or clothes iron can also be used **(see illustration 5.13)**. Alternatively, soak a rag in boiling water, wring it out and wrap it around the bearing housing.

> ⚠ **Warning: All of these methods require care in use to prevent scalding and burns to the hands. Wear protective gloves when handling hot components.**

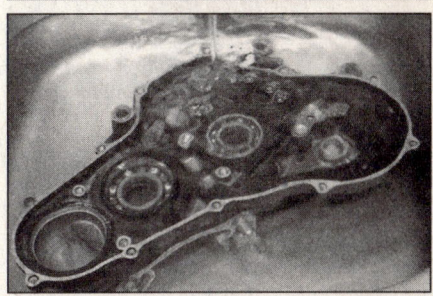

5.12 A casing can be immersed in a sink of boiling water to aid bearing removal

5.13 Using a localised heat source to aid bearing removal

● If heating the whole casing note that plastic components, such as the neutral switch, may suffer - remove them beforehand.

● After heating, remove the bearing as described above. You may find that the expansion is sufficient for the bearing to fall out of the casing under its own weight or with a light tap on the driver or socket.

● If necessary, the casing can be heated to aid bearing installation, and this is sometimes the recommended procedure if the motorcycle manufacturer has designed the housing and bearing fit with this intention.

REF•28 Tools and Workshop Tips

- Installation of bearings can be eased by placing them in a freezer the night before installation. The steel bearing will contract slightly, allowing easy insertion in its housing. This is often useful when installing steering head outer races in the frame.

Bearing types and markings

- Plain shell bearings, ball bearings, needle roller bearings and tapered roller bearings will all be found on motorcycles (see illustrations 5.14 and 5.15). The ball and roller types are usually caged between an inner and outer race, but uncaged variations may be found.

5.16 Typical bearing marking

5.18 Example of ball journal bearing with damaged balls and cages

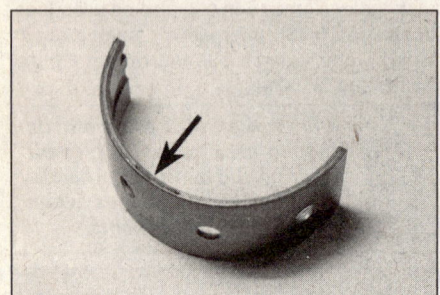

5.14 Shell bearings are either plain or grooved. They are usually identified by colour code (arrow)

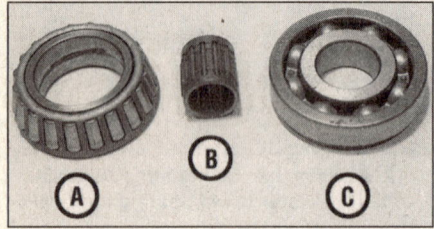

5.15 Tapered roller bearing (A), needle roller bearing (B) and ball journal bearing (C)

- Shell bearings (often called inserts) are usually found at the crankshaft main and connecting rod big-end where they are good at coping with high loads. They are made of a phosphor-bronze material and are impregnated with self-lubricating properties.
- Ball bearings and needle roller bearings consist of a steel inner and outer race with the balls or rollers between the races. They require constant lubrication by oil or grease and are good at coping with axial loads. Taper roller bearings consist of rollers set in a tapered cage set on the inner race; the outer race is separate. They are good at coping with axial loads and prevent movement along the shaft - a typical application is in the steering head.
- Bearing manufacturers produce bearings to ISO size standards and stamp one face of the bearing to indicate its internal and external diameter, load capacity and type (see illustration 5.16).
- Metal bushes are usually of phosphor-bronze material. Rubber bushes are used in suspension mounting eyes. Fibre bushes have also been used in suspension pivots.

Bearing fault finding

- If a bearing outer race has spun in its housing, the housing material will be damaged. You can use a bearing locking compound to bond the outer race in place if damage is not too severe.
- Shell bearings will fail due to damage of their working surface, as a result of lack of lubrication, corrosion or abrasive particles in the oil (see illustration 5.17). Small particles of dirt in the oil may embed in the bearing material whereas larger particles will score the bearing and shaft journal. If a number of short journeys are made, insufficient heat will be generated to drive off condensation which has built up on the bearings.

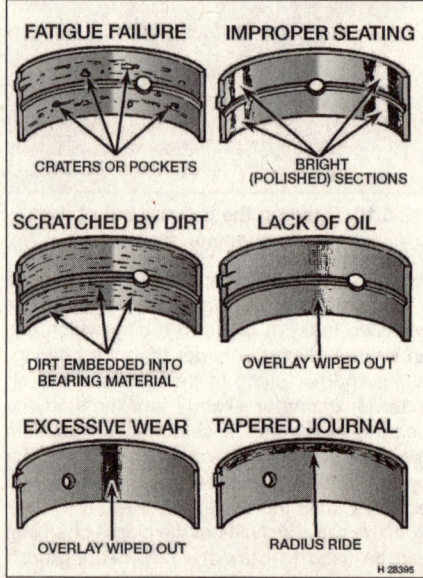

5.17 Typical bearing failures

- Ball and roller bearings will fail due to lack of lubrication or damage to the balls or rollers. Tapered-roller bearings can be damaged by overloading them. Unless the bearing is sealed on both sides, wash it in paraffin (kerosene) to remove all old grease then allow it to dry. Make a visual inspection looking to dented balls or rollers, damaged cages and worn or pitted races (see illustration 5.18).
- A ball bearing can be checked for wear by listening to it when spun. Apply a film of light oil to the bearing and hold it close to the ear - hold the outer race with one hand and spin the inner race with the other hand (see illustration 5.19). The bearing should be almost silent when spun; if it grates or rattles it is worn.

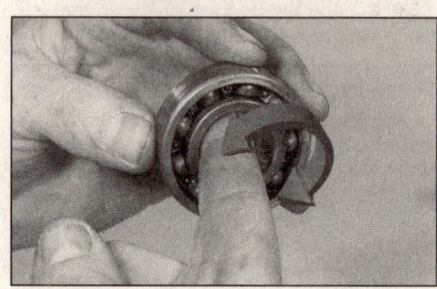

5.19 Hold outer race and listen to inner race when spun

6 Oil seals

Oil seal removal and installation

- Oil seals should be renewed every time a component is dismantled. This is because the seal lips will become set to the sealing surface and will not necessarily reseal.
- Oil seals can be prised out of position using a large flat-bladed screwdriver (see illustration 6.1). In the case of crankcase seals, check first that the seal is not lipped on the inside, preventing its removal with the crankcases joined.

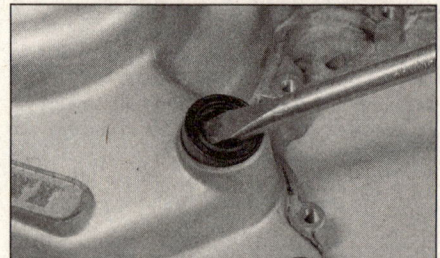

6.1 Prise out oil seals with a large flat-bladed screwdriver

- New seals are usually installed with their marked face (containing the seal reference code) outwards and the spring side towards the fluid being retained. In certain cases, such as a two-stroke engine crankshaft seal, a double lipped seal may be used due to there being fluid or gas on each side of the joint.

Tools and Workshop Tips

- Use a bearing driver or socket which bears only on the outer hard edge of the seal to install it in the casing - tapping on the inner edge will damage the sealing lip.

Oil seal types and markings

- Oil seals are usually of the single-lipped type. Double-lipped seals are found where a liquid or gas is on both sides of the joint.
- Oil seals can harden and lose their sealing ability if the motorcycle has been in storage for a long period - renewal is the only solution.
- Oil seal manufacturers also conform to the ISO markings for seal size - these are moulded into the outer face of the seal (see illustration 6.2).

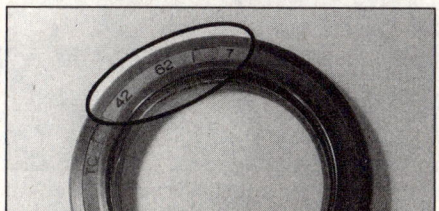

6.2 These oil seal markings indicate inside diameter, outside diameter and seal thickness

7 Gaskets and sealants

Types of gasket and sealant

- Gaskets are used to seal the mating surfaces between components and keep lubricants, fluids, vacuum or pressure contained within the assembly. Aluminium gaskets are sometimes found at the cylinder joints, but most gaskets are paper-based. If the mating surfaces of the components being joined are undamaged the gasket can be installed dry, although a dab of sealant or grease will be useful to hold it in place during assembly.
- RTV (Room Temperature Vulcanising) silicone rubber sealants cure when exposed to moisture in the atmosphere. These sealants are good at filling pits or irregular gasket faces, but will tend to be forced out of the joint under very high torque. They can be used to replace a paper gasket, but first make sure that the width of the paper gasket is not essential to the shimming of internal components. RTV sealants should not be used on components containing petrol (gasoline).
- Non-hardening, semi-hardening and hard setting liquid gasket compounds can be used with a gasket or between a metal-to-metal joint. Select the sealant to suit the application: universal non-hardening sealant can be used on virtually all joints; semi-hardening on joint faces which are rough or damaged; hard setting sealant on joints which require a permanent bond and are subjected to high temperature and pressure. **Note:** Check first if the paper gasket has a bead of sealant impregnated in its surface before applying additional sealant.
- When choosing a sealant, make sure it is suitable for the application, particularly if being applied in a high-temperature area or in the vicinity of fuel. Certain manufacturers produce sealants in either clear, silver or black colours to match the finish of the engine. This has a particular application on motorcycles where much of the engine is exposed.
- Do not over-apply sealant. That which is squeezed out on the outside of the joint can be wiped off, whereas an excess of sealant on the inside can break off and clog oilways.

Breaking a sealed joint

- Age, heat, pressure and the use of hard setting sealant can cause two components to stick together so tightly that they are difficult to separate using finger pressure alone. Do not resort to using levers unless there is a pry point provided for this purpose (see illustration 7.1) or else the gasket surfaces will be damaged.
- Use a soft-faced hammer (see illustration 7.2) or a wood block and conventional hammer to strike the component near the mating surface. Avoid hammering against cast extremities since they may break off. If this method fails, try using a wood wedge between the two components.

Caution: If the joint will not separate, double-check that you have removed all the fasteners.

7.1 If a pry point is provided, apply gently pressure with a flat-bladed screwdriver

7.2 Tap around the joint with a soft-faced mallet if necessary - don't strike cooling fins

Removal of old gasket and sealant

- Paper gaskets will most likely come away complete, leaving only a few traces stuck

Most components have one or two hollow locating dowels between the two gasket faces. If a dowel cannot be removed, do not resort to gripping it with pliers - it will almost certainly be distorted. Install a close-fitting socket or Phillips screwdriver into the dowel and then grip the outer edge of the dowel to free it.

on the sealing faces of the components. It is imperative that all traces are removed to ensure correct sealing of the new gasket.

- Very carefully scrape all traces of gasket away making sure that the sealing surfaces are not gouged or scored by the scraper (see illustrations 7.3, 7.4 and 7.5). Stubborn deposits can be removed by spraying with an aerosol gasket remover. Final preparation of

7.3 Paper gaskets can be scraped off with a gasket scraper tool . . .

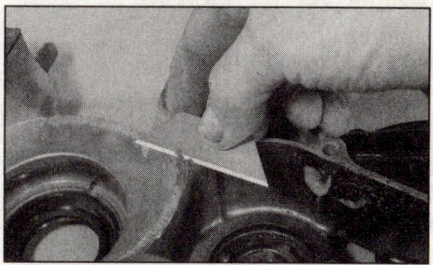

7.4 . . . a knife blade . . .

7.5 . . . or a household scraper

REF•30 Tools and Workshop Tips

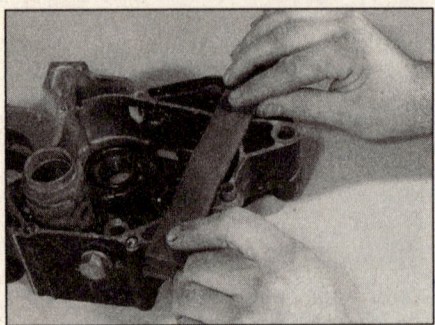

7.6 Fine abrasive paper is wrapped around a flat file to clean up the gasket face

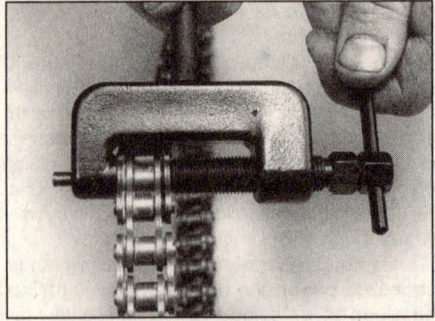

8.1 Tighten the chain breaker to push the pin out of the link . . .

8.4 Insert the new soft link, with O-rings, through the chain ends . . .

7.7 A kitchen scourer can be used on stubborn deposits

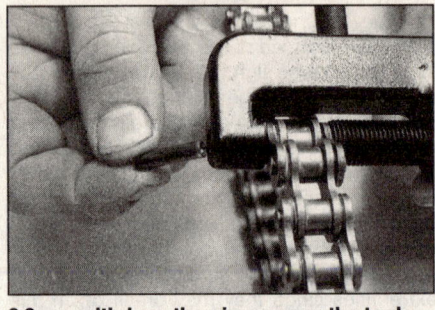

8.2 . . . withdraw the pin, remove the tool . . .

8.5 . . . install the O-rings over the pin ends . . .

8.6 . . . followed by the sideplate

the gasket surface can be made with very fine abrasive paper or a plastic kitchen scourer **(see illustrations 7.6 and 7.7).**

● Old sealant can be scraped or peeled off components, depending on the type originally used. Note that gasket removal compounds are available to avoid scraping the components clean; make sure the gasket remover suits the type of sealant used.

8 Chains

Breaking and joining final drive chains

● Drive chains for all but small bikes are continuous and do not have a clip-type connecting link. The chain must be broken using a chain breaker tool and the new chain securely riveted together using a new soft rivet-type link. Never use a clip-type connecting link instead of a rivet-type link, except in an emergency. Various chain breaking and riveting tools are available, either as separate tools or combined as illustrated in the accompanying photographs - read the instructions supplied with the tool carefully.

> ⚠️ **Warning:** The need to rivet the new link pins correctly cannot be overstressed - loss of control of the motorcycle is very likely to result if the chain breaks in use.

● Rotate the chain and look for the soft link. The soft link pins look like they have been

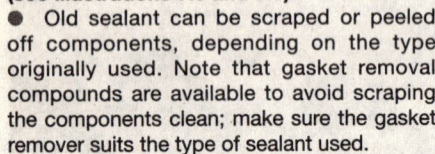

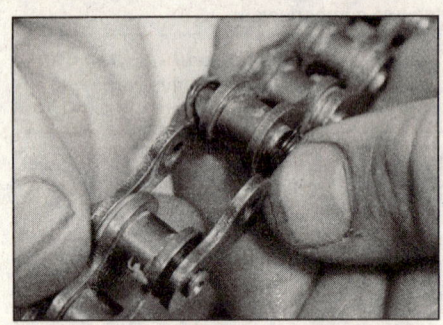

8.3 . . . and separate the chain link

deeply centre-punched instead of peened over like all the other pins **(see illustration 8.9)** and its sideplate may be a different colour. Position the soft link midway between the sprockets and assemble the chain breaker tool over one of the soft link pins **(see illustration 8.1)**. Operate the tool to push the pin out through the chain **(see illustration 8.2)**. On an O-ring chain, remove the O-rings **(see illustration 8.3)**. Carry out the same procedure on the other soft link pin.

> **Caution:** Certain soft link pins (particularly on the larger chains) may require their ends to be filed or ground off before they can be pressed out using the tool.

● Check that you have the correct size and strength (standard or heavy duty) new soft link - do not reuse the old link. Look for the size marking on the chain sideplates **(see illustration 8.10)**.

● Position the chain ends so that they are engaged over the rear sprocket. On an O-ring chain, install a new O-ring over each pin of the link and insert the link through the two chain ends **(see illustration 8.4)**. Install a new O-ring over the end of each pin, followed by the sideplate (with the chain manufacturer's marking facing outwards) **(see illustrations 8.5 and 8.6)**. On an unsealed chain, insert the link through the two chain ends, then install the sideplate with the chain manufacturer's marking facing outwards.

● Note that it may not be possible to install the sideplate using finger pressure alone. If using a joining tool, assemble it so that the plates of the tool clamp the link and press the sideplate over the pins **(see illustration 8.7)**. Otherwise, use two small sockets placed over

8.7 Push the sideplate into position using a clamp

Tools and Workshop Tips

8.8 Assemble the chain riveting tool over one pin at a time and tighten it fully

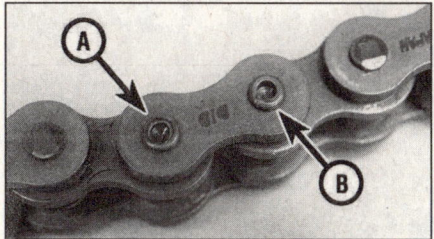

8.9 Pin end correctly riveted (A), pin end unriveted (B)

the rivet ends and two pieces of the wood between a G-clamp. Operate the clamp to press the sideplate over the pins.
● Assemble the joining tool over one pin (following the maker's instructions) and tighten the tool down to spread the pin end securely **(see illustrations 8.8 and 8.9)**. Do the same on the other pin.

> ⚠ **Warning: Check that the pin ends are secure and that there is no danger of the sideplate coming loose. If the pin ends are cracked the soft link must be renewed.**

Final drive chain sizing

● Chains are sized using a three digit number, followed by a suffix to denote the chain type **(see illustration 8.10)**. Chain type is either standard or heavy duty (thicker sideplates), and also unsealed or O-ring/X-ring type.
● The first digit of the number relates to the pitch of the chain, ie the distance from the centre of one pin to the centre of the next pin **(see illustration 8.11)**. Pitch is expressed in eighths of an inch, as follows:

8.10 Typical chain size and type marking

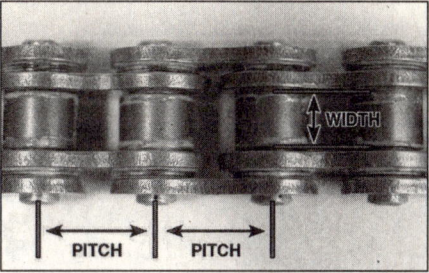

8.11 Chain dimensions

Sizes commencing with a 4 (eg 428) have a pitch of 1/2 inch (12.7 mm)

Sizes commencing with a 5 (eg 520) have a pitch of 5/8 inch (15.9 mm)

Sizes commencing with a 6 (eg 630) have a pitch of 3/4 inch (19.1 mm)

● The second and third digits of the chain size relate to the width of the rollers, again in imperial units, eg the 525 shown has 5/16 inch (7.94 mm) rollers **(see illustration 8.11)**.

9 Hoses

Clamping to prevent flow

● Small-bore flexible hoses can be clamped to prevent fluid flow whilst a component is worked on. Whichever method is used, ensure that the hose material is not permanently distorted or damaged by the clamp.
a) A brake hose clamp available from auto accessory shops **(see illustration 9.1)**.
b) A wingnut type hose clamp **(see illustration 9.2)**.

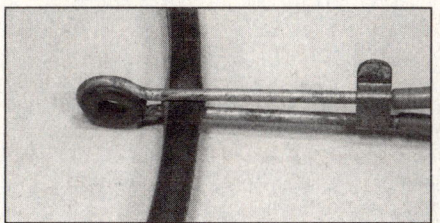

9.1 Hoses can be clamped with an automotive brake hose clamp . . .

9.2 . . . a wingnut type hose clamp . . .

c) Two sockets placed each side of the hose and held with straight-jawed self-locking grips **(see illustration 9.3)**.
d) Thick card each side of the hose held between straight-jawed self-locking grips **(see illustration 9.4)**.

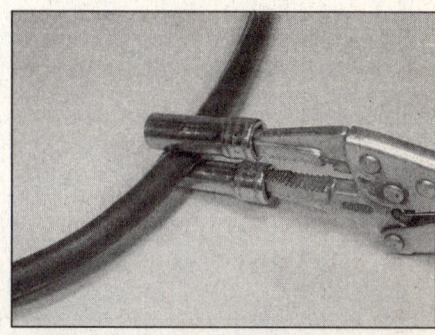

9.3 . . . two sockets and a pair of self-locking grips . . .

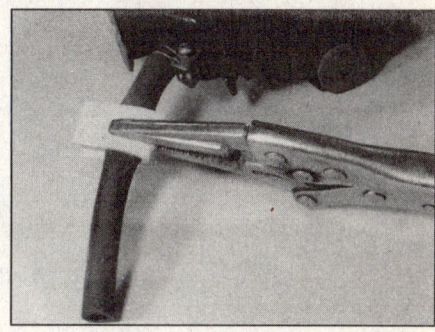

9.4 . . . or thick card and self-locking grips

Freeing and fitting hoses

● Always make sure the hose clamp is moved well clear of the hose end. Grip the hose with your hand and rotate it whilst pulling it off the union. If the hose has hardened due to age and will not move, slit it with a sharp knife and peel its ends off the union **(see illustration 9.5)**.
● Resist the temptation to use grease or soap on the unions to aid installation; although it helps the hose slip over the union it will equally aid the escape of fluid from the joint. It is preferable to soften the hose ends in hot water and wet the inside surface of the hose with water or a fluid which will evaporate.

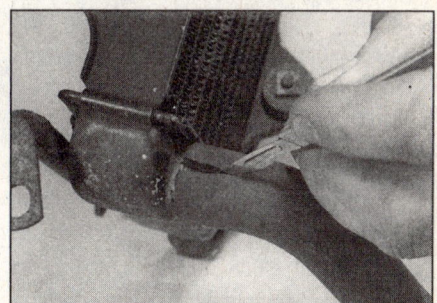

9.5 Cutting a coolant hose free with a sharp knife

Notes

Storage REF•33

Preparing for storage

Before you start

If repairs or an overhaul is needed, see that this is carried out now rather than left until you want to ride the bike again.

Give the bike a good wash and scrub all dirt from its underside. Make sure the bike dries completely before preparing for storage.

Engine

- Remove the spark plug(s) and lubricate the cylinder bores with approximately a teaspoon of motor oil using a spout-type oil can **(see illustration 1)**. Reinstall the spark plug(s). Crank the engine over a couple of times to coat the piston rings and bores with oil. If the bike has a kickstart, use this to turn the engine over. If not, flick the kill switch to OFF position and crank the engine over on the starter **(see illustration 2)**. If the nature on the ignition system prevents the starter operating with the kill switch in the OFF position, remove the spark plugs and fit them back in their caps; ensure that the plugs are earthed (grounded) against the cylinder head when the starter is operated **(see illustration 3)**.

 Warning: It is important that the plugs are earthed (grounded) away from the spark plug holes otherwise there is a risk of atomised fuel from the cylinders igniting.

HAYNES HiNT *On a single cylinder four-stroke engine, you can seal the combustion chamber completely by positioning the piston at TDC on the compression stroke.*

- Drain the carburettor(s) otherwise there is a risk of jets becoming blocked by gum deposits from the fuel **(see illustration 4)**.

- If the bike is going into long-term storage, consider adding a fuel stabiliser to the fuel in the tank. If the tank is drained completely, corrosion of its internal surfaces may occur if left unprotected for a long period. The tank can be treated with a rust preventative especially for this purpose. Alternatively, remove the tank and pour half a litre of motor oil into it, install the filler cap and shake the tank to coat its internals with oil before draining off the excess. The same effect can also be achieved by spraying WD40 or a similar water-dispersant around the inside of the tank via its flexible nozzle.

- Make sure the cooling system contains the correct mix of antifreeze. Antifreeze also contains important corrosion inhibitors.

- The air intakes and exhaust can be sealed off by covering or plugging the openings. Ensure that you do not seal in any condensation; run the engine until it is hot,

Squirt a drop of motor oil into each cylinder

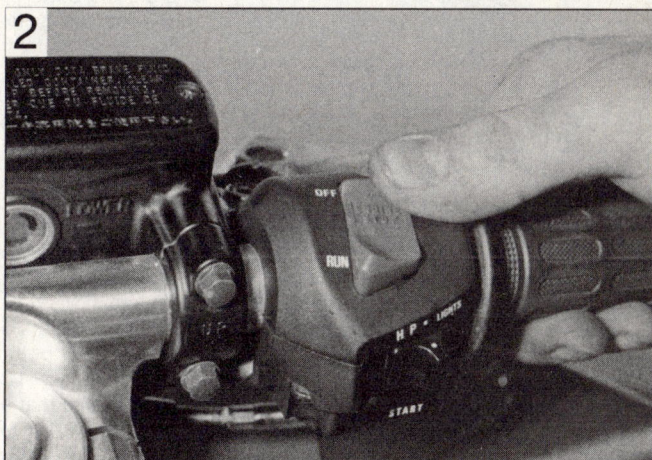

Flick the kill switch to OFF . . .

. . . and ensure that the metal bodies of the plugs (arrows) are earthed against the cylinder head

Connect a hose to the carburettor float chamber drain stub (arrow) and unscrew the drain screw

REF•34 Storage

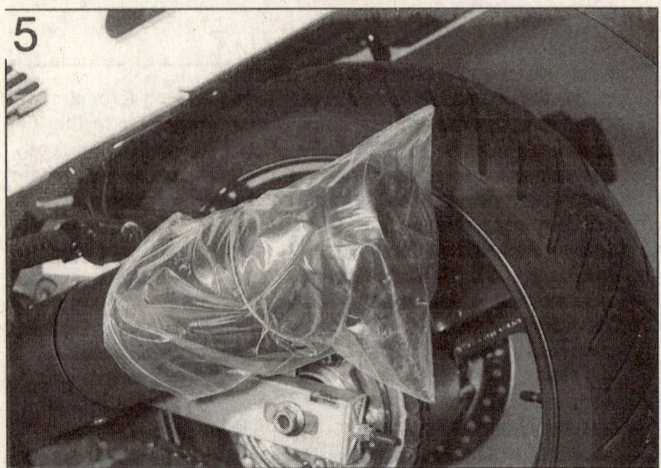
Exhausts can be sealed off with a plastic bag

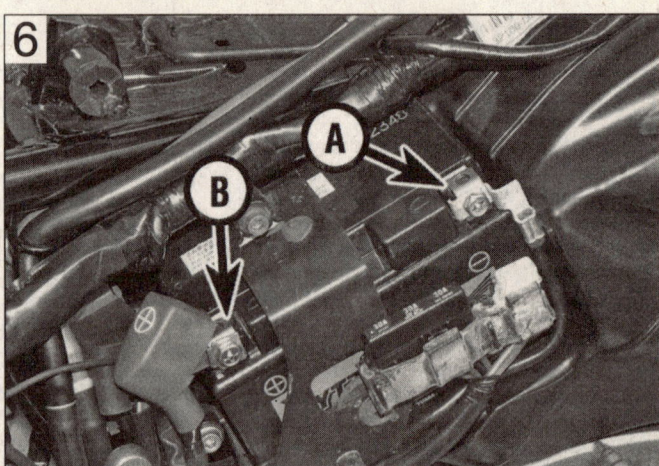
Disconnect the negative lead (A) first, followed by the positive lead (B)

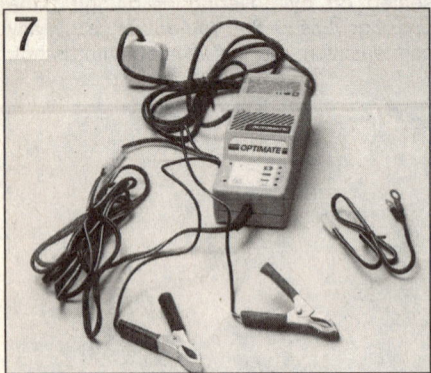
Use a suitable battery charger - this kit also assess battery condition

then switch off and allow to cool. Tape a piece of thick plastic over the silencer end(s) **(see illustration 5)**. Note that some advocate pouring a tablespoon of motor oil into the silencer(s) before sealing them off.

Battery
● Remove it from the bike - in extreme cases of cold the battery may freeze and crack its case **(see illustration 6)**.
● Check the electrolyte level and top up if necessary (conventional refillable batteries). Clean the terminals.
● Store the battery off the motorcycle and away from any sources of fire. Position a wooden block under the battery if it is to sit on the ground.
● Give the battery a trickle charge for a few hours every month **(see illustration 7)**.

Tyres
● Place the bike on its centrestand or an auxiliary stand which will support the motorcycle in an upright position. Position wood blocks under the tyres to keep them off the ground and to provide insulation from damp. If the bike is being put into long-term storage, ideally both tyres should be off the ground; not only will this protect the tyres, but will also ensure that no load is placed on the steering head or wheel bearings.
● Deflate each tyre by 5 to 10 psi, no more or the beads may unseat from the rim, making subsequent inflation difficult on tubeless tyres.

Pivots and controls
● Lubricate all lever, pedal, stand and footrest pivot points. If grease nipples are fitted to the rear suspension components, apply lubricant to the pivots.
● Lubricate all control cables.

Cycle components
● Apply a wax protectant to all painted and plastic components. Wipe off any excess, but don't polish to a shine. Where fitted, clean the screen with soap and water.
● Coat metal parts with Vaseline (petroleum jelly). When applying this to the fork tubes, do not compress the forks otherwise the seals will rot from contact with the Vaseline.
● Apply a vinyl cleaner to the seat.

Storage conditions
● Aim to store the bike in a shed or garage which does not leak and is free from damp.
● Drape an old blanket or bedspread over the bike to protect it from dust and direct contact with sunlight (which will fade paint). This also hides the bike from prying eyes. Beware of tight-fitting plastic covers which may allow condensation to form and settle on the bike.

Getting back on the road

Engine and transmission
● Change the oil and replace the oil filter. If this was done prior to storage, check that the oil hasn't emulsified - a thick whitish substance which occurs through condensation.
● Remove the spark plugs. Using a spout-type oil can, squirt a few drops of oil into the cylinder(s). This will provide initial lubrication as the piston rings and bores comes back into contact. Service the spark plugs, or fit new ones, and install them in the engine.

● Check that the clutch isn't stuck on. The plates can stick together if left standing for some time, preventing clutch operation. Engage a gear and try rocking the bike back and forth with the clutch lever held against the handlebar. If this doesn't work on cable-operated clutches, hold the clutch lever back against the handlebar with a strong elastic band or cable tie for a couple of hours **(see illustration 8)**.
● If the air intakes or silencer end(s) were blocked off, remove the bung or cover used.
● If the fuel tank was coated with a rust

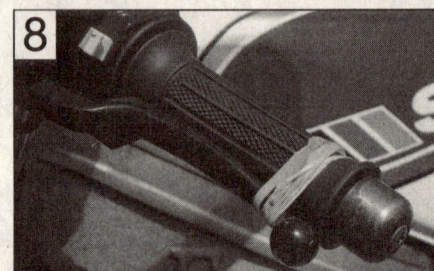
Hold clutch lever back against the handlebar with elastic bands or a cable tie

Storage REF•35

preventative, oil or a stabiliser added to the fuel, drain and flush the tank and dispose of the fuel sensibly. If no action was taken with the fuel tank prior to storage, it is advised that the old fuel is disposed of since it will go off over a period of time. Refill the fuel tank with fresh fuel.

Frame and running gear

● Oil all pivot points and cables.
● Check the tyre pressures. They will definitely need inflating if pressures were reduced for storage.
● Lubricate the final drive chain (where applicable).
● Remove any protective coating applied to the fork tubes (stanchions) since this may well destroy the fork seals. If the fork tubes weren't protected and have picked up rust spots, remove them with very fine abrasive paper and refinish with metal polish.
● Check that both brakes operate correctly. Apply each brake hard and check that it's not possible to move the motorcycle forwards, then check that the brake frees off again once released. Brake caliper pistons can stick due to corrosion around the piston head, or on the sliding caliper types, due to corrosion of the slider pins. If the brake doesn't free after repeated operation, take the caliper off for examination. Similarly drum brakes can stick due to a seized operating cam, cable or rod linkage.
● If the motorcycle has been in long-term storage, renew the brake fluid and clutch fluid (where applicable).
● Depending on where the bike has been stored, the wiring, cables and hoses may have been nibbled by rodents. Make a visual check and investigate disturbed wiring loom tape.

Battery

● If the battery has been previously removal and given top up charges it can simply be reconnected. Remember to connect the positive cable first and the negative cable last.
● On conventional refillable batteries, if the battery has not received any attention, remove it from the motorcycle and check its electrolyte level. Top up if necessary then charge the battery. If the battery fails to hold a charge and a visual checks show heavy white sulphation of the plates, the battery is probably defective and must be renewed. This is particularly likely if the battery is old. Confirm battery condition with a specific gravity check.
● On sealed (MF) batteries, if the battery has not received any attention, remove it from the motorcycle and charge it according to the information on the battery case - if the battery fails to hold a charge it must be renewed.

Starting procedure

● If a kickstart is fitted, turn the engine over a couple of times with the ignition OFF to distribute oil around the engine. If no kickstart is fitted, flick the engine kill switch OFF and the ignition ON and crank the engine over a couple of times to work oil around the upper cylinder components. If the nature of the ignition system is such that the starter won't work with the kill switch OFF, remove the spark plugs, fit them back into their caps and earth (ground) their bodies on the cylinder head. Reinstall the spark plugs afterwards.
● Switch the kill switch to RUN, operate the choke and start the engine. If the engine won't start don't continue cranking the engine - not only will this flatten the battery, but the starter motor will overheat. Switch the ignition off and try again later. If the engine refuses to start, go through the fault finding procedures in this manual. **Note:** *If the bike has been in storage for a long time, old fuel or a carburettor blockage may be the problem. Gum deposits in carburettors can block jets - if a carburettor cleaner doesn't prove successful the carburettors must be dismantled for cleaning.*

● Once the engine has started, check that the lights, turn signals and horn work properly.

● Treat the bike gently for the first ride and check all fluid levels on completion. Settle the bike back into the maintenance schedule.

Notes

Fault Finding REF•37

This Section provides an easy reference-guide to the more common faults that are likely to afflict your machine. Obviously, the opportunities are almost limitless for faults to occur as a result of obscure failures, and to try and cover all eventualities would require a book. Indeed, a number have been written on the subject.

Successful troubleshooting is not a mysterious 'black art' but the application of a bit of knowledge combined with a systematic and logical approach to the problem. Approach any troubleshooting by first accurately identifying the symptom and then checking through the list of possible causes, starting with the simplest or most obvious and progressing in stages to the most complex.

Take nothing for granted, but above all apply liberal quantities of common sense.

The main symptom of a fault is given in the text as a major heading below which are listed the various systems or areas which may contain the fault. Details of each possible cause for a fault and the remedial action to be taken are given, in brief, in the paragraphs below each heading. Further information should be sought in the relevant Chapter.

1 Engine doesn't start or is difficult to start
- [ ] Starter motor doesn't rotate
- [ ] Starter motor rotates but engine does not turn over
- [ ] Starter works but engine won't turn over (seized)
- [ ] No fuel flow
- [ ] Engine flooded
- [ ] No spark or weak spark
- [ ] Compression low
- [ ] Stalls after starting
- [ ] Rough idle

2 Poor running at low speed
- [ ] Spark weak
- [ ] Fuel/air mixture incorrect
- [ ] Compression low
- [ ] Poor acceleration

3 Poor running or no power at high speed
- [ ] Firing incorrect
- [ ] Fuel/air mixture incorrect
- [ ] Compression low
- [ ] Knocking or pinking
- [ ] Miscellaneous causes

4 Overheating
- [ ] Engine overheats
- [ ] Firing incorrect
- [ ] Fuel/air mixture incorrect
- [ ] Compression too high
- [ ] Engine load excessive
- [ ] Lubrication inadequate
- [ ] Miscellaneous causes

5 Clutch problems
- [ ] Clutch slipping
- [ ] Clutch not disengaging completely

6 Gearchange problems
- [ ] Doesn't go into gear, or lever doesn't return
- [ ] Jumps out of gear
- [ ] Overselects

7 Abnormal engine noise
- [ ] Knocking or pinking
- [ ] Piston slap or rattling
- [ ] Valve noise
- [ ] Other noise

8 Abnormal driveline noise
- [ ] Clutch noise
- [ ] Transmission noise
- [ ] Final drive noise

9 Abnormal frame and suspension noise
- [ ] Front end noise
- [ ] Shock absorber noise
- [ ] Brake noise

10 Oil pressure warning light comes on
- [ ] Engine lubrication system
- [ ] Electrical system

11 Excessive exhaust smoke
- [ ] White smoke
- [ ] Black smoke
- [ ] Brown smoke

12 Poor handling or stability
- [ ] Handlebar hard to turn
- [ ] Handlebar shakes or vibrates excessively
- [ ] Handlebar pulls to one side
- [ ] Poor shock absorbing qualities

13 Braking problems
- [ ] Brakes are spongy, don't hold
- [ ] Brake lever or pedal pulsates
- [ ] Brakes drag

14 Electrical problems
- [ ] Battery dead or weak
- [ ] Battery overcharged

Fault Finding

1 Engine doesn't start or is difficult to start

Starter motor doesn't rotate

- ☐ Engine kill switch OFF.
- ☐ Fuse blown. Check main, ignition and engine management fuses (Chapter 8).
- ☐ Battery voltage low. Check and recharge battery (Chapter 8).
- ☐ Starter motor defective. Make sure the wiring to the starter is secure. Make sure the starter solenoid clicks when the starter button is pushed. If the solenoid clicks, then the fault is in the wiring or motor.
- ☐ Starter solenoid or starter relay faulty. Check as described in Chapter 8.
- ☐ Starter button not contacting. The contacts could be wet, corroded or dirty. Disassemble and clean the switch (Chapter 8).
- ☐ Wiring open or shorted. Check all wiring connectors to make sure that they are dry, tight and not corroded. Also check for broken or frayed wires and wiring insulation that can cause a short to ground (earth) (see wiring diagrams, Chapter 8).
- ☐ Ignition switch defective. Check the switch as described in Chapter 8. Replace the switch with a new one if it is defective.
- ☐ Engine kill switch defective. Check for wet, dirty, corroded or broken contacts. Clean or renew the switch as necessary (Chapter 8).
- ☐ Faulty neutral, sidestand or clutch switch. Check the wiring to each switch and the switch itself as described in Chapter 8.

Starter motor rotates but engine does not turn over

- ☐ Starter clutch defective. Inspect and repair or renew (Chapter 2).
- ☐ Damaged idler or starter gears. Inspect and renew the damaged parts (Chapter 2).

No fuel flow

- ☐ No fuel in tank.
- ☐ Fuel tank breather hose obstructed.
- ☐ Fuel pump faulty, or strainer and/or filter is blocked (see Chapter 4).
- ☐ Fuel hose clogged, or connector not properly fitted onto union.
- ☐ Fuel injector clogged or faulty. For all of the injectors to be clogged, either a very bad batch of fuel with an unusual additive has been used, or some other foreign material has entered the tank. Many times after a machine has been stored for many months without running, the fuel turns to a varnish-like liquid.

Engine flooded

- ☐ Fuel injector stuck open. The Triumph diagnostic tool is required to check the injectors (see Chapter 4).
- ☐ Starting technique incorrect. Under normal circumstances (i.e., if the fuel injection system is sound) the machine should start with no throttle, whatever the temperature.

No spark or weak spark

- ☐ Ignition switch OFF.
- ☐ Engine kill switch turned to the OFF position.
- ☐ Battery voltage low. Check and recharge the battery as necessary (Chapter 8).
- ☐ Spark plugs dirty, defective or worn out. Locate reason for fouled plugs using spark plug condition chart on the inside rear cover and follow the plug maintenance procedures (Chapter 1).
- ☐ HT coil wiring faulty or connector loose. Check condition and connector fitting (Chapter 1).
- ☐ Electronic control module (ECM) defective. Check it, referring to Chapter 4 for details.
- ☐ Crankshaft position sensor defective. Check it, referring to Chapter 4 for details.
- ☐ Ignition HT coils defective. Check the coils, referring to Chapter 4.
- ☐ Ignition or kill switch shorted. This is usually caused by water, corrosion, damage or excessive wear. The switches can be disassembled and cleaned with electrical contact cleaner. If cleaning does not help, renew the switches (Chapter 8).
- ☐ Wiring shorted or broken in the ignition and starting circuit. Make sure that all connectors are clean, dry and tight. Look for chafed and broken wires (Chapters 4 and 8).

Compression low

- ☐ Spark plugs loose. Remove the plugs and inspect their threads. Reinstall and tighten to the specified torque (Chapter 1).
- ☐ Cylinder head not sufficiently tightened down. If the cylinder head is loose, then there's a chance that the gasket or head is damaged. Tighten the cylinder head bolts to the correct torque in the proper sequence (Chapter 2).
- ☐ Incorrect valve clearance. If the valve is not closing completely then engine pressure will leak past the valve. Check and adjust the valve clearances (Chapter 1).
- ☐ Cylinder and/or piston worn. Excessive wear will cause compression pressure to leak past the rings. This is usually accompanied by worn rings as well. A top-end overhaul is necessary (Chapter 2).
- ☐ Piston rings worn, weak, broken, or sticking. Broken or sticking piston rings usually indicate a lubrication or fuelling problem that causes excess carbon deposits to form on the pistons and rings. Top-end overhaul is necessary (Chapter 2).
- ☐ Piston ring-to-groove clearance excessive. This is caused by excessive wear of the piston ring lands. Piston renewal is necessary (Chapter 2).
- ☐ Cylinder head gasket damaged. If the head is allowed to become loose, or if excessive carbon build-up on the piston crown and combustion chamber causes extremely high compression, the head gasket may leak. Retorquing the head is not always sufficient to restore the seal, so gasket renewal is necessary (Chapter 2).
- ☐ Cylinder head warped. This is caused by overheating or improperly tightened head bolts. Machine shop resurfacing or head renewal is necessary (Chapter 2).
- ☐ Valve spring broken or weak. Caused by component failure or wear; the springs must be renewed (Chapter 2).
- ☐ Valve not seating properly. This is caused by a bent valve (from over-revving or improper valve adjustment), burned valve or seat (improper combustion) or an accumulation of carbon deposits on the seat (from combustion or lubrication problems). The valves must be cleaned and/or renewed and the seats serviced if possible (Chapter 2).

Stalls after starting

- ☐ Ignition malfunction. See Chapter 4.
- ☐ Fuel injection or engine management system malfunction. See Chapter 4.
- ☐ Fuel contaminated. The fuel can be contaminated with either dirt or water, or can change chemically if the machine is allowed to sit for several months or more. Drain the tank, fuel hoses and fuel rail (Chapter 4).
- ☐ Intake air leak. Check for loose throttle body-to-intake manifold connections or a leaking gasket (Chapter 4).
- ☐ Idle air control unit faulty. The unit can only be checked using the Triumph diagnostic tool (see Chapter 4).

Fault Finding   REF•39

1 Engine doesn't start or is difficult to start (continued)

Rough idle

- ☐ Ignition malfunction. See Chapter 4.
- ☐ Idle air control unit faulty. The unit can only be checked using the Triumph diagnostic tool (see Chapter 4).
- ☐ Throttle bodies not synchronised. Adjust them with vacuum gauge or manometer set as described in Chapter 1.
- ☐ Fuel injection or engine management system malfunction. See Chapter 4.
- ☐ Fuel contaminated. The fuel can be contaminated with either dirt or water, or can change chemically if the machine is allowed to sit for several months or more. Drain the tank, fuel hoses and fuel rail (Chapter 4).
- ☐ Intake air leak. Check for loose throttle body-to-intake manifold connections or a leaking gasket (Chapter 4).
- ☐ Air filter clogged. Renew the air filter element (Chapter 1).

2 Poor running at low speeds

Spark weak

- ☐ Battery voltage low. Check and recharge battery (Chapter 8).
- ☐ Spark plugs fouled, defective or worn out. Refer to Chapter 1 for spark plug maintenance.
- ☐ HT coil faulty or loose wiring. Check condition. Renew if cracks or deterioration are evident (Chapter 4).
- ☐ Electronic control module (ECM) defective. Check it, referring to Chapter 4 for details.

Fuel/air mixture incorrect

- ☐ Fuel injector clogged or fuel injection system malfunction (see Chapter 4).
- ☐ Air filter clogged, poorly sealed or missing (Chapter 1).
- ☐ Air filter housing poorly sealed. Look for cracks, holes or loose clamps and renew or repair defective parts.
- ☐ Fuel tank breather hose obstructed.
- ☐ Intake air leak. Check for loose throttle body-to-intake manifold connections or a leaking gasket (Chapter 4).
- ☐ Idle air control unit faulty. The unit can only be checked using the Triumph diagnostic tool (see Chapter 4).
- ☐ Fuel injection or engine management system malfunction. See Chapter 4.

Compression low

- ☐ Spark plugs loose. Remove the plugs and inspect their threads. Reinstall and tighten to the specified torque (Chapter 1).
- ☐ Cylinder head not sufficiently tightened down. If the cylinder head is loose, then there's a chance that the gasket or head is damaged. Tighten the cylinder head bolts to the correct torque in the proper sequence (Chapter 2).
- ☐ Incorrect valve clearance. If the valve is not closing completely then engine pressure will leak past the valve. Check and adjust the valve clearances (Chapter 1).
- ☐ Cylinder and/or piston worn. Excessive wear will cause compression pressure to leak past the rings. This is usually accompanied by worn rings as well. A top-end overhaul is necessary (Chapter 2).
- ☐ Piston rings worn, weak, broken, or sticking. Broken or sticking piston rings usually indicate a lubrication or fuelling problem that causes excess carbon deposits to form on the pistons and rings. Top-end overhaul is necessary (Chapter 2).
- ☐ Piston ring-to-groove clearance excessive. This is caused by excessive wear of the piston ring lands. Piston renewal is necessary (Chapter 2).
- ☐ Cylinder head gasket damaged. If the head is allowed to become loose, or if excessive carbon build-up on the piston crown and combustion chamber causes extremely high compression, the head gasket may leak. Retorquing the head is not always sufficient to restore the seal, so gasket renewal is necessary (Chapter 2).
- ☐ Cylinder head warped. This is caused by overheating or improperly tightened head bolts. Machine shop resurfacing or head renewal is necessary (Chapter 2).
- ☐ Valve spring broken or weak. Caused by component failure or wear; the springs must be renewed (Chapter 2).
- ☐ Valve not seating properly. This is caused by a bent valve (from over-revving or improper valve adjustment), burned valve or seat (improper combustion) or an accumulation of carbon deposits on the seat (from combustion or lubrication problems). The valves must be cleaned and/or renewed and the seats serviced if possible (Chapter 2).

Poor acceleration

- ☐ Intake air leak. Check for loose throttle body-to-intake manifold connections or a leaking gasket (Chapter 4).
- ☐ Timing not advancing. The ECM or a sensor in the engine management system may be defective. If so, they must be renewed as they can't be repaired. The systems can only be checked using the Triumph diagnostic tool – see Chapter 4 for details.
- ☐ Throttle bodies not synchronised. Adjust them with a vacuum gauge set or manometer (Chapter 1).
- ☐ Engine oil viscosity too high. Using a heavier oil than that recommended in Pre-ride checks can damage the oil pump or lubrication system and cause drag on the engine.
- ☐ Brakes dragging. Usually caused by debris which has entered the brake piston seals, or from a warped disc or bent axle. Repair as necessary (Chapter 6).

3 Poor running or no power at high speed

Firing incorrect

- [ ] Air filter restricted. Clean or renew the filter (Chapter 1).
- [ ] Spark plugs fouled, defective or worn out. See Chapter 1 for spark plug maintenance.
- [ ] HT coil or wiring defective. See Chapters 1 and 4 for details of the ignition system.
- [ ] Incorrect spark plugs. Wrong type, heat range or cap configuration. Check and install correct plugs listed in Chapter 1.
- [ ] Electronic control module (ECM) defective. Check it, referring to Chapter 4 for details.

Fuel/air mixture incorrect

- [ ] Fuel injector clogged or fuel injection system malfunction (see Chapter 4).
- [ ] Air filter clogged, poorly sealed or missing (Chapter 1).
- [ ] Air filter housing poorly sealed. Look for cracks, holes or loose clamps and renew or repair defective parts.
- [ ] Fuel tank breather hose obstructed.
- [ ] Intake air leak. Check for loose throttle body-to-intake manifold connections or a leaking gasket (Chapter 4).
- [ ] Idle air control unit faulty. The unit can only be checked using the Triumph diagnostic tool (see Chapter 4).
- [ ] Fuel injection or engine management system malfunction. See Chapter 4.

Compression low

- [ ] Spark plugs loose. Remove the plugs and inspect their threads. Reinstall and tighten to the specified torque (Chapter 1).
- [ ] Cylinder head not sufficiently tightened down. If the cylinder head is loose, then there's a chance that the gasket or head is damaged. Tighten the cylinder head bolts to the correct torque in the proper sequence (Chapter 2).
- [ ] Incorrect valve clearance. If the valve is not closing completely then engine pressure will leak past the valve. Check and adjust the valve clearances (Chapter 1).
- [ ] Cylinder and/or piston worn. Excessive wear will cause compression pressure to leak past the rings. This is usually accompanied by worn rings as well. A top-end overhaul is necessary (Chapter 2).
- [ ] Piston rings worn, weak, broken, or sticking. Broken or sticking piston rings usually indicate a lubrication or fuelling problem that causes excess carbon deposits to form on the pistons and rings. Top-end overhaul is necessary (Chapter 2).
- [ ] Piston ring-to-groove clearance excessive. This is caused by excessive wear of the piston ring lands. Piston renewal is necessary (Chapter 2).
- [ ] Cylinder head gasket damaged. If the head is allowed to become loose, or if excessive carbon build-up on the piston crown and combustion chamber causes extremely high compression, the head gasket may leak. Retorquing the head is not always sufficient to restore the seal, so gasket renewal is necessary (Chapter 2).
- [ ] Cylinder head warped. This is caused by overheating or improperly tightened head bolts. Machine shop resurfacing or head renewal is necessary (Chapter 2).
- [ ] Valve spring broken or weak. Caused by component failure or wear; the springs must be renewed (Chapter 2).
- [ ] Valve not seating properly. This is caused by a bent valve (from over-revving or improper valve adjustment), burned valve or seat (improper combustion) or an accumulation of carbon deposits on the seat (from combustion or lubrication problems). The valves must be cleaned and/or renewed and the seats serviced if possible (Chapter 2).

Knocking or pinking

- [ ] Carbon build-up in combustion chamber. Use of a fuel additive that will dissolve the adhesive bonding the carbon particles to the crown and chamber is the easiest way to remove the build-up. Otherwise, the cylinder head will have to be removed and decarbonised (Chapter 2).
- [ ] Incorrect or poor quality fuel. Old or improper grades of fuel can cause detonation. This causes the piston to rattle, thus the knocking or pinking sound. Drain old fuel and always use the recommended fuel grade.
- [ ] Spark plug heat range incorrect. Uncontrolled detonation indicates the plug heat range is too hot. The plug in effect becomes a glow plug, raising cylinder temperatures. Install the proper heat range plug (Chapter 1).
- [ ] Improper air/fuel mixture. This will cause the cylinders to run hot, which leads to detonation. Clogged injectors or an air leak can cause this imbalance, as could a fault in the engine management system which controls the fuel injection. See Chapter 4.

Miscellaneous causes

- [ ] Throttles don't open fully. Check the cable and the twistgrip, and then the throttle bodies themselves (Chapters 1 and 4).
- [ ] Clutch slipping. May be caused by loose or worn clutch components. Refer to Chapter 2 for clutch overhaul procedures.
- [ ] Timing not advancing. The ECM or a sensor in the engine management system may be defective. If so, they must be renewed with new ones, as they can't be repaired. The system can only be checked using the Triumph diagnostic tool – see Chapter 4 for details.
- [ ] Engine oil viscosity too high. Using a heavier oil than the one recommended in Chapter 1 can damage the oil pump or lubrication system and cause drag on the engine.
- [ ] Brakes dragging. Usually caused by debris which has entered the brake piston seals, or from a warped disc or bent axle. Repair as necessary.

Fault Finding REF•41

4 Overheating

Engine overheats

☐ Coolant level low. Check and add coolant (Pre-ride checks).
☐ Leak in cooling system. Check cooling system hoses and radiator for leaks and other damage. Repair or renew parts as necessary (Chapter 3).
☐ Thermostat sticking open or closed. Check and renew as described in Chapter 3.
☐ Faulty radiator cap. Remove the cap and have it pressure tested.
☐ Coolant passages clogged. Drain and flush the system, then refill with fresh coolant (Chapter 1).
☐ Water pump defective. Remove the pump and check the components (Chapter 3).
☐ Clogged radiator fins. Clean them by blowing compressed air through the fins from the rear of the radiator.
☐ Cooling fan not cutting in. Cooling fan or fan relay fault (Chapter 3). Coolant temperature sensor faulty or ECM faulty (Chapter 4).

Firing incorrect

☐ Air filter restricted. Clean or renew filter (Chapter 1).
☐ Spark plugs fouled, defective or worn out. See Chapter 1 for spark plug maintenance.
☐ Spark plug cap/coil or wiring defective. See Chapters 1 and 4 for details of the ignition system.
☐ Incorrect spark plugs. Wrong type, heat range or cap configuration. Check and install correct plugs listed in Chapter 1.
☐ Electronic control module (ECM) defective. Check it, referring to Chapter 4 for details.

Fuel/air mixture incorrect

☐ Fuel injector clogged or fuel injection system malfunction (see Chapter 4).
☐ Air filter clogged, poorly sealed or missing (Chapter 1).
☐ Air filter housing poorly sealed. Look for cracks, holes or loose clamps and renew or repair defective parts.
☐ Fuel tank breather hose obstructed.
☐ Intake air leak. Check for loose throttle body-to-intake manifold connections or a leaking gasket (Chapter 4).
☐ Idle air control unit faulty. The unit can only be checked using the Triumph diagnostic tool (see Chapter 4).
☐ Fuel injection or engine management system malfunction. See Chapter 4.

Compression too high

☐ Carbon build-up in combustion chamber. Use of a fuel additive that will dissolve the adhesive bonding the carbon particles to the piston crown and chamber is the easiest way to remove the build-up. Otherwise, the cylinder head will have to be removed and decarbonised (Chapter 2).
☐ Improperly machined head surface or installation of incorrect gasket during engine assembly.

Engine load excessive

☐ Clutch slipping. Can be caused by damaged, loose or worn clutch components. Refer to Chapter 2 for overhaul procedures.
☐ Engine oil level too high. The addition of too much oil will cause pressurisation of the crankcase and inefficient engine operation. Check Specifications and drain to proper level (Chapter 1).
☐ Engine oil viscosity too high. Using a heavier oil than the one recommended in *Pre-ride checks* can damage the oil pump or lubrication system as well as cause drag on the engine.
☐ Brakes dragging. Usually caused by debris which has entered the brake piston seals, or from a warped disc or bent axle. Repair as necessary.

Lubrication inadequate

☐ Engine oil level too low. Friction caused by intermittent lack of lubrication or from oil that is overworked can cause overheating. The oil provides a definite cooling function in the engine. Check the oil level (Pre-ride checks).
☐ Poor quality engine oil or incorrect viscosity or type. Oil is rated not only according to viscosity but also according to type. Some oils are not rated high enough for use in this engine. Change to the correct oil (Pre-ride checks).

Miscellaneous causes

☐ Modification to exhaust system. Most aftermarket exhaust systems cause the engine to run leaner, which make them run hotter. Before installing an accessory exhaust system, always check with the exhaust manufacturer or Triumph themselves, as you may well need an adjustment to the engine management system, which can only be done using a diagnostic tool.

5 Clutch problems

Clutch slipping
- ☐ Insufficient clutch cable freeplay. Check and adjust (Chapter 1).
- ☐ Friction plates worn or warped. Overhaul the clutch assembly (Chapter 2).
- ☐ Plain plates warped (Chapter 2).
- ☐ Clutch springs broken, sagged or weak. Replace the springs with new ones (Chapter 2).
- ☐ Clutch release mechanism defective. Remove the clutch cover and check the mechanism (Chapter 2).
- ☐ Clutch centre or housing unevenly worn. This causes improper engagement of the plates. Renew the damaged or worn parts (Chapter 2).

Clutch not disengaging completely
- ☐ Excessive clutch cable freeplay. Check and adjust (Chapter 1).
- ☐ Clutch plates warped or damaged. This will cause clutch drag, which in turn will cause the machine to creep. Overhaul the clutch assembly (Chapter 2).
- ☐ Clutch spring tension uneven. Usually caused by a sagged or broken spring. Check and renew the springs as a set (Chapter 2).
- ☐ Engine oil deteriorated. Old, thin, worn out oil will not provide proper lubrication for the plates, causing the clutch to drag. Change the oil and filter (Chapter 1).
- ☐ Engine oil viscosity too high. Using a heavier oil than recommended can cause the plates to stick together, putting a drag on the engine. Change to the correct weight oil (Pre-ride checks).
- ☐ Clutch housing sleeve seized on input shaft. Lack of lubrication, severe wear or damage can cause the sleeve to seize on the shaft. Overhaul of the clutch, and perhaps transmission, may be necessary to repair the damage (Chapter 2).
- ☐ Clutch release mechanism defective. Remove the clutch cover and check the mechanism (Chapter 2).
- ☐ Loose clutch centre nut. Causes housing and centre misalignment putting a drag on the engine. Engagement adjustment continually varies. Overhaul the clutch assembly (Chapter 2).

6 Gearchange problems

Doesn't go into gear or lever doesn't return
- ☐ Clutch not disengaging. See above.
- ☐ Selector fork(s) bent or seized. Often caused by dropping the machine or from lack of lubrication. Overhaul the transmission (Chapter 2).
- ☐ Gear pinion(s) stuck on shaft. Most often caused by a lack of lubrication or excessive wear in transmission bearings and bushings. Overhaul the transmission (Chapter 2).
- ☐ Selector drum binding. Caused by lubrication failure or excessive wear. Renew the drum and bearing (Chapter 2).
- ☐ Gearchange lever return spring weak or broken (Chapter 2).
- ☐ Gearchange lever broken. Splines stripped out of lever or shaft, caused by allowing the lever to get loose or from dropping the machine. Renew necessary parts (Chapter 2).
- ☐ Gearchange mechanism stopper arm broken or worn. Full engagement and rotary movement of selector drum results. Renew the arm (Chapter 2).
- ☐ Stopper arm spring broken. Allows arm to float, causing sporadic gearchange operation. Renew spring (Chapter 2).
- ☐ Gearchange mechanism selector arm pawl broken or worn. The selector arm pawls aren't engaging correctly with the pins on the selector drum cam plate. Check the entire mechanism (Chapter 2).

Jumps out of gear
- ☐ Selector fork(s) worn. Overhaul the transmission (Chapter 2).
- ☐ Gear groove(s) worn. Overhaul the transmission (Chapter 2).
- ☐ Gear dogs or dog slots worn or damaged. The gears should be inspected and renewed. No attempt should be made to service the worn parts.

Overselects
- ☐ Stopper arm spring weak or broken (Chapter 2).
- ☐ Gearchange shaft return spring post broken or distorted (Chapter 2).
- ☐ Gearchange mechanism stopper arm broken or worn. Full engagement and rotary movement of selector drum results. Renew the arm (Chapter 2).

Fault Finding REF•43

7 Abnormal engine noise

Knocking or pinking

- [ ] Carbon build-up in combustion chamber. Use of a fuel additive that will dissolve the adhesive bonding the carbon particles to the piston crown and chamber is the easiest way to remove the build-up. Otherwise, the cylinder head will have to be removed and decarbonised (Chapter 2).
- [ ] Incorrect or poor quality fuel. Old or improper fuel can cause detonation. This causes the pistons to rattle, thus the knocking or pinking sound. Drain the old fuel and always use the recommended grade fuel (Chapter 4).
- [ ] Spark plug heat range incorrect. Uncontrolled detonation indicates that the plug heat range is too hot. The plug in effect becomes a glow plug, raising cylinder temperatures. Install the proper heat range plug (Chapter 1).
- [ ] Improper air/fuel mixture. This will cause the cylinders to run hot and lead to detonation. Clogged injectors or an air leak can cause this imbalance. See Chapter 4.

Piston slap or rattling

- [ ] Cylinder-to-piston clearance excessive. Caused by improper assembly. Inspect and overhaul top-end parts (Chapter 2).
- [ ] Connecting rod bent. Caused by over-revving, trying to start a badly flooded engine or from ingesting a foreign object into the combustion chamber. Renew the damaged parts (Chapter 2).
- [ ] Piston pin or piston pin bore worn or seized from wear or lack of lubrication. Renew damaged parts (Chapter 2).
- [ ] Piston ring(s) worn, broken or sticking. Overhaul the top-end (Chapter 2).
- [ ] Piston seizure damage. Usually from lack of lubrication or overheating. Renew the pistons and cylinder liners, as necessary (Chapter 2).
- [ ] Connecting rod upper or lower end clearance excessive. Caused by excessive wear or lack of lubrication. Renew worn parts.

Valve noise

- [ ] Incorrect valve clearances. Adjust the clearances by referring to Chapter 1.
- [ ] Valve spring broken or weak. Check and renew weak valve springs (Chapter 2).
- [ ] Camshaft or cylinder head worn or damaged. Lack of lubrication at high rpm is usually the cause of damage. Insufficient oil or failure to change the oil at the recommended intervals are the chief causes. Since there are no replaceable bearings in the head, the head itself will have to be renewed if there is excessive wear or damage (Chapter 2).

Other noise

- [ ] Cylinder head gasket leaking.
- [ ] Exhaust pipe leaking at cylinder head connection. Caused by improper fit of pipe(s), loose nuts or broken gasket(s). All exhaust fasteners should be tightened evenly and carefully. Failure to do this will lead to a leak. If there is still a leak after tightening, remove the downpipe assembly and install new gaskets (Chapter 4).
- [ ] Crankshaft runout excessive. Caused by a bent crankshaft (from over-revving) or damage from a top-end component failure. Can also be attributed to dropping the machine on either of the crankshaft ends.
- [ ] Engine mounting bolts loose. Tighten all engine mount bolts (Chapter 2).
- [ ] Crankshaft bearings worn (Chapter 2).
- [ ] Camchain, guide blades or tensioner worn. Renew according to the procedure in Chapter 2.

REF•44 Fault Finding

8 Abnormal driveline noise

Clutch noise
- [ ] Clutch housing/friction plate clearance excessive (Chapter 2).
- [ ] Loose or damaged clutch pressure plate and/or bolts (Chapter 2).

Transmission noise
- [ ] Bearings worn. Also includes the possibility that the shafts are worn. Overhaul the transmission (Chapter 2).
- [ ] Gears worn or chipped (Chapter 2).
- [ ] Metal chips jammed in gear teeth. Probably pieces from a broken clutch, gear or selector mechanism that were picked up by the gears. This will cause early bearing failure (Chapter 2).
- [ ] Engine oil level too low. Causes a howl from transmission. Also affects engine power and clutch operation (Pre-ride checks).

Final drive noise
- [ ] Chain not adjusted properly (Chapter 1).
- [ ] Front or rear sprocket loose. Tighten fasteners (Chapter 5).
- [ ] Sprockets worn. Renew sprockets and chain (Chapter 5).
- [ ] Sprocket coupling or hub assembly bearings worn, or loose axle nut, or damaged cush drive. Check and tighten or renew, according to model (Chapter 5).

9 Abnormal frame and suspension noise

Front end noise
- [ ] Low fork oil level or improper viscosity. This can sound like spurting and is usually accompanied by irregular fork action (Chapter 5).
- [ ] Spring weak or broken. Makes a clicking or scraping sound. Fork oil, when drained, will have a lot of metal particles in it (Chapter 5).
- [ ] Steering head bearings loose or damaged. Clicks when braking. Check and adjust or renew as necessary (Chapters 1 and 5).
- [ ] Fork yokes loose. Make sure all clamp bolts are tightened to the specified torque (Chapter 5).
- [ ] Fork tube bent. Good possibility if machine has been dropped. Replace tube with a new one (Chapter 5).
- [ ] Front axle bolt or axle clamp bolts loose. Tighten them to the specified torque (Chapter 6).
- [ ] Loose or worn wheel bearings. Check and renew if necessary (Chapter 6).

Shock absorber noise
- [ ] Fluid level incorrect. Indicates a leak caused by defective seal. Shock will be covered with oil. Renew shock or seek advice on repair from a Triumph dealer or suspension specialist (Chapter 5).
- [ ] Defective shock absorber with internal damage. This is in the body of the shock and can't be remedied. The shock must be replaced with a new one (Chapter 5).
- [ ] Bent or damaged shock body. Replace the shock with a new one (Chapter 5).
- [ ] Loose or worn suspension linkage components. Check and renew if necessary (Chapter 5).

Brake noise
- [ ] Squeal caused by pad shim not installed or positioned correctly (where fitted) (Chapter 6).
- [ ] Squeal caused by dust on brake pads. Usually found in combination with glazed pads. Clean using brake cleaning solvent (Chapter 6).
- [ ] Contamination of brake pads. Oil, brake fluid or dirt causing brake to chatter or squeal. Clean or renew pads (Chapter 6).
- [ ] Pads glazed. Caused by excessive heat from prolonged use or from contamination. Do not use sandpaper, emery cloth, carborundum cloth or any other abrasive to roughen the pad surfaces as abrasives will stay in the pad material and damage the disc. A very fine flat file can be used, but pad renewal is suggested as a cure (Chapter 6).
- [ ] Disc warped. Can cause a chattering, clicking or intermittent squeal. Usually accompanied by a pulsating lever and uneven braking. Renew the disc (Chapter 6).
- [ ] Loose or worn wheel bearings. Check and renew if necessary (Chapter 6).

10 Oil pressure warning light comes on

Engine lubrication system
- [ ] Engine oil pump defective, blocked oil strainer gauze or failed relief valve. Carry out an oil pressure check (Chapter 2).
- [ ] Engine oil level low. Inspect for leak or other problem causing low oil level and add recommended oil (Pre-ride checks).
- [ ] Engine oil viscosity too low. Very old, thin oil or an improper weight of oil used in the engine. Change to correct oil (Pre-ride checks).
- [ ] Camshaft or journals worn. Excessive wear causing drop in oil pressure. Renew cam and/or cylinder head (Chapter 2). Abnormal wear could be caused by oil starvation at high rpm from low oil level or improper weight or type of oil.
- [ ] Crankshaft and/or bearings worn. Same problems as above. Check and renew crankshaft and/or bearings (Chapter 2).

Electrical system
- [ ] Oil pressure switch defective. Check the switch according to the procedure in Chapter 8. Renew it if it is defective.
- [ ] Oil pressure warning light circuit defective. Check for pinched, shorted, disconnected or damaged wiring (Chapter 8).

Fault Finding REF•45

11 Excessive exhaust smoke

White smoke
- ☐ Piston oil ring worn. The ring may be broken or damaged, causing oil from the crankcase to be pulled past the piston into the combustion chamber. Replace the rings with new ones (Chapter 2).
- ☐ Cylinders worn, cracked, or scored. Caused by overheating or oil starvation. Install new liners (Chapter 2).
- ☐ Valve stem seal damaged or worn. Remove valves and replace seals with new ones (Chapter 2).
- ☐ Valve guide worn. Perform a complete valve job (Chapter 2).
- ☐ Engine oil level too high, which causes the oil to be forced past the rings. Drain oil to the proper level (Chapter 1 and Pre-ride checks).
- ☐ Head gasket broken between oil return and cylinder. Causes oil to be pulled into the combustion chamber. Renew the head gasket and check the head for warpage (Chapter 2).
- ☐ Abnormal crankcase pressurisation, which forces oil past the rings. Clogged breather is usually the cause.

Black smoke
- ☐ Air filter clogged. Clean or renew the element (Chapter 1).
- ☐ Fuel injection system or idle air control unit malfunction (Chapter 4). These systems can only be checked using the Triumph diagnostic tool. Refer to Chapter 4 for further information.
- ☐ Fuel pressure too high. Check the fuel pressure regulator (Chapter 4).

Brown smoke
- ☐ Fuel pump faulty or pressure regulator stuck open (Chapter 4).
- ☐ Throttle body-to-intake manifold bolts loose or gasket broken (Chapter 4).
- ☐ Air filter poorly sealed or not installed (Chapter 1).
- ☐ Fuel injection system malfunction (Chapter 4).

12 Poor handling or stability

Handlebar hard to turn
- ☐ Steering head bearing adjuster nut too tight. Check adjustment as described in Chapter 1.
- ☐ Bearings damaged. Roughness can be felt as the bars are turned from side-to-side. Renew bearings and races (Chapter 5).
- ☐ Races dented or worn. Denting results from wear in only one position (e.g. straight-ahead), from a collision or hitting a pothole or from dropping the machine. Renew races and bearings (Chapter 5).
- ☐ Steering stem lubrication inadequate. Causes are grease getting hard from age or being washed out by high pressure car washes. Disassemble steering head and repack bearings (Chapter 5).
- ☐ Steering stem bent. Caused by a collision, hitting a pothole or by dropping the machine. Renew damaged part. Don't try to straighten the steering stem (Chapter 5).
- ☐ Front tyre air pressure too low (Pre-ride checks).

Handlebar shakes or vibrates excessively
- ☐ Tyres worn or out of balance (Chapter 6).
- ☐ Swingarm bearings worn. Renew worn bearings (Chapter 5).
- ☐ Wheel rim(s) warped or damaged. Inspect wheels for runout (Chapter 6).
- ☐ Wheel bearings worn. Worn front or rear wheel bearings can cause poor tracking. Worn front bearings will cause wobble (Chapter 6).
- ☐ Handlebar clamp bolts loose (Chapter 5).
- ☐ Fork clamp bolts loose in yoke(s). Tighten them to the specified torque (Chapter 5).
- ☐ Engine mounting bolts loose. Will cause excessive vibration with increased engine rpm (Chapter 2).

Handlebar pulls to one side
- ☐ Frame bent. Definitely suspect this if the machine has been dropped. May or may not be accompanied by cracking near the bend. Renew the frame (Chapter 5).
- ☐ Wheels out of alignment. Caused by improper location of axle spacers or from bent steering stem or frame (Chapter 5).
- ☐ Swingarm bent or twisted. Caused by age (metal fatigue) or impact damage. Renew the arm (Chapter 5).
- ☐ Steering stem bent. Caused by impact damage or by dropping the motorcycle. Renew the steering stem (Chapter 5).
- ☐ Fork tube bent. Disassemble the forks and renew the damaged parts (Chapter 5).
- ☐ Fork oil level uneven. Check and add or drain as necessary (Chapters 1 and 5).

Poor shock absorbing qualities
- ☐ Too hard:
  - a) Fork oil level too high (Chapter 5).
  - b) Fork oil viscosity too high. Use a lighter oil.
  - c) Fork tube bent. Causes a harsh, sticking feeling (Chapter 5).
  - d) Rear shock shaft or body bent or damaged (Chapter 5).
  - e) Fork internal damage (Chapter 5).
  - f) Rear shock internal damage.
  - g) Tyre pressure too high (Pre-ride checks).
- ☐ Too soft:
  - a) Fork or shock oil insufficient and/or leaking (Chapter 5).
  - b) Fork oil level too low (Chapter 5).
  - c) Fork oil viscosity too light (Chapter 5).
  - d) Fork springs weak or broken (Chapter 5).
  - e) Rear shock internal damage or leakage (Chapter 5).

REF•46 Fault Finding

13 Braking problems

Brakes are spongy, don't hold
- [ ] Air in brake line. Caused by inattention to master cylinder fluid level or by leakage. Locate problem and bleed brakes (Chapter 6).
- [ ] Pad or disc worn (Chapters 1 and 6).
- [ ] Brake fluid leak. Locate leak and renew faulty seals or hose as necessary (Chapter 6).
- [ ] Contaminated pads. Caused by contamination with oil, grease, brake fluid, etc. Renew the pads. Clean disc thoroughly with brake cleaner (Chapter 6).
- [ ] Brake fluid deteriorated. Fluid is old or contaminated. Drain system, replenish with new fluid and bleed the system (Chapter 6).
- [ ] Master cylinder internal parts worn or damaged causing fluid to bypass (Chapter 6).
- [ ] Master cylinder bore scratched by foreign material or broken spring. Repair or renew master cylinder (Chapter 6).
- [ ] Disc warped. Renew disc(s) (Chapter 6).

Brake lever or pedal pulsates
Note: *On models with ABS, under heavy braking and in the event of the ABS system cutting in, the lever or pedal will pulsate - do not confuse this with any of the problems listed below, which will be felt even with light braking.*

- [ ] Disc warped. Renew disc(s) (Chapter 6).
- [ ] Axle bent. Renew axle (Chapter 6).
- [ ] Brake caliper bolts loose (Chapter 6).
- [ ] Brake caliper slider pins damaged or sticking (rear caliper only), causing caliper to bind. Lubricate the sliders or renew them if they are corroded or bent (Chapter 6).
- [ ] Wheel warped or otherwise damaged (Chapter 6).
- [ ] Wheel bearings damaged or worn (Chapter 6).

Brakes drag
- [ ] Master cylinder piston seized. Caused by wear or damage to piston or cylinder bore (Chapter 6).
- [ ] Lever balky or stuck. Check pivot and lubricate (Chapter 6).
- [ ] Brake caliper binds (sliding type caliper only). Caused by corrosion or inadequate lubrication or damage on caliper slider pins (Chapter 6).
- [ ] Brake caliper piston seized in bore. Caused by wear or ingestion of dirt past deteriorated seal (Chapter 6).
- [ ] Brake pad damaged. Pad material separated from backing plate. Usually caused by faulty manufacturing process or from contact with chemicals. Renew pads (Chapter 6).
- [ ] Pads improperly installed (Chapter 6).

14 Electrical problems

Battery dead or weak
- [ ] Battery faulty. Caused by sulphated plates which are shorted through sedimentation. Also, broken battery terminal making only occasional contact (Chapter 8).
- [ ] Battery cables making poor contact (Chapter 8).
- [ ] Load excessive. Caused by addition of high wattage lights or other electrical accessories.
- [ ] Ignition switch defective. Switch either earths (grounds) internally or fails to shut off system. Renew the switch (Chapter 8).
- [ ] Regulator/rectifier defective (Chapter 8).
- [ ] Alternator defective (Chapter 8).
- [ ] Wiring faulty. Wiring earthed (grounded) or connections loose in ignition, charging or lighting circuits (Chapter 8).

Battery overcharged
- [ ] Regulator/rectifier defective. Overcharging is noticed when battery gets excessively warm (Chapter 8).
- [ ] Battery defective. Replace battery with a new one (Chapter 8).
- [ ] Battery amperage too low, wrong type or size. Install manufacturer's specified amp-hour battery to handle charging load (Chapter 8).

Technical Terms Explained

A

ABS (Anti-lock braking system) A system, usually electronically controlled, that senses incipient wheel lockup during braking and relieves hydraulic pressure at wheel which is about to skid.
Aftermarket Components suitable for the motorcycle, but not produced by the motorcycle manufacturer.
Allen key A hexagonal wrench which fits into a recessed hexagonal hole.
Alternating current (ac) Current produced by an alternator. Requires converting to direct current by a rectifier for charging purposes.
Alternator Converts mechanical energy from the engine into electrical energy to charge the battery and power the electrical system.
Ampere (amp) A unit of measurement for the flow of electrical current. Current = Volts ÷ Ohms.
Ampere-hour (Ah) Measure of battery capacity.
Angle-tightening A torque expressed in degrees. Often follows a conventional tightening torque for cylinder head or main bearing fasteners **(see illustration)**.

Angle-tightening con-rod bolts

Antifreeze A substance (usually ethylene glycol) mixed with water, and added to the cooling system, to prevent freezing of the coolant in winter. Antifreeze also contains chemicals to inhibit corrosion and the formation of rust and other deposits that would tend to clog the radiator and coolant passages and reduce cooling efficiency.
Anti-dive System attached to the fork lower leg (slider) to prevent fork dive when braking hard.
Anti-seize compound A coating that reduces the risk of seizing on fasteners that are subjected to high temperatures, such as exhaust clamp bolts and nuts.
API American Petroleum Institute. A quality standard for 4-stroke motor oils.
Asbestos A natural fibrous mineral with great heat resistance, commonly used in the composition of brake friction materials. Asbestos is a health hazard and the dust created by brake systems should never be inhaled or ingested.
ATF Automatic Transmission Fluid. Often used in front forks.
ATU Automatic Timing Unit. Mechanical device for advancing the ignition timing on early engines.
ATV All Terrain Vehicle. Often called a Quad.
Axial play Side-to-side movement.
Axle A shaft on which a wheel revolves. Also known as a spindle.

B

Backlash The amount of movement between meshed components when one component is held still. Usually applies to gear teeth.
Ball bearing A bearing consisting of a hardened inner and outer race with hardened steel balls between the two races.
Bearings Used between two working surfaces to prevent wear of the components and a build-up of heat. Four types of bearing are commonly used on motorcycles: plain shell bearings, ball bearings, tapered roller bearings and needle roller bearings.
Bevel gears Used to turn the drive through 90°. Typical applications are shaft final drive and camshaft drive **(see illustration)**.

Bevel gears are used to turn the drive through 90°

BHP Brake Horsepower. The British measurement for engine power output. Power output is now usually expressed in kilowatts (kW).
Bias-belted tyre Similar construction to radial tyre, but with outer belt running at an angle to the wheel rim.
Big-end bearing The bearing in the end of the connecting rod that's attached to the crankshaft.
Bleeding The process of removing air from an hydraulic system via a bleed nipple or bleed screw.
Bottom-end A description of an engine's crankcase components and all components contained there-in.
BTDC Before Top Dead Centre in terms of piston position. Ignition timing is often expressed in terms of degrees or millimetres BTDC.
Bush A cylindrical metal or rubber component used between two moving parts.
Burr Rough edge left on a component after machining or as a result of excessive wear.

C

Cam chain The chain which takes drive from the crankshaft to the camshaft(s).
Canister The main component in an evaporative emission control system (California market only); contains activated charcoal granules to trap vapours from the fuel system rather than allowing them to vent to the atmosphere.
Castellated Resembling the parapets along the top of a castle wall. For example, a castellated wheel axle or spindle nut.
Catalytic converter A device in the exhaust system of some machines which converts certain pollutants in the exhaust gases into less harmful substances.

Charging system Description of the components which charge the battery, ie the alternator, rectifer and regulator.
Circlip A ring-shaped clip used to prevent endwise movement of cylindrical parts and shafts. An internal circlip is installed in a groove in a housing; an external circlip fits into a groove on the outside of a cylindrical piece such as a shaft. Also known as a snap-ring.
Clearance The amount of space between two parts. For example, between a piston and a cylinder, between a bearing and a journal, etc.
Coil spring A spiral of elastic steel found in various sizes throughout a vehicle, for example as a springing medium in the suspension and in the valve train.
Compression Reduction in volume, and increase in pressure and temperature, of a gas, caused by squeezing it into a smaller space.
Compression damping Controls the speed the suspension compresses when hitting a bump.
Compression ratio The relationship between cylinder volume when the piston is at top dead centre and cylinder volume when the piston is at bottom dead centre.
Continuity The uninterrupted path in the flow of electricity. Little or no measurable resistance.
Continuity tester Self-powered bleeper or test light which indicates continuity.
Cp Candlepower. Bulb rating commonly found on US motorcycles.
Crossply tyre Tyre plies arranged in a criss-cross pattern. Usually four or six plies used, hence 4PR or 6PR in tyre size codes.
Cush drive Rubber damper segments fitted between the rear wheel and final drive sprocket to absorb transmission shocks **(see illustration)**.

Cush drive rubbers dampen out transmission shocks

D

Decarbonisation The process of removing carbon deposits - typically from the combustion chamber, valves and exhaust port/system.
Degree disc Calibrated disc for measuring piston position. Expressed in degrees.
Detonation Destructive and damaging explosion of fuel/air mixture in combustion chamber instead of controlled burning.
Dial gauge Clock-type gauge with adapters for measuring runout and piston position. Expressed in mm or inches.

Technical Terms Explained

Diaphragm The rubber membrane in a master cylinder or carburettor which seals the upper chamber.
Diaphragm spring A single sprung plate often used in clutches.
Direct current (dc) Current produced by a dc generator.
Diode An electrical valve which only allows current to flow in one direction. Commonly used in rectifiers and starter interlock systems.
Disc valve (or rotary valve) A induction system used on some two-stroke engines.
Double-overhead camshaft (DOHC) An engine that uses two overhead camshafts, one for the intake valves and one for the exhaust valves.
Drivebelt A toothed belt used to transmit drive to the rear wheel on some motorcycles. A drivebelt has also been used to drive the camshafts. Drivebelts are usually made of Kevlar.
Driveshaft Any shaft used to transmit motion. Commonly used when referring to the final driveshaft on shaft drive motorcycles.

E

Earth return The return path of an electrical circuit, utilising the motorcycle's frame.
ECU (Electronic Control Unit) A computer which controls (for instance) an ignition system, or an anti-lock braking system.
EGO Exhaust Gas Oxygen sensor. Sometimes called a Lambda sensor.
Electrolyte The fluid in a lead-acid battery.
EMS (Engine Management System) A computer controlled system which manages the fuel injection and the ignition systems in an integrated fashion.
Endfloat The amount of lengthways movement between two parts. As applied to a crankshaft, the distance that the crankshaft can move side-to-side in the crankcase.
Endless chain A chain having no joining link. Common use for cam chains and final drive chains.
EP (Extreme Pressure) Oil type used in locations where high loads are applied, such as between gear teeth.
Evaporative emission control system Describes a charcoal filled canister which stores fuel vapours from the tank rather than allowing them to vent to the atmosphere. Usually only fitted to California models and referred to as an EVAP system.
Expansion chamber Section of two-stroke engine exhaust system so designed to improve engine efficiency and boost power.

F

Feeler blade or gauge A thin strip or blade of hardened steel, ground to an exact thickness, used to check or measure clearances between parts.
Final drive Description of the drive from the transmission to the rear wheel. Usually by chain or shaft, but sometimes by belt.
Firing order The order in which the engine cylinders fire, or deliver their power strokes, beginning with the number one cylinder.
Flooding Term used to describe a high fuel level in the carburettor float chambers, leading to fuel overflow. Also refers to excess fuel in the combustion chamber due to incorrect starting technique.
Free length The no-load state of a component when measured. Clutch, valve and fork spring lengths are measured at rest, without any preload.
Freeplay The amount of travel before any action takes place. The looseness in a linkage, or an assembly of parts, between the initial application of force and actual movement. For example, the distance the rear brake pedal moves before the rear brake is actuated.
Fuel injection The fuel/air mixture is metered electronically and directed into the engine intake ports (indirect injection) or into the cylinders (direct injection). Sensors supply information on engine speed and conditions.
Fuel/air mixture The charge of fuel and air going into the engine. See Stoichiometric ratio.
Fuse An electrical device which protects a circuit against accidental overload. The typical fuse contains a soft piece of metal which is calibrated to melt at a predetermined current flow (expressed as amps) and break the circuit.

G

Gap The distance the spark must travel in jumping from the centre electrode to the side electrode in a spark plug. Also refers to the distance between the ignition rotor and the pickup coil in an electronic ignition system.
Gasket Any thin, soft material - usually cork, cardboard, asbestos or soft metal - installed between two metal surfaces to ensure a good seal. For instance, the cylinder head gasket seals the joint between the block and the cylinder head.
Gauge An instrument panel display used to monitor engine conditions. A gauge with a movable pointer on a dial or a fixed scale is an analogue gauge. A gauge with a numerical readout is called a digital gauge.
Gear ratios The drive ratio of a pair of gears in a gearbox, calculated on their number of teeth.
Glaze-busting see Honing
Grinding Process for renovating the valve face and valve seat contact area in the cylinder head.
Gudgeon pin The shaft which connects the connecting rod small-end with the piston. Often called a piston pin or wrist pin.

H

Helical gears Gear teeth are slightly curved and produce less gear noise that straight-cut gears. Often used for primary drives.
Helicoil A thread insert repair system. Commonly used as a repair for stripped spark plug threads **(see illustration)**.

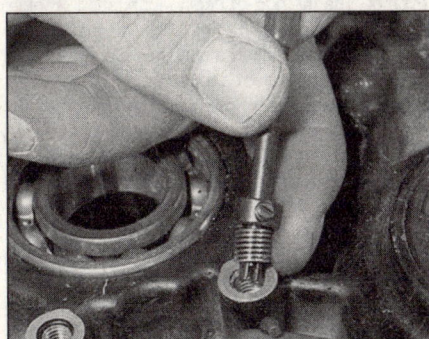
Installing a Helicoil thread insert

Honing A process used to break down the glaze on a cylinder bore (also called glaze-busting). Can also be carried out to roughen a rebored cylinder to aid ring bedding-in.
HT (High Tension) Description of the electrical circuit from the secondary winding of the ignition coil to the spark plug.
Hydraulic A liquid filled system used to transmit pressure from one component to another. Common uses on motorcycles are brakes and clutches.
Hydrometer An instrument for measuring the specific gravity of a lead-acid battery.
Hygroscopic Water absorbing. In motorcycle applications, braking efficiency will be reduced if DOT 3 or 4 hydraulic fluid absorbs water from the air - care must be taken to keep new brake fluid in tightly sealed containers.

I

lbf ft Pounds-force feet. An imperial unit of torque. Sometimes written as ft-lbs.
lbf in Pound-force inch. An imperial unit of torque, applied to components where a very low torque is required. Sometimes written as in-lbs.
IC Abbreviation for Integrated Circuit.
Ignition advance Means of increasing the timing of the spark at higher engine speeds. Done by mechanical means (ATU) on early engines or electronically by the ignition control unit on later engines.
Ignition timing The moment at which the spark plug fires, expressed in the number of crankshaft degrees before the piston reaches the top of its stroke, or in the number of millimetres before the piston reaches the top of its stroke.
Infinity (∞) Description of an open-circuit electrical state, where no continuity exists.
Inverted forks (upside down forks) The sliders or lower legs are held in the yokes and the fork tubes or stanchions are connected to the wheel axle (spindle). Less unsprung weight and stiffer construction than conventional forks.

J

JASO Quality standard for 2-stroke oils.
Joule The unit of electrical energy.
Journal The bearing surface of a shaft.

K

Kickstart Mechanical means of turning the engine over for starting purposes. Only usually fitted to mopeds, small capacity motorcycles and off-road motorcycles.
Kill switch Handebar-mounted switch for emergency ignition cut-out. Cuts the ignition circuit on all models, and additionally prevent starter motor operation on others.
km Symbol for kilometre.
kmh Abbreviation for kilometres per hour.

L

Lambda (λ) sensor A sensor fitted in the exhaust system to measure the exhaust gas oxygen content (excess air factor).

REF•50 Technical Terms Explained

Lapping see Grinding.
LCD Abbreviation for Liquid Crystal Display.
LED Abbreviation for Light Emitting Diode.
Liner A steel cylinder liner inserted in a aluminium alloy cylinder block.
Locknut A nut used to lock an adjustment nut, or other threaded component, in place.
Lockstops The lugs on the lower triple clamp (yoke) which abut those on the frame, preventing handlebar-to-fuel tank contact.
Lockwasher A form of washer designed to prevent an attaching nut from working loose.
LT Low Tension Description of the electrical circuit from the power supply to the primary winding of the ignition coil.

M

Main bearings The bearings between the crankshaft and crankcase.
Maintenance-free (MF) battery A sealed battery which cannot be topped up.
Manometer Mercury-filled calibrated tubes used to measure intake tract vacuum. Used to synchronise carburettors on multi-cylinder engines.
Micrometer A precision measuring instrument that measures component outside diameters **(see illustration)**.

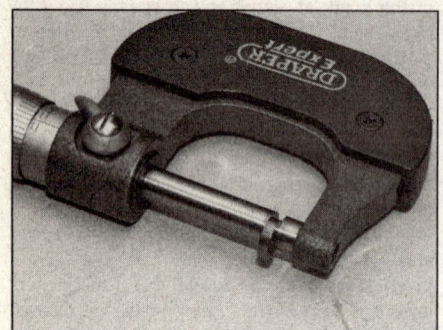

Tappet shims are measured with a micrometer

MON (Motor Octane Number) A measure of a fuel's resistance to knock.
Monograde oil An oil with a single viscosity, eg SAE80W.
Monoshock A single suspension unit linking the swingarm or suspension linkage to the frame.
mph Abbreviation for miles per hour.
Multigrade oil Having a wide viscosity range (eg 10W40). The W stands for Winter, thus the viscosity ranges from SAE10 when cold to SAE40 when hot.
Multimeter An electrical test instrument with the capability to measure voltage, current and resistance. Some meters also incorporate a continuity tester and buzzer.

N

Needle roller bearing Inner race of caged needle rollers and hardened outer race. Examples of uncaged needle rollers can be found on some engines. Commonly used in rear suspension applications and in two-stroke engines.
Nm Newton metres.
NOx Oxides of Nitrogen. A common toxic pollutant emitted by petrol engines at higher temperatures.

O

Octane The measure of a fuel's resistance to knock.
OE (Original Equipment) Relates to components fitted to a motorcycle as standard or replacement parts supplied by the motorcycle manufacturer.
Ohm The unit of electrical resistance. Ohms = Volts ÷ Current.
Ohmmeter An instrument for measuring electrical resistance.
Oil cooler System for diverting engine oil outside of the engine to a radiator for cooling purposes.
Oil injection A system of two-stroke engine lubrication where oil is pump-fed to the engine in accordance with throttle position.
Open-circuit An electrical condition where there is a break in the flow of electricity - no continuity (high resistance).
O-ring A type of sealing ring made of a special rubber-like material; in use, the O-ring is compressed into a groove to provide the sealing action.
Oversize (OS) Term used for piston and ring size options fitted to a rebored cylinder.
Overhead cam (sohc) engine An engine with single camshaft located on top of the cylinder head.
Overhead valve (ohv) engine An engine with the valves located in the cylinder head, but with the camshaft located in the engine block or crankcase.
Oxygen sensor A device installed in the exhaust system which senses the oxygen content in the exhaust and converts this information into an electric current. Also called a Lambda sensor.

P

Plastigauge A thin strip of plastic thread, available in different sizes, used for measuring clearances. For example, a strip of Plastigauge is laid across a bearing journal. The parts are assembled and dismantled; the width of the crushed strip indicates the clearance between journal and bearing.
Polarity Either negative or positive earth (ground), determined by which battery lead is connected to the frame (earth return). Modern motorcycles are usually negative earth.
Pre-ignition A situation where the fuel/air mixture ignites before the spark plug fires. Often due to a hot spot in the combustion chamber caused by carbon build-up. Engine has a tendency to 'run-on'.
Pre-load (suspension) The amount a spring is compressed when in the unloaded state. Preload can be applied by gas, spacer or mechanical adjuster.
Premix The method of engine lubrication on older two-stroke engines. Engine oil is mixed with the petrol in the fuel tank in a specific ratio. The fuel/oil mix is sometimes referred to as "petroil".
Primary drive Description of the drive from the crankshaft to the clutch. Usually by gear or chain.
PS Pfedestärke - a German interpretation of BHP.
PSI Pounds-force per square inch. Imperial measurement of tyre pressure and cylinder pressure measurement.
PTFE Polytetrafluroethylene. A low friction substance.
Pulse secondary air injection system A process of promoting the burning of excess fuel present in the exhaust gases by routing fresh air into the exhaust ports.

Q

Quartz halogen bulb Tungsten filament surrounded by a halogen gas. Typically used for the headlight **(see illustration)**.

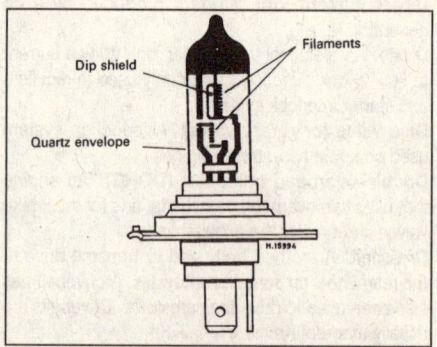

Quartz halogen headlight bulb construction

R

Rack-and-pinion A pinion gear on the end of a shaft that mates with a rack (think of a geared wheel opened up and laid flat). Sometimes used in clutch operating systems.
Radial play Up and down movement about a shaft.
Radial ply tyres Tyre plies run across the tyre (from bead to bead) and around the circumference of the tyre. Less resistant to tread distortion than other tyre types.
Radiator A liquid-to-air heat transfer device designed to reduce the temperature of the coolant in a liquid cooled engine.
Rake A feature of steering geometry - the angle of the steering head in relation to the vertical **(see illustration)**.

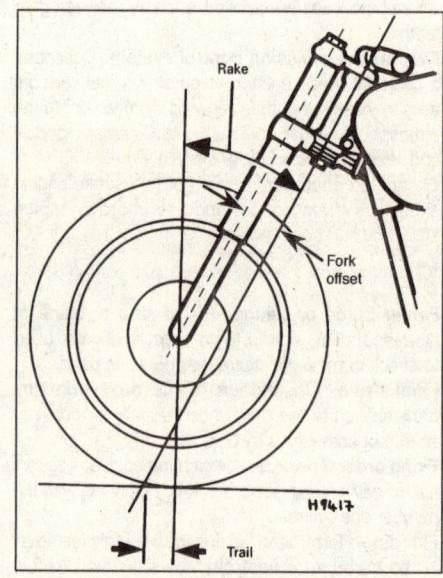

Steering geometry

Technical Terms Explained

Rebore Providing a new working surface to the cylinder bore by boring out the old surface. Necessitates the use of oversize piston and rings.
Rebound damping A means of controlling the oscillation of a suspension unit spring after it has been compressed. Resists the spring's natural tendency to bounce back after being compressed.
Rectifier Device for converting the ac output of an alternator into dc for battery charging.
Reed valve An induction system commonly used on two-stroke engines.
Regulator Device for maintaining the charging voltage from the generator or alternator within a specified range.
Relay A electrical device used to switch heavy current on and off by using a low current auxiliary circuit.
Resistance Measured in ohms. An electrical component's ability to pass electrical current.
RON (Research Octane Number) A measure of a fuel's resistance to knock.
rpm revolutions per minute.
Runout The amount of wobble (in-and-out movement) of a wheel or shaft as it's rotated. The amount a shaft rotates 'out-of-true'. The out-of-round condition of a rotating part.

S

SAE (Society of Automotive Engineers) A standard for the viscosity of a fluid.
Sealant A liquid or paste used to prevent leakage at a joint. Sometimes used in conjunction with a gasket.
Service limit Term for the point where a component is no longer useable and must be renewed.
Shaft drive A method of transmitting drive from the transmission to the rear wheel.
Shell bearings Plain bearings consisting of two shell halves. Most often used as big-end and main bearings in a four-stroke engine. Often called bearing inserts.
Shim Thin spacer, commonly used to adjust the clearance or relative positions between two parts. For example, shims inserted into or under tappets or followers to control valve clearances. Clearance is adjusted by changing the thickness of the shim.
Short-circuit An electrical condition where current shorts to earth (ground) bypassing the circuit components.
Skimming Process to correct warpage or repair a damaged surface, eg on brake discs or drums.
Slide-hammer A special puller that screws into or hooks onto a component such as a shaft or bearing; a heavy sliding handle on the shaft bottoms against the end of the shaft to knock the component free.
Small-end bearing The bearing in the upper end of the connecting rod at its joint with the gudgeon pin.
Spalling Damage to camshaft lobes or bearing journals shown as pitting of the working surface.
Specific gravity (SG) The state of charge of the electrolyte in a lead-acid battery. A measure of the electrolyte's density compared with water.
Straight-cut gears Common type gear used on gearbox shafts and for oil pump and water pump drives.
Stanchion The inner sliding part of the front forks, held by the yokes. Often called a fork tube.
Stoichiometric ratio The optimum chemical air/fuel ratio for a petrol engine, said to be 14.7 parts of air to 1 part of fuel.
Sulphuric acid The liquid (electrolyte) used in a lead-acid battery. Poisonous and extremely corrosive.
Surface grinding (lapping) Process to correct a warped gasket face, commonly used on cylinder heads.

T

Tapered-roller bearing Tapered inner race of caged needle rollers and separate tapered outer race. Examples of taper roller bearings can be found on steering heads.
Tappet A cylindrical component which transmits motion from the cam to the valve stem, either directly or via a pushrod and rocker arm. Also called a cam follower.
TCS Traction Control System. An electronically-controlled system which senses wheel spin and reduces engine speed accordingly.
TDC Top Dead Centre denotes that the piston is at its highest point in the cylinder.
Thread-locking compound Solution applied to fastener threads to prevent slackening. Select type to suit application.
Thrust washer A washer positioned between two moving components on a shaft. For example, between gear pinions on gearshaft.
Timing chain See **Cam Chain**.
Timing light Stroboscopic lamp for carrying out ignition timing checks with the engine running.
Top-end A description of an engine's cylinder block, head and valve gear components.
Torque Turning or twisting force about a shaft.
Torque setting A prescribed tightness specified by the motorcycle manufacturer to ensure that the bolt or nut is secured correctly. Undertightening can result in the bolt or nut coming loose or a surface not being sealed. Overtightening can result in stripped threads, distortion or damage to the component being retained.
Torx key A six-point wrench.
Tracer A stripe of a second colour applied to a wire insulator to distinguish that wire from another one with the same colour insulator. For example, Br/W is often used to denote a brown insulator with a white tracer.
Trail A feature of steering geometry. Distance from the steering head axis to the tyre's central contact point.
Triple clamps The cast components which extend from the steering head and support the fork stanchions or tubes. Often called fork yokes.
Turbocharger A centrifugal device, driven by exhaust gases, that pressurises the intake air. Normally used to increase the power output from a given engine displacement.
TWI Abbreviation for Tyre Wear Indicator. Indicates the location of the tread depth indicator bars on tyres.

U

Universal joint or U-joint (UJ) A double-pivoted connection for transmitting power from a driving to a driven shaft through an angle. Typically found in shaft drive assemblies.
Unsprung weight Anything not supported by the bike's suspension (ie the wheel, tyres, brakes, final drive and bottom (moving) part of the suspension).

V

Vacuum gauges Clock-type gauges for measuring intake tract vacuum. Used for carburettor synchronisation on multi-cylinder engines.
Valve A device through which the flow of liquid, gas or vacuum may be stopped, started or regulated by a moveable part that opens, shuts or partially obstructs one or more ports or passageways. The intake and exhaust valves in the cylinder head are of the poppet type.
Valve clearance The clearance between the valve tip (the end of the valve stem) and the rocker arm or tappet/follower. The valve clearance is measured when the valve is closed. The correct clearance is important - if too small the valve won't close fully and will burn out, whereas if too large noisy operation will result.
Valve lift The amount a valve is lifted off its seat by the camshaft lobe.
Valve timing The exact setting for the opening and closing of the valves in relation to piston position.
Vernier caliper A precision measuring instrument that measures inside and outside dimensions. Not quite as accurate as a micrometer, but more convenient.

Wet liner arrangement

VIN Vehicle Identification Number. Term for the bike's engine and frame numbers.
Viscosity The thickness of a liquid or its resistance to flow.
Volt A unit for expressing electrical "pressure" in a circuit. Volts = current x ohms.

W

Water pump A mechanically-driven device for moving coolant around the engine.
Watt A unit for expressing electrical power. Watts = volts x current.
Wear limit see **Service limit**
Wet liner A liquid-cooled engine design where the pistons run in liners which are directly surrounded by coolant **(see illustration)**.
Wheelbase Distance from the centre of the front wheel to the centre of the rear wheel.
Wiring harness or loom Describes the electrical wires running the length of the motorcycle and enclosed in tape or plastic sheathing. Wiring coming off the main harness is usually referred to as a sub harness.
Woodruff key A key of semi-circular or square section used to locate a gear to a shaft. Often used to locate the alternator rotor on the crankshaft.
Wrist pin Another name for gudgeon or piston pin.

REF•52 **Notes**

Index

Note: *References throughout this index are in the form - "Chapter number" • "Page number"*

A

Acknowledgements – 0•7
Air filter – 1•23
Air injection system – 1•24
Air temperature sensor – 4•25
Airbox – 4•7
Alternator – 8•35
Angle-tightening – REF•25
Antifreeze – REF•6
Anti-lock brake system (ABS) – 6•18
 modulator – 6•20
 wheel pulse ring – 6•20
 wheel sensor – 6•19
Atmospheric pressure sensor – 4•24

B

Balancer shaft – 2•55
Battery – 1•30
 charging – 8•6
 inspection and maintenance – 8•6
 removal and installation – 8•5
Bearings – 1•27, 2•50, REF•26
Belly pan – 7•9, 7•11
Bike spec – 0•16 *et seq*
 chassis – 0•17
 dimensions – 0•16
 engine – 0•17
 engine number – 0•8
 frame number – 0•8
 identification number – 0•8
 model development – 0•18
 spare parts – 0•18
 vehicle identification numbers – 0•8
 weights – 0•16
Bleeding brake fluid – 6•17
Bodywork – 7•1 *et seq*
 belly pan – 7•9, 7•11
 cockpit trim panels – 7•4, 7•9, 7•11
 fairing – 7•4, 7•5, 7•9, 7•10
 general information – 7•1
 mirrors – 7•11
 mudguard – 7•12
 radiator cowls – 7•7
 seat – 7•2
 seat cowling – 7•3, 7•8
 side panels – 7•3, 7•6, 7•7, 7•8, 7•10
 windshield – 7•12

Bolts – REF•17
 tightness – 1•19
Brakes, wheels and final drive – 1•17, 1•18, 6•1 *et seq*, REF•46
 anti-lock brake system – 6•18
 bleeding – 6•17
 calipers – 6•6, 6•11
 discs – 6•9, 6•12
 fluid – REF•6
  bleeding – 6•16
  change – 1•29, 6•18
  levels – 0•12
 general information – 6•3
 hoses, pipes and fittings – 1•19, 6•16
 lever – 5•8
 light – 8•15
  switches – 1•18, 8•22
 master cylinder – 6•9, 6•14
 modulator (ABS) – 6•20
 pads – 1•17, 6•3
 pedal – 5•4
Broken fasteners – REF•19
Bulbs
 brake/tail light – 8.15
 headlight – 8•9
 licence plate – 8.16
 sidelight – 8•9
 turn signal – 8•19
Buying spare parts – 0•8

C

Cables
 clutch – 1•19, 2•39
 lubrication – 1•28
 throttle – 1•14, 4•15
Calipers – 6•6, 6•11
 seals – 1•19
Cam chain
 guide blade – 2•24
 sprocket – 2•24
 tensioner – 2•17
 tensioner blade – 2•24, 2.25
 upper guide – 2•24
Camshafts and followers – 2•18
Catalytic converter – 4•28
Centrestand – 5•6

Chain – REF•30
 adjustment – 1•10
 cleaning – 1•11
 lubrication – 1•11, REF•6
 removal, cleaning and installation – 6•28
 slider – 1•20
 stretch – 1•11
Charging system test – 8•34
Circlips – REF•18
Clutch – 1•19, 2•34
 cable – 1•19, 2•39
 lever – 5•7
 switch – 8•28
Cockpit trim panels – 7•4, 7•9, 7•11
Coils – 4•20
Compression – 2•5
 gauge – REF•24
Connecting rods – 2•51
Continuity checks – 8•4
Conversion factors – REF•13
Coolant – 1•2
 change – 1•28
 hoses, pipes and unions – 3•8
 level – 0•10
 reservoir – 3•2
 temperature sensor – 4•25
Cooling fan – 3•3
 relay – 3•4
Cooling system – 1•15, 3•1 *et seq*
 coolant reservoir – 3•2
 cooling fan and relay – 3•3, 3•4
 general information – 3•2
 hoses, pipes and unions – 3•8
 pressure cap – 3•2
 radiator – 3•5
 thermostat – 3•5
 water pump – 3•7
Crankcase
 inspection – 2•50
 separation and reassembly – 2•48
Crankshaft – 2•53
 bearings – 2•51
 position sensor – 4•25
 sprocket – 2•24
Cylinder compression – 2•5
Cylinder head
 overhaul – 2•26
 removal and installation – 2•25
Cylinder liners – 2•29

Index

D

Degreasers – REF•7
Diagnostic tool – 4•21
Dial gauge – REF•24
Dimensions – 0•16
Discs – 6•9, 6•12
   locks – REF•3
Drawbolts – REF•27
Drive chain – REF•30
   adjustment – 1•10
   cleaning – 1•11
   lubrication – 1•11
   removal, cleaning and installation – 6•28
   slider – 1•20
   stretch – 1•11

E

Earth (ground) checks – 8•5
Electrical system – 8•1 *et seq*, REF•46
   alternator – 8•35
   battery – 1•30, 8•5, 8•6
   brake light – 8•15, 8•22
   clutch switch – 8•28
   continuity checks – 8•4
   earth (ground) checks – 8•5
   fault finding – 8•3
   fuses – 8•7
   general information – 8•3
   handlebar switches – 8•27
   headlight – 8•9, 8•13
      aim – 8•15
   horn – 8•29
   ignition switch – 8•26
   instrument cluster – 8•23
   licence plate light – 8•16
   lighting system – 8•8
   neutral switch – 8•27
   oil pressure switch – 8•29
   regulator/rectifier – 8•37
   relays – 8•24
   sidelight – 8•9
   sidestand switch – 8•28
   starter motor – 8•31
   starter solenoid – 8•30
   tail light – 8•17
   turn signals – 8•19
   voltage checks – 8•4
   wiring continuity checks – 8•4
   wiring diagrams – 8•38 *et seq*
Electronic control module (ECM) – 4•22
EMS relay – 4•23
Engine coolant temperature sensor – 4•25
Engine management system – 4•21
Engine management system (fuel and ignition) – 4•1 *et seq*
   air temperature sensor – 4•25
   airbox – 4•7
   atmospheric pressure sensor – 4•24
   catalytic converter – 4•28
   coils – 4•20
   coolant temperature sensor – 4•25
   crankshaft position sensor – 4•25
   diagnostic tool – 4•21
   electronic control module (ECM) – 4•22
   EMS relay – 4•23
   engine coolant temperature sensor – 4•25
   engine management system – 4•21
   EVAP system – 4•27
   exhaust system – 4•16
   fault codes – 4•21
   fuel injectors – 4•14
   fuel level sensor – 4•12
   fuel pressure and pressure regulator – 4•11
   fuel pump – 4•9
      relay – 4•11
   fuel rail – 4•14
   fuel tank – 4•3
   general information and precautions – 4•3
   idle air control unit – 4•27
   ignition coils – 4•20
   injectors – 4•14
   intake air temperature sensor – 4•25
   lambda sensor – 4•26
   manifold absolute pressure sensor – 4•25
   oxygen (lambda) sensor – 4•26
   sensors – 4•24
   speed sensor – 4•26
   throttle body – 4•12
   throttle cable – 4•15
   throttle position sensor – 4•26
   tip-over sensor – 4•26
Engine management system check – 1•14
Engine number – 0•8
Engine oil – 1•2
   change and filter – 1•13
   level – 0•11
Engine, clutch and transmission – 2•1 *et seq*
   balancer shaft – 2•55
   cam chain and tensioner/guide blades – 2•17, 2•24
   camshafts – 2•18
   clutch – 2•24
      cable – 2•39
   compression – 2•5
   connecting rods – 2•51
   crankcase – 2•48, 2•50
   crankshaft – 2•53
   cylinder compression – 2•5
   cylinder head – 2•25, 2•26
   cylinder liners – 2•29
   engine overhaul information – 2•14
   engine removal and installation – 2•6
   engine wear assessment – 2•5
   followers – 2•18
   gearchange mechanism – 2•43
   general information – 2•5
   main bearings – 2•50, 2•53
   oil cooler and hoses – 2•14
   oil pressure check – 2•6
   oil pump – 2•41
   oil strainer – 2•39
   piston and rings – 2•31
   selector drum and forks – 2•45
   starter clutch – 2•22
   sump – 2•39
   transmission shafts – 2•56
   valve cover – 2•17
   valves – 2•26
EVAP system (California market models) – 4•27
Exhaust system – 4•16, REF•45

F

Fairing – 7•4, 7•5, 7•9, 7•10
Fasteners – REF•17
Fault codes – 4•21
Fault Finding – REF•37 *et seq*
   electrical system – 8•3
Filter
   air – 1•23
   engine oil – 1•13
   fuel – 1•16
Fluids – 1•2, REF•5
Followers – 2•18
Footrests – 5•3

Index

Forks
  adjustment – 5•25
  oil – 5•1, REF•6
  oil change – 1•31, 5•9
  overhaul – 5•12
  removal and installation – 5•8
Frame – 5•3
Frame and suspension – 5•1 *et seq*
  brake lever – 5•8
  brake pedal – 5•4
  centrestand – 5•6
  clutch lever – 5•7
  footrests – 5•3
  forks – 5•8, 5•9, 5•12
  frame – 5•3
  gearchange lever – 5•5
  general information – 5•3
  handlebars – 5•6
  shock absorber – 5•20, 5•27
  sidestand – 5•6
  stands – 5•6
  steering head bearings – 5•19
  steering stem – 5•18
  suspension linkage – 5•25
  swingarm – 5•28, 5•33
Frame number – 0•8
Fuel – 4•1
Fuel filter – 1•16
Fuel hose renewal – 1•16
Fuel injectors – 4•14
Fuel level sensor – 4•12
Fuel pressure and regulator – 4•11
Fuel pump – 4•9
  relay – 4•11
Fuel rail – 4•14
Fuel strainer and filter – 1•16
Fuel tank – 4•3
  cleaning and repair – 4•7
Fuses – 8•2, 8•7

G

Gaskets and sealants – REF•7, REF•29
Gearbox – 2•56
Gearchange
  lever – 5•5
  mechanism – 2•43
Greases – 1•2, REF•7
Ground anchors – REF•4

H

Hand protection – REF16
Handlebars – 5•6
  switches – 8•27
Headlight – 8•7
  aim – 8•15, REF•8
  assembly – 8•13
  bulbs – 8•9
Horn – 8•29, REF•8
Hoses – REF•31
  brake – 1•19, 6•16
  coolant – 3•8
  fuel – 1•16
Hub bearings – 6•27

I

Identification Number – 0•8
Idle air control unit – 4•27
Idle speed – 1•21
Ignition coils – 4•20
Ignition switch – 8•26
Immobilisers – REF•3
Injectors – 4•14
Input shaft – 2•54
Instrument cluster – 8•23
Intake air temperature sensor – 4•25

L

Lambda sensor – 4•26
Legal – 0•15
Lever pivots lubrication – 1•27
Levers
  brake – 5•8
  clutch – 5•7
  gearchange – 5•5
Licence plate light – 8•16
Lighting – 0•16, REF•8
  system check – 8•8
Lubricants and fluids – REF•5 *et seq*
  recommended – 1•2

M

Main bearings – 2•50, 2•53
  oil clearance – 2•54
Maintenance schedule – 1•3
Manifold absolute pressure sensor – 4•25
Master cylinder
  brake – 6•9, 6•14
  seals – 1•19
Measuring tools and gauges – REF•21
Micrometers – REF•21
Mirrors – 7•11
Model development – 0•18
Modulator (ABS) – 6•20
MOT Test Checks – REF•8 *et seq*
Mudguard (front) – 7•12

N

Neutral switch – 8•27
Number plate light – 8•16
Nuts – REF•17
  tightness – 1•19

O

Oil cooler and hoses – 2•14
Oil
  engine – 0•11, 1•2
  fork – 5•1
Oil change
  engine – 1•13
  fork – 1•31, 5•9
Oil filter change – 1•13
Oil pressure – 2•6
  gauge – REF•24
  relief valve – 2•42
  switch – 8•29
Oil pump – 2•41
Oil seals – REF•29
Oil strainer – 2•39
Output shaft – 2•56
Oxygen (lambda) sensor – 4•26

Index

P

Pads
  renewal – 6•3
  wear – 1•17
Parts – 0•8
Pedal
  brake – 5•4
  gearchange – 5•5
Piston and rings – 2•31
Plastigauge – REF•23
Pre-ride checks – 0•10 et seq
  brake fluid levels – 0•12
  coolant level – 0•10
  engine oil level – 0•11
  final drive – 0•15
  fuel – 0•15
  legal – 0•15
  safety – 0•15
  steering – 0•15
  suspension – 0•15
  tyres – 0•15
Pressure cap – 3•2
Pullers – REF•26
Pump
  fuel – 4•9
  oil – 2•41
  water – 3•7

R

Radiator – 3•5
  pressure cap – 3•2
Rectifier – 8•37
Reference – REF•1 et seq
Regulator/rectifier – 8•37
Relays – 8•24
  cooling fan – 3•4
  EMS – 4•23
  fuel pump – 4•11
  headlight – 8•24
  starter solenoid – 8•30
  starter circuit – 8•24
  turn signal – 8•19
Routine maintenance and Servicing – 1•1 et seq
Running-in procedure – 2•61

S

Safety first! – 0•15, 0•9
Safety interlock circuit – 1•30
Screws – REF•17
Sealing compound – REF•7, REF•29
Seals – REF•29
Seat – 7•2
  cowling – 7•3, 7•8
Secondary air injection system (SAIS) – 1•24
Security – REF•2 et seq
Seized fasteners – REF•18
Selector drum and forks – 2•45
Sensors – 4•24
  atmospheric pressure sensor – 4•24
  coolant temperature sensor – 4•25
  crankshaft position sensor – 4•25
  intake air temperature sensor – 4•25
  manifold absolute pressure sensor – 4•25
  oxygen (lambda) sensor – 4•26
  speed sensor – 4•26
  throttle position sensor – 4•26
  tip-over sensor – 4•26
Shock absorber – 5•20, 5•27
Side panels – 7•3, 7•6, 7•7, 7•8, 7•10
Sidecars – REF•12
Sidelight – 8•9
Sidestand – 5•6
  switch – 8•28
Slide-hammers – REF•26
Solvents – REF•7
Spare parts – 0•8
Spark plugs – 1•1, 1•20
Speed sensor – 4•26
Split pins – REF•17
Spray lubricants – REF•7
Sprockets – 6•29
  coupling/rubber dampers – 6•30
  coupling bearing – 6•26
  cover – 6•29
  wear – 1•11
Stand(s) – 1•27, 5•6
  lubrication – 1•27
Starter circuit relay – 8•24
Starter clutch – 2•22
Starter motor – 8•31
Starter solenoid – 8•30
Steering – 0•16, REF•9
Steering head bearings – 1•21
  lubrication – 1•23
  overhaul – 5•19
Steering stem – 5•18
Storage – REF•33 et seq
Sump – 2•39
Suspension – 0•15, 1•16, REF•9
  adjustment – 5•25
  forks – 5•8, 5•19, 5•12
  linkage – 5•23
  rear shock – 5•20
Swingarm
  bearing lubrication – 1•17
  bearings – 5•33
  removal and installation – 5•28
Switches
  brake light – 8•22
  clutch – 8•28
  continuity checks – 8•4
  handlebar – 8•27
  ignition – 8•26
  neutral – 8•27
  oil pressure – 8•29
  sidestand – 8•28

Index

T

Tail light – 8•15, 8•17
Temperature sensor – 4•25
Thermostat – 3•5
Thread diameter and pitch – REF•18
Thread locking compound – REF•7, REF•21
Thread repair – REF•20
Throttle body
  removal, cleaning, inspection and installation – 4•12
  synchronisation – 1•21
Throttle cable – 1•14
  removal and installation – 4•15
Throttle position sensor – 4•26
Tip-over sensor – 4•26
Tools and Workshop Tips – REF•14 *et seq*
Torque and leverage – REF•25
Torque settings – 1•2, 2•3, 3•1, 4•2, 5•1, 6•2, 7•1, 8•3
Torque wrench – REF•25
Transmission shafts – 2•54
Turn signals – 8•19, REF•8
Tyres – 0•15, REF•11
  care, pressures and tread depth – 0•15
  information and fitting – 6•28
  sizes – 6.2

U

U-locks – REF•3

V

Valves
  clearance – 1•1, 1•26
  cover – 2•15
  overhaul – 2•26
Vehicle Identification Number – 0•8
Vernier caliper – REF•22
Voltage checks – 8•4

W

Washers – REF•17
Water pump – 3•7
Weights – 0•16
Wheel bearings – 1•23, 6•24
  lubrication – 1•23
Wheel pulse ring (ABS) – 6•20
Wheel sensor (ABS) – 6•19
Wheels – 1•19, 6•22, 6•23, REF•11
  alignment check – 6•21
  bearings – 1•27, 6•25
  inspection – 6•21
Windshield – 7•12
Wiring continuity checks – 8•4
Wiring diagrams – 8•38 *et seq*

Notes

Haynes Motorcycle Manuals – The Complete List

Title		Book No
APRILIA RS50 (99 – 06) & RS125 (93 – 06)		4298
Aprilia RSV1000 Mille (98 – 03)	◆	4255
Aprilia SR50		4755
BMW 2-valve Twins (70 -96)	◆	0249
BMW F650	◆	4761
BMW K100 & 75 2-valve models (83 - 96)	◆	1373
BMW F800 (F650) Twins (06 – 10)	◆	4872
BMW R850, 1100 & 1150 4-valve Twins (93 – 06)	◆	3466
BMW R1200 (04 – 09)	◆	4598
BMW R1200 dohc Twins (10 – 12)	◆	4925
BSA Bantam (48 – 71)		0117
BSA Unit Singles (58 – 72)		0127
BSA Pre-unit Singles (54 – 61)		0326
BSA A7 & A10 Twins (47 – 62)		0121
BSA A50 & A65 Twins (62 – 73)		0155
CHINESE, Taiwanese & Korean Scooters		4768
Chinese, Taiwanese & Korean 125cc motorcycles		4781
Pulse/Pioneer Adrenaline, Sinnis Apache, Superbyke RMR (07 – 14)	◇◆	5750
DUCATI 600, 620, 750 & 900 2-valve V-twins (91 – 05)	◆	3290
Ducati Mk III & Desmo singles (69 – 76)	◇	0445
Ducati 748, 916 & 996 4-valve V-twins (94 – 01)	◆	3756
GILERA Runner, DNA, Ice & SKP/Stalker (97 – 11)		4163
HARLEY-DAVIDSON Sportsters (70 – 10)	◆	2534
Harley-Davidson Shovelhead & Evolution Big Twins (70 -99)	◆	2536
Harley-Davidson Twin Cam 88, 96 & 103 models (99 – 10)	◆	2478
HONDA NB, ND, NP & NS50 Melody (81 -85)	◇	0622
Honda NE/NB50 Vision & SA50 Vision Met-in (85-95)	◇	1278
Honda MB, MBX, MT & MTX50 (80 – 93)		0731
Honda C50, C70 & C90 (67 – 03)		0324
Honda XR50/70/80/100R & CRF50/70/80/100F (85 – 07)		2218
Honda XL/XR 80, 100, 125, 185 & 200 2-valve models (78 – 87)		0566
Honda H100 & H100S Singles (80 – 92)	◇	0734
Honda 125 Scooters (00 – 09)		4873
Honda ANF125 Innova Scooters (03 -12)	◆	4926
Honda CB/CD125T & CM125C Twins (77 – 88)	◇	0571
Honda CBF125 (09 – 14)	◆	5540
Honda CG125 (76 – 07)	◇	0433
Honda NS125 (86 – 93)	◇	3056
Honda CBR125R (04 – 10)		4620
Honda CBR125R, CBR250R & CRF250L/M (11 – 14)	◆	5919
Honda MBX/MTX125 & MTX200 (83 – 93)	◇	1132
Honda XL125V & VT125C (99 – 11)		4899
Honda CD/CM185 200T & CM250C 2-valve Twins (77 – 85)		0572
Honda CMX250 Rebel & CB250 Nighthawk Twins (85 – 09)	◇	2756
Honda XL/XR 250 & 500 (78 – 84)		0567
Honda XR250L, XR250R & XR400R (86 – 04)		2219
Honda CB250 & CB400N Super Dreams (78 – 84)	◇	0540
Honda CR Motocross Bikes (86 – 07)		2222
Honda CRF250 & CRF450 (02 – 06)		2630
Honda CBR400RR Fours (88 – 99)	◇◆	3552
Honda VFR400 (NC30) & RVF400 (NC35) V-Fours (89 – 98)	◇◆	3496
Honda CB500 (93 – 02) & CBF500 (03 – 08)	◇	3753
Honda CB400 & CB550 Fours (73 – 77)		0262
Honda CX/GL500 & 650 V-Twins (78 – 86)		0442
Honda CBX550 Four (82 – 86)	◇	0940
Honda XL600R & XR600R (83 – 08)	◆	2183
Honda XL600/650V Transalp & XRV750 Africa Twin (87 – 07)	◆	3919
Honda CB600 Hornet, CBF600 & CBR600F (07 – 12)	◆	5572
Honda CBR600F1 & 1000F Fours (87 – 96)	◆	1730
Honda CBR600F2 & F3 Fours (91 – 98)	◆	2070
Honda CBR600F4 (99 – 06)	◆	3911
Honda CB600F Hornet & CBF600 (98 – 06)	◇◆	3915
Honda CBR600RR (03 – 06)	◆	4590
Honda CBR600RR (07 -12)	◆	4795
Honda CB650 sohc Fours (78 – 84)		0665
Honda NTV600 Revere, NTV650 & NT650V Deauville (88 – 05)	◇◆	3243
Honda Shadow VT600 & 750 (USA) (88 – 09)		2312
Honda NT700V Deauville & XL700V Transalp (06 -13)	◆	5541
Honda CB750 sohc Four (69 – 79)		0131
Honda V45/65 Sabre & Magna (82 – 88)		0820
Honda VFR750 & 700 V-Fours (86 – 97)	◆	2101
Honda VFR800 V-Fours (97 – 01)	◆	3703
Honda VFR800 V-Tec V-Fours (02 – 09)	◆	4196
Honda CB750 & CB900 dohc Fours (78 – 84)		0535
Honda CBF1000 (06 -10) & CB1000R (08 – 11)	◆	4927
Honda VTR1000 Firestorm, Super Hawk & XL1000V Varadero (97 – 08)	◆	3744
Honda CBR900RR Fireblade (92 – 99)	◆	2161
Honda CBR900RR Fireblade (00 – 03)	◆	4060
Honda CBR1000RR Fireblade (04 – 07)	◆	4604
Honda CBR1000RR Fireblade (08 – 13)	◆	5688
Honda CBR1100XX Super Blackbird (97 – 07)	◆	3901
Honda ST1100 Pan European V-Fours (90 – 02)	◆	3384
Honda ST1300 Pan European (02 -11)	◆	4908
Honda Shadow VT1100 (USA) (85 – 07)		2313

Title		Book No
Honda GL1000 Gold Wing (75 – 79)		0309
Honda GL1100 Gold Wing (79 – 81)		0669
Honda Gold Wing 1200 (USA) (84 - 87)		2199
Honda Gold Wing 1500 (USA) (88 – 00)		2225
Honda Goldwing GL1800	◆	2787
KAWASAKI AE/AR 50 & 80 (81 – 95)		1007
Kawasaki KC, KE & KH100 (75 – 99)		1371
Kawasaki KMX125 & 200 (86 – 02)	◇	3046
Kawasaki 250, 350 & 400 Triples (72 – 79)		0134
Kawasaki 400 & 440 Twins (74 – 81)		0281
Kawasaki 400, 500 & 550 Fours (79 – 91)		0910
Kawasaki EN450 & 500 Twins (Ltd/Vulcan) (85 – 07)		2053
Kawasaki ER-6F & ER-6N (06 -10)	◆	4874
Kawasaki EX500 (GPZ500S) & ER500 (ER-5) (87 – 08)	◆	2052
Kawasaki ZX600 (ZZ-R600 & Ninja ZX-6) (90 – 06)	◆	2146
Kawasaki ZX-6R Ninja Fours (95 – 02)	◆	3451
Kawasaki ZX-6R (03 – 06)	◆	4742
Kawasaki ZX600 (GPZ600R, GPX600R, Ninja 600R & RX) & ZX750 (GPX750R, Ninja 750R) (85 – 97)	◆	1780
Kawasaki 650 Four (76 – 78)		0373
Kawasaki Vulcan 700/750 & 800 (85 – 04)	◆	2457
Kawasaki Vulcan 1500 & 1600 (87 – 08)	◆	4913
Kawasaki 750 Air-cooled Fours		0574
Kawasaki ZR550 & 750 Zephyr Fours (90 – 97)	◆	3382
Kawasaki Z750 & Z1000 (03 – 08)	◆	4762
Kawasaki ZX750 (Ninja ZX-7 & ZXR750) Fours (89 – 96)	◆	2054
Kawasaki Ninja ZX-7R & ZX-9R (94 – 04)	◆	3721
Kawasaki 900 & 1000 Fours (73 – 77)		0222
Kawasaki ZX900, 1000 & 1100 Liquid-cooled Fours (83 – 97)	◆	1681
Kawasaki ZX-10R (04 – 10)	◆	5542
KTM EXC Enduro & SX Motocross (00 – 07)	◆	4629
LAMBRETTA Scooters (58 – 00)	◆	5573
MOTO GUZZI 750, 850 & 1000 V-Twins (74 – 78)		0339
MZ ETZ models (81 – 95)	◇	1680
NORTON 500, 600, 650 & 750 Twins (57 – 70)		0187
Norton Commando (68 – 77)		0125
PEUGEOT Speedfight, Trekker & Vivacity Scooters (96 – 08)	◇	3920
Peugeot V-Clic, Speedfight 3, Vivacity 3, Kisbee & Tweet (08 – 14)	◇◆	5751
PIAGGIO (Vespa) Scooters (91 – 09)	◇	3492
SUZUKI GT, ZR & TS50 (77 – 90)	◇	0799
Suzuki TS50X (84 – 00)	◇	1599
Suzuki 100, 125, 185 & 250 Air-cooled Trail bikes (79 – 89)		0797
Suzuki GP100 & 125 Singles (78 – 93)	◇	0576
Suzuki GS, GN, GZ & DR125 Singles (82 – 05)	◇	0888
Suzuki Burgman 250 & 400 (98 – 11)	◆	4909
Suzuki GSX-R600/750 (06 – 09)	◆	4790
Suzuki 250 & 350 Twins (68 – 78)		0120
Suzuki GT250X7, GT200X5 & SB200 Twins (78 – 83)	◇	0469
Suzuki DR-Z400 (00 – 10)	◆	2933
Suzuki GS/GSX250, 400 & 450 Twins (79 – 85)		0736
Suzuki GS500 Twin (89 – 08)	◆	3238
Suzuki GS550 (77 – 82) & GS750 Fours (76 – 79)		0363
Suzuki GS/GSX550 4-valve Fours (83 – 88)		1133
Suzuki SV650 & SV650S (99 – 08)	◆	3912
Suzuki DL650 V-Strom & SFV650 Gladius (04 – 13)	◆	5643
Suzuki GSX-R600 & 750 (96 – 00)	◆	3553
Suzuki GSX-R600 (01 – 03), GSX-R750 (00 – 03) & GSX-R1000 (01 – 02)	◆	3986
Suzuki GSX-R600/750 (04 – 05) & GSX-R1000 (03 – 06)	◆	4382
Suzuki GSF600, 650 & 1200 Bandit Fours (95 – 06)	◆	3367
Suzuki Intruder, Marauder, Volusia & Boulevard (85 – 09)	◆	2618
Suzuki GS850 Fours (78 – 88)		0536
Suzuki GS1000 Four (77 – 79)		0484
Suzuki GSX-R750, GSX-R1100 (85 – 92) GSX600F, GSX750F, GSX1100F (Katana) Fours (88 – 96)	◆	2055
Suzuki GSX600/750F & GSX750 (98 – 02)	◆	3987
Suzuki GS/GSX1000, 1100 & 1150 4-valve Fours (79 – 88)		0737
Suzuki TL1000S/R & DL V-Strom (97 – 04)	◆	4083
Suzuki GSF650/1250 Bandit & GSX650/1250F (07 – 14)	◆	4798
Suzuki GSX1300R Hayabusa (99 – 14)	◆	4184
Suzuki GSX1400 (02 – 08)	◆	4758
TRIUMPH Tiger Cub & Terrier (52 – 68)		0414
Triumph 350 & 500 Unit Twins (58 – 73)		0137
Triumph Pre-Unit Twins (47 – 62)		0251
Triumph 650 & 750 2-valve Unit Twins (63 – 83)		0122
Triumph 675 (06 – 10)	◆	4876
Triumph Tiger 800 (10 – 14)	◆	5752
Triumph 1050 Sprint, Speed Triple & Tiger (05 -13)	◆	4796
Triumph Trident & BSA Rocket 3 (69 – 75)		0136
Triumph Bonneville (01 – 12)	◆	4364
Triumph Daytona, Speed Triple, Sprint & Tiger (97 – 05)	◆	3755
Triumph Triples & Fours (carburetor engines) (91 – 04)	◆	2162
VESPA P/PX125, 150 & 200 Scooters (78 – 12)		0707
Vespa GTS125, 250 & 300 (05 – 10)		4898
Vespa Scooters (59 – 78)		0126

Title		Book No
YAMAHA DT50 & 80 Trail Bikes (78 – 95)	◇	0800
Yamaha T50 & 80 Townmate (83 – 95)	◇	1247
Yamaha YB100 Singles (73 – 91)	◇	0474
Yamaha RS/RXS 100 & 125 Singles (74 – 95)		0331
Yamaha RD & DT125LC (82 – 87)	◇	0887
Yamaha TZR125 (87 – 93) & DT125R (88 – 07)	◇	1655
Yamaha TY50, 80, 125 & 175 (74 – 84)	◇	0464
Yamaha XT & SR125 (82 – 03)	◇	1021
Yamaha YBR125 & XT125R/X (05 – 13)		4797
Yamaha YZF-R125 (08 – 11)	◆	5543
Yamaha Trail Bikes (81 – 03)		2350
Yamaha 2-stroke Motocross Bikes (86 – 06)		2662
Yamaha YZ & WR 4-stroke Motorcross Bikes (98 – 08)		2689
Yamaha 250 & 350 Twins (70 – 79)		0040
Yamaha XS250, 360 & 400 sohc Twins (75 – 84)		0378
Yamaha RD250 & 350LC Twins (80 – 82)		0803
Yamaha RD350 YPVS Twins (83 – 95)		1158
Yamaha RD400 Twin (75 – 79)		0333
Yamaha XT, TT & SR500 Singles (75 – 83)		0342
Yamaha XZ550 Vision V-Twins (82 – 85)		0821
Yamaha FJ, FX, XY & YX600 Radian (84 – 92)		2100
Yamaha XT660 & MT-03 (04 – 11)	◆	4910
Yamaha XJ600S (Diversion, Seca II) & XJ600N Fours (92 – 03)	◆	2145
Yamaha XJ6 & FZ6R (09 – 15)	◆	5889
Yamaha YZF600R Thundercat & FZS600 Fazer (96 – 03)	◆	3702
Yamaha FZ-6 Fazer (04 – 08)	◆	4751
Yamaha YZF-R6 (99 – 02)	◆	3900
Yamaha YZF-R6 (03 – 05)	◆	4601
Yamaha YZF-R6 (06 – 13)	◆	5544
Yamaha 650 Twins (70 – 83)		0341
Yamaha XJ650 & 750 Fours (80 – 84)		0738
Yamaha XS750 & 850 Triples (76 – 85)		0340
Yamaha TDM850, TRX850 & XTZ750 (89 – 99)	◇◆	3450
Yamaha YZF750R & YZF1000R Thunderace (93 – 00)	◆	3720
Yamaha FZR600, 750 & 1000 Fours (87 – 96)	◆	2056
Yamaha XV (Virago) V-Twins (81 – 03)	◆	0802
Yamaha XVS650 & 1100 Drag Star/V-Star (97 – 05)	◆	4195
Yamaha XJ900F Fours (83 – 94)	◆	3239
Yamaha XJ900S Diversion (94 – 01)	◆	3739
Yamaha YZF-R1 (98 – 03)	◆	3754
Yamaha YZF-R1 (04 – 06)	◆	4605
Yamaha FZS1000 Fazer (01 – 05)	◆	4287
Yamaha FJ1100 & 1200 Fours (84 – 96)	◆	2057
Yamaha FJR1300 (01 – 13)	◆	5607
Yamaha XJR1200 & 1300 (95 – 06)	◆	3981
Yamaha V-Max (85 – 03)	◆	4072
ATVs		
Honda ATC 70, 90, 110, 185 & 200 (71 – on)		0565
Honda Rancher, Recon & TRX250EX ATVs		2553
Honda TRX300 Shaft Drive ATVs (88 – 00)		2125
Honda Foreman (95 – 11)		2465
Honda TRX300EX, TRX400EX & TRX450R/ER ATVs (93 – 06)		2318
Kawasaki Bayou 220/250/300 & Prairie 300 ATVs (86 – 03)		2351
Polaris ATVs (85 – 97)		2302
Polaris ATVs (98 – 07)		2508
Suzuki/Kawasaki/Artic Cat ATVs (03 – 09)		2910
Yamaha YFS200 Blaster ATV (88 – 06)		2317
Yamaha YFM350 & YFM400 (ER & Big Bear) ATVs (87 – 09)		2126
Yamaha YFZ450 & YFZ450R (04 – 10)		2899
Yamaha Banshee and Warrior ATVs (87 – 10)		2314
Yamaha Kodiak and Grizzly ATVs (93 – 05)		2567
ATV Basics		10450
SCOOTERS		
Twist and Go (automatic transmission) Scooters Service and Repair Manual	◇	4082
TECHBOOK SERIES		
Motorcycle Basics Techbook (2nd edition)		3515
Motorcycle Electrical Techbook (3rd edition)		3471
Motorcycle Fuel Systems Techbook		3514
Motorcycle Maintenance Techbook		4071
Motorcycle Modifying		4272
Motorcycle Workshop Practice Techbook (2nd edition)		3470

◇ = not available in the USA ◆ = Superbike

The manuals on this page are available through good motorcycle dealers and accessory shops.
In case of difficulty, contact: **Haynes Publishing**
(UK) **+44 1963 442030** (USA) **+1 805 498 6703**
(SV) **+46 18 124016**
(Australia/New Zealand) **+61 2 8713 1400**

MCL 07.05.15

Preserving Our Motoring Heritage

< The Model J Duesenberg Derham Tourster. Only eight of these magnificent cars were ever built – this is the only example to be found outside the United States of America

Almost every car you've ever loved, loathed or desired is gathered under one roof at the Haynes Motor Museum. Over 300 immaculately presented cars and motorbikes represent every aspect of our motoring heritage, from elegant reminders of bygone days, such as the superb Model J Duesenberg to curiosities like the bug-eyed BMW Isetta. There are also many old friends and flames. Perhaps you remember the 1959 Ford Popular that you did your courting in? The magnificent 'Red Collection' is a spectacle of classic sports cars including AC, Alfa Romeo, Austin Healey, Ferrari, Lamborghini, Maserati, MG, Riley, Porsche and Triumph.

A Perfect Day Out

Each and every vehicle at the Haynes Motor Museum has played its part in the history and culture of Motoring. Today, they make a wonderful spectacle and a great day out for all the family. Bring the kids, bring Mum and Dad, but above all bring your camera to capture those golden memories for ever. You will also find an impressive array of motoring memorabilia, a comfortable 70 seat video cinema and one of the most extensive transport book shops in Britain. The Pit Stop Cafe serves everything from a cup of tea to wholesome, home-made meals or, if you prefer, you can enjoy the large picnic area nestled in the beautiful rural surroundings of Somerset.

> John Haynes O.B.E., Founder and Chairman of the museum at the wheel of a Haynes Light 12.

< The 1936 490cc sohc-engined International Norton – well known for its racing success

The Museum is situated on the A359 Yeovil to Frome road at Sparkford, just off the A303 in Somerset. It is about 40 miles south of Bristol, and 25 minutes drive from the M5 intersection at Taunton.
Open 9.30am - 5.30pm (10.00am - 4.00pm Winter) 7 days a week, *except Christmas Day, Boxing Day and New Years Day*
Special rates available for schools, coach parties and outings Charitable Trust No. 292048